Blackburn
College

Library

Development of Language

EIGHTH EDITION

The Development of Language

JEAN BERKO GLEASON
Boston University

NAN BERNSTEIN RATNER
University of Maryland, College Park

PEARSON

Boston • Columbus • Indianapolis • New York • San Francisco • Upper Saddle River
Amsterdam • Cape Town • Dubai • London • Madrid • Milan • Munich • Paris • Montreal • Toronto
Delhi • Mexico City • São Paulo • Sydney • Hong Kong • Seoul • Singapore • Taipei • Tokyo

Executive Editor and Publisher: Stephen D. Dragin
Editorial Assistant: Michelle Hochberg
Marketing Manager: Joanna Sabella
Production Editor: Paula Carroll
Editorial Production Service: Walsh & Associates, Inc.
Manufacturing Buyer: Megan Cochran
Electronic Composition: Jouve
Photo Research: Poyee Oster
Cover Designer: Jennifer Hart

Credits and acknowledgments borrowed from other sources and reproduced, with permission, in this textbook appear on the appropriate page 433.

Microsoft® and Windows® are registered trademarks of the Microsoft Corporation in the U.S.A. and other countries. Screen shots and icons reprinted with permission from the Microsoft Corporation. This book is not sponsored or endorsed by or affiliated with the Microsoft Corporation.

If you purchased this book within the United States or Canada, you should be aware that it has been imported without the approval of the Publisher or the Author.

10 9 8 7 6 5 4 3 2 1

ISBN-10: 0-13-298532-2
ISBN-13: 978-013-298532-1

To the memory of our dear friends and co-authors, Richard Ely and Barbara Alexander Pan.

About the Authors

Jean Berko Gleason is professor emerita in the Department of Psychology at Boston University, where she has served as chair and as director of the Graduate Program in Developmental Science. She is also a faculty member and former director of Boston University's Graduate Program in Applied Linguistics. She has been a visiting scholar at Harvard University, Stanford University, and at the Linguistics Institute of the Hungarian Academy of Sciences in Budapest. A fellow of the American Association for the Advancement of Science and of the American Psychological Association, she was elected president of the International Association for the Study of Child Language. She is also past president of the Gypsy Lore Society. Her background includes an undergraduate degree in history and literature and a Ph.D. in linguistics and psychology from Harvard. She is the author of leading works on psycholinguistics and creator of the Wug Test, the best known experimental study of children's language acquisition. She has continued to conduct research and publish in the areas of language development in children, aphasia, gender differences, and parent–child interaction. Her work is frequently cited in the professional literature, in the popular press, on television, and on the Internet, where she is featured in the award-winning NOVA series, The Secret Life of Scientists (www.pbs.org/wgbh/nova/secretlife/scientists/jean-berko-gleason).

Nan Bernstein Ratner, Ed.D., C.C.C., is professor and chair, the Department of Hearing and Speech Sciences, University of Maryland, College Park, where she has worked since 1983. She holds degrees in Child Study (Tufts University), Speech-Language Pathology (Temple University), and Applied Psycholinguistics (Boston University). With Jean Berko Gleason, she has also co-authored the text *Psycholinguistics*. Her research has centered on typical and atypical parent–child interaction and speech and language development in children, with an emphasis on children who stutter, and more recently, children with seizure disorder. She is Specialty Board recognized in child language and in fluency disorders.

Contents

4 SEMANTIC DEVELOPMENT   89

Paola Uccelli, *Harvard Graduate School of Education*

Barbara Alexander Pan, *Harvard Graduate School of Education*

5   PUTTING WORDS TOGETHER   120

Andrea Zukowski, *University of Maryland*

6   LANGUAGE IN SOCIAL CONTEXTS: DEVELOPMENT OF COMMUNICATIVE COMPETENCE   163

Judith Becker Bryant, *University of South Florida*

7   THEORETICAL APPROACHES TO LANGUAGE ACQUISITION   190

John N. Bohannon III, *Butler University*

John D. Bonvillian, *University of Virginia*

8   VARIATION IN LANGUAGE DEVELOPMENT: IMPLICATIONS FOR RESEARCH AND THEORY   241

Beverly A. Goldfield, *Rhode Island College*

Catherine E. Snow, *Harvard Graduate School of Education*

Ingrid A. Willenberg, *Macquarie University*

9 ATYPICAL LANGUAGE DEVELOPMENT   266

Nan Bernstein Ratner, *University of Maryland, College Park*

10 LANGUAGE AND LITERACY IN THE SCHOOL YEARS   329

Gigliana Melzi, *New York University*

Adina R. Schick, *New York University*

What's New to This Edition

The eighth edition of *The Development of Language* provides new information on language development in children who are learning languages other than English (with an emphasis on Spanish), as well as on children with risk factors for language delay or disorder. Additionally, the chapters address cultural influences that lead to group and individual variation in children's language environments and profiles of language development. It focuses even more completely on language acquisition throughout the lifespan, with new coverage of linguistic achievements in the first year of life, before children even produce their first words, through the middle school years, and into adulthood and the senior years.

New Features

1. New cross-linguistic coverage of language acquisition, with an emphasis on Spanish acquisition

   Benefit: Invaluable to students in all fields. This new feature recognizes that there is a growing non-English-speaking segment of the United States population, especially those learning Spanish as a first language.

   Location in text: All chapters, but see Chapter 3 for specific comparisons in phonological development.

2. New and expanded coverage of infant developmental precursors to language development

   Benefit: Emphasizes the importance of the first year of life in setting the stage for typical language development, particularly in the domains of perception and comprehension, topics often neglected by other texts.

   Location in text: Chapter 2

3. A concise summary of the newest research on the nature and most effective treatment of language disorders in children that provides understandable and up-to-date coverage of the thousands of research reports on autism spectrum disorder, hearing impairment and cochlear implants, children with SLI, and other populations that have appeared since the seventh edition.

   Benefit: Creates an applied transition between profiles of typical and atypical development likely to be seen by future teachers, speech–language pathologists, psychologists, and other constituencies that adopt this book.

   Location in text: Chapter 9

4. Expanded coverage of recent findings in language use in mature and older adults, including the latest findings on language following stroke and language in individuals with Alzheimer's disease.

Benefit: Provides a complete perspective on the life-long developmental nature of language development and use.
Location in text: Chapter 11

5. Freshly updated and expanded coverage of topics often neglected in other language development texts, such as communication in non-human primates and other animals, individual variation in human language development, the impacts of cultural and linguistic variation on profiles of typical language development.
Benefit: Allows reader to put language development into a larger biological, social, and cultural context.
Location in text: Throughout, but see Chapters 1 and 8

6. Revised and timely applied projects and activities designed to engage the reader in extended, hands-on application of text materials in order to solidify text concepts and expand them to real-world applications.
Benefit: More involved, dynamic applications of text concepts permit both instructor and student to gauge the degree to which information can be applied in the real-life situations likely to be encountered by students in professional settings.
Location in text: End of each chapter, teacher's manual

7. Thorough updating of research in each topic area; roughly 20 percent of the references are new to this edition
Benefit: Newer references not only update content in chapters but convey scientific advances in understanding the bases of language acquisition, including the newest paradigms in infant testing, brain imaging, neuropsychology, and genetics.
Location in text: Throughout

Preface

This is the eighth edition of *The Development of Language,* which we have written for any-one with an interest in how children acquire language and in how language develops over the life span. Readers will learn about what the fetus hears prenatally, what happens to language in the aging brain, and everything in between. The field has changed substan-tially the since our last edition, and we are very pleased to present the new perspectives and new information that have evolved over the past several years.

Our goal in writing this book is to provide an authoritative, interesting text that in-cludes concepts and research findings that are both important and useful. The eighth edi-tion places a substantial emphasis on language development in children who are learning languages other than, or in addition, to English, as well as children with risk factors for language delay or disorder. Additionally, the chapters address cultural influences that lead to group and individual variation in children's language. It focuses even more completely on language acquisition throughout the life span, with new coverage of linguistic achieve-ments in the first year of life, before children even produce their first words, through the middle school years, and into adulthood and the senior years. Some new features include:

- Cross-linguistic coverage of language acquisition, with an emphasis on Spanish acquisition. This is invaluable to students in all fields, with the growing non–English speaking segment of the U.S. population, particularly those learning Span-ish as a first language. Included in all relevant chapters, for instance in Chapter 3, which provides comparative information on phonological development, Chapter 4, which discusses vocabulary and assessment, and Chapter 10, which describes differ-ences in the language of school age children.

- Increased coverage of developmental precursors to language development in infancy that set the stage for normal or atypical development. New information on the first year of life, particularly in the perception and comprehension domains, topics often neglected by other texts. These topics are covered in Chapter 2.

- A summary of the newest research on the nature and most effective treatment of language disorders in children. This provides understandable and up-to-date cov-erage of the thousands of research reports on autism spectrum disorder, hearing impairment, and cochlear implants, children with SLI and other populations that have appeared since the seventh edition. Profiles of typical and atypical develop-ment likely to be seen by future teachers, speech-language pathologists, psycholo-gists, and other constituencies that adopt this book are in Chapter 9.

- Freshly updated and expanded coverage of topics frequently not included in other language development texts, such as communication in non-human primates and other animals, individual variation in human language development, and the impacts of cultural and linguistic variation on typical language development.

This allows the reader to put language development into a larger biological and social context. Found throughout the book but especially in Chapter 1 and Chapter 8.

- Expanded coverage of recent research on language in mature and older adults, including the latest findings on language following stroke and language in individuals with Alzheimer's disease. This provides the student with a comprehensive introduction to language in aging, along with an understanding of the lifelong development of language. Found in Chapter 11.

- Revised and timely applied projects and activities that provide the reader with hands-on application of text materials. This helps the student to solidify concepts and expand them to real-world applications. Dynamic application of text concepts permits both instructor and student to see how research information can be applied in professional settings. New projects and ideas are at the ends of every chapter and in the instructor's manual.

- Thorough updating of references in each topic area. Approximately 20 percent of the references are new to this edition. The new citations not only update content in chapters but convey scientific advances in understanding the bases of language acquisition, including the newest paradigms in infant testing, brain imaging, neuropsychology, and genetics.

As in the past, each chapter is written by outstanding scholars who are known for their expertise in the areas that they discuss. For students, each chapter provides a helpful summary, suggested readings, and a list of key words used in the chapter. The book includes a comprehensive glossary that clearly explains each key term in the text.

The book is intended as a text for upper-level undergraduate or graduate courses in language development, or as readings for courses in psycholinguistics, cognition, developmental psychology, speech pathology, and related subjects. The book also serves as a resource for professionals in all of the fields just noted.

In order to benefit from the book, readers do not need previous knowledge of linguistics; each chapter presents its material along with whatever linguistic background information is relevant. This means that there will be some repetition of major concepts, which will help to reinforce them and make them clearer. On the other hand, we assume that readers are familiar with basic concepts in psychology (e.g., *object permanence*) and with the work of major figures such as Jean Piaget and B. F. Skinner. Many books on language development are concerned only with language acquisition by children and have tended to assume that development is complete when the most complex syntactic structures have been attained. But linguistic development, like psychological development, is a life-long process, and so we have set out to illuminate the nature of language development over the life span.

This book is written by a number of authors, and we believe that is one of its strengths: The study of language development has grown rapidly in recent years, and there are now many topics that are highly specialized. Not many researchers are experts in all areas of this expanding field. For instance, there are few investigators who are authorities on the language of both toddlers and people in their 70s and older, yet both topics are covered here. Fortunately, a number of leading researchers in their fields have agreed to contribute to the book; the chapters, therefore, are written by authors who not only know their topic well, but are known for their research in it. They present what they consider to be the salient ideas and the most recent and relevant studies in their own areas.

Since development is always the result of an interaction between innate capacities and environmental forces, we take an interactive perspective, one that takes into account both the biological endowment that makes language possible and the environmental factors that foster development.

Instructors who adopt the text will be happy to learn that a new instructor's manual prepared by Pam Gleason is available. The manual provides Internet resources, exam questions, and helpful outlines of the chapters that can be used in structuring lectures. It emphasizes key points and provides suggestions for classroom activities.

Acknowledgments

We are indebted to many people who helped make this book possible. We are grateful, first of all, to our co-authors, who devoted so much time and thought to their chapters. Thanks also to Steve Dragin, our editor at Pearson Education, and to Jamie Bushell, Paula Carroll, and Kathy Whittier. We thank the following reviewers for their comments and suggestions:

Michael Casby
Michigan State University

Harriet S. Magen
Rhode Island College

Julie McGory
The Ohio State University

The Development of Language

An Overview and a Preview

Jean Berko Gleason
Boston University

By the time they are 3 or 4 years old, children everywhere in the world have acquired the major elements of the languages spoken around them, regardless of how complex they may be. The development of language is an amazing, yet basically universal, human achievement. It poses some of the most challenging theoretical and practical questions of our times: Does an infant, or even the developing fetus, process language? If so, what aspects of speech and language can they perceive? What if no one spoke to them—would children invent language by themselves? How do young children acquire complex grammar? Are humans unique, or do other animals have language as we define it? What if we raised a chimp as if it were our own child—would it learn to use language in the same way that a human child does? Do parrots who talk know what they are saying? Are there theories that can adequately account for language development? Is language a separate capacity, or is it simply one facet of our general cognitive ability? What is it that individuals actually must know in order to have full adult competence in language, and to what extent is the development of those skills representative of universal processes? What about individual differences? What happens when language develops atypically, and is there anything we can do about it? What happens to language skills as one grows older: What do we lose, and what, if anything, gets better as we age? These are some of the questions that intrigue researchers in language development, and they have led to the plan of this book.

Once children begin to acquire language, they make rapid progress. By the time they are of school age and even before they can read, they can vary their speech to suit the social and communicative nature of a situation; they know the meaning and pronunciation of literally thousands of words, and they use the major sentence types and grammatical forms—subjects, objects, verbs, plurals, and tenses—of their language quite correctly. Language development, however, does not cease when people reach school age, nor, for that matter, adolescence or maturity; language development continues throughout our lives. The reorganization and reintegration of mental processes that are typical of other intellectual functions can also be seen in language, as the changes that accompany maturity lead to modification of linguistic capacity. This book, therefore, is written from a developmental perspective that covers the entire life span. Although most studies of language development have centered on children, the questions we ask require the study of mature and aging individuals as well.

This chapter is divided into four major sections. The first section provides a brief overview of *the course of language development* from early infancy to old age. It serves as a preview of the chapters that follow.

The second section notes some of the unique *biological foundations* for language that make its development possible in humans. Our biological endowment is necessary but not sufficient to ensure language development, which does not occur without social interaction.

The third section describes the major *linguistic systems* that individuals must acquire. Rather than endorsing any particular linguistic theory, we present descriptive information that has provided the framework for much basic research in language acquisition. More technical linguistic material is presented in the chapters devoted to particular topics such as the acquisition of syntax or of the sound system. If there is a unifying perspective that the authors of this book share, it is the view that individuals acquire during their lives an **internalized representation** of language that is systematic in nature and amenable to study.

The fourth and final section of this chapter focuses on the background and methods of the *study of language development.*

An Overview of the Course of Language Development

Communication Development in Infancy

Even before babies are born, they are listening to the language spoken around them: Research shows that newborns prefer to hear the language or languages they heard while *in utero*. During their first months, infants have communicative abilities that underlie language, long before they say their first words. Babies are intensely social beings: They gaze into the eyes of their caregivers and are sensitive to the emotional tone of the voices around them. They pay attention to the language spoken to them; they take their turn in conversation, even if that turn is only a burble. If they want something, they learn to make their intentions known. In addition to possessing the social motivations that are evidenced so early in life, infants are also physiologically equipped to process incoming speech signals; they are even capable of making fine distinctions among speech sounds. By the age of 6 months, babies have already begun to categorize the sounds of their own language, much as adult speakers do. By the age of about 11 months, many babies understand 50 or more common words, and point happily at the right person when someone asks, "Where's Daddy?"

At approximately the same age that they take their first steps, many infants produce their first words. Like walking, early language appears at around the same age and in much the same way all over the world, regardless of their society or culture or the characteristics of the language that is being acquired. The precursors of language development that emerge before infants begin to speak are discussed in Chapter 2.

Phonological Development: Learning Sounds and Sound Patterns

Midway through their first year, infants begin to babble, playing with sound much as they play with their fingers and toes. Early in their second year, for most children, the babbling of the prelinguistic infant gives way to words. There has been considerable controversy over the relation between babbling and talking, but most researchers now agree that babbling blends into early speech and may continue even after the appearance of recognizable words. Once infants have begun to speak, the course of language development appears to have some universal characteristics. Typically, toddlers' early utterances contain only one word, usually a word that is simple to pronounce and concrete in meaning. It is important to recognize that different constraints act upon the child's **comprehension** and **production** of a particular form and that children may comprehend things more sophisticated than what they are able to say. Some sounds are more difficult to pronounce than others, and combinations of consonants may prove particularly problematic. Within a given language, or when acquiring more than one language, children solve the phonological problems they encounter in varying ways. A framework for the study of children's acquisition of the phonology, or sound system, of their language is provided in Chapter 3.

Semantic Development: Learning the Meanings of Words

The ways in which speakers relate words to their referents and their meanings are the subject matter of **semantic development**. Just as there are constraints on the phonological shapes of children's early words, there appear to be limits on the kinds of meanings of those early words; for instance, very young children's vocabularies are more likely to contain words that refer to objects that move *(bus)* than objects that are immobile *(bench)*. Their vocabularies reflect their daily lives and are unlikely to refer to events that are distant in time or space or to anything of an abstract nature. Early words like *hi, doggie, Mommy,* and *juice* refer to the objects, events, and people in the child's immediate surroundings. As they enter the school years, children's words become increasingly complex and interconnected, and children also gain a new kind of knowledge: **metalinguistic awareness**. This new ability makes it possible for them to think about their language, understand what words are, and even define them. Investigations of children's early words and their meanings, as well as the ways that meaning systems develop into complex semantic networks, are discussed in Chapter 4.

Putting Words Together: Morphology and Syntax in the Preschool Years

Sometime during their second year, after they know about fifty words, most children progress to a stage of two-word combinations. Words that they said in the one-word stage are now combined into these brief utterances, without articles, prepositions, inflections, or any of the other grammatical modifications that adult language requires. The child can now say such things as "That doggie," meaning "That is a doggie," and "Mommy juice," meaning "Mommy's juice," or "Mommy, give me my juice," or "Mommy is drinking her juice."

An examination of children's two-word utterances in many different language communities has shown that everywhere in the world children at this age are expressing the same kinds of thoughts and intentions in the same kinds of utterances. They ask for more of something; they say no to something; they notice something, or they notice that it has disappeared. This leads them to produce utterances like "More milk!" "No bed!" "Hi, kitty!" and "All-gone cookie!"

A little later in the two-word stage, another dozen or so kinds of meanings appear. For instance, children may name an actor and a verb: "Daddy eat." They may modify a noun: "Bad doggie." They may specify a location: "Kitty table." They may name a verb and an object, leaving out the subject: "Eat lunch." At this stage children are expressing these basic meanings, but they cannot use the language forms that indicate number, gender, and tense. Toddler language is in the here and now; there is no tomorrow and no yesterday in language at the two-word stage. What children can say is closely related to their level of cognitive and social development, and a child who cannot conceive of the past is unlikely to speak of it. As the child's utterances grow longer, grammatical forms begin to appear. In English, articles, prepositions, and inflections representing number, person, and tense begin to be heard. Although the two-word stage has some universal characteristics across all languages, what is acquired next depends on the features of the language being learned. English-speaking children learn the articles *a* and *the,* but in a language such as Russian, there are no articles. Russian grammar, on the other hand, has features that English grammar does not. One remarkable finding has been that children acquiring a given language do so in essentially the same order. In English, for instance, children learn *in* and *on* before other prepositions such as *under.* After they learn regular plurals and pasts, like *juices* and *heated,* they create some **overregularized** forms of their own, like *gooses* and *eated.*

Researchers account for children's early utterances in varying ways. Research in the field that was originally inspired by the linguistic theories that began to emerge in the 1960s interpreted early word combinations as evidence that the child was a young cryptographer, endowed with a cognitive impetus to develop syntax and a grammatical system. In more recent times, the child's intentions and need to communicate them to others have been offered as explanations of grammatical development. However, children's unique ability to acquire complex grammar, regardless of the motivation behind it, remains at the heart of linguistic inquiry. Early sentences and the acquisition of morphology are examined in Chapter 5.

Language in Social Contexts: Development of Communicative Competence

Language development includes acquiring the ability to use language appropriately in a multiplicity of social situations. This complex ability is often referred to as **communicative competence**. The system of rules that dictates the way language is used to accomplish social ends is often called **pragmatics**. An individual who acquires the phonology, morphology, syntax, and semantics of a language has acquired **linguistic competence**. A sentence such as "Pardon me, sir, but might I borrow your pencil for a moment?" certainly shows that the speaker has linguistic competence, since it is perfectly grammatical. If, however, this sentence is addressed to your grandmother, it is just as certainly inappropriate. Linguistic competence is not sufficient; speakers must also acquire communicative competence, which goes beyond linguistic competence to include the ability to use language appropriately in many different situations. In other words, it requires knowledge of the social rules for language use, or pragmatics. During the preschool years, young children learn to respond to social situations by making polite requests or clarifying their own utterances. Their parents are typically eager that they learn to be polite. Parents' intuitions about the importance of using language in socially appropriate ways are borne out by research that shows that inappropriate children are often unpopular or disliked. Speakers ultimately learn important variations in language that serve to mark their gender, regional origin, social class, and occupation. Other necessary variations are associated with such things as the social setting, topic of discourse, and characteristics of the person being addressed. The development of communicative competence is discussed in Chapter 6.

Theoretical Approaches to Language Acquisition

In general, explaining what it is that children acquire during the course of language development is easier than explaining how they do it. Do parents shape their children's early babbling into speech through reinforcement and teaching strategies? Or is language perhaps an independent and **innate** faculty, built into the human biobehavioral system? Learning theorists and linguistic theorists do not agree on these basic principles. Between the theoretical poles represented by learning theorists on the one hand and linguistic theorists on the other lie three different interactionist perspectives.

1. *Cognitive interactionists* who rely primarily on the theories of Piaget believe that language is just one facet of human cognition and that children in acquiring language are basically learning to pair words with concepts they have already acquired. Other, more recent, cognitive interactionists study language from the perspective of the neural architecture that supports it. They see children as processors of information, and

they use computers to model the ways neural connections supporting language are strengthened through exposure to adult speech.

2. *Social interactionists* emphasize the child's motivation to communicate with others. They emphasize the role that the special features of **child-directed speech (CDS)** may play in facilitating children's language acquisition.

3. *Gestural and usage-based theorists* are more concerned with the roots of language that are demonstrated when even very young children begin to communicate through gestures, pointing, shared attention, and other nonverbal but goal-directed and social behaviors. A discussion and an evaluation of language development theories are included in Chapter 7.

Variation in Language Development: Implications for Research and Theory

Even though this brief overview has emphasized the regularities and continuities that have been observed in the development of language, it is important to know that individual differences have been found in almost every aspect of the process, even during the earliest period of development. In the acquisition of phonology, for instance, some children are quite conservative and avoid words they have difficulty pronouncing; others are willing to take a chance. Early words and early word combinations reveal different strategies in acquiring language. Although much research has been devoted to finding commonalities in language acquisition across children, it is important to remember that there is also variation in the onset of speech, the rate at which language develops, and the style of language used by the child. This should not surprise us; we know that babies differ in temperament, cognitive style, and in many other ways. In addition, children's early language may reflect their social class, their gender, whether they are growing up mono- or bilingual, and preferences of adults in their society; for instance, American parents stress the names of things, but nouns are not so important in all societies. Any comprehensive theory of language development must account for individual differences; those who work with children must be aware of them. Individual differences are the topic of Chapter 8.

Atypical Language Development

Language has been a human endowment for so many millennia that it is exceptionally robust. There are conditions, however, that may lead to atypical language development—for instance, sensory problems such as deafness. In this case the capacity for language is intact, but lack of accessible auditory input makes the acquisition of oral language difficult. In some cases, technology can provide access to the auditory signal using hearing aids or cochlear implants; in other cases, children with hearing impairment who learn a manual language such as **American Sign Language (ASL)** are able to communicate in a complete and sophisticated language.

Children who are diagnosed with intellectual disability, such as most children with **Down syndrome**, may show rather standard patterns of language development, but at a slower rate than typically developing children. On the other hand, children with **autism spectrum disorder** and those with **pervasive developmental disorder** frequently exhibit patterns of language development that are atypical in multiple ways; they may have particular problems, for instance, in understanding what other people know and in adjusting their language accordingly. Occasionally children suffer from **specific language impairment**, problems in language development accompanied by no other obvious physical, sensory, or emotional difficulties. Still other children have particular problems producing speech, even though their internal representation of language is intact: They may stutter or have motor or physical impairments. Atypical language development, as well as its relation to the processes described in earlier chapters, is the subject of Chapter 9.

Language and Literacy in the School Years

By the time they get to kindergarten, children have amassed a vocabulary of about 8,000 words, and they can handle questions, negative statements, dependent clauses, compound sentences, and a great variety of other constructions. They have also learned much more than vocabulary and grammar—they have learned to use language in many different social situations. They can, for instance, talk baby talk to babies, tell jokes to their friends, and speak politely to strangers. Their communicative competence is growing.

During the school years, children are increasingly called upon to interact with peers; peer speech is quite different from speech to parents, and it is often both humorous and inventive. Jokes, riddles, and play with language constitute a substantial portion of school-children's spontaneous speech. Faced with many new models, school-age children also learn from television and films, and their speech may be marked by expressions from their favorite entertainments.

New cognitive attainments in the school years make it possible for children to talk in ways that they could not as preschoolers, and they develop **metalinguistic awareness,** the ability to think about language itself. They become increasingly adept at producing connected, multi-utterance speech and can create narratives that describe their past experiences. To succeed in school, children must also learn to use **decontextualized language**: language that is not tied to the here and now. They develop the ability to provide explanations and descriptions using decontextualized language.

The attainment of literacy marks a major milestone in children's development, and it calls upon both their metalinguistic abilities (for instance, they must understand what a word is) and their new abilities to use decontextualized language. Study of the cognitive processes involved in reading and the development of adequate models that represent the acquisition of this skill are two topics that actively involve researchers in developmental psycholinguistics.

Children who come from literate households know a great deal about reading and writing before formal instruction begins and thus are at an advantage in school. Children who are bilingual may have some advantages in the acquisition of the metalinguistic knowledge that develops in the school years. Once children have acquired the ability to read and write, these new skills, in turn, have profound effects upon their spoken language. Learning to read is not an easy task for all children; this extremely complex activity requires intricate coordination of a number of separate abilities. Humans have been speaking since the earliest days of our prehistory, but reading has been a common requirement only in very modern times; we should not be surprised, therefore, that reading skills vary greatly in the population. Reading problems, such as **dyslexia**, pose serious theoretical and practical problems for the psycholinguistic researcher. The acquisition of literacy skills and increasingly complex language during the school years and through adolescence are discussed in Chapter 10.

Developments in the Adult Years

In the normal course of events, language development, like cognitive development, moral development, or psychological development, continues beyond the point where the individual has assumed the outward appearance of an adult. During the teen years, young people acquire their own special style, and part of being a successful teenager rests in knowing how to talk like one. Then, in adulthood, there are new linguistic attainments.

Language is involved in psychological development, and one of the major life tasks facing young people is the formation of an identity—a sense of who they are. A distinct personal linguistic style is part of one's special identity. Further psychological goals of early adulthood that call for new or expanded linguistic skills include both entering the world of work and establishing intimate adult relations with others. Language development during the adult years varies greatly among individuals, depending on such things as their education and social and occupational roles. Actors, for instance, must learn not only to be heard by large audiences but to speak the words of others using varying voices and regional dialects. Working people learn the special tones of voice and terminology associated with their own occupational register or code.

With advancing age, numerous linguistic changes take place. For instance, some word-finding difficulty is inevitable; the inability to produce a name that is "on the tip of the tongue" is a phenomenon that becomes increasingly familiar as one gets older. Hearing loss and memory impairment can affect an older person's ability to communicate. However, not all changes are for the worse: Vocabulary increases, as does narrative skill. In preliterate societies, for instance, the official storytellers are typically older members of the community. Although most individuals remain linguistically vigorous in their later years, language deterioration becomes severe for some, and they may lose both comprehension and voluntary speech. The **aphasias** and **dementias** exact their linguistic toll on affected individuals, whose speech may become as limited as that of young children. Language development in adulthood and the later years is described in Chapter 11.

The Biological Bases of Language

Animal Communication Systems

Human language has special properties that have led many researchers to conclude that it is both **species specific** and **species uniform**; that is, it is unique (specific) in the human species and essentially similar, or uniform in all of members of our human species (Lenneberg, 1967; Pääbo, 2003). The characteristics that distinguish human language are illuminated when they are compared with those of nonhuman animal communication systems. Other animals are clearly able to communicate at some level with one another as well as with humans. Cats and dogs meow and bark in varied ways and are able to convey a variety of messages to us by methods such as scratching at the door or looking expectantly at their dishes. These signals are limited in scope and clearly not language, although one enterprising Japanese inventor has devised an electronic collar intended to translate your dog's different barks (Gregory, 2009). (It is not clear how well this device, called BowLingual, works, but in 2002 its inventors received an Ig Nobel Prize for "promoting peace and harmony between the species.")

Bee Communication.   Bees have been shown to have an elaborate communication system. The ethologist Karl von Frisch (1950) began to study bees in the 1920s and won a Nobel Prize in 1973 for his studies of bee communication. Unlike the expressive meowing of a hungry cat, in many senses the communication system of the bee is referential—it tells other bees about, or refers to, something in the outside world. A bee returning to the hive after finding nectar-filled flowers collects an audience and then performs a dance that indicates the direction and the approximate distance of the nectar from the hive. Other bees watch, join the dance, and then head for the flowers. The bee's dance is actually a miniature form of the trip to the flowers rather than a symbolic statement. There is nothing symbolic or arbitrary about dancing toward the north to indicate that other bees should fly in that direction. Moreover, although the movements of the dance have structure and meaning, there is only one possible conversational topic: where to find nectar. Even this repertoire is seriously limited; bees cannot, for instance, tell one another that the flowers are pretty or that they are bored with their job.

Nonprimate Mammals and Birds.   Many animals have ways of communicating with other members of their species. Dolphins, who are intelligent and social mammals, employ elaborate systems of whistles that can be heard at a distance by other dolphins under water. This vocal communication reflects highly developed skills on which dolphins rely in surroundings that would make visual interactions difficult. During the first year of its life, each baby bottlenose dolphin learns a "signature whistle" by which it can be recognized (Tyack, 2000). Later on, bottlenose dolphins display vocal learning behaviors that are seen in birds but not in other nonhuman mammals. They are able to imitate the whistles of other dolphins and use this "whistle matching" when they address one another (Janik, 2000).

African elephants communicate with one another in many ways, including seismically. They have as many as twenty-five different vocal calls and a number of "rumbles" that are below the threshold of human hearing. These subsonic communications are carried through the ground and can be sensed and understood by other elephants as much as a dozen miles away. In one study, Namibian elephants reacted to long-distance predator warnings given by members of their own group, but were unimpressed by similar warnings issued by unfamiliar Kenyan elephants (O'Connell, 2007).

Some birds use a variety of meaningful calls to court one another, to warn of danger, or to indicate that it is time to fly home. The eerie cry of the loon is just one of a number of distinct and meaningful calls made by these inhabitants of northern lakes. Recent research reveals that male loons convey information about their size to potential rivals through the auditory frequency of their yodels (Piper, Mager, & Walcott, 2011).

All of these communication systems are useful for the creatures that use them, and each one resembles human language in some respect, but they are all tied to the stimulus situation, limited to the "here and now" and to a restricted set of messages. Human language has characteristics not found in their entirety in these other systems.

Not all researchers agree on the list of criteria that should be used in describing true *language*. However, most would agree on at least these three, cited by Roger Brown (1973):

1. True language is marked by *productivity* in the sense that speakers can make many new utterances and can recombine or expand the forms they already know to say things they have never heard before. This feature is also called *recombination, recursion,* or *generativity,* depending on the author and emphasis.
2. It also has *semanticity* (or *symbolism*); that is, language represents ideas, events, and objects symbolically. A word is a symbol that stands for something else.
3. Language offers the possibility of *displacement*—messages need not be tied to the immediate context.

human *

Human language is unique because it enables its users to comment on any aspect of their experience and to consider the past and the future, as well as referents that may be continents away or only in the imagination. The natural communication systems of nonhumans do not meet these criteria of language.

Attempts to teach human language to talking birds, however, have produced some extremely provocative results. For instance, an African grey parrot named Alex knew the word *yummy* and he knew the word *bread*. When someone brought in a birthday cake, something he had never seen before, he tasted his portion and exclaimed, "Yummy bread!" The ability to combine communicative concepts as shown in this example has long been thought to be exclusive to humans. Alex could recognize the colors, shapes, and numbers of objects and answer novel questions about them in English. Faced with an array of blocks, he was asked, "How many blue blocks?" Alex correctly answered, "six." He was right about 80 percent of the time (Pepperberg & Gordon, 2005).

Experiments with a number of young grey parrots have shown that they can learn to label common objects if they have human tutors who provide interactive lessons; they do

Alex could tell you what color these blocks are, and he could count them as well.

not learn from passive listening to lessons on audio recordings or from watching videos, but do best when the words are presented in context by a friendly and informative person. Interacting with a parrot can be an unnerving experience—one that makes us marvel that a bird whose brain is the size of a walnut can speak to us in clear and appropriate human language. Do African grey parrots have the same sort of linguistic skill human children do? One view is that they do not and that the birds are responding to complex learned cues. Another interpretation of the evidence is that language is not a unitary set of features, but a continuum on which grey parrots have clearly alighted. Although Alex died unexpectedly at the relatively young age of 31 in 2007, further research with African grey parrots continues.

Dogs have recently made their entrance into the comprehension side of the human language arena. Dogs are not able to produce human words, except, after much coaxing, some very limited approximations to expressions such as "I love you." A version of this modified yowling by a husky named Mishka has been viewed approximately 48 million times on YouTube (**www.youtube .com/watch?v=qXo3NFqkaRM**). There is, however some recent intriguing research on language comprehension by a breed often viewed as the smartest of all pups, the border collie. In one set of studies, a border collie named Chaser acquired the names of 1,022 objects during a three-year training period and could very accurately select a toy with the right name from a large array. Even more impressive, Chaser was able to infer that a name she had never heard before belonged to a new, unnamed object among the ones she already knew. For instance, an unfamiliar doll was included among her toys. When asked to bring "Darwin," a name she had not heard before, she correctly inferred that the unfamiliar name belonged to the unfamiliar object and promptly delivered the doll (Pilley & Reid, 2011). By inferring that a new name must belong to a novel object, Chaser was demonstrating a principle of vocabulary acquisition commonly ascribed to human children.

Dominic knows the names of his toys and will bring you the right one if you ask him for the alligator.

Primate Language.   Researchers have long wondered if primates are capable of learning human language. Chimpanzees, in particular, have been the subject of much research. Chimpanzees are intelligent, social, and communicative animals. They use a variety of vocal cries in the wild, including a food bark and a danger cry. There have been numerous attempts to teach language to chimpanzees, who possess genetic structures very similar to our own and are our closest relatives in the animal world, and at least one major gorilla language project is still ongoing (Tanner, Patterson, & Byrne, 2006). Koko the gorilla is now more than 40 years old and knows thousands of signs and words. Her trainer, Francine Patterson, has also reported that Koko is able to express very human-like feelings, such as her sadness at the death of a kitten. Koko is featured in books and films and on her own web site. The chimpanzee studies have provided us with much useful and controversial data on the ability of nonhumans to acquire human language.

Gua and Viki.   In 1931 Indiana University professor Winthrop Kellogg and his wife, Luella, became the first American family to raise a chimpanzee and a child together (Kellogg, 1980). The Kelloggs brought an infant chimpanzee named Gua into their home; she stayed with them and their infant son, Donald, for 9 months. No special effort was made to teach Gua to talk, and although she was ahead of Donald in her motor development, she did not babble and did not learn to say any words. Some wonderful old films comparing Donald and Gua are available on the Internet. See, for instance, **www.archive.org/details/comparative_tests_on_human_chimp_infants**.

In the 1940s psychologists Catherine and Keith Hayes (Hayes, 1951) set out to raise a baby chimpanzee named Viki as if she were their own child. This included outfitting her in little dresses and introducing her to strangers as their daughter. (One horrified motel owner actually believed that Catherine Hayes had given birth to Viki.) The Hayeses tried to teach language to Viki. They assumed that chimpanzees were rather like children with developmental delays and that with love and patient instruction Viki would learn to talk. After six years of training, Viki understood a great deal, but she was able to produce, with great difficulty, only four words: *mama, papa, cup,* and *up*. She was never able to say more, and in order to pronounce a /p/, she had to hold her lips together with her fingers. The Hayeses' research with Viki showed that chimpanzees do not have the specialized articulatory and physiological abilities that make spoken language possible.

After these failed experiments, other researchers began to realize that true language need not be spoken. The Deaf community in the United States, for instance, uses a gestural rather than a spoken language, American Sign Language (ASL). ASL is a complete language, with its own grammar and a rich vocabulary, all of which can be conveyed by facial expression, movements of the upper torso, and the shape and movement of the hands in front of the body; it is the equal of vocal language in its capacity to communicate complex human thought (Klima & Bellugi, 1979; Hoza, 2008). A new appreciation of the richness of ASL led to innovative experiments with chimpanzees.

Washoe.   The first attempt to capitalize on the ability to comprehend language and the natural gestural ability of a chimpanzee by teaching her signed human language was made by Beatrice and Allen Gardner at the University of Nevada in 1966 (Gardner & Gardner, 1969). The Gardners moved a 10-month-old chimpanzee named Washoe into a trailer behind their house and began to teach her ASL. Washoe became a chimp celebrity. During the time she was involved in this project, she learned over 130 ASL signs, as well as how to combine them into utterances of several signs (Gardner & Gardner, 1994). On seeing her trainer, she was able to sign "Please tickle hug hurry," "Gimme food drink," and similar requests.

Washoe was able to sign many of the same things that are said by children in the early stages of language acquisition before they learn the grammatical refinements of their own language (Brown, 1970; Van Cantfort & Rimpau, 1982). Unlike English-speaking children, she did not pay attention to word order, and at the time her training ceased in the fifty-first month, it was not clear whether her sign language was actually grammatically structured in the sense that even a young child's is (Brown, 1970; Klima & Bellugi, 1972). However, through vocabulary tests of Washoe, as well as of several other chimpanzees they worked with, the Gardners were able to demonstrate that children's and chimpanzees' first 50 words are very similar.

The chimpanzees studied by the Gardners also extended, or generalized, their words in much the same way that humans do—for instance, calling a hat they had never seen before *hat*. The question of whether a chimpanzee is capable of syntax remained open. This is an important theoretical question, because syntax makes *productivity*—one of the hallmarks of human language—possible. On the practical side, the remarkable successes attained with chimps led to innovative programs that teach sign language to children with communication disorders (Toth, 2009).

Nim Chimpsky.   An attempt to answer the question of whether chimpanzees can make grammatical sentences was made by a professor at Columbia University, Herbert S. Terrace (1980). Terrace adopted a young male chimp, whom he named Nim Chimpsky (a play on the name of Noam Chomsky, the well-known linguist who emphasizes the uniquely human ability to use language). The plan was to raise Nim in a rich human environment, teach him ASL, and then analyze the chimp's emerging ability to combine signs into utterances, paying special attention to any evidence that he could indeed produce grammatical signed sentences. Nim began to sign early: He produced his first sign, "drink," when he was only 4 months old. However, his later utterances never progressed much beyond the two- or three-sign stage. He signed "Eat Nim" and "Banana me eat," but when he made four-sign utterances, he added no new information, and unlike even young children, he used no particular word order. He signed "Banana me eat banana," in which the additional word is merely repetitive. Analyzing the extensive data collected in this project, Terrace concluded that there was no evidence that the chimp could produce anything that might be called a sentence.

An even more serious question regarding the chimpanzee's linguistic capability was raised after Terrace and his associates studied the videotaped interactions of young Nim and his many teachers. They found that Nim understood little about conversational turn taking, often interrupting his teachers, and that very little of what Nim signed actually originated with the chimp. Most of what he signed was prompted by the teacher and contained major constituents of the teacher's prior signed utterance to him.

Terrace carried his study further by analyzing films made available to him by other ape-language projects and arrived at the same conclusion: Much of what the chimps signed had just been signed to them. The signing chimps appeared to be responding at least in part to subtle cues from their trainers. Armed with this information, some critics went so far as to suggest that the chimps were modern equivalents of Clever Hans. Clever Hans was a horse who was famous for his mental powers in early twentieth-century Germany, until it was discovered that, rather than doing arithmetic, he was sensitive to minute physical cues in the people around him who knew the answers to the questions he was being asked. The question of the apes' potential was not completely settled by this study, since, as other researchers pointed out, children also interrupt and repeat parts of what adults say. Also, as Terrace himself was aware, the project had various shortcomings; for instance, Nim may have had too many trainers, and not all of them were equally proficient in ASL. Nim Chimpsky died in 2000 at the age of 26. The story of the project was recently chronicled by Hess (2008), and a major Hollywood film about this experiment, called *Project Nim,* came out in 2011.

Kanzi.   Although it may be true that apes are not capable of adult language as we know it, the chimpanzee studies have indicated that there are substantial similarities between very young children's and chimpanzees' abilities to engage in symbolic communication. Early chimpanzee studies used the common chimp *(Pan troglodytes)* and had the same self-limiting characteristic: The common chimp can become difficult, even dangerous, to work with once sexual maturity is attained.

Research by D. M. Rumbaugh and E. S. Savage-Rumbaugh with a pygmy chimp, or bonobo *(P. paniscus)* named Kanzi, who was born in 1980 and now lives at the Great Ape Trust of Iowa in Des Moines (Rumbaugh, Savage-Rumbaugh, King, & Taglialatela , 2011), led to new speculation about primate cultural and linguistic abilities. The bonobo was virtually unheard of until the mid-1970s, when they were found in the remote rain forests of the Democratic Republic of Congo. Bonobos are smaller, less aggressive, more social, more intelligent, and more communicative than the common chimp. Kanzi surprised his trainers when he acquired some manual signs merely by observing his mother's lessons. He has been the subject of an intensive longitudinal study, and he understands complex language and at least 500 spoken words. Studies of his understanding of spoken English show that he comprehends word order and basic syntax. For instance, if asked to "Put the milk in the jelly" or to "Put the jelly in the milk," Kanzi obligingly does so, proving that he is attending to language word order and not simply carrying out activities that are evident from the nonverbal situation. He became a father in 2010 with the birth of his son, Teco. Kanzi now has a complex social life; he makes tools and engages in artistic and musical activities, and his accomplishments have gone far beyond those of any of the earlier chimps. Kanzi's linguistic abilities remain at the level of a 2- or 3-year-old child. It is not clear whether his (or any nonhuman's) linguistic skills are on the same continuum as our own, or if they are qualitatively different (Trachsel, 2010). You can read about Kanzi and his companions online at **www.greatapetrust.org**.

The Biological Base: Humans

Language in humans is clearly dependent on their having a society in which to learn it, other humans to speak to, and the emotional motivation and intelligence to make it possible; humans have also evolved with specialized capacities for speech and neural mechanisms related to language. Recent work in genetics has pointed to a specific gene, *FOXP2*, that is related to speech and language and that may have been the result of a mutation that occurred in our ancestors about 120,000 years ago (Pääbo, 2003). It is clear, however, that no single gene could account for the complexity and robustness of human language. Other genes have also been implicated in language development, such as those referred to as ASPM and MCPH1, and current thinking in the molecular genetics world is that these genes are regulatory in nature and that they are part of a complex signaling system that affects many different traits (Misyak & Christiansen, 2011).

Children who are physiologically and psychologically intact will acquire the language of those around them if they grow up among people who speak to them. This human social interaction is necessary; there is no evidence that infants can acquire language from watching television, for instance. There are some strong arguments for the case that language is biologically determined—that it owes its existence to specialized structures in the brain and in the neurological systems of humans. Some of these biological specifications underlie the social and affective characteristics of infants that tie them to the adults around them and serve as precursors to language development. For instance, infants are intensely interested in human faces, and there is evidence that the infant brain contains neurons that are specialized for the identification of human faces and for the recognition of emotions in faces (Locke, 1993). As they interact with the people around them, infants build a social brain that helps direct them to the information that is important to process—speech sounds, for instance, and not a variety of environmental noises.

Researchers are currently intrigued by the discovery of **mirror neurons** and their possible role in cognitive, linguistic, and social development (Fogassi & Ferarri, 2007). Mirror neurons are a class of neurons that activate when an individual either engages in an activity or observes another engage in that activity, or hears associated sounds (Kohler, Keysers, Umiltà, Fogassi, Gallese, & Rizzolatti, 2002). Mirror neurons may be an integral part of what we recognize as empathy and imitation—the explanation, for instance, for why it is that when you stick your tongue out at a newborn baby, she then sticks her tongue out at you! One of the many implications for language development is the likelihood that when adults speak to babies, they are actually activating the infants' neural patterns for language.

Language-Sensitive Areas in the Brain.   Unlike our relatives the apes, humans have areas in the cerebral cortex that are known to be associated with language. Language, however, is not *in* those areas of the brain. The contemporary view is very much that language localization patterns result from the dynamic activity of neural networks that are constantly optimizing the storage and retrieval of information (Ross, 2010). The two hemispheres of the brain are not symmetrical (Geschwind, 1982). Most individuals, about 85 percent of the population, are right-handed, and almost all right-handers have their language functions represented in their left hemisphere. Of the left-handed population, perhaps half also have their language sensitive areas in the left hemisphere; therefore, the vast majority of the populace is **lateralized** for language in the left hemisphere. The right hemisphere, however, also participates in some aspects of language processing. For instance, recognition of the emotional tone of speech appears to be a right-hemisphere function.

Imaging techniques such as functional magnetic resonance imaging (fMRI) have made it possible to study the normal brain in action. Before imaging techniques were developed, most of our information about specialized areas came from the study of what happens when the brain is injured, through an accident, for instance, or as a result of a stroke. Damage to the language-sensitive areas of the brain results in **aphasia**, a generalized communication disorder with varying characteristics depending on the site of the lesion

(Goodglass, 1993). There are at least three well-established major language-related areas in the left hemisphere (see Figure 1.1).

- **Broca's area** in the left frontal region (inferior frontal gyrus) is very near to that part of the motor strip that controls the tongue and lips, and damage to Broca's area results in a typical aphasic syndrome, called *Broca's aphasia,* in which the patient has good comprehension but much difficulty with pronunciation and producing the little words of the language, such as articles and prepositions. For instance, when one patient seen in Boston was asked how he planned to spend the weekend at home, he replied, with labored articulation, "Boston College. Football. Saturday."

- **Wernicke's area** is located in the posterior left temporal lobe, near the auditory association areas of the brain. Damage to Wernicke's area produces an aphasia that is characterized by fluent speech with many **neologisms** (nonsense words) and poor comprehension. One patient with Wernicke's aphasia, when asked to name an ashtray, said, "That's a fremser." When he was later asked to point to the fremser, however, he had no idea what the examiner meant.

- The **arcuate fasciculus** is a band of subcortical fibers that connects Wernicke's area with Broca's area (see Figure 1.1). If you ask someone to repeat what you say, the incoming message is processed in Wernicke's area and then sent out over the arcuate fasciculus to Broca's area, where it is programmed for production. Patients with lesions in the arcuate fasciculus are unable to repeat; their disorder is called **conduction aphasia**. There are also areas of the brain known to be associated with written language; damage to the angular gyrus, for instance, impairs the ability to read.

---

figure 1.1   **Language Areas in the Left Hemisphere.**   Broca's area, at the foot of the motor strip, is involved in the programming of speech for production. Wernicke's area, adjacent to the auditory cortex, is involved in the comprehension of language we hear. The arcuate fasciculus is a bundle of subcortical fibers that connects Broca's and Wernicke's areas. In order to repeat a word we hear (e.g., *cat*), we process it first in Wernicke's area, and then send a representation of it via the arcuate fasciculus to Broca's area, where its spoken form is organized. Damage to the arcuate fasciculus results in conduction aphasia, characterized by an inability to repeat words.

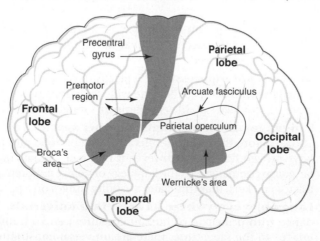

A child aged 5 or 6 who suffers left-brain damage will in all likelihood recover complete use and comprehension of language. However, adults who become aphasic are liable to remain so if they do not recover in the first half-year after their injury. Specialized language areas of the brain are found in adults, but there is evidence that in young children, the neural circuits are not yet so firmly committed, and the nonlanguage hemisphere can take over in the event of damage to the dominant hemisphere.

The brains of infants are not fully formed and organized at birth. The brains of newborns have many fewer synapses (connections) than those of adults. By the age of about 2 years, the number of synapses reaches adult levels, and then increases rapidly between the ages of 4 and 10, far exceeding adult levels. During this period of synaptic growth, there is a concurrent pruning process as connections that are not used die off. This process may help to explain the neurological bases of sensitive or critical periods in development. If, for instance, an infant does not hear language or does not establish an emotional bond with an adult, the neural networks that underlie language and emotion may be weakened. By the age of 15 or 16, the number of synapses has returned to adult levels.

humans *

Special Characteristics.   In examining the attempts to teach language to apes, we saw that language is probably unique to our species; the specialized areas of the brain contribute to that uniqueness. Human beings, of course, also have unique cognitive abilities and unique social settings in which to acquire language. These are discussed in later chapters—the intent here is to describe briefly the neuroanatomical foundations that make language acquisition possible. As Eric Lenneberg (1967) pointed out, language development in humans is associated with other maturational events. The appearance of language is a developmental milestone, roughly correlated with the onset of walking.

In addition to possessing specialized brain structures, humans, unlike other creatures, have a long list of adaptations in such things as the development of their heads, faces, vocal cords, and larynxes, and the ability to coordinate making speech sounds with breathing and swallowing. Humans perform a remarkably complex (and dangerous) set of actions when they engage in everyday activities such as having a talk over lunch. As noted earlier, our ape relatives do not have the capacity for speech; vocal tract reconstructions have also shown that even Neanderthal men and women had quite limited vocalizing capacity and would have been incapable of the rapidly articulated speech common to all modern humans, who typically produce about 140 words a minute in ordinary conversation. With the evolution of *Homo sapiens,* the position of the larynx was lowered, and rapid, clear speech became a physical possibility (Lieberman, 2011).

Lenneberg (1967) listed a number of additional features as evidence that language is specific to humans and uniform across our species in its major characteristics:

1. **The onset of speech is regular.** The order of appearance of developmental milestones, including speech, is regular in the species—it is not affected by culture or the language to be learned.
2. **Speech is not suppressible.** Typically developing children learn to talk if they are in contact with older speakers. The wide variations that exist within and across cultures have all provided suitable environments for children to learn language.
3. **Language cannot be taught to other species.** Lenneberg made this claim in the 1960s, before there were results from the bonobo and parrot studies, and time may have proven him right. However, it is also clear that chimpanzees can be taught sign language comparable to the language of young children and parrots can do more than ask for crackers; thus this claim's validity hinges on a particular definition of language.
4. **Languages everywhere have certain universals.** They are structured in accordance with principles of human cognition, and a human infant can learn any language. At the same time, there are universal constraints on the kinds of rules that children can learn. The universals that are found in all languages include phonology,

grammar, and semantics. These systematic aspects of language, along with another universal, the existence of social rules for language use, provide the research arena for developmental psycholinguistics.

The Structure of Language: Learning the System

Competence and Performance

A speaker who knows the syntactic rules of a language is said to have *linguistic competence*. Competence in this case refers to the inner, largely unconscious, knowledge of the rules, not to the way the person speaks on any particular occasion. The expression of the rules in everyday speech is *performance*. In the normal course of events, speakers produce utterances that include false starts, slips of the tongue, and various other errors. These are performance errors and are not thought to reflect the speakers' underlying competence. There is also a general assumption among linguists that, within a given linguistic community, all adults who are native speakers of the language and not neurologically impaired in some way share linguistic competence; this claim, however, has never been substantiated and there is increasing evidence that, though all typically developing children acquire language, they do not all do so in the same way, nor do they all arrive at the same level of competence (Arnon & Clark, 2011) It is possible to find out a great deal about adults' syntax by asking them to judge the grammatical acceptability of a sentence. However, in studying children, researchers must either rely on performance for clues to competence or design clever experiments to probe inner knowledge, since young children do not have the metalinguistic ability required to discuss questions of "grammaticality."

When children learn language, what is it that they must learn? Language has many subsystems having to do with sound, grammar, meaning, vocabulary, and knowing the right way to say something on a particular occasion in order to accomplish a specific purpose. Knowing the language entails knowing its **phonology**, **morphology**, **syntax**, and **semantics**, as well as its social rules, or **pragmatics**. The speaker who knows all this has acquired *communicative competence*.

Phonology

What are the sounds of English? Although we all speak the language, without specific training it is difficult to describe the sounds we make when we speak, and even harder to explain the rules for their combination. Phonology includes all of the important sounds, the rules for combining them to make words, and such things as the stress and intonation patterns that accompany them. Each language has its own set of important sounds, which are actually categories of sounds that include a number of variations. For instance, in English we pronounce the sound /t/ many different ways: At the beginning of a word like *top* it is pronounced with a strong aspiration, or puff of air (you can check this by holding the back of your hand near your mouth and saying *top* vigorously). We pronounce a word like *stop* without the puff of air, unaspirated. Some speakers produce a different, unreleased /t/ when they say a word like *hat* at the end of a sentence: They leave their tongues in place at the point of articulation. Many speakers pronounce yet another kind of /t/ in a word like *Manhattan* by releasing the air through their noses at the end. A phonetician would hear these /t/ sounds as four different sounds: aspirated, unaspirated, unreleased, and nasally released. For ordinary English speakers, however, these are all just one sound. A group of similar sounds that are regarded as all the same by the speakers of a language are called **phonemes**. The different /t/ sounds just described are all part of one /t/ phoneme in English. Children have to learn to recognize and produce the phonemes of their own language and to combine those phonemes into words and sentences with the right sorts of intonational patterns. Some parts of the system, such as consonant-vowel combinations, are acquired early on. Others are not acquired until well into the elementary school years: for instance, the ability to distinguish between the stress patterns of *HOT dog* (frankfurter, at the picnic) and *hot DOG* (Ruby, at the beach) when the words are presented without a context (Vogel & Raimy, 2002).

English has some sounds that are rarely found in other languages of the world, such as the *th* sound in *this*. Many African languages contain phonemic clicks rather similar to the sounds we make in English when we say what is written as "tsk tsk" or when we encourage a horse to go faster. In some languages, tone is a phoneme: In Chinese, a rising or falling tone on a word can change its meaning entirely. When the tones are produced correctly, the sentence "Mama ma ma ma?" means "Did mother chide the horse?"

Morphology

When a new word like *abdominoplasty* comes into the English language, adult speakers can immediately tell what its plural is; they do not have to look it up in a dictionary or consult with an expert. They are able to pluralize a word that they have never heard before because they know the English inflectional morphological system. A **morpheme** is the smallest unit of meaning in a language; it cannot be broken into any smaller parts that have meaning. Words can consist of one or more morphemes. The words *cat* and *danger* each consist of one morpheme, which is called a **free morpheme** because it can stand alone. **Bound morphemes,** on the other hand, cannot stand alone and are always found attached to free morphemes; they appear affixed to free morphemes as prefixes, suffixes, or within the word as infixes. *Happiness, unclear,* and *singing* contain the bound morphemes *-ness, un-,* and *-ing*. Bound morphemes can be used to change one word into another word that may be a different part of speech; for instance, *-ness* turns the adjective *happy* into the noun *happiness*. In this case, they are called **derivational morphemes** because they can be used to derive new words.

Other bound morphemes do not change the basic word's meaning so much as they modify it to indicate such things as tense, person, number, case, and gender. These variations on a basic word are *inflections,* and the morphemes that signal these changes are *inflectional morphemes*. Languages like Latin, Russian, and Hungarian are highly inflected. The verb *to love (amare)* in Latin has six separate forms in the present tense: the singular forms *amo, amas,* and *amat* (I love, you love, he/she loves) and the plural forms *amamus, amatis,* and *amant* (we love, you love, they love).

Compared with Latin, English has few verb inflections in the present tense: an added *-s* for the third person (he *loves*) and no inflection for other persons (I, we, you, they *love*). Latin indicates the subject and object of its sentences using case inflections—*agricola amat puellam* and *puellam amat agricola* both mean "The farmer loves the girl." The endings of the words mark the subject and the object. English does not have case endings on its nouns: Whether the girl loves the farmer or the farmer loves the girl is indicated entirely by word order. Grammar teachers, perhaps influenced by their knowledge of Latin, have tended to confuse the issue in English by referring to nouns as being in the subjective or objective case when, in fact, there are no separate noun case forms in English. Pronouns, on the other hand, have subjective, objective, and possessive forms: *I, me,* and *my*.

English inflectional morphology includes the progressive of the verb (e.g., *singing*); the past, pronounced with /d/, /t/, or /əd/ *(played, hopped, landed);* and the third-person singular verb and the noun plural and possessive, all of which use /z/, /s/, or /əz/ in spoken language *(dogs, cats, watches)*. Whether one says, "He dogs my steps" (verb), "It's the dog's dish" (possessive), or "I have ten dogs" (plural), the inflected form is pronounced in exactly the same way. The forms of the inflections vary depending on the last sound of the word being inflected, and there is a complex set of rules that adult speakers know (at some level) that enables them to make a plural or past tense of a word that they have never heard before.

One task for the student of language development is to determine whether children have knowledge of morphology and, if so, how it is acquired and to what extent it resembles the rule system that adults follow.

Syntax

The syntactic system includes the rules for how to combine words into acceptable phrases and sentences and how to transform sentences into other sentences. A competent speaker can take a basic sentence like "The cat bites the dog" and make a number of transformations of it: "The cat bit the dog," "The cat didn't bite the dog," "Did the cat bite the dog?," and "Wasn't the dog bitten by the cat?" Knowledge of syntax allows the speaker to generate an almost endless number of new sentences and to recognize those that are not grammatically acceptable. If you heard a nonsense sentence like "The daksy wug wasn't miggled by the mimsy zibber," you could not know what happened because the vocabulary is unfamiliar. On the other hand, the morphology and syntax of the sentence convey a great deal of information, and with this information you could make a number of new, perfectly grammatical sentences: "The wug is daksy," "The zibber did not miggle the wug," and "The zibber is mimsy."

There is a great deal of controversy among researchers as to whether young children just learning language are acquiring syntactic structures, that is, grammatical rules, or whether it is more reasonable to characterize their early utterances in terms of the semantic relations they are trying to express. The child who says, "Mommy eat lunch," can be said to have learned to produce subject–verb–object constructions and to be following English syntactic rules specifying that the subject comes first in active sentences. (Even very young children do not say, "Lunch eat Mommy.") To describe the language of young children, however, it is probably more useful to note the kinds of semantic relations the children are using. In this case the child is expressing knowledge that an action (eat) is taking place and that there is an agent (Mom) and an object (lunch).

Once children begin to produce longer sentences, however, they add the grammatical words of the language and begin to build sentences according to syntactic rules. They learn how to make negatives, questions, compound sentences, passives, and imperatives. Later, they add very complex structures, including embedded forms. The child who early on was limited to sentences like "Mommy eat lunch" can eventually comprehend and produce "The lunch that Grandpa cooked the baby sitter was eaten by Mommy" in full confidence that the caregiver was neither cooked by Grandpa nor eaten by Mom.

Semantics

The semantic system includes our mental dictionary, or lexicon. Word meanings are complicated to learn; words are related to one another in complex networks, and awareness of words—for example, the ability to think about words, comes later than does word use. A very young child may use a word that occurs in adult language, but that word does not mean exactly the same thing, nor does it have the same internal status for the child as it does for the adult. Two-year-olds who say "doggie," for instance, may call sheep, cows, cats, and horses "doggie," or they may use the word in reference to a particular dog, without knowing that it refers to a whole class of animals. Vocabulary is structured hierarchically, and words are attached to one another in semantic networks. Dogs are a class of animals, and the adult who knows the meaning of *dog* also knows, for instance, that it belongs to a group known as domestic animals, it is a pet, it is related to wolves, it is animate, and so on. Studying semantic development in children involves examining how they acquire the semantic system, beginning with simple vocabulary. Ultimately, it includes studying their metalinguistic knowledge, which enables them to notice the words in their language and comment on them.

The Social Rules for Language Use

Linguistic competence involves knowing how to construct grammatically acceptable sentences. Language, however, must be used in a social setting to accomplish various ends.

Speakers who know how to use language *appropriately* have more than linguistic competence; they have communicative competence, a term first used by Dell Hymes (1972). Pragmatics, another term for the social uses of language, refers to the use of language to express one's intentions and get things done in the world. Adult pragmatics may include many interpersonal or social functions such as denying, refusing, blaming, offering condolences, and flattering, and even very young children use pragmatic functions such as labeling and demanding.

Communicative competence includes being able to express one's intent appropriately in varying social situations. The importance of knowing the right forms becomes obvious when social rules are violated. Consider the use of directives. If you are seated in an aisle seat of a bus, next to a stranger, and you are cold because the window is open, you can express your intent in a syntactically correct sentence: "Shut that window." This could lead to an angry reaction or, at the very least, to the impression that you are a rude person. If, instead, you say, "I wonder if you would mind shutting the window?" compliance and the beginning of a pleasant conversation will probably follow. Knowing the politeness rules of language is part of communicative competence.

Communicative competence includes important topics such as the ability to make conversation. Making conversation requires various skills, including, for instance, knowing something about what your listener already knows. Some conversational principles we follow include the following (Grice, 1975):

1. **Say as much as you need to, but not too much.** For instance, if a mother asks a child where her notebook is, and the child answers, "Julie has it," this is fine if her mother knows who Julie is. If the child says "Julie has it. She's my sister and also your daughter," she is being sarcastic or humorous.
2. **Be truthful.** Participants in a conversation expect one another not to lie or embellish the facts.
3. **Be relevant.** Contributions to the conversation are expected to be relevant. If a child responds to the question, "What do you like for lunch?" by saying, "I like my kitty," she is violating the relevance principle (or exhibiting serious antisocial tendencies).
4. **Present information in a logical order.** To say, "We put on our pajamas and took a bath," violates this principle of logical order, since presumably bathing precedes putting on pajamas.

Adults, of course, violate these conversational rules in order to achieve certain very human ends: to be ironic, for instance, or to make a joke, or perhaps to be deceptive or insulting. Every type of interaction between individuals requires observance of social conventions, and adults do not leave children's development of these rules to chance: Whereas they may not correct syntactic violations except in the most superficial cases (see Chapter 5), they are active participants in their children's use of the appropriate (often polite) forms (Ely & Gleason, 2006). Just as there are phonological and grammatical rules, there are also rules for the use of language in social context. Mature language users know how to speak like men or women, to conduct discourse, and to speak in appropriate ways to different people. They can talk baby talk to babies and be formal and deferential when appearing in court. All of these are part of communicative competence, which is the goal of language development.

The Study of Language Development

The Ancient Roots of Child Language Study

Probably the first recorded account of a language acquisition study is found in the work of the Greek historian Herodotus. Herodotus, sometimes called the father of history, lived from about 484 to 425 B.C.E. In Book 2 of his *History,* he relates the story of the ancient

Egyptian king Psamtik I (664–610 B.C.E.), also called Psammetichus, who wanted to prove that the Egyptians were the original human race.

In order to do this, Psamtik ordered a shepherd to raise two children, caring for their needs but not speaking to them. "His object herein was to know, after the indistinct babblings of infancy were over, what word they would first articulate." The king believed that the children would begin to speak in the language of the oldest group of humans, without ever hearing any language. This is perhaps the strongest version of a nativist theory of language development that one could have: Babies arrive in the world with a specific language already in their brains.

When the children were about 2 years old, the shepherd went to their quarters one day. They ran up to him with their hands outstretched, saying "Becos." *Becos* was not a word that anyone recognized. The king, according to Herodotus, asked around the kingdom and eventually was told that *becos* meant "bread" in the Phrygian language, whereupon the Egyptians gave up their claim to being the oldest race of humans and decided that they were in *second* place, behind the Phrygians.

Even though interest in language development has ancient roots, the systematic study of children's language is fairly recent, in part because the science of linguistics, with its special analytic techniques, came of age in the twentieth century. In earlier times the structural nature of language was not well understood, and research tended to concentrate on the kinds of things that children said rather than on their acquisition of productive linguistic subsystems.

Studies in the Nineteenth and Twentieth Centuries

Many studies of children, including notes on their language, were published in Germany, France, and England during the latter half of the nineteenth century and the early years of the twentieth century. One of the main early figures in the United States in the field of developmental psychology, G. Stanley Hall, taught at Clark University in Worcester, Massachusetts. Hall (1907) was interested in "the content of children's minds." Hall inspired a school of American students of child language.

The kinds of questions that child language researchers asked during this period were related primarily to philosophical inquiries into human nature. This was true of Charles Darwin (1877), who kept careful diaries on the language development of one of his sons. Many of these early investigations included valuable insights into language. The early studies were typically in the form of diaries with observations of the authors' own children. Notable exceptions were studies of "wild children" and isolated children who had failed to acquire language. Just as in antiquity, there was philosophical interest in the effects of isolation on language development; that interest has been sustained to the present day. *The Wild Boy of Aveyron,* a landmark study of a feral child, Victor, was written in the eighteenth century (and retold by Lane, 1979), and the study of Genie, an American girl who was kept isolated from other humans, was published not too long ago (Curtiss, 1977; Lapointe, 2005).

During the first half of the twentieth century, many psychologists still kept diary records of their children. In the field of education, children's language was studied in order to arrive at norms, to describe gender and social class differences, and to search for the causes and cures of developmental difficulties. Educational psychologists frequently used group tests with large numbers of children, and there was a great interest in such things as the average sentence length used by children at different grade levels, or the kinds of errors they made in grammar or pronunciation (McCarthy, 1954).

Research from the 1950s to the Present

The mid-1950s saw a revolution in child language studies. Work on descriptive linguistics (Gleason, 1955) and the early work of Noam Chomsky (1957) provided new models of

One of the first child language research subjects, "Adam" grew up to be an author and public speaker.

language for researchers to explore. At the same time, a behaviorist theory of language put forth by B. F. Skinner (1957) inspired other groups of investigators to design studies aimed at testing this learning theory.

Psycholinguistics came into being as a field when linguists and psychologists combined the techniques of their disciplines to investigate whether the systems described by the linguist had psychological reality in the minds of speakers. The linguistic description of English might, for instance, point out that the plural of words ending in /s/ or /z/ is formed by adding /əz/, as, for example, in *kiss* and *kisses*. A task for the psycholinguist was to demonstrate that the linguistic description matched what speakers actually do, that speakers have a "rule" for the formation of the plural that is isomorphic (i.e., identical in form) with the linguist's descriptive rule. Some of the earliest questions in cognitive science dealt with the mental representation of the units of language.

In the decade of the 1960s, after the powerful grammatical model advanced by Chomsky became widely known, there was an explosion of research into children's acquisition of syntax. The 1960s were characterized by studies of grammar; many projects studied a small number of children over a period of time, writing grammars of the children's developing language. At Harvard University, for instance, a group of researchers, many of whom were to become prominent individually, worked with Roger Brown (1973) on a project that studied the language development of three children called Adam, Eve, and Sarah (not their real names). Members of Brown's research group visited the children once a month in their homes and made tape recordings of each child with his or her parents, engaged in everyday activities. The recordings were brought back to the laboratory and transcribed, and the resulting transcriptions were studied by a team of faculty and graduate students that met in a weekly seminar. Adam, Eve, and Sarah became very famous in the linguistics community. Although the ethics of research require us to maintain the anonymity of participants unless they agree otherwise, we were recently in touch with grownup Adam, who gave us permission to provide an update about him. Adam grew up to be a prolific author, public speaker, CEO, and philanthropist, who himself has offered a unique framework on effective human interaction called Intelligent Influence.

As the 1960s drew to a close, the dominance of syntax in research gave way to a broadening interest that included the context in which children's language emerges and an emphasis on the kinds of semantic relations children are trying to express in their early utterances. The early 1970s saw a spate of studies on the language addressed to children; many of these were conducted to shed light on the innateness controversy. Researchers wanted to know whether children were innately programmed to discover the rules of language all by themselves, or whether adults provided them with help or even with language learning lessons.

Studies of the 1980s and 1990s included all of the traditional linguistic topics: phonology, morphology, syntax, semantics, and pragmatics. Now, in the second decade of the twenty-first century, there is growing interest in cross-cultural research in language development and in understanding how language development interfaces with other aspects of children's social and psychological development; in acquiring a language, children become members of a society, with all of its unique cultural practices and belief systems.

Cross-cultural studies and studies of children in nontypical developmental situations are also vital to our ultimate understanding of the process of language acquisition. What happens, for instance, if a child spends her first year in one language community and then, just as she is about to begin speaking, she finds herself in a new family that speaks a new and totally unrelated language? This is the case with international adoptions. In the past few years, thousands of young children have come to the United States from a variety of countries. These children are of great interest to the linguistics community. A recent meta-analysis of a number of studies of internationally adopted children points out that these children are essentially learning a first language for the second time; there is great variability in their language outcomes, with adoption before the age of one year one of the best predictors that their language will be comparable to that of their non-adopted peers (Scott, Roberts & Glennon, 2011.)

In addition to basic linguistic studies, social class and gender differences in language, bilingualism, stylistic variation in acquisition and use, and the language addressed to children are examples of topics found in current journals and on the programs of professional meetings. While historically, research with typical and atypical language learners often was conducted and reported in different settings and journals, researchers are increasingly integrating work across populations to gain better insights into the bases of normal and disordered language development.

The study of language acquisition has obviously changed in major ways in the twenty-first century. It has become more international and interdisciplinary, and researchers now make use of sophisticated contemporary technology. Early studies were typically of monolingual, middle-class, English-speaking children. There is now a community of scholars from all over the world, many of whom are members of the International Association for the Study of Child Language (IASCL). Study of many different languages and cultures is changing our ideas about what might be universal in acquisition. The inclusion of atypical populations and dual language learners is helping build theory. At the same time this research provides information that has real-world applications in the development of both remedial programs for children at risk and educational programs for children who, for example, speak different languages at home and at school. Language development researchers now acknowledge that most children in the world are not monolingual.

Research Methods

Modern technology has made it possible to collect accurate data on language development and for researchers around the world to share data and data analysis programs. In collecting new data, researchers must obtain informed consent from the participants (or their parents) and follow the strict ethical guidelines set down by their institutions and by government funding agencies. Psamtik's study could never be conducted under current scientific research guidelines.

Equipment.   Increasingly sophisticated audio and video equipment has greatly simplified data collection. Powerful computers with immense memory capacity make it possible to conduct research that was unimaginable just a few years ago. For instance, in a remarkable recent project, Deb Roy, a researcher at MIT with an engineering background, has recorded 230,000 hours of the home life of his son over the first three years of his life, including everything that was said to the child as well as every child utterance, making it possible to follow the evolution, in context, of every word that the child acquired. Deb Roy's data are not yet fully analyzed, but you can hear him talk about the study and see some striking computer landscapes of the child's early words online at **www.ted.com/talks/ deb_roy_the_birth_of_a_word.html**. The Internet includes many video clips of typical child language, as well as samples from people who have impaired or exceptional language skills. These illustrate a variety of the concepts that we will cover in this text. In addition, several other excellent TED talks on language development, including one by Patricia Kuhl, can be seen online. TED is an acronym for Technology, Entertainment, Design, and the name of a nonprofit organization devoted to promoting "Ideas Worth Spreading."

Studies of prelinguistic infants or of cortical reactions to linguistic stimuli at any age require especially sensitive recording equipment and may use sophisticated imaging technology. Imaging is a way of observing mental activity related to language. It can show if a very young infant is able to distinguish among speech sounds, because if the infant notices a difference, there will be some kind of reaction in the brain that can be measured (Kuhl, 2010). Imaging devices are able to do this in various noninvasive ways:

They can measure *electrical changes* in the brain, because brain activity produces electrical current; **event-related potentials (ERPs)** measure changes in current. **Magnetoencephalography (MEG)** measures the tiny magnetic changes that accompany changes in electrical activity.

They can measure *blood flow,* because increased brain activity is accompanied by increased blood flow to the area that is activated; **functional magnetic resonance imaging (fMRI)** measures changes in oxygen; increased blood flow to an activated area carries more oxygen with it. **Near-Infrared Spectroscopy (NIRS)** also measures blood changes, but in this case the machine records the changes in hemoglobin that accompany increased blood flow.

With the exception of event-related potential equipment, imaging is expensive and not easily accessible. Imaging studies also require rather restricted and careful experimental tasks, rather than observation of natural language use in context. Many language development studies, however, use standard laboratory equipment, and others are conducted with easily acquired video and audio recorders. This makes it possible to film in the laboratory or in participants' homes with a minimum of intrusion. Regardless of the method of recording, it is necessary to make a transcription of the data for analysis. This involves writing down as exactly as possible everything that is said on the recording, preferably following a standard format that makes computer analysis possible (see Figure 1.2). The major program that researchers use to analyze language samples is called CLAN (Computerized Language ANalysis), a tool developed by the CHILDES (Child Language Data Exchange System) project (you can visit the project and its open-access databases and freely distributed software at **http://childes.psy.cmu.edu/**).

Research Design.   Language development studies can be either *cross-sectional* or *longitudinal* in their design. Cross-sectional studies use two or more groups of participants. If, for instance, you wanted to study the development of the negative between the ages of 2 and 4, you could study a group of 2-year-olds and a group of 4-year-olds and then describe the differences in the two groups' use of negation. Longitudinal studies follow individual participants over time; one might study the same children's use of negatives at specified periods between the ages of 2 and 4.

Cross-sectional studies make it possible to obtain a great deal of data about a large number of participants in a short time; one doesn't have to wait two years to get results. Longitudinal designs are used to study individuals over time when questions such as the persistence of traits or the effects of early experience are relevant. If, for instance, you wanted to know whether children who are late talkers have problems learning to read, you would have to use a longitudinal design.

Both cross-sectional and longitudinal studies can be either *observational* or *experimental*. Observational studies involve a minimum of intrusion by the researcher. Naturalistic observational studies attempt to capture behavior as it occurs in real life; for instance, one might record and analyze family speech at the dinner table. Controlled observational studies can be carried out in various settings, including the laboratory, where the researcher provides certain constants for all participants. Fathers might come to the laboratory with their daughters and be observed reading them a book provided by the researcher. Observational research can indicate what kinds of behaviors correlate with one another, but it cannot reveal which behavior might cause another.

In experimental research, the researcher has some control and can manipulate variables. Typical experimental research includes:

- Hypotheses about what will happen
- An experimental group of participants that receives the treatment (training, for instance) and a control group that receives no special treatment
- Independent variables, manipulated by the experimenter (training, exposure to a TV program, etc.)
- Dependent variables: the behaviors that are measured (for instance, the participants' use of a particular grammatical form)
- Randomization: assignment of participants at random to control or experimental conditions
- Standardization of procedures (all participants receive the same instructions, etc.)

---

figure 1.2   **Sample Transcript.**   This excerpt from CHILDES can be analyzed by a number of CLAN programs that can automatically compute MLU, list all vocabulary by speaker, and derive many standardized measures.

@Begin
@Participants: CHI Charlie Child, MOT Mother, FAT Father
@Date: 7-JUL-1996
@Filename: CHARLIE.CHA
@Situation: Home Dinner Conversation.
*MOT: did you tell Dad what we did today?
*MOT: who'd we see?
*CHI: who?
*MOT: remember?
*CHI: Judy and my friend.
*MOT: did we see Michael?
*CHI: yes.
*FAT: was Mike at the beach?
*CHI: no.
*FAT: that's because he had work to do.
*FAT: do you remember the name of the beach you went to?
*CHI: not this time.
*FAT: you don't remember it this time?
*FAT: it was Winger-: what?
*FAT: Winger-Beach?
*CHI: yes.
*FAT: Winger Sheek Beach.
*CHI: Winger Sheek Beach.
*FAT: that's the one.
*CHI: Winger Beach.
*MOT: did you go swimming, Charlie?
*CHI: I went swimming, Dad.
*FAT: you did?
*FAT: did you wear water wings?
*CHI: no.
*FAT: no?
@End

If you wanted to see whether training makes a difference in the acquisition of the passive voice, for instance, you might take a group of thirty 3-year-olds and randomly assign them to two groups, a control group and an experimental group of fifteen children each. The experimental group would receive training in the passive; the control group, no special treatment. Finally, both groups could be asked to describe some pictures they had never seen before, and differential use of the passive would be recorded. If the trained group used passives and the control group did not, there would be evidence that training causes accelerated acquisition of one aspect of grammar. Experimental research can easily be replicated in the laboratory, but it may not be easily generalized to the outside world.

In addition to clear-cut observational and experimental methods, language development researchers use a variety of research techniques. These include *standard assessment measures,* in which participants can be compared or evaluated on the basis of their responses to published standardized language tests. These are useful for indicating whether a participant's language is developing at a typical rate or whether some facet of development is out of line with the others.

Imitation is a technique used by many researchers: You simply ask the child to say what you say. Imitation reveals a great deal about children's language, since they typically cannot imitate sentences that are beyond their stage of development. This is true of adults as well—try imitating a few sentences in Bulgarian the next time you meet someone from Sofia who is willing to say them to you.

Elicitation is a technique that works well when a particular language form is the target and you want to give your participants all the help they need (short of the answer itself). In investigating the plural through elicitation, you might show your participants a picture, first of one and then of two birdlike creatures, and say, "This is a wug. Now there is another one. There are two of them. There are two?" The participant obligingly fills in "wugs." This technique works well with aphasic patients, especially severe Broca's aphasics who have very little voluntary speech.

The *interview* is an old technique, but one that can be very effective if the researcher has the time to do more than ask a list of questions and fill in a form. Researchers of the Piagetian school frequently use an interview type called the *clinical method.* This is an open-ended interview in which the sequence of questions depends on the answers the participant has given. In studying metalinguistic awareness, the investigator might ask a series of questions, such as "Is *horse* a word? Why? (Or why not?) What is a word? How do you know? What is your favorite word? Why?" The choice of method depends very much on the theoretical inclination of the investigator. Since without some sort of intervention on the part of the researcher it might take a very long time before participants say the kinds of things that interest us, many ingenious methods for studying language production have been designed (Menn & Bernstein Ratner, 2000).

CHILDES

As noted earlier, one of the most significant events in language development research has been the creation of the Child Language Data Exchange System **CHILDES**. CHILDES was launched in 1984 at Carnegie Mellon University under the direction of Brian MacWhinney and Catherine Snow (Berko Gleason & Thompson, 2002; MacWhinney, 2000). The system is made up of three main parts:

1. Transcription rules for transcribing spoken language in a standardized way that makes computer analysis possible. The rules are called **CHAT** (acronym for Codes for the Human Analysis of Transcripts). Figure 1.2 shows a sample transcript.
2. Computer programs that can run on the CHAT files to do such things as instantly list every word used by a child. The programs are called **CLAN** (acronym for Computerized Language Analysis programs). They can also search for groups of words, compute

linguistic attributes of utterances, and analyze discourse patterns between participants in conversations.

3. The database: Digital files in 25 different languages, containing language data that have been contributed from over one hundred research projects around the world.

CHILDES is web-based and available without cost to researchers everywhere. A visit to its main website at **http://childes.psy.cmu.edu** is recommended. There you will find the programs and data, as well as much useful information. Many powerful computer programs are included in CLAN (MacWhinney, 2000). Some of the advantages of CHILDES are that it allows (1) data sharing among researchers, who can test their hypotheses on many more participants, (2) increased precision and standardization in coding, and (3) automation of many coding procedures. CLAN programs can operate on any or all speakers' output and can automatically derive the mean length of utterance (see Chapter 5), a total list of words used as well as their frequency, and other data of immense value to the language researcher. Data from many studies in English and other languages are available; even older studies, such as Brown's famous work on Adam, Eve, and Sarah from the 1960s, have been scanned and entered, thus making these data available to anyone who wants them.

One of the most recent developments in CHILDES is an interactive Internet resource that links transcripts with digitized video and audio data: It is possible to read the transcript online, view the participants, and hear the actual speech, all at the same time (MacWhinney, 2001).

SUMMARY

Babies seek the love and attention of their caregivers. Before they are even 1 year old, they are able to make fine discriminations among the speech sounds they hear, and they begin to communicate nonverbally with those around them. Young children acquire the basic components of their native language in just a few years: *phonology, morphology, semantics, syntax,* and the social rules for language use, often called *pragmatics.* By the time they are of school age, children control all of the major grammatical and semantic features. Language development, however, proceeds throughout the life cycle; as individuals grow older, they acquire new skills at every stage of their lives, and in the declining years they are vulnerable to a specific set of language disabilities. To elucidate both the scope and the nature of language development, this book is written from a life-span perspective.

Babies begin to acquire language during their first months, long before they say their first words; language is built upon an earlier affective communicative base. Midway through the first year, infants begin to babble, an event seen by many researchers as evidence of linguistic capacity. Near their first birthdays, infants say their first words. Early words, word meanings, and word combinations have universal characteristics, since toddlers' language is similar across cultures. Children's progress toward learning the particular grammatical structure of their own language follows a predictable order that is common to all children learning that language.

Although there are universal characteristics, there are also patterns of individual variation in language development. Different theories of language development emphasize *innate mechanisms, learning principles, cognitive characteristics, social interaction,* and the *gestural-usage* bases of language.

During the school years, children perfect their knowledge of complex grammar, and they learn to use language in many different social situations. They develop *metalinguistic awareness,* the ability to consider language as an object. At the same time, they learn another major linguistic system: the written language. The demands of literacy remove a child's language from the here and now and emphasize *decontextualized language.* Not all children learn to read with ease.

Teenagers develop a distinct personal linguistic style, and young adults must acquire the linguistic register common to their occupations. With advancing age, numerous linguistic changes take place; there is some inevitable loss of word-finding ability, but vocabulary and narrative skill may improve.

Human language has special properties that have led many researchers to conclude that it is *species specific* and *species uniform.* Humans can talk about any part of their experience. Sea mammals employ communicative systems of whistles and grunts, and many birds have been shown to have a variety of meaningful calls. None of these systems equals human language, however, which is *productive,* has *semanticity,* and offers the possibility of *displacement.*

During the past seventy-five years, many researchers have attempted to discover whether language is really unique to humans or if it can be learned by other species. Recent studies have shown that African grey parrots and dogs have some sophisticated linguistic abilities. Early studies that tried to teach spoken language to chimpanzees showed conclusively that primates cannot speak as humans do. More recent studies have taught American Sign Language (ASL) to chimpanzees and have met with mixed results. The signing chimps may be responding at least in part to subtle cues from their trainers, but the question of the apes' potential is not completely settled. These studies have shown that there are substantial similarities between very young children's and chimpanzees' abilities to engage in symbolic communication.

Language development requires social interaction, but spoken language in humans is possible only because we have evolved with specialized neural mechanisms that subserve language. These include special areas in the brain, such as *Broca's area, Wernicke's area,* and the *arcuate fasciculus.* Other evidence of humans' biological disposition for language includes the regular onset of speech and the facts that speech is not suppressible, language cannot be taught to other species, and languages everywhere have universals.

The study of language development includes research into major linguistic subsystems. The *phonological system* is composed of the significant sounds of the language and the rules for their combination; the *morphological system* includes the minimal units that carry meaning; *syntax* refers to the rules by which sentences are constructed in a given language; and the *semantic systems* contain the meanings of words and the relationships between them. Finally, to function in society, speakers must know the social or *pragmatic rules* for language use. Individuals must be able to comprehend and produce all of these systems in order to attain *communicative competence.*

Although interest in language development has ancient roots, the scientific study of this subject began in the 1950s, with the appearance of new linguistic and psychological theories of language that gave birth to the combined discipline now known as *developmental psycholinguistics.* Developmental psycholinguists use all of the research techniques, designs, and resources employed by psychologists and linguists, as well as a few that are unique, such as CHILDES, a shared computerized bank of language data, as well as specialized transcription formats and computer programs for analyzing language.

SUGGESTED PROJECTS

1. Choose three related articles on language development from the *Journal of Child Language,* or from another journal, such as *Applied Psycholinguistics.* Write an introduction, explaining what the major questions of the research are, and then, for each article, describe the methods used by the authors, the participants, any special equipment that was needed, and the nature of the results. In a separate discussion section, compare the results of the studies.

2. List some stereotypic notions people have about language development. For instance: Girls talk more than boys. Babies say "goo goo, ga ga." Children call rabbits "wabbits." Children can learn a language watching television, and so on. Pick one of these beliefs

and design a study to find out if it is true. Since this is a thought experiment, you don't have to worry about how long it would take or how much it would cost, but be explicit in describing exactly how you would proceed, what data you would need to collect, and how you would analyze it in order to answer your question.

3. Read papers on studies with the border collie Chaser, the gorilla Koko, the chimp Kanzi, and the parrot Alex. Summarize the language claims that are made for each of these animals and draw some conclusions of your own about which of them you think comes closest to having language.

SUGGESTED READINGS

Berko Gleason, J., & Thompson, R. B. (2002). Out of the baby book and into the computer: Child language research comes of age. *Contemporary Psychology, APA Review of Books, 47,* 4, 391–394.

Brown, R. W. (1970). The first sentences of child and chimpanzee. In

R. W. Brown (Ed.), *Psycholinguistics.* New York: Macmillan.

Pilley, J. W., & Reid, A. K. (2011). Border collie comprehends object names as verbal referents. *Behavioural Processes,* 86(2), 184-195.

KEY WORDS

American Sign Language (ASL)
aphasia
arcuate fasciculus
autism spectrum disorder
bound morpheme
Broca's area
CHAT
child-directed speech (CDS)
CHILDES
CLAN
communicative competence
comprehension
conduction aphasia
decontextualized language
dementia
derivational morpheme
Down syndrome

dyslexia
event-related potentials (ERPs)
free morpheme
functional magnetic resonance imaging (fMRI)
innate
internalized representation
lateralized
linguistic competence
magnetocncephalography (MEG)
metalinguistic awareness
mirror neurons
morpheme
morphology
Near-Infrared Spectroscopy (NIRS)

neologisms
overregularized
pervasive developmental disorder
phoneme
phonology
pragmatics
production
semantic development
semantics
species specific
species uniform
specific language impairment
speech acts
syntax
Wernicke's area

REFERENCES

Arnon, I., & Clark, E. (Eds.). (2011). *Experience, variation and generalization: Learning a first language.* Amsterdam: Benjamins.

Berko Gleason, J., & Thompson, R. B. (2002). Out of the baby book and into the computer: Child language research comes of age. *Contemporary Psychology, APA Review of Books, 47,* 4, 391–394.

Brown, R. W. (1970). The first sentences of child and chimpanzee. In R. W. Brown (Ed.), *Psycholinguistics.* New York: Macmillan.

Brown, R. W. (1973). *A first language.* Cambridge, MA: Harvard University Press.

Chomsky, N. (1957). *Syntactic structures.* The Hague: Mouton.

Curtiss, S. (1977). *Genie: A psycholinguistic study of a modern day "wild" child.* New York: Academic Press.

Darwin, C. (1877). A biographical sketch of an infant. *Mind, 2,* 285–294.

Ely, R., & Berko Gleason, J. (2006). I'm sorry I said that: Apologies in young children's discourse. *Journal of Child Language, 33,* 599–620.

Fogassi, L., & Ferrari, P. F. (2007). Mirror neurons and the evolution of embodied language. *Current Directions in Psychological Science, 16,* 3, 136–141.

Gardner, R. A., & Gardner, B. T. (1969). Teaching sign language to a chimpanzee. *Science, 165,* 664–672.

Gardner, R. A., & Gardner, B. T. (1994). Development of phrases in the utterances of children and cross-fostered chimpanzees. In R. A. Gardner, B. T. Gardner, B. Chiarelli, & F. X. Plooij (Eds.), *The ethological roots of culture.* NATO ASI series D: Behavioural and Social Sciences (Vol. 78, pp. 223–255). Dordrecht, The Netherlands: Kluwer Academic.

Geschwind, N. (1982). Specializations of the brain. In W. S.-Y. Wang (Ed.), *Human communication: Language and its psychobiological bases.* San Francisco: W. H. Freeman.

Gleason, H. A. (1955). *An introduction to descriptive linguistics.* New York: Henry Holt.

Goodglass, H. (1993). *Understanding aphasia.* San Diego, CA: Academic Press.

Gregory, L. (2009). *Stupid science: Weird experiments, mad scientists, and idiots in the lab.* Riverside, NJ: McMeel.

Grice, H. P. (1975). Logic and conversation. In P. Cole & J. Morgan (Eds.), *Syntax and semantics* (Vol. 3). New York: Academic Press.

Hall, G. S. (1907). *Aspects of child life and education.* New York: Appleton.

Hayes, C. (1951). *The ape in our house.* New York: Harper.

Hess, E. (2008). *Nim Chimpsky: The chimp who would be human.* New York: Bantam Books.

Hoza, J. (2008). Five nonmanual modifiers that mitigate requests and rejections in American sign language. *Sign Language Studies,* 8(3), 264–288.

Hymes, D. (1972). On communicative competence. In J. Pride & J. Holmes (Eds.), *Sociolinguistics.* Hammondsworth, UK: Penguin.

Janik, V. M. (2000). Whistle matching in wild bottlenose dolphins *(Tursiops truncatus). Science, 289,* 1355–1357.

Kellogg, W. N. (1980). Communication and language in the home raised chimpanzee. In T. Sebeok & J. Umiker Sebeok (Eds.), *Speaking of apes.* New York: Plenum Press.

Klima, E. S., & Bellugi, U. (1972). The signs of language in child and chimpanzee. In R. Alloway, L. Krames, & P. Pliner (Eds.), *Communication and affect: A comparative approach.* New York: Academic Press.

Klima, E. S., & Bellugi, U. (1979). *The signs of language.* Cambridge, MA: Harvard University Press.

Kohler, E., Keysers, C., Umiltà, M. A., Fogassi, L., Gallese, V., & Rizzolatti, G. (2002). Hearing sounds, understanding actions: Action representation in mirror neurons. *Science, 297,* 846–848.

Kuhl, P. K. (2010). Brain mechanisms in early language acquisition. *Neuron, 67,* 713.

Lane, H. (1979). *The wild boy of Aveyron.* Cambridge, MA: Harvard University Press.

LaPointe, L. (2005). Feral children. *Journal of Medical Speech-Language Pathology, 13*(1), vii–ix.

Lenneberg, E. (1967). *The biological foundations of language.* New York: Wiley.

Lieberman, D. E. (2011). *The evolution of the human head.* Cambridge, MA: Harvard University Press.

Locke, J. L. (1993). *The child's path to spoken language.* Cambridge, MA: Harvard University Press.

MacWhinney, B. (2000). *The CHILDES Project: Tools for analyzing talk: Transcription format and programs, Vol. I* (3rd ed.) and *The CHILDES Project: Tools for analyzing talk: The database, Vol. II* (3rd ed.). Mahwah, NJ: Erlbaum.

MacWhinney, B. (2001). From CHILDES to TalkBank: New systems for studying human communication. In M. Almgren, A. Barreña, M. Ezeizaberrena, I. Idiazabal, and B. MacWhinney (Eds.), *Research on child language acquisition* (pp. 17–34). Somerville, MA: Cascadilla.

McCarthy, D. (1954). Language development in children. In P. Mussen (Ed.), *Carmichael's manual of child psychology.* New York: Wiley.

Menn, L., & Bernstein Ratner, N. (Eds.). (2000). *Methods for studying language production.* Mahwah, NJ: Erlbaum.

Misyak, J. & Christiansen, M. (2011). Genetic variation and individual differences in language. In I. Arnon and E. Clark (Eds.), *Experience, variation and generalization: Learning a first language* (pp. 223–238). Amsterdam: Benjamins.

O'Connell, C. (2007). *The elephant's secret sense: The hidden life of the wild herds of Africa.* New York: Free Press.

Pääbo, S. (2003). The mosaic that is our genome. *Nature, 421,* 409–412.

Pepperberg, I. M., & Gordon, J. D. (2005). Number comprehension by a grey parrot (*Psittacus erithacus*), including a zero-like concept. *Journal of Comparative Psychology, 119,* 2, 197–209.

Pilley, J. W., & Reid, A. K. (2011). Border collie comprehends object names as verbal referents. *Behavioural Processes,* 86(2), 184–195.

Piper, W., Mager, J., & Walcott, C. (2011). Marking loons, making progress. *American Scientist,* 99(3), 220–227.

Ross, E. D. (2010). Cerebral localization of functions and the neurology of language: Fact versus fiction or is it something else? *Neuroscientist,* 16(3), 222–243.

Rumbaugh, D. E., Savage-Rumbaugh, S. E., King, J. E. & Taglialatela, J. P. (2011). The foundations of primate intelligence and language skills. In *The Human Brain Evolving: Paleoneurological Studies in Honor of Ralph L. Holloway.*

Bloomington, IN: Stone Age Institute Press.

Scott, K. A., Roberts, J. A. & Glennen, S. (2011). How well do children who are internationally adopted acquire language? A meta-analysis. *Journal of Speech, Language and Hearing Research, 54,* 1153–1169.

Skinner, B. F. (1957). *Verbal behavior.* Englewood, NJ: Prentice-Hall.

Tanner, J. E., Patterson, F.G. & Byrne, R.W. (2006) . The development of spontaneous gestures in zoo-living gorillas and sign-taught gorillas: From action and location to object representation. *Journal of Developmental Processes, 1,* 69–102.

Terrace, H. S. (1980). *Nim: A chimpanzee who learned sign language.* New York: Knopf.

Toth, A. (2009). Bridge of signs: Can sign language empower non-deaf children to triumph over their communication disabilities? *American Annals of the Deaf, 154*(2), 85–95.

Trachsel, M. (2010). Human uniqueness in the age of ape language research. *Society & Animals,* 18(4), 397–412.

Tyack, P. L. (2000). Dolphins whistle a signature tune. *Science, 289,* 1310–1311.

Van Cantfort, T. E., & Rimpau, J. G. (1982). Sign language studies with children and chimpanzees. *Sign Language Studies, 34,* 15–72.

Vogel, I., & Raimy, E. (2002). The acquisition of compound vs. phrasal stress in English. *Journal of Child Language, 29,* 225–250.

von Frisch, K. (1950). *Bees, their vision, chemical senses, and language.* Ithaca, NY: Cornell University Press.

Communication Development in Infancy

Rochelle Newman
University of Maryland

Jacqueline Sachs
University of Connecticut

If you ask parents about their child's early language development, they will often mention their child's first words, or perhaps first sentences. But well before children begin to talk, they are building a set of skills that they will need for later communication. The current chapter focuses on these **prelinguistic** abilities that serve as the foundation for later stages in the acquisition of language. These skills can be divided into two primary domains: infants' perceptual ability to recognize patterns in the language input they hear around them and their early attempts to communicate preverbally (through nonword vocalizations and gestures).

In Chapter 1 we learned that there is a biological basis for language: The infant's brain and sensory systems are prepared for the task of acquiring a language. But infants begin learning their language even before they are born; by the third trimester, the fetus can hear sounds produced by the mother. The speech sounds produced by the mother travel via bone conduction throughout her body, including into the womb. As a result, infants come into the world having had several months of exposure to their native language, and newborns already prefer listening both to their mothers' voices and to the sounds of their native language more generally (DeCasper & Fifer, 1980; Mehler et al., 1988). For example, when French newborns were played samples of French and Japanese speech, they listened more attentively to the French (Nazzi, Bertoncini, & Mehler, 1998). Infants even prefer listening to particular stories their mothers had read to them *in utero* (DeCasper & Spence, 1986). Recent work even suggests that newborns may cry differently depending on the language they heard *in utero* (Mampe, Friederici, Christophe, & Wermke, 2009).

This prenatal exposure sets the stage for further language development: Infants prefer listening to familiar sounds, and this greater attention to their native language (and to language in general) provides them with more opportunities to learn from it. This, in turn, induces yet further attention and further learning. Although infants are able to learn their native language even without this prenatal exposure (as demonstrated in infants born of Deaf parents who do not speak and infants who are adopted into a different language environment), this early exposure gives children a head start on acquiring their language by facilitating their attention to the appropriate signals.

As infants continue to listen, their preferences begin to narrow, and their speech-perception abilities gradually become shaped by the language they hear. As a result, their perception becomes "tuned" to their native language. The following section examines these perceptual changes in more detail.

Perceptual "Tuning" to Speech

Most of the sounds that are used in speech, including those in languages that the infant has never heard, are perceived well by young infants. This has been shown using a technique known as the **high-amplitude sucking paradigm** (HASP). In this method, a machine measures how often infants suck on a pacifier in response to different sounds. Infants begin by hearing a single sound—if they are interested, they will increase their sucking rate. As the same sound continues to play, they become less interested in it, and their sucking rate drops. This decreased response rate is known as **habituation**. Once the infants are habituated to the original stimulus, the experimenter changes the sound. If the infants start sucking harder on the pacifier, we can take this to mean that they could tell the difference between the prior (boring) sound and the new sound.

Using this paradigm, researchers have found that infants discriminate different phonemes in much the same way as adults do: for example, even at 1 month of age, American infants can distinguish a "b" from a "p," even though they are very similar sounds acoustically (Eimas et al., 1971). (See Chapter 3 for more on the difference between these two sounds.) Follow-up studies have shown that infants can distinguish a wide range of different speech sounds well before they are producing speech themselves. They can even distinguish speech sounds that do not occur in their native language: For example, infants learning English and infants learning Japanese can both distinguish between /r/ and /l/, even though these sounds are very difficult for Japanese-speaking adults to distinguish (Eimas, 1975; Tsushima et al., 1994).

Even though infants start out the language-acquisition process being able to perceive a wide variety of phonetic distinctions, the ability to hear the differences among many of the sounds that are not used in their language is lost by about 1 year of age. That is, if French babies have not heard any Japanese, by the time they begin to say words they will not hear Japanese sounds in exactly the same way that a Japanese infant would (Kuhl, Williams, Lacerda, Stevens, & Lindbloom, 1992). Werker and Tees (1984) presented English-learning infants with two contrasts that English-speaking adults fail to distinguish, one from Hindi and one from a Native American language known as Nlaka'pamux. Infants aged 6 to 8 months were able to distinguish both contrasts. But infants only a little bit older, between 10 and 12 months of age, failed to do so. This suggests that during their first year of life, infants' perception becomes attuned to the language they hear around them. While infants may begin being able to identify many different sounds, their perception gradually becomes focused on just those phonemes that are important for their native language.

This focusing begins during the first year of life, but takes many years before it is completely set. It likely provides a number of advantages for the language learner. But it also poses a distinct disadvantage if an individual wishes to learn a new language later in life: It is very hard to learn to correctly produce a sound distinction that you have difficulty hearing! This perceptual attunement is not limited to just phonemes. Languages also differ from one another in their use of lexical tone. Nearly half the people in the world speak a tone language (Yip, 2002), such as Chinese, in which differences in pitch serve to distinguish meanings, much the same way phonetic differences do. Infants show early discrimination of tone categories regardless of their native language, but infants learning non-tonal languages, such as English, begin to lose this sensitivity by 9 months of age (Mattock, Molnar, Polka, & Burnham, 2008), similar to the time point at which they begin to lose their ability to distinguish non-native phonemes. Infants of this same age also begin to attend

table 2.1	Examples of the Typical Order of Emergence of Prelinguistic Skills in the First Year, with Approximate Ages
Newborn	Turns head to look in the direction of sound
	Prefers listening to native language
	Prefers mother's voice to a stranger's
	Discriminates many of the sounds used in speech
1–2 mos.	Smiles when spoken to
4–6 mos.	Shows recognition of own name and first words in a laboratory setting
6–8 mos.	Is able to segment words from fluent speech
8–10 mos.	Begins to lose the ability to discriminate non-native speech sounds
	Starts responding to own name and familiar routines (e.g., waves to "bye-bye")
	Shows clear recognition of first words

preferentially to common phoneme combinations in their native language (Jusczyk, Luce, & Charles-Luce, 1994) as compared to legal but less common ones. (Thus, infants learning English will listen longer to lists of nonsense words such as *pem* and *dal* than to lists of items such as *jowt* and *zooj,* which contain less common sounds.) In general, the picture that emerges is that of a gradual shaping of infants' attention toward native-language patterns during the second half of their first year of life.

Segmentation

Infants' recognition of the sounds in their language is only a first step to learning language; after all, the underlying goal of communication is to understand a speaker's meaning, and this requires recognizing words, not just sounds. One of the first steps in learning words is to recognize where each word starts and stops. If you listen to someone speaking to an infant, you will notice that he or she generally speaks in complete phrases or sentences, not individual words: that is, a parent may say, "Can you pet the kitty?" but he or she is far less likely to simply say, "Kitty!" by itself.

This poses a potential problem for the infant, because unlike this typewritten text, fluent speech does not have obvious pauses or breaks to indicate where one word ends and another begins. (Try listening to someone speak a language you do not understand—chances are that you'll have a hard time identifying the individual words!)

Thus, in order to learn the words from a sentence such as "*lookatthekitty,*" the infant first needs to learn how to **segment**, or break up, the fluent speech. Laboratory studies suggest that infants begin learning to segment speech into individual words during the second half of their first year of life (Jusczyk & Aslin, 1995), but that this skill takes time to develop fully. These studies have used a technique known as the **Headturn-Preference Procedure** (or HPP), a method intended for testing slightly older infants (aged 4 months+) than the High-Amplitude Sucking Paradigm described earlier (Kemler Nelson et al., 1995). In HPP, the infant sits on his or her caregiver's lap in the center of a three-sided testing booth. Sounds are played on either the right or left side of the booth, along with a flashing light; infants typically turn their heads to face the "source" of a sound they are attending to (here, the flashing light). When the infant becomes bored with the sound, he or she typically will look away; thus, by measuring the amount of time the infant spends looking at the light, we can infer how much interest the infant has in that sound. This paradigm can be used to measure general infant preferences for one sound over another, but it can also be used to measure children's segmentation by first playing them a fluent speech passage, and then comparing their listening times to individual words that had either occurred in that passage or had not occurred. Jusczyk and Aslin found that after listening to a story about a dog, infants listened longer to repeated instances of the word "dog" than to the word "bike," suggesting that they had pulled the relevant word out from the fluent passage. However, this depended critically on the age of the infants: Infants aged 6 months and younger did not succeed at this task, even though older infants did.

Infants who are better at segmentation tasks have been shown to develop a larger vocabulary and greater language skills later in life (Junge et al., 2010; Newman et al., 2006). Moreover, there is evidence to suggest that segmentation abilities may be delayed in some clinical populations, such as children with Williams Syndrome (Nazzi et al., 2003), a genetic condition that results in cognitive impairment (see chapter 9). These results

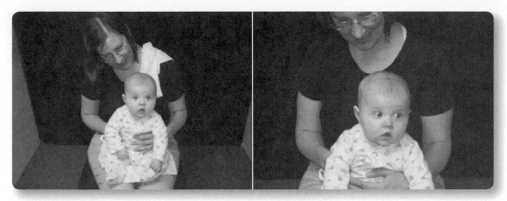

In the Headturn-Preference Procedure, infants sit on their parents' lap in a three-sided booth. The amount of time the infant spends looking toward the source of a sound is taken as a measure of interest in that sound.

suggest that being able to identify word boundaries is a critical prerequisite for language acquisition.

Statistical Learning

Answer quickly: What color car is more common, blue or yellow? Most people will quickly say that blue cars are more common and will do so with little or no hesitation or uncertainty. Yet chances are that you have never actively counted the number of blue and yellow cars on the road. The fact that you recognize the frequency of car colors is an indication that you have picked up on a statistical pattern in the world around you. These types of statistical patterns are seen not only in the frequency of objects in the environment, but also in the frequency of different patterns in the language input. For example, in English, a word ending in *–ing* is far more likely to occur after the word *is* than after the word *can* (*is running* vs. *can running*), and the syllable *tee* is particularly common after hearing *prih* (*pretty*).

Infants are able to identify these types of statistical patterns and use them to learn both grammatical and lexical aspects of their native language. In fact, this **statistical learning** ability is a critical component of many aspects of children's language development. Infants appear to track the statistical patterns among sounds, syllables, and words, and they use this information to help them learn their native language. For example, Saffran, Aslin, and Newport (1996) presented 8-month-old infants with a continuous stream of sound, in which some syllables always occurred adjacent to one another; infants later demonstrated that they had grouped those syllables together as being a single word. (That is, the infants used statistical patterns to segment the fluent speech.) Infants also identify statistical patterns among words and can use them to start learning the basics of their native language grammar (Gómez & Gerken, 2000; Marcus, Vijayan, Bandi Rao, & Vishton, 1999; Santelmann & Jusczyk, 1998). This sensitivity to statistical patterns may be the first step in many aspects of infants' early language development.

Thus, infants in the second half of their first year of life demonstrate a remarkable array of perceptual skills that allow them to identify patterns in the language they hear around them. These perceptual skills are not sudden changes, but develop gradually as the child gains more exposure to her native language. Yet these abilities serve as critical building blocks for the more advanced language skills that will develop later on. This highlights the importance of infant hearing and infant language exposure during the first year of life.

One thing to note is that most of the work on early infant perceptual abilities has focused on monolingual infants learning either English or a European language. Although a few studies have examined how the shaping of attention might differ in infants raised bilingually (Bosch & Sebastián-Gallés, 2003; Sundara et al., 2008), much less is known about how their perceptual development may differ from that of infants raised monolingually. Given the high rate of bilingualism around the world, this is a critical gap in our knowledge.

Early Communicative Attempts

The ability of infants to vocalize changes dramatically in the first year of life. Just as infants' perception becomes shaped by exposure to their native language, so too does their production. Infants' earliest babbling is relatively comparable across languages, but by the end of the first year, most babies make sounds that reflect the sound patterns in the language they have heard (Boysson-Bardies, Sagart & Durand, 1984). Chapter 3 will provide more detail on sound production during this period as it relates to the development of the ability to produce speech sounds.

Yet communication involves more than just production and perception of sounds—it involves interactions between two individuals. Although infants may seem helpless and dependent in many ways, they are not simply passive recipients of stimulation. Instead, infants are active interactional partners and their actions affect the subsequent behavior of the caregivers. For example, caregivers expect infants to make eye contact with them, and most adults find interacting with a baby who will not look at them frustrating. In fact, the parents of an autistic infant often will notice eye aversion as the very first sign of abnormality. (See Trevarthan & Aiken, 2001, and Chapter 9, for more discussion of early adult–infant interaction and autism.)

In vocal interaction, infants' behavior also affects the caregivers. For example, in the course of carrying out research on young babies' vocalizations, Bloom (1990) noticed that occasionally students and staff members who overheard a tape made remarks like "That baby is really talking up a storm!" (p. 131). Suspecting that perhaps the adults were responding to specific sorts of infant vocalizations, Bloom and Lo (1990) had adults rate videotapes of babies who were making sounds that were more speechlike or less speechlike. The adults preferred the babies who produced sounds that were more like speech, rating them "cuddlier," "more fun," and generally more likable.

The pleasant cooing sounds like "ooh" or "aah" that infants make also draw caregivers into "conversations" with them. If an adult then responds vocally to a baby's sounds, even a 3-month-old baby will begin to produce more speechlike sounds in turn. Furthermore, babies learn to wait for the adult's response after they have vocalized. Thus, both the adult and the infant are constantly influencing one another in establishing conversation-like vocal interactions during a period well before the child uses words (Masataka, 1993). By 8 months, merely the approach, smile, or touch of an adult will increase the quality of vocalizations (Goldstein, King, & West, 2003).

From the beginning, the crying, cooing, and babbling of young infants are communicative only in the sense that the infant is a member of a social species and caregivers are alert to those signals. However, in the latter part of the first year of life, the normally developing infant makes a very important discovery that provides a transition to language: that one can intentionally make a signal (a vocalization or a gesture) and expect that it will have a specific effect on the caregiver. Thus, signals begin to have meanings arising out of the shared experiences of the child and the caregiver.

In the next section we will look in more detail at what typically occurs in the emergence of **intentional communication.** After that, we will look at some aspects of the social context of the emergence of these behaviors. Although we have divided what the infants do and what caregivers do into two sections for organizational purposes, keep in mind that the behaviors of infants and their caregivers are always mutually affecting one another.

The Expression of Communicative Intent before Speech

Characteristics of Intentional Communication

Many parents view all infants' vocalizations as communicative and meaningful. Goldman (2001) interviewed mothers and found that many of them thought their babies were saying "mama" as early as 2 months of age and they interpreted "mama" as meaning "wanting something." However, there is no indication at that age that the child is doing anything *intentionally* to obtain the caregiver's attention and help. In contrast, at 11 months, an infant might point to an object out of reach, make eye contact with the caregiver, look at the object again, and make a sound. How is this sequence of actions different from merely crying or fussing or making a babbling sound that the mother interprets as "mama"?

Deciding whether any one instance of behavior is intentionally communicative is very difficult. Think, for example, of a dog barking by the kitchen door. The owner may interpret that signal as meaning that the animal wants to be let out. Is the barking intentional communication or a behavior that simply is repeated because in the past it has led to the desired event? How would one decide? There has been much debate about the characteristics of intentional communication and the issue of when an infant deliberately vocalizes or gestures in order to get a caregiver's help. Trying to establish a single crucial criterion for deciding whether a particular behavior is intentionally communicative seems hopeless. However, if we use a set of criteria, applying them to the infant's entire behavioral repertoire at a particular point in development, we can feel some confidence in judging whether the infant is beginning to communicate with intentionality (Sugarman, 1984).

The following criteria are often applied to decide whether a baby is engaging in *intentional communication:*

1. The child makes eye contact with the partner while gesturing or vocalizing, often alternating his or her gaze between an object and the partner.
2. Some gestures have become consistent and ritualized. For example, one baby used a gesture of opening and closing her hand whenever she wanted something, rather than attempting to reach the object herself.
3. Some vocalizations have become consistent and ritualized. An infant might make the sound "eh eh" whenever she wants something. Another child would probably use a different sound in the same situation, because this sound was not copied from adult speech but was a signal developed by the infant.
4. After a gesture or vocalization, the child pauses to wait for a response from the partner.
5. The child persists in attempting to communicate if he or she is not understood and sometimes even modifies behavior to communicate more clearly.

When an infant's behaviors are viewed in terms of such criteria, there is not a distinct boundary between behavior without communicative intent and intentional communication, nor an exact age at which we classify the infant as intentionally communicative. Rather, the child moves gradually toward an understanding of goals and the potential role of others in achieving them. For example, in one study the mothers of infants ranging from 6 to 13 months of age held a desirable toy out of reach. Observers videotaped and scored the infants' gaze, gestures, and vocalizations for signs that the infants were trying to influence their mothers, rather than simply attempting to get the toy or expressing frustration. In this situation, even some 6-month-old infants were judged as deliberately using their mothers to meet their goals (Mosier & Rogoff, 1994).

For the average baby, we expect that the first signs of intentional communication will emerge between 8 and 10 months of age. When we try to determine whether an infant has begun to communicate intentionally, even small differences in the situations observed or the criteria used to classify gestures or vocalizations as intentional will affect our judgments, but certainly the transition from inadvertent communicator to intentional communicator is a major one for both the child and that child's caregivers (Camaioni, 2001; Legerstee & Barillas, 2003).

This is not to say that the infant who is not yet using words understands the communicative process in the same way an older child does. A full realization of how words or gestures affect the knowledge and beliefs of others is a much later development, and even a talkative 4-year-old is still learning about how communication takes place.

The Forms and Functions of Early Communicative Behaviors

Early communication takes place using both gestures and sounds. These early communicative behaviors can serve a variety of different functions, all of which are expressed by normally developing infants well before they begin to use words (Wetherby, Cain, Yonclas, & Walker, 1988). Infants use vocalizations and gestures to request objects or actions (such as an infant lifting her arms to indicate that she wants to be picked up), to indicate rejection (such as pushing away an object), and to gain the caregiver's attention.

Infants also use these behaviors to direct the partner's attention for the purpose of jointly noticing an object or event. For example, the infant might "show" an object to the caregiver by holding it out and vocalizing, or the infant might give an object to the caregiver. Pointing might be used not for the purpose of obtaining an object, but for directing the partner's attention to an object. Most infants begin pointing at objects or pictures between 6 and 10 months of age. They also learn to interpret the pointing gestures of others; infants learn that the appropriate response to a caregiver's point is to look in the direction indicated by the finger, not at the end of the finger itself. (When you have a chance, contrast the response of a pet dog or cat to pointing.) Babies usually begin responding appropriately to points by others between 9 and 12 months. By 12 months, many infants will point at an object themselves and then shift their gaze to make eye contact with the listener, checking whether their points have been noticed (Masur, 1983). See Chapter 9 for more information on initiating and responding to joint attention.

You may wonder why a book about *language* development includes a discussion of pointing. For an adult speaker, although gestures typically accompany speech, they do not seem a part of "language" in the same way sounds, words, or sentences are. For an infant, however, both gestures and sounds can, and normally do, serve as symbols.

The emergence of both types of symbols reflects an important developmental change in the child's mental ability. For example, babies who discover early how to communicate by pointing tend to be early in other aspects of language development as well, such as beginning to understand words (Butterworth, 2003). As a result, when children begin to talk using real words from their language, these words emerge within a rich framework of communicative functions that have been established through the use of gestures and other communicative acts.

These gestures are not limited to just pointing. While pointing continues to be a part of nonverbal communication throughout life, most infants develop unique gestures that are used before the first words are learned. Acredolo and Goodwyn (1988) observed that babies attempted to convey a whole range of communicative functions through "invented gestures." Since the babies' caregivers were not typically watching for gestural comunication, many times they did not even realize that consistent gestures were being used. As babies begin to pick

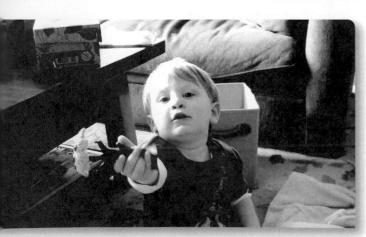

Showing an object is an early communicative behavior.

up words from the language spoken to them, they come to depend increasingly on vocal communication, and the invented gestures fade away (Messinger & Fogel, 1998).

There has been a recent move toward teaching infants a more conventional set of gestures. Goodwyn, Acredolo, and Brown (2000) taught a group of parents to use gestures of their own choosing while speaking to their infants starting about 11 months of age. For example, while saying "See the birdie," the parent might "flap arms." The babies began using these gestures slightly before they began using words, perhaps because the motor movements required to produce the gestures are easier for infants than are the motor movements required to produce intelligible words. More interestingly, the children taught the gestures had better scores on tests of language development at various ages up to 36 months. On the basis of this research, Acredolo and Goodwyn (1998) published a book for parents in which they stated that gesturing provides advantages for babies and their parents and showed parents how to teach signs to their babies. Since then, many similar books, videotapes, and products have emerged on the marketplace.

However, some question the value of so much emphasis on teaching gestures. They argue that one is, after all, altering the normal course of development by teaching signs, without knowing whether there could be negative consequences (Johnston, Durieux-Smith, & Bloom, 2005). There is not yet enough research on the long-term effects of "baby signing" systems to make recommendations about whether parents should or should not use signs. Parents who do decide to try signing may appreciate having another way to interact with their baby, but they should not try to teach signs if their baby is not also enjoying it, and they certainly should not be doing it to turn their infant into a "baby genius."

The vocalizations used by children shortly before they begin learning conventional words have received much attention, because they form an interesting link between prelinguistic communication and speech. Vocalizations that contain consistent sound patterns and are used in consistent situations, but are unique to the child rather than based on the adult language, are referred to as **protowords.** For example, an infant might start using some vocalization (let us imagine that it sounds like "lala") when rubbing his blanket against his cheek, and then at a later time use "lala" when he wants his blanket. Sometimes the family even adopts the baby's "word" for a while, saying things that would be a mystery to strangers, like "I think he wants his lala." Often, these preverbal vocalizations are initially linked with a particular gesture; over time, the vocalizations become more consistent and less tied to a particular action. (Chapter 3 will contain more about protowords.)

The Assessment of Communicative Intent

One might wish to assess a child's communicative abilities as a part of carrying out research on communication development, or in a clinical evaluation in order to find out whether that child is atypical in the pace of language development (see Chapter 9). In research, a method called **low-structured observation** is sometimes used. The caregiver is instructed to play with the child in a natural way, and a trained observer scores the child's behavior either during the session or from a videotape. For example, the observer would look for instances of commenting, as indicated by the child's pointing at, showing, or giving objects, sometimes accompanied by consistent vocalizations (Coggins, Olswang, & Guthrie, 1987).

In a **structured observation,** one manipulates the situation somewhat to increase the likelihood of observing the behavior of interest. For example, a **communicative temptation task** could be used to entice the child to produce requests. The child might be presented with an attractive toy inside a tightly covered plastic container. An infant who is not yet communicating intentionally might bang the container and fuss or cry in frustration, while another preverbal infant might hand the container to an adult, make eye contact, point to the toy and/or vocalize, and persist in such behaviors that seem to be directed toward the adult (Casby & Cumpata, 1986). Similarly, one could see how the child expresses rejection by presenting the child with a less desirable toy while more desirable toys are in view but out of reach (Olswang, Bain, Dunn, & Cooper, 1983).

To aid in a clinical evaluation, there are norms available for various aspects of language development, including the period before words are used, based on a large study that collected mothers' reports on their children's communicative behaviors (Fenson et al., 1994). The questions used in the study are available as two scales called the **MacArthur-Bates Communicative Development Inventories (CDI)**, one used for infants 8 to 16 months of age and the other for toddlers 16 to 30 months of age (Fenson et al., 2007). Typically, the child's caregiver is asked to report on words comprehended or said and is asked specific questions about his or her child's communicative behavior. Meadows, Elias, and Bain (2000) have reported that caregivers are able to identify their children's communicative acts consistently. Studies using a similar (but briefer) vocabulary assessment, the **Language Development Survey** (**LDS**; Rescorla, 1989; Rescorla & Alley, 2001) have shown it to be a reliable and valid screening tool for identifying children with expressive language delay.

Another assessment device, the **Communication and Symbolic Behavior Scales (CSBS;** Wetherby & Prizant, 2002), was used in a study of almost 2,000 infants, including those with risk factors (prematurity, multiple birth, family history of speech-language difficulties, low socioeconomic status, and others). There was little variation in the pattern of development of communicative behaviors, even when there were differences in the age of acquisition of a particular behavior (Reilly et al., 2006).

A continuing goal in research is to find reliable early clues that would predict whether a child is having difficulty acquiring language. For example, if a baby seems somewhat slow in beginning to speak but is understanding language and attempting to communicate with gestures or protowords, there would be less concern than there would be about a baby the same age who showed no interest in communication (Watt, Wetherby, & Shumway, 2006). (See also Chapter 9 regarding atypical language development.) For that reason, research has recently focused on some of the perceptual skills described earlier in this chapter; if infants fail to notice patterns in the language they hear, they are highly unlikely to then learn those patterns. Examining infants' early perceptual skills might provide an important clue to the children's subsequent language outcomes.

The Social Context of the Preverbal Infant

Here we will look at some aspects of early communicative interaction between caregivers and preverbal infants. We will see that caregivers speak to infants in special ways, that they create situations in which their babies will have an opportunity to take their turns at talking, and that they behave in other ways that may be supportive of infants' attempts to communicate. We will not be able to describe all of the ways in which adults and infants communicate, but we will concentrate on those aspects of communication that seem most closely related to later language development.

In describing the social context in which communication emerges, we are not arguing that social interaction causes the child to begin to communicate or that adults teach their infants to communicate. Think, for example, of trying to teach a cat or a dog to react like a baby! The infant has the **biological capacity** for certain sorts of behaviors and abilities to develop. However, that biological capacity will not be fully realized without certain kinds of social supports. An important goal of research concerning the social context of communicative development is to find out what kinds of experiences are sufficient to allow normal development and how variations in experiences ultimately affect the language abilities of the child.

Consider, as an example, the learning of a sound distinction. As was noted earlier in this chapter, the specific language that babies hear changes their ability to discriminate sounds. But what constitutes "hearing" a language? Kuhl, Tsao, and Liu (2003) found that 10-month-old infants regained their ability to discriminate certain sounds used in Chinese but not in English after only a few hours of interaction with Chinese-speaking adults. When infants were exposed to the same sort of language by television, rather than live interaction, they did not discriminate the sounds correctly. Kuhl (2007) has suggested, on the basis of this and other studies, that language learning requires social interaction. We will now explore various aspects of that social context.

The Sound of the Caregiver's Speech: "Listen to Me!"

Speech addressed to babies is typically quite unlike the speech directed to adults. We even have a name for it: **baby talk**. You will also see the terms **infant-directed speech (IDS)**, **child-directed speech (CDS),** and **motherese** (or *parentese*) used to refer to this speech style.

The term *baby talk* in particular may merely bring to mind adult imitations of childlike speech ("Is ooo my tweetie-pie?") and special vocabulary words like *choo-choo* and *pottie,* along with strong denials that *you* would ever "use baby talk." However, as we will see here and in later chapters, there are actually many very interesting aspects of speech and language that are modified when we talk to infants and young children, and we make most of these modifications without even being aware of them.

One of the most dramatic characteristics of talk to babies in English is its **prosodic features**, such as higher pitch, more variable pitch, and exaggerated stress. These features have been found in baby talk in many different languages, and some researchers have suggested that special prosodic patterns (although not identical to those mentioned above) may be a universal characteristic of baby talk (e.g., Fernald, 1992).

Since variations in the prosodic features in speech to babies are common across many languages, it may be that these characteristics are used because they are especially appropriate. We can find out about babies' perceptual abilities and preferences by devising experiments in which they can "tell" us what they want to listen to. Infants cannot talk or press buttons, but they can turn their heads and control their eye movements, so a researcher might set up a situation in which a message plays only when the baby's head turns in a certain direction or when the eyes are fixated on a pattern and measure the amount of time the baby thereby "chooses" to listen to one message or another. (A very important application of such techniques is for the testing of hearing in young infants.) A number of studies have shown that babies prefer IDS patterns, even when they are only 2 days old (Cooper & Aslin, 1990).

Some studies have called into question whether high and variable pitch and exaggerated stress are the crucial elements in the baby talk to which infants respond. In an experiment, speech stimuli were constructed with these baby-talk characteristics, but without the positive affect that generally accompanies them. Conversely, messages spoken in an adult-to-adult style were created that did have positive affect. Six-month-old babies preferred the positive affect, whether it had the typical baby-talk features or not, leading the researchers to conclude that babies prefer "happy talk" rather than baby talk (Singh, Morgan, & Best, 2002).

There are also some differences in IDS across cultures. The prosodic changes found in American English are more extreme than those found even in other dialects of English (such as British English), let alone in other languages (Fernald et al., 1989). Higher pitch and exaggerated intonation to infants were not found to be characteristic of rural African American families in North Carolina (Heath, 1983), Kaluli families in New Guinea (Schieffelin, 1990), and Quiche-Mayan families in Guatemala (Bernstein Ratner & Pye, 1984). Perhaps there are alternative ways of marking IDS (Ingram, 1995).

If babies are naturally responsive to speech that has certain features, adults may use these characteristics because they discover that infants pay more attention to them when they do. Here, too, the infants play a role in the type of input they receive: Their attentiveness (or lack thereof) can encourage certain types of speech changes to be repeated. In fact, recent studies demonstrate that adults' speech changes depending on the type of feedback they receive from infants (Smith & Trainor, 2008). Thus, parents tend to alter their speech so as to maintain infants' attention, and doing so may help to cement the emotional bond between caregiver and child.

Children can learn language even if they are not in loving interactions, given their resilient language abilities, but adult–infant attachment may be involved in their optimal development. One large study investigating the effect of learning environment examined children in Romanian institutions: Children were randomly assigned to either enter foster care or to remain in the institution. Those who entered foster care later showed greater expressive and receptive language skills than did children who remained in the institutional setting (Windsor, Glaze, Koga, & the Bucharest Early Intervention Project Core Group, 2007). Even within biological families, adult–infant attachment is important for language learning. Kaplan, Bachorowski, Smoski, and Hudenko (2002) found that depressed mothers used less of the exaggerated prosody that characterizes baby talk when they spoke to their 4-month-old infants. This result is not surprising, since flat affect is a common symptom of depression. Interestingly, the infants of the depressed mothers also showed poorer learning of a response from that speech, although they readily learned when spoken to by unfamiliar nondepressed mothers. However, note that this study, published the same year as the one by Singh and colleagues (2002), described above, could also be interpreted as showing that babies learn best from "happy talk." (For further discussion of the relation between affective development and communicative development, see Prizant & Wetherby, 1990.)

The emotional component of IDS thus encourages infant attention, and this provides infants with opportunities to learn other aspects of their native language. In addition to providing them with information on the sounds of the language, discussed earlier, word learning and sentence grammar acquisition might also be facilitated. Labels are spoken with exaggerated stress and higher, more variable pitch, perhaps encouraging infants' attention to these words (Fernald & Mazzie, 1991). Some studies suggest that there may be a tendency to pronounce labels for objects more distinctly in IDS (Kuhl et al., 1997), although other studies have found contradictory results (Bard & Anderson, 1994). However, at least one study suggests that even adults show better word learning from talkers using IDS than ADS speech (Golinkoff & Alioto, 1995), and infants are better able to identify clausal boundaries in infant-directed than adult-directed speech. These studies suggest the possibility that aspects of the input may enhance children's language development.

A word of caution: Most studies to date have been carried out in the United States with babies of middle-class families. Since babies everywhere learn to speak, one must be cautious about concluding that some particular feature of baby talk is necessary (or even useful) for babies. Moreover, most research on IDS has looked at "infants" as a group; IDS clearly changes with the child's own development, and some of the advantages of IDS may be specific to children of a particular level of linguistic development. We do not know enough yet to tell caregivers how they *should* talk. Research on language-learning environments in a wide variety of cultures and at a wide range of ages is needed, as is research to discover whether there are causal links between certain features of the linguistic environment and language learning.

The Conversational Nature of the Caregiver's Speech: "Talk to Me!"

Caregivers talk to infants in a way that is not only engaging but also encourages the baby to participate. Based on her observations of mothers interacting with babies in England, Snow (1977) argued that the mothers' primary goal in talking with their infants was to have a "conversation" with them. Even when the adult knows that the infant does not yet understand language, the adult behaves as if the child's response is a turn in the conversation. Here is a little "conversation" between a mother and her 3-month-old daughter, Ann (p. 12):

Mother	Ann
	(smiles)
Oh what a nice little smile.	
Yes, isn't that nice?	
There. There's a nice little smile.	
	(burps)
What a nice little wind as well!	

In this example, the mother spoke in short, simple utterances, although of course the 3-month-old could not understand the content of the speech. The mother responded to whatever her infant did, commenting on the various nonverbal and vocal behaviors that occurred and incorporating them into the conversation. It is as if she allowed the infant's behaviors to stand for a turn in the interaction and treated the behavior, whether a vocalization or a burp, as if it were intentional communication on the part of the infant.

The mothers devoted many of their utterances to attempting to elicit some kind of behavior from the infant, such as coos and smiles. In contrast to adult–adult conversations, where we often must try very hard to get our own turn, each mother seemed intent on giving her child many turns in the conversation. Often the mothers' utterances were followed by pauses, providing the opportunity for responses from the infant, as in this example (Snow, 1977, p. 13):

Oh you are a funny little one, aren't you, hmm? (pause)

Aren't you a funny little one? (pause)

Hmm? (pause)

Although the mothers had accepted almost any behavior on the part of their 3-month-olds as if it were an attempt to communicate, as the infants grew older, the mothers changed in what they accepted as a turn in the conversation. By 7 months, when the babies had begun to be more active partners in the interactions, the mothers responded only to higher-quality vocalizations, such as a babbled sound, and not to sounds such as burps. At 12 months the mothers' criteria for a turn had changed again, and they began to interpret their children's vocalizations as words, as in the following example (Snow, 1977, p. 17):

Mother	Ann
	abaabaa
Baba.	
Yes that's you, what you are.	

Having seen that adults interact conversationally in certain ways with infants in the first year of life, we now consider the effect of this interaction. The adult's behavior certainly has an effect on the infant's behavior in the immediate situation. When mothers speak to 3-month-old infants, the most common response is a vocalization, and if the caregiver uses a conversational pattern of interaction—in which the adult responds in a turn-taking manner to infant vocalizations—the type of sound a 3-month-old baby will produce becomes more speechlike in response (Bloom, 1988).

The adult's interpretation of the infant's vocalizations may help the child get the idea that communication is possible. Adults interpret infants' behaviors as communicative long before the children have an intention to communicate. A 2-month-old baby who is crying may be described by her mother as "wanting her diaper changed." The infant at this age is not actually intending a particular message but is crying because of discomfort. However, the fact that the mother accepts the cry as conveying a particular message creates the possibility for the child to begin to communicate different messages with different cries and eventually perhaps notice the correspondence between the vocalizations and the effect they have on others (Harding, 1983).

What about the long-term effects of the caregiver's interactive style? We cannot yet conclude that any particular style of caregiver–infant interaction is necessary for language development. Children learn to talk with a wide range of linguistic experiences. For example, Ochs (1988) observed childrearing in Samoa and found that infants were typically not spoken to until they began to speak themselves (however, of course, they heard the speech going on around them).

However, some research carried out on U.S. families suggests that caregivers' language usage does at least affect the rate of language learning. When infants were between 9 and 18 months old, the amount of talking that a mother did directly with her child (but not the amount of speech to others) was highly correlated with measures of the child's later linguistic competence. This result suggests that the overall quantity of speech that the child overhears is not so important for the rate of language development, but the quantity of direct adult-to-child speech is (Clarke-Stewart, 1973). Furthermore, infants whose mothers talked to them frequently using short utterances at 9 months of age performed better on tests of receptive language abilities at 18 months than did infants of less vocally responsive mothers (Murray, Johnson, & Peters, 1990).

In the United States, maternal communication style may vary by socioeconomic status (SES). High-SES mothers tend to use longer sentences and a greater variety of vocabulary than do low-SES mothers (Hoff, 2003; Hart & Risley, 1995). Such changes in the input that children hear has a marked effect on their vocabulary development (Hoff & Naigles, 2002; Huttenlocher, Haight, Bryk, Seltzer & Lyons, 1991; Pan, Rowe, Singer, & Snow, 2005). As a result, children from high-SES homes show a faster growth in vocabulary than do children from low-SES homes. Some of these differences may be tied to parents' knowledge of child development, in that parents with a greater understanding about children's language development are likely able to better gauge their child's abilities and adjust their speech accordingly (Rowe, 2008). If this is the case, it may be possible to improve children's communicative abilities by teaching parents more about language development; perhaps textbooks like this one would be a good starting point!

Contexts for the Emergence of Object Reference: "Look at That!"

At about 6 months of age, infants begin to show a great interest in objects, perhaps reflecting both advances in their visual ability to scan their environment and their motor ability to grasp and manipulate objects. Younger infants were entertained by face-to-face social interactions, but now they are drawn to investigate their surroundings. At this point, the caregivers usually begin to change the strategy of interacting with their infants, encouraging their interest in objects while they continue interpersonal interactions by jointly exploring objects and their potential (Adamson & Bakeman, 1984). For example, one might see a playful interaction in which a mother wiggles a toy cow dramatically, saying, "Look at the cow! What does the cow say? The cow says '*mooooo.*'" Caregivers label objects (and also the actions or characteristics of objects). These learning contexts can be found in any activity: playing, looking at pictures in books, and carrying out everyday routines such as bathing and feeding.

Around 9 months of age, an important change occurs in infants' **social cognition** (Meltzoff, 2007; Mundy & Acra, 2006). They begin to understand that other people are intentional beings, have thoughts and goals, and that there can be a sharing of minds. They look in the direction of a point, and, at around 10 months, they even look in the direction that their caregiver looks (Brooks & Meltzoff, 2005).

Children whose mothers encourage **joint attention** to objects and supply labels for them increase their vocabularies faster in the early language-acquisition period (Campbell & Namy, 2003). Words are most likely to be learned if the caregiver focuses on what the *child* is interested in, providing a word at that moment, rather than trying to direct the child's attention and actively teach the child vocabulary (Tomasello, 1988, 1999).

Joint attention is based on a positive and affectionate relationship between the infant and caregiver, in which one can say that the pair are truly sharing an experience (Adamson & Russell, 1999; Harding, Weissmann, Kromelow, & Stilson, 1997). Infants learn best in a social context, and it is not productive to go around simply naming objects. Thus, gimmicks like flashcards or any other kind of "drills" for infant vocabulary learning are highly suspect and may even be counterproductive!

Child-centered interactions can affect more than just vocabulary. Rollins (2003) looked at mothers' use of language with their children at 9 months of age and found that higher use of **contingent comments** (comments made "when the mother discussed an object of joint focus of attention or narrated an ongoing activity," p. 225) predicted better language skills at 12, 18, and 30 months of age.

When the caregiver uses contingent comments, follows the child's interest, and bases the next utterances on what the child is focusing on, the caregiver is employing a verbally **sensitive** or **responsive interactional style,** as contrasted with a style that is constantly redirecting the child's attention (a verbally **intrusive** or **controlling interactional style**). For example, if the baby points at his bottle and the mother says "bottle," her utterance would be coded as responsive. If she tries to redirect the child's attention, saying, "Look at your book," in the same situation, the utterance would be coded as intrusive. Verbal sensitivity in mothers of preverbal infants predicts better language skills (e.g., Baumwell, Tamis-Lemonda, & Bornstein, 1997; Carpenter, Nagell, & Tomasello, 1998), particularly among low-birth-weight infants at risk for developmental delays (Landry, Smith, & Miller-Loncar, 1997).

Pointing to objects or events is one way that children initiate joint interaction with caregivers.

Of course, as in other areas we have considered, there can be cultural differences in the pattern of joint attention involving objects. For instance, one set of studies revealed differences between mothers in the United States and Japan in the way they interacted with babies, even though both cultures are similar in paying a great deal of attention to infants and children. The U.S. mothers encouraged their young infants when they looked away from them with comments such as "Want to look around? There you go," whereas Japanese mothers discouraged such looking away by saying things like "Say, look at me," and "What's wrong with you?" (Morikawa, Shand, & Kosawa, 1988, pp. 248–249). Also, U.S. mothers often provided a name when the infants looked at objects, whereas Japanese mothers used those objects to engage their infants in social routines (Fernald & Morikawa, 1993). The authors of these reports noted that Americans tend to encourage independence in their children more than the Japanese do. Cultural values may begin to be transmitted by mother–infant interaction at a very early age, affecting subtle aspects of the child's socialization.

In another observation in a different culture, !Kung San caregivers in Botswana were more likely to interact with an infant when he or she was not focusing on an object. If the infant was attending to an object, the caregivers did not try to join in that interaction in the way seen in many studies of U.S. mothers (Bakeman, Adamson, Konner, & Barr, 1990).

We have seen that joint attention to objects accompanied by labeling by the caregiver provides an opportunity for the infant to learn names for things. Studies in the United States have found that infants generally comprehend many words before they begin to say words themselves. For most children, the first evidence of word understanding that is observable by parents occurs between 8 and 10 months. At 8 months, more than half of a large sample of infants responded to three words that referred to people ("mommy," "daddy," and their own names), to "bottle," and to some words from games and routines, such as "peekaboo." By 11 months, a child typically responded to about fifty words, including many names for common objects (Fenson et al., 1994). However, some laboratory research suggests that infants may recognize words even earlier; infants will listen longer to their name than to other names by the age of 4 months, and they will look at the appropriate image when they hear "*mommy*" or "*daddy*" by 6 months (Mandel, Jusczyk, & Pisoni, 1995; Tincoff & Jusczyk, 1999).

Talk in Structured Situations: "Here's What We Say"

Early communication with infants often takes place in highly structured situations, such as games or routines, which can provide **formats** for the development of early communication signals (e.g., Bruner, 1983; Ratner & Bruner, 1978). These include games, such as pat-a-cake and peekaboo, as well as frequent interactions; for example, there may be certain things that are typically said when the infant is fed, dressed, or put down for a nap. In these routine interactions, the child learns what is said in particular communicative situations and such settings may provide another way for the infant to begin noticing correspondences between sounds and meaning, leading to comprehension of words or phrases in the period just before the child will begin to say words.

Another highly structured situation is picture-book reading. Sometimes people are astonished by the notion of reading books to infants. Infants can't understand the words, after all! But book reading, especially with the kind of sturdy books that encourage activities (touching something soft or smelling something), brings parent and child together, encourages an appreciation of reading, and provides an excellent opportunity for language growth. Reading the same book over and over is helpful, because, as in the games described earlier, the child learns from routines. In fact, once the child is old enough to choose what he wants read to him, the parent may be surprised that the child still has favorites that he wants to hear again and again. They may get very boring to the adult, but they are just the right thing for the child—a structured situation with repeated elements.

A complete explanation of the emergence of intentional communication in the infant undoubtedly will have to consider the interaction of many factors, including at least the biological basis for language, the changes that take place because of maturation, the social cognitive development of the child, and the types of experiences the child has had with caregivers. It is likely that there is both an inborn predisposition toward symbolic communication in the human infant and particular environmental experiences that normally interact with this predisposition to help bring about this important milestone in language development.

SUMMARY

The first year of life—though infants may not say a single word—is a very important period for communicative development. Infants are inherently social, responsive to caregivers, and draw caregivers into communicational interaction. Moreover, infants are receiving the language in the surrounding environment and identifying patterns and sounds that are common. This learning about the input serves as a building block for their later linguistic development.

Perhaps one reason that children enter so naturally into communication is that they are well equipped for perceiving speech sounds. Even before birth, children are hearing the language spoken by their mothers. By the time they are born, infants appear to hear and discriminate speech sounds very well and are thus prepared to begin the process of acquiring language.

Because infants can also discriminate sounds that they have not heard before, it seems likely that they are born with the ability to hear many sound categories that are used in different languages. As they interact with others who speak to them, their perceptual abilities become shaped by the language they hear. They also learn to pick up patterns within the input and to identify pieces of the signal within these larger patterns. All of this learning becomes gradually attuned to the particular language they hear around them.

Toward the end of the first year, children begin to behave in ways that seem intentionally communicative. They make gestures and vocalizations in a consistent and persistent manner to achieve goals. These early gestures and vocalizations are not learned from adults but are the child's own inventions. Through such means a child can express various communicative functions, such as rejecting, requesting, or commenting. It seems likely that children achieve the milestone of intentional communication through maturation, changes in their underlying social cognition, and through their experiences with others.

Caregivers in many cultures talk to infants in special ways, typically with higher pitch and more variable intonation patterns. Such speech provides one source of affectionate stimulation for the young child, and babies are responsive to such stimulation. This attention holding speech may also help the child to become aware of the linguistic function of vocalizations. The caregiver, in turn, accepts the child's responses to speech as early attempts at communication. Thus, caregivers and infants can engage in "conversations" well before infants begin using language. The adult can establish object- and situationally focused contexts in which the correspondence to vocabulary can be discovered. Thus, language begins in a rich social context that will continue when a child's own speech emerges. Through research in this culture and others, we are coming to understand the ways in which parents and other caregivers naturally provide a setting for their children's acquisition of communicative competence

At the end of the first year, the child is finally ready for the accomplishment that caregivers view as the beginning of language—the first word!—but the child has been preparing for that day from the very beginning.

SUGGESTED PROJECTS

1. Locate infants of different ages and observe the speech of the parents or caregivers to them. It is preferable to make video or tape recordings, so that transcripts can be made and segments can be heard repeatedly. (It is difficult to listen for a number of features of speech at one time during a live observation session.) Choose particular features such as pitch, intonation patterns, rhythmic patterns, or repetition and compare them in the tapes made at different ages. You might also want to compare caregivers; for example, observe both the mother and the father playing with the infant.

2. Locate babies at different ages, such as 1, 4, 8, and 12 months. Make video or tape recordings in social settings with a caregiver. It is difficult to make transcriptions of infants' sounds even if you have had training in phonetic transcription. If you have had such training, attempt to transcribe some samples and see what problems you encounter. If you have not had such training, listen to the tapes and attempt to compare the sounds the babies make with the sounds used in your language. Do you hear changes in the types of sounds from age to age?

3. Go to **youtube.com**, and search for infant speech perception studies. (Alternatively, search for the names of some of the researchers mentioned in this chapter, such as Janet Werker or Patricia Kuhl.) You should be able to find videos of infants participating in the studies discussed in this chapter.

4. Locate two babies, one about 7 months old and one about 11 months old but not yet using words. Observe these babies interacting with caregivers in a relatively unstructured, playful situation. Take notes on each baby's vocalizations and behaviors, watching for signs of intentional communication (described on pages 35–37). Do you notice any differences between the two ages?

SUGGESTED READINGS

Adamson, L. B., & Russell, C. L. (1999). Emotion regulation and the emergence of joint attention. In P. Rochat (Ed.), *Early social cognition: Understanding others in the first months of life* (pp. 281–297). Mahwah, NJ: Erlbaum.

Campbell, A. L., & Namy, L. L. (2003). The role of social referential context and verbal and nonverbal symbol learning. *Child Development, 74,* 549–563.

Gómez, R. L. & Gerken, L.A. (2000). Infant artificial language learning and language acquisition. *Trends in Cognitive Sciences, 4,* 178–186.

Werker, J. F., & Yeung, H. H. (2005). Infant speech perception bootstraps word learning. *Trends in Cognitive Science, 9*(11), 519–527.

KEY WORDS

baby talk
biological capacity
child-directed speech (CDS)
comment
Communication and Symbolic Behavior Scales (CSBS)
communicative functions
communicative temptation task
contingent comments
controlling interactional style

high-amplitude sucking paradigm (HASP)
head-turn preference procedure (HPP)
infant-directed speech (IDS)
intentional communication
intrusive interactional style
joint attention
low-structured observation
MacArthur-Bates Communicative

Development Inventories (CDI)
prelinguistic
prosodic features
protoword
rejection
request
responsive or sensitive interactional style
segmentation
social cognition
statistical learning
structured observation

REFERENCES

Acredolo, L., & Goodwyn, S. (1988). Symbolic gesturing in normal infants. *Child Development, 59,* 450–466.

Adamson, L. B., & Bakeman, R. (1984). Mothers' communicative acts: Changes during infancy. *Infant Behavior and Development, 7,* 467–478.

Adamson, L. B., & Russell, C. L. (1999). Emotion regulation and the emergence of joint attention. In P. Rochat (Ed.), *Early social cognition: Understanding others in the first months of life* (pp. 281–297). Mahwah, NJ: Erlbaum.

Bakeman, R., Adamson, L. B., Konner, M., & Barr, R. (1990). !Kung infancy: The social context of object exploration. *Child Development, 61,* 794–809.

Bard, E. G., & Anderson, A. H. (1994). The unintelligibility of speech to children: Effects of referent availability. *Journal of Child Language, 21,* 623–648.

Baumwell, L., Tamis-Lemonda, C. S., & Bornstein, M. H. (1997). Maternal verbal sensitivity and child language comprehension. *Infant Behavior and Development, 20,* 247–258.

Bernstein Ratner, N., & Pye, C. (1984). Higher pitch in BT is not universal: Acoustic evidence from Quiche Mayan. *Journal of Child Language, 11,* 515–522.

Bloom, K. (1988). Quality of adult vocalizations affects the quality of infant vocalizations. *Journal of Child Language, 15,* 469–480.

Bloom, K. (1990). Selectivity and early infant vocalization. In J. R. Enns (Ed.), *The development of attention: Research and theory* (pp. 121–136). Amsterdam: Elsevier/North-Holland.

Bloom, K., & Lo, E. (1990). Adult perceptions of vocalizing infants. *Infant Behavior and Development, 13,* 209–219.

Bosch, L., & Sebastián-Gallés, N. (2003). Simultaneous bilingualism and the perception of a language-specific vowel contrast in the first year of life. *Language and Speech, 46,* 217–243.

Boysson-Bardies, B. de, Sagart, L., & Durand, C. (1984). Discernable differences in the babbling of infants according to target language. *Journal of Child Language, 11,* 1–15.

Brooks, R., & Meltzoff, A. N. (2005). The development of gaze following and its relation to language. *Developmental Science, 8,* 535–543.

Bruner, J. (1983). *Child's talk: Learning to use language.* New York: W. W. Norton.

Butterworth, G. (2003). Pointing is the royal road to language for babies. In S. Kita (Ed.), *Pointing: Where language, culture, and cognition meet* (pp. 9–33). Mahwah, NJ: Erlbaum.

Camaioni, L. (2001). Early language. In G. Bremner & A. Fogel (Eds.), *Blackwell handbook of infant development: Handbooks of developmental psychology* (pp. 404–426). Malden, MA: Blackwell.

Campbell, A. L., & Namy, L. L. (2003). The role of social referential context and verbal and nonverbal symbol learning. *Child Development, 74,* 549–563.

Carpenter, M., Nagell, K., & Tomasello, M. (1998). Social cognition, joint attention, and communicative competence from 9 to 15 months of age. *Monographs of the Society for Research in Child Development, 63* (Serial No. 255).

Casby, M. W., & Cumpata, J. F. (1986). A protocol for the assessment of prelinguistic intentional communication. *Journal of Communication Disorders, 19,* 251–260.

Clarke-Stewart, K. A. (1973). Interactions between mothers and their young children: Characteristics and consequences. *Monographs of the Society for Research in Child Development, 38* (Serial No. 153).

Coggins, T. E., Olswang, L. B., & Guthrie, J. (1987). Assessing communicative intents in young children: Low structured observation or elicitation tasks. *Journal of Speech and Hearing Disorders, 52,* 44–49.

Cooper, R. P., & Aslin, R. N. (1990). Preference for infant-directed speech in the first month after birth. *Child Development, 61,* 1584–1595.

DeCasper A. J., & Spence M. J. (1986). Prenatal maternal speech influences newborns'perception of speech sounds. *Infant Behavior & Development, 9,* 133–150.

Eimas, P. D. (1975). Auditory and phonetic coding of the cues for speech: Discrimination of the [r-l] distinction by young infants. *Perception & Psychophysics, 18,* 341–347.

Eimas, P. D., Siqueland, E. R., Jusczyk, P. W., & Vigorrito, J. (1971). Speech perception in infants. *Science, 171,* 303–306.

Fenson, L., Dale, P. S., Reznick, J. S., Bates, E., Thal, D. J., & Pethick, S. J. (1994). Variability in early communicative development. *Monographs of the Society for Research in Child Development, 59* (Serial No. 242).

Fenson, L., Marchman, V., Thal, D., Dale, P., Reznick, S., & Bates, E. (2007). *The MacArthur-Bates Communicative Development Inventories: User's guide and technical manual* (2nd ed.). Baltimore, MD: Paul Brookes.

Fernald, A. (1992). Human maternal vocalizations to infants as biologically relevant signals: An evolutionary perspective. In J. H. Barkov, L. Cosmides, & J. Tooby (Eds.), *The adapted mind: Evolutionary psychology and the generation of culture* (pp. 391–428). New York: Oxford University Press.

Fernald, A., & Mazzie, C. (1991). Prosody and focus in speech to infants and adults. *Developmental Psychology, 27,* 209–221.

Fernald, A., & Morikawa, H. (1993). Common themes and cultural variation in Japanese and American mothers' speech to infants. *Child Development, 64,* 637–656.

Fernald, A., Taeschner, T., Dunn, J., Papousek, M., Boysson-Bardies, B. de, & Fukui, I. (1989). A cross-language study of prosodic modifications in mothers' and fathers' speech to preverbal infants. *Journal of Child Language, 16,* 477–501.

Goldman, H. J. (2001). Parental reports of "MAMA" sounds in infants: An exploratory study. *Journal of Child Language, 28,* 497–506.

Goldstein, M. H., King, A. P., & West, M. J. (2003). Social interaction shapes babbling: Testing parallels between birdsong and speech. *Proceedings of the National Academy of Sciences, 100,* 8030–8035.

Golinkoff, R. M., & Alioto, A. (1995). Infant-directed speech facilitates lexical learning in adults learning Chinese: Implications for language acquisition. *Journal of Child Language, 22,* 703–726.

Gómez, R. L., & Gerken, L.A. (2000). Infant artificial language learning and language acquisition. *Trends in Cognitive Sciences, 4,* 178–186.

Goodwyn, S., Acredolo, L., & Brown, C. (2000). Impact of symbolic gesturing on early language development. *Journal of Nonverbal Behavior, 24,* 81–103.

Harding, C. G. (1983). Setting the stage for language acquisition: Communication development in the first year. In R. M. Golinkoff (Ed.), *The transition from prelinguistic to linguistic communication* (pp. 93–115). Hillsdale, NJ: Erlbaum.

Harding, C. G., Weissman, L., Kromelow, S., & Stilson, S. R. (1997). Shared minds: How mothers and infants co-construct early patterns of choice within intentional communication partnerships. *Infant Mental Health Journal, 18,* 24–39.

Hart, B., & Risley, T. (1995). Meaningful differences in the everyday experience of young American children. Baltimore: Brookes.

Heath, S. B. (1983). *Ways with words: Language, life and work in communities and classrooms.* Cambridge, UK: Cambridge University Press.

Hoff, E. (2003). The specificity of environmental influence: Socioeconomic status affects early vocabulary development via maternal speech. *Child Development, 74,* 1368–1378.

Hoff, E., & Naigles, L. (2002). How children use input in acquiring a lexicon. *Child Development, 73,* 418–433.

Huttenlocher, J., Haight, W., Bryk, A., Seltzer, M., & Lyons, T. (1991). Early vocabulary growth: Relation to language input and gender. *Developmental Psychology, 27,* 236–248.

Ingram, D. (1995). The cultural basis of prosodic modifications to infants and children: A response to Fernald's universalist theory. *Journal of Child Language, 22,* 223–233.

Johnston, J. C., Durieux-Smith, A., & Bloom, K. A. (2005). Teaching gestural signs to infants to advance child development: A review of the evidence. *First Language, 25,* 235–251.

Junge, C., Hagoort, P., Kooijman, V., & Cutler, A. (2010). Brain potentials for word segmentation at seven months predict later language development. In K. Franich, K. M. Iserman, & L. L. Keil (Eds.), *Proceedings of the 34th annual Boston University Conference on Language Development* (Vol. 1, pp. 209–220). Somerville, MA: Cascadilla Press.

Jusczyk, P. W., & Aslin, R.N. (1995). Infants' detection of the sound patterns of words in fluent speech. *Cognitive Psychology, 29,* 1–23.

Jusczyk, P. W., Luce, P. A., & Charles-Luce, J. (1994). Infants' sensitivity to phonotactic patterns in the native language. *Journal of Memory and Language, 33,* 630–645.

Kaplan, P., Bachorowski, J. A., Smoski, M. J., & Hudenko, W. J. (2002). Infants of depressed mothers, although competent learners, fail to learn in response to their own mothers' infant-directed speech. *Psychological Science, 13,* 268–271.

Kemler Nelson, D. G., Jusczyk, P. W., Mandel, D. R., Myers, J., Turk, A., & Gerken, L. A. (1995). The Headturn Preference Procedure for testing auditory perception. *Infant Behavior and Development, 18,* 111–116.

Kuhl, P. K. (2007). Is speech learning "gated" by the social brain? *Developmental Science, 10,* 110–120.

Kuhl, P. K., Andruski, J. E., Christovich, I. A., Christovich, L. A., Kozhevnikova, E. V., Ryskina, V. L., Stolyarova, E. I., Sundberg, U., & Lacerda, F. (1997). Cross-language analysis of phonetic units in language addressed to infants. *Science, 277,* 684–686.

Kuhl, P. K., Tsao, F.-M., & Liu, H.-M. (2003). Foreign-language experience in infancy: Effects of short-term exposure and social interaction on phonetic learning. *Proceedings of the National Academy of Sciences, USA, 100,* 9096–9101.

Kuhl, P. K., Williams, K. A., Lacerda, F., Stevens, K. N., & Lindblom, B. (1992). Linguistic experience alters phonetic perception in infants by 6 months of age. *Science, 255,* 606–608.

Landry, S. H., Smith, K. E., & Miller-Loncar, C. (1997). Predicting cognitive-language and social growth curves from early maternal behaviors in children at varying degrees of biological risk. *Developmental Psychology, 33,* 1040–1053.

Legerstee, M., & Barillas, Y. (2003). Sharing attention and pointing to objects at 12 months: Is the intentional stance implied? *Cognitive Development, 18,* 91–110.

Mampe, B., Friederici, A. D., Christophe, A. & Wermke, K. (2009). Newborns' cry melody is shaped by their native language. *Current Biology, 19,* 1994–1997.

Mandel, D. R., Jusczyk, P. W., & Pisoni, D. B. (1995). Infants' recognition of the sound patterns of their own names. *Psychological Science, 6*(5), 314–317.

Marcus, G. F., Vijayan, S., Bandi Rao, S., & Vishton, P. M. (1999). Rule learning by seven-month-old infants. *Science, 283,* 77–80.

Masataka, N. (1993). Effects of contingent and noncontigent maternal stimulation on the vocal behavior of three- to four-month-old Japanese infants. *Journal of Child Language, 20,* 303–312.

Masur, E. F. (1983). Gestural development, dual-directional signaling and the transition to words. *Journal of Psycholinguistic Research, 12,* 93–109.

Mattock, K., Molnar, M., Polka, L., & Burnham, D. (2008). The developmental course of lexical tone perception in the first year of life. *Cognition, 106,* 1367–1381.

Meadows, D., Elias, G., & Bain, J. (2000). Mothers' ability to identify infants' communicative acts. *Journal of Child Language, 27,* 393–406.

Mehler, J., Jusczyk, P. W., Lambertz, G., Halsted, N., Bertoncini, J. & Amiel-Tison, C. (1988). A precursor of language acquisition in young infants. *Cognition, 29,* 143–178.

Meltzoff, A. N. (2007). "Like me": A foundation for social cognition. *Developmental Science, 10, 126–134.*

Messinger, D. S., & Fogel, A. (1998). Give and take: The development of conventional infant gestures. *Merrill-Palmer Quarterly, 44,* 566–590.

Morikawa, H., Shand, N., & Kosawa, Y. (1988). Maternal speech to prelingual infants in Japan and the United States: Relationships among functions, forms and referents. *Journal of Child Language, 15,* 237–256.

Mosier, C. E., & Rogoff, B. (1994). Infants' instrumental use of their mothers to achieve their goals. *Child Development, 65,* 70–79.

Mundy, P., & Acra, F. (2006). Joint attention, social engagement, and the development of social competence. In P. Marshall & N. Fox (Eds.), *The development of social engagement: Neurological perspectives* (pp. 81–117). New York: Oxford University Press.

Murray, A. D., Johnson, J., & Peters, J. (1990). Fine-tuning of utterance length to preverbal infants: Effects on later language development. *Journal of Child Language, 17,* 511–526.

Nazzi, T., Bertoncini, J., & Mehler, J. (1998). Language discrimination by newborns: Toward an understanding of the role of rhythm. *Journal of Experimental*

Psychology: Human Perception and Performance, 24, 756–766.

Nazzi, T., Paterson, S., & Karmiloff-Smith, A. (2003). Early word segmentation by infants and toddlers with Williams Syndrome. *Infancy, 4,* 251–271.

Newman, R. S., Bernstein Ratner, N., Jusczyk, A. M., Jusczyk, P. W., & Dow, K. A. (2006). Infants' early ability to segment the conversational speech signal predicts later language development: a retrospective analysis. *Developmental Psychology, 42,* 643–655.

Ochs, E. (1988). *Culture and language development. Language acquisition and language socialization in a Samoan village.* New York: Cambridge University Press.

Olswang, L., Bain, B., Dunn, C., & Cooper, J. (1983). The effects of stimulus variation on lexical learning. *Journal of Speech and Hearing Disorders, 48,* 192–201.

Pan, B. A., Rowe, M. L., Singer, J. D. & Snow, C. E. (2005). Maternal correlates of growth in toddler vocabulary production in low-income families. *Child Development, 76,* 763–82.

Prizant, B. M., & Wetherby, A. M. (1990). Toward an integrated view of early language and communicative development and socioemotional development. *Topics in Language Disorders, 10,* 1–16.

Ratner, N. K., & Bruner, J. S. (1978). Games, social exchange and the acquisition of language. *Journal of Child Language, 5,* 391–401.

Reilly, S., Eadie, P., Bavin, E. L., Wake, M., Prior, M., Williams, J., Bretherton, I., Barrett, Y., & Ukoumunne, O. C. (2006). Growth of infant communication between 8 and 12 months: A population study. *Journal of Paediatrics and Child Health, 42,* 764–770.

Rescorla, L. (1989). The Language Development Survey: A screening tool for delayed language in toddlers. *Journal of Speech and Hearing Disorders, 54,* 567–699.

Rescorla, L., & Alley, A. (2001). Validation of the Language Development Survey (LDS): A parent report tool for identifying language delay in toddlers. *Journal of Speech, Language, and Hearing Research, 44,* 434–445.

Rollins, P. R. (2003). Caregivers' contingent comments to 9-month-old infants: Relationship with later language. *Applied Psycholinguistics, 24,* 221–234.

Rowe, M. L. (2008). Child-directed speech: relation to socioeconomic status, knowledge of child development and child vocabulary skill. *Journal of Child Language, 35,* 185–205.

Saffran, J. R., Aslin, R. N., & Newport, E. L. (1996). Statistical learning by 8-month-old infants. *Science, 274,* 1926–1928.

Santelmann, L. M., & Jusczyk, P. W. (1998). Sensitivity to discontinuous dependencies in language learners: Evidence for limitations in processing space. *Cognition, 69,* 105–134.

Schieffelin, B. B. (1990). *The give and take of everyday life: Language socialization of Kaluli children.* Cambridge, UK: Cambridge University Press.

Singh, L., Morgan, J. L., & Best, C. T. (2002). Infants' listening preferences: Baby talk or happy talk? *Infancy, 3,* 365–394.

Smith, N. A., & Trainor, L. J. (2008). Infant-directed speech is modulated by infant feedback. *Infancy, 13,* 410–420.

Snow, C. (1977). The development of conversation between mothers and babies. *Journal of Child Language, 4,* 1–22.

Sugarman, S. (1984). The development of preverbal communication. In R. Schiefelbusch & J. Pickar (Eds.), *The acquisition of communicative competence* (pp. 23–67). Baltimore: University Park Press.

Sundara, M., Polka, L., & Molnar, M. (2008). Development of coronal stop perception: Bilingual infants keep pace with their monolingual peers. *Cognition, 108,* 232–242.

Tincoff, R., & Jusczyk, P. W. (1999). Some beginnings of word comprehension in 6-month-olds. *Psychological Science, 10*(2), 172–175.

Tomasello, M. (1988). The role of joint attentional processes in early language development. *Language Sciences, 10,* 69–88.

Tomasello, M. (1999). Social cognition before the revolution. In P. Rochat (Ed.), *Early social cognition: Understanding others in the first months of life* (pp. 301–314). Mahwah, NJ: Erlbaum.

Trevarthen, C., & Aiken, K. J. (2001). Infant intersubjectivity: Research, theory, and clinical applications. *Journal of Child Psychology and Psychiatry and Allied Disciplines, 42,* 3–48.

Tsushima, T., Takizawa, O., Sasaki, M., Shiraki, S., Nishi, K., Kohno, M., Menyuk, P., & Best, C. T. (1994). *Discrimination of English /r-l/ and /w-y/ by Japanese infants at 6-12 months: Language specific developmental changes in speech perception abilities.* Paper presented at the International Conference on Spoken Language Processing (ICLSP), Yokohama, Japan.

Watt, N., Wetherby, A., & Shumway, S. (2006). Prelinguistic predictors of language outcome at 3 years of age. *Journal of Speech, Language and Hearing Research, 49,* 1224–1237.

Werker, J. F., & Tees, R. C. (1984). Cross-language speech perception: Evidence for perceptual reorganization during the first year of life. *Infant Behavior & Development, 7,* 49–63.

Wetherby, A., Cain, D., Yonclas, D., & Walker, V. (1988). Analysis of intentional communication of normal children from the prelinguistic to the multi-word stage. *Journal of Speech and Hearing Research, 31,* 240–252.

Wetherby, A., & Prizant, B. (2002). *Communication and symbolic behavior scales.* Baltimore: Paul A. Brookes.

Windsor, J., Glaze, L. E., Koga, S. F., & the Bucharest Early Intervention Core Group (2007). Language acquisition with limited input: Romanian institution and foster care. *Journal of Speech, Language, and Hearing Research, 50,* 1365–1381.

Yip, M. (2002). *Tone.* Cambridge: Cambridge University Press.

Phonological Development

Learning Sounds and Sound Patterns

Carol Stoel-Gammon
University of Washington

Lise Menn
University of Colorado

Why do children's early attempts at words sound so different from adult pronunciations? It seems obvious that *tore* is easier to say than *store*, but why do some toddlers say *gig* instead of *pig*? And if most children learning English say *tore* for *store*, why do some of them say it as *sore* or *door*?

In this chapter we describe how children move from babbling to speaking. Before we start, however, we need to study the speech sounds themselves, so that you can see the enormous amount of coordination that children need to master in learning to say them. Pronunciation of words is an incredible skill, but it becomes so automatic that as adults we are unaware of it—until we try to analyze it, try to pronounce words in a new language, or watch X-ray videos of people's tongue, lips, and lower jaw moving while they are speaking (look at **http://psyc.queensu.ca/faculty/munhall/x-ray**).

English Speech Sounds and Sound Patterns

We need the International Phonetic Alphabet because our English spelling system is full of ambiguities and thus is a poor tool for describing speech sounds. Does "A" mean its sound in *Sam*, its sound in *same*, or one of its two sounds in *Martha*? School grammar terms like hard and soft "g" or long and short "a" are clumsy. And there are multiple ways of spelling almost any sound; for example, the *f* in *fat* can also be spelled *ff*, *ph*, and even *gh* (as in *cough*). Because sounds and letters match up so poorly, linguists and speech scientists describe spoken words as being composed of speech sounds or **segments** rather than "letters." And instead of the English alphabet, we use a system called the **International Phonetic Alphabet (IPA)**. The IPA symbols presented in Table 3.1 are enough for the basic speech sounds of general American English, plus some that are needed for other dialects and other languages spoken in the United States. For the full chart, go to the International Phonetics Association website, **www.langsci.ucl.ac.uk/ipa**. To hear pronunciations for these and many other sounds, click on the IPA chart at **http://web.uvic.ca/ling/resources/ipa**

table 3.1			Phoneme Symbols for Speech Sounds of General American English							
Vowels				Consonants						
Symbol	Example	Symbol	Example	Symbol	Example	Symbol	Example	Symbol	Example	
/i/	bead	/ʊ/	put	/p/	pill	/f/	fie	/h/	high	
/ɪ/	bid	/u/	boot	/t/	till	/θ/	thigh	/m/	ram	
/eɪ/	bait	/ʌ/	putt	/k/	kill	/s/	sigh	/n/	ran	
/ɛ/	bet	/ɝ/	bird	/b/	bow	/ʃ/	shy	/ŋ/	rang	
/æ/	bat	/aɪ/	bite	/d/	doe	/v/	vat	/l/	led	
/a/	tot	/æʊ/	bout[a]	/g/	go	/ð/	that	/r/	red	
/ɔ/	taught	/ɔɪ/	boy	/tʃ/	chill	/z/	Caesar	/j/	yet	
/oʊ/	tote	/ə/	about[b]	/dʒ/	Jill	/ʒ/	seizure	/w/	wet	

[a]This vowel is also transcribed /aʊ/.

[b]This vowel occurs in unstressed syllables only.

handbook.htm. A few hours' practice in using the IPA to rewrite English words with the sounds you really use when you say them will give you a good start on mastering it.

Phonetics: The Production and Description of Speech Sounds

Linguists and speech scientists group the sounds of language primarily by what our mouths do in order to produce them. For example, the sounds /p/, /b/, and /m/ are all made with your lips closed, so they are classed together as **labial** (lip) consonants. (In this chapter, we will usually put IPA symbols for the sounds of adult words in / / brackets, and sounds of children's pronunciations in [ ] brackets. We also use [ ] brackets when we discuss the fine details of adult pronunciations.) Sounds like /f/, /s/, and "sh" are all made with airstream friction (say them—they all sound like air hissing out of a hose), so they are classed together as **fricative** (friction) consonants. Understanding such similarities and differences among the groups of speech sounds is the key to understanding young children's speech patterns, and also dialect differences and foreign accents.

Descriptive Features: Classifying Sounds by How They Are Produced

There are two main kinds of descriptive terms or features. Some, like "labial," help to describe the shape of your vocal tract during sound production; others, like "fricative," describe the source of the sound in the vocal tract.

The source of most speech sounds is the hiss of airstream turbulence or the buzz of **vocal fold** vibration or both of these together. Turbulence occurs when air is forced through a narrow opening. In the vocal tract, the narrow opening is usually made by bringing one of your **lower articulators** (lower lip, teeth, and tongue) close to one of your **upper articulators** (upper lip, teeth, and roof of the mouth). However, when you make an /h/, the narrow passage may be the opening between your vocal folds, which is called the **glottis**. (The common term "vocal cords" for the vibratory sound source in your larynx is misleading, because the structure that is set into vibration by air flowing through the larynx is a pair of folds of connective tissue, not a pair of cords.)

If the source of a speech sound is partly or entirely vocal fold vibration, it is called a **voiced** sound; if there's no vocal fold vibration, the sound is called **voiceless** or **unvoiced**. Your vocal folds have to vibrate to make a singing tone, so that gives you a way to tell whether a sound is voiced: Voiced sounds like /m/ or /v/ can be hummed or sung, but unvoiced sounds like /p/ or /f/ can't be hummed at all. (/b/ can be hummed for a short time: keep your lips closed tightly and let your mouth fill up with the air coming from your lungs.)

The sounds produced by the vocal folds or by airstream friction take on different qualities depending on the exact position of your lips, jaws, and tongue; that's why /f/ sounds different from /s/ even though both have friction as their source, and /a/ sounds different from /i/ even though both have the vibration of vocal folds as their source. The study of how the shape of the vocal tract gives sounds their distinct identities is **articulatory phonetics**.

The Major Sound Classes: Vowels and Consonants

We make **vowel** sounds with the vocal tract relatively unobstructed, so air flows through it smoothly. Different vowel sounds result from varying the positions of your articulators: how wide your jaw opening is, whether the bulk of the tongue is held toward the front or the back of your mouth, and whether your lips are pursed, relaxed, or pulled out into a smile position.

Consonant sounds are made with a more constricted vocal tract than vowels. They are usually classified by three descriptive features. The first is the **place of articulation**, which means the place where the constriction is tightest—roughly, which upper articulator is closest to which lower articulator. The other two features give information about the consonant's sound source: the **manner of articulation** (how the air flows while the sound is being made), and the **voicing** (presence or absence of vocal fold vibration during production). Table 3.2 gives a classification of the consonants of American English.

The **stops** are the consonants made with the tightest vocal tract constriction; they are produced with upper and lower articulators pressed together so tightly that no air can escape from the mouth. The English unvoiced stops are /p/, /t/, and /k/; our voiced stops are /b/, /d/, and /g/.

We have already mentioned some of the **fricatives**. English has eight **oral fricatives**, which are made with lips, tongue, and/or teeth. The four voiceless oral fricatives are /f/, /s/, "sh" (as in *shy*), written in IPA as /ʃ/, and /θ/ (as in *thigh*). The four English **voiced fricatives**, made with both vocal fold vibration and oral airstream turbulence, are /v/, /z/, /ð/ (as in *the*), and /ʒ/ (the consonant in the middle of the word *seizure*). /h/ is our ninth friction-based sound; it's a voiceless consonant that is sometimes produced with light fric-

table 3.2	Classification of Consonants by Place of Articulation and Manner of Articulation						
Place	**Bilabial**	**Labiodental**	**Interdental**	**Alveolar**	**(Pre)-Palatal**	**Velar**	**Glottal**
Manner							
Stop	p b			t d		k g	
Fricative		f v	θ ð	s z	ʃ ʒ		h
Affricate					tʃ dʒ		
Nasal	m			n		ŋ	
Liquid				l	r		
Glide	w				j		

tion in the **glottis** (the space between the vocal folds), so it is called a **glottal fricative**. This name isn't perfect, though, because /h/ is often made with light friction in your mouth instead of your glottis; its actual place of articulation depends on the sound that follows it.

Two English consonants begin like a stop and end like a fricative; they are called **affricates**. /tʃ/, as in *chill,* is a voiceless affricate; /dʒ/, as in *Jill,* is a voiced affricate.

When we breathe normally, our mouths are closed and air from the lungs goes up through the pharynx into the nasal cavity and out through our nostrils. In making the speech sounds that we have described so far, however, we close off passage from the pharynx to the nose by raising the **velum** (soft palate), a soft-tissue extension of the roof of the mouth (hard palate). When the velum is raised, the air can't get into the nasal passage, so it must go out of the mouth, as shown in Figure 3.1. But three speech sounds of English, the **nasal stops** /m/, /n/, and /ŋ/, are made with your velum lowered so that air can escape through the nose. Wet the side of your finger and hold it under your nose while you hum these three consonants; the wet spot on your finger will be slightly cooled by the air flowing from your nose. (English speakers are often unaware of the third nasal stop, the /ŋ/, because it does not have its own symbol in our alphabet. It is the sound spelled *n* in *finger,* and it is also the final sound in words that end with the letters *ng*—in most varieties of English, there is no real /g/ in *ring* or *sing*).

Together, oral (i.e., non-nasal) stop, fricative, and affricate consonants are referred to as **obstruents**, because they fully or partially obstruct the airflow. The three nasal stops are not obstruents, however, because air flows smoothly out of the nose when we say /m, n, ŋ/.

The **liquids** /r/ and /l/ and the **glides** /j/ and /w/ are made with less constriction than the fricatives. Their airflow is smooth, without friction noise. Because glides and liquids have phonetic characteristics intermediate between the vowels and the obstruent consonants, they are often called **semivowels**. One vowel-like characteristic of liquids is the role

---

figure 3.1   **The Vocal Tract**

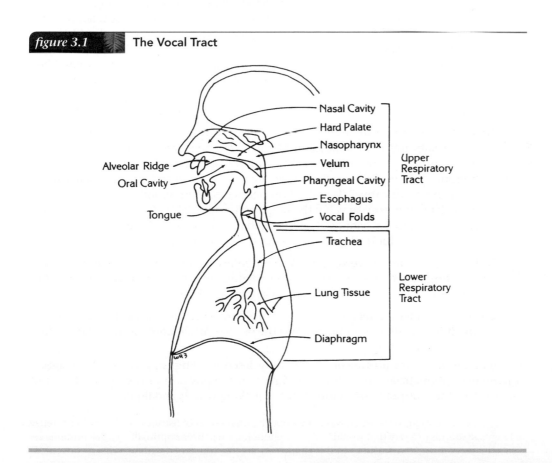

that they can play in syllable structure: We usually think of a syllable as having to contain a vowel, but English has syllables in which a liquid is used just like a vowel. For example, the second syllable of *legal* is spelled with an *a*, but what we say is /li-gl/ or /lig-l/; and in most varieties of American English, the noun *record* is /rɛ-krd/. The nasal consonants also can serve in place of vowels: consider *random* /ræn-dm/ and *season* /si-zn/.

The Shape of the Vocal Tract: Position of Articulation

As we said, the point at which the upper and lower articulators (upper lip, upper teeth, roof of the mouth; lower lip, lower teeth, tongue) touch or approach each other most closely is usually called the **position of articulation** or **place of articulation**. The sounds /p/, /b/, and /m/ are all produced with closed lips, so their place of articulation is called **labial** (or **bilabial**).

Moving from your lips toward the back of your mouth, the other positions usually used in describing English sounds are shown in Figure 3.1 and listed across the top of Table 3.2.

Labiodental: /f/ and /v/. These sounds are articulated with your lower lip resting lightly against your upper teeth, leaving a slight space between the lip and teeth for air to escape from your mouth.

Interdental: /θ/, as in *thigh*, and /ð/, as in *thy*. This term describes sounds made with your tongue lightly touching the upper teeth, perhaps projecting out slightly beyond them.

Alveolar: /t, d, n, s, z, l/ These are sounds made by bringing the front part of your tongue in contact with or very close to the alveolar ridge (the gum ridge behind your upper teeth). The fricatives /s/ and /z/ are also alveolar; they are made with the tongue in essentially the same position as /t, d/, and /n/, but of course not quite in contact with the alveolar ridge, since they have to let the air hiss out. The sound /l/ (at the beginnings of syllables) is made with the front of your tongue touching the alveolar ridge, but /l/ is not a stop, because when you make it, air escapes from your mouth by flowing out around the side of your tongue. Check this by saying /l/ and then breathing in without changing the position of your tongue. It will feel cool on one or both sides, where the incoming air flows over it.

(Pre-)Palatal: These are sounds articulated with your tongue near or contacting the hard palate and/or the slope leading up to it from the alveolar ridge. English has no palatal stops, but your tongue makes contact just in front of the palatal area at the beginning of the affricates /tʃ/ and /dʒ/, and it almost touches the hard palate when you make the fricatives /ʃ/ and /ʒ/ (in phonetics, these sounds are properly called pre-palatal or alveopalatal, but the simpler term "palatal" will do here). Your tongue is fairly close to the hard palate for the glide /j/ (remember, this is pronounced "y") and sometimes for the liquid /r/, but not close enough to cause airstream friction.

Velar: /k/, /g/, and the velar nasal /ŋ/. Velar refers to sounds made when the back of your tongue touches your velum (soft palate). English has no velar fricatives, but many other languages do, including German and Russian.

Glottal: This term refers to sounds produced by narrowing or closing your glottis, and it is sometimes (but not always) the place of articulation of the fricative /h/.

Some additional features are needed for fully describing English and other languages—in particular, phoneticians have been learning that the position of the low-back part of your tongue, the **tongue root**, is important in making vowels and liquids.[1]

---

[1] A classical goal of linguistic research was to describe the smallest set of features needed to characterize all language sounds in a way that would bring out phonological patterns optimally; such a minimal set is called a set of distinctive features. In this chapter we are not concerned with whether a convenient descriptive feature is distinctive.

Contrast: The Phoneme

How do we know that two audibly different sounds are both kinds of /t/, but that another sound, objectively similar to them, is a /d/ or a /k/? Native speakers of a language find such a question odd; we are normally quite sure that some pairs of sounds are "the same" and other pairs are "different." But confusion sometimes arises when two different sounds are spelled alike, for example, the two sounds /θ/ and /ð/, both spelled *th*. Remember what we did to clear up that confusion: To show that these are two different speech sounds, we looked at a pair of words, *thigh* and *thy*, that are kept distinct merely by the difference in pronunciation of these two sounds. We could also have used the pair *wreath* and *wreathe*, where the contrasting sounds are at the ends of the words. A pair of words that differs only with respect to one pair of sounds, like *thigh* and *thy* or *chill* and *Jill* or *wreath* and *wreathe*, is called a **minimal pair**. Two sounds are said to **contrast** if there is a minimal pair of words that displays the fact that simply changing from one sound to the other produces a change in meaning, or changes a word to a nonword—for example, changing the English word *thistle* /θɪsl/ to the nonword /ðɪsl/ (as in "*this'll* be okay"). The set of contrasting sounds in a language are its **phonemes**, so the unvoiced /θ/ and the voiced /ð/ are separate phonemes in English, even though they are both spelled with *th*.

Phonotactics: Constraints on Possible Words

Not every sequence of speech sounds is a possible word: There are **phonotactic constraints** on the possible sequences of speech sounds. No English word begins with the sound /ŋ/, which is why a set like *ram, ran, rang* had to be used to present the nasals in Table 3.1. If a new product were to be called Ngicekreem, it might be pronounced /nəgaɪskrim/ or /ɛŋgaɪskrim/, but few English speakers would be able to say /ŋaɪskrim/. We have the same problem with African names like Nkomo /ŋkomo/; this name is usually turned into /n-komo/ or /ɛŋkomo/. Linguists say that English has a phonotactic constraint on the position of /ŋ/: No word can begin with that sound. But many languages don't have this constraint, and some children learning to speak English don't have it either.

Many phonotactic constraints concern consonant clusters and their possible positions in words. For example, English words frequently end with consonant clusters such as *lp* or *rt*, but no English word can begin with these sound sequences. We can say *trap* and *part*, *plot* and *pulp*, but we cannot have a word like *lpot* or *rtup*. However, Russian has words beginning with /lb/ or /rt/; *lba* means "of the forehead" and *rta* means "of the mouth."

In learning a first or second language, mastering a new cluster or a new word position for a familiar sound may require as much work as mastering a new sound. English speakers learning Russian usually have problems with words like *rta* and *lba,* as well as the truly impressive consonant cluster in *vzglyad* ("glance"). Breaking through **constraints** on what sequences of sounds can be pronounced is just as central to acquisition of phonology as learning to pronounce individual phonemes.

Suprasegmental Aspects of Speech: Stress and Intonation Contour

Compare the noun *record* in "Make a record of that!" and the verb in *record* in "Let's record that!" The differences between these two words come from the fact that noun /**rɛ**-krd/ is accented or **stressed** on the first syllable, but the verb /rə-**kɔrd**/ is stressed on the second syllable. Voice pitch, loudness, and timing are all involved in the correct production of English stress: The stressed or accented syllables in a word are usually higher in pitch, longer, and louder than they would be if they were unaccented. Pitch, loudness, and timing are called **suprasegmental** phenomena because they basically concern the way groups of segments are pronounced, rather than focusing on single segments.

The pitch or melody of your voice naturally rises and falls during speaking; the pattern of pitch changes accompanying a phrase or sentence is called its **intonation**

contour. Strong final rises in pitch are found in many (but not all!) types of questions, and smaller rises are often found in tentative polite statements. A rise in pitch corresponds to an increase in frequency of vocal fold vibration; this can easily be measured with computer programs for speech sound analysis, such as PRAAT, which can be downloaded from the Internet.

Production: The Prelinguistic Period

Now we can turn to how children learn to produce speech sounds. Chapter 2 introduced the development of children's vocalizations during the first year of life. Newborn infants begin with simple cries. Prelinguistic vocalizations can be divided into two categories: (1) **reflexive vocalizations**—cries, coughs, burps, and involuntary grunts that seem to be automatic responses reflecting the physical state of the infant, and that don't change much over the first year—and (2) **nonreflexive** (or **non-automatic vocalizations**, like cooing, voluntary grunts, or jargon babbling, which develop over the first year of life. These non-automatic productions contain some of the phonetic features found in adult languages.

All infants seem to pass through the same stages of vocal development. But these stages do not have sharp boundaries, and vocalization types typically overlap from one stage to another. A new stage is marked by the appearance of vocal behaviors that are not observed in the preceding period, but the older behaviors may not disappear until weeks or months after the new ones have started. (For a comprehensive review, see Oller, 2000; Vihman, 1996.)

> **Stage 1. Reflexive vocalizations (birth to 2 months).** Most vocalizations in this stage are reflexive, such as crying and fussing, or vegetative sounds like coughing, burping, and sneezing. In addition, the baby may make some vowel-like sounds. The small size of the oral cavity and the position of the larynx limit the types of sound that can be produced (Lieberman, Crelin, & Klatt, 1972).
>
> **Stage 2. Cooing and laughter (2 to 4 months).** During and after this stage, rapid growth of the head and neck area allows production of a greater variety of sounds. Infants begin to make some comfort-state vocalizations, often called "cooing" or "gooing." These vocalizations seem to be made in the back of the mouth, with velar consonants and back vowels. Crying typically becomes less frequent, and, much to parents' delight, sustained laughter and infant chuckles appear.
>
> **Stage 3. Vocal play (4 to 6 months).** In this period babies seem to be testing their vocal apparatus. They may produce very loud and very soft sounds (yells and whispers), and very high and very low sounds (squeals and growls). Some babies produce long series of raspberries (bilabial trills) and sustained vowels, and occasionally some rudimentary consonant-plus-vowel syllables.
>
> **Stage 4. Canonical babbling (6 months and older).** The prime feature of this period is the appearance of canonical babble—that is, sequences of consonant–vowel syllables with adultlike timing. For the first time, babies sound as though they are trying to produce words, and if they happen to produce [mama] or [dada], parents may feel that their baby has begun to call them by name. Two types of multi-syllable utterances usually occur in this period: **reduplicated babbles** (strings of identical syllables, like [bababa]) and **variegated babbles** (syllable strings with varying consonants and vowels, like [bagidabu]). Reduplicated babbles predominate initially, but around 12 or 13 months, variegated babbles become the more frequent type.

During this period, infants start to notice similarities and differences between the sounds they hear and the sounds they produce (Goldstein & Schwabe, 2008; Stoel-Gammon, 1998a; 2011). Infants with hearing loss are generally delayed in the production of canonical syllables and are slower to move through the stages of prelinguistic development (Moeller et al., 2007; Oller, 2000; Stoel-Gammon & Otomo, 1986).

Stage 5. Jargon stage (10 months and older). The last stage of babbling generally overlaps with the early period of meaningful speech. It is characterized by strings of sounds and syllables uttered with a rich variety of stress and intonational patterns. This kind of output is also called conversational babble, or **jargon**.

Some children seem to enjoy playing with sounds when they do not appear to be "talking" to anyone or to be playing with a toy that might have "sound effects." Their **sound play** may contain recurring favorite sound sequences, or even early words. Jargon vocalizations, in contrast, are delivered with eye contact, gesture, and intonation so rich and appropriate that the person addressed typically feels compelled to respond, at least with "You don't say!" A child producing jargon vocalizations seems to grasp the social nature of conversation and has merely missed the fact that the sounds in it have particular meanings. Sometimes, the gestures and the context make it clear that the intonation—the rise and fall of the pitch of the child's voice—is carrying interactional meaning (greeting, demanding, complaining, offering), even if the articulated sounds are not. At other times, however, the child is apparently not conveying any meaning by her eloquent pitch modulation; instead, she appears to be imitating the outward form of adult conversation—for example, in pretended telephone conversations. (A Web search on terms like "babbling baby" will yield many examples on YouTube.)

Sounds of Babbling

The speech-like sounds used by infants change dramatically during the first year of life. In the first six months, vowel articulations tend to predominate, as mentioned earlier, most of the consonantal sounds are produced in the back of the mouth (i.e., sounds like [k] or [g]). With the onset of the canonical babbling stage, there is a marked shift toward front consonants, particularly [m], [h], and [d].

Between 6 and 12 months of age, the sound repertoire expands considerably. During the first part of this expansion period, all babies sound similar, even with input languages as different as English, Arabic, Spanish, Japanese, and Chinese (Lee, Davis, & MacNeilage, 2009; Locke, 1983), as shown by studies examining whether listeners or spectrographic analyses could distinguish the babble of babies who have been exposed to different languages. As children approach the end of the first year, however, their babbling becomes more and more like the language(s) they are hearing. They gradually stop using sounds that they do not hear around them, such as /h/ in French, and they start to produce relatively more of the sounds that are relatively more frequent in their language (de Boysson-Bardies & Vihman, 1991; Vihman, 1996).

Languages also differ in the pitch contour and timing of syllables. During the canonical babbling stage, children's syllables start to acquire the timing and pitch contour of the language around them. Listeners can use this information to recognize babies from their own speech communities (de Boysson-Bardies, Sagart, & Durand, 1984). French infants' babble shows more lengthening of the final syllable of a babble sequence than U.S. infants' babble does, and this pattern is also found when the adult languages are contrasted (Levitt & Wang, 1991).

A relatively small set of consonants accounts for the great majority of consonantal sounds that are produced in babbling. In his review of babbling data from 129 infants aged 11 to 12 months, Locke (1983) showed that twelve of the twenty-four consonantal sounds of English accounted for nearly 95 percent of their consonants. These twelve consonants were the six stops ([p, b, t, d, k, g]), two of the nasals ([m, n]), the glides ([w, j]), the fricative [s], and the glottal [h]. The consonants that are frequent in late babbling (the stops, nasals, and glides) are nearly identical to those that appear in the first adult-based words (Stoel-Gammon, 2011), while fricatives like [v] or [ð], affricates like [tʃ], and liquids ([l] and [r]) tend to appear in words later, although there is a fair amount of individual variation

(Menn & Vihman, 2011). So it seems that the consonants of late babbling may serve as the building blocks for the production of words.

The Relationship between Babbling and Speech

As we have just seen, babble has a limited range of sounds that are gradually brought under voluntary control, and most early speech sounds and sound sequences develop directly from these babbled sounds, without a sharp break between babble and speech. Early speech usually coexists with babbling for several months, and some children produce utterances that contain mixtures of babble and words, or that consist of non-communicative sound play based on the sounds of real adult words. Longitudinal studies of prelinguistic vocalizations have shown that it is not only the sounds that tend to carry over from late babble to early speech, it's also the child's preferred sequences of sounds; Vihman (1996) calls these preferred sound sequences **vocal motor schemes**. Early words tend to use the same sounds and sound sequences that the child has preferred in babbling, because she can hear that these words fit the vocal motor schemes that she has managed to bring under voluntary control (see Stoel-Gammon, 1998a, b; 2011).

One factor that predicts early language development is the quality and complexity of canonical babble. Among children with typical development, frequent use of canonical syllables correlates with earlier onset of words, a larger productive vocabulary, and more accurate word productions at 24 to 36 months (Stoel-Gammon, 1998b; Vihman & Greenlee, 1987). A similar relationship has been observed among children with hearing loss: The production of canonical syllables during the prelinguistic period (which is often protracted in this population) partially predicts the quality of phonological development between the ages of 24 and 36 months (see Ertmer & Mellon, 2001; Moeller et al., 2007).

🗨Learning to Make Words

The Beginning of Phonological Development: Protowords

The beginning of speech seems easy to identify for some children: One day they make a sequence of sounds that resembles an adult word, and they do it when that word would be appropriate. These first recognizable words are often greetings, farewells, or other social phrases, like *peekaboo*. Sometimes, however, a child repeatedly uses a form that does not resemble any appropriate adult word; for example, Halliday's (1975) subject Nigel created the form *na* to indicate that he wanted an object. Is a word that the child has made up—a **protoword**—"speech"?

It is, in at least two respects. First, the child who uses a made-up protoword has some voluntary control over his vocalizations. Second, a child using one or two invented words has moved beyond jargon, because she has acquired the difficult concept that specific sequences of sounds have specific meanings. She is now unclear only about the fact that you are supposed to find out what words already exist, instead of making them up for yourself.

The sounds of protowords may be very poorly controlled, and individual instances may vary much more than repeated uses of a word do in adult usage. For example, Menn's (1976) subject Jacob had a protoword that he used to accompany the action of turning something (a wheel, a knob, a page of a book); the form of this "spinning song" varied from *ioioio* to *weeaweeaweea*.

Words and Sounds: Vocabulary and Phonology Interact

As noted above, the sounds and syllables of babble form the building blocks for word productions in young children. The link is especially obvious in some of the first words to appear in the vocabularies of many children acquiring English, specifically *daddy, mommy, baby, hi*. The sounds of these words closely resemble (non-meaningful) babbles like [mama] and [dada]. As adult speakers of English, we know other words for parents: *father* and *mother*. These words do not resemble babble and, in fact, are acquired many months after the more familiar forms *daddy* and *mommy*.

Many people think that children learn words because they are useful in some way, allowing the child to name things they like (*cookie, bottle*) or to request or refuse something (*more, no*). But the sounds of adult words also have an influence on word acquisition. For example, one little girl liked to use words with "sibilant" consonants, that is, words with /s/ and /ʃ/-like sounds (Ferguson & Farwell, 1975). Among her earliest words were *ice, shoes, cereal, cheese, juice, eyes, sit*; she was able to produce the words fairly accurately even though sibilants occur rarely in babble and are not among the "early-acquired" consonants of English. Another child had a preference for words ending with a velar stop ([k] or [g]), a consonant he could produce correctly. His very early vocabulary included a high proportion of words *milk, clock, talk, walk, frog, block, quack, whack, sock*, and *yuk*, all pronounced as [gak] (Stoel-Gammon & Cooper, 1984). Preference for words containing "favorite sounds" is called **lexical selection** and has been documented for many children (see Stoel-Gammon, 2011; Vihman, 1996 for summaries).

When the notion of lexical selection was first introduced, some people wondered whether the words children chose were just those that they heard especially frequently. Perhaps the girl was exposed to many instances of the words *ice, shoes, cereal, cheese, juice, eyes*, while the boy heard the words *milk, clock, talk, walk, frog* many times. To prove that phonological factors played a role in vocabulary acquisition, one would need to be sure that the number of exposures to a set of words was carefully controlled. So researchers designed an experiment in which they analyzed very early word productions of a group of young children and determined, for each child, which sounds they were able to produce (Leonard, Schwartz, Morris, & Chapman, 1981; Schwartz & Leonard, 1982). The researchers then created a set of nonsense forms for each child to see whether that child could learn to say them; some of the forms contained sounds that occurred in the child's productions (e.g., /p/ and /m/ to make the nonword *pim*), but other words contained sounds that did not occur in the productions; e.g., /z/ and /l/ in the nonword *zool*. These nonwords were used as the names of novel items (a funny-looking doll; an unusual cooking implement): "Look Joey, here is a *pim*. . . We can put the *pim* in the bucket!" or "Look Joey, here is a *zool* . . . We can put the *zool* in the bucket!" Each nonword was presented the same number of times. After ten experimental sessions, researchers reported that children were more likely to produce novel words that contained only the sounds they already knew how to make (IN words) than words with sounds not yet in their repertoire (OUT words). Word comprehension was also assessed, using a pointing task: "Okay, Joey, can you show me the *zool*? (Word comprehension was not affected by the child's productive capabilities; that is, there were no differences in their ability to point to toys named by IN nonwords versus OUT nonwords.) These studies show that phonology can influence production vocabulary in the early stages of word learning.

Accuracy of Perception. Do children fail to pronounce particular sounds correctly because they have failed to perceive them accurately? This seems unlikely in most cases—in the experiment we just described, the children learned to point to items with names like *zool* even when they couldn't pronounce the words. Confusing two similar adult phonemes may sometimes happen with pairs of extremely similar sounds, such as /f/ and /θ/; this may contribute to the generally late acquisition of [θ] (Velleman, 1988). Usually, however, children with normal hearing are able to tell the difference between pairs of similar speech sounds like /r/ and /w/, even though they pronounce them both the same way as far as adult listeners can tell; for example, children can point correctly to a picture of a ring or a picture of a wing, even if they say "wing" for both words. (And sometimes, measurements of their speech sounds show that they are actually using a different [w] for *wing* than they are using for *ring*, even though adults can't hear this difference.)

A Cognitive Approach to the Acquisition of Phonology

Several theories of the acquisition of phonology predict that a child's pronunciation should just improve steadily until it matches the adult model. In fact, however, there are cases of **regression**—getting worse instead of better—in the acquisition of phonology (as there are in other areas of language and cognitive development). Regression seems to happen when a child finds new and (presumably) more efficient ways of producing an utterance; when this happens, some correct aspects of their older ways of saying things may get lost temporarily. An early report of regression comes from the case study of Daniel (Menn, 1971). At a certain point, he reliably said the words *down* and *stone* as [dæwn] (correct) and [don] ("doan"). But some days later, when he first tried to say some other words that also begin with oral stops and end with nasals, he produced them with nasals at both beginning and end: He said *beans* as [minz] ("means") and *dance* as [næns] ("nance"). After a few weeks this "nasal assimilation" pattern spread to his correct established forms for *down* and *stone*: He began to say [næwn] ("noun") and [non] ("noan") along with [minz] and [næns]. So his originally correct pronunciation of *down* was replaced by the incorrect form [næwn], and [don], his old fairly close approximation to *stone,* was now replaced by [non].

Another type of regression does not involve a particular word getting worse; instead, the child seems to lose her the ability to say a particular sound in new words, even though she maintains the correct pronunciation in earlier-learned words. For example, Menn's Daniel had initial [h] on his second and third words, *hi* and *hello;* he said all other adult words beginning with /h/ (for example *horse, hose, hat)* without the initial /h/. So for many months, he could say [h] in those two words, but in no others.

The kind of theory of phonological development that deals best with regression data is a cognitive (or problem-solving) theory. In a cognitive theory of phonological development, the child is seen as an intelligent creature trying to solve a problem: how to talk like the people around her (Macken & Ferguson, 1983). She may adopt general strategies that can provide temporary solutions: **avoidance** of difficult sounds or sound sequences, **selection** of favorite sounds (as noted in the section on words and sounds, above), and replacement or rearrangement of the sounds in the target word. Within a child's general strategy, we can see characteristic components of problem solving: first, trial-and-error articulation attempts, then the use of existing solutions to deal with new problems (generalization), and sometimes the temporary extension of these behaviors to situations in which they are not quite the needed response (overgeneralization), like Daniel's use of "noun" for *down.* This general sequence of events can be found in all areas of linguistic and cognitive development, not just in phonology.

A child's phonological problem solving is constrained not just by the language she is learning and her interaction with the people around her, but also by her **physiological substrate for language**—that is, her brain and her perceptual and motor systems, which develop rapidly during her first two years. For example, the perceptual system will respond to the acoustic similarities between the fricatives /s/ and /ʃ/, so a child learning to say them by trial and error may be temporarily satisfied by the same sound for both of them. As another example, stops seem easier to produce than fricatives—perhaps because a stop can be produced by a fairly clumsy lip or tongue gesture that blocks off airflow through her mouth at the right point. However, making a fricative needs more delicate motor control: The child must maintain just the right distance between her upper and lower articulators along with enough airflow to cause airstream turbulence.

Considering auditory similarities between sounds and differences in how they are produced can be helpful when are trying to explain what children tend to have in common. However, because children also have substantial individual differences, we can only make statements about how they will produce particular kinds of sounds in probabilistic terms, for example, "It is more likely that a child will use a stop for a fricative than vice versa." The exact order of acquisition of phonemes varies across children, and the actual ages of acquisition vary even more (see the section on norms and measures). The specific language or dialect that a child is learning also affects which sounds are mastered first; /l/, a rather late sound in English, is mastered early in K'iché Mayan, where it is a very important phoneme (Pye, Ingram, & List, 1987).

Children need to hear how their own sound productions differ from the speech of adults in order to learn phonology. Prelingually deaf children in oral training programs get intensive feedback, yet many of them never learn to produce a useful amount of intelligible speech unless they have cochlear implants to restore partial hearing (see Chapter 9). In contrast, children learn manual sign language rapidly if they have parents and companions who communicate with one of the sign languages used by the Deaf community. The reason for this difference is obvious: A deaf child can judge the accuracy of his signs because he can see his hands as well as the hands of others, but he cannot judge the accuracy of his sounds, because he cannot hear his words or compare them to the words of others. More formally, what the deaf child is missing for spoken language is the internal feedback that he needs to assess his own performance. (Imagine learning to play tennis if you had to rely on someone else to tell you where the ball went!) Learning the intricate motor skill of speaking, like any other fine motor skill (see Kent, 1993; Stoel-Gammon, 1992, 2011), requires internal feedback.

Why is there such a difference in effectiveness between internal and external feedback? Probably because there are literally dozens—even hundreds—of phonetic details that must fall within narrow tolerances for production of an adult-sounding word. The language learner must be able to tell what part of a word is wrong, consciously or unconsciously, and to play around with it, listening to it until she gets it better.

Learning to Pronounce

How Real Children Pronounce Words

Let's consider the examples from published literature in Table 3.3. Some productions are quite accurate, others show overall resemblances between the target and the attempt, and some seem far-fetched. There are three principal ways of describing at least some of the orderliness behind this variety: writing **rules** to relate adult target sounds to the sounds the child actually produces; describing the child's limitations in terms of **constraints** (Bernhardt & Stemberger, 1998); and describing the child's preferred output (and input) forms in terms of phonological **templates** (Vihman & Croft, 2007). All three of these approaches can be useful in understanding normal and disordered phonological development, and none of them can really do the job alone.

How to Describe Regularity in Children's Renditions of Adult Words

Many of the young children who have been studied have developed rather systematic approaches to the reproduction of adult target words.[2] That is, they have a core of early words that show clear patterns that can be described using phonetic features. Let's begin with two hypothetical, simplified examples. Suppose that Child A uses these pronunciations:

Child A

pot [bat] ("bot")	back [bæk] (correct)
top [dap] ("dop")	day [deɪ] (correct)
cat [gæt] ("gat")	game [geɪm] (correct)

[2]Sometimes a particular word does seem to evoke an unsystematic series of potshots; the difference between these words and others can be very striking. Ferguson and Farwell (1975) recorded a little girl's repeated attempts to say the word pen over the course of a half an hour; they included the forms [mã^{a}], [dɛ^{dn}], [hɪn], [^{m}bõ], [pɪn], [tntntn], [ba^{h}], [d^{h}au^{n}], and [buã]. (Transcription is simplified from the original; raised symbols indicate weakly produced sounds, and the tilde [˜] over a vowel indicates a nasalized pronunciation, i.e., with air coming out of both nose and mouth.)

table 3.3	Examples of Early Pronunciation of Common Words				
	Jacob (approx. 19 months)	Hildegard (approx. 24 months)	Daniel (approx. 25 months)	Amahl (A) (approx. 25 months)	Amahl (B) (approx. 32 months)
apple /æpl/	[æpw]	[ʔapa]	[æpu]	[ɛbu]	[æpəl]
bottle /badl/	[ɡʌɡʌ]	[balu]	[baw]	[bɔgu]	[bɔkəl]
water /wɔdr/[a]	—	[walu]	[ɔərs]	[wɔːdə]	[wɔːtə]
house / haʊs /	—	[haʊs]	[æʊs]	[aut]	[haut]
dog/doggie /dɔg/ /dɔgi/	[dadi]	[doti]	[ɡɔɡ]	[ɡɔɡi]	[dɔɡ]
cookie /kʊki/	[kikʌ] [kʌki]	[tuti]	[ɡuki]	—	—
shoe /ʃu/	[du] [ʃu]	[ʒu]	[u]	[duː]	[tuː]
sock /sak/	[sak]	—	[ak]	[ɡɔk]	[tɔk]
stone /stoʊn/	—	[doiʃ]	[non]	[duːn]	—

Note: ʔ is the glottal closure phone (the "glottal stop") heard between the syllables of the expression "uh-oh" /ʌʔoʊ/.
     ː indicates lengthening of preceding sound.
[a] Amahl's model was British "Received Pronunciation" /wɔtə/.
Sources: Amahl's data are from Smith, 1973; Hildegard's are from Leopold, 1939–1949, and may also be found in Moskowitz, 1970.

As you see, Child A uses voiced stops in word-initial position, whether they are appropriate (in the right-hand column) or whether the adult word has the corresponding unvoiced stop (in the left-hand column). The place of articulation in all of these consonants is correct, however.

Another hypothetical child might pronounce those words this way:

Child B

pot [pat] (correct)	back [bæt] ("bat")
top [tap] (correct)	day [deɪ] (correct)
cat [tæt] ("tat")	game [deɪm] ("dame")

Child B has voicing correct but is unable to manage the velar place of articulation; she produces adult words containing /k/ with a [t], and words containing /g/ with [d].

These simplified examples show two benefits of describing children's pronunciations in terms of phonological features. First, we can see how their attempts to say a sound may be partly right and partly wrong. Child A gets the feature "position of articulation" right for all her stops, but the feature "voicing" wrong for the word-initial unvoiced ones; Child B gets "voicing" correct for all his stops but hasn't learned to make the velar position of articulation. Learners in general get things partly right before they get them fully correct; using features helps us to describe what aspect of a partly correct speech sound is right and what part is still not adultlike.

The second benefit of using features is that they can help us to see what several different-looking errors have in common. For example, the three mistakes of Child A are essentially identical: They are all errors in which word-initial unvoiced stops are replaced by voiced stops because she has not yet learned to produce voiceless stops at the beginning of a word. Similarly, the three mistakes of Child B are all cases of using an alveolar articulation when the target word requires a velar. Patterns or families of errors like this are very common in child language (and in second-language acquisition).

Patterns are not always so regular, however. Sometimes a child may learn to get voicing correct for, say, /t/ and /d/, and yet still use [b] for /p/; another child may follow the general pattern of using voiced stops for unvoiced stops at the beginnings of words, but have one or two words in which a word-initial /t/ is produced correctly. A good theory of the acquisition of phonology must be able to accommodate both the regular and irregular relations between the child's attempt and the target word. What happens to individual phonemes and individual words must be taken into account; this means that theories that try to describe the acquisition of phonology only in terms of acquiring features or overcoming constraints will be inadequate.

Cluster Reductions. **Consonant clusters** (sequences of two or more consonants) appear to cause problems for most young speakers. This is sometimes described by saying that young children start out with a constraint against having two consonants in a row. This constraint has to be overcome by children learning English, German, or Russian. However, if they are learning only Hawai'ian, which has no consonant clusters, they would not have to overcome this constraint.

Children follow different patterns in dealing with consonant clusters. Many children satisfy the constraint against consonant clusters by just leaving out one of the sounds. Daniel's speech, for example, satisfied the constraint "No sequences of two consonants" by producing the forms given in the first column of examples.

	Daniel	**Stephen**
spill	[pɪl] ("pill")	[fɪl] ("fill")
store	[tɔr] ("tore")	[sɔr] ("sore")
school	[kul] ("cool")	[sul] ("sool")

A less common way of satisfying this constraint, found in perhaps 10 percent of children learning English, is to leave out the stop consonant, as we see in the treatment of *store* and *school* in the second column. Children who omit alveolar and velar stops in these clusters often do something special, like Stephen, with their /sp/ clusters: Instead of just leaving out the /p/, they replace the /sp/ cluster with [f]. This looks like an attempt to match the sound of the whole cluster within a single consonant, and it brings them closer to satisfying another, very basic constraint: Be **faithful** to the adult phonology: Produce sounds accurately. An [f] is a good compromise between "no consonant clusters" and "be accurate," because it is a single consonant that is fricative, like /s/, but labial, like /p/.

If a child has not yet learned to make particular consonant clusters, she can also approximate the words she wants to say by inserting an unstressed vowel between the consonants, as in column 2, or by using a different sound for one of them, as in column 3, where /r/ is replaced by [w].

table 3.4	Ways to Deal with Consonant Clusters		
	1	**2**	**3**
bread	[bɛd] ("bed")	[bərɛd] ("buh-RED")	[bwɛd] ("bwed")
blue	[bu] ("boo")	[bəlu] ("buh-LOO")	[bwu] ("bwoo")

Suprasegmental-Segmental Interactions. Word pronunciations are often affected by length of the word and its accent or **stress patterns**. For example, young children often omit the initial syllable of a multisyllabic word when that syllable is unstressed, producing forms like "mato" for *tomato,* "zert" for *dessert,* and "posed" for *supposed.* Unstressed syllables in the middle of a word may also be omitted, for example in *telephone* [tɛfon] and *elephant* [ɛfənt]. At the end of a word, however, it is much less common for unstressed syllables to be omitted. Children may do better with final unstressed syllables than with the initial and medial ones because most two-syllable words in English have stress on the first syllable; children hear and produce many words of the type *DAddy, BAby, TAble, DOggy* (where the capital letters represent the stressed syllable). So when they are faced with a long word like *baNAna* or *toMAto,* they may reduce it to the familiar pattern of a stressed and an unstressed syllable.

Assimilation. Many of the ways in which children adapt adult words cannot be explained without considering the sounds of the whole target word. Daniel (Menn, 1971) showed the following pattern:

Initial voiced stops usually showed correct position of stop articulation and correct voicing:

Set 1

bump	[bʌmp]	(correct)
down	[dæʊn]	(correct)
gone	[gɔn]	(correct)

Initial unvoiced stops usually had the correct position of articulation but were voiced:

Set 2

pipe	[baɪp]	("bipe")
toad	[doʊd]	("dode")
car	[gar]	("gar")

However, when Daniel attempted to say a word that begins with a stop in one place of articulation and ends with a stop in a different place of articulation, a very striking kind of error occurred:

Initial labial stops became [g] when the target word ended with a velar stop:

Set 3

bug	[gʌg]	("gug")
big	[gɪg]	("gig")
book	[gʊk]	("gook")
bike	[gaɪk]	("gike")
pig	[gɪg]	("gig")

Initial alveolar stops and *s* + stop clusters also became [g] when the target word ended with a velar stop:

Set 4

dog	[gɑg]	("gog")
Doug	[gʌg]	("gug")
duck	[gʌk]	("guck")
stick	[gɪk]	("gick")

Initial alveolar stops and *s* + stop clusters became [b] when the target word ended with a labial stop:

Set 5

tub	[bʌb]	("bub")
top	[bap]	("bop")
step	[bɛp]	("bep")
stop	[bap]	("bop")

We know that Daniel could pronounce the stops /p/, /b/, /t/, and /d/—as well as /g/ and /k/, because he got the labials and alveolars correct in words like *bump* and *toad* in sets 1 and 2. His problem was with adult words that contain two stops with different places of articulation: In a word like *pig* or *tub,* he could get only one of the places of articulation correct. Apparently, he hadn't figured out how to make two different positions of articulation within a single word. In other words, he had the constraint that all the stops in a word had to have the same place of articulation. He satisfied this constraint by changing the place of articulation of the initial stop to match the place of articulation of the final stop.

A change in one sound to make it more like another is called **assimilation**. Assimilation may also involve a sound's manner of articulation rather than its place of articulation. We've already seen one kind of manner assimilation, **nasal assimilation**, in the section on regression. Remember that after learning to say the two words *down* and *stone* using both nasal and non-nasal consonants, Daniel began to do something different: If the sound at the beginning of the word wasn't already nasal, he changed it into a nasal sound (without changing its place of articulation):

bump	[mʌmp]	("mump")
beans	[minz]	("means")
dance	[næns]	("nance")
going	[ŋowɪŋ]	(cannot be spelled with English orthography)

Nasal assimilation is simple if we think about it in articulatory terms: Daniel let his velum drop at the very beginning of a word if the word had a nasal consonant anywhere in it.

You can see from these examples that tests or speech samples used for study of articulation need to consider all the sounds in a target word. It would be incorrect to say that Daniel could not pronounce word-initial /b/ or /d/, but you might come to that conclusion if you only looked at his versions of *big, dog, duck, beans,* and *dance.* It is important to use test words that have only one position and one manner of stop articulation—words like *pipe, bib, daddy, papa, do, go, cake*—to assess stop production, because a child's problem may be managing words with sound sequences that use two different places or manners of articulation, not in articulating the sounds themselves. Texts on functional articulation disorders (phonological disability) in children (Grunwell, 1987; Ingram, 1989; Stoel-Gammon & Dunn, 1985) make this point clearly.

Rules, Templates, and Strategies

The Discovery of Rules.   We have seen that many children have regular ways of replacing sounds in adult words, and if there is a regularity, we can write a rule to describe it.

So far, we have discussed several error patterns that are regular enough to be abbreviated as rules: a rule making all initial stops voiced (hypothetical Child A), a rule replacing all velar stops by alveolar ones (hypothetical Child B), a rule omitting [s] in word-initial consonant clusters, a rule changing initial stops to nasals if there is a nasal at the end of the word, and Daniel's more complex pattern involving rules of velar and labial assimilation. In general, it appears, as common sense suggests, that children produce these patterns because they cannot yet produce an accurate match to the adult target sound or sound sequence (except perhaps during imitation). More formally, they cannot yet be faithful to the adult phonological form because they cannot yet overcome their constraints against the sounds or sound sequences that the adult word demands.

However, a child who has finally learned to overcome enough constraints to be able to say a sound or sound sequence in her new words may continue in her habit of complying with the old constraints, especially in her older words. Rules, once acquired, appear to have a life of their own; as Bernhardt and Stemberger (1998) say, in such cases the child has strengthened the connections between the way she remembers the sound of the word and the incorrect way she has been saying it, to the point where she can't substitute the correct sound for the incorrect one.

A child's first handful of words are often not regular enough for rule writing. Early words typically include a few **phonological idioms** (words that are unexpectedly accurate or inaccurate compared to the rest of the child's pronunciations) and also a few grossly variable and inaccurate forms (e.g., *bye-bye* produced as [bæbæ], [gaga], and [ɣæɣæ]; the symbol [ɣ] (gamma) denotes a voiced velar fricative). It generally takes a child some time to develop regular ways—accurate or inaccurate—of dealing with adult sounds. This suggests that rules are discovered by trial and error; they don't come into play automatically as the child starts to speak (Menn & Vihman, 2011).

This child's "tat" doesn't care what he calls it. But what would you have to know in order to tell whether he says "tat" because of assimilation or because of difficulty with velars in general like Child B in the text?

Canonical Forms and Word Templates.   We concluded earlier that children learn sound sequences, not just sounds. After a beginning speaker discovers how to say a few word-length sequences of sounds, she is likely to use these sequences to say other words that are similar to her initial conquests. We say that a child who is doing this has mastered some word-length **template** (Vihman & Croft, 2007); when she tries to say an adult word that sounds like her one of her templates, she uses that template to help approximate it. In cognitive terms, she generalizes the solution to a problem—how to say a particular word—to similar problems. This procedure results in the development of little groups of words; each group consists of the child's renditions of adult words that are somewhat similar in adult language and become even more similar in the child's versions. The following sets of words from Waterson (1971) are classic examples of a child using two different templates to approximate English words:

Set 1		**Set 2**	
Randall	[ɲa ɲø]	fish	[ɪʃ/ʊʃ]
window	[ɲe: ɲe:]	dish	[dɪʃ]
finger	[ɲe: ɲe:] or [ɲi: ɲɪ]	vest	[ʊʃ]
another	[ɲaɲa]	brush	[byʃ]
		fetch	[ɪʃ]

Note: [ɲ] represents a palatal nasal, roughly the sound of *ny* in *canyon*.
[y] is the front rounded vowel spelled *u* in French and *ü* in German.
: indicates that the preceding sound was of relatively long duration.

The template for each little group can be described by abstracting out what the child's renditions have in common. The words in the first column are disyllables consisting of two palatal nasals [ɲ] and two vowels. The words in the second column all end with the fricative [ʃ], contain a vowel made with the tongue relatively high in the mouth, and begin with either a stop or that vowel. Using V to stand for any vowel and C to stand for any stop consonant, we can abbreviate the two patterns just presented: The first is [ɲVɲV], and the second is [(C)V$_{[high]}$ʃ]. (Putting the C in parentheses indicates that it is sometimes omitted.)

These abstracted patterns for sets of words are the templates (also called **canonical forms**), and each word that conforms to a particular pattern is an instance of that template. The output of children who have more than about five but fewer than perhaps 100 words often consists of a majority of words that belong to several sets of templates, plus a handful of other, relatively isolated words that are usually phonological idioms.

The template-based organization of children's early vocabulary is the key to understanding most of their ways of dealing with adult words. A child's templates represent the kinds of sound sequences that she has learned to produce up to that point. Her rules, if she has them, are the regular ways that she adjusts adult words to fit into those templates. Remember that not all children arrive at regular ways to make these adjustments; Daniel had rules, but Waterson's child did not, and neither did the children reported in other classic studies, such as Macken (1979) and Priestly (1977).

Children who do use rules may start to do so at different points in their development. Some researchers distinguish a pre-rule period, "the stage of the first fifty words," from a later, rule-governed period; but there is a great amount of individual variation across children, and on top of that, some aspects of a child's phonology can be quite rule-governed while other aspects remain irregular.

Strategies in Learning to Pronounce.   If we look at the strategies that children adopt to deal with the problem of producing words, we see another type of individual difference. Some children seem to be relatively conservative: They avoid certain sounds (Ferguson & Farwell, 1975), relying heavily on sounds that they can produce well, and rarely use a word unless they can produce it fairly accurately. For example, Jacob, who has been cited several times in this chapter, understood many words beginning with /b/, /k/, and /d/, but for several months, he only attempted to say words beginning with /d/, plus *thank you* and his own name (except for *bye-bye*, which he said under social pressure and which came out [dada]). Next, quite suddenly, he produced a group of /k/-initial words, all with a correct first segment, and then he finally mastered initial /b/. Jacob stuck to

Initial consonant clusters can make a word like "spaghetti" difficult for preschoolers to pronounce.

what he knew how to pronounce and avoided other words until he had figured out how to produce them to his own satisfaction.

Other children, often 2 years old or older, try to say a variety of words, regardless of whether they can pronounce them accurately; they seem blissfully unaware of the discrepancy between what they are saying and the adult target. Most children probably fall between the extremes of those who select only what they can say and those who casually rearrange any adult word so that it fits one of their output templates (see Schwartz & Leonard, 1982).

Another variation in acquisition strategy seems closely related to Katherine Nelson's (1973) referential/expressive dimension (see Chapter 8 for further discussion). Some children attempt one word at a time, and those words generally have relatively clear and consistent (although possibly quite incorrect) pronunciation. Other children use a more global approach to speech, approximating whole phrases with much less clear or consistent articulation (Peters, 1977). The meaning of these phrases may be understandable from context and tone of voice, and there may be enough recognizable phonetic material in the utterance to make it clear that particular words are intended; yet the phrase may be reduced to a virtually untranscribable mess.

Some children combine these approaches; for example, some embed one or two clear words in long, otherwise unintelligible strings. However, as the selectors and the adaptors learn more sounds, as the one-worders start to put words together, and as the phrase-approximators become more precise in their articulation, the distinctions in strategy eventually blur and disappear.

Children learning languages with different adult sound patterns—for example, children learning Spanish, Finnish, Japanese, and other languages that have relatively few one-syllable words—may have different strategies and patterns from children learning English, which has so many monosyllables. In particular, they use longer words from the beginning, sometimes at a cost in phonetic accuracy (Vihman, 1996, p. 201).

Phonological Development: Norms and Measures

We have seen that children vary in their pathways toward achieving adultlike pronunciations. At the same time, when we look across children, we can see common features of acquisition and, using these, can establish a general picture of phonological development. Data from studies of large groups of children are often referred to as "normative" data, and they serve as the basis of guidelines for speech-language pathologists who need to identify children with atypical phonological development (see Chapter 9). The guidelines are based on a variety of measures related to different aspects of development. Three different measures are presented in this section: a phonetic inventory measure that focuses on speech sounds and word shapes, a measure of accuracy focusing on consonants, and a general measure of age and order of acquisition.

Phonetic Inventories of Young Children

A phonetic inventory is basically a list of speech sounds and word patterns that occur in word productions. The unique aspect of this measure is that it does not involve accuracy of production; there is no attempt to compare the child's form with the adult word—only the child's production is analyzed. To give a small example, let's look at the phonetic inventory for twelve words produced by a child around 22 months of age. This child pronounced the vowels in these words correctly.

Word	Child's form	Word	Child's form
ball	[ba]	cup	[tʌp]
doggy	[dadi]	three	[wi]
juice	[dus]	chicken	[tɪkɪn]
milk	[mɪk]	that	[dæt]
bananas	[nænæ]	pat	[pæt]
woof	[wʊf]	lip	[jɪp]

For this analysis, our inventory has three parts: (a) a list of consonants that occur at the beginning of words; (b) a list of consonant that occur at the end of words; and (c) a list of word "shapes" in terms of consonants (C) and vowels (V). In making an inventory, we are not interested in whether a consonant matches the consonant of the adult form; we are only interested in the fact that it occurred. Thus, the word *jump* produced as [dʌp] "dup" would be analyzed as having initial [d], final [p], and the word shape consonant-vowel-consonant (CVC). An inventory analysis of the twelve words provides the following:

(a) word-initial consonants: [b d p t m n w j]
(b) word-final consonants: [p t k n t s]
(c) word shapes: CV (in the child's pronunciation of *ball*); CVC; CVCV; CVCVC

This analysis tells us that this child begins words with a small set of consonants: the voiced and voiceless stops [b d] and [p t], two nasal consonants [m n] and two glides [w j]. In an inventory analysis, it is important to note the types of consonants that do not occur as well as those that do. In the inventory of initial consonants above, there are no fricatives (e.g., [s z] etc.), no affricates: [tʃ dʒ], no liquids: [l r] and no velar stops: [k g].

In word-final position, we see that there are fewer consonants than in initial position; for these 12 words, the inventory contains three voiceless stops: [p t k], one nasal [n], and two voiceless fricatives [f s]. Comparing the inventories for initial and final position, we see [k] and two fricatives in the inventory of final consonants, although these did not occur in the inventory of initial consonants. The differences between this set of initial and final consonants are typical—both voiced and voiceless stops occur in initial position, only voiceless in final position; fricatives occur in final position but not initial; velars occur in final position but not in initial. So the ability to produce a particular consonant is affected by its position within the word—some consonants tend to occur in word-initial position and others in word-final position. If we analyze these productions in terms of word shapes, we see that this child can produce words of one or two syllables (e.g., CVC; CVCV); final consonants are present but there are no consonant clusters.

Inventory analyses allow us to examine children's productions and compare them in terms of size (number of word-initial and word-final consonants) and nature of the phonetic inventories. Remember that the example above is for illustration only. In reality, we would need to examine many more words with a greater variety of target consonants and word shapes. At 24 months, most children with typical development have nine to ten consonants in the initial inventory, mostly voiced and voiceless stops, nasals, and glides; the final inventory is usually five to six consonants, containing nasals, and voiceless stops and fricatives (Dyson, 1988; Stoel-Gammon, 1985). Word shapes that are present in the productions of typically developing 2-year-olds include CV, CVC, CVCV, and CVCVC and some instances of consonant clusters (e.g., tw-).

Accuracy of Production

Another way of measuring a child's productions is to examine overall accuracy; in this case, we do not look at the accuracy of specific consonants or vowels, but at all phonemes with a measure called **Percent of Consonants Correct (PCC)**, which has been widely adopted as a way to compare one child's performance with another. PCC is calculated by comparing the accuracy of consonants in the child's word productions with the adult pronunciation (Shriberg & Kwiatkowski, 1982). For example, if the child produced [tæt] for the word *cat*, comparison of her pronunciation with the adult form [kæt]) would show that she produced one of two consonants correctly, so the PCC for this word would be 50 percent (one consonant out of two were produced correctly). A sample PCC analysis is provided at the end of this chapter (see page 83). A review of PCC scores from conversational samples (not articulation tests) of children aged 18 months to 14 years (Campbell, Dollaghan, Janosky, & Adelson, 2007) showed that PCC for the youngest group (18 months) was 53 percent. PCC was 70 percent at 24 months, and 85 percent at 36 months; by 43 months, PCCs exceeded 90 percent. So consonantal accuracy in children's speech increases dramatically between 1½ and 3½ years. PCC measures are useful in comparing one child to another and in determining if a child's pronunciations fall within the expected range given her age.

Ages and Stages of Acquisition

Parents often ask, "When should Susie be able to pronounce the 'r' of rabbit?" or "When should Larry be able to say his name correctly?" Primary school teachers similarly ask, "At what age should my students be able to produce all the sounds of English?" The answers to these questions come from studies of large groups of children aged 2 to 9 years on the basis of productions of a carefully selected set of words. To carry out the studies, researchers create a list of "test" words that contain all, or nearly all, the consonants and vowels of English in various word positions. Selecting the words for these tests is not easy, in part because they should be familiar to children as young as 2 or 2½ years, a time when vocabulary is still quite limited. Because most tests use pictures to elicit word productions (the examiner shows the picture and says, "Tell me what this is"), most words are nouns. Can you think of an appropriate test word for the sound /v/ in word-initial position? Remember the words must be picturable, so the form *very* (a word likely to be familiar to 2-year-old children) cannot be used. Some possibilities are *violin, vest, vase,* or *van*; they can be elicited by pictures, but may not be in the vocabulary of a 2-year-old.

Studies of groups of children tested at different ages (e.g., Prather, Hedrick, & Kern, 1975; Smit, Hand, Freilinger, Bernthal, & Bird, 1990; Templin, 1957) provide information about the acquisition of English phonemes. However, the precise order (and age) of acquisition of the consonants of English varies somewhat from one study to another, presumably because the tests are based on different words, use different groups of children and different scoring protocols. One important finding from Smit and colleagues (1990), who analyzed productions of 997 children aged 3 to 9 years, was that, for some phonemes, production accuracy of boys was different than that of girls of the same age. In most cases, accuracy levels for girls was higher; for example, 75 percent of 4-year-old girls produced /ʃ/ correctly, but the boys did not reach the 75 percent accuracy level for this phoneme until age 5.

Table 3.5 provides information based on Sander's re-analysis (1972) of data from three studies of large groups of children: Poole (1934), Wellman and colleagues (Wellman, Case, Mengert, & Bradbury, 1931), and Templin (1957). Rather than using a single age for the acquisition of each consonant, Sander identified two stages: (1) the age at which half the children tested produced the consonant correctly at least half the time (across word positions); this benchmark is referred to as the age of "customary production"; and (2) the age at which at least 90 percent of children produced the consonant correctly in all word positions (i.e., word-initial, medial, final), referred to as the "age of mastery." Although these oft-cited norms are based on speech samples taken years ago, the findings are similar to those of more recent studies (e.g., Prather et al., 1975; Smit et al., 1990; Shriberg, 1993).

This table shows that correct production of consonants belonging to the manner classes of stops, nasal, and glides is achieved early, while correct production of fricatives, affricates, and liquids occurs much later. The table also shows that the time span between the age of customary production and the age of mastery varies considerably across the consonants; for example, /p,m,n,w,h/ are customarily produced before age 2;0 and mastered by age 3;0; in contrast, the period between customary production and mastery for the phonemes /s, z, v/ is 4 to 5 years.

As noted above, Table 3.5 focuses on the accuracy of single consonants in various word positions. Consonant clusters (e.g., [fl-] at the beginning of the word *fly*) are usually acquired relatively late. A child who can produce the individual phonemes within a cluster may not be able to put them together in a sequence. Thus, the /f/ of *four* and the /l/ of *look* could be pronounced correctly, but the /fl-/ combination in *fly* would be produced without the /l/ or without the /f/. According to Smit and colleagues (Smit, 1993; Smit et al., 1990) accurate production of two-consonant clusters at the beginning of words (e.g., /tw-, sm-, pl-, br-/) occurs by age 7; three consonant clusters (/spl-, str-, skw-/) are accurate by age 8.

The measures and timelines described above provide a general picture of phonological development in children acquiring English. As such, they serve as the basis for assessing development in children and for determining if a given child is developing within the normal range. Further aspects of this approach are discussed in Chapter 9 on atypical development.

Atypical Development

In spite of normal development in other areas (e.g., cognitive and motor development), some children fail to acquire their phonological system in the typical manner. In most cases, these children exhibit "delayed" development, meaning that phonological acquisition is following the normal course but is slower than expected. One indicator of speech development is "intelligibility," a term used to describe the extent to which a child's speech can be understood by a stranger. By the age of 4, most children are fully intelligible. This does not mean that they have adultlike pronunciation, but that the errors they make (like substituting [w] for /r/) do not have a great effect on the listener's ability to understand what is being said. In contrast, many children with delayed or deviant speech development cannot be understood at the age of 4 or 5 years. As a result of their atypical speech, these children may have difficulties participating in social activities with peers and may have problems when they enter school. Speech-language pathologists are trained to assess phonological disorders and to provide treatment when needed.

Even though children can pronounce the phonemes of English correctly when they are 7 or 8 years old, they still don't sound like adults when they talk. They tend to speak more slowly than adults and with

table 3.5	Ages of Customary Production and Mastery of Consonantal Phonemes of English	
Age (yrs)	**Customary production**	**Mastery**
Before 2;0	p b m n w h[a]	
2;0	t d k g ŋ	
3;0	f s r l j	p m n w h
4;0	v z ʃ tʃ dʒ	b d k g f j
5;0	θ ð	
6;0	ʒ[b]	t ŋ r l
7;0		θ ʃ tʃ dʒ
8;0		v ð s z

Adapted from Sander (1972), Stoel-Gammon and Dunn (1985).

[a]*These* consonants exceeded 70 percent correct production at 2;0.

[b]*This* consonant was not mastered by age 8;0 and does not appear in the right column.

greater variability in pronunciation and timing, and of course, their voices are higher, particularly boys' voices when compared to adult male voices. Finally, children may adopt speech styles that are used by their "group"; in some regions of the country they may use rising intonation on both questions and statements, whereas adults in that region do not.

The Acquisition of English Morphophonology

Morphophonology concerns the kind of variation that we see when we compare the pronunciation of the *nat-* in sets of related words like *nation, native, nativity,* and *nationality,* or the pronunciation of *knife* as compared to *knives.* How do children master these sound-variation patterns?

Words often consist of smaller meaningful parts; the smallest units that carry meaning are called **morphemes**. Any word that cannot be subdivided into smaller parts with meaning is therefore one morpheme: *cat, run, big, how, elephant.* A morpheme may be a single phoneme, like the /s/ that signals plural in *cats* or the /d/ that indicates past tense in *waved.* Or it may be several syllables long, like the whole word *elephant. Cats, waved, hatband, runner, biggest,* and *however* consist of two morphemes each. Like the plural and past tense endings of *cats* and *waved,* the *-er* of *runner* and the *-est* of *biggest* are separable, meaningful elements; *-er* here means "one who," and *-est* means "most."

Some inflectional endings have the same shape regardless of the words to which they are attached, like the progressive *-ing* of verbs like *giving;* others have different shapes depending on the sound of the word or stem to which they are attached. These different shapes are called the **allomorphs** of the morpheme, and morphophonology describes the way that the choice among allomorphs is determined. The plural morpheme, for example, sounds like /s/ when it follows unvoiced stops: *cats, rocks.* When the plural morpheme follows a vowel or most voiced stops, its sound is /z/: *days, kids, dogs.* There is one group of final sounds that requires still a third variant of this morpheme. Words ending in the hissing (sibilant) sounds /s/, /z/, /ʃ/, /ʒ/, /tʃ/, or /dʒ/ take the variant /əz/: *kisses, sneezes, fishes, garages, churches,* and *judges.* These three variants of the plural morpheme are referred to as its *regular allomorphs;* regular, in this case, means that if one knows the sound of the singular noun, the choice among the three plural endings is automatic. There are also some irregular plural allomorphs, which have to be learned separately: for example, the *-en* of *oxen,* the *-ren* of *children,* and the internal vowel changes that signal the plural of words like *man.* (*Men,* therefore, consists of two morphemes, *man* and the plural, even though it cannot be separated into stem and ending as *cats* can.) There are also some words, like *sheep* and *deer,* that are unchanged in the plural; such words are said to have a "zero" plural allomorph when they are used with plural meaning.

As a child's vocabulary grows, the target words become longer and phonetically more complex and, as she gets older, the child must learn to deal with variations in the production of related word forms. For example, the words *photograph, photography,* and *photographic* are related but differ substantially in stress and pronunciation of certain sounds. In *photograph,* the first syllable is stressed (PHOtograph); in the word *photography,* the second syllable is stressed (phoTOgraphy); and in the word *photographic,* stress falls on the third syllable (photoGRAphic). In addition to the change in stress placement, pronunciation of the vowels changes across the three words. Pronunciation of words like *electric* and *electricity, nation* and *nationality, confess* and *confession* are additional examples of pronunciation patterns that must be learned as the child moves toward mastery of the phonological system of English.

Parents' Role in Phonological Development

Parents not only slow down and use shorter sentences for children who are starting to produce words (see Chapter 2 and look at **www.ted.com/talks/deb_roy_the_birth_of_a_word.html**), they seem to improve the precision of their articulation above normal conversational levels, presumably to help their children learn to speak. Two researchers, Malsheen (1980) and Bernstein Ratner (1984a, 1984b), showed this with acoustic measurements of the fine details of mothers' articulation when they were speaking to their children. Malsheen found that mothers clarified their pronunciation of initial consonants in speech to the children at the one-word stage, but not to the prelingual children or to the older ones. Bernstein Ratner (1984a, 1984b) studied vowel production of nine mothers speaking to their children, and what she found was that speech to children at the one-word stage showed clarification of vowels in nouns, verbs, and adjectives—that is, the sort of words being used most by the children themselves. Speech directed to children who were using several-word utterances showed clarification not only in nouns, verbs, and adjectives, but also in the function words that these children were just beginning to use: pronouns, prepositions, and conjunctions. This increased precision of articulation is probably not conscious, but it seems to be very precisely attuned to the child's level of language development.

Language Variation in the United States: Languages, Dialects, and Speech Styles

Most Americans speak only one language, although we may learn other languages at school. Consequently, we tend to think that the ability to communicate in more than one language is relatively rare. In the United States, the proportion of children who are raised learning more than one language is estimated to be about 20 percent, with Spanish being the most common second language (2009 American Community Survey). In contrast, across all countries of the world, approximately two out of three children in the world are raised as bilingual speakers (Worldwatch Institute, 2001), which means that the United States is unusual because of its large proportion of monolingual speakers. In India and Africa, nearly all children learn more than one language; in many cases, one language is spoken in the home, another at elementary school, and perhaps a third at university. So learning two languages should not be viewed as special, but as the norm. Bilingual children do not need be gifted in terms of language abilities, they simply need to have regular exposure to both languages.

Spanish in the United States

The number of Spanish speakers in the United States has increased dramatically. According to figures published by the Census Bureau, the Hispanic population was estimated to be 22.4 million in 1990; the population more than doubled in twenty years, rising to about 50 million in 2010 (16 percent of the U.S. population). Current projections indicate the population will continue to increase rapidly, reaching nearly 133 million (30 percent of the U.S. population) by 2050. Although Spanish is spoken by the great majority of individuals who identify themselves as Hispanic, researchers, educators, and speech-language clinicians have only recently begun to examine the acquisition of Spanish. Studies of phonological acquisition in children acquiring Spanish are complicated by the fact that families in the United States come from a variety of geographical locales, and their speech reflects a variety of dialects. The majority of Hispanic-origin people in the United States are from Mexico, 66 percent in 2008, most of whom live in the western and southwestern states. In the eastern part of the United States, significant numbers of speakers (9 percent) are of Puerto Rican background, along with those from Cuban (3.4 percent), Salvadoran (3.4 percent), and Dominican (2.8 percent) backgrounds. In most cases, children raised in Hispanic-origin homes learn Spanish as their first language. Data from the 2008 American Community Survey indicate that 35 million U.S. residents age 5 and older spoke Spanish at home; this represents 12 percent of all U.S. residents. According to self-report, more than half the Spanish speakers spoke English "very well."

Issues in Studying the Development of Spanish Phonology.   Almost all language acquisition research in the United States has focused on children from monolingual homes acquiring English. If we want to study the acquisition of Spanish, some issues must be considered: (1) What dialect of Spanish are the children learning? (2) If children are being raised in a bilingual home environment, how much English and how much Spanish are they hearing? Are they exposed to both languages from birth? (3) Are bilingual children exposed to one language when they are very young (under 3 years) and then to the other? Do they speak one language at home and another at preschool/school?

Studies of phonological development have focused primarily on two areas: (1) the acquisition of Spanish in young monolingual children raised in Spanish-speaking environments and (2) the acquisition of Spanish and English among children who are learning both languages, either at the same time (simultaneous bilinguals) or one after the other (sequential bilinguals). The findings are especially important to teachers who work with these children in the classroom, to speech-language pathologists who must identify children who are delayed in language acquisition, and to linguists and phonologists interested in comparing monolingual and bilingual phonological development.

The Phonology of North American Spanish.   We started this chapter with a description of the consonants and vowels (phonemes) and of the phonotactic patterns (possible sequences of sounds) of General American English. Similarly, before presenting findings on the acquisition of North American Spanish, we must consider the phonological system of Spanish, keeping in mind that there are major differences across dialects. As shown in Table 3.2, there are forty phonemes of American English, twenty-four consonants and sixteen vowels. By comparison, Mexican Spanish has eighteen consonants and five vowels: /i,e,a,o,u/. The place and manner of the consonant phonemes are shown in Table 3.6.

If you compare the consonants of English and Spanish (Tables 3.2 and 3.6), you will note several differences: (1) English has a **velar** nasal ("ng" of *sing*), whereas Spanish has a **palatal** nasal (the first "n" of *mañana*); (2) English has a **voiceless palatal fricative**

---

table 3.6	Classification of Consonants of North American Spanish by Place and Manner of Articulation

Place	Bilabial	Labiodental	Alveolar	Palatal	Velar
Manner					
Stop	p b		t d		k g
Fricative		f	s		x
Affricate				tʃ	
Nasal	m		n	ŋ	
Glide	w			j	
Lateral			l		
Tap			ɾ[a]		
Trill			r[b]		

[a] *The* symbol [ɾ] represents an apical (tongue-tip) tap. English has something close to this sound, but in English the tap is not a phoneme on its own, so we have not introduced this symbol for it. See the text for more information.

[b] *The* symbol [r] represents an apical (tongue-tip) trill in Spanish; the same symbol appeared in the table of English consonants (Table 3.2), where it represented a palatal liquid.

("sh" of shoe), whereas Spanish has a **voiceless velar fricative** ("x" in *Quixote*); (3) Spanish has two "r" sounds - a **tap** (similar to the second consonant in *water* or *ladder*), and a tongue-tip **trill** that occurs in the Spanish word *perro* ("dog"); and (4) the **voiced fricatives** of English /v, z, ð, ʒ/ (the consonants that occur at the beginning *vine, they, zoo,* and in the middle of the word *leisure)* are not phonemes in Spanish (even though Spanish has a "v" in written forms, e.g., *vaca* "cow"). However, the voiced stops /b, d, g/ of Spanish are pronounced as voiced fricatives [β, ð, ɣ], respectively, when they occur between vowels.

In addition to differences in the number of types of phonemes, Spanish and English differ in their phonotactic patterning, that is, in the way sounds can occur within a word. Here are two examples: (1) Nearly all consonants of English can occur at the end of a word, while in Spanish, only five of the eighteen consonants occur in this position. (2) English has over twenty-five different word-initial **consonant clusters** (sequences of two to three consonants), for example, the sp- of *spin,* spr- of *spring,* st- of *stone,* tr- of *try,* fl- of *flu,* gr- of *gray*; in addition, many types of clusters can occur in word-final position. In comparison, Spanish has twelve different types of consonant clusters in word-initial position, all formed of two consonants, and no clusters at the end of words. Additionally, in English, the great majority of words in children's vocabularies are relatively short, composed of one or two syllables, but in Spanish, words of one syllable are rare, and those of three or four syllables occur commonly in the speech of 2-year-olds.

As with English, the pronunciation of North American Spanish varies extensively from one region to another. However, in English, dialect differences lie mainly in the pronunciation of vowels (see the section on dialects below), while in Spanish, they occur in the pronunciation of consonants, making it difficult to generalize about consonant acquisition among children from different dialect areas. A difference that is particularly important for creating age-of-acquisition norms is that some dialects of Spanish replace word final /s/ with [h].

Phonological Acquisition in Monolingual Children: Comparing Spanish and English.

One interpretation of the summary above is that the phonology of Spanish is somehow simpler than the phonology of English—Spanish has a smaller inventory of consonants and vowels, fewer words ending in a consonant (and we know final consonants are later-acquired than initial consonants), fewer types of word-initial consonant clusters, and no clusters at the end of words. Given these differences, we might expect that phonological development in Spanish will be faster than in English. This is not the case, possibly because Spanish words are longer than English, on average. Monolingual children learning Spanish appeared to follow the same general timetable as those acquiring English (Catano, Barlow, & Moyna, 2009; Goldstein & Iglesias, 1996; Jimenez, 1987), and comparisons of accuracy using a measure of Percent Consonants Correct indicated that accuracy of consonants in single words and in conversational speech was high for both groups of monolingual children.

Although overall performance is similar, differences are apparent if we look at the timeline of acquisition of the consonants that tend to be in error. Correct production of the fricative /s/, the tap "r" of *pero* ("but"), and the trill "r" of *perro* ("dog") occurs relatively late for children learning Spanish; for children learning English, late-acquired consonants include the voiced fricatives / ð, ʒ/ and the liquids /l, r/. Note that although "r" appears in the list for both groups, the pronunciation of "r" in English is very different from either the tap or trill "r" of Spanish.

Phonological Acquisition in Bilingual Children: Comparing Spanish and English.

We might expect that phonological acquisition among children learning both Spanish and English will be slower than that of children acquiring a single language; support for this view is mixed. Most studies have shown that bilingual children are comparable to their monolingual peers in terms of accuracy, as measured by Percent Consonants Correct (Goldstein, Fabiano, & Washington, 2005; Goldstein & Washington, 2001). Differences are observed, however, in the nature of errors produced in the two languages. For example, the

4-year-olds studied by Goldstein and Washington (2001) were more likely to omit a consonant when attempting to produce a **consonant cluster** when speaking Spanish than when speaking English and were also more likely to omit a final consonant when speaking Spanish compared with English. Some studies of children between the ages 3 and 4 years show differences between monolingual and bilingual acquisition. Fabiano-Smith and colleagues (Fabiano-Smith & Barlow, 2010; Fabiano-Smith & Goldstein, 2010) found that overall consonant accuracy was the same in both mono- and bilingual groups when speaking English; however, accuracy levels were higher among monolinguals than bilinguals when speaking Spanish. In spite of these differences, the bilingual children were not delayed in their acquisition—their performance fell within the "typical" range for their ages. A study focusing on English (Gildersleeve, Kester, Davis, & Peña, 2008) indicated that acquisition of English phonology was different among bilinguals than among monolingual English speakers, with more errors and more uncommon error patterns. Overall, these studies suggest that learning two languages is not more difficult than learning a single language, although some aspects of acquisition may take a bit longer.

Regional and Ethnic Dialectal Differences in English

Most of us know only the geographical and ethnic varieties of English that surrounded us while we were growing up. But the study of geographical and ethnic dialect variation (part of the field of **sociolinguistics**) and understanding the language varieties that children are learning is important for educators and speech-language pathologists. Here is why: Not only do people from different places and ethnic groups pronounce things differently, they also hear speech sounds differently. In the section on the development of speech perception, you learned that between 10 and 12 months, children become much less able to distinguish sounds that don't contrast in their native language (which of course means their native dialect of their native language), although if they start using a new language or dialect early enough (roughly, before age 5), they can regain their earlier abilities naturally.

Adults who actually pronounce pairs of words like *pin* and *pen* identically may think that they say them differently because they are spelled differently. Reading teachers need to know how words are really pronounced by themselves and by the people they are teaching, so they can figure out which words their students should be able to sound out and which ones they will have to memorize. If, say, *pin* and *pen* or *cot* and *caught* or *merry* and *marry* are pronounced identically by the teacher or the students, their spellings will have to be memorized (just as we all have to memorize *pair, pare,* and *pear* or *to, two,* and *too*). The children cannot hear differences in pronunciation that are not present in their native dialect, and the teacher is unlikely to be able to hear differences that are not present in her own dialect.

Speech-language pathologists also need to know which pronunciations are normal for the language variety that their clients are learning, so that they don't try to "correct" speech that is in fact normal for a person's region and ethnic group (unless the person is an "accent reduction" client who wants to learn to sound like a speaker of "General American" English). We often cannot tell whether a child's form that differs from our own is correct or incorrect until we compare it with how the child's parents and/or slightly older friends say the same word in the same setting. A child with parents from New York who pronounces *bang* as [bɪəŋ] or one from the West who says it as [beŋ] is just as correct as one from the Middle Atlantic who says [bæŋ].

And of course, if you are learning to transcribe speech phonetically, or teaching some else to do so, you need to be aware of dialect differences in pronunciation. The two authors of this chapter are from different parts of the United States; for CSG, *dog* is [dɑg], and it rhymes with *log* [lɑg], while for LM, it is [dɔg] and does not rhyme with [lɑg] at all. Some of the IPA transcriptions in this chapter reflect these differences; what counts as a "correct" transcription is one that accurately captures the speech of the person being transcribed, not one that matches a dictionary pronunciation.

So far we have been talking about regional dialects, but ethnic ones are just as important, especially African American English (AAE), also known as AAVE (African American Vernacular English) and BAE (Black American English). Adult and adolescent speakers of AAE may choose to use more or fewer of the distinctive AAE patterns, depending on who they are talking to and how formal the situation is, but young children are likely to be learning the more relaxed patterns first. Some of these are relevant to assessment of the language development as well as to teaching reading in a way that makes sense to the child. Coppedge, Conner, Mason, and Velleman (2009) report that because AAE tends to omit some General American English (GAE) word-final consonants and simplify word-final consonant clusters, children learning AAE produce fewer word-final consonants than children at the same vocabulary level who are learning GAE. Velleman and colleagues found that most common AAE patterns in the speech of the mothers in their study were:

- using the alveolar nasal [n] (e.g., [duwɪn] for *doing*) where GAE has velar nasal [ŋ]; in casual conversation GAE speakers may also say [duwɪn] for *doing*
- using [v] or [d] where GAE has voiced /ð/ and using /f/ where GAE has voiceless /θ/
- deleting GAE unstressed syllables, especially initial ones (e.g., [kʌz] for *because* and [baʊt] for *about*)
- reducing GAE word-final clusters to a single consonant (e.g., [kɛp] for *kept*); more common in clusters in which both consonants are voiceless
- deleting GAE final consonants (e.g., [ko] for *coat*)

The toddlers in their study, who were just beginning to talk, used fewer word-final consonants than children with the same vocabulary size who were learning GAE and attempted fewer adult words that have final consonants. Pearson and colleagues (Pearson, Velleman, Bryant, & Charko, 2009), working with children somewhat older, found a trade-off. Four-year-old children learning AAE tended to produce "later-developing consonants" such as /s/, /r/, and /z/ earlier than children learning GAE, and they also mastered word-initial consonant clusters earlier than children learning GAE. A possible explanation for this finding is that children learning AAE have to master relatively fewer consonants or consonant clusters in final position and thus are able to focus on other aspects of the phonology.

Pronunciation in Conversational Speech

The pronunciation of a word depends on the speech style being used. There is considerable variation between the highly self-monitored speech styles that speakers use for reading word lists aloud or presenting a new word to a young child and the very unmonitored styles that they use in a deeply involving conversation among family members or old friends. The most distinctive regional and ethnic variations are most likely to be heard in the less monitored style.

Speakers are generally unaware how much the pronunciation of words in conversational speech may differ from the way the same words are produced when they are read aloud carefully from a list. For example, in the phrase "I have to leave now," the *have* and *to* are always run together as a single word, pronounced [hæftə]. *Want to* and *going to* are rendered as *wanna* or *wannu* and *gonna* or *gonnu*, except when they are being specially emphasized. In the conversational insert phrase *y'know*, many speakers reduce the sounds to something like [jõ]. Americans are especially likely to be fooled by the spelling of words with the letter *t* between two vowels, like *water*; many people think that they should (and that they do) say [watɛr], but in fact, the normal, correct American pronunciation is closer to [wadr] or [wada] or [wɔdɚ], depending on where you are from. The consonant in the middle is not the [t] of *Tina*; it is a "flap" or "tap" similar to the [ɾ] that we introduced in discussing Spanish, and that symbol is usually used for it instead of [d] in more advanced texts.

English speakers of all dialects also simplify various word-final consonant clusters, especially if the next word begins with a consonant ("George an' Mary"; "cann' peaches"). We omit vowels in unstressed syllables, partially devoice phrase-final voiced stops and fricatives, omit /ð/ and /h/ in unstressed object pronouns ("I see *'er*"; "Push *'em* over here"), and so on. Although young children often hear nouns in isolation in naming routines, they usually hear most other words in phrases, and the "targets" that they are trying to pronounce must be considered to be these phrasal forms (i.e., forms like *hafta, wan'em, couldja,* and so on). So these pronunciations of *have, want,* and *you* are not errors unless they are being used in the wrong context, as in *I haf a cat, What does he wan, I see dja.*

SUMMARY

Phonology concerns the relations among the speech sounds of a language: Their phonetic resemblances due to the way they are produced, their contrasts as shown by minimal pairs, the possible phonotactic sequences in which they occur, and the way that distinct phonemes correspond to one another in the several variant forms that a morpheme can have. Children learning to talk must learn to produce the right sounds, to put them in the sequences demanded by the language(s) that they are learning, and to recognize variant phones as representative of the same phoneme. If they are learning two languages or two different dialects of the same language, either simultaneously or sequentially, they need to learn the phonology of both ways of speaking.

Humans have an innate, biological basis for hearing and producing speech sounds, and this basis is continually being reshaped by language experience, including reactions to difficult sounds and sound-sequences. Normal infants are born with the ability to hear many distinctions between speech sounds, but around age 10 to 12 months their auditory perceptions become adultlike—that is, they become less sensitive to those differences that are not phonemic in whatever language is around them. Infants also appear to progress through the first few months of sound production in a biologically determined way, because the detrimental effects of deafness on production start to appear only after babbling has begun. Individual differences and ambient language effects gradually appear in later babbling. The transition from babbling to speech is gradual; early words tend to use the same sounds and sequences of sounds that the child has been favoring in late babbling.

Descriptive features are used to assess children's partial successes in pronunciation and to see similarities linking their attempts at related sounds. Common patterns in English child phonology include rendering all initial stops as voiced, using alveolar place of articulation for both alveolar and velar consonants, assimilating nasality and/or place of articulation, and cluster simplification. These patterns can be described, respectively, as constraints against initial voiceless stops, against velar consonants, against having two different values for nasality/places of articulation, and against having two successive consonants within a given word. When patterns of correspondence between adult and child sounds occur regularly in a given child's speech, we can write rules to describe the relation between the adult word and the child's form, for both correct and incorrect renditions. Even when the adult–child correspondences are not regular enough to be called rules, the constraints that the child's words obey may be easy to see.

Early child words typically occur in little groups whose common properties can be abstracted as templates and written in formulas called canonical forms. Often there are a few isolated words whose pronunciation is much more adultlike than others; these forms do not belong to any of the child's templates and they are exceptions to his rules. A child's earliest words also often do not obey the rules or constraints that she uses later.

Some of a child's progress cannot be assessed correctly just by listening; instrumental studies of audio recordings show that children's earliest steps toward mastering adult phonemic distinctions may be inaudible to adults.

Individual variation among children is found in the strategies they adopt in complying with phonological constraints, as well as in their individual rules and canonical forms. Some children attempt whole phrases, others try words singly; some avoid (public) attempts at words they cannot pronounce, others rearrange adult words freely to fit them into their existing repertoire.

Eventually, the child overcomes constraints against difficult sound patterns and learns to put more different kinds of speech sounds together within one word, becoming more faithful to the adult model. The small groups of words expand and merge, so that templates become less useful as descriptors, while rules become more useful.

In the elementary school years, children learn to distinguish certain aspects of the English stress system, and in the later school years they become acquainted with some of the relationships that are found among words in the Latin-based portion of the English lexicon. These relationships are important because they reduce the memory load required for learning new words.

Overt parental correction of pronunciation has perhaps the same (lack of) effect on children as correction of any other habitual behavior. Yet mothers appear to increase the accuracy of their production of word-initial consonants and vowels in content words just as children are learning to pronounce single words. Furthermore, when their children are beginning to express the grammatical relations that adult grammar encodes in function words, they pronounce their function words more clearly. Probably these subtle changes in adult speech do help children to learn the language around them.

CHILD PHONOLOGY PROBLEMS

1. Consider Child A from the chapter text.

   pot [bat]   back [bæk]
   top [dap]   day [deɪ]
   cat [gæt]   game [geɪm]

   As we said, she uses voiced stops in word-initial position both when they are appropriate (in the right-hand column) and when the corresponding unvoiced stop is required (in the left-hand column). So we see that she has not yet learned to produce voiceless stops at the beginning of a word, although the place of articulation is correct. (We can say that she has a constraint against producing word-initial voiceless stops that is stronger than her constraint to be faithful to the voicing of the adult model word.)

   If she follows the pattern that you see above, how will she most likely pronounce the following words so that they conform to her constraint? Give your answer in IPA, not in English spelling. Will she get any of them correct?

   (a) pull   (b) tummy   (c) kiss   (d) baby

2. There are several ways Child A might modify words with final voiced stops so that she can say them. The most common strategies are to omit or to devoice the final stop. Or, instead of modifying anything, she could avoid the words that she finds difficult—that is, she could simply refuse to try to say any adult words that have final voiced stops.

   (a) We already know that she does not mind changing initial voiceless stops to their voiced counterparts, but we don't know if she's so relaxed about the voicing of final stops. Which of the following words would Child A refuse to say if she didn't want to omit or devoice word-final voiced stops?

      (a) dog   (b) bad   (c) duck   (d) buzz   (e) top   (f) pig

   (b) Suppose instead that Child A had been willing to omit final voiced stops. Write out in IPA how she would say the words in Problem 2(a) that violate her constraints in that case. (Assume that she will reliably change initial voiceless stops to voiced ones, as in Problem 1.)

(c) Now suppose she had preferred to devoice the final voiced stops. In that case, how would she produce the words in Problem 2(a) that violate her constraints? Write her pronunciations in IPA.

3. Consider Child B from the chapter text. Here is what he does with the first six words:

   pot [pat] (correct)   back [bæt]
   top [tap] (correct)   day [deɪ]
   cat [tæt]   game [deɪm]

   What will he probably do with the following words?

   (a) pull   (b) tummy   (c) kiss   (d) baby

4. If Child B has no other difficulties besides the inability to make velars as discussed in the text, how will he produce the following words?

   (a) bed   (b) car   (c) pig   (d) pick   (e) big   (f) bike   (g) get

The data set below provides a phonemic transcription of the target form of adult words followed by the phonetic form of the child's productions. Use this information to answer questions 5–7.

List A			**List B**		
Word	Target Form	Child's Form	Word	Target Form	Child's Form
smoke	/smoʊk/	[moʊk]	blue	/blu/	[bu]
snow	/snoʊ/	[noʊ]	green	/grin/	[gin]
spot	/spat/	[bat]	stuck	/stʌk/	[dʌk]
star	/star/	[da]	played	/pleɪd/	[beɪt]
skinny	/skɪni/	[gɪni]	drop	/drap/	[dap]
grab	/græb/	[gaep]	broken	/broʊkɪn/	[boʊkɪn]
small	/smal/	[ma]	pretty	/prɪdi/	[bɪdi]

5a. Look at the child's forms in both lists and determine the inventory of word-initial and word-final consonants that occur in the child's productions

   Initial consonants: _____

   Final consonants: _____

5b. What place and manner classes are present in the child's productions?

   Word-initial manner classes_____

   Word-initial place classes_____

   Word-final manner classes _____

   Word-final place classes_____

   What differences do you see in the sound classes for word-initial and word-final positions?

5c. Consider the **word shapes** of the words in both lists, that is, occurrences of consonants (C) and vowels (V) in the forms. (Note: Two vowels together—a diphthong—as in *smoke* /smoʊk/ can be analyzed as V, yielding CCVC for this word.)

   List the word shapes in the child's production _____

   List the word shapes in the target forms_____

6. All the target words begin with a consonant cluster (a sequence of consonants), but the child's productions have no clusters.

   a. Look at the words in List A and write a rule describing how the child produces consonant clusters that begin with /s/. Your description should refer to manner classes and voicing changes rather than individual phonemes.

b. Look at the words in List B and write a rule describing how the child produces consonant clusters. Once again, your description should refer to manner classes and voicing changes rather than individual phonemes.

c. Given your description above, how would the child produce the words *spring* and *scream?*

7. Calculate Percent Consonants Correct (PCC) for these words using the procedures outlined below.

Special Interest Sections

For people especially interested in linguistics:

More about constraints. Optimality theory formalizes the idea of constraints on pronounceable sounds and sound sequences (Bernhardt & Stemberger, 1998; Stemberger & Bernhardt, 1999). Optimality theory sets up a list of typical preferences as constraints that speakers prefer not to violate. For example, constraints like "every syllable should begin with one consonant followed by a vowel" (true for a fair number of human languages, and also a preference for most children learning English, although not so strong for children learning Welsh or Finnish) or "stop consonants within a cluster should have the same position of articulation" (true for many adult languages and, again, a preference for children). Constraints that are hard to overcome for a particular speaker or language are said to be "ranked higher" than ones that are easier to overcome. Optimality theory formalizes the process of overcoming a constraint by moving it lower in the constraint ranking.

Optimality theory describes the child who uses the column 3 pattern in Table 3.4 by saying that the child has been able to rank faithfulness to the adult syllable structure as more important than the constraint against having two consonants in a row—as long as one of those consonants is a /w/.

For people especially interested in speech-language pathology:

Rules for calculating Percent Consonants Correct (PCC) are shown below (using words from page 77 as an example):

Word	Child's Form	Target Form	PCC
ball	[ba]	[bal]	1/2 (child produces 1 of 2 consonants correctly)
doggy	[dadi]	[dagi]	1/2
juice	[dus]	[dʒus]	1/2
milk	[mɪk]	[mɪlk]	2/3
bananas	[nænæ]	[bənænəz]	2/4
woof	[wʊf]	[wʊf]	2/2

1. For each word, determine how many consonants are produced correctly by the child and how many consonants occur in the adult form and make a ratio of child-to-adult consonants; the ratios are shown in the PCC column above.

2. Determine the total number of correct consonants in the child's forms by adding the numbers in the numerator of the PCC column; in this case, the total is 9.

3. Determine the total number of consonants in the target words by adding the numbers in the denominator of the PCC column: The number is 15.

4. Using the totals from steps 2 and 3, create an overall ratio of child-to-adult consonants; the ratio is 9/15; and (5) express the ratio to a percentage; for these words, the percentage is 60 percent.

Thus in this set of words, 60 percent of consonants were produced correctly by the child. As an exercise, you can calculate PCC for the words in the second half of the list from page 71); your answer should be 54 percent (7/13). (As you make this calculation, remember that two letters in the English written form are sometimes a single sound in IPA, that is, in the spoken form; for instance, the word *three* begins with two consonants, θ and r.)

SUGGESTED PROJECTS

These activities are time-consuming and, if carried out in full detail, might well take several weeks to complete.

1. Record the babbling or speech of a child between the ages of 12 and 30 months, keeping notes of the child's accompanying activities. As soon as possible after this session, transcribe the sounds the child made and try to classify them into the types of vocalizations discussed in the chapter: sound play, conversational babble, proto-words, and words. What problems, if any, do you face in making these distinctions? What additional information do you need? Are there any utterances about which you could never be sure? Are there any utterances that are none of the above? If yes, what keeps them from fitting into each of the four major categories? What would you call them?

2. Find a child whose speech is somewhat intelligible, but whose pronunciation of words is still babyish. Record and transcribe a half-hour of the child's speech during a play session. Alternatively, you could find a sample (with good audio) on YouTube.

   Can you find regularities in the way the child renders adult words? What constraints does the child seem to be obeying that cause her words to sound different from the adult models? Can you find canonical output forms that the child seems to rely on? Are any adult sounds or sequences of sounds especially variable in the way the child produces them? If you do find some regularities, write rules to describe them. Do these rules have exceptions? Are the forms of these exceptions closer to the adult word or farther from it?

SUGGESTED WEBSITES

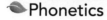Phonetics

http://web.uvic.ca/ling/resources/ipa/handbook.htm
www.praat.org
www.uiowa.edu/~acadtech/phonetics/ (for both English and Spanish)
http://psyc.queensu.ca/faculty/munhall/x-ray

Dialects

www.utexas.edu/courses/linguistics/resources/socioling
http://accent.gmu.edu
www.evoca.com/news/2010/11/02/yale-linguistics-project-collects-north-american-english-dialect-recordings

Early Phonological Development

www.hulu.com/watch/223331/tedtalks-deb-roy-the-birth-of-a-word#s-p1-sr-i0
www.ted.com/talks/patricia_kuhl_the_linguistic_genius_of_babies.html
http://childes.psy.cmu.edu/data

SUGGESTED READINGS

Bernhardt, B., & Stemberger, J. (1998). *Handbook of phonological development.* New York: Academic Press.

Ferguson, C. A., Menn, L., & Stoel-Gammon, C. (Eds.). (1992). *Phonological development: Models, research, implications.* Timonium, MD: York Press.

Jusczyk, P. W. (1997). *The discovery of spoken language.* Cambridge, MA: MIT Press.

Stoel-Gammon, C. (2011). Relationships between lexical and phonological development in young children. *Journal of Child Language, 38,* 1–34. (see also related articles, pp. 35–86).

Vihman, M. M. (1996). *Phonological development: The origins of language in the child.* Oxford: Blackwell.

KEY WORDS

AAE (African American English), AAVE, BAE
affricate
allomorph
alveolar
articulatory phonetics
assimilation
avoidance
bilabial
canonical form
cluster reduction
consonant
consonant cluster
constraint
contrast
faithful
fricative
GAE (General American English)
glide
glottal
glottis
IPA (International Phonetic Alphabet)
interdental
intonation contour
jargon
labial
labiodental

lexical selection
liquid
lower articulators
manner of articulation
minimal pair
morpheme
morphophonology
nasal stop
nasal assimilation
nonreflexive vocalizations
obstruent
Optimality Theory
oral
palatal, pre-palatal
Percent of Consonants Correct (PCC)
phone
phoneme
phonetic inventory
phonology
phonotactic constraint
physiological substrate for language
place of articulation
phonological idiom
position of articulation
protoword
reduplicated babble
reflexive vocalization

regression
rule
segment
selection
semivowel
sociolinguistics
sound play
stop
stress, stress pattern
suprasegmental
tap
template
trill
tongue root
unvoiced
upper articulators
variegated babble
velar
velar fricative
velum
vocal fold
vocal play
vocal motor scheme
voiced
voice onset time (VOT)
voiceless
voicing
vowel

REFERENCES

Bernhardt, B., & Stemberger, J. P. (1998). *Handbook of phonological development: From the perspective of constraint-based non-linear phonology.* San Diego, CA: Academic Press.

Bernstein Ratner, N. (1984a). Patterns of vowel modification in mother–child speech. *Journal of Child Language, 11,* 557–578.

Bernstein Ratner, N. (1984b). Cues to post-vocalic voicing in mother–child speech. *Journal of Phonetics, 12,* 285–289.

Campbell, T., Dollaghan, C., Janosky, J., & Adelsen, P. (2007). A performance curve for assessing change in Percentage of Consonants Correct Revised (PCC-R). *Journal of Speech, Language, and Hearing Research, 44,* 192–206.

Catano, L., Barlow, J., Moyna, M. (2009). A retrospective study of phonetic inventory complexity in acquisition of Spanish: Implications for phonological universals. *Clinical Linguistics and Phonetics, 23,* 446–472.

Coppedge, H., Conner, T., Mason, J., & Velleman, S. L. (2009, November 19). Phonotactics in Early AAE. Paper presented at the American Speech-Language-Hearing Association, New Orleans, LA.

de Boysson-Bardies, B., Sagart, L., & Durand, C. (1984). Discernible differences in the babbling of infants according to target language. *Journal of Child Language, 11,* 1–15.

de Boysson-Bardies, B., & Vihman, M. M. (1991). Adaptation to language: Evidence from babbling and first words in four languages. *Language, 67,* 297–319.

Dyson, A. (1988). Phonetic inventories of 2- and 3-year-old children. *Journal of Speech and Hearing Disorders, 53,* 89–93.

Ertmer, D. J., & Mellon, J. A. (2001). Beginning to talk at 20 months: Early vocal development in a young cochlear implant recipient. *Journal of Speech, Language, and Hearing Research, 44,* 192–206.

Fabiano-Smith, L., & Barlow, J. (2010). Interaction in bilingual phonological acquisition: Evidence from phonetic inventories. *International Journal of Bilingual Education and Bilingualism, 13,* 81–97.

Fabiano-Smith, L., & Goldstein, B. (2010). Phonological acquisition in bilingual Spanish–English speaking children. *Journal of Speech, Language, and Hearing Research, 53,* 160–178.

Ferguson, C. A., & Farwell, C. B. (1975). Words and sounds in early language acquisition. *Language, 51,* 439–491. Reprinted in Vihman, M. M., & Keren-Portnoy, T. (in press, Cambridge University Press).

Gildersleeve, C., Kester, E., Davis, B., & Peña, E. (2008). English speech-sound development in preschool children from bilingual Spanish-English environments. *Language, Speech, and Hearing Services in Schools, 39,* 314–328.

Goldstein, B., Fabiano, L., & Washington, P. (2005). Phonological skills in predominantly English-speaking, predominantly Spanish-speaking, and Spanish-English bilingual children. *Language, Speech, and Hearing Services in Schools, 36,* 201–218.

Goldstein, B., & Iglesias, A. (1996). Phonological patterns in normally developing Spanish-speaking 3- and 4-year-olds of Puerto Rican descent. *Language, Speech, and Hearing Services in Schools, 27,* 82–90.

Goldstein, M., & Schwabe, J. (2008) Social feedback to infants' babbling facilitates rapid phonological learning. *Psychological Sciences, 19,* 515–523.

Goldstein, B., & Washington, P. (2001). An initial investigation of phonological patterns in typically-developing 4-year-old Spanish-English bilingual children. *Language, Speech, and Hearing Services in Schools, 32,* 153–164.

Grunwell, P. (1987). *Clinical phonology* (2nd ed.). Baltimore: Williams and Wilkins.

Halliday, M. A. K. (1975). *Learning how to mean: Explorations in the development of language.* London: Edward Arnold.

Ingram, D. (1989). *Phonological disabilities in children* (2nd ed.). London: Cole and Whurr.

Jimenez, B. (1987). Acquisition of Spanish consonants in children aged 3–5 years, 7 months. *Language, Speech, and Hearing Services in Schools, 18,* 357–363.

Kent, R. D. (1993). Infants and speech: Seeking patterns. *Journal of Phonetics, 21,* 117–123.

Lee, S., Davis, B. L., & MacNeilage, P.F. (2009). Universal production patterns and ambient language influences in babbling: A cross-linguistic study of Korean- and English-learning infants. *Journal of Child Language, 35,* 591–617.

Leonard, L., Schwartz, R., Morris, B., & Chapman, K. (1981). Factors influencing early lexical acquisition: Lexical orientation and phonological composition. *Child Development, 52,* 882–887.

Leopold, W. (1939–1949). *Speech development of a bilingual child.* Evanston, IL: Northwestern University Press.

Levitt, A., & Wang, Q. (1991). Evidence for language-specific rhythmic influences in the reduplicative babbling of French- and English-learning infants. *Language and Speech, 34,* 235–249.

Lieberman, P., Crelin, E. S., & Klatt, D. H. (1972). Phonetic ability and related anatomy of the newborn, adult human, Neanderthal man, and the chimpanzee. *American Anthropologist, 74,* 287–307.

Locke, J. L. (1983). *Phonological acquisition and change.* New York: Academic Press.

Macken, M. A. (1979). Developmental reorganization of phonology: A hierarchy of basic units of acquisition. *Lingua, 49,* 11–49.

Macken, M. A., & Ferguson, C. A. (1983). Cognitive aspects of phonological development. Model, evidence, and issues. In K. E. Nelson (Ed.), *Children's language* (Vol. 4). Hillsdale, NJ: Erlbaum. pp. 256–282.

Malsheen, B. (1980). Two hypotheses for phonetic clarification in the speech of mothers to children. In G. Yeni-Komshian, J. F. Kavanagh, & C. A. Ferguson (Eds.), *Child phonology, Vol. 2: Perception.* New York: Academic Press. 173–184.

Menn, L. (1971). Phonotactic rules in beginning speech. *Lingua, 26,* 225–241.

Menn, L. (1976). *Pattern, control, and contrast in beginning speech: A case study in the acquisition of word form and function.* Unpublished doctoral dissertation, University of Illinois, Urbana-Champaign.

Menn, L. & Vihman, M.M. (2011). Features in child phonology: inherent, emergent, or artefacts of analysis? In N. Clements & R. Ridouane (Eds.), *Where do phonological contrasts come from?* Amsterdam: Benjamins. pp. 261–301.

Moeller, M. P., Stelmachowitz, P., Hoover, B., Putman, C., Arbataitis, K., Bohnenkamp, G., Wood, S., & Lewis, D. (2007). Vocalizations of infants with hearing loss and normal hearing: Part one—phonetic development. *Ear and Hearing, 28,* 605–627.

Moskowitz, B. A. (1970). The two-year-old stage in the acquisition of phonology. *Language, 46,* 426–441.

Oller, D. K. (2000). *The emergence of the speech capacity.* Mahwah, NJ: Lawrence Erlbaum.

Nelson, K. (1973). Structure and strategy in learning to talk. *Monographs of the Society for Research in Child Development, 38.*

Pearson, B. Z., Velleman, S. L., Bryant, T. J., & Charko, T. (2009). Phonological milestones for African American English-speaking children learning Mainstream American English as a second dialect. *Language, Speech, and Hearing Services in the Schools, 40,* 229–244.

Peters, A. M. (1977). Language learning strategies. *Language, 53,* 560–573.

Poole, I. (1934). Genetic development of articulation of consonant sounds in speech. *Elementary English Review, 11,* 159–161.

Prather, E., Hedrick, D., & Kern, C. (1975). Articulation development in children aged two to four years. *Journal of Speech and Hearing Disorders, 40,* 179–191.

Priestly, T. M. S. (1977). One idiosyncratic strategy in the acquisition of phonology. *Journal of Child Language, 4,* 45–66.

Pye, C., Ingram, D., & List, H. (1987). A comparison of initial consonant acquisition in English and Quiché. In K. E. Nelson & A. Van Kleeck (Eds.), *Children's language* (Vol. 6, pp. 175–190). Hillsdale, NJ: Erlbaum.

Sander, E. (1972). When are speech sounds learned? *Journal of Speech and Hearing Disorders, 37,* 55–63.

Schwartz, R. G., & Leonard, L. B. (1982). Do children pick and choose? An examination of phonological selection and avoidance in early lexical acquisition. *Journal of Child Language, 9,* 319–336.

Shriberg, L. (1993). Four new speech and voice-prosody measures for genetics research and other studies in developmental phonological disorders. *Journal of Speech, Language, and Hearing Research, 36,* 105–140.

Shriberg, L. & Kwiatkowski, J. (1982). Phonological disorders III. A procedure for assessing the severity of involvement. *Journal of Speech and Hearing Disorders, 47,* 256–270.

Smit, A. (1993). Phonological error distributions in the Iowa-Nebraska articulation norms project: Word-initial consonant clusters. *Journal of Speech and Hearing Research, 36,* 533–547.

Smit, A., Hand, L., Freilinger, F., Bernthal, J., & Bird, A. (1990). The Iowa articulation norms project and its Nebraska replication. *Journal of Speech and Hearing Disorders, 55,* 779–798.

Smith, N. V. (1973). *The acquisition of phonology: A case study.* Cambridge, UK: Cambridge University Press.

Stemberger, J. P., & Bernhardt, B. H. (1999). The emergence of faithfulness. In B. MacWhinney (Ed.), *The emergence of language* (pp. 417–446). Mahwah, NJ: Erlbaum.

Stoel-Gammon, C. (1985). Phonetic inventories, 15–24 months: A longitudinal study. *Journal of Speech and Hearing Research, 28,* 505–512.

Stoel-Gammon, C. (1992). Research on phonological development: Recent advances. In C. A. Ferguson, L. Menn, & C. Stoel-Gammon (Eds.), *Phonological development: Models, research, implications* (pp. 273–282). Timonium, MD: York Press.

Stoel-Gammon, C. (1998a). The role of babbling and phonology in early linguistic development. In A. M. Wetherby, S. F. Warren, & J. Reichle (Eds.), *Transitions in prelinguistic communication: Preintentional to intentional and presymbolic to symbolic* (pp. 87–110). Baltimore, MD: Paul H. Brookes.

Stoel-Gammon, C. (1998b). Sounds and words in early language acquisition: The relationship between lexical and phonological development. In R. Paul (Ed.), *Exploring the speech-language connection* (pp. 25–52). Baltimore, MD: Paul H. Brookes.

Stoel-Gammon, C. (2011). Relationships between lexical and phonological development in young children. *Journal of Child Language, 38,* 1–34.

Stoel-Gammon, C., & Cooper, J. (1984). Patterns of early lexical and phonological development. *Journal of Child Language, 11,* 247–271.

Stoel-Gammon, C., & Dunn, C. (1985). *Normal and disordered phonology in children.* Austin, TX: Pro-Ed.

Stoel-Gammon, C., & Otomo, K. (1986). Babbling development of hearing-impaired and normally hearing subjects. *Journal of Speech and Hearing Disorders, 51,* 33–41.

Templin, M. C. (1957). *Institute of child welfare monographs* (Vol. 26). Minneapolis: University of Minnesota.

Velleman, S. (1988). The role of linguistic perception in later phonological development. *Applied Psycholinguistics, 9,* 221–236.

Velleman, S. L., Coppedge, H., Conner, T., Mason, J., Dragan, C., & Bryant, T. (in press). African American English phonotactic development. In M. M. Vihman (Ed.), *Child phonology: Whole word approaches, cross-linguistic evidence.* Cambridge, UK: Cambridge University Press.

Vihman, M. M., (1996). *Phonological development.* Oxford, UK: Blackwell.

Vihman, M. M., & Croft, W. (2007). Phonological development: Toward a "radical" templatic phonology. *Linguistics, 45,* 683–725. Reprinted in Vihman, M. M. & Keren-Portnoy, T. (in press, Cambridge University Press).

Vihman, M., & Greenlee, M. (1987). Individual differences in phonological development: Ages one and three years. *Journal of Speech and Hearing Research, 30,* 503–521.

Waterson, N. (1971). Child phonology: A prosodic view. *Journal of Linguistics, 7,* 179–221.

Wellman, B., Case, I., Mengert, I., & Bradbury, D. (1931). Speech sounds of young children. *University of Iowa Studies in Child Welfare, 5,* 1–82.

Worldwatch Institute (2001). www.worldwatch.org/node/748.

Semantic Development

Learning the Meanings of Words

Paola Uccelli
Harvard Graduate School of Education

*Barbara Alexander Pan
Harvard Graduate School of Education

Very young children understand the pragmatic intent of adults' utterances before they can understand the words themselves. This earliest comprehension is at the emotional, social, and contextual levels. The prosodic contours of their parents' speech carry varied messages of comfort, excitement, or displeasure (Fernald, 1992; Locke, 1993) situated in particular contexts. A toddler who rushes to the door on hearing his father ask, "Wanna go outside and play with Spot?" may be responding to a variety of situational cues: the time of day, the family dog bounding playfully around the backyard, Dad holding a ball and perhaps pointing to the door. Only very slowly do children come to understand and use words in adult fashion, to break them free of context and use them flexibly in a variety of situations. The acquisition of words and their meanings does not happen all at once. During the course of this process, which is usually called **semantic development**, children's strategies for learning word meanings and relating them to one another change as their internal representation of language constantly grows and becomes reorganized.

In this chapter we describe the relationship between words and their referents, and some of the theories that attempt to explain how children acquire and represent meaning. We address what is known about early words and the ways that contemporary researchers have attempted to interpret the data on children's early words and word meanings. We also present research on later semantic development that examines how the semantic system is elaborated as words become related to one another in more complex semantic networks. Finally, we describe children's growing awareness of words as physical entities independent of their meanings, and discuss the implications of this metalinguistic development for a variety of language uses. The relevance of these skills for the academic success of monolingual and bilingual children is taken into consideration throughout the chapter.

*Previously contributed by Barbara Alexander Pan.

The Relations between Words and Their Referents

What does it mean to say that children acquire meaning? And what is it that adults have in common when they know the meaning of a word? First, it is important to note that the meaning of a word resides in the speakers of a common language, not in the world of objects. The word is a sign that signifies a **referent**, but the referent is not the meaning of the word. If, for example, you say to a child, "Look at the doggie," the dog is the referent, but not the meaning of *doggie*—if the dog ran away or were run over by a truck, the word would still have meaning because meaning is a cognitive construct.

Let us assume that the child learns that the word *doggie* refers to her dog. What is the relationship between the word and the dog? Dogs can be called *doggie, Hund, perro,* or *gou,* depending on whether one is speaking English, German, Spanish, or Mandarin. There is nothing intrinsic to dogs that makes one name or another more appropriate or fitting: The relationship between the name and the thing is thus *arbitrary,* and it is by social convention in a particular language that speakers agree to call the animal by a particular word (Morris, 1946). This arbitrary relationship between the referent (the dog) and the sign for it (the word *dog*) is *symbolic.* Nonverbal signs can also share this symbolic nature; the red light that means stop, for instance, is purely symbolic because there is no obvious connection between the color red and the action of stopping. We could agree to have blue lights or even green lights mean *stop,* as long as we all agreed on the meaning of the light.

For a few words, the relation between word and referent is not arbitrary. If one says, for example, "The book fell with a *thud,*" the relationship between the word *thud* and the actual sound referred to is not arbitrary, since the word is an attempt to resemble the real sound. Nor is the name of the cuckoo bird arbitrary: It represents the sound that the bird actually makes. Use of words that resemble real sounds is called onomatopoeia. However, even onomatopoeia reflects some cultural conventions when we compare its characteristics across languages. For instance, ask yourself: What sound does a rooster make? In English, a rooster says: *Cock-a-doodle-doo!* However, in Spanish a rooster says: *Kikirikí!* As noted by the linguist Ferdinand de Saussure, even though roosters around the world produce very similar sounds, different languages have opted for slightly different onomatopoeic sounds. Despite this cultural arbitrariness, onomatopoeia, in contrast to other types of words, attempts to imitate or recreate the sound of their referents. Even though they are less arbitrary than other types of words, onomatopoeias still need to be learned.

We should not be surprised to learn that many of children's earliest words or proto-words have a less-than-arbitrary relation to their referents; trains are called *choo-choos* and dogs are *bow-wows.* Some of these words are in the baby-talk lexicon that adults use when attempting to communicate with babies, and others are the children's own creations. It is probably easier for children to learn a word that is more directly related to its referent than one that is totally arbitrary and symbolic, and as some research has shown, young children believe that the name and the referent are intrinsically related. They think that one cannot change the name of something without changing its nature as well; for instance, many children believe that if we decided to call a dog a *cow,* it would begin to moo (Vygotsky, 1962).

This belief in the essential appropriateness of names was a subject of argument among ancient philosophers as well. Plato, writing in the fourth century B.C.E., discussed the question of whether there is a natural relation between names and referents in his Cratylus dialogue. The Anomalists of Plato's day believed that the relation was inexplicable, but the Analogists believed that through careful etymology the essential nature of words could be revealed (Bloomfield, 1933). Using English examples, we might show that a blueberry is so called because it is a berry that is blue, and a bedroom is so named because it is a room containing a bed. The ancient Greek Analogists would also claim that if we only looked hard enough, we would find the natural connections behind *gooseberry* and *mushroom* as well. This altogether human desire to produce order can be seen in many **folk etymologies** today and explains why college students as well as young children may believe that a handkerchief is so named "Because you hold it in your hand and go *kerchoo*" (Berko, 1958).

Mental Images

Although meaning is a mental representation, or concept, that is not to say that meaning is a mental picture. Even though it is true that many people are able to visualize words, many words, such as *happy* or *jealousy,* do not have picturable referents, and still we know their meanings. Even if one has an image for a word, it is likely to be quite individualized: *Dog,* for instance, might evoke a picture of a brown cocker spaniel for one person and a golden retriever for another. Furthermore, images tend to be quite idiosyncratic; speakers who share meaning may hold very different internal images. One speaker's mental house may look like a mansion, whereas another's may be a simple cottage, yet both speakers recognize new instances of houses when they encounter them. Finally, to be useful for communication, meaning cannot reside solely in the mind of the individual, but must be shared by a speech community. Thus, meaning is a social construct.

Concepts. One of the child's primary tasks in semantic development is to acquire categorical concepts (e.g., to learn that the word *dog* refers to a whole class of animals) and to be able to extend the word to appropriate new instances of the category. How, for instance, might a toddler who knows that her family's Irish setter is a dog know when she first encounters a tiny Yorkshire terrier that this is also a dog? Theorists differ as to how to characterize the nature of children's categorical concept acquisition. One view is that children acquire categories by learning the essential semantic features of the category; a second is that they first learn prototypical examples of a category; yet another is that they use a probabilistic strategy in assigning category membership.

The **semantic feature** view is that children learn a set of distinguishing features for each categorical concept (Clark, 1974). At first the word *dog* may be understood to apply only to the child's own dog, but the child soon comes to understand that other creatures may also be called *dog* as long as they share a small set of critical features: Dogs are animate, warm-blooded, have four legs, and bark. Other theorists propose that categories are defined by a set of weighted, rather than equally critical, features. The child's task, then, is to sort out which features are most important for membership in a particular category. For example, the feature "bark" might be weighted relatively heavily for the concept *dog,* because most dogs do bark, whereas other warm-blooded, four-legged mammals do not.

How might a child know that both of these animals should be called "dog"?

According to prototype theory (see Figure 4.1), children acquire **prototypes**, or very good examples of concepts, when they acquire meaning and only later come to recognize category members that are distant from the prototypes. Apples, collies, and roses are examples of prototypical fruits, dogs, and flowers. For adults, prototypical members of a category are more accessible in memory (Rosch, 1973). A robin has more typical *bird* characteristics than does a penguin; therefore, people see robins as better examples of birds, and they also can classify them faster when asked if a robin is a bird.

A slightly different view is that children assign category membership not on the basis of essential features or on prototypes, but on probabilistic grounds. Upon first seeing a penguin, children (and adults) would decide that it is *probably* a bird, because it has many birdlike features, such as a beak and wings. Thus, even though it does not fly or chirp, it still qualifies for membership in the bird category.

Some researchers, notably Smith and Medin (1981), have pointed out that even if children are acquiring their concepts as categories, there are differences in the nature of the

figure 4.1	Prototypical and Nonprototypical Category Members	
Category	**Prototypical Member**	**Nonprototypical Member**
Vegetable	Carrot	Eggplant
Dog	Collie	Chihuahua
Fruit	Apple	Tomato
Bird	Robin	Penguin
Flower	Rose	Gladiolus
Chair	Armchair	Throne

concepts themselves. For instance, there are **classical concepts**, such as *triangle,* which can be unambiguously defined: All triangles must have three angles, or they are simply not triangles. *Bird,* on the other hand, is an example of a **probabilistic concept.** Most, but not all, birds have many features in common, but there is not a single set of essential features. Furthermore, some concepts have fairly sharp boundaries and are hierarchically organized, while others are not; for instance, most adults can agree on what is and is not a dog and know that dogs belong to the superordinate category of animals. By contrast, color concepts have fuzzy boundaries. Even adults find it difficult to agree on color names for non-focal shades (Braisby & Dockrell, 1999). Given these differences among concepts, it is unlikely that any one theory can account for the nature of children's categorical concepts.

Next we consider behavioral and developmental theories of how children acquire words and their meanings.

Theoretical Perspectives on Semantic Development

Learning Theory

One of the simplest explanations of how children acquire the meanings of their first words is that they do so through associative learning. Learning theory predicts that repeated exposure to a stimulus (for example, hearing the parent say the word *kitty*) paired with a particular experience (seeing the family cat appear) will result in the child associating the sound of the word *kitty* with the family cat. Eventually, the infant will react to the word alone as if the cat were there—looking around for it or getting excited and ready for play. For learning to have taken place, it suffices that the word *kitty* and the actual cat have been associated, so that they evoke at least some of the same responses (see Chapter 7 for further discussion of learning theory).

Learning theory may explain the earliest and simplest kinds of linking between words and objects. Children are especially sensitive to novelty in their environment and predisposed to apply new words to new objects (Smith, 1999). Thus, it is likely that many of their earliest words, such as *bottle* and *blanket,* which have concrete referents, could be learned through association. Exclusive reliance on associative learning, however, would be slow, effortful, idiosyncratic, and result in many errors. As we will see, beyond the initial stages, young children's word learning is not slow and error laden. Rather, it is rapid, predictable, and remarkably accurate. If children do not learn words only through association, how do they do it?

Developmental Theories

In contrast to the behavioral model, developmental theories consider semantic development within the wider context of the child's unfolding social, cognitive, and linguistic skills. Children learn the meanings of words by drawing on skills in multiple domains. During the first few months of life, before they actually begin producing words, infants are laying the foundation for language development. Clark (1993) theorizes that by the time they start learning language, all children have developed a set of **ontological categories;** these are concepts about how the world is organized. Ontological categories include objects, actions, events, relations, states, and properties. These are the basic categories in all languages that speakers refer to when they use language.

Even equipped with a set of ontological categories, the infant's task is still quite daunting. Developmental theories attempt to explain how the child acquires first words, why the scope of reference of children's early words may not match that of adults, and how children's semantic systems become more adult-like over time. Consider what an infant must understand about verbal communication in order to begin mapping words she hears to referents. Let us say, for instance, that the infant is in her home, and the family dog, Rufus, is lying nearby on a rug with a bone. The baby hears her mother say words such as *Rufus, dog, bone,* and *look.* An infant may initially assume that the word *dog* applies only to the family dog. Eventually, however, young children must come to understand that a single label can be applied to more than one specific case (that is, *dog* refers not only to their own Rufus, but to many different dogs, seen in the park, pictured in books and on dog food boxes, etc.). Without this insight, infants cannot begin to understand the nature of reference, or to communicate about objects, actions, and properties (Clark, 1993; 2009). However, this understanding is only one step in cracking the mapping puzzle. Not only does the label *dog* refer to many different dogs, a particular dog may be labeled in many different ways *(Rufus, dog, setter, pet, puppy).* Moreover, when a child hears a new word, the word could refer to an action such as barking, a property or state such as sleeping, or even a part of an object, such as the dog's tail.

One way that young children may avoid this mapping nightmare is to rely on their rudimentary understanding of other people's attentional and intentional states and how those states relate to what is likely to be communicated (Tomasello, 2003). In order to become efficient word learners, young children must come to understand, for example, that a novel word they hear probably relates to an object or event that the *speaker* is paying attention to. If the infant simply assumes that the word she hears relates to whatever is present or that it refers to whatever she herself is attending to, she will be relying solely on associative learning and no doubt make many mismappings. Graham, Nilsen, Collins, and Olineck (2010) have shown that by 24 months of age infants hearing an adult produce an unfamiliar label check to see whether the adult is attending to the same object or event they themselves are, and if not, adjust their own focus of attention to match the adult's. Similarly, Tomasello and Barton (1994) have shown that when 2-year-olds hear an adult say, "Let's go find the toma!" they expect *toma* to refer to the object the adult shows satisfaction finding, and not those she rejects along the way. The ability to establish and maintain joint focus of attention with those around them, as well as a basic understanding of others' intentions and goal-directed actions, is crucial for children's efficient word learning (L. Bloom, 2000; Tomasello, 2003).

Other theorists have suggested that children are aided by a number of lexical **principles** that constrain the number of possible word–referent mappings. For example, young children may tend to assume that a new word they hear refers to an object (Golinkoff, Mervis, & Hirsh-Pasek, 1994), and further, that the word refers to the *whole* object rather than to its parts (Markman & Wachtel, 1988). These two tendencies together may predispose the child to eliminate the family dog's floppy ears or the way he runs around the living room as likely referents for the label *dog*. Other lexical principles suggest that children tend to avoid two labels for one referent (Hansen & Markman, 2009). According to this **principle of mutual exclusivity**, the child in our example will be inclined to eliminate Rufus as a possible referent for *bone,* because Rufus already has a name. Although it may be useful in some contexts and especially for early word learning, this propensity may make the subsequent learning of superordinate or subordinate terms and synonyms for known words more difficult. Clark (2007) proposes a slightly different child principle, that is, that words contrast in meaning. According to this **principle of contrast**, the child will not completely eliminate Rufus as a possible referent for a new label, *bone,* but will assume that the meaning of the word *bone* does not overlap perfectly with the meaning of the word *Rufus*.

Although children may rely in part on lexical principles, such default assumptions can be overridden by their linguistic and world knowledge. For example, Akhtar (2002) showed that young children rely on discourse context to decide whether a novel word refers to shape or texture. When told, "This is a round one; this is a square one; this is a *dacky* one," children interpreted the novel word as referring to shape. However, when told, "This is a smooth one; this is a fuzzy one; this is a *dacky* one," they discarded any shape or whole-object bias and instead interpreted *dacky* as referring to texture. Bélanger & Hall (2006) found that, by 20 months, most toddlers can use the presence or absence of an article to distinguish between proper names ("that's Daxy") and count nouns ("that's a Daxy"). As they get older, Hall (1994a) showed that children used their world knowledge that dogs often have proper names, whereas caterpillars do not, to interpret *zav* as a proper name in a sentence such as "This dog is Zav," but as an adjective in the sentence, "This caterpillar is zav." According to Hollich, Hirsh-Pasek, and Golinkoff (2000), children take advantage of multiple cues in learning words and weight those cues differently at different points in development. At the beginning of word learning, children may give more weight to perceptual information, such as the concreteness of an action, or the visible shape of an object, and only later draw more heavily on social and linguistic cues. By the preschool years, children adhere less strictly to lexical principles such as the whole-object bias. For example, they may be particularly likely to learn the word *fur* when hearing it used in conjunction with a familiar object and marked with possessive syntax: "Look at the doggie's fur!" (Saylor & Sabbagh, 2004). Regardless of the hypotheses children adopt and the sources of social and world knowledge they employ, their initial mappings will occasionally be incorrect. As we will see later, children rely on input and feedback from mature speakers to test and revise their label-to-referent mappings.

Fast Mapping

Despite the challenges of word mapping, children as young as 18 months old can make an initial word–referent mapping after only a few exposures to a new word, often also without explicit instruction by an adult (Houston-Price, Plunkett, & Harris, 2005). This phenomenon, called **fast mapping**, has spawned a wealth of research in recent years. Researchers are investigating such questions as: What exactly do children learn about words after only limited exposure? Do their initial mappings differ in predictable ways from adult usage? How many exposures are necessary for children to make an initial mapping? How long do they remember such mappings? Are different types of words (nouns, verbs, descriptors) learned equally easily? Are there any age differences in fast mapping? Is incidental learning as effective as direct teaching?

Carey and Bartlett (1978) first demonstrated fast mapping by providing 3- and 4-year-olds with exposure to unfamiliar words in the course of classroom activities. Children were not taught the words explicitly, but were simply asked, for example, "Bring me the chromium tray, not the blue one, the chromium one." The researchers found that most children remembered something about the sound and meaning of the target word (such as that it was a color word) a week later. Later research showed that fast-mapped labels are remembered by preschoolers for at least a month (Markson & Bloom, 1997), a capacity that probably helps ensure that new words will not be forgotten quickly if they are encountered infrequently. Although children's memory for nonlinguistic facts is inferior to adults', Markson and Bloom found that children remembered fast-mapped words over several weeks' time as well as adults. As with most other kinds of learning, exposure distributed over several days makes for more successful word learning than the same number of exposures concentrated in a single day (Childers & Tomasello, 2002). In this respect, 2-year-olds learning novel words and college students studying for exams seem to adhere to similar learning principles.

Finally, there is evidence that children ages 2 and older may learn nouns as effectively through incidental learning as through **ostension** (that is, when objects are labeled explicitly) (Jaswel & Markman, 2001). One theory for this finding is that, in the absence of labeling or pointing by adults, children may attend more closely to semantic and grammatical information in the input (Hall, Quantz, & Persoage, 2000). For example, upon hearing a sentence like "Mother is feeding the ferret," they may use what they know about the meaning of the word *feed* (that one only feeds animate objects) to seek out an animate referent for the word *ferret*.

Early Words

By early in their second year, most children have begun to produce some words themselves. They begin with words related to what is intellectually and socially most meaningful to them (Anglin, 1995), such as names for important people and objects in their lives. Thus *mommy, daddy, doggie,* and *blankie* are common early words, and *tree, vase,* and *policeman* are not. Subsequent patterns of word meaning and use reflect development not only within children's semantic systems, but also in other areas such as their cognition and memory, in addition to widened experience.

The Study of Vocabulary

Examination of children's vocabulary is probably the oldest approach to the study of language acquisition. Beginning word use signals that children have a new tool that will enable them to learn about and participate more fully in their societies. Furthermore, word use is thought to provide tangible indication of the makeup and workings of children's minds. The first studies—some as early as the eighteenth century (e.g., Tiedemann, 1787)—were almost invariably based on observations of the authors' own children and were kept in the form of diaries. During the nineteenth century and the first half of the twentieth century, many psychologists kept diary records of their children's development. This remains a valuable way to trace the development of language in individual children. By themselves, however, diaries can be misleading, since the temptation to write what is unusual or interesting, rather than what is daily and ordinary, is hard to resist. More recently, a number of researchers have found ways to augment and improve diary studies by giving parents participating in research studies checklists of the words that their children are likely to acquire during their first years (Dale, Bates, Reznick, & Morisset, 1989) and then comparing parental reports with the children's actual language in order to validate their judgments. One of the most commonly used is the *MacArthur-Bates Communicative Development Inventories* (Fenson et al., 2007). Such checklists, now standardized across a broad variety of languages, help parents organize their observations and remind them of the more ordinary, but important, things their children understand and say that they might otherwise overlook.

What Are Early Words Like?

By the time children begin to acquire a vocabulary, they have already been exposed to a great deal of language and have had a wide range of experiences. Children's earliest words usually appear in the context of labeling objects, participating in routine game formats, and imitations. Many children's early words tend to fulfill a social purpose. In other words, children tend to start using language to connect to other people or to engage in ritual or playful speech, such as saying *bye-bye* or *peek-a-boo* (Ninio & Snow, 1996). When early words are used to refer to the outside world, they may be used in unconventional ways. For example, Halliday's son, Nigel, would use *syrup* to refer to maple syrup for his pancakes in the morning, but not in any other context.

During the second year of life, children start learning approximately one word per week, and then one word per day. After this initial outset and throughout the first five years of life, this rate accelerates intensely, so that children learn an average of one new word every two waking hours (Tomasello, 2003; Fenson, Dale, Reznick, & Bates, 1994). Some researchers have identified a **vocabulary spurt**, a rapid increase in the number of words learned that occurs around age 18 months. However, other studies suggest that vocabulary acquisition is best characterized as a gradual process during which children become more skillful as word learners (P. Bloom, 2000). A vocabulary spurt may be apparent for some children, but research has shown that not all children display an abrupt increase in their production of words (Ganger & Brent, 2004).

The words children acquire in their early productive vocabularies are influenced by many factors. Early words tend to share phonetic features, occur frequently in speech, and be shorter in length than later-acquired words (Storkel, 2004). Researchers have analyzed the phonology of children's first fifty words, studied children's imitations of words, and tried to teach new words to 1-year-olds (Schwartz & Leonard, 1982). The results of these studies show that words that are easier for children to pronounce are more likely to be included in their early productive vocabularies and that favored sound patterns vary greatly across children.

Research suggests that at around 20 months of age, children can use specific phonetic information in learning similar words. Experimental studies carried out with English and French monolingual children have shown that 20-month-olds were able to learn two words that display a consonantal contrast, such as [du**k**] and [du**t**]. However, these same children were not yet able to learn simultaneously two new words that display only vowel contrasts, such as [d**a**]/[d**i**] or [dr**o**]/[dr**y**] (Nazzi, 2005; Werker, Fennell, Corcoran, & Stager, 2002). Interestingly, even though young children learn to produce vowel sounds before consonants, they are able to benefit from consonantal contrasts before vowel contrasts in early word learning. Nespor, Peña, and Mehler (2003) have proposed that vowels and consonants play different roles in speech processing and language acquisition, arguing that consonants are more salient in word identification.

From the beginning, children's vocabularies appear to include words from a variety of grammatical classes; their first fifty words represent all of the major grammatical classes found in adult language (see Table 4.1). Nonetheless, common nouns account for nearly 40 percent of the average English-speaking child's first fifty words, whereas verbs, adjectives, and function words each account for less than 10 percent. By the time children's productive vocabularies exceed 600 words, about 40 percent are nouns, 25 percent verbs and adjectives, and about 15 percent are function words (Bates et al., 1994).

Among nouns, those that are the easiest to distinguish from the surroundings, such as animate beings or things that move, are the earliest learned (Gentner, 2006). Most English-speaking children learn more *different* nouns than verbs or other relational words early on, but they make more frequent and consistent *use* of relational words such as *that, there, no, more,* and *uh-oh* (Gopnik & Choi, 1995). The number of nouns reported using checklists is somewhat inflated relative to children's actual use, perhaps because mothers are more likely to notice nouns in their children's speech (Pine, Lieven, & Rowland, 1996). Estimations of children's noun use also vary by context, with somewhat higher use observed in book reading than in toy play across languages (Tardif, Gelman, & Xu, 1999; Ogura, Dale, Yamashita, Murase & Mahieu, 2006). Proportions vary from child to child as well (see Chapter 8) and differ somewhat across languages. For example, some research shows less marked noun preference in the early vocabularies of children learning Mandarin or Korean (Choi & Gopnik, 1995; Tardif et al., 1999). However, the *noun bias* seems to be a fairly robust phenomenon, with parents of young children learning Spanish, Dutch, French, Hebrew, Italian, Korean, and American English all reporting greater proportions of nouns than other word classes, despite striking structural differences across languages (Bornstein & Cote, 2004).

Why should nouns initially be acquired more rapidly than other types of words? Several possible explanations have been suggested. One hypothesis holds that children's vocabularies reflect the input directed to them; studies have shown that in adult speech to English-speaking children, labels for different kinds of objects are more numerous than labels for actions, properties, or relations (Goldfield, 1993). Additionally, nouns are often highlighted in the first or last position of mothers' utterances to children, making them more salient (Wai Han & Nicoladis, 2010). An alternative explanation is that nouns are favored over verbs in acquisition because nouns tend to refer to clearer, more concrete, and more readily identifiable referents than verbs. The linguistic and conceptual complexity of verbs may be one reason that children initially rely on general-purpose verbs such as *do, go, make,* and *get* (Clark, 1993). Apparently, children are not

 **table 4.1**	Children's Earliest Words: Examples from the Vocabularies of Children Younger than 20 Months

Sound effects
baa baa, meow, moo, ouch, uh-oh, woof, yum-yum

Food and drink
apple, banana, cookie, cheese, cracker, juice, milk, water

Animals
bear, bird, bunny, dog, cat, cow, duck, fish, kitty, horse, pig, puppy

Body parts and clothing
diaper, ear, eye, foot, hair, hand, hat, mouth, nose, toe, tooth, shoe

House and outdoors
blanket, chair, cup, door, flower, keys, outside, spoon, tree, tv

People
baby, daddy, gramma, grampa, mommy, [child's own name]

Toys and vehicles
ball, balloon, bike, boat, book, bubbles, plane, truck, toy

Actions
down, eat, go, sit, up

Games and routines
bath, bye, hi, night-night, no, peekaboo, please, shhh, thank you, yes

Adjectives and descriptives
all gone, cold, dirty, hot

the only ones who find mapping verbs difficult. Gillette, Gleitman, Gleitman, and Lederer (1999) showed adults video clips of mother–child interactions in which a noun or a verb had been replaced with a beep. The participants' task was simply to guess the omitted word. When the word was a noun, adults guessed the word correctly 45 percent of the time. When the beep obscured a verb, however, adults guessed correctly only 15 percent of the time. Correct responses for mental verbs such as *think* or *see* were even fewer. These results suggest that identifying the proper referent for verbs may be generally more challenging than it is for nouns. A recent proposal for a "unified developmental theory of word learning" (Maguire, Hirsh-Pasek, & Golinkoff, 2006) argues that grammatical categories do not offer the best explanation to understand early word learning. Maguire, Hirsh-Pasek, and Golinkoff have proposed the "SICI continuum" of Shape, Individuability, Concreteness, and Imageability. Instead of debating whether children first learn nouns or verbs, this theory proposes a more comprehensive explanation, arguing that, regardless of grammatical form, children's early words tend to refer to concepts with a reliable and consistent shape,

Imitating a waitress carrying a plate, this young child says the Spanish word pan *(bread), a word she uses to refer to many types of food.*

that can more easily be distinguished from others (individuability), that are more perceptually salient and concrete (concreteness) and that can easily yield a mental image (imageability). Taking into consideration the many different types of nouns and verbs in a language, this theory predicts why nouns that are highly abstract (such as *idea* or *justice)* tend to be learned much later in life than other nouns (such as *dog* or *cup); as* well as why many concrete verbs, such as *dance* or *eat,* are learned early in development.

Unconventional Word/Meaning Mappings

An **overextension** is said to occur when a child uses a word in a context or manner that is inconsistent with, but in some way related to, the adult meaning of the word, as when a dog is called *kitty* or a cotton ball *snow,* or when a visitor is greeted with a hearty *bye-bye!* Thus, the term *overextension* derives from the fact that the child is extending the term beyond the adult word concept. An **underextension** is said to occur when a child uses a particular word for only a limited subset of the contexts allowed by the adult concept. A child who uses *duck* for birds that swim, *bird* for those that fly, and *chicken* for those that do not fly appears to be using the term *bird* for a reduced set of referents (Clark, 2007) Both overextensions and underextensions are common in 1- and 2-year-old children's speech, accounting for up to one-third of their production vocabulary (Clark, 1993). Beyond age 2¼, however, such unconventional mappings become less frequently observable, unless elicited experimentally (Bloomquist, 2007).

What do children's extensions of words tell us? At most, they reveal how children categorize the world and what aspects of their experiences they find relevant to certain words. Mervis and Mervis (1988) and others have pointed out that children's categories may not initially match those of adults. At the same time, some caution must be exercised. As some researchers (e.g., Hoek, Ingram, & Gibson, 1986) have noted, the extent to which the child's spoken word should be considered an accurate representation of her inner structuring of the world remains unclear. Although some of children's unconventional mappings occur because their underlying word concepts differ from those of adults, there are other plausible explanations for overextensions and underextensions:

- As noted earlier, not all categories have clear-cut boundaries. Carabine (1991) found that most of the inappropriate labeling by 2- and 3-year-old children he studied consisted of labels applied to objects that were not uniformly categorized by adults either.

- Some of children's overextensions may reflect retrieval problems, such that an older, better-known label (e.g., *dog*) may be inappropriately used in place of a more recently acquired but more appropriate one such as *moose* (Hoek, Ingram, & Gibson, 1986).

- At other times, children may not yet have acquired the proper label, even though their concepts match those of adults. They may then opt to use words as semantic stand-ins for the words they do not know. Gelman and her colleagues, for example, have shown that children are much more likely to overextend in production—when they must come up with the appropriate word themselves—than in comprehension—when they need only choose the appropriate referent for a given word (Gelman, Croft, Fu, Clausner, & Gottfried, 1998).

- Children may use their single words analogically to comment on similarities they have noticed (Nelson, Benedict, Gruendel, & Rescorla, 1977). Thus, the child who points to a Saint Bernard and says "cow" may mean only that the dog is like a cow. Additional evidence that children are using analogy comes from the fact that they are seldom observed using words in this fashion after they acquire syntax and can explain what they mean.

- In other situations, children seem to overextend words as a humorous gesture. When a 2-year-old who routinely uses the word *hat* puts an overturned bowl on his head, giggles, and says "hat," we can be fairly certain that he is making a joke.

Determining what a child's early words mean requires attention to the contexts in which they are spoken and understood, as well as information about how the child has referred to the concepts or used the words before. Research thus shows that children's unconventional mappings are only sometimes a reflection of incomplete categorization skills (McDonough, 2002). Other times, overextensions and underextensions may reflect the structure of the category; alternatively, they may be retrieval errors, semantic stand-ins, analogies, or even jokes.

Invented Words

In an early study, Berko (1958) found that preschoolers and first-graders were often able to invent words to refer to meanings that were specified by an experimenter. In this structured situation, children and adults were asked questions like, "What would you call a man whose job is to 'zib'?" Although children only rarely employed the typical adult strategy of creating **derived words** by adding suffixes (a *zibber* zibs for a living), they were frequently able to create words by using alternative techniques (e.g., making **compound words** like *zib-man*).

Children also often invent or coin words spontaneously in their own speech. Sometimes invented words are used interchangeably with conventional words, as, for example, when a child uses *bee-house* and *bee-hive* in the same sentence (Becker, 1994). At other times, children may invent new words to fill gaps in their vocabularies. Clark (1981) found that these gaps occurred when the child had forgotten or did not know the usual word. Inventions such as *pourer* for *cup* and *plant-man* for *gardener* were common. Preschoolers frequently created needed verbs from nouns they knew, as when one child said, while putting crackers in her soup, "I'm crackering my soup" (Clark, 1981, p. 304).

Clark found that children's lexical innovations follow fairly regular principles.

- ***Simplicity.*** **Simplicity** is reflected in children's use of a conventional word in an unconventional, but totally obvious, role (for example, *to pillow,* meaning *to throw a pillow at;* Clark, 1993, p. 120).

- ***Semantic transparency.*** **Semantic transparency** is evident in innovations such as *plant-man* for *gardener;* the meaning of the invented word is more apparent and more easily remembered than the conventional one.

- ***Productivity.*** **Productivity** is shown in children's use of forms that are frequently used by adults as the basis of new words. Many English words meaning *people who do something,* for instance, end in *-er (teacher, player).* Thus, children create agentival nouns such as *cooker* and *bicycler.*

Differences between Comprehension and Production

According to Nelson and her colleagues (1977), comprehension of a word requires that a child, on hearing the word, anticipate or do something. Production of a word requires on its most basic level that the child speak the word at an appropriate time and place. Productive vocabularies typically lag behind receptive vocabularies. According to maternal reports, for example, most 16-month-olds comprehend between 100 and 200 different words, but produce fewer than fifty (Bates et al., 1994).

For many years, researchers interested in investigating young children's vocabulary comprehension relied on tasks requiring the child to select or point to an object or picture labeled by the researcher. This methodology was less than ideal for at least two reasons. First, referents for some words, such as action verbs, are often difficult to depict. Second, infants and young children often do not reliably touch or point to the referent requested, even when their looking behaviors suggest they recognize the referent being labeled. More recently, researchers have begun using a new method, called the **preferential looking paradigm**, to test infants' and toddlers' vocabulary comprehension (Golinkoff, Hirsh-Pasek, Cauley, & Gordon, 1987). In this paradigm, the infant is seated on his blindfolded mother's lap facing two video monitors (see Chapter 5). Words or sentences are played over a centrally located speaker. At the same time, brief segments of videotape are shown on the two monitors. The object or action sequence shown on one monitor matches the word or sentence the child hears, while that shown on the other screen does not. Because children prefer to gaze at video segments matching what they hear, they will look longer at the matching screen if they understand the word or sentence. Using this method, Naigles and Gelman (1995) showed that children who call *cow* "doggie" nonetheless look longer at the picture of a cow than the competing picture of a dog, suggesting that young children's underlying concepts may be more adult-like than their productive vocabulary may indicate. Receptive vocabulary, then, rather than productive vocabulary, may be a more accurate reflection of children's conceptual knowledge (Gershkoff-Stowe, Thal, Smith, & Namy, 1997). Clearly, the receptive and expressive systems do not overlap perfectly, and a complete understanding of the dimensions and features of each requires careful study.

How Adult Speech Influences Children's Semantic Development

Even before children begin using words themselves, adults' labeling and gaze behaviors serve to focus children's attention on objects; similarly, babies' vocalizations and visual behaviors provide adults with clues as to what the child is interested in communicating about. Much of adult speech addressed to young children deals with the here and now (Shatz & Gelman, 1973; Snow, 1972) or with events that are about to happen (Bloom, 2000). Many of these words are accompanied by gestures that additionally aid children in mapping object referents (Zammit & Schafer, 2011). When adults look at and label objects that are visible to children, children assume that the label refers to the adult focus of attention and make an initial object-label mapping (Baldwin, 1995). This dovetailing of adults' and children's predispositions may help explain how children as young as 13 months learn to comprehend new words after only a few exposures (Woodward, Markman, & Fitzsimmons, 1994). Adults also give children many opportunities to practice producing object labels themselves by engaging them in naming games (Ninio & Snow, 1996). In these interactions, the parent points to and names specific objects for the child and then helps the child say the name. As children acquire language, parents' speech to them incorporates increasingly rich information about the categories they are acquiring. For instance, in book reading, parents go beyond labeling ("That's a bat") to explain that "Bats live in caves. Bats have big wings" (Gelman, Coley, Rosengran, Hartman, & Pappas, 1998).

The labels adults provide for children are not always the ones they would use with adults or older children. Adults sometimes mislabel objects when speaking to very young children, teaching them in some cases to use labels that are incorrect by adult standards. Mervis and Mervis (1982) gave ten mothers and their 13-month-olds sets of toys to play with and recorded their speech. The mothers named almost all of the toys for their children and were observed quite often to misname some of them according to how their children might have categorized them. For example, a toy leopard was commonly referred to as *kitty-cat,* and a toy tow truck was referred to as *car.* Why would parents mislabel objects for their children? According to Mervis and Mervis, children provide their parents with signals indicating how they might categorize objects. Although babies first treat all objects in the same ways (mouthing, touching, shaking, and banging them), eventually they begin treating them differentially. At this point a doll might be held and a toy car pushed on the floor. Children's differential treatment of objects indicates on a fundamental level how they are categorizing the objects. By labeling the objects for children according to the children's own categories, parents are probably showing how words are used. That is, objects that differ in minor ways but are of the same category share names.

The naming practices of mothers, then, seem to be based on children's own ways of categorizing the world (Golinkoff, Shuff-Bailey, Olguin, & Ruan, 1995). (Fathers, by contrast, seem to engage in this behavior less often [Bernstein Ratner, 1988].) The names that mothers choose tend to follow what Rosch and colleagues (1976) have called **basic-level categories.** The first principle underlying such categories is that similarities within categories are emphasized, rather than similarities between categories. Thus, because leopards are more like cats than other objects, they are labeled "cats." The second principle defining the basic level is that it is the most general level at which objects are similar because of their forms, functions, component parts (Poulin-Dubois, 1995), or motions. Thus, although an owl bank and a Christmas ornament share neither name nor function for adults, because they are round objects that would most likely be treated similarly (i.e., rolled) by very young children, they were grouped with balls and identified as *balls* by the mothers studied by the Mervises.

Mothers of young children use different strategies when teaching their children basic-level terms than when they teach either more general or more specific terms (Hall, 1994b). For basic-level words, mothers use ostension; they may point and say, "That's a tractor." When asked to teach superordinates, however, they employ a strategy of *inclusion,* mentioning both basic-level terms and the superordinate term. For instance, they say things such as, "A car and a bus and a train. All of them are kinds of *vehicles.*" When teaching terms such as *passenger,* which are more specific than basic-level terms, mothers provide an explanation that includes a basic-level term as well as the new word. For example, they may say, "The pig is a passenger because he's riding in a car," or, "A passenger is a person when he is riding in a car." Parents provide particular help with rare words by explaining them explicitly or embedding them in a context that calls on the child's prior knowledge or real-world experience. For instance, at dinner, 4-year-old George's mother explained what *cramps* are: "Cramps are when your stomach feels all tight and it hurts 'cause you have food in it" (Beals, 1997, p. 682).

Mothers' speech has also been shown to have an effect on the ways that children come to understand and use vocabulary relating to their own inner states (Tingley, Gleason, & Hooshyar, 1994). In a study conducted in Great Britain, Dunn, Bretherton, and Munn (1987) found that mothers talking with their young children routinely labeled a variety of children's inner states, including quality of consciousness (e.g., *bored*), physiological states *(dizzy),* and emotional states *(happy).* By the age of 2, the children used many of these inner-state words themselves, particularly those relating to sleep, distress, dislike, temperature, pain, and pleasure. An even more intriguing finding of this study was that mothers used more of these labels with daughters, and by the age of 2, girls themselves referred to feeling states significantly more frequently than boys did. Infants' own communication skills tend to impact the frequency with which mothers will use mental state words. For example, as children begin to point and vocalize, mothers are more apt to comment on what the child "wants" or "needs" (Slaughter, Peterson, & Carpenter, 2009). Thus, as in many aspects of development, parents and children's communicative styles are bi-directional: parents respond to children and vice versa.

In addition to the special vocabulary directed to young children, adults and even older children in many cultures seem to tailor other aspects of their language to the child's ability level (Shatz & Gelman, 1973); some of the characteristics of input language may facilitate semantic development. Input language, especially when young children begin to understand and use words, is more clearly and slowly enunciated and is characterized by exaggerated intonation and clear pauses between utterances (Liu, Tsao, & Kuhl, 2009; Soderstrom, 2007). In addition, single-word utterances are common (Ninio, 1992), and words that are being taught or focused on tend to be placed in sentence-final position with especially marked pitch and stress (Wai Han & Nicoladis, 2010). Brent and Siskind (2001) observed that mothers talking to their 9- to 15-month-olds at home often produce words in isolation and do so several times within a short space of time. They also found that hearing a word in isolation, rather than simply the number of times the word was heard overall, predicted whether the word would be learned by the infant. Thus, speech directed to young children tends to be better formed and more intelligible than speech to other adults, which tends to be fraught with sloppily pronounced words, false starts, and ill-formed or incomplete sentences with unclear boundaries between words. This clearer, more precise, and simpler input language could assist children in separating words from the flow of speech and in perceiving correct pronunciation. Similarly, the consistent pronunciation could aid them in becoming familiar with new words and in picking out those words that map onto meanings they wish to express.

Adults communicate with young children in order to share information about social, emotional, and physical topics, but in so doing, they provide children with feedback about their own language. Some feedback is nonverbal, as, for example, when a mother appears when her child calls *mama* from the crib or brings the child a saltine when he asks for a *cracker.* If the child really wanted a cookie instead of a cracker, he will have made a useful (if disappointing) discovery. Corrective feedback can also be in verbal form. For example, when a child labels a yo-yo a *ball,* the adult may provide the correct label, accompanied by a description of critical features (e.g., *That's a yo-yo. See? It goes up and down*). Such contrastive recasts of children's language errors appear to help typical language learners (Saxton, 2005).

Children's vocabulary development is also affected by the amount of speech that is directed to them. As we have seen, children can quickly form an initial hypothesis about a word's meaning after hearing it only once or twice. However, in-depth learning requires multiple exposures to the word in many different contexts (Hoff-Ginsberg & Naigles, 1999). It should not be surprising, then, that children exposed to larger amounts of adult input develop larger, richer vocabularies than children exposed to more limited input (Hoff & Naigles, 2002; Huttenlocher, Haight, Bryk, Seltzer, & Lysons, 1991).

As noted so far, most research on language input focuses exclusively on one-to-one parent–child interactions, those typical of many Western middle-class families. **Joint attention** (mutual engagement between child and parent) and **joint focus** (focus on the same object or event) are factors recognized as essential for effective learning in these well-documented linguistic interactions (Tomasello, 2003). However, the language environment surrounding young children is not always dominated by one-to-one interactions with speech directly addressed to the child. In many cultures around the world adults do not address young children as conversational partners, but instead children learn mostly as observers or listeners (Rogoff, 2003). The Kaluli children from Papua New Guinea, for example, have been shown to develop language successfully despite almost never participating in one-to-one conversations with an adult (Schieffelin & Ochs, 1986). Recently, a promising and intriguing line of research is expanding the communicative contexts under study by focusing on the effect of overheard speech in children's vocabulary learning. Instead of stressing *joint attention* (or mutual engagement) between adult and child, some research suggests that in some circumstances joint focus alone might be sufficient for effective language learning. In other words, children seem to be able to learn words from overheard speech only by sharing *joint focus* and without directly participating in the conversation. Children as young as 18 months are able to learn from overheard speech if the memory load is not too high (Floor & Akhtar, 2006). Interestingly, some research suggests that children with prior experience observing multiple adults in their everyday lives might be better equipped to pay attention to third-party conversations and, consequently, better able to learn words from overheard speech (Shneidman, Buresh, Shimpi, Knight-Schwarz, & Woodward, 2009). This line of research is expanding our understanding of the range of contextual factors that can influence word learning throughout development.

Later Semantic Development

Vocabulary is crucial not only because a larger and deeper lexical repertoire allows speakers to express themselves with more preciseness, flexibility, and effectiveness, but also because of the strong association between vocabulary and reading comprehension. If students do not understand the words in a text, they will not understand what they read and, consequently, will not be able to learn the content-area material needed for academic success. In fact, numerous students struggle in particular because their word knowledge is insufficient for understanding the oral and written language of school (Snow & Uccelli, 2009).

In the study of later vocabulary acquisition, researchers distinguish between two constructs: breadth and depth of vocabulary. **Vocabulary breadth** refers to the number of words known. **Vocabulary depth** encompasses the degree of various kinds of word knowledge: (1) the sound and spelling of a word, (2) its morphological structure, (3) the types of sentences in which it can occur, (4) its multiple meanings and word associations, (5) the situations in which its use is appropriate, and (6) the origin of its form and meaning(s). Speakers have different degrees of knowledge about words. Fourth graders might know that *bitter* means "unpleasant taste," but they might not know that *bitter* can also refer to feelings

Children's exposure to rare words such as handlebars and spokes often occurs in the context of shared activity with adults.

of anger and resentment, or to piercingly cold weather, or that it can also be used as a noun. With repeated exposures and multiple contexts of use, speakers accumulate increasing levels of knowledge about a word.

The most reliable estimates of vocabulary breadth are based on word families, because researchers assume that if speakers know one of the words in a family, they also know the others. A **word family** includes a base word, its inflections, and some regular derived forms (for example, *drive, drives, driving, driver*). Children face an enormous vocabulary-learning task over the school years. A 5-year-old native English speaker is presumed to have a vocabulary of approximately 4,000 to 5,000 word families. Once in school, students learn between 2,000 and 4,000 words a year, reaching approximately 40,000 to 50,000 words by the end of high school (Graves, 2006; Stahl & Nagy, 2006).

However, as we have suggested, vocabulary acquisition consists not just of adding new words and concepts to an ever-expanding list. Semantic development is also reflected in the incrementality of various kinds of knowledge about already acquired words (Stahl & Nagy, 2006). The difficulty of assessing children's semantic knowledge arises, of course, because children's semantic systems themselves are becoming more complex. Not only do children learn new words and new concepts, they also enrich and solidify their knowledge of known words by establishing multiple links among words and concepts. For example, children learn that the words *walk, walks, walking,* and *walked* refer to similar actions that differ in tense or duration, while *eat* and *devour* refer to actions that differ in manner. *Compete, win,* and *lose* share some semantic components, but they differ in the outcome each conveys. *Pain* and *pane* are linked phonologically, as are *pane, mane,* and *lane,* though each has a different referent. *Oak, spruce,* and *birch* are linked by virtue of their co-membership in the superordinate category *tree*. These types of connections among words and concepts form what are called **semantic networks.**

Although formation of semantic networks continues throughout the life span, there is evidence that children begin forming rudimentary semantic networks very early in development. Clark (1993), for example, notes that children often add several new words for one semantic domain all at once, as when 1-year-old Damon learned *ant, bug,* and *ladybug* all in one week, and *frog, snake,* and *alligator* the next. Semantic networking can also be observed using preferential looking paradigms. Styles and Plunkett (2009) observed that priming a target with a related semantic category member attracted more sustained looking behavior than when the target was preceded by an unrelated noun. Children seek links, relationships, and conceptual wholes in everything they experience, including language. As such, it is not surprising that children's earliest words can be predicted by the numbers of word associates that they have in the input; that is, the more semantic neighbors that a word has in the parent's input to a child, the faster such items are learned (Hills, Maouene, Riordan, & Smith, 2010). Semantic links are also evident in young children's inappropriate use of certain words after they have learned the appropriate use. In such cases, Bowerman (1978) observed that there was some semantic overlap between the word used incorrectly and the correct word. An example of this phenomenon was when 2-year-old Christy said, "Daddy take his pants on" (p. 986), after having previously used *put* correctly in similar circumstances. Both *put* and *take* refer to actions that result in a change of location for an object. Bowerman suggests that such substitutions can be interpreted most adequately as "incorrect choices among semantically related words that compete for selection in a particular speech context" (p. 979).

Another indication that words in children's vocabularies are becoming interconnected is developmental change in children's **word associations.** These changes have been demonstrated using a variety of word-association tasks. In an early example of such a task, Nelson (1974) gave children the name of a category, such as "animals" or "furniture," and asked them to supply names of as many category members as possible. With this **set task**, Nelson found that 8-year-olds were able to supply nearly twice as many category members as 5-year-olds. Moreover, only the 5-year-olds included *meat* and *ice cream* in the vegetable category and *wall* and *door* in the furniture category, evidence that their categories were not as well defined as those of older children. Semantic networks grow steadily and undergo reorganization over childhood; tasks such as those Nelson used are now typically called **semantic verbal fluency** tests. They are robustly normed across many languages and are used in a number of psycho-educational and language tests to distinguish typical from delayed language development (Crowe & Prescott, 2003).

Brown and Berko (1960), using a **free-word association** task, found evidence of a **syntagmatic-paradigmatic shift** in children's responses. Given a particular word and instructed to give the next word that comes to mind, young children tend to respond with words that are related in syntax to the stimulus word; that is, they give words that would typically follow the stimulus word in a normal sentence (a syntagmatic response). For example, in response to the stimulus word *eat,* a child might say *lunch.* Around age 7, children begin to respond instead with words that are of the same grammatical category as the stimulus word (e.g., *eat—drink*). Although this trend in response pattern continues to evolve from first grade to college, it shows by far the greatest change between first and second grade. Explanations for the shift include general cognitive strategy shifts, developmental changes in children's interpretation of the task, changes in knowledge of the features that define words, and cognitive reorganization that accompanies the acquisition of reading (Cronin, 2002).

Home and School Factors Influencing Vocabulary Development

Vocabulary is a language domain that is characterized by extreme individual variability. Variability certainly comes both from individual and contextual factors. A child who is skillful at remembering phonological representations, who already knows numerous words and concepts, and who understands the concepts of "word" and "definition" (Nagy, 2007) will learn new words more efficiently. However, these individual characteristics are in turn highly influenced by contextual factors. A study conducted in Canada found that *first graders* who scored at the top 25th percentile in vocabulary scores and who attended an economically privileged school outperformed some *fourth graders* from an underprivileged school (Biemiller & Slonim, 2001).

Research on home language environments has identified the quantity, variety, and contextual richness of the words heard as key predictors of children's vocabulary acquisition (see "Literacy Experiences at Home" in Chapter 10). In a classic study, Hart and Risley (1995) documented that in comparison to middle-class parents, less educated parents with very low socioeconomic status (SES) tended to use a reduced quantity and variety of words in their child-directed speech, which resulted in their children's reduced vocabularies. In line with these findings, research has shown that bilingual children from low-SES families in the United States tend to display vocabularies that lag considerably behind their English-speaking monolingual peers, with the gap persisting as children grow older (Tabors, Pàez, & López, 2003; Uccelli & Paéz, 2007). Research, however, also suggests that there is considerable within-group variation and considerable overlap in the distribution of vocabulary skills across monolingual and bilingual children from different socioeconomic levels. For instance, Pan, Rowe, Singer, and Snow's (2005) longitudinal study of 108 monolingual children from low-SES rural families revealed considerable variability in children's productive vocabulary at 14, 24, and 36 months of age. Children's vocabulary growth was found to be positively associated with mothers' diversity of vocabulary (i.e., number of different words) and maternal language and literacy skills. In addition, children's vocabulary growth was negatively associated with maternal depression. In other words, low-SES mothers who used a higher diversity of words, had more advanced literacy skills, and were not depressed had children with higher rates of vocabulary growth. Expanding the range of factors under study for low-SES families, Rodríguez and colleagues found that by 3 years of age, children's vocabulary could be predicted by the frequency of their participation in literacy activities (e.g., book reading, storytelling), the quality of maternal engagement, and the availability in the home of age-appropriate learning materials (Rodríguez, Tamis-LeMonde, Spellman, Pan, Raikes, et al., 2009). Finally, while most studies have traditionally focused on mother–child interactions, a recent study by Duursma, Pan, and Raikes (2008) focused instead on the father's role in low-SES families. These authors found that the frequency of their fathers' book reading to them at 24 months predicted children's receptive vocabulary scores a year later.

Over time, sources of vocabulary knowledge expand from primarily the home and caregivers to include a variety of other sources, such as classroom environments, peer interactions, and exposure to reading and other media. Vocabulary knowledge is a key predictor of literacy development and subsequent academic success. When students do not have enough vocabulary to understand what they read, it is unrealistic to expect them to learn vocabulary from reading, and therefore explicit instruction is required. Whereas many monolingual and bilingual students struggle with the demands of school, other bilingual students and students who have overcome socioeconomic disparities achieve the highest levels of lexical proficiency. Bilingualism or socioeconomic conditions per se are not barriers to advanced vocabulary. If optimal environmental conditions are provided at home and at school, children can indeed achieve adequate vocabulary repertoires in one or more languages. How to offer optimal instructional conditions that provide effective opportunities to develop high levels of language and literacy skills for *all students* is a challenging question that is currently testing the creativity of researchers, educators, and policy makers. Research suggests that rich vocabulary instruction that focuses on content learning, depth of vocabulary, contextualized words, frequent exposure, and recurrent use of taught words in the context of high-quality instructional language is the most effective (Beck, McKeown, & Kucan, 2002).

Assessing Vocabulary in Bilingual Children

Many people assume that being monolingual is the "typical" language status, but it is worth remembering that bilingualism or multilingualism is the natural way of life for hun-

In an early investigation of the ability to define, Wehren, DeLisi, and Arnold (1981) found a developmental progression in word definitions among children aged 5 to 11 and college students, beginning with an emphasis on personal experience and moving toward information of a more general, socially shared nature. During the early school years, children's definitions are concrete (descriptions of the referent's appearance or function), personal, and incidental (Snow, 1990). Asked to define the word *cat*, a 5-year-old might offer, "My cat had kittens under my bed." During the elementary school years, such functional and personal definitions are gradually replaced by abstract types of responses: synonyms, explanations, and specifications of categorical relationships (Kurland & Snow, 1997; Skwarchuk & Anglin, 1997).

Developmental changes in the mastery of the definitional genre have also been identified as children move toward better-structured and more conventional formats (Benelli et al., 2006; Snow, 1990). These changes probably reflect children's increased awareness of definitions as a conventional genre, as well as increasing specificity of word meanings in the mental lexicon.

An additional factor that has proven highly relevant in the development of definitional skill is exposure to this genre, in particular through reading and school activities. In many contexts, students are asked to derive definitions for new words embedded in their reading materials; this process requires developing sophistication in the ability to use both semantic and syntactic cues in the surrounding materials (Marinellie, 2010). In others, they are asked to create definitions, more typically a skill required in school, but not other settings. Thus, it is not surprising that, in one study, sixth graders performed better than adults who had not attended high school, but not as well as adults with high levels of education (Benelli et al., 2006). Similarly, researchers studying English-speaking teenagers found that strong readers gave better definitions than weak readers (Nippold, Hegel, & Sohlberg, 1999). In keeping with these findings, Snow (1990) showed that knowledge of the conventional form for good definitions (the definitional genre), combined with frequent opportunities to practice hearing and giving definitions, are necessary for the development of adult-like definitional skills.

A Life-Long Enterprise

Although vocabulary acquisition is most rapid between the ages of 6 and 18, semantic development continues throughout the life span. Not only do we as adults continue to add new words to our lexicons, we also continue to fine-tune the extensions of old words in response to widening experience and to social and cultural changes in our linguistic community. Reflection on and analysis of language result in continual lexical reorganization, a flexibility that is essential if we are to use our language in the most adaptive and effective way to address a wide variety of communicative tasks throughout our lives.

SUMMARY

Words are related to their referents in an arbitrary and symbolic way, defined by social convention. Thus learning word meanings involves learning how one's own language community labels the physical and mental world. Developmental theorists suggest that very young children have a rudimentary understanding of others' intentions and that they also have some predispositions, or principles, that help them quickly make initial word-to-referent mappings. For example, children may assume that words refer to whole objects rather than to their parts. Feedback from more competent speakers allows children to confirm or disprove their initial hypotheses and gradually make their mappings conform to those of their speech community.

English-speaking children's early vocabularies typically include more nouns than verbs or function words, perhaps because the referents of nouns are more concrete and more easily identifiable, or perhaps because they are more common in the speech addressed to young children. Unconventional word-to-meaning mappings (overextensions and underextensions) in children's early speech may reflect processing limitations such as retrieval errors, underlying conceptual differences, or even analogical use of limited vocabulary. Even very young children use language creatively to draw analogies, make jokes, and to invent their own words in systematic ways.

Many features of adult speech to young children are thought to facilitate children's semantic development. Slow, clear enunciation and exaggerated intonation may help children segment the speech stream and identify new words. Talk about the here and now and labeling of objects at the basic level may also simplify the mapping task. Parents' speech provides children with rich information about the words they are acquiring, and children who hear more of this elaborated speech develop larger vocabularies.

As they get older, children not only continue to acquire new words and to learn new meanings for familiar words, they also make connections among words. They learn, among other things, which words are similar in meaning, which contrast, which are subordinate to others, and which are phonologically related. In addition to semantic knowledge of words, children begin to develop the metalinguistic understanding that words themselves have properties that can be reflected on and discussed. The development of semantic networks, along with the continual reorganization of our inner lexicon, is a life-long process.

SUGGESTED PROJECTS

1. Go on the Internet to the Child Language Data Exchange System (MacWhinney, 2000); find the English USA-Providence dataset; open the video and transcript for Naima at 28 months (Demuth, Culbertson, & Alter, 2006) using the link: **http://childes.psy.cmu .edu/browser/index.php?url=Eng-USA/Providence/Naima/nai28.cha**, and identify two segments in the nai28.cha transcript: (a) book reading (lines 99–221 in transcript), and (b) mealtime conversation (lines 1691–1775 in transcript). Finally, compare the segments (a) and (b) to answer the following questions:

   a. How many total words does the mother (MOT) produce in the book reading vs. the mealtime conversation segment? And the child?

   b. How many different words does the mother (MOT) produce in the book reading vs. the mealtime conversation segment? And the child?

   c. Does one activity—book reading vs. mealtime conversation—seem to offer a better scaffolding for word learning at 28 months of age? Why?

2. Using the transcript described above, nai28.cha, first, sort the words into three groups: nouns, verbs, and other, and describe any patterns that you observe. For instance: Are nouns more frequent in this girl's vocabulary production as she interacts with her mother? Does the mother use more nouns than verbs? Then, classify the nouns and verbs into a continuum from most concrete to most abstract meanings. Describe any patterns that you observe and interpret your findings using the concepts learned in the "Early Words" section of this chapter.

3. Ask children from third through fifth grade about the following words: *bitter, brilliant, country, similar,* and *structure.* For each of the words, ask the children to complete the following tasks.

   a. How well do you know this word? Choose one answer: I don't know it, I know it a little bit, I know it very well.

   b. Can you write a sentence using this word?

   c. Write all the words that you can think of that are connected to these words. (Give them 3 minutes to write them.)

   d. Can you define the meaning or meanings of this word?

When you have the responses, reflect upon the constructs of breadth and depth of vocabulary. How well did the students know the words? Were there differences across grades? Were there differences across words? How informative and well structured were the definitions? Did their answers about how well they knew the words relate to their performance on the other tasks?

4. Find a children's picture book with few or no words. Ask a parent of a child 12 to 18 months old to spend 10 or 15 minutes using the book with the child. Ask a parent of a $3^1/_2$- to 4-year-old child to do the same thing. Record and compare the words the parents use with the two children. Does the parent of the older child produce the same number of words in isolation (i.e., one-word utterances) as the parent of the younger? In what other ways does their language differ?

5. Ask children of different ages to tell their favorite words and things and explain their choices. Compare their choices and explanations.

SUGGESTED READINGS

Bates, E., Marchman, V., Thal, D., Fenson, L., Dale, P., Reznick, S., Reilly, J., & Hartung, J. (1994). Developmental and stylistic variation in the composition of early vocabulary. *Journal of Child Language, 21,* 85–123.

Bélanger, J., & Hall, D. (2006). Learning proper names and count nouns: Evidence from 16- and 20-month-olds. *Journal of Cognition & Development*, 7(1), 45–72.

Bialystok, E. (2007). Acquisition of literacy in bilingual children: A framework for research. *Language Learning, 57,* 45–77.

Bloom, P. (2000). *How children learn the meanings of words*. Cambridge, MA: MIT Press.

Tomasello, M. (2003). *Constructing a language: A usage-based theory of language acquisition*. Cambridge, MA: Harvard University Press.

KEY WORDS

basic-level category
classical concept
compound word
derived word
fast mapping
folk etymology
free-word association
joint attention
joint focus
irony
metalinguistic awareness
metaphor
onset and rime
ontological categories
ostension

overextension
phoneme
phonological awareness
preferential looking
    paradigm
principle of contrast
principle of mutual
    exclusivity
principles
probabilistic concept
productivity
prototypes
referent
sarcasm
semantic development

semantic feature
semantic network
semantic transparency
set task
simplicity
syntagmatic-paradigmatic
    shift
underextension
vocabulary breadth
vocabulary depth
vocabulary spurt
word associations
word family

REFERENCES

Akhtar, N. (2002). Relevance and early word learning. *Journal of Child Language, 29,* 677–686.

Anglin, J. (1995). Classifying the world through language: Functional relevance, cultural significance, and category name learning. *International Journal of Intercultural Relations, 19,* 161–181.

Baldwin, D. (1995). Understanding the link between joint attention and language. In C. Moore & P. Dunham (Eds.), *Joint attention: Its origins and role in development* (pp. 131–158). Hillsdale, NJ: Erlbaum.

Bates, E., Marchman, V., Thal, D., Fenson, L., Dale, P., Reznick, S., Reilly, J., & Hartung, J. (1994). Developmental and stylistic variation in the composition of early vocabulary. *Journal of Child Language, 21,* 85–123.

Beals, D. (1997). Sources of support for learning words in conversation: Evidence from mealtimes. *Journal of Child Language, 24,* 673–694.

Beck, I., McKeown, M., & Kucan, L. (2002). *Bringing words to life: Robust vocabulary instruction.* New York: Guilford Press.

Becker, J. (1994). Sneak-shoes, sworders, and nose-beards: A case study of lexical innovation. *First Language, 14,* 195–211.

Bedore, L., Peña, E. D., & García, M. (2005). Clinical forum: Conceptual versus monolingual scoring: When does it make a difference? *Language, Speech, and Hearing Services in Schools, 36,* 188–200.

Bélanger, J., & Hall, D. (2006). Learning proper names and count nouns: Evidence from 16- and 20-month-olds. *Journal of Cognition & Development, 7*(1), 45–72.

Benelli, B., Belacchi, C., Gini, G., & Lucangeli, D. (2006). "To define means to say what you know about things": The development of definitional skills as metalinguistic acquisition. *Journal of Child Language, 33,* 71–98.

Bergen, Doris (2006). Play as the context for humor development. In D. P. Fromberg & D. Bergen (eds.) *Play from birth to twelve* (2nd ed.). New York: Routledge.

Bergen, D. (2009). Gifted children's humor preferences, sense of humor, and comprehension of riddles. *Humor: International Journal of Humor Research, 22*(4), 419–436.

Berko, J. (1958). The child's learning of English morphology. *Word, 14,* 150–177.

Berninger, V., Abbott, R., Nagy, W., & Carlisle, J. (2010). Growth in phonological, orthographic, and morphological awareness in grades 1 to 6. *Journal of Psycholinguistic Research, 39*(2), 141–163.

Bernstein Ratner, N. (1988). Patterns of parental vocabulary selection in speech to very young children. *Journal of Child Language, 15*(3), 481–492.

Bialystok, E. (2007). Acquisition of literacy in bilingual children: A framework for research. *Language Learning, 57,* 45–77.

Biemiller, A., & Slonim, N. (2001). Estimating root word vocabulary growth in normative and advantaged populations: Evidence for a common sequence of vocabulary acquisition. *Journal of Educational Psychology, 93,* 498–520.

Bloom, L. (2000). The intentionality model of word learning: How to learn a word, any word. In R. M. Golinkoff, K. Hirsh-Pasek, L. Bloom, L. B. Smith, A. Woodward, N. Akhtar, M. Tomasello, & G. Hollich, *Becoming a word learner* (pp. 19–50). Oxford: Oxford University Press.

Bloom, P. (2000). *How children learn the meanings of words.* Cambridge, MA: MIT Press.

Bloomfield, L. (1933). *Language.* New York: Henry Holt.

Bloomquist, J. (2007). Developmental trends in semantic acquisition: Evidence from over-extensions in child language. *First Language, 27*(4), 407–420.

Bornstein, M., & Cote, L. (2004). Cross-linguistic analysis of vocabulary in young children: Spanish, Dutch, French, Hebrew, Italian, Korean, and American English. *Child Development, 75,* 1115–1139.

Bowerman, M. (1978). Systematizing semantic knowledge: Changes over time in the child's organization of word meaning. *Child Development, 49,* 977–987.

Braisby, N., & Dockrell, J. (1999). Why is colour naming difficult? *Journal of Child Language, 26,* 23–48.

Brent, M. R., & Siskind, J. M. (2001). The role of exposure to isolated words in early vocabulary development. *Cognition, 81,* B33–B44.

Brown, R., & Berko, J. (1960). Word association and the acquisition of grammar. *Child Development, 31,* 1–14.

Carabine, B. (1991). Fuzzy boundaries and the extension of object words. *Journal of Child Language, 18,* 355–372.

Carey, S., & Bartlett, E. (1978). Acquiring a single new word. *Papers and Reports on Child Language Development, 15,* 17–29.

Chaney, C. (1989). I pledge a legiance to the flag: Three studies in word segmentation. *Applied Psycholinguistics, 10,* 261–282.

Chaney, C. (1992). Language development, metalinguistic skills, and print awareness in three-year-old children. *Applied Psycholinguistics, 13,* 485–514.

Childers, J. B., & Tomasello, M. (2002). Two-year-olds learn novel nouns, verbs, and conventional actions from massed or distributed exposures. *Developmental Psychology, 38,* 967–978.

Choi, S., & Gopnik, A. (1995). Early acquisition of verbs in Korean: A cross-linguistic study. *Journal of Child Language, 22,* 497–529.

Clark, E. (1974). Some aspects of the conceptual basis for first language acquisition. In R. L. Schiefelbusch & L. L. Lloyd (Eds.), *Language perspectives—Acquisition, retardation, and intervention.* Baltimore: University Park Press.

Clark, E. (1981). Lexical innovations: How children learn to create new words. In W. Deutsch (Ed.), *The child's construction of language.* London: Academic Press.

Clark, E. (1993). *The lexicon in acquisition.* Cambridge, UK: Cambridge University Press.

Clark, E. V. (2007). Conventionality and contrast in language and language acquisition. *New Directions for Child & Adolescent Development, 115,* 11–23.

Clark, E. (2009). *First language acquisition.* Cambridge, UK: Cambridge University Press.

Cronin, V. (2002). The syntagmatic-paradigmatic shift and reading development. *Journal of Child Language, 29,* 189–204.

Crowe, S. J., & Prescott, T. J. (2003). Continuity and change in the development of category structure: Insights from the semantic fluency task. *International Journal of Behavioral Development, 27*(5), 467–479.

Dale, P., Bates, E., Reznick, J., & Morisset, C. (1989). The validity of a parent report instrument of child language at twenty months. *Journal of Child Language, 16,* 239–250.

Demuth, K., Culbertson, J., & Alter, J. 2006. Word-minimality, epenthesis, and coda licensing in the acquisition of English. *Language & Speech, 49,* 137–174.

Dews, S., Winner, E., Kaplan, J., Rosenblatt, E., Hunt, M., Lim, K., McGovern, A., Qualter, A., & Smarsh, B. (1996). Children's understanding of the meaning and functions of verbal irony. *Child Development, 67,* 3071–3085.

Dunn, J., Bretherton, I., & Munn, R. (1987). Conversations about feeling states between mothers and their young children. *Developmental Psychology, 23,* 132–139.

Duursma, E., Pan, B. A., & Raikes, H. (2008). Predictors and outcomes of low-income fathers' reading with their toddlers. *Early Childhood Research Quarterly, 23,* 351–365.

Fenson, L., Dale, P., Reznick, J., & Bates, E. (1994). Variability in early communicative development. *Monographs of the Society for Research in Child Development, 59,* v–173.

Fenson, L., Marchman, V., Thal, D., Dale, P., Reznick, J., & Bates, E. (2007). *MacArthur Communicative Development Inventories: Users' guide and technical manual, 2nd edition.* Baltimore: Brookes.

Fernald, A. (1992). Meaningful melodies in mothers' speech to infants. In H. Papousek, U. Jurgens, and M. Papousek (Eds.), *Origins and development of nonverbal vocal communication: Evolutionary, comparative, and methodological aspects.* Cambridge, UK: Cambridge University Press.

Floor, P., & Akhtar, N. (2006). Can 18-month-old infants learn words by listening in on conversations? *Infancy, 9,* 327–339.

Ganger, J., & Brent, M. (2004). Reexamining the vocabulary spurt. *Developmental Psychology, 40,* 621–632.

Gelman, S., Coley, J., Rosengran, K., Hartman, E., & Pappas, A. (1998). Beyond labeling: The role of maternal input in the acquisition of richly structured categories. *Monographs of the Society for Research in Child Development, 63* (253).

Gelman, S., Croft, W., Fu, P., Clausner, T., & Gottfried, G. (1998). Why is a pomegranate an *apple*? The role of shape, taxonomic relatedness, and prior lexical knowledge in children's overextensions of *apple* and *dog*. *Journal of Child Language, 25,* 267–291.

Gentner, D. (2006). Why verbs are hard to learn. In K. Hirsh-Pasek, R. Golinkoff, K. Hirsh-Pasek, R. Golinkoff (Eds.). *Action meets word: How children learn verbs* (pp. 544–564). New York: Oxford University Press.

Gershkoff-Stowe, L., Thal, D., Smith, L., & Namy, L. (1997). Categorization and its developmental relation to early language. *Child Development, 68,* 843–859.

Gillette, J., Gleitman, H., Gleitman, L., & Lederer, A. (1999). Human simulations of vocabulary learning. *Cognition, 73,* 135–176.

Glenwright, M., & Pexman, P. (2010). Development of children's ability to distinguish sarcasm and verbal irony. *Journal of Child Language,* 37(2), 429–451.

Goldfield, B. (1993). Noun bias in maternal speech to one-year-olds. *Journal of Child Language, 20,* 85–99.

Golinkoff, R., Hirsh-Pasek, K., Cauley, K., & Gordon, P. (1987). The eyes have it: Lexical and syntactic comprehension in a new paradigm. *Journal of Child Language, 14,* 23–46.

Golinkoff, R., Mervis, C., & Hirsh-Pasek, K. (1994). Early object labels: The case for a developmental lexical principles framework. *Journal of Child Language, 21,* 125–155.

Golinkoff, R., Shuff-Bailey, M., Olguin, R., & Ruan, W. (1995). Young children extend novel words at the basic level: Evidence for the principle of categorical scope. *Developmental Psychology, 31,* 494–507.

Gopnik, A., & Choi, S. (1995). Names, relational words, and cognitive development in English and Korean speakers:

Nouns are not always learned before verbs. In M. Tomasello & W. Merriman (Eds.), *Beyond names for things: Young children's acquisition of verbs.* Hillsdale, NJ: Erlbaum.

Goswami, U. (2001). Early phonological development and the acquisition of literacy. In *Handbook of early literacy research* (pp. 111–125). New York: Guilford Press.

Graham, S. A., Nilsen, E. S., Collins, S., & Olineck, K. (2010). The role of gaze direction and mutual exclusivity in guiding 24-month-olds' word mappings. *British Journal of Developmental Psychology, 28*(2), 449–465.

Graves, M. (2006). *The vocabulary book: Learning and instruction.* New York: Teachers College Press.

Hall, D. (1994a). Semantic constraints on word learning: Proper names and adjectives. *Child Development, 65,* 1299–1317.

Hall, D. (1994b). How mothers teach basic level and situation-restricted count nouns. *Journal of Child Language, 21,* 391–414.

Hall, D. G., Quantz, D. H., & Persoage, K. A. (2000). Preschoolers' use of form class cues in word learning. *Developmental Psychology, 36,* 449–462.

Hansen, M. B., & Markman, E. M. (2009). Children's use of mutual exclusivity to learn labels for parts of objects. *Developmental Psychology, 45*(2), 592–596.

Hart, B., & Risley, T. (1995). *Meaningful differences in the everyday experience of young American children.* Baltimore: Brookes.

Hills, T. T., Maouene, J., Riordan, B., & Smith, L. B. (2010). The associative structure of language: Contextual diversity in early word learning. *Journal of Memory and Language, 63*(3), 259–273.

Hoek, D., Ingram, D., & Gibson, D. (1986). Some possible causes of children's early word overextensions. *Journal of Child Language, 13,* 477–494.

Hoff, E., & Naigles, L. (2002). How children use input to acquire a lexicon. *Child Development, 73,* 418–433.

Hoff-Ginsberg, E., & Naigles, L. (1999). *Fast mapping is only the beginning: Complete word learning requires multiple expo-sures.* Paper presented at the VIIIth International Congress for the Study of Child Language, July 12–16, San Sebastian, Spain.

Hoicka, E., Jutsum, S., & Gattis, M. (2008). Humor, abstraction, and disbelief. *Cognitive Science, 32*(6), 985–1002.

Hollich, G., Hirsh-Pasek, K., & Golinkoff, R. (2000). What does it take to learn a word? *Monographs of the Society for Research in Child Development, 65,* 1–16.

Horgan, D. (1981). Learning to tell jokes: A case study of metalinguistic abilities. *Journal of Child Language, 8,* 217–227.

Houston-Price, C., Plunkett, K., & Harris, P. (2005). "Word-learning wizardry" at 1;6. *Journal of Child Language, 32,* 175–189.

Huttenlocher, J. (1964). Children's lan-guage: Word-phrase relationship. *Science, 143,* 264–265.

Huttenlocher, J., Haight, W., Bryk, A., Seltzer, M., & Lysons, T. (1991). Early vocabulary growth: Relation to lan-guage input and gender. *Developmental Psychology, 27,* 236–248.

Jaswal, V. K., & Markman, E. M. (2001). Learning proper and common names in inferential versus ostensive contexts. *Child Development, 72,* 768–786.

Johnson, C. J., & Anglin, J. M. (1995). Qualitative developments in the con-tent and form of children's definitions. *Journal of Speech and Hearing Research, 36,* 612–629.

Kurland, B., & Snow, C. (1997). Longitudinal measurement of growth in definitional skill. *Journal of Child Language, 24,* 603–625.

Liu, H., Tsao, F., Kuhl, P. K. (2009). Age-related changes in acoustic modifica-tions of Mandarin maternal speech to preverbal infants and five-year-old chil-dren: A longitudinal study. *Journal of Child Language, 36,* 909–922.

Locke, J. (1993) *The child's path to spo-ken language.* Cambridge, MA: Harvard University Press.

MacWhinney, B. (2000). *The CHILDES Project: Transcription format and pro-grams.* Mahwah, NJ: Erlbaum.

Maguire, M., Hirsh-Pasek, K., & Golinkoff, R. M. (2006). A unified theory of word learning: Putting verb acquisition in context. In K. Hirsh-Pasek & R. M. Golinkoff (Eds.), *Action meets word: How children learn verbs* (pp. 364–391). New York, NY: Oxford University Press.

Marinellie, S. A. (2010). The understand-ing of word definitions in school-age children. *Journal of Psycholinguistic Research, 39*(3), 179–197.

Markman, E., & Wachtel, G. (1988). Children's use of mutual exclusivity to constrain the meanings of words. *Cognition, 20,* 121–157.

Markson, L., & Bloom, P. (1997). Evidence against a dedicated system for word learn-ing in children. *Nature, 385,* 813–815.

McDonough, L. (2002). Basic-level nouns: First learned but misunderstood. *Journal of Child Language, 29,* 357–377.

McGhee, P. (1979). *Humor: Its origin and development.* San Francisco: W. H. Freeman.

McNeill, D. (1966). A study of word as-sociation. *Journal of Verbal Learning and Verbal Behavior, 5,* 548–557.

Mervis, C. B., & Mervis, C. A. (1982). Leopards are kitty-cats: Object labeling by mothers for their thirteen-month-olds. *Child Development, 53,* 267–273.

Mervis, C., & Mervis, C. (1988). Role of adult input in young children's cat-egory evolution, I: An observational study. *Journal of Child Language, 15,* 257–272.

Morris, C. (1946). *Signs, language, and be-havior.* New York: Prentice-Hall.

Nagy, W. (2007). Metalinguistic awareness and the vocabulary-comprehension connection. In R. Wagner, A. Muse, & K. Tannenbaum (Eds.), *Vocabulary ac-quisition: implications for reading compre-hension.* New York: Guilford Press.

Naigles, L., & Gelman, S. (1995). Overextensions in comprehension and production revisited: Preferential looking in a study of dog, cat, and cow. *Journal of Child Language, 22,* 19–46.

Nazzi, T. (2005). Use of phonetic speci-ficity during the acquisition of new words: Differences between consonants and vowels. *Cognition, 98,* 13–30.

Nelson, K. (1974). Variations in children's concepts by age and category. *Child Development, 45,* 577–584.

Nelson, K. (1977). The syntagmatic-paradigmatic shift revisited: A review of research and theory. *Psychological Bulletin, 84,* 93–116.

Nelson, K., Benedict, H., Gruendel, J., & Rescorla, L. (1977). *Lessons from early lexicons.* Paper presented at the meeting of the Society for Research in Child Development, New Orleans.

Nespor, M., Peña, M., & Mehler, J. (2003). On the different roles of vowels and consonants in speech processing and language acquisition. *Lingue e Linguaggio, 2,* 2221–2247.

Newport, E. (1975). *Motherese: The speech of mothers to young children* (Technical Report 52). San Diego: University of California, Center for Human Information Processing.

Ninio, A. (1992). The relation of children's single word utterances to single word utterances in the input. *Journal of Child Language, 19*(1), 87–110.

Ninio, A., & Snow, C. (1996). *Pragmatic development.* Boulder, CO: Westview Press.

Nippold, M., Hegel, S., & Sohlberg, M. (1999). Defining abstract entitites: Development in pre-adolescents, adolescents, and young adults. *Journal of Speech, Language, and Hearing Research, 42,* 473–481.

Ogura, T., Dale, P. S., Yamashita, Y., Murase, T., & Mahieu, A. (2006). The use of nouns and verbs by Japanese children and their caregivers in book-reading and toy-playing contexts. *Journal of Child Language, 33*(1), 1–29.

Pan, B. (2011). Language and literacy insights from research based on Early Head Start. In D. Dickinson and S. Neuman (Eds.), *Handbook of early literacy research, vol. 3.* New York: Guilford Press.

Pan, B., Rowe, M., Singer, J., & Snow, C. (2005). Maternal correlates of toddler vocabulary production in low-income families. *Child Development, 76,* 763–782.

Papandropoulou, I., & Sinclair, H. (1974). What is a word? *Human Development, 17,* 241–258.

Parra, M., Hoff, E., & Core, C. (2011). Relations among language exposure, phonological memory, and language development in Spanish–English bilingually developing 2-year-olds. *Journal of Experimental Child Psychology, 108*(1), 113–125.

Pearson, B. (2002). Bilingual infants: What we know, what we need to know. In M. Suarez-Orozco & M. Pàez (Eds.), *Latinos: Remaking America* (pp. 306–320). Berkeley: University of California Press.

Pexman, P. M. (2008). It's fascinating research: The cognition of verbal irony. *Current Directions in Psychological Science, 17*(4), 286–290

Pine, J., Lieven, E., & Rowland, C. (1996). Observational and checklist measures of vocabulary composition: What do they mean? *Journal of Child Language, 23,* 573–589.

Poulin-Dubois, D. (1995). Object parts and the acquisition of the meaning of names. In K. Nelson & Z. Réger (Eds.), *Children's language* (Vol. 8). Hillsdale, NJ: Erlbaum.

Pufpaff, L. A. (2009). A developmental continuum of phonological sensitivity skills. *Psychology in the Schools, 46*(7), 679–691.

Recchia, H., Howe, N., Ross, H., & Alexander, S. (2010). Children's understanding and production of verbal irony in family conversations. *The British Journal Of Developmental Psychology, 28*(p. 2), 255–274.

Rodriguez, E. T., Tamis-LeMonda, C. S., Spellmann, M. E., Pan, B. A., Raikes, H., Lugo-Gil, J., et al. (2009). The formative role of home literacy experiences across the first three years of life in children from low-income families. *Journal of Applied Developmental Psychology, 30*(6), 677–694

Rogoff, B. (2003). *The cultural nature of human development.* New York: Oxford University Press.

Rosch, E. (1973). Natural categories. *Cognitive Psychology, 4,* 328–350.

Rosch, E., Mervis, C., Gray, W., Johnson, D., & Boyes-Braem, P. (1976). Basic objects in natural categories. *Cognitive Psychology, 8,* 382–439.

Rundblad, G., & Annaz, D. (2010). Development of metaphor and metonymy comprehension: Receptive vocabulary and conceptual knowledge. *British Journal of Developmental Psychology, 28*(3), 547–563.

Saxton, M. (2005). "Recast" in a new light: Insights for practice from typical language studies. *Child Language Teaching and Therapy, 21*(1), 23–38.

Saylor, M., & Sabbagh, M. (2004). Different kinds of information affect word learning in the preschool years: The case of part-term learning. *Child Development, 75,* 395–408.

Schieffelin, B., & Ochs, E. (1986). *Language socialization across cultures.* New York: Cambridge University Press.

Schmale, R., Cristia, A., Seidl, A., & Johnson, E. K. (2010). Developmental changes in infants' ability to cope with dialect variation in word recognition. *Infancy,* 15, 650–662.

Schultz, T. (1976). A cognitive-developmental analysis of humor. In A. Chapman & M. Foot (Eds.), *Humor and laughter: Theory, research, and applications.* New York: Wiley.

Schwartz, R., & Leonard, L. (1982). Do children pick and choose? An examination of phonological selection and avoidance in early lexical acquisition. *Journal of Child Language, 9,* 319–336.

Shatz, M., & Gelman, R. (1973). The development of communication skills: Modifications in the speech of young children as a function of the listener. *Monographs of the Society for Research in Child Development, 38* (152).

Shneidman, L. A., Buresh, J. Sootsman, Shimpi, P. M., Knight-Schwarz, J. & Woodward, A. L. (2009). Social experience, social attention and word learning in an overhearing paradigm. *Language Learning and Development, 5,* 266–281.

Skwarchuk, S., & Anglin, J. (1997). Expression of superordinates in children's word definitions. *Journal of Educational Psychology, 89,* 298–308.

Slaughter, V., Peterson, C. C., & Carpenter, M. (2009). Maternal mental state talk and infants' early gestural communication. *Journal of Child Language,* 36(5), 1053–1074.

Slobin, D. (1978). A case study of early language awareness. In A. Sinclair, R. Jarvella, & W. Levelt (Eds.), *The child's conception of language.* New York: Wiley.

Smith, L. (1999). Children's noun learning: How general learning processes make specialized learning mechanisms. In B. MacWhinney (Ed.), *The emergence of language* (pp. 227–305). Mahwah, NJ: Erlbaum.

Smith, E., & Medin, D. (1981). *Categories and concepts.* Cambridge, MA: Harvard University Press.

Snow, C. (1972). Mothers' speech to children learning language. *Child Development, 43,* 549–585.

Snow, C. (1990). The development of definitional skill. *Journal of Child Language, 17,* 697–710.

Snow, C. E., & Uccelli, P. (2009). The challenge of academic language. In Olson, D. R., & N. Torrance (Eds) *The Cambridge handbook of literacy* (pp. 112–133). Cambridge, UK: Cambridge University Press.

Soderstrom, M. (2007). Beyond babytalk: Re-evaluating the nature and content of speech input to preverbal infants. *Developmental Review, 27*(4), 501–532.

Stahl, S. A., & Nagy, W. E. (2006). *Teaching word meanings.* Mahwah, NJ: Erlbaum.

Storkel, H. (2004). Do children acquire dense neighborhoods? An investigation of similarity neighborhoods in lexical acquisition. *Applied Psycholinguistics, 25,* 201–222.

Styles, S. J., & Plunkett, K. (2009). How do infants build a semantic system? *Language & Cognition, 1*(1), 1–24.

Tabors, P., Paéz, M., & López, M. (2003). Dual language abilities of bilingual four-year olds: Initial findings from the Early Childhood Study of Language and Literacy Development of Spanish-speaking children. *NABE Journal of Research and Practice, 1,* 70–91.

Tardif, T., Gelman, S., & Xu, F. (1999). Putting the "noun bias" in context: A comparison of English and Mandarin. *Child Development, 70,* 620–635.

Tiedemann, D. (1787). Über die Entwicklung der Seelenfähigkeiten bei Kindern. *Hessiche Beiträge zur Gelehrsamkeit und Kunst.* Reprinted in English in A. Bar-Adon & W. Leopold (Eds.), (1971), *Child language: A book of readings.* Englewood Cliffs, NJ: Prentice-Hall.

Tingley, E., Gleason, J., & Hooshyar, N. (1994). Mothers' lexicon of internal state words in speech to children with Down syndrome and to nonhandi-capped children at mealtime. *Journal of Communication Disorders, 27,* 135–155.

Tomasello, M. (1995). Pragmatic contexts for early verb learning. In M. Tomasello & W. Merriman (Eds.), *Beyond names for things: Young children's acquisition of verbs.* Hillsdale, NJ: Erlbaum.

Tomasello, M. (2003). *Constructing a language: A usage-based theory of language acquisition.* Cambridge, MA: Harvard University Press.

Tomasello, M., & Barton, M. (1994). Learning words in non-ostensive contexts. *Developmental Psychology, 30,* 639–650.

Torgesen, J., Wagner, R., & Rashotte, C. (1994). Longitudinal studies of phono-logical processing and reading. *Journal of Learning Disabilities, 27,* 276–286.

Treiman, R., & Zukowski, A. (1991). Levels of phonological awareness. In S. Brady & D. Shankweiler (Eds.), *Phonological processes in literacy* (pp. 67–83). Hillsdale, NJ: Erlbaum.

Uccelli, P., & Paéz, M. (2007). Narrative and vocabulary development of bilingual children from kindergarten to first grade: Developmental changes and asso-ciations among English and Spanish lan-guage skills. *Language, Speech, and Hearing Services in Schools, 38*(3), 225–236.

Vagh, S., Pan, B., & Mancilla-Martinez, J. (2007). *Measuring children's productive vocabulary: The utility of combining par-ent and teacher report.* Poster presented at the Biennial Meeting of the Society for Research in Child Development, Boston, MA.

Vygotsky, L. (1962). *Thought and language.* Cambridge, MA: MIT Press.

Wai Han, C., & Nicoladis, E. (2010). Predicting two Mandarin-English bi-lingual children's first 50 words: Effects of frequency and relative exposure in the input. *International Journal of Bilingualism, 14*(2), 237–270.

Wehren, A., DeLisi, R., & Arnold, M. (1981). The development of noun definition. *Journal of Child Language, 8,* 165–175.

Werker, J., Fennell, C., Corcoran, K., & Stager, C. (2002). Infants' ability to learn phonetically similar words: Effects of age and vocabulary size. *Infancy, 3,* 1–30.

Winner, E. (1988). *The point of words: Children's understanding of metaphor and irony.* Cambridge, MA: Harvard University Press.

Woodward, A., Markman, E., & Fitzsimmons, C. (1994). Rapid word learning in 13- and 18-month-olds. *Developmental Psychology, 30,* 553–566.

Zammit, M., & Schafer, G. (2011). Maternal label and gesture use affects acquisition of specific object names. *Journal of Child Language, 38*(1), 201–221.

Putting Words Together

Morphology and Syntax in the Preschool Years

Andrea Zukowski
University of Maryland

After months of waiting and wondering when their children will begin to talk, and what they might say when they do, parents are finally rewarded when the first word is produced. Several weeks after this important milestone is duly recorded, vocabulary begins to grow quite rapidly, as new words are learned daily. At this initial stage young children use their words in a variety of contexts, most frequently to label objects or to interact socially, but they always limit their messages by speaking one word at a time. Still, parents and children together delight in showing off these earliest linguistic accomplishments, which mark the beginning of the journey toward full mastery of language.

Within a few months, usually in the latter half of the second year, children reach the next important milestone: They begin putting words together to form their first "sentences." This new stage marks a crucial turning point, for even the simplest two-word utterances show evidence of **syntax**; that is, the child combines words in a systematic way to create sentences that appear to follow rules rather than combining words in random fashion. Research on the timing of first word combinations has found that it is related to several developmental factors. These include the timing of children's first words, the time at which they understand about fifty words, and the responsiveness of mothers to their children's communications at around the first birthday (Tamis-Lemonda, Bornstein, Kahana-Kalman, Baumwell, & Cyphers, 1998).

The importance of syntax is that it allows the child to express countless novel messages, even with a very limited vocabulary. One of the remarkable features about the development of grammatical rules is that it seems to take place almost unnoticed, with no explicit instruction. Parents who quite consciously and conscientiously teach their children new concepts and words never presume to teach syntax. And when parents correct their children's early non-adult-like multiword utterances, their corrections focus more on *what* the child said rather than *how* the child said it (Brown & Hanlon, 1970).

*The author and editors wish to thank Helen Tager-Flusberg for her creation of and contributions to previous editions of this chapter.

Even though parents and others have essentially ignored the child's use and occasional misuse of grammatical rules, child language researchers and linguists have studied that usage closely all over the world. Years of careful and painstaking research have yielded a detailed descriptive picture of the course of syntactic development in English and other languages, although the mechanisms that account for these accomplishments are still being hotly debated (see Chapter 7). In this chapter we describe the main stages of grammatical development that take place during the preschool years, focusing on the order in which various constructions are acquired. At each stage we are concerned with extracting the universal and invariant features of children's language and characterizing the underlying knowledge of linguistic rules and categories that fit the language at that point in development. Debate continues in the theoretical literature, however, about whether children's earliest sentences are based on adult-like linguistic categories (containing nouns, determiners, etc.) or something shallower (lexically based combinations of words) and, more generally, about how similar early child grammars and mature adult grammars really are (e.g., Valian, Solt, & Stewart, 2009; Tomasello, 2003).

The Nature of Syntactic Rules

Despite theoretical disagreements among child language researchers, everyone agrees that as surely as children become adults, child grammars eventually become adult grammars. Therefore, knowledge of the adult system is important because it provides a frame of reference against which to compare a child's developing language.

Much of our understanding of the nature of syntactic rules has come from linguists who have been concerned primarily with characterizing the rules that underlie the well-formed sentences of adult language users—the natural end point of the acquisition process. The most influential linguistic framework is the one developed by Noam Chomsky, called the theory of **universal grammar**, or UG. Chomsky began developing this framework in 1957, but it has undergone several revisions since. One prominent version is known as **government and binding theory**, or GB (Chomsky, 1981, 1982). Although an even newer theoretical program has been developed (Chomsky, 1995), in this chapter we focus on the GB version, because it continues to have a significant influence on research on grammatical development. We shall first describe briefly some of the major concepts and characteristics of this linguistic approach.

According to Chomsky, the goals of any theory of grammar, such as universal grammar, are that it is compatible with the grammars of all the world's languages (the goal of **universality**) and that it must, in principle, be compatible with the fact that children worldwide acquire the grammar of their language within a few short years, usually with little or no explicit training or correction (the goal of **learnability**). According to Chomsky, a theory of syntax is a theory of language knowledge; essentially, it is a theory of how we represent language as a set of principles in our minds. Chomsky believes that our mental representation of grammar is autonomous of other cognitive systems, which means that the principles and rules of grammar are not shared with other cognitive systems but are in fact highly specialized.

The central tenet of GB theory is that there are several components of the grammar that are linked at different levels of representation. Figure 5.1 provides a simplified view of the main components. Of key interest are the two levels: **d-structure**, which captures the underlying relationships between subject and object in a sentence (the basic unit of grammar); and **s-structure**, which captures the surface linear arrangements of words in a sentence. In order to see why these two levels are necessary, consider the following sentences:

John is easy to please.

John is eager to please.

Both sentences have virtually the same s-structures:

noun–verb–adjective–infinitive verb

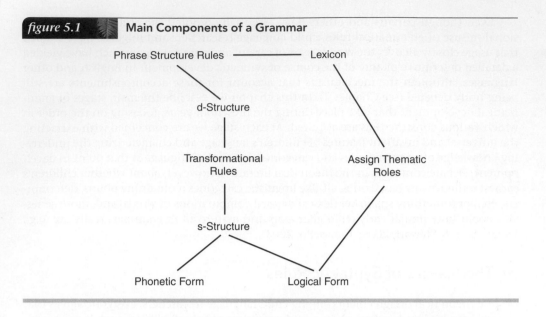

figure 5.1 **Main Components of a Grammar**

However, they mean quite different things. The subject of the verb *to please* is John in the second sentence, but someone else in the first. This difference in the underlying grammatical relationships of subject, predicate, and so forth, would be captured by very different d-structures. From a developmental point of view, we must ask how children come to grasp the underlying grammatical relations of sentences they hear (d-structures) when they are presented only with s-structures.

Figure 5.1 also shows that each level, s-structure and d-structure, has several components. The s-structure has two parts: **phonetic form**, which is the actual sound structure of the sentence; and **logical form**, which captures the meaning of sentences (this component connects the grammar to other aspects of cognition). The d-structure is fed by two other components of the grammar: **phrase structure rules an**d the *lexicon*. Phrase structure rules are rules that dictate how to construct phrases and sentences out of words. The lexicon specifies a number of important features (morphophonological, syntactic) for each lexical item in a sentence. Together, the lexicon and the phrase structure rules generate the d-structure of a sentence.

Phrase structure rules are sometimes represented as "rewrite rules" such as these:

NP → N

NP → Determiner N

VP → V

VP → V NP

These examples show two different ways of constructing a noun phrase or NP and a verb phrase or VP. Phrase structure rules dictate ways of combining not particular words, such as *dogs* and *that dog*, but words and phrases of a particular syntactic category, such as nouns and noun phrases. Hence they are abstract templates for phrases. Notice that both NPs have a noun as a central component and both VPs have a verb as a central component. In syntactic theory, it is thought that all phrases have a central component or **head**, whose syntactic category defines the syntactic category of the phrase (all XPs have a head of category X). Furthermore, it is thought that whole sentences or clauses are also a type of phrase with a head. The head of a clause is thought to be a syntactic category called **Infl**, which stands for inflection. The Infl head contains information about the tense of a clause, such as whether the clause is present or past tense. The Infl position is also the position in which auxiliary verbs such as *could* and *will* occur; this is because auxiliary verbs, unlike main verbs, are thought to be inherently tensed (which is why, in sentences with both an auxiliary verb and a main verb, the main verb is never inflected for tense). The phrase structure rule for building an Infl phrase (i.e., a clause or a sentence) is

InflP (or S) → NP Infl VP

The NP in this rule is the subject of the clause, and the Infl and VP together constitute the predicate of the clause. Infl is considered to be a **functional category**, which contrasts with **lexical categories** such as V and N, whose members are content words. Another example of a functional category is **Comp** or complementizer. A complementizer (a word like *that, if,* or *whether*) is a word that is used to embed a clause (an InflP) inside another clause, such as when a clause is the direct object of a verb, as in the two VPs "hope that the Red Sox are winning the game" and "doubt whether the train will be on time." A complementizer phrase (CompP) is constructed of a Comp and an InflP, as shown in this rule:

CompP → Comp InflP

VPs headed by verbs like *hope* and *doubt,* which take a whole clause as a direct object, are constructed from this phrase structure rule:

VP → V CompP

Complementizer phrases or CompPs are also thought to be involved in the construction of questions, as will be discussed.

Phrase structure rules can also be represented as tree diagrams, as in Figure 5.2, which contains individual tree diagrams corresponding to some of the preceding rewrite rules. Phrase structure rules and tree diagrams are different ways of representing the same information, and they are freely interchangeable. Tree diagrams corresponding to different phrase structure rules can be connected up like interlocking pieces of a puzzle, to represent all of the hierarchical structural relationships in a given sentence, as shown in the large tree structure in Figure 5.2. Despite the protestations that most people would make that they do not know how to "diagram a sentence," the sentences that people produce and understand every day demonstrate that they have implicit knowledge of hierarchical structures such as those in Figure 5.2.

The lexicon provides the specific "words" or lexical items that get inserted at the bottom of the phrase structure trees as shown in Figure 5.2. The lexicon contains information for each item about its syntactic category (noun, verb, adjective, etc.), much like a dictionary. It also contains information about what kinds of sentence structures the item requires, which is especially important for verbs. Consider the following set of verbs:

run

see

put

The lexicon would include different information for each verb because they all appear in different sentence structures, or *argument structures*. The verb *run* requires only a subject:

John runs.

The verb *see* requires both a subject and an object, and it can take as an object either a simple noun phrase or a complete sentence:

John sees Mary (writing her book).

The verb *put* requires not only a subject and an object, but also a specified location:

John put the book on the shelf.

figure 5.2   Tree Diagrams Corresponding to Different Phrases and an Example of How They Combine to Form One Complex Sentence

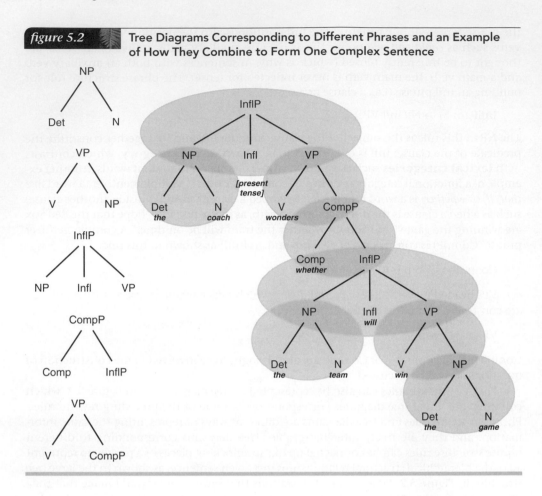

This information about the argument structure of different verbs is all contained in the lexicon and is critical in organizing appropriate phrase structures. In addition to required arguments, additional optional phrases may also be added to other phrases in a sentence. For example,

John put the book on the shelf *last night*.

This optional phrase is referred to as an *adjunct*.

The d-structure is connected to the s-structure by **transformational rules**—rules that specify how one sentence can be transformed to create a closely related sentence. For example, all human languages provide a systematic means for taking a statement like "The team will win the game" and transforming it into closely related questions, such as "Will the team win the game?" and "What will the team win?" Transformational rules involve the movement of heads (lexical items) and whole phrases from one position in a tree structure to another, which typically results in a rearrangement of the linear order of words in a sentence. The movement thought to underlie the question "What will the team win?" is illustrated in Figure 5.3. Another example of a transformation is the formation of a passive sentence (e.g., "The window was shattered") from an active sentence (e.g., "Someone shattered the window").

The lexicon is also connected to the logical form component of s-structure (see Figure 5.1) via the assignment of **thematic roles** or **semantic roles**. Verbs from the lexicon assign to each of the main noun phrases a role in the sentence, like agent, patient, recipient, and location:

John	gave	the book	to Mary	at school.
agent		*patient*	*recipient*	*location*

All these components and rule systems are considered to be universal in UG. Besides these universals, the grammar also has a system for handling the kind of syntactic and morphological variations that exist across languages of the world: **parameters**. Parameters are features of grammar that vary in a highly limited way, showing perhaps only two or three options or "settings" across all languages. One example of a parameter is called the **null-subject parameter**. In English, every sentence is required to have an explicit subject (option 1); however, languages such as Italian or Spanish allow subjects to be dropped in the s-structure, resulting in an "empty" subject in the phonetic form of the sentence (option 2). So, for example, one can say in Italian:

Sta piovendo. (Is raining.)

For this sentence to be grammatical in English, we must add an *It* as the subject, although the pronoun does not refer to anything at all. This kind of pronoun is called an *expletive,* and only languages that require subjects also have expletive pronouns. There are other differences between Italian and English that all co-vary under the null-subject parameter. In this way language variation is captured by an economical system that considers a range of correlated syntactic features under a single parameter.

In theory, at least, each language's grammar is captured by a unique combination of settings for a variety of parameters. One hypothesis that has been proposed is that children are born with implicit knowledge of both the universals of language and of parameters like the null-subject parameter, along with knowledge of the possible settings for each parameter. It is thought that as a child is exposed to her native language, the evidence from this input is used to choose the proper setting for each parameter. We shall see later in this chapter how this idea of parameters, especially the null-subject parameter, has motivated some interesting though not uncontroversial research into early child language.

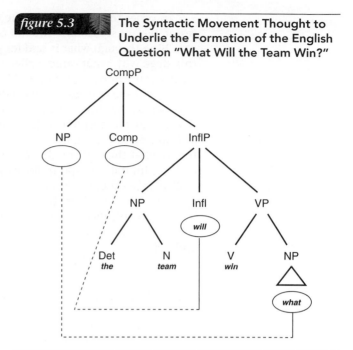

figure 5.3 The Syntactic Movement Thought to Underlie the Formation of the English Question "What Will the Team Win?"

Studying Syntactic Development

Much of what we know about the development of syntax comes, of course, from studying what children actually say. Longitudinal studies of children in their homes, talking with their mothers or fathers, have produced vast quantities of raw data in the form of transcripts. They have been an especially rich source of information about language development in children from many different cultures and language-learning environments. Brian MacWhinney (see Chapter 7) at Carnegie Mellon University has created a major databank containing hundreds of transcripts from children learning many different languages. This system, called CHILDES, also includes computer programs (CLAN) for analyzing these transcripts (MacWhinney, 2000). The data and programs are publicly available at **http://childes.psy.cmu.edu.**

In order to find out what the child knows of syntactic rules at any given stage, the researcher must examine the full corpus of speech, looking for patterns and regularities, searching through what is said for what is left unspoken, and contrasting the language at this stage with what came earlier and what will come later. Spontaneous speech data are an especially important source of information about the kinds of errors that children make at different stages of grammatical development; these errors are often the most interesting clues about the child's underlying linguistic knowledge (Stromswold, 1996). These studies of spontaneous speech can tell us a great deal about the language produced by the child, but they do not reveal much about what the child can or cannot understand. Nor do they tell us what the child might have been able to say if the opportunity had arisen. Because of these limitations, spontaneous speech data need to be complemented with more controlled, experimental studies that are designed to test children's comprehension of various syntactic forms or their ability to produce or judge particular constructions in less natural but more controlled situations. Menn and Bernstein Ratner (2000) provide a comprehensive review of a variety of methods that can be used to study language production in young children.

Entering the Complex Linguistic System

One of the most difficult issues about acquiring language that the child faces is how to break into the system. How do children manage to break up the steady stream of sounds they hear into basic units like words and morphemes? How do they learn to map specific sound sequences onto meanings? And how do they learn to figure out the basic grammatical categories of their language, such as nouns, verbs, and adjectives? These are some of the fundamental questions about language acquisition that child language researchers must also address in their theories, even though young children at the earliest stages of development provide us with few clues.

One interesting hypothesis that has received some empirical support has been suggested by Morgan (1986), among others. According to Morgan, if adults provided information in their speech to children about where boundaries exist, not only between words but also between phrases, the task of acquiring language would become feasible and simplified.

There does appear to be evidence that mothers and fathers provide strong intonational or prosodic evidence about word and phrase boundaries, not only in English, but also in other languages, such as French and Japanese (Fernald et al., 1989). More important, there is also evidence that infants are sensitive to the salience of the information sent in pauses (Jusczyk, 1997). Shady and Gerken (1999) found that very young English-speaking children are sensitive to prosodic cues as well as other cues provided by their caregivers in experiments that tested their ability to understand spoken language. Extending this research to children learning other languages, Shi, Morgan, and Allopena (1998) found that caregivers' speech to infants acquiring both Turkish and Mandarin Chinese contained similar kinds of phonological and acoustic cues that allowed them to distinguish different lexical and grammatical categories.

Once the child has broken the stream of speech into words, he or she may use other information in order to identify the syntactic categories of words (e.g., noun, verb) and phrases (e.g., noun phrase, verb phrase). Some researchers have suggested that children can use meaning, or *semantics,* to help determine the syntactic category of words (e.g., Pinker, 1984) by exploiting innate knowledge that objects tend to be nouns and actions tend to be verbs. Others have suggested that distributional information would help children with this task (Mintz, 2003), and indeed analyses have shown for English, Spanish, and French that words that fall within the same "frequent frame" (e.g., after the word *the* and before the word *on*) consistently belong to the same category (a noun in this example; Chemla, Mintz, Bernal, & Christophe, 2009; Weisleder & Waxman, 2010). Still others have suggested that a combination of prosodic information and distributional information about frequently occurring function words could allow children to build a a rough syntactic skeleton of utterances even before they know many content words, and that infants do indeed use these cues when listening to speech (Christophe, Millotte, Brusini, & Cauvet, 2010). It is possible that children exploit all of this information in the earliest stages of syntactic development.

Measuring Syntactic Growth

As children grow older, their sentences get longer. Studies of large numbers of children have provided excellent normative data on the age at which English-speaking children make the transition to combining words and using simple sentences. These data come from a set of parental report measures called the *MacArthur-Bates Communicative Development Inventories* (Fenson et al., 2007), which provide highly reliable information about children's language abilities at the early stages. These *inventories* are now available in forty different languages and dialects. There is wide variability in the onset of combinatorial language. Some children begin as early as 15 months; the average seems to be at about 18 months, and by the age of 2 almost all children are producing some word combinations (Bates, Dale, & Thal, 1995). Although age itself is not the best predictor of language development since children develop at vastly different rates, the length of a child's sentences is an excellent indicator of syntactic development; each new element of syntactic knowledge adds length to a child's utterances.

Roger Brown (1973), in his classic studies of Adam, Eve, and Sarah, introduced a measure of the length of a child's utterances called the **mean length of utterance (MLU)**, which has come to be widely used as an index of syntactic development in early childhood. MLU is based on the average length of a child's sentences scored on transcripts of spontaneous speech. Length is determined by the number of meaningful units, or *morphemes*, rather than words. Morphemes include simple content words such as *cat, play, do, red;* function words such as *no, the, you, this;* and affixes or grammatical inflections such as *un-, -s, -ed*. The addition of each morpheme (or minimal unit carrying meaning) reflects the acquisition of new linguistic knowledge. So children who have similar MLUs can be expected to have language that is at the same level of complexity.

In order to calculate the MLU of a particular child, one needs a transcript of a half-hour conversation. The child's language must be divided into separate utterances, and these utterances must be divided into morphemes. Brown (1973) provided detailed rules for judging what constitutes a morpheme for the child learning English (see Figure 5.4). These rules have become widespread conventions in the analysis of children's language and have been adopted by the CHILDES Project (see Chapter 1).

In longitudinal studies, the MLUs calculated at successive points in time gradually increase. Figure 5.5 shows the MLU plotted against chronological age for the three children studied by Brown and his colleagues. Clearly, MLU grows at different rates in different children. Of the children followed by Brown, Eve's MLU rose most sharply, indicating very rapid language development, whereas Sarah and Adam showed more gradual and less consistent increments in their MLU. Review Chapter 1 to see Adam as he is today.

Using the MLU, Brown subdivided the major period of syntactic growth into five stages, beginning with Stage I, when the MLU is between 1.0 and 2.0. Successive stages are marked by increments of 0.5. Thus, Stage II goes from 2.0 to 2.5; Stage III is from 2.5 to 3.0; Stage IV is from 3.0 to 3.5; and Stage V is from 3.5 to 4.0. Beyond an MLU of about 4.0, some of the assumptions on which the measure is based are no longer valid, and longer sentences do not simply reflect what the child knows about language; therefore, MLU loses value as an index of language development after this stage.

Some questions arise in calculating MLUs in foreign languages, especially highly inflected and synthetic languages such as German, Russian, or Hebrew. In these cases it becomes difficult to decide what functions as a morpheme in the child's speech, and it is easy to obtain inflated numbers. Still, there have been attempts to extend the concept

---

figure 5.4   **Rules for Calculating Mean Length of Utterance**

1. Start with the second page of the transcription unless that page involves a recitation of some kind. In this latter case, start with the first recitation-free stretch. Count the first 100 utterances satisfying the following rules.

2. Only fully transcribed utterances are used, none with blanks. Portions of utterances, entered in parentheses to indicate doubtful transcription, are used.

3. Include all exact utterance repetitions (marked with a plus sign in records). Stuttering is marked as repeated efforts at a single word; count the word once in the most complete form produced. In the few cases where a word is produced for emphasis or the like *(no, no, no)* count each occurrence.

4. Do not count such fillers as *mm* or *oh*, but do count *no, yeah,* and *hi.*

5. All compound words (two or more free morphemes), proper names, and ritualized reduplications count as single words. Examples: *birthday, rackety-boom, choo-choo, quack-quack, night-night, pocketbook, see saw.* Justification is that no evidence exists that the constituent morphemes function as such for these children.

6. Count as one morpheme all irregular pasts of the verb *(got, did, went, saw).* Justification is that there is no evidence that the child relates these to present forms.

7. Count as one morpheme all diminutives *(doggie, mommy)* because these children at least do not seem to use the suffix productively. Diminutives are the standard forms used by the child.

8. Count as separate morphemes all auxiliaries *(is, have, will, can, must, would).* Also all catenatives: *gonna, wanna, hafta.* These latter counted as single morphemes rather than as *going to* or *want to* because evidence is that they function so for the children. Count as separate morphemes all inflections, for example, possessive {s}, plural {s}, third person singular {s}, regular past {d}, progressive {ing}.

9. The range count follows the above rules but is always calculated for the total transcription rather than for 100 utterances. Divide the number of morphemes by the number of utterances to get the mean length of utterance (MLU).

---

of MLU to structurally varied languages (Bowerman, 1973) or to modify the measure to account for cross-linguistic differences (Dromi & Berman, 1982). In some languages, calculating the length of utterances in words, rather than morphemes, has proven to be quite useful (e.g., Hickey, 1991). By using a similar index to chart language growth across a range of languages, we can search for the universal and invariant features that characterize the main stages of syntactic development.

Other measures of syntactic development have also been developed. One example is the **Index of Productive Syntax (IPSyn)**, introduced by Hollis Scarborough (1989). For this measure one also needs a transcript of one hundred spontaneous speech utterances from a child. Using the scoresheet provided by Scarborough, the researcher marks the use, up to a maximum of two very different uses, of a variety of structures in four categories: in noun phrases (e.g., nouns, pronouns, articles, plural endings, compound nouns), verb phrases (verbs, prepositions, verb endings, auxiliaries, modals, tense), questions and negation forms (at various levels of complexity), and sentence structure (simple, complex, complements, conjunctions, infinitive forms). The score received is simply the total number of points, with points awarded for each structure used. The IPSyn measure correlates highly with MLU, demonstrating its validity as a measure of grammatical development. However, it has the advantage of providing a measure that remains useful far beyond the MLU limit of 4.0, at least until around 5 years of age, and it has the potential for being adapted to other languages.

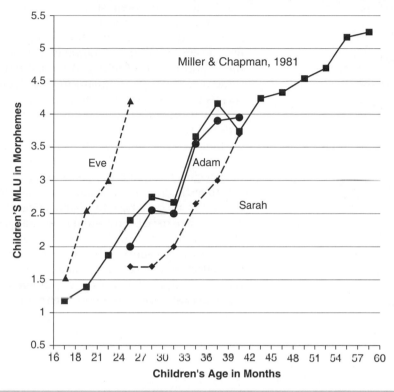

figure 5.5 **The Relation between Mean Length of Utterance and Chronological Age.**
A comparison of the age-MLU relation for three children studied longitudinally by Roger Brown and for a group of 123 children studied by Miller and Chapman (1981). Datapoints from Miller and Chapman are means based on four to twelve children each, in a cross-sectional study.

Two-Word Utterances

The first stage defined by Brown follows children through their earliest attempts at multi-word utterances, as the MLU grows from 1.0 to 2.0. Most of the child's sentences are two words long, although a few may be as long as three or even four words. Table 5.1 lists examples of two-word sentences taken from separate children acquiring English as their first language. Children learning other languages produce utterances that are remarkably similar to these.

Looking at these examples, we can note a number of interesting features about children's early sentences. First, from the beginning, the child's language is truly creative; many of these sentences would never have been spoken in exactly the same way by an adult. The particular word combinations spoken by Stage I children are unique and novel rather than mere imitations of adult sentences. Lieven and her colleagues found that children's early utterances are built around "schemas" in which many sentence elements are fixed (e.g., "I want") and only one or two words vary (Lieven, Behrens, Speares, & Tomasello, 2003). Second, these sentences are simple, compared to adult sentences, and simplicity is accomplished in a systematic way. Certain words called *content words*, or **open-class words**, dominate the children's language. Thus, their sentences are composed primarily of nouns, verbs, and adjectives. These large word classes are called open since they freely admit new items and drop old ones as a language evolves. The most

table 5.1	Examples of Two-Word Utterances
Andrew	**Eve**
more car	bye-bye baby
more cereal	Daddy bear
more high	Daddy book
more read	Daddy honey
outside more	there Daddy
no more	there potty
no pee	more pudding
no wet	Mommy stair
all wet	Mommy dimple
all gone	Mommy do
bye-bye Calico	Mommy bear
bye-bye back	eat it
bye-bye car	read it
bye-bye Papa	see boy
Mama come	more cookie
See pretty	

Note: Utterances in column 1 are from Braine, 1976; those in column 2 are from Eve's transcripts and from Brown and Fraser, 1963.

frequent open-class words are nouns, which dominate most very young children's language at this stage (Imai & Gentner, 1997). In contrast, *function words,* or **closed-class words**, are usually missing at this stage of language development. The closed-class words (including prepositions, conjunctions, articles, pronouns, auxiliaries, and inflections) are much smaller and do not change their composition readily. The absence of these grammatical terms lends to the impression of simplicity. We can also notice that some words are very frequent in a particular child's corpus (Andrew uses *more* and *bye-bye* often and in combination with many different words), and the order of the words appears quite regular. Finally, if we look at what the children are talking about, we can see that certain topics (such as possession, location, recurrence) are very prevalent.

Investigators of child language have long been interested in how best to characterize Stage I language. There have been a number of changes in these characterizations as the focus shifted from one significant feature to another. However, these changes do not reflect differences in the data but in the kinds of categories imposed on the data by different researchers. The challenge is to ascribe neither too little nor too much knowledge of syntactic categories or rules to the child just beginning to acquire syntax.

Telegraphic Speech

One early characterization of Stage I language focused on the contrast between the open-class and closed-class words. Brown and Fraser (1963) called these two-word utterances **telegraphic speech**, because the omission of closed-class words makes them resemble telegrams. Telegrams, of course, are well on their way to becoming an anachronism, as Western Union transmitted its last one ever in February 2006. However, much like today's instant messaging (IM), telegrams encouraged message senders to economize in their word choices, which led to messages like "Broke—send money." (If Brown and Fraser's work had begun fifty years later than it did, perhaps children's early simplified word combinations would have been called IM speech!)

Gleitman and Wanner (1982) have suggested that children, in fact, learn open- and closed-class words quite separately. The earlier acquisition of open-class words is based on their perceptual salience, according to Gleitman and Wanner, and thus represents a good example of prosodic features helping the child to discover basic language structure.

The idea that Stage I language consists primarily of open-class words comes from research on the acquisition of English. More recent studies that have looked at children acquiring other languages, for example, Italian (Caselli, Casadio, & Bates, 1999), Turkish (Aksu-Koc, 1988), or Hebrew (Levy, 1988), which have much richer morphological systems and may be less reliant on words to express basic grammatical relations, have shown that even at the earliest stages, children acquiring these kinds of languages are also beginning to acquire some of the closed-class morphology. Hung and Peters (1997) found that prosody helps children learning Mandarin and Taiwanese to acquire closed-class morphology at this developmental stage. Studies on the acquisition of other languages have also led some to question whether nouns really are acquired before verbs, as suggested by Imai and Gentner (1987). While the English pattern of an early advantage for nouns has been observed for children learning a variety of languages (Klammler & Schneider, 2011; Bornstein et al., 2006), some researchers report that verbs do not emerge later than nouns in other languages, such as Korean (Gopnik & Choi, 1995) and Mandarin Chinese (Tardiff, 1996).

Semantic Relations

Studies of children from around the world in Stage I, using two-word utterances, have shown that one universal feature of this stage is that only a small group of meanings, or **semantic relations**, is expressed in the children's language. Bloom (1970) first observed this in her study of three American children. Later, Brown (1973) extended her findings to children acquiring Finnish, Swedish, Samoan, Spanish, French, Russian, Korean, Japanese, and Hebrew. Table 5.2 lists the eight most prevalent combinatorial meanings found by Brown (1973, pp. 193–197) along with some examples of each. From these examples we see that during Stage I, children talk a great deal about objects: They point them out and name them (demonstrative) and they talk about where the objects are (location), what they are like (attributive), who owns them (possession), and who is doing things to them (agent–object). They also talk about actions performed by people (agent–action), performed on objects (action–object), and oriented toward certain locations (action–location). Objects, people, and actions and their interrelationships thus preoccupy the toddler universally, and, as Brown (1970, 1973) points out, these are precisely the concepts that the child has just completed differentiating during what Piaget called the sensorimotor stage of cognitive development.

table 5.2	Set of Prevalent Semantic Relations in Stage I
Semantic Relation	**Examples**
agent + action	mommy come; daddy sit
action + object	drive car; eat grape
agent + object	mommy sock; baby book
action + location	go park; sit chair
entity + location	cup table; toy floor
possessor + possession	my teddy; mommy dress
entity + attribute	box shiny; crayon big
Demonstrative + entity	dat money; dis telephone

Early Grammar

Another important feature of children's two-word utterances is their consistent word order. Braine (1976) documented the early productive use of word order rules for children acquiring a variety of languages. He noted, however, that early two-word combinations had more limited, lexical-specific scope than either Bloom or Brown had suggested, which he called **limited scope formulae**. Moreover, Braine (1976) showed that there were large individual differences in the order in which different semantic relations were acquired. In an interesting study, Tomasello and his colleagues taught novel nouns or verbs to very young children at this stage of language acquisition (Tomasello, Akhtar, Dodson, & Rekau, 1997). They found that while the children were able to combine the novel nouns with other words, they were not able to combine the novel verbs with other words. This is reminiscent of the lag between the acquisition of nouns and verbs observed for children learning English and several other languages.

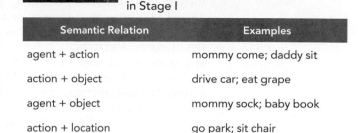

"My doggie." Possessor + possession is one of the semantic relations expressed by children who are just beginning to combine two words in Stage I speech.

Pinker (1984, 1987) has taken the findings about Stage I speech to argue that children use semantics as a way to bootstrap themselves into the linguistic system. If, as Pinker has argued, children expect there to be a correspondence between concrete objects and nouns and between actions and verbs, they can use this knowledge to guess the syntactic categories of words. And if children expect there to be a correspondence between semantic agents and grammatical subjects, this can help them to identify the subject of a sentence, first in sentences with agentive subjects (e.g., Mary threw the frisbee) and later, once they have learned the distrubutional properties of subjects, in sentences with non-agentive subjects (e.g., Mary received a letter).

How does the evidence about very early child language fit in with the linguistic theory proposed in GB theory? One answer to this question comes from a British linguist, Andrew Radford (1990), who argues that much of the linguistic system is absent in Stage I, but what the child does have at this stage is a lexicon and a limited set of phrase structure rules in d-structure. Specifically, Radford claims that English-speaking children at Stage I have only lexical categories; what is missing from their grammars are the functional categories such as Infl and Comp. There is also no transformational rule; however, the d-structure does get assigned semantic roles to yield the s-structure. These ideas are very similar to the other descriptions of Stage I language that we discussed earlier, but Radford uses the terminology and framework of the GB theory.

Another use of the GB framework to explain Stage I grammar has been proposed by Hyams (1986, 1989). If one looks at the examples of Stage I utterances in Table 5.1 that contain verbs (e.g., *eat it*), one notices that many of these utterances lack a subject. According to Hyams, such utterances are the result of the null-subject parameter, which starts out in all children in the position that allows sentences without subjects (the setting for Italian and Spanish). If this is correct, then English-speaking children eventually have to switch the setting of the parameter to the other position. In contrast, children learning a null subject language (like Italian or Spanish) have the parameter set correctly from the beginning, and so this corner of grammar is already complete for them. However, one question of interest is what happens to children in a bilingual learning environment. In null subject languages like Spanish and Italian, the contexts in which adult speakers leave a subject null are exactly the contexts in which adult speakers of non-null subject languages use pronouns. For example, the English sentence "While John is eating, he (John) is talking on the phone" is equivalent to the Italian sentence "Mentre Gianni mangia, parla al telefono" (literally: "While Gianni eats, talks on the phone"; Sorace & Serratrice, 2009). In fact, it has been shown that bilingual children acquiring a null-subject language alongside English overuse subject pronouns in their null subject language compared to monolingual child speakers of the same null subject language. This is true for Spanish-English bilingual children (Paradis & Navarro, 2003), as well as Italian-English bilinguals (Serratrice, 2007), Hebrew-English bilinguals (Argyri & Sorace, 2007), and Greek-English bilinguals (Argyi & Sorace, 2007).

Although Hyams's hypothesis is attractive because it is theoretically grounded, some important criticisms have been raised by other researchers. Valian (1990) points out some logical problems with the claim that parameters start off in one particular setting. She also provides evidence that even though U.S. children at the early stages of language development omit subjects, they do, in fact, include a sentence subject significantly more often than do Italian children at the same stage of development, suggesting that they know that subjects need to be expressed. Additionally, Ingham (1992) reports a case study that found that the acquisition of obligatory sentence subjects in English was not tied to other developments in the child's grammar, as would be predicted by Hyams's theory.

Controversies about the nature of children's early grammars, the role of GB theory, and the best way to conceptualize the child's early linguistic system have yet to be resolved. This extensive look at one stage in the acquisition of grammar highlights the importance of both theory and detailed observations of child language in the quest to understand language development.

Children's Early Comprehension of Syntax

Thus far we have presented a picture of early language development that is based entirely on studies of spontaneous speech production. These studies, however, leave unanswered a host of questions about young children's comprehension of syntax. We might ask, for example, when children begin to comprehend two-or-more-word utterances. Is comprehension in advance of production or vice versa? What is the relationship between comprehension and production?

Parents generally believe that their children understand multiword utterances almost from the time they begin using their first words and that comprehension is clearly in advance of production. Unfortunately, until very recently, research on this issue yielded conflicting results. Of course, one difficulty in comparing different studies is that researchers have used very different methods for assessing comprehension while ensuring that children could not be relying on context to interpret the linguistic message. Different methods that have been used to assess comprehension include diary studies (which document conditions under which the child can or cannot understand), act-out tasks (in which the experimenter asks the child to act out a sentence using toys (e.g., "Make the girl kiss the duck"), direction tasks (in which the child is asked to carry out a direction, such as "Tickle the duck," or answer questions), and picture-choice tasks (in which the child must select the picture that best represents the linguistic form being tested). McDaniel, McKee, and Cairns (1996) provide an excellent review of these and other methods for studying children's grammatical knowledge at different developmental stages.

In recent years, Golinkoff and Hirsh-Pasek have pioneered the use of the **preferential looking paradigm** for assessing language comprehension in infants as young as 12 months old. Using this method, these researchers have found that even in the single-word stage, 17-month-old children can use word order to comprehend multiword utterances (Hirsh-Pasek & Golinkoff, 1996). Their method involves setting the child on a parent's lap equidistant from two video displays (see Figure 5.6). While the parent closes his or her

---

figure 5.6   **Testing Young Children's Language Abilities.**   *Researchers can now gain insight into the language abilities of very young children, using techniques such as preferential looking (a), which assesses the child's attention to visual stimuli in the presence of an accompanying speech signal, and conditioned head turn (b), which assesses attention to auditory stimuli.*

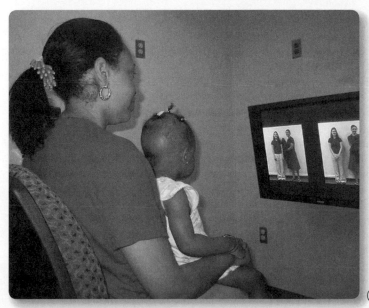

(a)

(b)

eyes or is blindfolded and makes no attempt to communicate with the child, the child watches two simultaneously presented color videos. The linguistic message, presented over a centrally placed loudspeaker in synchrony with the videotaped scenes, directs the child to attend to one of the monitors. A hidden experimenter directly observes the child's eye movements and records the amount of time spent watching the two videos on each trial.

Hirsh-Pasek and Golinkoff (1993) have used this paradigm to assess comprehension of various language features. For example, one key comparison they used to test comprehension of word order involved observing very young children while they heard the sentence, "Cookie Monster is tickling Big Bird." One of the video scenes had Cookie Monster tickling Big Bird, while in the other scene, presented simultaneously, Big Bird was tickling Cookie Monster. Because children at 17 months of age reliably spent longer looking at the former scene, Golinkoff and Hirsh-Pasek (1995) concluded that children can comprehend word order before they even begin using two-word sentences. Moreover, Hirsh-Pasek (2000) found that when children begin using two-word utterances they already recognize bound morphemes (morphemes that must attach to another word or morpheme, such as the –*ing* in the Cookie Monster examples above), which may be used to assist in constructing the grammar of their language.

More recently, researchers have been able to examine what young children do and do not understand by using electrophysiological methods, such as Event Related Potentials or ERPs (see "Knowledge vs. Processing" later in this chapter for further discussion of this method). Bernal, Dehaene-Lambertz, Millotte, and Christophe (2010) found that 24-month-old French children, who are just beginning to produce multiword utterances, show different brain responses to grammatical and ungrammatical sentences that are otherwise identical (ungrammatical sentences contained a noun where the preceding syntactic context would lead to the expectation of a verb, or vice-versa). French 2-year-olds do not generally produce sentences as complex as those used in this study until at least one year later, suggesting that sentence production lags behind sentence comprehension in early development.

These findings suggest that comprehension is indeed in advance of production, as parents have always believed. Hirsh-Pasek and Golinkoff (1996) propose that very young children use a number of cues to help them comprehend grammatical forms. These cues include prosody, semantics, and syntax, as well as the environmental and social context in which they hear utterances. Children are thus able to exploit knowledge gained from listening to adult speech in context to guide the acquisition of grammatical forms.

Developing Grammatical Morphemes

When we look at children's language as it develops beyond Stage I, we notice two important changes. One is that sentences get longer as children begin combining two or more basic semantic relations. For example, *agent + action* and *action + object* may be combined to yield *agent + action + object,* as in "Adam hit ball."

The second change is the gradual appearance of a few inflections and other closed-class terms that, "like an intricate sort of ivy, begin to grow up between and upon the major construction blocks, the nouns and verbs, to which Stage I is largely limited" (Brown, 1973, p. 249). The process of acquiring the major *grammatical morphemes* in English is gradual and lengthy. Some are still not fully controlled until the child enters school (for example, certain irregular past-tense verbs). Nevertheless, the process begins early, as soon as the MLU approaches 2.0, and we will discuss the main research findings on the acquisition of a small subset of fourteen English grammatical morphemes.

The development of these morphemes was studied by Brown and his colleague Courtney Cazden (1968) using the longitudinal data from Adam, Eve, and Sarah (Brown, 1973). The fourteen morphemes were selected both because they were very frequent and because one can easily identify the contexts in which they are needed to produce a grammatically well-formed sentence.

Brown's Fourteen Morphemes

Grammatical morphemes, even though they do not carry independent meaning, do subtly shade the meaning of sentences. The morpheme group studied by Brown included two prepositions *(in, on)*, two articles *(a, the)*, noun inflections marking possessive *('s)* and plural *(-s)*, verb inflections marking progressive *(-ing)*, third-person present tense of regular verbs (e.g., he walk*s*) or irregular verbs (e.g., he *has*), past tense of regular verbs (e.g., he walk*ed*) and irregular verbs (e.g., *had*), and the main uses of the verb *to be:* as auxiliary, both when it can be contracted (e.g., I *am* walking or I*'m* walking) and when it cannot be contracted (e.g., I *was* walking), and as a main verb or *copula* in its contractible form (e.g., I *am* happy or I*'m* happy) and its uncontractible form (e.g., This *is* it), where you cannot contract the two /s/ sounds without losing the inflection.

In order to chart the development of these morphemes, Brown closely examined each child utterance to identify whether it required any of the morphemes to make it fully grammatical by adult standards. Both the linguistic context (the utterance itself) and the nonlinguistic context can be used to decide which morphemes are necessary. For example, when a child says "that book" while pointing out a book, we know that there should be a copula *('s* or *is)* and an article *(a)*. Or if a child says "two book table" when there are several books lying on the table, we know that *book* should have a plural *-s* and the preposition *on* and article *the* are required before the word *table*. In this way Brown went through the transcripts of his three subjects from Stage I to Stage V and identified all of the obligatory contexts for each morpheme. Then he checked how many of these contexts were actually filled with the appropriate morphemes at the different stages of development. From this, he calculated the percentage of each morpheme actually supplied in its obligatory context for each child for each sample of spontaneous speech. This measure has the advantage of being independent of actual frequency of use since frequency may vary considerably from one child to another and from one point in time to the next.

The process of acquiring each of these grammatical morphemes is a gradual one—they do not suddenly appear in their required contexts all of the time. Rather, their appearance fluctuates, sometimes quite sharply, during the period when they are being acquired until they are almost always present.

Order of Acquisition

The most important finding that Brown reports is the remarkable similarity among his three subjects in the order in which these morphemes were acquired. Brown defined "acquisition" as the time when the morpheme was supplied in 90 percent of its obligatory contexts. The first set of morphemes to be acquired included the two prepositions, the plural, and the present progressive inflection. The last morphemes were the contractible copula and auxiliary, which had not yet reached the acquisition criterion by Stage V. Table 5.3 shows the average order of acquisition of all fourteen morphemes.

Explaining the Order of Acquisition.   What accounts for this invariant sequence of development? Why do all children find the progressive inflection *(-ing)* easier than the past tense inflection *(-ed)* and articles *(a, the)* harder than the plural ending? One possible explanation is that the morphemes the children hear most often are acquired earlier. Brown tested this *frequency hypothesis* in the following way. He examined the speech of each child's parents just before the child reached Stage II and began using the morphemes. He tallied the number of times each morpheme was used by each parent and compared these frequencies with the order in which the morphemes were acquired by the children. But there was no relationship between these figures. For example, the most frequent morphemes in the parents' speech were the articles, but these were not among the earliest to be acquired. And even though prepositions were not so frequent in the parents' samples, they

---

table 5.3 Average Order of Acquisition of Fourteen Grammatical Morphemes by Three Children Studied by Brown

1. present progressive	(sing*ing*; play*ing*)
2/3. prepositions	(*in* the cup; *on* the floor)
4. plural	(book*s*; doll*s*)
5. irregular past tense	(*broke*; *went*)
6. possessive	(Mommy*'s* chair; Susie*'s* teddy)
7. copula (uncontractible)	(This *is* my book)
8. articles	(*The* teddy; *A* table)
9. regular past tense	(walk*ed*; play*ed*)
10. third-person present tense regular	(he climb*s*; Mommy cook*s*)
11. third-person present tense irregular	(John *has* three cookies)
12. auxiliary (uncontractible)	(She *was* going to school; *Do* you like me?)
13. copula (contractible)	(I*'m* happy; you *are* special)
14. auxiliary (contractible)	(Mommy*'s* going shopping)

---

were acquired very early by all the children. So, overall, frequency does not account well for the particular order in which the 14 morphemes develop.

On the other hand, Brown (1973) did find that *linguistic complexity* predicted the order of acquisition very well. Complexity can be defined in two ways: *semantic* (the number of meanings encoded in the morpheme) and *syntactic* (the number of rules required for the morpheme). Brown defined complexity in a conservative way that he called cumulative complexity. Only morphemes that share common meanings or grammatical rules can be fairly compared. A morpheme that requires knowledge of both *x* and *y* is defined as more complex than a morpheme requiring knowledge of only *x* or *y,* but it cannot be compared to a morpheme requiring knowledge of *w.*

If we look at cumulative semantic complexity, the plural morpheme encodes only number, the past-tense (regular or irregular) morphemes encode "earlierness," and the present progressive morpheme encodes temporary duration. Since the copula verb and the third-person singular morphemes encode both number and "earlierness," we would predict that these morphemes would be acquired later. This prediction is borne out by the order shown in Table 5.3. We would also predict that the auxiliary—which encodes number, "earlierness," and temporary duration—would be acquired after all of these since it entails all of these meanings. This prediction, too, is confirmed by the data.

From a syntactic point of view, it is interesting to note that the morphemes that are acquired early involve only lexical categories, whereas the later-acquired morphemes all involve functional categories, particularly Infl (present and past tense; auxiliary verbs). In fact, an extensive line of empirical inquiry has led to the hypothesis that young children go through a stage during which they believe that tense is optional in main clauses—the so-called "optional infinitive stage." Since Brown's order of acquisition is based on 90 percent production of morphemes in obligatory contexts, if children do go through a stage in which they think tense is not obligatory, this would explain why tense-related morphemes appear later in development than other morphemes.

Optional Infinitives

Young children learning English often produce sentences that lack tense (past, present progressive, etc.) and person markers (in English, the only regular person marker is the third person singular, as in "he goes"). Thus, they produce utterances such as "Elephant fall down and camel fall down" (Abe, age 2 years and 5 months; Kuczaj, 1976) and "I bump my head" (Naomi, age 2 years and 0 months; Sachs, 1983). Although untensed verbs (also called non-finite verbs) like this are possible when they are embedded inside another clause (e.g., "I didn't see *the elephant fall down*"), main clauses (unembedded clauses) require a tense marker. Early errors like these may not seem too surprising, because there must be a stage during which children do not yet know what the tensed forms of verbs look like. However, more interestingly, there appears to be a stage during which children simultaneously produce sentences with untensed verbs and sentences with tensed forms of the very same verbs. For example, a few seconds after Abe produced the sentence containing untensed *fall*, he produced a sentence containing a tensed version of *fall:* "He fell down!" (there had been no adult modeling of the correct form nor any feedback given between the two utterances). Importantly, when children do provide a tensed verb form during this stage, they almost always choose the correct tensed form. This kind of evidence has been interpreted as showing that children under age 3 know a great deal about the inflectional system for English. It has been argued that the only thing children do not know at this stage is that tense must be obligatorily marked in main clauses (Wexler, 1994). For this reason, this stage has been called the **optional infinitive stage** (untensed verbs may also be called infinitives; Pierce, 1992). Using multiple research methods (elicited production, spontaneous production and grammaticality judgment), researchers have shown that English-speaking children are still actively producing non-finite (uninflected) main clauses at age 3 years, and finally stop producing them at about age 4 and a half years (Rice, Wexler, & Hershberger, 1998). However, it has been argued that children with Specific Language Impairment go through an extended optional infinitive stage (Rice & Wexler, 1996; see Chapter 9).

Productivity of Children's Morphology

Even though it is generally accepted that children cannot and do not learn the morphology of a language by repeating specific examples they have heard from others, some researchers believe that at the initial stages, children's use of grammatical morphemes is tied to particular lexical forms and does not reflect the same degree of complexity or the same syntactic categories as the mature adult system. For example, Pine and Lieven (1997) argue that children's early use of determiners such as *a* and *the* is initially tied to particular nouns and does not reflect any deeper understanding that both are examples of the syntactic category of determiners. However, the empirical facts on which this argument is based are challenged by Valian, Solt, and Stewart (2008), who argue that a proper analysis of the data demonstrates just the opposite. Despite ongoing debate about how best to characterize the developing language system in its earliest stages, there is clear evidence that by age 3 or 4, children are indeed acquiring a rule-governed system. To start with, there are the charming mistakes that children make—mistakes in applying a morphological rule when it should not be applied. For example, children frequently add the plural *-s* to exceptional nouns (man*s*, foot*s*, teeth*s*, people*s*) or use the regular past tense *-ed* on irregular verbs (fall*ed*, go*ed*, brok*ed*), even when the correct irregular form has previously been used. **Overregularization errors** like these are an excellent source of evidence for the productivity and creativity of the child's morphology; these are the forms no child would have heard from an adult.

    Other evidence for the productive use of morphological rules came from a pioneering study by Berko (1958). Berko designed an elicited-production task in which children were shown novel creatures and actions that were given invented names. The children were then provided with the linguistic context for adding plural and possessive inflections

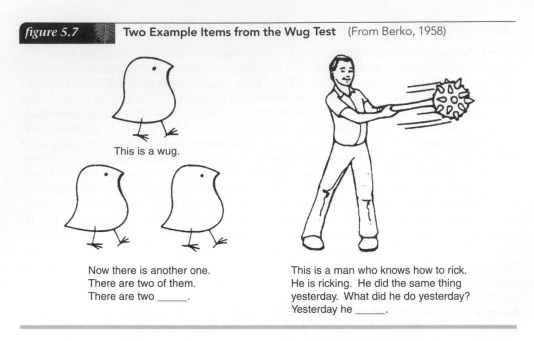

figure 5.7 **Two Example Items from the Wug Test** (From Berko, 1958)

This is a wug.

Now there is another one.
There are two of them.
There are two _____.

This is a man who knows how to rick.
He is ricking. He did the same thing
yesterday. What did he do yesterday?
Yesterday he _____.

to the novel nouns and progressive, third-person present tense, and past-tense endings to the novel verbs. Figure 5.7 shows two examples from this study. Overall, Berko found that preschool and first-grade children performed well with the nonsense words, although their performance was clearly constrained by the controlled, somewhat artificial conditions of the experiment. Nevertheless, the ability to supply correct morphemes on novel nouns and verbs demonstrates beyond doubt that children have internalized knowledge about English morphological rules and have not simply learned the morphemes in a rote fashion by imitating others.

Children's knowledge of both regular and irregular forms of English, particularly the past-tense ending, has been the focus of a number of important studies by Pinker and his associates (Marcus et al., 1992). Their findings, based on spontaneous speech analyses and experimental studies, suggest that past-tense overregularization errors are, in fact, relatively rare (between 5 and 10 percent), but they persist well into middle childhood for particular types of verbs. Based on these findings, Pinker (1999) argues that two different mechanisms are involved in acquiring regular and irregular forms. Regular forms involve a rule-governed mechanism that applies the -*ed* ending in contexts requiring the expression of a past tense, whereas irregular forms are retrieved directly from the lexicon and thus involve a memory storage system. Ullman (2001) combines these mechanisms in what he calls the declarative-procedural model of language. This dual-mechanism hypothesis has come under attack from models developed within a *connectionist* framework (see Chapter 7), in which only a single mechanism is needed to compute the correct past tense ending (Rumelhart & McClelland, 1986). Connectionist models learn the verb endings based on the input they receive. The debate between the dual-mechanism and connectionist camps continues in a lively fashion in the current psycholinguistic literature (McClelland & Patterson, 2002; Pinker & Ullman, 2002).

An example of an overregularization error is when a child says, "The importantest thing to do is to not look down," when explaining how to balance.

Cross-Linguistic Data

There is by now a growing body of literature on the acquisition of grammatical morphology in other languages. Some of the findings on English have been supported by data on children's acquisition of other languages. For example, records of children's acquisition of the morphology of Polish (Dabrowska, 2001), Hebrew (Berent, Pinker, & Shimron, 2002), Spanish (Clahsen, Aveledo, & Roca, 2002), and many other languages all include abundant examples of overgeneralization errors.

An optional infinitive stage is also observed in children learning languages other than English, such as French, Danish, Swedish, German, Dutch, and Russian (French: Pierce, 1992; Danish: Hamann & Plunkett, 1998; Swedish: Platzack, 1990; German: Behrens, 1993; Dutch: Haegeman, 1994; Russian; Bar-Shalom & Snyder, 1997). In these languages, evidence that many of children's early sentences contain infinitives is even clearer than it is in English, because in these cases the verb forms that children produce when they do not inflect the verb for tense are special infinitive forms (e.g., French *dormir,* meaning "to sleep"). As in the case of English, when young children speaking one of these languages do produce a tensed form, it is nearly always an appropriate form for the context, suggesting that children know a lot about how tense works in their language, but that the one thing lacking is knowledge that tense is obligatory in main clauses.

It has been believed for many years that children learning Italian and other Romance languages, such as Spanish, do not go through an optional infinitive stage (Guasti, 1992). However, Grinstead, De la Mora, Vega-Mendoza, and Flores (2009) argue that this may be incorrect. Researchers looking for optional infinitives in the speech of Spanish- or Italian-speaking children have assumed that these non-finite forms would take the form of an actual infinitive verb (e.g., Spanish *cantar;* "to sleep") as they do in German-speaking children, and indeed when counted in this way, rates of optional infinitives are very low for Spanish-speaking children. What they have ignored, according to Grinstead and colleagues, is that non-finite forms in Spanish- or Italian-speaking children might take the form of bare verbs. Grinstead and colleagues have argued that the problem of determining what should be counted as a non-finite form is exacerbated by the fact that languages like Spanish and Italian are null subject languages; thus a child utterance such as "Canta" might represent a correctly inflected present-tense verb with a null subject that is third-person singular (e.g., a null *el* or *ella*), or it might represent a bare verb stem with a null subject that is not third-person singular (e.g., a null *yo* or *Usted*). To avoid this inevitable problem with spontaneous production data, Grinstead and colleagues have used a receptive Grammaticality Choice paradigm (Pratt & Grinstead, 2007) where they present children with two utterances and ask them which is better. Using this technique, Grinstead, Vega-Mendoza, and Goodall (2010) have shown that some Spanish-speaking 3-year-olds accept uninflected main clause verbs as often as 37 percent of the time.

Different Sentence Modalities

After Stage II, when the grammatical morphemes begin to appear, the major changes in children's language are in the development of different types of sentences, such as negatives, questions, and imperatives. Although children most certainly say no, ask questions, and make demands at the very earliest stages of language development, it is not until about Stage III (when the MLU reaches 2.5) that they begin to acquire the adult forms for their expression. During earlier stages of language development, children rely on different intonation patterns, closely matching those used by adults, to mark different sentence modalities (Bassano & Mendes-Maillochon, 1994). Gradually, children begin to master the morphosyntactic devices that mark **sentence modality**, and these come to complement the earlier-acquired prosodic devices. In this section we will follow the course of development of two different sentence modalities: negatives and questions.

Negatives

Ursula Bellugi, one of Brown's students, undertook the analysis of the expression of **negation** in the longitudinal transcripts of Adam, Eve, and Sarah (Bellugi, 1967). She identified three main periods in the acquisition of the full negative. In the first period a sentence was made negative by placing the negative marker, *no* or *not,* outside the sentence, usually preceding it. There were many utterances of this form:

> No go movies.
>
> No sit down.
>
> No Mommy do it.

In the next period, the negative word was moved inside the sentence and placed next to the main verb; however, there was no productive use of the auxiliary system. During this period Bellugi reports examples such as these:

> I no like it.
>
> Don't go.
>
> I no want book.

The final period (which is not usually reached until Stage V) was marked by the appearance of different auxiliaries, and the child's negative sentences then approximated the adult forms. Negatives such as these are produced during this final period:

> You can't have this.
>
> I don't have money.
>
> I'm not sad now.

Bellugi's analysis of negation focused on the development of its syntactic form. Because of the complexity of the English auxiliary system, children take a long time to acquire full mastery over the expression of negation in English.

Bloom (1970) soon criticized Bellugi's approach. She argued that almost all of the sentences produced during the first period had no subjects anyway, and so, in fact, the negative marker was correctly placed next to the verb or predicate. In those few instances where there was a sentence subject and the *no* was outside the sentence (as in "No Mommy do it"), Bloom inferred that *no* was not negating the sentence but was *anaphoric;* that is, it referred back to a preceding utterance. In this example the meaning of the sentence would be, "No, I want Mommy to do it." The thrust of Bloom's argument, then, was to question the existence of the first period of negative acquisition. However, de Villiers and de Villiers (1979) pointed out that there were too few critical sentences in the existent literature on which to judge the issue. Fortunately, their own children had learned how to say *no* and, in the process, provided large numbers of these critical sentences (de Villiers & de Villiers, 1979).

The de Villierses found that their son, Nicholas, produced two kinds of negative sentences during the first period. One kind confirmed Bellugi's analysis of a *no* + sentence rule, where the *no* was not anaphoric but negated the sentence. However, at the same time, Nicholas produced sentences that had the negative marker placed internally, next to the verb or predicate. He therefore appeared to use two different rules to generate negatives. He used the *no* + sentence form to express rejection and the internal *no* form to express denial. This same pattern was confirmed in their second child, Charlotte, and in Eve, but they did not find it in Adam's speech.

Where did this pattern come from? De Villiers and de Villiers suggest that the children picked it up from their parents' speech. Both Eve's parents and Nicholas and Charlotte's parents (but not Adam's) used a polite but indirect form to express rejection, which inadvertently modeled a *no* + sentence form. For example, they would say, "No, I don't think you should do that."

We see, then, that the development of negation reflects a complex interaction of syntactic, semantic, and input factors that may combine in different ways for different children learning various languages in the early stages. The acquisition of negation has now been examined in a wide variety of languages, including Italian, Turkish, Hebrew, Japanese, Korean, French, Russian, German, Dutch, ASL, Mandarin, Cantonese, Swedish, Polish, and Latvian (see Dimroth, 2010, for a summary of the cross-linguistic findings, with references to all of this work). Taken together, these studies illustrate the complex interplay of universal and language-specific factors that determine the rate at which children achieve full mastery of the ability to express negation in all its forms and meanings.

Questions

Single-Clause Questions.   In English and other languages we can ask different kinds of questions for different purposes in a number of ways. For example, we can simply use rising intonation on a declarative sentence to signal that we are asking a question: "Mommy is tired?" Children seem to rely on rising intonation in the earliest stages (Klima & Bellugi, 1966). We can also form this question, called a **yes/no question** since these are the responses that are called for, by reversing the subject of the sentence (*Mommy*) and the auxiliary verb (*is*), as in "Is Mommy going?" This syntactic rule is much more complex, and children only begin to master it in Stage III.

A different group of questions is used for obtaining more than a simple *yes/no* answer. They are called the **wh-questions** in English since they begin with *what, where, which, who, whose, when, why,* and *how.* Answers to these questions will be more complex and contain more information. These questions also require the rule of inverting the subject and the auxiliary, as well as the correct placement of the appropriate *wh*-word at the beginning: for example, "When is dinner?" or "Why are we staying home?" Children initially ask *wh*-questions omitting the auxiliary altogether:

What that?

Where Daddy go?

They then include the auxiliary but do not consistently switch it around with the subject:

Where are you going?

What she is playing?

Finally, children are able to incorporate all of the syntactic rules necessary to produce well-formed *wh*-questions.

Klima and Bellugi (1966) hypothesized that since *yes/no* questions involve only one rule (inverting subject and auxiliary) and *wh*-questions require two rules (*wh*-word placement and subject–auxiliary inversion), one should find that children produce correctly inverted *yes/no* questions earlier than inverted *wh*-questions. Their analysis of questions asked by Adam, Eve, and Sarah supported this hypothesis; however, later studies using larger groups of children found no evidence for this late development of inversion (Santelmann, Berk, Austin, Somashekar, & Lust, 2002). Instead, many children employ the inversion rule for both kinds of questions at about the same time. A careful analysis of the emergence of the auxiliary verb in *wh*-questions has found that if it appears, it is generally inverted; otherwise it is most often absent from the question altogether (Stromswold, 1995; Valian, 1992). De Villiers and colleagues (1990) explored the spontaneous speech of a few children and found that for each child the presence of inverted auxiliaries in *wh*-questions emerged at separate points for each *wh*-term *(what, how, why),* and that there was a close developmental relationship between inverting auxiliaries and expressing embedded *wh*-questions (e.g., "How did you know that?" or "I saw how you played the game."). De Villiers (1995) argues that these developments reflect the acquisition of the functional category of Comp (cf. the section at the beginning of this chapter on "The Nature of Syntactic Rules"). Rowland and

Pine (2000), however, argue that questions emerge based on lexical combinations and there is no need to posit abstract functional categories in the child's grammar.

There is more agreement among researchers concerning the order in which children acquire the various *wh*-questions. Wootten, Merkin, Hood, and Bloom (1979) found that *what, where,* and *who* were the first questions asked by the children they followed longitudinally. Only later did their subjects ask questions about *when, how,* and *why.* And studies of children's comprehension of different *wh*-questions have found that *what, where,* and *who* are easier to understand and respond to correctly than *how, why,* and *when* (Winzemer, 1980).

What factors account for this invariant acquisition order? One plausible determinant is semantic or cognitive complexity. The concepts that are required for encoding *how, when,* and *why* questions, including manner, time, and causality, are more abstract and develop later than the concepts encoded in *what, where,* and *who* questions, which are already incorporated into early Stage I speech.

Negative Questions. An interesting finding originally observed by Bellugi (1971) is that even after children consistently invert the subject and the auxiliary in their affirmative questions, they may fail to do so in their negative questions, producing non-adult forms like "What you don't like?" in contexts in which adults typically produce "What don't you like?" These errors are not often obvious in spontaneous speech because negative questions are quite rarely produced, even by adults. However, such errors have now been robustly observed in elicited-production studies, even with some children as old as age 5 (Guasti, Thornton, & Wexler, 1995). It seems that the difficulty of these questions is due specifically to the auxiliary having a contracted negative joined to it, because during this stage children never fail to invert the subject and auxiliary if the negative is not contracted to the auxiliary. That is, they do not produce questions like "What you do not like?" or "What you not like?" but rather the well-formed "What do you not like?" A related error that some children produce during the same stage is doubling of the auxiliary in negative questions, as in "What do you don't like?" This error seems to represent a compromise between reluctance to invert *don't* with the subject and the understanding that questions require subject–auxiliary inversion. It is not currently known how children eventually overcome this problem.

Long-Distance Questions. *Wh*-questions can also be formed from complex sentences, including multi-clause sentences. For example, *wh*-movement can apply to multiclause sentences like "Mary told Jane that we should get something" and "I think Mary told Jane that we should get something," to form these **long-distance questions**:

> What did Mary tell Jane that we should get?
>
> What do you think Mary told Jane that we should get?

In these examples, the *wh*-phrase—*what*—has moved *long distance* (i.e., over more than one clause) from the end of the most embedded clause (i.e., "we should get what"). The long-distance movement of *wh*-phrases is subject to a number of constraints to which adult speakers seem to adhere. For example, some syntacticians believe that long-distance *wh*-questions involve multiple steps of movement: a *wh*-phrase must move one clause at a time in successive jumps or cycles, landing in a position inside of a complementizer phrase (CompP) at the top of each clause on its way to the topmost CompP position at the beginning of the sentence. If another *wh*-phrase already fills this position inside the CompP of an embedded clause, a *wh*-word cannot pass through that position, and hence this will block long-distance *wh*-movement.

Children as young as age 3 have shown evidence that they have knowledge of these features of complex questions. One piece of evidence comes from a mistake that some children make in producing long-distance questions. Crain and Thornton (1998) have shown that a small minority of children aged 3 to 5 years seem to go through a stage during which they produce the *wh*-word in the CompP of both the topmost clause and the embedded clause. This results in questions like "Who do you think who is in the box?" (meaning "Who do you think is in the box?") and "What do you think what Cookie Monster eats?" (meaning "What do you think Cookie Monster eats?"). These non-adult questions seem to show that children do understand that part of the procedure for forming a long-distance question involves moving a *wh*-phrase in small jumps from one CompP position to the next. The only mistake is in pronouncing the *wh*-phrase in its temporary (sentence-medial) position as well as in the final (sentence-initial) position.

Young children also seem to know that a *wh*-word cannot move (temporarily) into an embedded CompP position if the position is already filled with another *wh*-phrase. Evidence for this comes from comprehension studies by de Villiers et al. (1990). These researchers first showed that between the ages of 3 and 6, children understand that some *wh*-questions are ambiguous; they can have more than one interpretation. For example,

> When did Jane say she ripped her dress?

On one reading of this question, the answer might be

> (She said it) when she was in the bath.

On a different reading of this question, the answer might be

> (She ripped it) when she was climbing out of the tree.

De Villers et al. found that young children freely give both types of answers to these ambiguous questions, including the second one, suggesting that they do allow long-distance interpretations of *when* questions. However, children respond differently to a subtly different *when* question if the CompP of the embedded clause already contains a *wh*-phrase, as in this example:

> When did Jane say how she ripped her dress?

In response to questions like this, children aged 3 to 6 years restrict their answers to when Jane said it, and mostly avoid answers concerning when the dress was ripped. That is, children seem to understand that in this example, the *when* question cannot be a long-distance question. This suggests that children know that the presence of *how* in the CompP of the embedded clause blocks the movement of other *wh*-phrases out of that clause.

Different languages form *wh*-questions in different ways, and there are variations in the rules that allow long-distance movement across clauses. A key question in language acquisition is how children acquire these highly complex rules that are specific to their language (de Villiers et al., 1990). This question continues to be investigated by many researchers.

Later Developments in Preschoolers

By the time children begin school, they have acquired most of the morphological and syntactic rules of their language. They can use language in a variety of ways, and their simple sentences, questions, negatives, and imperatives are much like those of adults. There are more complex grammatical constructions that children begin using and understanding during the preschool years, by early Stage IV, but their acquisition is not complete until some years later. In this section we briefly consider three such constructions: passives, coordination, and relative clauses.

Passives

The **passive** construction is used relatively rarely in English, to highlight the object of a sentence or the recipient of an action. For example, one

Some types of children's errors are rarely heard outside of elicited production experiments, but occasionally, if you listen carefully and get lucky, you might hear a spontaneous example. The child in this picture produced this long-distance question error: "What do you wanna tell me what's on it?" The adult version of this sentence would be "What do you wanna tell me is on it?"

might say, "The window was broken by a dog," if the focus is on the window. Not surprisingly, passives are extremely rare in transcripts of children's spontaneous speech—too rare to study unless the researcher specifically tries to elicit them in an experimental situation. Nevertheless, a great deal of attention has been paid to how children handle passive sentences. Because the order of the agent and the object is reversed in passives in English, this particular construction can reveal a great deal about how children acquire word-order rules that play a major role in English syntax.

One of the earliest studies of children's facility with passive sentences was a production study carried out by Horgan (1978). She used a set of pictures to elicit passives from a group of children who ranged in age from 2 to 13. She found that the younger children produced full passives far less frequently than *truncated* passives, in which no agent is specified, as in "The window was broken." She also found that there were topic differences between the children's full and truncated passives. Full passives almost always had animate subjects (e.g., *girl, boy, cat*), whereas truncated passives almost always had inanimate subjects (e.g., *lamp, windows*). Because of these differences, Horgan argued that full and truncated passives develop separately and, at least for the young child, are unrelated.

In fact, some researchers have argued that children's truncated passives are not true passives at all, which would explain why they pattern differently than full passives in children's early productions. The suggestion is that when children produce a sentence like "The window was broken," *broken* is being used as an adjective, not as a passive participle of break. "Adjectival passives" are thought to be generated in the lexicon, differing crucially from true passives, which are thought to be generated by a syntactic transformation (Wasow, 1977).

Most research has focused on children's *comprehension* of passive sentences. One of the earliest studies on passive sentence comprehension was conducted by Bever (1970). He compared children aged 2, 3, and 4 on their understanding of active and passive sentences. Some of the sentences were semantically reversible; that is, both nouns could plausibly act as agent or object: "The boy kissed the girl" (active) or "The boy was kissed by the girl" (passive). And some of the sentences were semantically irreversible; that is, only one of the nouns could plausibly act as agent: "The girl patted the dog" or "The dog was patted by the girl."

Not surprisingly, Bever found that children could understand the irreversible passives earlier than the reversible ones. It was not until children were about 4 or 5 that they could correctly act out the reversible passive sentences, making passives quite a late development for English-speaking children. The most interesting aspect of Bever's results were the systematic mistakes that the 3- and some of the 4-year-olds made on the reversible passive sentences. They consistently reversed the agent and object. When they were given a sentence like "The car was pushed by the truck," they made the car push the truck, as if they had heard an active sentence.

Subsequent comprehension research has confirmed that children learning English do not master passive sentences with **actional verbs** like *kiss* and *pat* until age 4 or 5, and, interestingly, mastery of passives comes even later for sentences containing so-called **psychological verbs**, such as *see* and *like* (Fox & Grodzinsky, 1998; Hirsch & Wexler, 2007). For example, Hirsch and Wexler (2007) found that children performed at chance level in comprehending sentences like "Bart was seen by Marge" up until age 7, and they only reached 90 percent correct at age 9.

Bever proposed that by 3 or 4 years of age, children have developed a generalized abstract rule that the order of words in English signals the main sentence relations. They know that English uses predominantly noun–verb–noun sequences that, in the active voice, mean agent–action–object. Consequently, when they hear a passive sentence, they ignore the *was* and *by* and infer the meaning of the passive noun–verb–noun sequence to be active.

Many subsequent experiments have confirmed Bever's findings, and the strategy that children use at about 3 or 4 is usually called the word-order strategy. However, research conducted on children learning languages other than English has shown that this is not a universal strategy.

Studies of the development of some non–Indo-European languages have also found that children learning these languages in fact acquire the passive construction very much earlier than children learning languages like English (e.g., Demuth, 1990; Suzman, 1987). Thus, children acquiring Inuktitut use passives frequently by age 3 (Allen & Crago, 1996), and Demuth's study of children acquiring Sesotho, a language spoken in southern Africa, found that these children began using the passive in everyday conversation by the time they were 2 years old, and it was quite frequent by the time they were 4. Demuth (1990) suggests this is because in Sesotho, where subjects always mark the topic of a sentence, the passive is a very basic and quite frequent construction since most verbs can be passivized. She argues that the typology of a language, and the importance of the passive to a particular language, influences the timing of its development.

Coordinations

At very young ages, as early as 2½ years, children begin combining sentences to express complex or compound propositions. The simplest and most frequent way children combine sentences is to conjoin two propositions with *and*. Research on young children's development of **coordination** with *and* has demonstrated that, like many of the other constructions we have considered, its development depends not only on linguistic complexity but also on semantic and contextual factors.

There have been a number of independent studies on the development of coordination in spontaneous speech. One of the questions that has interested researchers is the order in which different coordination constructions enter the child's speech. There are two main forms of coordination according to linguists: *sentential coordination,* in which two (or more) complete sentences are conjoined, as in "I'm pushing the wagon and I'm pulling the train," and *phrasal coordination,* in which phrases within the sentence are conjoined, as in "I'm pushing the wagon and the train." There does not seem to be a strict sequence of acquisition for these two forms. Bloom and her colleagues (Bloom, Lahey, Hood, Lifter, & Fiess, 1980) reported that for three of the children they studied longitudinally, both forms entered the children's speech at the same time. Their fourth subject, as well as Adam, Eve, and Sarah, who were studied by de Villiers, Tager-Flusberg, and Hakuta (1977), all used phrasal coordination before sentential coordination. The only constraint on acquisition order is that sentential coordination generally does not develop before phrasal coordination.

In their longitudinal study, Bloom and her colleagues (1980) found that the course of acquisition of coordination was also influenced by semantic factors. All four of their subjects used *and* to encode a variety of meanings, and these meanings developed in a fixed order. The earliest meaning to develop was additive (no dependency relation between the conjoined clauses), as in "Maybe you can carry this and I can carry that." Several months later children began using *and* to encode temporal relations (the two clauses were related by temporal sequence or simultaneity), for example, "Jocelyn's going home and take her sweater off." Later still, *and* was used to encode causal relations, for example, "She put a bandage on her shoe and it maked it feel better." Some of the children went on to use *and* to encode other meanings, for example, object specification—"It looks like a fishing thing and you fish with it"—and adversative relation (expressing opposition)—"Cause I was tired and now I'm not tired"—but these were less frequent and more variable among the children. This study is important since it highlights the variety of meanings encoded by the single connective *and*. Thus, at the early stage of coordination development, children use *and* in a semantically limited way; however, as they progress, children add greater semantic flexibility as well as syntactic complexity to their language.

Relative Clauses

Children begin producing and understanding some sentences with embedded **relative clauses** when they are about 3 years old, in Stage IV. In their longitudinal study, Bloom and colleagues (1980) reported that relativization developed much later than coordination, and it was used exclusively to present information about an object or person, as in "It's the one you went to last night" (Peter, age 2 years and 10 months; Bloom, Hood, & Lightbown, 1974).

Studies on relative clauses that have depended on spontaneous speech samples find that the actual number of sentences with relative clauses in child speech is disappointingly small. Perhaps children avoid them since they are syntactically complex, or they may lack the occasion to use them in a naturalistic setting, where knowledge about the context is shared by listener and speaker and need not be made explicit. Whatever the reason for this gap, the small samples yielded from early spontaneous speech make it difficult to evaluate how knowledge of these structures develops.

To get around these problems, researchers have used elicitation techniques that increase the probability of children attempting to produce a relative clause. Elicited-production studies have allowed researchers to probe for a variety of types of relative clauses in a variety of locations within a sentence. In these studies, children are asked to describe a scene containing two identical objects to a listener who cannot observe the scene. In order to communicate successfully, the children need to use a relative clause or similar construction to specify the correct object. A sample stimulus picture for eliciting a relative clause is shown in Figure 5.8.

Hamburger and Crain (1982) confirmed the earlier research on spontaneous speech and found that 4-year-olds could successfully produce relative clauses modifying the object of a sentence, such as "Pick up the walrus that is tickling the zebra." In English these are

---

figure 5.8   **Sample Stimulus for Eliciting a Relative Clause.**   The experimenter first describes the picture with "This man is running past an elephant and this man is talking to an elephant." Then one of the men turns blue, and the experimenter asks, "Which man turned blue?" The target response (*The man who is running past the elephant*) is a subject-gap relative clause.

sometimes called **right-branching relative clauses**. (Figures 5.2 and 5.3 showed that one way of representing a sentence structure is as a tree with branches; extending this metaphor, a right-branching relative clause is one that is added to the NP to the right of a verb—the direct object of the verb—and that thereby expands the number of branches on the right side of the tree.)

Tager-Flusberg (1982) provided children with the opportunity to produce both right-branching relative clauses and **center-embedded relative clauses**. Center-embedded relative clauses modify the main clause subject, and hence in English they appear in the center of the main clause between the subject and the predicate, as in "The bear who is sitting in a chair jumped up and down." In this example the main clause is "The bear jumped up and down," and the center-embedded relative clause is "who is sitting in a chair."

Tager-Flusberg found that once children used relative clauses (at about age 4), they could produce them in both positions equally well. However, Tager-Flusberg also found that if the main sentence was more complex and included a direct object and an indirect object phrase, such as "The boy gave the dog to the bear," the 4-year-olds could add a relative clause only to the final object (the bear) and not to the subject or direct object. So they would say, "The boy gave the dog to the bear who is holding the wagon." It seems that children initially find it easiest to add a clause at the end of a sentence rather than in the middle, since this minimizes constraints on processing (see Hakuta, de Villiers, & Tager-Flusberg, 1982).

None of the results from the elicited-production studies we have discussed involved **object-gap relative clauses**. Relative clauses, regardless of whether they appear in a right-branching or a center-embedded position, can be classified on the basis of where they "contain" a gap inside of them. In the noun phrase, "the horse that the boy rode," the relative clause "that the boy rode" is missing a direct object, which is required by the verb *ride*, and thus this type of relative clause is called an object-gap relative clause. Psycholinguistic work with adults has shown that object-gap relative clauses are much more difficult to comprehend than **subject-gap relative clauses**, those that have a gap in the position of the subject, as in "the walrus that is tickling the zebra" (Gibson, Desmet, Grodner, Watson, & Ko, 2005; Traxler, Morris, & Seeley, 2002). Not surprisingly, then, in elicited-production studies, young children are less successful at producing object-gap relative clauses than subject-gap relative clauses, and some children do not produce any of the more difficult type in a testing session (Bar-Shalom, Crain, & Shankweiler, 1993; McDaniel, McKee, & Bernstein, 1998, Zukowski, 2009). Also, in comprehension studies, sentences containing object-gap relative clauses in center-embedded position are very difficult for young children to interpret correctly, whereas sentences containing subject-gap relative clauses in the same position are comparatively easy to interpret (de Villiers, Tager-Flusberg, Hakuta, & Cohen, 1979).

More and more studies are being conducted on the acquisition of relative clauses in other languages. The special difficulty of object-gap relatives compared to subject-gap relatives has been repeatedly observed in studies of elicited production of children speaking a variety of typologically distinct langauges: Spanish, Mandarin, and Jakartan Indonesian (e.g., Cole, Hermon, & Tjung, 2005; Perez-Leroux, 1993; Tjung, 2006). Interestingly, this order of difficulty is mirrored in the grammatical patterns observed in languages of the world: No language seems to have object-gap relative clauses unless it also has subject-gap relative clauses, yet many languages have only subject-gap relative clauses (Keenan & Comrie, 1977). Many people believe that this pattern is linked to the greater processing difficulty of object-gap relatives.

The research conducted thus far shows that young preschoolers who are just beginning to produce relative clauses continue to experience difficulty producing and comprehending certain types of relative clauses for some time. Their actual performance with relative-clause sentences is highly constrained by processing limitations, and this makes it very difficult to evaluate their knowledge of the syntactic structure of this construction (cf. the final section of this chapter, "Knowledge versus Processing").

Beyond the Preschool Years

Before we leave the topic of syntactic and morphological development, we should note that even during the school years, children continue to develop in this domain of language. Certain constructions are not yet fully controlled by children at the time they enter school. One area that has received much attention in recent years, because of its centrality to GB theory, is the child's knowledge of **anaphora**—how different pronoun forms link up with their referents in a sentence. Additionally, several constructions in which an infinitive clause has no overt subject cause problems for children well beyond the preschool years. We discuss one of these problematic constructions: "John is easy to please."

Anaphora

Consider the following sentences:

John said that Robert hurt himself.

John said that Robert hurt him.

We know that in the first sentence Robert was hurt—the reflexive pronoun *himself* is "bound" to the referent *Robert*. In the second sentence, Robert cannot be the one to get hurt; it must be John—here we note that the pronoun *him* is bound to the referent *John*. According to GB theory, this knowledge is encompassed in the **binding principles**, which are a part of our grammar. These sentences illustrate two of the binding principles (A and B), which are loosely defined here:

Principle A: A reflexive is always bound to a referent that is within the same clause.

Principle B: An anaphoric pronoun cannot be bound to a referent within the same clause.

These two principles explain our intuitions about the meanings of the two sentences above. The third binding principle (C) is concerned with "backwards" sentences, in which the pronoun comes before the referent. The following two sentences illustrate this principle:

When he came home John made dinner.

He made dinner when John came home.

In the first sentence, *he* can refer to John, or we could say that the pronoun is bound to the referent in the same sentence (backward co-reference), but in the second sentence *he* cannot be John: Here, backward co-reference is not allowed. These intuitions are explained by the third binding principle:

Principle C: Backward co-reference is allowed only if the pronoun is in a subordinate clause to the main referent.

From a developmental perspective, we can ask when children seem to know these principles. Dozens of experiments have been conducted on children's knowledge of all three principles, using a variety of tasks and paradigms. One example is a study by Chien and Wexler (1990), which looked at children's knowledge of Principles A and B. In one experiment, children were asked to judge the truth of sentences paired with pictures. (Some of the test pictures and sentences used are shown in Figure 5.9.)

In this study, the researchers found that by age 6, children knew Principle A but were still making errors on pronouns (Principle B), for example, saying "yes" to the question accompanying illustration (46). Some have argued that the grammatical knowledge of Principle B is absent until after the age of 6 or 7 (the "Delay of Principle B Effect"); others *figure 5.9*   **A Test of Anaphora—How Pronouns Must Be Used in a Sentence.**   *(From Y.-C. Chein & K. Wexler, Children's knowledge of locality conditions in binding as evidence for the modularity of syntax and pragmatics. Language Acquisition* [1990], *3,* 225–295. © Lawrence Erlbaum Associates. Reprinted with permission.)

The "Match" Cases	The "Mismatch" Cases

Name-Reflexive

(41) This is Goldilocks; this is Mama Bear.
Is Mama Bear <u>touching </u>herself?

Name-Reflexive

(45) This is Goldilocks; this is Mama Bear.
Is Mama Bear <u>touching </u>herself?

Name-Pronoun

(42) This is Mama Bear; this is Goldilocks.
Is Mama Bear <u>touching </u>her?

Name-Pronoun

(46) This is Mama Bear; this is Goldilocks.
Is Mama Bear touching her?

argue that children lack some important pragmatic knowledge (Foster-Cohen, 1994). Very many studies of Principle B have now been conducted with mixed results, with some studies confirming difficulty, and others not. Conroy, Takahashi, Lidz, and Phillips (2009) summarize all of these studies and conclude that a consideration of the differences among the methods used suggests that experimental factors may explain children's failure in Principle B studies, and they report three new studies showing that even 4-year-olds obey Principle B when the problematic experimental conditions are avoided (and they fail when the problematic conditions are reintroduced into the experiment). This suggests that knowledge of Principle B may indeed be present from an early age.

It also used to be thought that Principle C is not firmly controlled by children until the middle-school years (Hsu, Cairns, Eisenberg, & Schlisselberg, 1991), but it has since been shown in multiple studies that Principle C is mastered quite early (Crain & Thornton, 1998; Kazanina & Phillips, 2001; Leddon & Lidz, 2006). These studies demonstrate the dynamic nature of our understanding of the facts about early language development.

Interpreting "Empty" Subjects in Infinitive Clauses

It was noted at the beginning of this chapter that despite the surface similarity between "John is eager to please" and "John is easy to please," these two sentences are very different structurally. In one case, John is understood as the subject of the embedded clause "to please," and in the other case, John is understood as the object of the embedded clause, while the subject is left unspecified. Cromer (1970) gave children two puppets (a wolf and a duck) and asked them to act out sentences just like this ("The wolf is glad to bite" versus "The wolf is easy to bite"). He found that at a young age children act out both types of sentences by making the wolf (the named animal in the sentence) bite the duck. By age 6, children sometimes made the non-named animal do the biting, but they still had not learned which adjectives require this interpretation and which ones disallow it. Subsequent work with older age groups (Cromer, 1972) demonstrated that children do not reach adult levels of performance until age 10 or 11.

Although the reason for the special difficulty of these structures is not known, a fascinating longitudinal study has shown that children's development of these structures may be accelerated by merely asking them periodically to act out examples of the two types of sentences, without any feedback being given at all. Cromer (1987) first tested a group of thirty-three 8-year-olds and found a typical poor level of performance: Only 15 percent of them interpreted sentences like "The wolf is easy to bite" in an adult-like manner. He then administered the same test to them every three months for one year. No feedback was ever given on their performance. In this now 9-year-old age group, 54 percent of children performed like adults. By contrast, in cross-sectional studies, no more than 20 percent of 9-year-olds performed like adults. Cromer's findings seem to suggest that, while children are doing most of the work of development by themselves, in some cases simple manipulations of the input, such as merely providing children with extra opportunities to "work on" particular constructions, can accelerate their development (see Chapter 7).

Knowledge versus Processing

During early childhood, a child's grammar is not the only system that is undergoing development. At the same time, a child's ability to comprehend and produce sentences in real time is developing. Even if children have the grammatical knowledge necessary to generate a particular sentence, more than this is needed to produce it successfully or to comprehend it. Utterances are linear strings of words that unfold one word at a time. In order to produce a sentence, a child has to map an idea onto a sentence structure that expresses that idea, insert lexical items into appropriate parts of that structure, and utter those lexical items in correct left-to-right order. Similarly, in order to comprehend a sentence, a child has to transform a linear string of words that she hears onto a hierarchical structure that cannot be heard in the speech signal and, from this, compute the speaker's intended message.

It is still poorly understood, even for adults, how these language-processing systems interface with the grammatical system—how, for example, speakers "find" structures that are appropriate for expressing their ideas, how they manage, most of the time, to avoid producing sentences that violate the rules of the grammar, and how they manage to "recover" on those occasions when they realize they have made a mistake (see Levelt, 1989, for the most articulated model of language production in adults). Children's production and comprehension processing systems surely undergo development and improve over time, but work examining such development has only just begun. (See Trueswell, Sekerina, Hill, &

Logrip, 1999, for work on child–adult differences in the ability to reanalyze the meaning of a sentence during sentence comprehension; and see Rispoli & Hadley, 2001, for work showing that rates of disfluencies in children's sentences may reflect differences in how automatized the production of different syntactic structures has become.)

Some of the patterns that are observed in young children's syntax may reflect immature processing systems instead of, or in addition to, an immature grammatical system. For example, recall that passive sentences with actional verbs are not produced until age 4 or 5 by children learning English. The late development of passives could reflect an immature grammar (not knowing the passive structure), or it could reflect an immature processing system (one that has difficulty "finding" or accessing the passive structure, because it is so infrequent in English). Evidence for a processing explanation comes from a structural priming study with young 3-year-olds (2;11 to 3;6). Bencini & Valian (2006) showed that if children are first asked to repeat a full passive sentence, they are more likely than children who repeated an active sentence to subsequently describe a new event (with no overlapping lexical items) using a full passive. This result dovetails nicely with the cross-linguistic results showing that children learning languages in which the passive is very frequent are able to produce passives easily by age 3. That is, passives seem to be within the grammatical abilities of 3-year-olds, but these structures may be difficult to access for children who have very little occasion to hear them, due to their low frequency in the language.

Researchers interested in child language processing have recently begun to use technologies that measure rapid responses that are not under a child's conscious control, such as eye movements and patterns of electrical activity in the brain, which are measured with **electroencephalography (EEG)**. For example, in studies of adults, researchers have found robust evidence for specific brain responses to a variety of components of language processing. These responses are changes in scalp voltages that are time-locked to the presentation of particular types of linguistic stimuli, and they are measured noninvasively via electrode caps placed on the head. For example, when adults hear a word that is semantically incongruent with the beginning of a sentence, as in "I take my coffee with cream and DOG," their response to the unexpected word *(dog)* is reflected in a negative voltage deflection that peaks approximately 400 milliseconds after the onset of the word (the "N400"), and which is largest over central regions of the scalp (Kutas & Hillyard, 1980, 1984). The amplitude of the N400 varies with word expectancy, with highly unexpected words yielding a larger N400 than moderately unexpected words. The N400 reflects processes involved in semantic processing, and may be related to a listener's ability to predict semantic information about upcoming words (Kutas & Federmeier, 2000). A very different brain response is observed when adults hear a word whose syntactic category is unexpected, as in "The broker persuaded TO sell the stock" or "The dog ate Max's OF picture his grandmother." In this case, adult brains respond with activity that presents as a positive voltage deflection over posterior scalp sites that peaks approximately 600 milliseconds after the first syntactically unexpected word (Friederici & Weissenborn, 2007). This response is known as the "P600." The P600 reflects processes involved in syntactic processing. Since these electrical potentials occur in response to particular language "events" such as the appearance of an unexpected word, they are called **event-related potentials (ERPs)**. The existence of these two distinct brain responses provides evidence that as adults process a sentence, both the semantic and the syntactic "fit" of each word is quickly and automatically evaluated with respect to the context, and that different brain processes are involved in calculating these two types of fit.

Child language researchers have recently become interested in whether young children exhibit N400-like and P600-like responses to semantically and syntactically unexpected words, and if so, at what age these components first appear, and how they change during development. At this time, the best

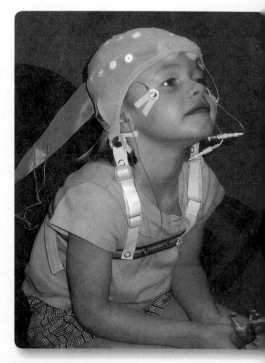

A 5-year-old child ready for an EEG experiment.

figure 5.10 **Age-Related Differences in Brain Responses.** These were measured at an anterior temporal scalp location to "best completion" words (e.g., "We saw elephants and monkeys at the ZOO") vs. anomolous words (e.g., "Kids learn to read and write in FINGER"). (From P. J. Holcomb, S. A. Coffey, & H. J. Neville, Visual and auditory sentence processing: A developmental analysis using event-related brain potentials. *Developmental Neuropsychology* [1992], *8*, 203–241.)

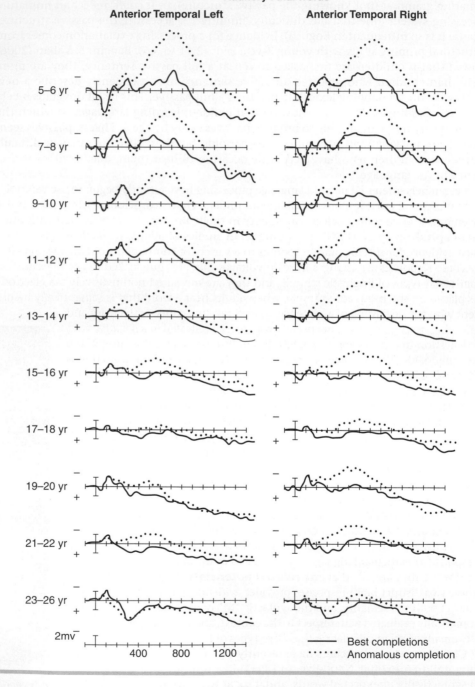

Auditory Final Words

Anterior Temporal Left · Anterior Temporal Right

5–6 yr · 7–8 yr · 9–10 yr · 11–12 yr · 13–14 yr · 15–16 yr · 17–18 yr · 19–20 yr · 21–22 yr · 23–26 yr

2mv · 400 · 800 · 1200

—— Best completions
· · · · Anomalous completion

investigated ERP component in both adults and children is the N400. In one of the earliest developmental studies of the N400, Holcomb, Coffey, and Neville (1992) examined children and adults from ages 5 to 26, using sentences ending with semantically anomalous words ("Kids learn to read and write in finger") versus sentences ending with "best completion" words ("We saw elephants and monkeys at the zoo"). Best completion words were those that more than 80 percent of second- and third-grade children had chosen when asked to fill in the final word of the sentence. Sentences were presented in auditory form in one study (for all ages) and in written form for another study (for age 7 and up). An N400-like component was observed for all age groups and for both modes of presentation, but some interesting differences were also found. The youngest children exhibited the highest-amplitude N400 to anomalous words (i.e., the largest N400), and the latest peak latency to the anomalous words (i.e., the slowest-peaking N400). Both the peak amplitude and the peak latency of the N400 component decreased markedly and linearly from age 5 to 15, and then stabilized. These patterns can be observed in Figure 5.10. These age-related changes in the N400 component may indicate developmental changes in the ability of children to predict semantic information about upcoming words, which may contribute to developmental changes in the speed and effort involved in comprehending sentences.

Surprisingly little subsequent work has examined the N400 as a response to unexpected words in a sentence context (one recent exception is work with 10-year-olds by Benau, Morris, & Couperus, 2011); most developmental work on the N400 in children has focused on words that are unexpected because they do not match a picture. Although this area of research is still in its infancy, the early findings suggest that this method can be used successfully with young children, and can reveal developmental changes in language processing. We can look forward to more of this work in the years to come.

SUMMARY

We have followed the course of children's acquisition of syntax and morphology from its very beginnings in Stage I until the end of the preschool years. During these few years children develop an extremely rich and intricate linguistic system. They go from expressing just a few simple meanings in two words to expressing abstract and complex ideas in multiword sentences. Yet the journey is not quite complete: Children continue in the early school years to acquire full structural knowledge of constructions such as passives, coordinations, and relative clauses. And all of this is accomplished with no formal instruction and little informal guidance or correction. The course of development is influenced by linguistic, semantic, and contextual factors that together determine the order of grammatical development. The acquisition of grammar is, indeed, one of the most remarkable and mysterious achievements of childhood.

SUGGESTED PROJECTS

1. This project is highly recommended in order to appreciate fully the richness of a spontaneous speech sample and its utility as a source of data and insight into the child's linguistic system. First, you need to collect a speech sample, or you could download transcripts from the CHILDES system. Most researchers rely on audio recordings of naturalistic interactions between children and their mothers. About one hour is long enough to obtain a useful sample of child speech. If you wish to collect your own sample, you should assemble a group of toys, such as a dollhouse with furniture and suitable occupants, a set of blocks, animals and a farmhouse, and play dough—toys that will elicit comment by both mother and child. After a few minutes warming up, during which the child can get used to your presence, turn on your audio recording device and allow the child and mother to play naturally. Make sure that you are not intrusive.

To facilitate coding later on, it is important to make detailed notes about the ongoing activity and context associated with the child's remarks.

After the session is over, the recording should be transcribed as soon as possible, while your memories of the activities and the conversation are as fresh as possible. Divide the page down the middle into two halves. Keep the mother's speech on the right and the child's on the left. Contextual notes can be placed wherever relevant. Each new utterance should begin on a new line, to make a transcript that is both easy to read and easy to code. It is not always simple to judge when a new utterance or sentence begins. Try using falling intonation and pauses to mark breaks between utterances.

Once you have created the transcript in this way, it is ready for analysis. First, you could compute the mean length of utterance (MLU) for the child in the sample. Just follow the rules set out in Figure 5.4. The MLU will provide some indication about the child's current stage. If the child speaks a language other than English, calculating the MLU will be much trickier. You will have to come up with a new set of rules, comparable to those for English, that will provide objective criteria for deciding what functions as a morpheme in the child's language.

The transcript can be used to analyze any number of syntactic forms, depending on the child's stage. For example, you could look in detail at how children are able to talk about the past. First you must decide, for each child utterance, whether it refers to the past, using the context or the mother's prior utterance. If it does, mark this utterance as an obligatory context for a past-tense verb. Then code the verb for whether it marks the past correctly. You can address many different questions in this analysis, for example: Do children mark the past more often for regular verbs or irregular verbs? Do the children use the past tense more frequently if the mother has been using the past tense in her preceding utterances? Do children make overregularization errors?

2. It is becoming increasingly popular to use an elicited-production technique to complement spontaneous speech samples as a source of production data. The main advantage of this method is that the experimenter can control which forms the children should produce, so that one can test the children to their limits. One way of eliciting forms reliably is to use a puppet that is manipulated by a second experimenter. In this project it is suggested that you use a puppet to elicit questions from children.

Select a sample of children between about 2½ and 5 years old. You should see each child individually. Introduce the child to the puppet and explain that he's afraid of grown-ups and will only talk to children and that you have some questions that you would like to ask him. Ask the child to help, and then prompt the child to ask particular questions by whispering the elicitation prompts below. The examples show how to elicit a yes/no question, a *wh*-question, and a negative *wh*-question. The target response for each question is also provided in the examples. For these examples, assume that the puppet's name is Elmo.

Experimenter:	I think Elmo can drive, but I'm not sure. Ask him for me.
Target Response:	Can you drive?
Experimenter:	Elmo likes so many foods—applesauce, pizza, carrots. But that's not all. Ask him what else he likes.
Target Response:	What (else) do you like?
Experimenter:	Elmo sure likes a lot of different foods. But I'm sure he doesn't like everything. Ask him what he doesn't like.
Target Response:	What don't you like?

You can continue to use this method to elicit questions of your own choosing. If you find that a child makes a particular type of mistake, such as a negative-question error like "What do you don't like?" you might want to follow up with additional prompts for negative questions in order to better determine the child's pattern.

Provide the child with plenty of encouragement and praise. Present the test sentences in random order and record what the child says.

You will need to transcribe your recordings before the data can be analyzed. Check which sentences the children get right and which ones have errors. Look for improvements with age. Examine the kinds of errors that children make at different age levels. Look for systematic patterns of correct and incorrect responses, both by subject and by age group. What do your findings tell about the developmental course of the syntax of questions?

3. One of the most suitable ways for assessing children's understanding of language is to have them act out sentences or phrases, using toys. This project can be done with very young children (2- and early 3-year-olds) who are still in the process of acquiring grammatical morphology. The purpose of this project is to find out whether children who omit inflections and function words (such as articles, tense endings, and prepositions) understand equally well sentences that are presented with and without such elements.

You will need to select children who are still in their early stages of language development and are still omitting inflections. Try recording several young 2- and 3-year-olds for about 10 minutes and examine their speech for the presence or absence of the morphemes listed in Table 5.3. When you have your subjects picked out, you will need to demonstrate the procedure. You will need to see each child one at a time. First, give the child two toys and then tell the child that you will say something that she should show you with the toys. Then give a sample sentence: "The boy pats the dog." If the child doesn't know what to do, show her, and then have her repeat the action. Give several more examples using correct syntax.

Once the child understands the task, present your test sentences. Half of these should be presented normally, including all of the relevant morphology. Because your subjects will be very young, you will need to make the sentences simple, with only a single clause. The other half of the sentences should be presented without relevant morphology, but in other respects they should be like the normal sentences.

Normal:	The boy puts the ball on the table.
No inflections:	Girl put book chair.
Normal:	The cow pushes the kangaroo.
No inflections:	Dog hit horse.

Make up about eight sentences of each kind (complete and without inflections) and collect the toys you will need for all of them. Before giving the sentence, place the relevant toys in front of the child. Write down exactly what the child does with the toys.

Code the children's responses as correct/incorrect. Compare within and across ages the percentage correct on normal sentences and that on sentences without inflections. What do your results tell you about young children's use of morphology in comprehension before they can produce that morphology?

SUGGESTED READINGS

Brown, R. (1973). *A first language.* Cambridge, MA: Harvard University Press.

Christophe, A., Milotte, S., Bernal, S., & Lidz, J. (2008). Bootstrapping lexical and syntactic acquisition. *Language and Speech, 51,* 61–75.

McDaniel, D., McKee, C., & Cairns, H. S. (Eds.). (1996). *Methods for assessing children's syntax.* Cambridge, MA: MIT Press.

Menn, L., & Bernstein Ratner, N. (Eds.). (2000). *Methods for studying language production.* Mahwah, NJ: Erlbaum.

Montrul, S. A. (2004). *The acquisition of Spanish: Morphosyntactic development in monolingual and bilingual L1 acquisition and adult L2 acquisition.* Philadelphia: John Benjamins.

KEY WORDS

actional verbs
anaphora
binding principles
center-embedded relative
   clause
closed-class words
Comp
coordination
d-structure
electroencephalography
   (EEG)
event-related potentials
   (ERPs)
functional category
government and binding
   theory
head
Index of Productive Syntax
   (IPSyn)

Infl
learnability
lexical category
limited scope formulae
logical form
long-distance question
mean length of utterance
   (MLU)
negation
null-subject parameter
object-gap relative clause
open-class word
optional infinitive stage
overregularization
   errors
parameters
passive
phonetic form
phrase structure rule

preferential looking
   paradigm
psychological verbs
relative clauses
right-branching relative
   clause
semantic relations
semantic roles
sentence modality
s-structure
subject-gap relativeclause
syntax
telegraphic speech
thematic roles
transformational rule
universal grammar
universality
wh-question
yes/no question

REFERENCES

Aksu-Koc, A. A. (1988). *The acquisition of aspect and modality.* Cambridge, UK: Cambridge University Press.

Allen, S. E. M., & Crago, M. (1996). Early passive acquisition in Inuktitut. *Journal of Child Language, 23,* 129–156.

Argyri, E., & Sorace, A. (2007). Crosslinguistic influence and language dominance in older bilingual children. *Bilingualism: Language and Cognition, 10,* 77–99.

Bar-Shalom, E., Crain, S., & Shankweiler, D. (1993). A comparison of comprehension and production abilities of good and poor readers. *Applied Psycholinguistics, 14,* 197–227.

Bar-Shalom, E., & Snyder, W. (1997). Optional infinitives in child Russian and their implications for the pro-drop debate. In M. Lindseth and S. Franks (Eds.), *Formal approaches to Slavic linguistics: The Indiana Meeting 1996.* Ann Arbor: MI: Slavic Publications.

Bassano, D., & Mendes-Maillochon, I. (1994). Early grammatical and prosodic marking of utterance modality in French: A longitudinal case study. *Journal of Child Language, 21,* 649–675.

Bates, E., Dale, P., & Thal, D. (1995). Individual differences and their implications for theories of language development. In P. Fletcher & B. MacWhinney (Eds.), *The handbook of child language* (pp. 96–151). Oxford: Blackwell.

Behrens, H. (1993). *Temporal reference in German child language.* Unpublished Ph.D. dissertation. Amsterdam, The Netherlands: University of Amsterdam.

Bellugi, U. (1967). *The acquisition of negation.* Unpublished doctoral dissertation. Cambridge, MA: Harvard University.

Bellugi, U. (1971). Simplification in children's language. In R. Huxley and E. Ingram (Eds.), *Methods and models in language acquisition.* New York: Academic Press.

Benau, E. M., Morris, J., & Couperus, J. W. (2011). Semantic processing in children and adults: Incongruity and the N400. *Journal of Psycholinguistic Research, 40*(3), 225–239.

Bencini, G., & Valian, V. (2006, November). *Abstract sentence representations in*

3-year-olds: Evidence from language comprehension and production. Boston University Conference on Language Development, Boston, MA.

Berent, I., Pinker, S., & Shimron, J. (2002). The nature of regularity and irregularity: Evidence from Hebrew nominal inflection. *Journal of Psycholinguistic Research, 31,* 459–502.

Berko, J. (1958). The child's learning of English morphology. *Word, 14,* 150–177.

Bernal, S., Dehaene-Lambertz, G., Millotte, S., & Christophe, A. (2010). Two-year-olds compute syntactic structure online. *Developmental Science,* 13(1), 69–76.

Betancur, C. (2011). Etiological heterogeneity in autism spectrum disorders: More than 100 genetic and genomic disorders and still counting. *Brain Research,* 138042–138077.

Bever, T. G. (1970). The cognitive basis for linguistic structure. In J. R. Hayes (Ed.), *Cognition and the development of language.* New York: Wiley.

Bloom, L. (1970). *Language development: Form and function in emerging grammars.* Cambridge, MA: MIT Press.

Bloom, L., Hood, L., & Lightbown, P. (1974). Imitation in language development: If, when and why. *Cognitive Psychology, 6,* 380–420.

Bloom, L., Lahey, J., Hood, L., Lifter, K., & Fiess, K. (1980). Complex sentences: Acquisition of syntactic connectives and the semantic relations they encode. *Journal of Child Language, 7,* 235–261.

Bornstein, M. H., Cote, L. R., Maital, S., Painter, K., Sung-Yun, P., Pascual, L., & Vyt, A. (2004). Cross-linguistic analysis of vocabulary in young children: Spanish, Dutch, French, Hebrew, Italian, Korean, and American English. *Child Development,* 75(4), 1115–1139.

Bowerman, M. (1973). *Early syntactic development. A cross-linguistic study with special reference to Finnish.* Cambridge, UK: Cambridge University Press.

Braine, M. D. S. (1976). Children's first word combinations. *Monographs of the Society for Research in Child Development, 41* (Serial No. 164).

Brown, R. (1973). *A first language.* Cambridge, MA: Harvard University Press.

Brown, R., & Fraser, C. (1963). The acquisition of syntax. In C. N. Cofer & B. Musgrave (Eds.), *Verbal behavior and learning: Problems and processes.* New York: McGraw-Hill.

Brown, R., & Hanlon, C. (1970). Derivational complexity and the order of acquisition in child speech. In J. R. Hayes (Ed.), *Cognition and the development of language.* New York: Wiley.

Caselli, M. C., Casadio, P., & Bates, E. (1999). A comparison of the transition from first words to grammar in English and Italian. *Journal of Child Language, 26,* 69–111.

Cazden, C. (1968). The acquisition of noun and verb inflections. *Child Development, 39,* 433–448.

Chemla, E., Mintz, T., Bernal, S., & Christophe, A. (2009). Categorizing words using "frequent frames": What cross-linguistic analyses reveal about distributional acquisition strategies. *Developmental Science,* 12(3), 396–406.

Chien, Y.-C., & Wexler, K. (1990). Children's knowledge of locality conditions in binding as evidence for the modularity of syntax and pragmatics. *Language Acquisition, 3,* 225–295.

Chomsky, N. (1981). *Lectures on government and binding.* Dordrecht, The Netherlands: Foris.

Chomsky, N. (1982). *Some concepts and consequences of the theory of government and binding.* Cambridge, MA: MIT Press.

Chomsky, N. (1995). *The minimalist program.* Cambridge, MA: MIT Press.

Christophe, A., Millotte, S., Brusini, P., & Cauvet, E. (2010). Early bootstrapping of syntactic acquisition. In M. Kail & M. Hickmann (Eds.), *Language acquisition across linguistic and cognitive systems* (pp. 53–66). Amsterdam, The Netherlands: Benjamins.

Clahsen, H., Aveledo, F., & Roca, I. (2002). The development of regular and irregular verb inflection in Spanish child language. *Journal of Child Language, 29,* 591–622.

Cole, P., Hermon, G., & Tjung, Y. (2005). The formation of relative clauses in Jakarta Indonesian: Data from adults and children. In A. van Engelenhoven

& H. Steinhauer (Eds.), *Selected studies on Indonesian/Malay linguistics*. Leiden/Amsterdam: International Institute for Asian Studies.

Conroy, S., Takahashi, E., Lidz, J., & Phillips, C. (2009). Equal treatment for all antecedents: How children succeed with Principle B. *Linguistic Inquiry, 40,* 446–486.

Crain, S., & Thornton, R. (1998). *Investigations in universal grammar.* Cambridge, MA: MIT Press.

Cromer, R. F. (1970). Children are nice to understand: Surface structure clues for the recovery of a deep structure. *British Journal of Psychology, 61,* 397–408.

Cromer, R. F. (1972). The learning of surface structure clues to deep structure by a puppet show techique. *Quarterly Journal of Experimental Psychology, 24,* 66–76.

Cromer, R. F. (1987). Language growth with experience without feedback. *Journal of Psycholinguistic Research, 16,* 3, 223–231.

Dabrowska, E. (2001). Learning a morphological system without a default: The Polish genitive. *Journal of Child Language, 28,* 545–574.

Demuth, K. (1990). Subject, topic and Sesotho passive. *Journal of Child Language, 17,* 67–84.

de Villiers, J. G. (1995). Empty categories and complex sentences: The case of *wh*-questions. In P. Fletcher & B. MacWhinney (Eds.), *The handbook of child language* (pp. 508–540). Oxford, UK: Blackwell.

de Villiers, J. G., Roeper, T., & Vainikka, A. (1990). The acquisition of long distance rules. In L. Frazier & J. G. de Villiers (Eds.), *Language processing and acquisition.* Dordrecht, The Netherlands: Kluwer Academic.

de Villiers, J. G., Tager-Flusberg, H., & Hakuta, K. (1977). Deciding among theories of the development of coordination in child speech. *Papers and Reports on Child Language Development, 13,* 118–125.

de Villiers, J. G., Tager-Flusberg, H. B., Hakuta, K., & Cohen, M. (1979). Children's comprehension of relative clauses. *Journal of Psycholinguistic Research, 17,* 57–64.

de Villiers, P. A., & de Villiers, J. G. (1979). Form and function in the development of sentence negation. *Papers and Reports on Child Language Development, 17,* 56–64.

Dimroth, C. (2010). The acquisition of negation. In L. Horn (Ed.), *The expression of negation.* Walter de Gruyter: New York.

Dromi, E., & Berman, R. A. (1982). A morphemic measure of early language development: Data from modern Hebrew. *Journal of Child Language, 9,* 403–424.

Fenson, L., Marchman, V., Thal, D., Dale, P., Reznick, S., & Bates, E. (2007). *The MacArthur-Bates Communicative Development Inventories: User's guide and technical manual* (2nd ed.). Baltimore, MD: Paul Brookes.

Fernald, A., Taeschner, T., Dunn, J., Papousek, M., de Boysson-Bardies, B., & Fukui, I. (1989). A cross-language study of prosodic modifications in mothers' and fathers' speech to preverbal infants. *Journal of Child Language, 16,* 477–501.

Foster-Cohen, S. (1994). Exploring the boundary between syntax and pragmatics: Relevance and the binding of pronouns. *Journal of Child Language, 21,* 237–255.

Fox, D., & Grodzinsky, Y. (1998). Children's passive: A view from the by-phrase. *Linguistic Inquiry, 29,* 311–332.

Friederici, A. D., & Weissenborn, J. (2007). Mapping sentence form onto meaning: The syntax-semantic interface. *Brain Research, 1146,* 50–58.

Gibson, E., Desmet, T., Grodner, D., Watson, D., & Ko, K. (2005). Reading relative clauses in English. *Cognitive Linguistics 16,* 2, 313–353.

Gleitman, L. R., & Wanner, E. (1982). Language acquisition: The state of the art. In E. Wanner & L. R. Gleitman (Eds.), *Language acquisition: The state of the art.* Cambridge, MA: Harvard University Press.

Golinkoff, R. M., & Hirsh-Pasek, K. (1995). Reinterpreting children's sentence comprehension: Toward a new framework. In P. Fletcher & B. MacWhinney (Eds.), *The handbook of child language* (pp. 430–461). Oxford, UK: Blackwell.

Gopnik, A., & Choi, S. (1995). Names, relational words, and cognitive development in English and Korean speakers: Nouns are not always learned before words. In M. Tomasello & W. Merriman (Eds.), *Beyond names for things: Young children's acquisition of verbs*. Hillsdale, NJ: Erlbaum.

Grinstead, J. (2000). Case, inflection and subject licensing in child Catalan and Spanish. *Journal of Child Language, 27*, 119–155.

Grinstead, J., De la Mora, J., Vega-Mendoza, M., & Flores, B. (2009). An elicited production test of the optional infinitive stage in child Spanish. In J. Crawford, K. Otaki, & M. Takahashi (Eds.), *Generative approaches to language acquisition—North America* (GALANA 2008), p. 36–45. Somerville, MA: Cascadilla Press.

Grinstead, Vega-Mendoza, & Goodall (2010). *Subject-verb inversion and verb finiteness are independent in Spanish*. Presented at the Boston University Conference on Language Development.

Guasti, M. (1992). Verb syntax in Italian child grammar. *Geneva Generative Papers, 1–2*, 115–122.

Guasti, M., Thornton, R., & Wexler, K. (1995). Negation in children's questions: The case of English. In D. MacLaughlin and S. McEwen (Eds.), *Proceedings of the 19th Annual Boston University Conference on Language Development*. Cambridge, MA: Cascadilla Press.

Haegeman, L. (1995). Root infinitives, tense, and truncated structures in Dutch. *Language Acquisition, 4*, 3, 205–255.

Hakuta, K., de Villiers, J. G., & Tager-Flusberg, H. (1982). Sentence coordination in Japanese and English. *Journal of Child Language, 9*, 193–207.

Hamann, C., & Plunkett, K. (1998). Subjectless sentences in child Danish. *Cognition, 69*, 1, 35–72.

Hamburger, H., & Crain, S. (1982). Relative acquisition. In S. A. Kuczaj (Ed.), *Language development, Vol. 1: Syntax and semantics*. Hillsdale, NJ: Erlbaum.

Hickey, T. (1991). Mean length of utterance and the acquisition of Irish. *Journal of Child Language, 18*, 553–569.

Hirsch, C., & Wexler, K. (2007). The late development of raising: What children seem to think about seem. In W. Davies & S. Dubinsky (Eds.), *New horizons in the analysis of control and raising*. Dordrecht: Springer.

Hirsh-Pasek, K. (2000). Beyond Shipley, Smith, and Gleitman: Young children's comprehension of bound morphemes. In B. Landau, J. Sabini, J. Jonides, & E. Newport (Eds.), *Perception, cognition and language: Essays in honor of Henry and Lila Gleitman* (pp. 191–208). Cambridge, MA: MIT Press.

Hirsh-Pasek, K., & Golinkoff, R. M. (1993). Skeletal supports for grammatical learning: What the infant brings to the language learning task. In C. K. Rovee-Collier (Ed.), *Advances in infancy research* (Vol. 10). Norwood, NJ: Ablex.

Hirsh-Pasek, K., & Golinkoff, R. M. (1996). *The origins of grammar: Evidence from early language comprehension*. Cambridge, MA: MIT Press.

Holcomb, P. J., Coffey, S. A., & Neville, H. J. (1992). Visual and auditory sentence processing: A developmental analysis using event-related brain potentials. *Developmental Neuropsychology, 8*, 203–241.

Horgan, D. (1978). The development of the full passive. *Journal of Child Language, 5*, 65–80.

Hsu, J. R., Cairns, H. S., Eisenberg, S., & Schlisselberg, G. (1991). When do children avoid backwards co-reference? *Journal of Child Language, 18*, 339–353.

Hung, F.-S., & Peters, A. M. (1997). The role of prosody in the acquisition of grammatical morphemes: Evidence from two Chinese languages. *Journal of Child Language, 24*, 627–650.

Hyams, N. M. (1986). *Language acquisition and the theory of parameters*. Dordrecht, The Netherlands: D. Reidel.

Hyams, N. M. (1989). The null-subject parameter in language acquisition. In O. Jaeggli & K. Safir (Eds.), *The null-subject parameter*. Dordrecht, The Netherlands: Kluwer Academic.

Imai, M., & Gentner, D. (1997). A crosslinguistic study of early word meaning: Universal ontology and linguistic influence. *Cognition, 62*, 169–200.

Ingham, R. (1992). The optional subject phenomenon in young children's English: A case study. *Journal of Child Language, 19,* 133–151.

Jusczyk, P. W. (1997). *The discovery of spoken language.* Cambridge, MA: MIT Press.

Kazanina, N., & Phillips, C. (2001). Coreference in child Russian: Distinguishing syntactic and discourse constraints. In A. H.-J. Do, L. Dominguez & A. Johansen (Eds), *Proceedings of the 25th annual Boston University Conference on Language Development.* Somerville, MA: Cascadilla Press.

Keenan, E. L., & Comrie, B. (1977). NP accessibility and universal grammar. *Linguistic Inquiry, 8,* 63–100.

Klammler, A., & Schneider, S. (2011). The size and composition of the productive holophrastic lexicon: German-Italian bilingual acquisition vs. Italian monolingual acquisition. *International Journal of Bilingual Education and Bilingualism, 14*(1), 69–88.

Klima, E., & Bellugi, U. (1966). Syntactic regularities in the speech of children. In J. Lyons & R. Wales (Eds.), *Psycholinguistic papers.* Edinburgh, UK: Edinburgh University Press.

Kuczaj, S. (1976). *-ing, -s and -ed: A study of the acquisition of certain verb inflections.* Unpublished doctoral dissertation. Minneapolis: University of Minnesota.

Kutas, M., & Federmeier, K. D. (2000). Electrophysiology reveals semantic memory use in language comprehension, *Trends in Cognitive Science, 12,* 4, pp. 463–470.

Kutas, M., & Hillyard, S. A. (1980). Reading senseless sentences: Brain potentials reflect semantic incongruity. *Science, 207,* 203–205.

Kutas, M., & Hillyard, S. A. (1984). Event-related brain potentials (ERPs) elicited by "novel" stimuli during sentence processing. In R. Karrer, J. Cohen, & P. Tueting (Eds.), *Brain information: Event-related potentials* (pp. 236–241). New York: New York Academy of Sciences, Vol. 425.

Leddon, E., & Lidz, J. (2006). Reconstruction effects in child language. In D. Bamman, T. Magnitskaia,

& C. Zaller (Eds), *Proceedings of the 30th annual Boston University Conference on Language Development.* Somerville, MA: Cascadilla Press.

Levelt, W. J. M. (1989). *Speaking: From intention to articulation.* Cambridge, MA: MIT Press.

Levy, Y. (1988). On the early learning of formal grammatical systems: Evidence from studies of the acquisition of gender and countability. *Journal of Child Language, 15,* 179–187.

Lieven, E., Behrens, H., Speares, J., & Tomasello, M. (2003). Early syntactic creativity: A usage-based approach. *Journal of Child Language, 30,* 333–370.

MacWhinney, B. (2000). *The CHILDES Project: Tools for analyzing talk.* Mahwah, NJ: Erlbaum.

Marcus, G., Pinker, S., Ullman, M., Hollander, M., Rosen, J., & Xu, F. (1992). Overregularization in language acquisition. *Monographs of the Society for Research in Child Development, 57* (Serial No. 228).

McClelland, J., & Patterson, K. (2002). Rules or connections in past-tense inflections: What does the evidence rule out? *Trends in Cognitive Sciences, 6,* 465–472.

McDaniel, D., McKee, C., & Bernstein, J. B. (1998). How children's relatives solve a problem for minimalism. *Language, 74,* 308–334.

McDaniel, D., McKee, C., & Cairns, H. (Eds.). (1996). *Methods for assessing children's syntax.* Cambridge, MA: MIT Press.

Menn, L., & Bernstein Ratner, N. (Eds.). (2000). *Methods for studying language production.* Mahwah, NJ: Erlbaum.

Miller, J. F., & Chapman, R. S. (1981). The relation between age and mean length of utterance in morphemes. *Journal of Speech and Hearing Research, 24,* 154–161.

Mintz, T. H. (2003). Frequent frames as a cue for grammatical categories in child directed speech. *Cognition, 90*(1), 91–117.

Morgan, J. L. (1986). *From simple input to complex grammar.* Cambridge, MA: MIT Press.

Paradis, J., & Navarro, S. (2003). Subject realization and crosslinguistic interference in the bilingual acquisition of Spanish and English: What is the role of input? *Journal of Child Language, 30,* 1–23.

Perez-Leroux, A. T. (1993). *Empty categories and the acquisition of wh-movement.* Unpublished Ph.D. dissertation. Amherst: University of Massachusetts.

Pierce, A. (1992) *Language acquisition and syntactic theory: A comparative analysis of French and English child grammars.* Dordrecht, The Netherlands: Kluwer Academic.

Pine, J., & Lieven, E. (1997). Slot-frame patterns and the development of the determiner category. *Applied Psycholinguistics, 18,* 123–138.

Pinker, S. (1984). *Language learnability and language development.* Cambridge, MA: Harvard University Press.

Pinker, S. (1987). Constraint satisfaction networks as implementations of nativist theories of language acquisition. In B. MacWhinney (Ed.), *Mechanisms of language learning.* Hillsdale, NJ: Erlbaum.

Pinker, S. (1999). *Words and rules.* New York: Basic Books

Pinker, S., & Ullman, M. (2002). The past and future of the past tense. *Trends in Cognitive Sciences, 6,* 456–463.

Platzack, C. (1990). A grammar without functional categories: A syntactic study of early Swedish child language. *Working Papers in Scandinavian Syntax, 45,* 13–34. Lund, Sweden: University of Lund.

Pratt, A. & Grinstead, J. (2008). Receptive measures of the optional infinitive stage in child Spanish. In J. B. d. Garavito & E. Valenzuela (Eds.), *Proceedings of the Hispanic Linguistic Symposium,* 120–133. University of Western Ontario, London, Ontario. Cascadilla Press.

Radford, A. (1990). *Syntactic theory and the acquisition of English syntax.* Oxford: Blackwell.

Rice, M. L., & Wexler, K. (1996). Toward tense as a clinical marker of specific language impairment in English-speaking children. *Journal of Speech and Hearing Research, 39,* 1239–1257.

Rice, M. L., Wexler, K., & Hershberger, S. (1998). Tense over time: The longitudinal course of tense acquisition in children with specific language impairment. *Journal of Speech, Language, and Hearing Research, 41*(6), 1412–1431.

Rispoli, M., & Hadley, P. (2001). The leading edge: The significance of sentence disruptions in the development of grammar. *Journal of Speech, Language and Hearing Research, 44,* 1131–1143.

Rowland, C. F., & Pine, J. (2000). Subject–auxiliary inversion errors and *wh-*question acquisition: "What children do know?" *Journal of Child Language, 27,* 157–182.

Rumelhart, D., & McClelland, J. (1986). On learning the past tense of English verbs. In J. McClelland, D. Rumelhart, and the PDP Research Group (Eds.), *Parallel distributed processing: Explorations in the microstructure of cognition, Vol. 2: Psychological and biological models* (pp. 216–271). Cambridge, MA: MIT/Bradford.

Sachs, J. (1983). Talking about the there and then: The emergence of displaced reference in parent–child discourse. In K. E. Nelson (Ed.), *Children's language, Vol. 4.* Mahwah, NJ: Erlbaum.

Santelmann, L., Berk, S., Austin, J., Somashekar, S., & Lust, B. (2002). Continuity and development in the acquisition of inversion in yes/no questions: Dissociating movement and inflection. *Journal of Child Language, 29,* 813–842.

Scarborough, H. (1989). Index of productive syntax. *Applied Psycholinguistics, 11,* 1–22.

Serratrice, L. (2007). Cross-linguistic influence in the interpretation of anaphoric and cataphoric pronouns in English–Italian bilingual children. *Bilingualism: Language and Cognition, 10,* 225–238.

Shady, M., & Gerken, L. (1999). Grammatical and caregiver cues in early sentence comprehension. *Journal of Child Language, 26,* 163–175.

Shi, R., Morgan, J., & Allopena, P. (1998). Phonological and acoustic bases for earliest grammatical category assignment: A cross-linguistic perspective. *Journal of Child Language, 25,* 169–201.

Sorace, A., & Serratrice, L. (2009). Internal and external interfaces in bilingual language development: Beyond structural overlap. *International Journal of Bilingualism, 13,* 195–210.

Stromswold, K. (1995). The acquisition of subject and object *wh*-questions. *Language Acquisition, 4,* 5–48.

Stromswold, K. (1996). Analyzing children's spontaneous speech. In D. McDaniel, C. McKee, & H. S. Cairns (Eds.), *Methods for assessing children's syntax* (pp. 23–53). Cambridge, MA: MIT Press.

Suzman, S. (1987). Passives and proto-types in Zulu children's speech. *African Studies, 46,* 241–254.

Tager-Flusberg, H. (1982). The development of relative clauses in child speech. *Papers and Reports on Child Language Development, 21,* 104–111.

Tamis-Lemonda, C. S., Bornstein, M. H., Kahana-Kalman, R., Baumwell, L., & Cyphers, L. (1998). Predicting variation in the timing of language milestones in the second year: An events history approach. *Journal of Child Language, 25,* 675–700.

Tardiff, T. (1996). Nouns are not always learned before verbs: Evidence from Mandarin speakers' early vocabularies. *Developmental Psychology, 32,* 492–504.

Tjung, Y. (2006). *Relative clause formation in Jakarta Indonsian: Subject/object asymmetries.* Unpublished doctoral dissertation, Newark: University of Delaware.

Tomasello, M. (2003). *Constructing a language: A usage-based theory of language acquisition.* Cambridge, MA: Harvard University Press.

Tomasello, M., Akhtar, N., Dodson, K., & Rekau, L. (1997). Differential productivity in young children's use of nouns and verbs. *Journal of Child Language, 24,* 373–387.

Traxler, M., Morris, R., & Seely, R. (2002). Processing subject and object relative clauses: Evidence from eye movements. *Journal of Memory and Language 47,* 69–90.

Trueswell, J., Sekerina, I., Hill, N., & Logrip, M. (1999). The kindergarten-path effect: Studying on-line sentence processing in young children. *Cognition, 73,* 89–134.

Ullman, M. (2001). A neurocognitive perspective on language: The declarative/procedural model. *Nature Reviews Neuroscience, 2,* 717–726.

Valian, V. (1990). Null subjects: A problem for parameter-setting models of language acquisition. *Cognition, 35,* 105–122.

Valian, V. V. (1992). Categories of first syntax: Be, being, and nothingness. In J. Meisel (Ed)., *The acquisition of verb placement: Functional categories and V–2 phenomena.* Dordrecht, The Netherlands: Kluwer Academic.

Valian, V., Solt, S., & Stewart, J. (2009). Abstract categories or limited-scope formulae? The case of children's determiners. *Journal of Child Language, 36*(4), 743–778.

Wasow, T. (1977). Transformations and the lexicon. In P. Culicover (Ed.), *Formal syntax.* New York: Academic Press.

Weisleder, A., & Waxman, S. R. (2010). What's in the input? Frequent frames in child-directed speech offer distributional cues to grammatical categories in Spanish and English. *Journal of Child Language, 37*(5), 1089–1108.

Wexler, K. (1994). Optional infinitives, head movement, and economy of derivation. In N. Hornstein & D. Lightfoot (Eds.), *Verb movement.* Cambridge, UK: Cambridge University Press.

Winzemer, J. A. (1980, October). *A lexical expectation model for children's comprehension of wh-questions.* Paper presented at the Fifth Annual Boston University Conference on Language Development.

Wootten, J., Merkin, S., Hood, L., & Bloom, L. (1979, March). *Wh-questions: Linguistic evidence to explain the sequence of acquisition.* Paper presented at the biennial meeting of the Society for Research in Child Development, San Francisco.

Zukowski, A. (2009). Elicited production of relative clauses in children with Williams Syndrome. *Language and Cognitive Processes, 24,* 1–43.

Language in Social Contexts

Development of Communicative Competence

Judith Becker Bryant
University of South Florida

This chapter explores the concept of communicative competence. Consider the following interaction between two 4-year-olds. Child A is approaching a large toy car on which Child B has been sitting (Garvey, 1975, p. 42):

Child A:	Pretend this was my car.
Child B:	No!
Child A:	Pretend this was our car.
Child B:	(reluctantly) All right.
Child A:	Can I drive your car?
Child B:	Yes, okay. (smiles and moves away from the car)
Child A:	(turns wheel and makes driving noises)

Four-year-old Child A has already learned to modify her language to get what she wants—in this case to get her peer to let her use a toy car. When her first strategy fails, she rephrases herself until she succeeds. This example illustrates the fact that, when children are learning language, it is important for them to learn more than just phonology, semantics, and syntax. As is probably apparent, being a skilled language user means knowing how to use one's language appropriately and strategically in social situations. Children need to acquire **communicative competence** (Hymes, 1967). They must learn how to make language work in interactions with their families, peers, teachers, and others.

Now imagine a 4-year-old boy saying to someone, "I went cough and [food] went flying right there." This might be an effective way to initiate conversation with a peer (O'Neill, Main, & Ziemski, 2009). However, the sentence would not be appropriate if he said it to a stranger in a restaurant. Whether language is appropriate depends on how it is used in particular contexts. As Hymes put it, appropriateness is a function of the interaction of language and social setting. This is one of the main themes explored in this chapter.

Many skills are involved in communicative competence because we use language for so many purposes. Children need to learn to ask questions, make requests, give orders, express agreement or disagreement, apologize, refuse, joke, praise, and tell stories. They must learn **routines** and polite terms such as "trick or treat," "please" and "thank you," "hello" and "goodbye," "excuse me," and ways to address others. They must learn to initiate, maintain, and conclude conversations; know when to speak or be quiet and how to take turns; to provide and respond effectively to feedback; and to stay on topic. They must know and use the appropriate volume and tone of voice. They need to learn how the meanings of terms such as "I" and "you" and "here" and "there" vary in meaning according to who is speaking and who is listening. They must learn what styles of speech to use and appreciate the ways that speech styles signal membership in social groups; when to use jargon or particular dialects and languages; and when and whether to talk about certain subjects. In some languages other than English, children acquire polite and informal pronouns (e.g., *tu* and *usted* in Spanish) or several systems of words and expressions (e.g., to convey degrees of respect and social distance in Japanese). Bilingual children must learn which language to use with different conversational partners. With all of these skills, children must learn to be sensitive to their audience and to the situations in which they are communicating.

We can think about audience and situation (i.e., communicative context) as involving many levels. There is the immediate context that includes prior conversation, task and setting, relationship between speaker and listener, and listener characteristics. There are also broader contexts such as the culture or cultures in which children develop and communicate. To be competent and effective, speakers must learn to take all of these contexts into account.

In this chapter, I refer to the appropriate use of language in social situations using the broad term *communicative competence*. Others refer to the same and similar behaviors with other terms such as *pragmatics, discourse,* and *sociolinguistics*.

Routines such as "trick or treat" are essential aspects of children's growing communicative competence.

Clearly, the acquisition of communicative competence is complex because it involves so many different skills and requires that children be responsive to many contextual variations. Yet, remarkably, even very young children demonstrate some degree of competence.

This chapter begins with a section on the development of particular language skills in social contexts. Then there is a discussion of why acquisition is difficult for young children. Following this is evidence concerning how children acquire communicative competence. The chapter concludes with a section on why it is important for children to acquire communicative competence.

Language in Social Contexts

Communicative competence entails the appropriate use of language in social contexts. It is precisely because communicative behaviors are so contextually sensitive that it is difficult to describe clear developmental progressions for each of them (although see Resnick & Snow, 2009, for general developmental guidelines). Preschoolers usually perform differently in laboratory experiments than in everyday interaction and converse differently with strangers than with those who are more familiar, making it hard to define and assess their level of competence. This section therefore focuses on several domains that provide relatively clear information about development: nonegocentric language, requests, conversational skills, and language varieties.

Nonegocentric Language

One of the earliest researchers to assess young children's communicative competence was Jean Piaget, a Swiss biologist who formulated influential theories of cognitive development (also see Chapter 7). In his 1926 book, *The Language and Thought of the Child* (1926/1974), Piaget argued that young children think and act more egocentrically than adults. To Piaget, **egocentrism** is the inability to take another person's point of view; the inability to recognize that others have different knowledge, feelings, thoughts, and perceptions or to know what the different knowledge, feelings, thoughts, and perceptions might be. An example of egocentric behavior is when a child waves at the telephone rather than saying "hello" to Grandma or talks about "the show" she saw on television without explaining which program it was.

Piaget drew his conclusions after observing the language of twenty-two 4- to 7-year-olds in everyday activities in their schools. He and his colleagues classified the children's sentences as examples of egocentric speech (e.g., when a child twice asks someone, "What did you say?" but never listens for an answer; Piaget, 1926/1974, p. 41) or nonegocentric sentences that included requests and threats as well as information adapted to the listener's point of view. Egocentric speech comprised nearly half of the children's spontaneous language. There also appeared to be stages in the development of socialized speech, with the amount of socialized speech increasing with age.

To test his ideas further, Piaget also conducted more formal experiments in which he asked children between the ages of 6 and 8 years to retell stories, relay messages, and explain to a same-aged peer how a faucet or syringe works. Once again, children's language was relatively egocentric. For example, children called story characters "she" or "it" without explaining to whom they were referring, left out important information, and did not present events in the correct order, as if they assumed that their listeners already understood what they were talking about. From these data, Piaget concluded that preschoolers are egocentric and unable to take their listeners' perspectives, that "the effort to understand other people and to communicate one's thought objectively does not appear in children before the age of about 7 or 7½" (1926/1974, p. 139).

Using research procedures modeled after Piaget's, more recent researchers demonstrated that young children have the capacity to take the perspective of the listener in certain circumstances. These studies investigated **referential communication,** the ability to describe an item from a set of similar items so that a listener can identify it. An example of referential communication is a child describing a specific T-shirt he wants his mother to find in a crowded dresser drawer.

O'Neill (1996) had 2-year-olds ask a parent for help retrieving a toy. Children were more likely to name the toy or its location or to point to it when parents did not know its location than when they did. In other words, the children took the parents' knowledge into account when communicating. Preschoolers generally perform better in everyday situations than in experimental situations (Ninio & Snow, 1999) and with familiar items (e.g., sets of animals) than with unusual items (e.g., abstract shapes) (Yule, 1997). Providing an eyewitness account of an accident or crime might, therefore, prove to be especially challenging for preschoolers.

Taking a different approach to the question of egocentrism, Hoff (2010) investigated whether children between the ages of 1½ and 3 years would speak differently depending on who their listeners were. Children were video recorded in dyadic toy play with a 5-year-old sibling, an 8-year-old sibling, and their mother. Children produced richer vocabulary conversing with their mothers than with their siblings. They were also most likely to reply to their mothers' questions and more likely to reply to questions from the 8-year-old than 5-year-old siblings. Hoff suggests that her findings may be explained at least in part by differences in the extent to which mothers and siblings **scaffold** or support young children's language. Thus, we should be cautious in interpreting her data as clear evidence of nonegocentrism.

Further evidence relevant to the question of egocentrism comes from bilingual children. Genesee and his colleagues (Genesee & Nicoladis, 2007) demonstrated that 2- to 3-year-old French-English bilinguals appropriately switch between French and English with parents who habitually speak one or the other language with them. Children this age can also select the appropriate language to converse with strangers and adjust the amount of French and English they mix depending on the extent to which an adult mixes those languages.

So *are* preschoolers egocentric in their attempts to communicate? The answer depends on context, in these cases the type of task. When preschoolers are familiar with a fairly simple task and are motivated to do it, their language does not appear to be completely egocentric. Although it may seem that this conclusion is inconsistent with Piaget's theory, it is not. Piaget observed that preschoolers sometimes use egocentric language and sometimes use more social language. They are not inherently egocentric. Rather, they may *behave* egocentrically in certain situations and are more likely to behave egocentrically than older children and adults, especially when the cognitive, linguistic, and social demands on them are great.

Requests

Requests are interesting parts of communicative competence for at least two reasons. First, listeners must appreciate that very different request forms may have the same purpose and effect (and, conversely, that the same form might serve different functions) depending on context. This can be the case for sentences intended to get a listener to hand the speaker a book. Some sentences make such a request indirectly (e.g., "I'm bored," "Do you remember that book I lent you?"), whereas others make it very directly and explicitly (e.g., "Give me that book"). Adults are thought to infer the meaning of **indirect requests** by considering both their form and the context of their use. Researchers are interested in whether young children have this understanding and therefore investigate children's comprehension of indirect requests.

Second, effective speakers take context into account by varying the requests they use in different situations. Speakers have many forms of requests at their disposal, not only in terms of their direct and indirect structure, but in terms of whether they include words or phrases that intensify the request (e.g., "or else," "right now") or soften the request (e.g., "please" or reasons). Researchers are thus interested in how children produce requests and whether they recognize the relationship between the forms and functions of requests (see Becker, 1982).

Comprehension of Indirect Requests. Both observational and experimental studies indicate that preschoolers respond to indirect requests as requests for action. Two-year-olds respond as appropriately to requests their mothers phrase as questions as to those phrased directly (Shatz, 1978), and 3- and 4-year-olds respond with appropriate actions when, for instance, telephone callers ask, "Is your Daddy there?" and when someone hints, "It's noisy in here" (Ervin-Tripp, 1977).

Other evidence that preschoolers understand indirect requests to be requests for action is found in the way children normally refuse such requests. Garvey (1975) observed thirty-six preschool dyads. When children did not want to comply with indirect requests, they often justified and explained in terms of their inability to perform the requested act (e.g., "I can't"), lack of willingness (e.g., "I don't want to"), lack of obligation to comply (e.g., "I don't have to"), or their inappropriateness as the person being asked to comply (e.g., "No, you"). Their comments reveal not only that they viewed indirect requests as requests, but that they understood the conditions under which they could legitimately make requests and the conditions under which they should respond.

Experiments also show that preschoolers understand the intent of indirect requests. Leonard and his colleagues (Leonard, Wilcox, Fulmer, & Davis, 1978) assessed children's comprehension of embedded imperatives such as "Can you X?" and "Will you X?" Children watched videotapes of everyday interactions in which an adult used an embedded imperative to make a request of another adult. Children judged whether the listener's subsequent behavior was in compliance with the request. Even 4- and 5-year-olds performed at better than chance on these requests, even when the requests were that the listener stop or change a behavior.

It may be that indirect requests like hints are not very difficult for young children to understand. Because some indirect requests are so common in everyday speech, they may not require logical reasoning or the conscious consideration of form and context (Gordon & Ervin-Tripp, 1984). Preschoolers may routinely hear requests such as "Lunch time" (meaning "Clean up and wash your hands"), so that their intent has become obvious and the response automatic. Furthermore, accompanying nonverbal behavior may help disambiguate the intent of indirect requests (Kelly, 2001).

Production of Requests.   Many contextual factors affect the forms of requests adults use in different situations. They include the roles of the two people conversing, whether the setting is personal or involves a transaction of some sort, whether the requested action can normally be expected of the listener, and the relative status or power of the two people. Most of the research on children has focused on status.

In general, like adults, children tend to address direct requests with semantic intensifiers to listeners of lower status and indirect requests with semantic softeners to listeners of higher status. For example, preschoolers are more likely to use an imperative (e.g., "Gimme an X") with a peer and a more indirect request (e.g., "May I have an X?" "Do you have an X?") with an adult (Ervin-Tripp, 1977; Gordon & Ervin-Tripp, 1984). During role play, they have dominant puppets enact more direct requests than submissive puppets do (Andersen, 2000). They even make more subtle differentiations, using requests that are more indirect with more dominant, bigger peers than with less powerful peers (Wood & Gardner, 1980).

Preschoolers are, at least to some degree, aware of the association between request forms and the relative status of speakers and listeners and can recognize the social messages that requests convey. Preschool-age children reported that direct requests with semantic intensifiers were "bossier" than less direct requests with semantic softeners, which were seen as "nicer" (Becker, 1986). When asked to make bossy and nice requests, these children produced bossy requests that were more direct and aggravated than their nice requests. In other words, a peer who requests the way a higher-status person requests is bossy, whereas one who requests the way a lower-status person requests is nice. Requests themselves are not inherently bossy or nice. Rather, it is the use of the forms in particular contexts by particular people that imbues them with social nuances.

In summary, preschoolers are quite adept at comprehending and producing different request forms. They respond appropriately to indirect requests and understand conditions of their use. They also vary the forms of their requests systematically when speaking with individuals who are more or less powerful than they are.

Conversational Skills

The abilities to take others' perspectives while communicating and to use requests are components of conversations, which are even more complex communicative behaviors. Conversations require children to take turns, stay on topic, and repair misunderstandings.

Taking Turns.   Even young infants can alternate turns while communicating with adults. By preschool, they rarely overlap turns. However, preschoolers lack the precise timing of turns that older children and adults exhibit. They tend to rely on obvious cues that a speaker is done, rather than anticipating upcoming conversational boundaries, which often results in long pauses between turns (Garvey, 1984) or interruptions with comments that are no longer relevant (Ervin-Tripp, 1979).

Markers such as "uh," "um," and "y'know" help older children get and hold the floor more effectively (Garvey, 1984; Kam & Edwards, 2008). They are able to time their turns more precisely and have shorter pauses in their conversations. Skilled interrupting continues to develop at least through adolescence.

Managing turns is challenging in face-to-face dyadic conversations. It is even more difficult for children when there are more than two speakers (Blum-Kulka & Snow, 2002). And when older children are simultaneously using different modes of communication such as text messaging and social networking, some not in real time, the challenges become greater yet.

Maintaining the Topic. Whereas toddlers rely on simple strategies such as sound play and repetition to keep verbal interactions going, preschoolers' conversations are increasingly collaborative (Pan & Snow, 1999). They become better able to elaborate on topics and themes (Ninio & Snow, 1996). They can have discussions about their day's activities, get into prolonged debates about the relative merits of different super heroes, and enjoy long bouts of pretend play.

Some types of conversations are particularly challenging for preschoolers, however. Conversations over the telephone pose problems even though preschoolers have many experiences using telephones (Warren & Tate, 1992).

One way to maintain a face-to-face conversation is to use **cohesive devices.** These provide ways to link talk to earlier parts of a conversation. Comprehension depends on making the link. For example, 4-year-old Ben asks, "Where's the dog?" and his brother Sam replies, "He's here." The pronoun "he" helps connect parts of the conversation without the need to repeat a prior phrase ("The dog is here"). Another such device is **ellipsis,** in which a speaker omits part of what was said before. For example, Ben wonders, "Did that roach run into the house?" When Sam says, "No, it didn't," the missing information ("run into the house") can be found by referring to a more complete form earlier in the conversation. These cohesive devices as well as others such as connectives (e.g., *because, so, then*) become more frequent and diverse over the preschool years (Garvey, 1984) and beyond (Berman, 2009, and see discussion of anaphora in Chapter 5).

Giving and Responding to Feedback. In order for a conversation to progress smoothly, listeners must provide informative feedback if they are confused, and speakers must respond appropriately to that feedback. Toddlers can repeat or verify their utterances when asked to do so. Both monolingual and bilingual 2- to 3-year-olds can repair conversational breakdowns due to ambiguity, choice of words, mispronunciation, and inaudibility (Comeau, Genesee, & Mendelson, 2010). By later in preschool, many children can issue as well as respond to queries requesting more specific responses, as in the following example of an interaction between two 3½-year-olds, drawn from Garvey (1984, p. 46):

Girl: "But . . . uh . . . driver man. I have to drive this car."

Boy: "What car? This car?" (touches a wooden car)

Girl: "Yes."

However, preschoolers are inconsistent and often inept at asking for clarification when others' communication is unclear and at repairing their own speech, especially when their listener's feedback is not explicit or when the situation is unfamiliar or unnatural (Garvey, 1984). Elementary-age children are better able to achieve mutual understanding in conversations.

It is not until later that children are able to insert "uh-huhs," "rights," "I sees," and head nods at appropriate moments to indicate continuing attention and satisfactory comprehension (Garvey, 1984; Turkstra, Ciccia, & Seaton, 2003). This type of response is referred to as **back-channel feedback**.

Over the course of the preschool years, children become increasingly skilled at taking turns, maintaining the topic of conversations, and dealing with misunderstandings and conversational breakdown. Although preschoolers are remarkably good conversationalists, older children require less conversational support from adults and are better able to conduct coherent, sustained conversations. Middle school–aged and older children provide more feedback to listeners, including encouraging interjections such as "I know what you mean," that promote conversation. Even subtle feedback (e.g., listeners' quizzical expressions) elicits clarifications. Such communicative competence continues to develop through adulthood (see Chapter 10 as well as Berman, 2004; Ninio & Snow, 1999; and Pan & Snow, 1999).

Choices among Language Varieties

Another aspect of communicative competence involves the choices speakers make among language varieties. For example, one would speak differently while giving a formal speech at school than when playing in one's neighborhood; when talking to fellow gamers about strategy than when talking with younger siblings about television shows; when talking face-to-face than when text messaging; or when talking with one's elderly Cuban grandparents than with younger, European-American neighbors. These language varieties include **registers**, **dialects,** and languages. Registers (sometimes called *speech codes* or *styles*) are usually thought of as forms of language that vary according to participants, settings, and topics. Dialects are usually thought of as mutually intelligible forms of language associated with particular regions or defined groups of people. And languages are forms that are typically not intelligible across groups. The distinctions among these three forms are not always great; they are often based on social and political, rather than linguistic, considerations (Linguistic Society of America, 2011). The Linguistic Society of America notes, for example, that different varieties of Chinese are considered dialects even though speakers of these different forms cannot understand each other and that Swedish and Norwegian are separate languages but users of each do understand the other.

No one language variety is inherently more appropriate than another (although listeners have many stereotypes and prejudices concerning them). Examples of language varieties include those associated with ethnicity, gender, and social group identity. Keep in mind that these varieties are only *associated* with particular groups; there are tremendous differences across group members. Also, as with other aspects of communicative competence, whether a given variety is appropriate and effective depends on the context in which it is used.

Language and Ethnicity: African American English.   **African American English (AAE)**, a variety of English spoken by many African Americans, is characterized in adult usage by its phonological, syntactic (Rickford, 2011; Wolfram, 2005; see Table 6.1), and pragmatic features. Phonological features that best distinguish it from most other varieties of English include simplification processes such as consonant reversals and final-consonant cluster reduction. For example, *ask* changes to *aks* and the word *past* reduces to *pas*. Syntactic features include the addition of the simple past tense *had* to a verb as in "They had went outside" and subject–verb disagreement, as in *she say* for *she says*. Some slang is unique to or has its origins in AAE. Such terms include *phat* (excellent), *ashy* (pale, whitish color), and *kitchen* (kinky hair at the nape of the neck; Rickford, 2011). There are also pragmatic features such as the use of **signifying** (also referred to as *sounding, capping,* and *playing the dozens*). Signifying is a type of sarcastic or witty language play that allows users to initiate a verbal "war" or make indirect comments on socially significant topics. For example, one can describe someone by saying, "He is so cool that he even stops for green lights" (Smitherman, 2007). Rap and hip-hop language are related speech events. Another pragmatic characteristic of AAE is the use of topic-associating (rather than topic-focused) narratives, which you will read more about in Chapter 10.

Like any other form of English, children's production of AAE differs from that of adults. Unfortunately, little research has been devoted to developmental change in the use of this form. Preschoolers have been observed in pragmatic performances such as signifying (Wyatt, 1995). Children enter school being able to produce many of the phonological and syntactic features of AAE. Although the capacity to produce AAE features may

Many African Americans speak a variety of English characterized by its phonological, syntactic, and pragmatic features.

continue to develop over the primary school years, the amount AAE that speakers use decreases over those years (Van Hofwegen & Wolfram, 2010).

In addition to age, factors such as socioeconomic status, gender, and context affect how often children use AAE and which features they produce. It is more commonly used among lower-income than middle-income African Americans and by boys more than girls, but these group differences disappear by the age of 10 or 11 years (Craig & Washington, 2005).

Language and Gender. Some research has suggested that there are feminine and masculine speech registers. For example, women are said to be more likely than men to use standard phonetic forms (e.g., pronouncing the final *-ing* in words), use polite forms of requests, and react rather than initiate in conversations; women are said to use uncertainty markers such as tag questions ("It's hot in here, isn't it?"), and to use particular lexical items (e.g., intensifiers, meaningless particles, politeness markers, rare color terms, expressive adjectives, and euphemisms). There is a great deal of controversy about whether, in fact, there are such gender differences or

table 6.1	Sample Differences between Standard English (SE) and African American English (AAE)		
		SE	AAE
Phonology			
Consonant deletions			
Final-consonant cluster reduction		past	pas
Initial and final-consonant deletion		don't	'on
Consonant substitutions			
Final stop devoicing		good	goot
/f/ and /v/ for medial and final /th/		bath	baf
Consonant reversals			
Transposed *sk* and *sp*		ask	aks
Syntax			
Deletion of present tense *is/are*		they are all right	they all right
Deletion of plural *-s*		a lot of times	a lot of time
Simple past tense *had* + verb		They went outside	They had went outside
Deletion of copula		He is nice	He nice
Subject–verb disagreement		she says	she say
Habitual "be"		She usually drives	She be driving
Ain't for *didn't*		He didn't go there	He ain't go there

Source: Based on Rickford (2011) and Wolfram (2005).

whether these characteristics are more stereotypes or a function of role and activity rather than of gender per se. See Chapter 11 for a further discussion of gender differences in adult speech.

Overall, the language boys and girls produce is more similar than different. The most consistent difference with respect to communicative competence is that young girls tend to use more collaborative, supportive, and mitigated speech styles, whereas young boys tend to use more controlling and unmitigated speech styles in interaction with peers (Leaper & Smith, 2004; Leman, Ahmed, & Ozarow, 2005; Sheldon, 1990) (although note that Kyratzis, 2007, demonstrates preschool girls' capacity to use quite aggravated speech with peers). Girls are more likely to ask something collaborative like, "I'm gonna set up the table, OK?" In contrast, boys are more likely to produce such phrases as, "you have to" and "if you don't" (Sheldon, 1990). Similarly, preschool girls' stories are more likely to describe stable, harmonious relationships (e.g., in families), whereas boys' stories are more likely to involve conflict, action, and disruption (Nicolopoulou, 2002; Sheldon & Rohleder, 1996).

Some stylistic differences in girls' and boys' conversations are nicely illustrated in DeHart's (1999) observations of same-sex, dyadic interactions. In the following examples, both sets of 4-year-olds are playing with a toy village. Consider first a collaborative conversation between girls:

Jennifer:	Could I have the table?
Patricia:	Okay. (gives Jennifer the table)
Jennifer:	Thanks. What if . . .
Patricia:	Oh, here's another biddy bed for me. (picks up a new piece)
Jennifer:	Yeah, you got a biddy biddy bed.
Patricia:	There's two biddy beds for me, for the daddy and the mommy.
Jennifer:	No, that one is mine. I dropped it.
Patricia:	Whoops. (drops a piece) Oh yeah. (gives piece back to Jennifer) It's yours.

Contrast that example with one involving two boys:

Michael:	(teasing) Ha ha ha ha. I got the person. I got the person ha ha.
Alan:	I ha ha ha ha ha ha I got the person.
Michael:	(teasing) I got both of the brown dogs. I got both of the pups. I got one of the puppies.
Alan:	I got a brown dog. (pulls toys toward himself) Ah ha ha ha ha. I got . . .
Michael:	Hey, you have to spread 'em out (messes up Alan's toys; Alan pulls them back) and take 'em.
Alan:	Ah.
Michael:	Don't. (hits Alan on the head) Alan, it's not just yours. Don't be a pig. Let's set 'em up. (swings lake from play set at Michael) Whoa, give me that. (holds hand out to block)
Alan:	No.

There are many differences among children in the extent to which they use these gender-related speech styles. Moreover, their tendency to use these styles varies contextually. Preschoolers are more likely to use them with peers of the same gender than with peers of the other gender (Killen & Naigles, 1995) and more with peers than with siblings (DeHart, 1996).

Language of Different Roles.   Another indication that children understand the connection between different language forms and context is the way they role-play. That is, by speaking differently when enacting the roles, they reveal their knowledge of language registers. Andersen (2000) asked eighteen 4-, 5-, and 6- to 8-year-olds to enact a family situation using mother, father, and young child puppets; a classroom situation with a teacher and two child puppets; and a doctor situation with a patient puppet and male and female puppets in medical attire. Children marked the different roles prosodically (mostly through pitch differences, but also through intonation, volume, rate, and voice quality), lexically (e.g., some use of technical medical terminology), and syntactically. In the family situation, for example, children used deep, loud voices as fathers, higher pitch for mothers, and even higher pitch and often nasalization or whining for children. When pretending to have the child address the father, they used more indirect requests such as, "Would you button me?" than they did when pretending to address the mother. To her, they were more likely to use direct requests such as, "Gimme Daddy's flashlight" (Andersen, 2000, p. 236). When pretending to be fathers, children often used speech that was straightforward, unqualified, and forceful, and for mothers they used speech that was more polite, qualified, and indirect (e.g., using many hints such as "Baby's sleepy"). Andersen, Brizuela, DuPuy, and Gonnerman (1999) observed comparable behavior in 4- to 10-year-old middle-class French monolingual and working-class Spanish-English bilingual children.

With age, children were able to use more linguistic devices to differentiate among the roles (Andersen, 2000; Andersen et al., 1999). Initially, they relied on prosodic features and different speech acts, then added differentiated vocabulary and topics, and finally utilized syntax. Older children were also better able to maintain these contrasts throughout their role-play.

Language and Social Identity.   Older children become increasingly aware of the social significance of their choices among language varieties. African American children may use less of the AAE register in school as they get older if they believe that it is stigmatized or ineffective in that context (Alim, 2005). Bilingual children may choose in some situations to speak the language of school in order to fit in with the majority, whereas in other situations they may choose to speak their native language in order to identify with their cultural heritage (Liang, 2006; Pagett, 2006).

Adolescents use different language registers to mark their identity as a *jock*, *nerd*, *preppie,* or *stoner* and to distinguish themselves from those in other social categories as well as from younger children and adults. Think, for example, about the vocabulary and tone associated with the "valley girl" or "surfer dude" registers. Teens employ language both to connect to some and to marginalize others through teasing, insulting, sincere and sarcastic complimenting, labeling, and verbal forms of relational aggression (Eckert, 2003; Roberto & Eden, 2010).

Instant messaging, text messaging, posts to social networking sites and discussion forums, comments on blogs, and participation in multiplayer online role-playing games allow users to continually construct (and reconstruct) their identities using registers in complex ways not possible in face-to-face, real-time conversation. From usernames to abbreviations and emoticons, there are many meaning-laden choices available during the period of adolescent identity development (Subrahmanyam & Šmahel, 2011).

As you have seen, children have many varieties of language at their disposal, including dialects and registers. Many African American preschoolers are beginning to acquire the features of African American English and to use them differently in different settings. Girls and boys are developing somewhat different styles, with girls often communicating more collaboratively with peers than boys do. During play, young children demonstrate basic knowledge of the registers associated with different roles. By the time they enter school, children clearly have a command of some of the culturally determined components of communication. Language takes on even greater social significance as children move through adolescence.

The Challenge of Acquiring Communicative Competence

The preceding discussion shows that children must adapt their language to different contexts. They must learn, for example, that they may yell when they are playing outdoors but must use quieter voices inside and perhaps not even talk at all in settings such as movie theaters and churches. Similarly, they must learn that they may discuss toileting matters and details of recent illnesses with family members and physicians, but not with strangers, and that members of their chess team may understand chess jargon but that they must use other terminology with non-players. Not only must children acquire a repertoire of communicative behaviors, they must be able to recognize characteristics of different contexts and then use the behaviors that are expected, appropriate, and effective. This is clearly a difficult task for them.

In contrast with the morphological and syntactic rules described in Chapter 5, there are usually not strict rules for communicative competence (Abbeduto & Short-Myerson, 2002; Becker, 1990). Rather, in specific contexts, using or omitting a particular communicative behavior is seen as relatively appropriate or inappropriate. For example, children do not always have to say *please* in order to be polite and appropriate. There are other ways to make polite requests, such as saying, "May I have a tissue?" The lack of hard-and-fast rules probably makes it difficult for children to learn whether and when to exhibit different behaviors.

A second factor that makes acquisition of communicative competence difficult is that many polite forms have no clear referents. That is, it is not obvious what a form such as *please* means. Furthermore, some forms, such as *thank you*, that seem to have a meaning (in this case, being thankful) are often expected to be used in situations when their meaning is contradicted (such as when it is appropriate to thank elderly Aunt Gertrude for the hideous socks she sent for one's birthday). Therefore, the learning process is probably different from that described for other words in Chapter 4.

Third, the conventions for competent communication in one setting (e.g., home) are often different from those in other settings (e.g., school). To the extent that these conventions are different, children may have trouble learning and adjusting to institutional settings and may also be judged negatively. The implications of this mismatch between home and school are dramatically illustrated by children whose cultures are different from those of teachers and the classroom.

Communicative variations across cultures include the ways that silence, eye contact, volume, tempo, questioning, and turn-taking are used in conversations. For example, some young Canadian Inuit children spend a great deal of time playing with peers, frequently with many children talking at the same time. They are less experienced at speaking with adults. When these children begin school and talk without raising their hands, often simultaneously, non-Inuit teachers may view them as rude (Genesee, Paradis, & Crago, 2004). Non-native English speakers and children in other cultural groups may encounter similar difficulties in typical American classrooms (Gratier, Greenfield, & Isaac, 2011; Snow & Blum-Kulka, 2002). Teachers, speech-language pathologists (American Speech-Language-Hearing Association, 1998), medical staff, and other professionals can obtain more comprehensive and valid samples of behavior and evaluate it more appropriately when they appreciate such cultural differences and modify their practices accordingly.

How Do Children Acquire Communicative Competence?

Acquiring communicative competence is difficult, but children have some help. There are a number of ways families and schools contribute to the acquisition process. Furthermore, children's knowledge, cognitive abilities, and efforts to learn about communication also facilitate their communicative development.

Family Influences

In general, it can be said that caregivers "socialize" language. They use language to help their children become competent members of their societies and cultures, competence reflected in part in the children's language usage (Schieffelin & Ochs, 1996).

Virtually from birth, infants begin to receive information about some of the communicative behaviors that will help them meet their social needs. You have probably seen many parents wave the hands of their little preverbal infants and say things like "Say 'hi' to Mrs. Stanley" or "Bye-bye, Grandpa."

Much of the structure of conversations may be learned in early interactions between infants and caregivers, as indicated in Chapter 2. Actions and talk (e.g., the use of *hello, please,* and *thank you*) are highly organized and predictable during social games or routines such as peekaboo and in give-and-take with objects. Such games provide children clear and consistent information about a small number of socially significant phrases. In these interactions, infants also learn about taking turns, the responsibilities of both participants to keep the interaction going, how to focus on a theme or topic, and how to make the interaction cohere. Caregivers find ways to pull their infants into the interaction, to help infants respond and participate, much as if they are having a conversation (Ninio & Snow, 1996).

Once children exhibit some basic communicative competence, begin to participate more actively in interactions, and can anticipate sequences of behavior in the routines, caregivers adapt their interactions (Becker, 1990). A number of interesting studies have been conducted on how they do this during the preschool years.

In a simple and clever study, Gleason and Weintraub (1976) tape-recorded what happened at two homes as trick-or-treaters arrived on Halloween evening. They also followed two mothers and their children as they went trick-or-treating door to door. Many parents insisted that their children say "trick or treat" and "thank you," often using the prompt *say.* Their teaching is illustrated in the following example (Gleason & Weintraub, 1976, p. 134):

Girl's mother:	(approaching a house) Don't forget to say "thank you." (children go to door and return to sidewalk) Did you say "thank you," Sue, did you say "thank you"?
Sue:	Ya.
Girl's mother:	Good.
Boy's mother:	Ricky, did *you* say "thank you"?
Girl's mother:	Did you say "trick or treat," Sue?
Boy's mother:	(approaching another house) Will you remember to say "trick or treat" and "thank you"?
Girl's mother:	(children have walked to door; she calls to them from the sidewalk) Don't forget to say "thank you"!

In order to replicate and extend these findings I conducted a one-year longitudinal study of five families (Becker, 1994). Parents audiotaped everyday interactions between themselves and their preschoolers in their homes, particularly at the dinner table, an especially rich context for language socialization (Snow & Beals, 2006).

First, parents commented about a wide variety of communicative behaviors. They provided input about what children were expected to say (e.g., *please,* polite requests, *goodbye,* routines such as "trick or treat," address terms, slang), how children were expected to speak (using the appropriate volume, tone of voice, and clarity), when children should speak, and how to stay on topic.

Parents also used a variety of strategies in their comments about and reactions to their preschoolers' communicative behaviors. They prompted in several different ways, modeled, reinforced, occasionally posed hypothetical situations, evaluated behavior after the fact, addressed children's comments about communication, and evaluated others' communicative behavior (see Table 6.2).

One of the provocative aspects of these findings is that most of the parents' input was indirect. Specifically, parents' indirect comments on errors and omissions composed an average of 61 percent of the total input (49–91 percent across the families). Indirectness seems a risky way to teach communicative competence, because children might not understand what they are supposed to do. The finding that so much parental input is indirect is counterintuitive, because parents believe that displaying competence is important and

---

table 6.2   Categories of Parental Input Regarding Preschoolers' Communicative Competence

Prompts

Direct comment on omission
Explicitly point out the omitted behavior or that the child must produce this behavior; e.g., "Say 'excuse me' when you cough."

Indirect comment on omission
Allude to the omission; e.g., "What's the magic word?"

Direct comment on error
Explicitly point out the child's error or that the child must correct behavior; e.g., "Don't talk with your mouth full."

Indirect comment on error
Allude to the error; e.g., "What did you say?"

Anticipatory suggestion
Suggest a behavior prior to an omission or error, e.g., "Don't forget to say 'night-night' to Daddy."

Modeling

Modeling
Provide the appropriate behavior before the child has the opportunity to produce it; e.g., "Excuse me" as the child coughs.

Teaching sibling
Modeling for the preschooler by commenting on younger sibling's behavior; e.g., Mother: "What do you say?" Sibling: "Thank you." Mother: "You're welcome. Very good!"

Parents demonstrate
Parents demonstrate prompts and behaviors as instruction; e.g., Father: "Go get my milk." Mother: "Well, what do you say?" Father: "Please."

Reinforcement

Verbal reinforcement following preschoolers' appropriate usage; e.g., "I like the way you say [X]."

Other forms of input

Hypothetical situation
Pose a hypothetical situation for didactic purposes; e.g., "What would you say if that ape came up to you and said 'hi'?"

Retroactive evaluation
Comment on child's appropriateness well after the fact; e.g., "She said her prayers [earlier at lunch] all by herself! Word for word, too. I'm really happy about that."

Address child's comment
Respond to child's question, statement, or prompt about communicative competence; e.g., Child: "It's a bad word, 'ugly.'" Mother: "It's not a bad word, you just use it wrong."

Evaluate another
Seek child's evaluation of another person's behavior; e.g., "Right, Jane?"

Source: adapted from Becker (1994), pp. 136–137.

a reflection of their own socialization abilities (Becker & Hall, 1989; Bryant, 1999). One would think that parents would be explicit in order to maximize the chances of their children performing correctly. Although these are not experimental findings and therefore causal conclusions cannot be drawn, it is likely that indirectness challenges children more cognitively and provides more information about communicative conventions than does direct, explicit input (Ely & Gleason, 2006). In fact, mothers of preschoolers believe that indirect responses place cognitive burdens on children by helping them "to think rather than just parrot" and "figure it out on [their] own" (Bryant, 1999, p. 134).

Parents are not the only family members who socialize communicative competence. Siblings in several cultures have been observed to prompt appropriate behavior (Gleason, Hay, & Cain, 1989). For example, a 5-year-old American girl instructed her younger sister, "Don't talk while you're eating" (Gleason et al., 1989).

A number of researchers have suggested that different family members contribute to the acquisition of communicative competence in different and potentially important ways. That is, family members who know the child less intimately (e.g., fathers who are secondary caregivers) or who lack the capacity and motivation to tune in to the child's needs (e.g., older siblings) may pressure the child to communicate clearly and appropriately more than would family members who know the child most intimately (e.g., mothers who are primary caregivers) (Barton & Tomasello, 1994; Gleason, 1975). Fathers and siblings, in this view, challenge children to adapt and broaden their communicative skills and thus prepare them to talk with strangers and about unfamiliar topics. Thus, fathers and siblings may serve as "bridges" to the outside world, "leading the child to change her or his language in order to be understood" (Gleason, 1975, p. 293).

There is some evidence to support this bridge hypothesis. Relative to mothers, fathers of infants have been observed to have more breakdowns in communication, spend less time focused on the same object or action, be less successful at tuning in to their children's current focus of attention, make more off-topic replies, and request clarification more often (Tomasello, Conti-Ramsden, & Ewert, 1990). Fathers of preschoolers also use more imperatives with their children than do mothers (Gleason, 1975). A meta-analysis (a statistical review of many studies) demonstrated that, across studies, mothers are more supportive (e.g., they praise, acknowledge) in their speech than fathers (Leaper, Anderson, & Sanders, 1998). In general, fathers appear to be less tuned in to children than mothers are.

Note that less supportive conversational interaction is not necessarily a good thing: Parents who fail to give their preschoolers time to respond to requests tend to have children with poor turn-taking skills (Black & Logan, 1995). In general, parents nurture communicative development by showing interest and encouraging conversations with their children (Resnick & Snow, 2009).

Not surprisingly, older siblings are even less tuned in and conversationally responsive than fathers. Hoff-Ginsberg and Krueger (1991) observed toddlers interacting with preschool-age siblings, 7- to 8-year-old siblings, and their mothers. The older siblings were conversationally more like their mothers than were the preschoolers, but neither group of siblings adapted their speech adequately to their younger siblings' age. Likewise, Tomasello and Mannle (1985) found that preschool-age siblings of infants acknowledged fewer utterances than did their mothers. Mannle, Barton, and Tomasello (1991) observed those differences even when infants conversed similarly with their mothers and siblings. In general, siblings are more directive, less responsive, and less adept than their mothers at using techniques for maintaining conversations with younger siblings and at taking into account the infants' conversational immaturity.

Siblings can affect communicative competence in additional ways. Some researchers argue that children are motivated to participate in conversations between their mothers and older siblings. Therefore, they learn how to enter conversations effectively (Barton & Tomasello, 1991), as well as to maintain a topic and take turns in such complex, triadic conversations (Barton & Tomasello, 1994; Hoff-Ginsberg & Krueger, 1991). Younger siblings also have the opportunity to observe conversations between their mothers and older siblings and are thereby exposed to a variety of communicative styles.

If siblings affect the acquisition of communicative competence, one would expect first-born children to differ from later-born children in their communicative skills. Hoff-Ginsberg (1998) investigated this possibility with 1½- to 2½-year-olds. Although, as previous research has shown, the first-born children exhibited more advanced lexical and grammatical development, the later-born children had more advanced conversational skills in interactions with their mothers.

Even if they do not have siblings, preschoolers may be part of conversations with several children and adults at the dinner table, a party, or at school, for example. These multi-party conversations operate differently than do dyadic conversations (Blum-Kulka & Snow, 2002). Multiparty conversations allow children to hear more talk, hear greater varieties of talk, and observe and assume different conversational roles. Such conversations require children to deal with participants' varying degrees of background knowledge and to be assertive and clever in finding ways to participate.

This section has focused primarily on literature describing middle-class U.S. families because that is the population on which most of the research has been conducted. However, societies and cultures vary greatly in the communicative behaviors that adults value and the ways that they socialize those behaviors. For example, Canadian Inuit parents do not believe children can reason until they are 5 years old. These mothers do not typically converse with their infants or view their vocalizations as talk. They do not drill or rehearse language forms (Genesee et al., 2004). Insofar as those children ultimately acquire communicative competence, it is clear that they learn by monitoring the conversations of speakers around them. (See Aukrust, 2004; Blum-Kulka & Snow, 2002; and Schieffelin & Ochs, 1986, for information about the socialization of communicative competence in other cultures.)

Family mealtimes are rich contexts for communicative development.

There are several limitations in this literature that should be noted. First, causal conclusions cannot be drawn because the research is descriptive and correlational. Neither experimental studies nor interventions have been done on the ways families influence the acquisition of communicative competence. Second, there are many variations across families with similar configurations. Not all mothers behave the same way, nor do all fathers or all siblings. For example, Davidson and Snow (1996) failed to find that middle-class, highly educated fathers of kindergartners used more challenging language than mothers, contrary to the findings of some earlier research. We must also exercise caution in generalizing results of studies of relatively few families. Third, context influences parental behavior to a greater extent than parental gender does (Lewis, 1997). The setting, the task, and other situational characteristics strongly affect how family members interact with children.

Schools' and Peers' Influence

Teachers who provide opportunities and encourage children to talk for a wide variety of purposes, in different situations, and with different audiences also help children learn to communicate effectively (Resnick & Snow, 2009). More specifically, children need a variety of experiences communicating in order to learn the functions of language, different forms of discourse, and the conventions for using language appropriately. Valuable experiences include informal conversations between children and teachers and among children (not to mention with the principal, other teachers, parents, and members of the community), games, small-group projects, storytelling, role playing, and the integration of communication across the curriculum. Children also need to be able to listen to fluent, responsive adults. Children should not just be talked *to;* they should be able to develop communicative competence in relevant, purposeful, interesting, everyday situations. Having access to a variety of materials, interacting in small areas or centers within the classroom, and having extended opportunities for interaction also appear to promote communicative competence in the early school years.

Furthermore, teachers explicitly teach some rules governing communicative behavior specific to the classroom (Yifat & Zadunaisky-Ehrlich, 2008) and prompt, model, and comment on children's polite and impolite language (Burdelski, 2010). Effective teachers announce both restrictive rules (e.g., no screaming) and prescriptive rules (e.g., pay attention, follow routines) from the beginning of the school year and attempt to correct children's violations of these rules. In contrast, there are other rules that children must infer from the ongoing interaction. For example, teachers do not usually explicitly teach children that only teachers can initiate topics.

School also affords children opportunities to interact with peers. Peers probably affect communicative competence in a variety of ways. They may be similar to siblings as relatively uncooperative conversational partners and thus contribute to the pressure children feel to communicate more clearly and effectively. Interactions with peers are frequent, sustained, and emotionally engaging, and so provide a developmental context that promotes narrative and other communicative skills (Nicolopoulou & Richner, 2004). Peers also participate in forms of communication that are different from those of adult–child speech (Blum-Kulka & Snow, 2004), but, like adults, may correct and prompt peers' communicative behavior (Burdelski, 2010; Stude, 2007). Their special kinds of humor and disagreements, the topics about which they talk, and their explicit socialization about language provide communicative experiences that no doubt complement those experienced with adults. Chapter 10 explores further aspects of the language of peers.

Children's Cognitions and Efforts to Achieve Communicative Competence

Families and schools influence acquisition in part because they support and build on children's cognitive abilities and social predispositions (Snow, 1999).

Knowledge and Cognitive Abilities. Communicative competence requires a great deal of knowledge. Speakers must have a repertoire of terms and routines as well as language varieties. They must know something about situations and about relationships. Particular cognitive skills are thought to underlie specific communicative skills (e.g., spatial perspective taking as a prerequisite for the acquisition of deictic uses of *I* and *you;* Loveland, 1984). Other general skills that appear to influence communicative competence are knowledge of scripts and the ability to test hypotheses about communication.

Scripts. When children possess abstract knowledge about a familiar, everyday event, they are better able to communicate (Goodman, Duchan, & Sonnenmeier, 1994). This abstract knowledge is referred to as a **script.** Scripts are the way we represent familiar events in our memories. These representations contain information about sequences of actions, the usual functions of objects, roles of the people involved, and the kind of language used during the events—what one sees, does, and says in what order. For example, a script about going to a birthday party might contain information about wrapping a gift and preparing a card, getting dressed up, greeting the hosts at the door, playing party games, singing "Happy Birthday," eating cake and ice cream, watching presents get opened, and thanking the hosts as one is leaving. Familiarity with scripts reduces cognitive demands so children can concentrate more on their conversations. Familiarity also supports comprehension. Finally, to the extent that conversational partners have mutual knowledge of events, their communication is more effective. Preschoolers are better able to maintain topics, and they have fewer misunderstandings, if they share script knowledge (Short-Myerson & Abbeduto, 1997).

Hypothesis Testing.   It is important to remember that children are not passive acquirers of communicative competence (or much else, for that matter) (Becker, 1990). They naturally notice regularities across their experiences and organize those experiences. They associate communicative behaviors, conventions, and meanings with specific situational and contextual conditions and thereby "develop a sense of what is preferred and expected" (Schieffelin & Ochs, 1996, p. 258). They form hypotheses about communicative conventions and then test these hypotheses through trial and error and by asking questions and commenting on communicative behavior. Just as they overextend vocabulary and overregularize grammatical rules, young children sometimes misapply communicative conventions. It is common for infants to use *thank you* both when receiving and giving objects and to interchange *hello* and *good-bye* (Gopnik & Meltzoff, 1986). Overextensions suggest that infants are going beyond the evidence their environments have provided and are formulating generalizations about communicative behaviors.

When they are older, children may seek verification for their hypotheses. For example, one of the preschool girls in my research had been taught to say "yes, Daddy" and "yes, Mommy." One day she said to her father, "Daddy, I just made up another one: 'No, Daddy. No, Mommy.' Is that right?" (Becker, 1990).

It is apparent that preschoolers know there are specific aspects of communicative conventions to be learned, including what words to say and when, how, and why one should say them. Their active, conscious efforts to obtain this information are illustrated in the following excerpt from a conversation about events that will occur in the future on Christmas. Keep in mind that the preschooler in this example had had limited experience with Christmas and had relatively recently celebrated Halloween.

Girl:	Maybe somebody, we are gonna coming in say "trick or treat"?
Mother:	(laughs) No. They're not going to say "trick or treat" on Christmas.
Girl:	. . . What say then?
Mother:	Say "Merry Christmas."
Girl:	"Merry Christmas"?
Mother:	At Christmas time you say . . . And wish everybody a merry Christmas. That means you hope they have a good time on Christmas day.
Girl:	When they're sleeping, huh?
Mother:	No, when they're awake. (Becker, 1994, p. 141)

The daughter first attempts to ascertain what the appropriate verbal routine is for this occasion and then wonders what the phrase might mean. Finally, she inquires about the appropriate time at which one would use the phrase.

Evidence from Atypical Populations.   Research with atypical populations provides evidence that theory of mind, social orientation, and general linguistic ability are also relevant for the development of communicative competence. (See Chapter 9.) Impairment in communicative competence is one of the most central features of children with autism spectrum disorder (ASD; Luyster & Lord, 2009). These children have significant limitations in theory of mind. Their difficulty understanding others' intentions, motivations, and beliefs makes it hard to take listeners' needs into account (Hale & Tager-Flusberg, 2005b). They tend to use words idiosyncratically and certain phrases repeatedly. Children with ASDs tend to use language for a limited number of social functions. They have trouble initiating conversations, responding reciprocally and adding new information to sustain conversations, taking turns, and responding appropriately to requests for clarification. Nonverbal behaviors such as gaze and gestures tend not to be integrated with their language. The greater the degree of symptomatology, the greater the conversational impairment, regardless of children's overall language skill (Hale & Tager-Flusberg, 2005a).

Children with Down syndrome have better theory of mind and are more sociable than children with ASD. As one might expect, they demonstrate better conversational skills.

Communicative competence is an area of strength relative to their other language skills, though their degree of competence is related to mental age (Richardson & Thomas, 2009). For example, children with Down syndrome use language for a range of social purposes, can maintain the topic of conversations, respond appropriately to others, and are reasonably good at responding to feedback to make conversational repairs.

Deaf children of hearing parents may experience an environment that is limited in opportunities for rich, communicative interaction even when those interactions are loving and positive. Although, like hearing children, these young deaf children can initiate conversations, they often have difficulty making their communicative intentions clear, commenting, asking questions, maintaining and repairing conversations, and producing cohesive narratives (Lederberg, 2006). Semantic and syntactic improvements are associated with greater communicative competence (Lederberg & Everhart, 2000). Given the importance of very early conversational experience, some researchers advocate substantial contact with native signers or early implantation of cochlear implants (Surian, Tedoldi, & Siegal, 2010). (Note, by the way, that the communicative development of deaf children of deaf parents tends to be more like that of hearing children.)

To summarize, families and schools afford opportunities for children to learn about the language considered appropriate in different contexts. Mothers, fathers, siblings, teachers, and peers appear to contribute differently to the acquisition of communicative competence by providing different types of information, feedback, opportunities, and pressure. To varying degrees, children bring to these interactions their knowledge, interest in learning about communication, cognitive and language skills, and social orientation. There are many influences on the acquisition of communicative competence and no doubt many possible paths to its achievement, a view consistent with the social interaction approach to language acquisition you will read about in Chapter 7.

Why Does Communicative Competence Matter?

There are several reasons that communicative competence is important to children's lives. Communicative competence is necessary for understanding and functioning in the classroom, predicts later literacy skills, and is associated with greater liking by peers and adults. Not surprisingly, later in life, communicative competence is essential for obtaining a job and being successful in the workplace.

First, some degree of communicative competence is necessary for children to do well in school (Greenwood, Walker, & Utley, 2002; Resnick & Snow, 2009; Snow & Blum-Kulka, 2002). Talk is a mechanism for gaining as well as displaying knowledge. Children must learn the communicative practices valued in their schools. These practices include knowing when and how to speak and respond to teachers and peers, how to address teachers, to display their knowledge and obtain information appropriately, to comprehend indirect language (such as knowing that when preschool teachers say, "Use your words," they usually intend that children solve disputes verbally rather than physically), and to shift their behavior appropriately in different school settings (e.g., playground, lunch, lesson time). Communicative competence (or the lack thereof) affects children's opportunities for learning through interactions with peers and teachers as well as teachers' judgments of children's abilities and motivations (Becker, Place, Tenzer, & Frueh, 1991; Reaser & Adger, 2010). (Interestingly, speech and language clinicians also make social judgments about children on the basis of communicative competence; American Speech-Language-Hearing Association Joint Subcommittee of the Executive Board on English Language Proficiency, 1998).

A second way in which communicative competence is important is that some of its components in the early school years are predictive of (and may in fact prepare children for) later academic skills (Reeder, Shapiro, Watson, & Goelman, 1996). For example, narrative skills may provide a bridge to print literacy because they promote the enjoyment of stories and help children learn about the conceptual organization, purposes, and linguistic conventions of stories (Griffin, Hemphill, Camp, & Wolf, 2004; Snow, Porche, Tabors, & Harris, 2007). Reeder and his colleagues have found a relationship between pragmatic awareness and early writing ability (Reeder & Shapiro, 1997). They argue that having the metalinguistic skills to attribute intentions and motives to speakers, to differentiate what is said from what is meant, may help children develop the ability to understand written language that provides no clues from social interactions (Reeder & Shapiro, 1996). Children's ability to shift dialects appropriately across social contexts predicts reading ability, perhaps because both require metalinguistic awareness skills (Craig, Zhang, Hensel, & Quinn, 2009; Terry, Connor, Thomas-Tate, & Love, 2010). Similarly, Snow and Blum-Kulka (2002) suggest that the ability to take multiple perspectives in multiparty conversations aids in text comprehension. Perspective-taking skills underlying narrative may also explain why narrative production at 3 and 4 years of age even predicts math achievement two years later (O'Neill, Pearce, & Pick, 2004).

A third way in which communicative competence is important is that competent children are better liked than those who are less skilled. One author of your textbook, Jean Berko Gleason (Gleason et al., 1989) recalls driving in a car pool when her children were young. One boy never said "thank you" when she dropped him off at his house. Many years later, said Gleason, "It is impossible to think of him with anything but distaste." As we all know, people who are rude, who demand and interrupt, are not very pleasant to be around. Wrote Dell Hymes, the apparent originator of the term *communicative competence,* "A child capable of any and all grammatical utterances, but not knowing which to use, not knowing even when to talk and when to stop, would be a cultural monstrosity" (1967, p. 16).

There is empirical evidence for Gleason's and Hymes's impressions about the relationship between communicative competence and likableness. Many researchers have shown that children who are skilled at gaining entry to ongoing social interactions and who are verbally responsive are more popular than children who are less skilled (Samter, 2003). That is, it is advantageous to be able to employ such verbal strategies as greeting, suggesting, requesting to join in, and making substantive contributions to the interaction (Craig & Washington, 1993). Kemple, Speranza, and Hazen (1992) observed that 3½- to 5½-year-olds who are well liked by their peers (as contrasted with those who are disliked) are better able to initiate and maintain coherent conversations. These children clearly direct their communication to specific peers, respond appropriately when others try to communicate with them, and can attend to two playmates rather than focusing on just one of them. Furthermore, when interacting with unfamiliar children, popular preschoolers are also more responsive and better able to carry on a coherent conversation than are unpopular children. Other researchers have obtained similar findings (Black & Logan, 1995; Gertner, Rice, & Hadley, 1994). Rice and her colleagues have even suggested that something as simple as being able to address peers by name rather than as "hey, you" has implications for popularity.

The causal relationship between communicative competence and popularity is complex (Black & Logan, 1995). Kemple et al. (1992) argued that some communication skills (such as the ability to make relevant comments and respond positively and contingently to peers) contribute to young children's initial popularity. Then, further differences in communication skills emerge after children's reputations as being popular or unpopular are established. That is, unpopular children may avoid communicating with peers in order to avoid rejection. Their poor communication skills serve to maintain their lower status and may preclude their involvement in positive interactions that would help them learn better skills and develop better self-concepts.

In elementary school, skills such as being able to adjust messages to meet listeners' needs, ask appropriate questions, initiate and maintain conversations, communicate intentions clearly, address all participants when joining a group, make more positive than negative comments, and persuade and verbally comfort are all related to popularity with peers (Brinton & Fujiki, 1995). The effect of communicative competence on popularity is further supported by experimental work Place and I conducted (Place & Becker, 1991), in which elementary-age girls reported liking an unfamiliar girl who displayed communicative competence better than they liked unfamiliar girls who made rude requests, interrupted, or strayed off topic.

How well children get along with others is not a trivial matter. The quality of peer relationships has implications for future psychological well-being. Difficulty with peers puts children at risk for subsequent academic problems and psychological maladjustment.

This chapter opened with an example of preschoolers' conversation that illustrated the importance of communicative competence. Let's close with another. In this example, friends David and Josh, both 4 years old, are walking around pretending to be robots (Rubin, 1980, p. 55):

David: I'm a missile robot who can shoot missiles out of my fingers. I can shoot them out of everywhere—even out of my legs. I'm a missile robot.

Josh: (tauntingly) No, you're a fart robot.

David: (protestingly) No, I'm a missile robot.

Josh: No, you're a fart robot.

David: (hurt, almost in tears) No, Josh!

Josh: (recognizing that David is upset) And I'm a poo-poo robot.

David: (in good spirits again) I'm a pee-pee robot.

Josh's competent ability to modify his language shows us again just how powerful young children's language may be in social contexts.

SUMMARY

Communicative competence is the ability to use language appropriately and strategically in social contexts. That is, it involves knowing what, where, how, and with whom one should communicate. Communicative behaviors include routines, polite terms, conversational skills, and language varieties such as dialects and registers. It is important that children acquire communicative competence, because it helps children succeed in school, predicts later literacy skills, and is associated with popularity among peers.

Research indicates that preschoolers are able to use a wide range of communicative behaviors and adjust their communication for different listeners and in different situations. They comprehend indirect requests in which form does not obviously match function and produce different request forms for listeners of different statuses, suggesting that they have some understanding of the relationship between form and power. They can take turns and maintain topics in conversations and have basic skills that enable them to give and respond to feedback. Preschoolers are also acquiring language varieties associated with ethnicity, gender, and social roles and identities. Although they are communicatively competent in many respects, their abilities become more sophisticated with age.

The task of acquiring communicative competence is difficult, and families and schools both appear to play a role in acquisition. Mothers, fathers, and siblings socialize communicative behaviors, each pressuring preschoolers in complementary ways to communicate appropriately. Teachers and peers also offer opportunities for communicative development. Children's experiences as well as their knowledge and cognitive abilities and their natural tendency to form hypotheses about communication help drive the acquisition process.

SUGGESTED PROJECTS

1. Consider the ways that the meaning of a particular utterance varies according to context. For example, the sentence "It's hot in here" could be a request for the listener to open a window or an ironic statement about a cold room. Write a sentence and describe different contexts (e.g., in terms of settings or participants) in which it could be

produced. Also, explain how listeners consider the contexts and the sentence in determining the sentence's meanings.

Now think about how a particular meaning (e.g., agreement) may be expressed differently in different contexts (e.g., "Yeah" to a friend; "Aye, aye, sir" to a Navy superior; "Okeydokey" to an old-fashioned uncle). If a speaker used one of these expressions in an unexpected context, more meaning would be conveyed than just agreement. For example, if my 6-year-old responds to a simple request by saying "Yes, Sir," he would not simply be agreeing to do what I asked! Consider the following situations: When I get email from my father, he usually signs "love" at the end. My students usually sign with just their names, whereas applicants to my graduate program tend to sign "sincerely." How might I interpret unexpected email closings? Explain your answer.

2. Observe preschoolers at a playground. Compare and contrast their language with adults versus peers and in different activities (e.g., playing make-believe versus using playground equipment). Note, for example, children's topics, requests, volume, tone of voice, and turn-taking in these different contexts.

3. In 1918, the Chicago Woman's Club promulgated a pledge for children as part of the "better-speech movement" (Robbins, 1918). Children were asked to pledge "That I will say a good American 'yes' and 'no' in place of an Indian grunt 'um-hum' or a foreign 'ya' or 'yeh' and 'nope'" and "That I will do my best to improve American speech by avoiding loud, rough tones, by enunciating distinctly, and by speaking pleasantly, clearly, and sincerely" (p. 175). First, use material in the chapter to argue why "proper American speech" might be advantageous for children. Second, take the opposite position and use information from this chapter to argue why this was a misguided effort.

4. Think about occasions in which you were judged negatively because of the way you used language or about times when you saw others being judged for their language use. Analyze what it was about the language (e.g., vocabulary, grammar, dialect, accent, language, communicative competence) that may have led to these reactions. Why do you think others reacted in these ways? Think about times when you consciously changed the way you talked in order to get a more positive (or negative) reaction from others. What assumptions did you make about the social significance of language in those situations?

5. Prepare a handout about communicative competence for parents and teachers of young children. Describe what communicative competence is, make specific suggestions for ways that teachers and parents can help in its development, and explain why it is important for children to acquire. Try to use everyday language in your explanations. Give the handout to several teachers and parents and get their feedback about it. Submit your work to a local preschool or elementary school for possible inclusion in their school newsletter or website.

6. Interview a teacher or speech-language pathologist who works with young children. Ask about her or his experiences with children who have varying degrees of communicative competence or children whose home communication practices are different from those of white, middle class, English-speaking classrooms. Find out what strategies they employ, if any, to help children develop communicative competence. Write about the communicative behaviors they identify and their strategies in light of what you learned in this chapter.

SUGGESTED READINGS

Becker, J. (1994). Pragmatic socialization: Parental input to preschoolers. *Discourse Processes, 17,* 131–148.

Blum-Kulka, S., & Snow, C. (Eds.). (2002). *Talking to adults: The contribution of* *multi-party discourse to language acquisition.* Mahwah, NJ: Erlbaum.

Genesee, F., Paradis, J., & Crago, M. (2004). *Dual language development and disorders.* Baltimore: Paul H. Brookes.

O'Neill, D., Main, R., & Ziemski, R. (2009). 'I like Barney': Preschoolers' spontaneous conversational initiations with peers. *First Language, 29*, 401–425.

Reaser, J., & Adger, C. (2010). Vernacular language varieties in educational settings: Research and development. In S. Bernard & F. Hult (Eds.), *Handbook of educational linguistics* (pp. 161–173). Malden, MA: Wiley-Blackwell.

Resnick, L., & Snow, C. (Eds.) (2009), *Speaking and listening for preschool through third grade* (Rev.Ed.). Newark, DE: National Center on Education and the Economy and University of Pittsburgh.

KEY WORDS

African American English (AAE)	dialect	routine
back-channel feedback	egocentrism	scaffold
cohesive devices	ellipsis	script
communicative competence	indirect request	signifying
	referential communication	speech act
	register	

REFERENCES

Abbeduto, L., & Short-Myerson, K. (2002). Linguistic influences on social interaction. In H. Goldstein, L. Kaczmarek, & K. English (Eds.), *Promoting social communication* (pp. 27–54). Baltimore: Paul H. Brookes.

Alim, S. (2005). Critical language awareness in the United States. *Educational Researcher, 34*, 24–31.

American Speech-Language-Hearing Association (1998). *Students and professionals who speak English with accents and nonstandard dialects: Issues and recommendations.* Position statement [online]. Available: www.asha.org/docs/html/PS1998-00117.html

Andersen, E. (2000). Exploring register knowledge: The value of "controlled improvisation." In L. Menn & N. B. Ratner (Eds.), *Methods for studying language production* (pp. 225–248). Mahwah, NJ: Erlbaum.

Andersen, E., Brizuela, M., DuPuy, B., & Gonnerman, L. (1999). Cross-linguistic evidence for the early acquisition of discourse markers as register variables. *Journal of Pragmatics, 31*, 1339–1351.

Aukrust, V. (2004). Talk about talk with young children. *Journal of Child Language, 31*, 177–201.

Barton, M., & Tomasello, M. (1991). Joint attention and conversation in mother–infant–sibling triads. *Child Development, 62*, 517–529.

Barton, M., & Tomasello, M. (1994). The rest of the family: The role of fathers and siblings in early language development. In C. Gallaway & B. Richards (Eds.), *Input and interaction in language acquisition* (pp. 109–134). New York: Cambridge University Press.

Becker, J. (1982). Children's strategic use of requests to mark and manipulate social status. In S. Kuczaj (Ed.), *Language development: Language, thought, and culture* (pp. 1–35). Hillsdale, NJ: Erlbaum.

Becker, J. (1986). Bossy and nice requests: Children's production and interpretation. *Merrill-Palmer Quarterly, 32*, 393–413.

Becker, J. (1990). Processes in the acquisition of pragmatic competence. In G. Conti-Ramsden & C. Snow (Eds.), *Children's language* (Vol. 7, pp. 7–24). Hillsdale, NJ: Erlbaum.

Becker, J. (1994). Pragmatic socialization: Parental input to preschoolers. *Discourse Processes, 17*, 131–148.

Becker, J., & Hall, M. (1989). Adult beliefs about pragmatic development. *Journal of Applied Developmental Psychology, 10*, 1–17.

Becker, J., Place, K., Tenzer, S., & Frueh, C. (1991). Teachers' impressions of children varying in pragmatic skills. *Journal of Applied Developmental Psychology, 12,* 397–412.

Berman, R. (Ed.). (2004). *Language development across childhood and adolescence.* Philadelphia: John Benjamins.

Berman, R. (2009). Language development in narrative contexts. In E. Bavin (Ed.), *The Cambridge handbook of child language* (pp. 355–375). New York: Cambridge University Press.

Black, B., & Logan, A. (1995). Links between communication patterns in mother–child, father–child, and child–peer interactions and children's social status. *Child Development, 66,* 255–271.

Blum-Kulka, S., & Snow, C. (Eds.). (2002). *Talking to adults: The contribution of multi-party discourse to language acquisition.* Mahwah, NJ: Erlbaum.

Blum-Kulka, S., & Snow, C. (2004). Introduction: The potential of peer talk. *Discourse Studies, 6,* 291–306.

Brinton, B., & Fujiki, M. (1995). Conversational intervention with children with specific language impairment. In M. Fey, J. Windsor, & S. Warren (Eds.), *Language intervention: Preschool through the elementary years* (Vol. 5, Communication and Language Intervention Series) (pp. 183–212). Baltimore: Paul H. Brookes.

Bryant, J. B. (1999). Perspectives on pragmatic socialization. In A. Greenhill (Ed.), *Proceedings of the 23rd Annual Boston University Conference on Language Development* (Vol. 1, pp. 132–137). Somerville, MA: Cascadilla Press.

Burdelski, M. (2010). Socializing politeness routines: Action, other-orientation, and embodiment in a Japanese preschool. *Journal of Pragmatics, 42,* 1606–1621.

Comeau, L., Genesee, F., & Mendelson, M. (2010). A comparison of bilingual and monolingual children's conversational repairs. *First Language, 30,* 354–374.

Craig, H., & Washington, J. (1993). Access behaviors of children with specific language impairment. *Journal of Speech and Hearing Research, 36,* 322–337.

Craig, H., & Washington, J. (2005). Recent research on the language and literacy skills of African American students in the early years. In D. Dickinson & S. Neuman (Eds.), *Handbook of early literacy research* (Vol. 2, pp. 198–210). New York: Guilford.

Craig, H., Zhang, L., Hensel, S., & Quinn, E. (2009). African American English-speaking students: An examination of the relationship between dialect shifting and reading outcomes. *Journal of Speech, Language, and Hearing Research, 52,* 839–855.

Davidson, R., & Snow, C. (1996). Five-year-olds' interactions with fathers versus mothers. *First Language, 16,* 223–242.

DeHart, G. (1996). Gender and mitigation in four-year-olds' pretend play talk with siblings. *Research on Language and Social Interaction, 29,* 81–96.

DeHart, G. (1999). Conflict and averted conflict in preschoolers' interactions with siblings and friends. In W. A. Collins & B. Laursen (Eds.), *Relationships as developmental contexts. Minnesota Symposia on Child Psychology* (Vol. 30, pp. 281–303). Mahwah, NJ: Erlbaum.

Eckert, P. (2003). Language and gender in adolescence. In J. Holmes & M. Meyerhoff (Eds.), *The handbook of language and gender* (pp. 381–400). Malden, MA: Blackwell.

Ely, R., & Gleason, J. B. (2006). 'I'm sorry I said that': Apologies in young children's discourse. *Journal of Child Language, 33,* 599–620.

Ervin-Tripp, S. (1977). Wait for me, roller skate! In S. Ervin-Tripp & C. Mitchell-Kernan (Eds.), *Child discourse* (pp. 165–188). New York: Academic Press.

Ervin-Tripp, S. (1979). Children's verbal turn-taking. In E. Ochs & B. Schieffelin (Eds.), *Developmental pragmatics* (pp. 391–413). New York: Academic Press.

Garvey, C. (1975). Requests and responses in children's speech. *Journal of Child Language, 2,* 41–63.

Garvey, C. (1984). *Children's talk.* Cambridge, MA: Harvard University Press.

Genesee, F., & Nicoladis, E. (2007). Bilingual first language acquisition. In E. Hoff & M. Shatz (Eds.), *Blackwell handbook of language development* (pp. 324–342). Malden, MA: Blackwell.

Genesee, F., Paradis, J., & Crago, M. (2004). *Dual language development and disorders.* Baltimore: Paul H. Brookes.

Gertner, B., Rice, M., & Hadley, P. (1994). Influence of communicative competence on peer preferences in a preschool classroom. *Journal of Speech and Hearing Research, 37,* 913–923.

Gleason, J. B. (1975). Fathers and other strangers: Men's speech to young children. In D. Dato (Ed.), *Developmental psycholinguistics: Theory and applications. Georgetown University Roundtable on Language and Linguistics* (pp. 289–297). Washington, DC: Georgetown University Press.

Gleason, J. B., Hay, D., & Cain, L. (1989). Social and affective determinants of language acquisition. In M. Rice & R. Schiefelbusch (Eds.), *The teachability of language* (pp. 171–186). Baltimore: Paul H. Brookes.

Gleason, J. B., & Weintraub, S. (1976). The acquisition of routines in child language. *Language in Society, 5,* 129–136.

Goodman, G., Duchan, J., & Sonnenmeier, R. (1994). Children's development of scriptal knowledge. In J. Duchan & R. Sonnenmeier (Eds.), *Pragmatics: From theory to practice* (pp. 120–133). Englewood Cliffs, NJ: Prentice-Hall.

Gopnik, A., & Meltzoff, A. (1986). Words, plans, things, and locations: Interactions between semantic and cognitive development in the one-word stage. In S. Kuczaj & M. Barrett (Eds.), *The development of word meaning* (pp. 199–223). New York: Springer-Verlag.

Gordon, D., & Ervin-Tripp, S. (1984). The structure of children's requests. In R. Schiefelbusch & J. Pickar (Eds.), *The acquisition of communicative competence* (Vol. VIII, Language Intervention Series) (pp. 295–321). Baltimore: University Park Press.

Gratier, M., Greenfield, P., & Isaac, A. (2011). Tacit communicative style and cultural attunement in classroom interaction. *Mind, Culture, and Activity, 16,* 296–316.

Greenwood, C., Walker, D., & Utley, C. (2002). Relationships between

social-communicative skills and life achievements. In H. Goldstein, L. Kaczmarek, & K. English (Eds.), *Promoting social communication: Children with developmental disabilities from birth to adolescence* (pp. 345–370). Baltimore: Paul H. Brookes.

Griffin, R., Hemphill, L., Camp, L., & Wolf, D. (2004). Oral discourse in the preschool years and later literacy skills. *First Language, 24,* 123–147.

Hale, C., & Tager-Flusberg, H. (2005a). Brief report: The relationship between discourse deficits and autism symptomatology. *Journal of Autism and Developmental Disorders, 35,* 519–524.

Hale, C., & Tager-Flusberg, H. (2005b). Social communication in children with autism: The relationship between theory of mind and discourse development. *Autism, 9,* 157–178.

Hoff, E. (2010). Context effects on young children's language use: The influence of conversational setting and partner. *First Language, 30,* 461–472.

Hoff-Ginsberg, E. (1998). The relation of birth order and socioeconomic status to children's language experience and language development. *Applied Psycholinguistics, 19,* 603–629.

Hoff-Ginsberg, E., & Krueger, W. (1991). Older siblings as conversational partners. *Merrill-Palmer Quarterly, 37,* 465–482.

Hymes, D. (1967). Models of the interaction of language and social setting. *Journal of Social Issues, 23 (2),* 8–28.

Kam, C., & Edwards, N. (2008). The use of *uh* and *um* by 3- and 4-year-old native English-speaking children: Not quite right but not completely wrong. *First Language, 28,* 313–317.

Kelly, S. (2001). Broadening the units of analysis in communication: speech and nonverbal behaviours in pragmatic comprehension. *Journal of Child Language, 28,* 325–349.

Kemple, K., Speranza, H., & Hazen, N. (1992). Cohesive discourse and peer acceptance: Longitudinal relationships in the preschool years. *Merrill-Palmer Quarterly, 38,* 364–381.

Killen, M., & Naigles, L. (1995). Preschool children pay attention to their addressees: Effects of gender composition on peer disputes. *Discourse Processes, 19,* 329–346.

Kyratzis, A. (2007). Using the social organizational affordances of pretend play in American preschool girls' interactions. *Research on Language and Social Interaction, 40,* 321–352.

Leaper, C., Anderson, K., & Sanders, P. (1998). Moderators of gender effects on parents' talk to their children: A meta-analysis. *Developmental Psychology, 34,* 3–27.

Leaper, C., & Smith, T. (2004). A meta-analytic review of gender variations in children's language use. *Developmental Psychology, 40,* 993–1027.

Lederberg, A. (2006). Language development of deaf children with hearing parents. In K. Brown (Ed.), *Encyclopedia of language and linguistics* (2nd ed.) (pp. 361–368). Oxford, UK: Elsevier.

Lederberg, A., & Everhart, V. (2000). Conversations between deaf children and their hearing mothers: Pragmatic and dialogic characteristics. *Journal of Deaf Studies and Deaf Education, 5,* 303–322.

Leman, P., Ahmed., S., & Ozarow, L. (2005). Gender, gender relations, and the social dynamics of children's conversations. *Developmental Psychology, 41,* 64–74.

Leonard, L., Wilcox, J., Fulmer, K., & Davis, A. (1978). Understanding indirect requests: An investigation of children's comprehension of pragmatic meanings. *Journal of Speech and Hearing Research, 21,* 528–537.

Lewis, C. (1997). Fathers and preschoolers. In M. Lamb (Ed.), *The role of fathers in child development* (pp. 121–142). New York: Wiley.

Liang, X. (2006). Identity and language functions. *Journal of Language, Identity, and Education, 5,* 143–167.

Linguistic Society of America. (2011). *LSA resolution on the Oakland "Ebonics" issue* [Online]. Available: www.lsadc.org/info/lsa-res-ebonics.cfm.

Loveland, K. (1984). Learning about points of view: Spatial perspective and the acquisition of "I/you." *Journal of Child Language, 11,* 535–556.

Luyster, R., & Lord, C. (2009). The language of children with autism. In E. Bavin (Ed.), *The Cambridge handbook of child language* (pp. 447–458). New York: Cambridge University Press.

Mannle, S., Barton, M., & Tomasello, M. (1991). Two-year-olds' conversations with their mothers and preschool-aged siblings. *First Language, 12,* 57–71.

Nicolopoulou, A. (2002). Peer-group culture and narrative development. In S. Blum-Kulka & C. E. Snow (Eds.), *Talking to adults* (pp. 117–152). Mahwah, NJ: Erlbaum.

Nicolopoulou, A., & Richner, E. (2004). "When your powers combine, I am Captain Planet": The developmental significance of individual- and group-authored stories by preschoolers. *Discourse Studies, 6,* 347–371.

Ninio, A., & Snow, C. (1996). *Pragmatic development.* Boulder, CO: Westview Press.

Ninio, A., & Snow, C. (1999). The development of pragmatics: Learning to use language appropriately. In W. Ritchie & T. Bhatia (Eds.), *Handbook of child language acquisition* (pp. 347–383). San Diego, CA: Academic Press.

O'Neill, D. (1996). Two-year-old children's sensitivity to a parent's knowledge state when making requests. *Child Development, 67,* 659–677.

O'Neill, D., Main, R., & Ziemski, R. (2009). 'I like Barney': Preschoolers' spontaneous conversational initiations with peers. *First Language, 29,* 401–425.

O'Neill, D., Pearce, M., & Pick, J. (2004). Preschool children's narratives and performance on the Peabody Individualized Achievement Test – Revised: Evidence of a relation between early narrative and later mathematical ability. *First Language, 24,* 149–183.

Pagett, L. (2006). Mum and Dad prefer me to speak Bengali at home: Code switching and parallel speech in a primary school setting. *Literacy, 40,* 137–145.

Piaget, J. (1926/1974). *The language and thought of the child* (M. Gabains, Trans.). New York: New American Library.

Place, K., & Becker, J. (1991). The influence of pragmatic competence on the likeability of grade-school children. *Discourse Processes, 14,* 227–241.

Reaser, J., & Adger, C. (2010). Vernacular language varieties in educational settings: Research and development. In S. Bernard & F. Hult (Eds.), *Handbook of educational linguistics* (pp. 161–173). Malden, MA: Wiley-Blackwell.

Reeder, K., & Shapiro, J. (1996). A portrait of the literate apprentice. In K. Reeder, J. Shapiro, R. Watson, & H. Goelman (Eds.), *Literate apprenticeships: The emergence of language and literacy in the preschool years* (pp. 119–133). Norwood, NJ: Ablex.

Reeder, K., & Shapiro, J. (1997). Children's attributions of pragmatic intentions and early literacy. *Language Awareness, 6,* 17–31.

Reeder, K., Shapiro, J., Watson, R., & Goelman, H. (Eds.). (1996). *Literate apprenticeships: The emergence of language and literacy in the preschool years.* Norwood, NJ: Ablex.

Resnick, L., & Snow, C. (Eds.) (2009), *Speaking and listening for preschool through third grade* (Rev.Ed.). Newark, DE: National Center on Education and the Economy and University of Pittsburgh.

Richardson, F., & Thomas, M. (2009). Language development in genetic disorders. In E. Bavin (Ed.), *The Cambridge handbook of child language* (pp. 459–471). New York: Cambridge University Press.

Rickford, J. (2011). What is ebonics? (African American Vernacular English). [Online]. Available: www.lsadc.org/info/pdf_files/Ebonics.pdf

Robbins, K. (1918). The work of the American Speech Committee of the Chicago Woman's Club, and notes upon its school survey. *The English Journal, 7,* 163–176.

Roberto, A., & Eden, J. (2010). Cyberbullying: Aggressive communication in the digital age. In T. Avtgis & A. Rancer (Eds.), *Arguments, aggression, and conflict* (pp. 198–216). Florence, KY: Routledge.

Rubin, Z. (1980). *Children's friendships.* Cambridge, MA: Harvard University Press.

Samter, W. (2003). Friendship interaction skills across the life span. In J. Greene & P. Burleson (Eds.), *Handbook of com-munication and social interaction skills* (pp. 637–684). Mahwah, NJ: Erlbaum.

Schieffelin, B., & Ochs, E. (Eds.). (1986). *Language socialization across cultures.* New York: Cambridge University Press.

Schieffelin, B., & Ochs, E. (1996). The microgenesis of competence: Methodology in language socialization. In D. Slobin, J. Gerhardt, A. Kyratzis, & J. Guo (Eds.), *Social interaction, social context, and language: Essays in honor of Susan Ervin-Tripp* (pp. 251–263). Mahwah, NJ: Erlbaum.

Shatz, M. (1978). Children's comprehension of their mothers' question directives. *Journal of Child Language, 5,* 39–46.

Sheldon, A., & Rohleder, L. (1996). Sharing the same world, telling different stories: Gender differences in co-constructed pretend narratives. In D. Slobin, J. Gerhardt, A. Kyratzis, & J. Guo (Eds.), *Social interaction, social context, and language* (pp. 613–632). Mahwah, NJ: Erlbaum.

Short-Myerson, K., & Abbeduto, L. (1997). Preschoolers' communication during scripted interactions. *Journal of Child Language, 24,* 469–493.

Smitherman, G. (2007). The power of the rap. In H. S. Alim & J. Baugh (Eds.), *Talkin black talk: Language, education, and social change* (pp. 77–91). New York: Teachers College Press.

Snow, C. (1999). Social perspectives on the emergence of language. In B. MacWhinney (Ed.), *The emergence of language* (pp. 257–276). Mahwah, NJ: Erlbaum.

Snow, C., & Beals, D. (2006). Mealtime talk that supports literacy development. *New Directions for Child and Adolescent Development, No. 111,* 51–66.

Snow, C., & Blum-Kulka, S. (2002). From home to school: School-age children talking with adults. In S. Blum-Kulka & C. Snow (Eds.), *Talking to adults: The contribution of multi-party discourse to language acquisition* (pp. 327–341). Mahwah, NJ: Erlbaum.

Snow, C., Porche, M., Tabors, P., & Harris, S. R. (2007). *Is literacy enough?* Baltimore: Paul. H. Brookes.

Stude, J. (2007). The acquisition of metapragmatic abilities in preschool children. In W. Bublitz & A. Hübler (Eds.), *Metapragmatics in use* (pp. 199–220). Philadelphia: John Benjamins.

Subrahmanyam, K., & Šmahel, D. (2011). *Digital youth: The role of media in development*. New York: Springer.

Surian, L., Tedoldi, M., & Siegal, M. (2010). Sensitivity to conversational maxims in deaf and hearing children. *Journal of Child Language, 37*, 929–943.

Terry, N., Connor, C., Thomas-Tate, S., & Love, M. (2010). Examining relationships among dialect variation, literacy skills, and school context in first grade. *Journal of Speech, Language, and Hearing Research, 53*, 126–145.

Tomasello, M., Conti-Ramsden, G., & Ewert, B. (1990). Young children's conversations with their mothers and fathers: Differences in breakdown and repair. *Journal of Child Language, 17*, 115–130.

Tomasello, M., & Mannle, S. (1985). Pragmatics of sibling speech to one-year-olds. *Child Development, 56*, 911–917.

Turkstra, L., Ciccia, A., & Seaton, C. (2003). Interactive behaviors in adolescent conversation dyads. *Language,*

Speech, and Hearing Services in Schools, 34, 117–127.

Van Hofwegen, J., & Wolfram, W. (2010). Coming of age in African American English: A longitudinal study. *Journal of Sociolinguistics, 14*, 427–455,

Warren, A., & Tate, C. (1992). Egocentrism in children's telephone conversations. In R. Diaz & L. Berk (Eds.), *Private speech: From social interaction to self-regulation* (pp. 245–264). Hillsdale, NJ: Erlbaum.

Wolfram, W. (2005). African American English. In M. Ball (Ed.), *Clinical sociolinguistics* (pp. 87–100). Malden, MA: Blackwell.

Wood, B., & Gardner, R. (1980). How children "get their way": Directives in communication. *Communication Education, 29*, 264–272.

Wyatt, T. (1995). Language development in African American English child speech. *Linguistics and Education, 7*, 7–22.

Yifat, R., & Zadunaisky-Ehrlich, S. (2008). Metapragmatic comments indexing conversational practices of preschool children in institutional discourse. *First Language, 28*, 329–347.

Yule, G. (1997). *Referential communication tasks*. Mahwah, NJ: Erlbaum.

Theoretical Approaches to Language Acquisition

John N. Bohannon III
Butler University

John D. Bonvillian
University of Virginia

Most of the chapters in this book cover what children do in the process of learning language. This chapter, however, adopts a different approach: It describes theories and models that attempt to explain *how* children manage this extraordinary feat. The noted linguist Noam Chomsky (1957, 1965) proposed that descriptions, models, and theories are all part of an overall taxonomy of theoretical adequacy:

> *Descriptive adequacy,* Chomsky's first level, requires separating language behaviors from nonlanguage behaviors. Language acquisition research has gone a long way toward fulfilling this descriptive goal. On the other hand, children's language is creative and, potentially, infinitely variable. Therefore, an exhaustive list of all possible language productions, even from children, might be impossible to complete. Even if an exhaustive list were compiled, it would lack explanatory power, conveying little understanding of the mechanisms that produced the behavior.

> *Model adequacy,* the second level, is achieved when some finite number of unifying principles are identified that account for the emerging language behaviors. These principles predict the known facts of development, but are not necessarily the principles by which language-learning children actually operate. This second level is exemplified by learnability approaches. Most grammars written from transcripts of children's speech are attempts to determine the rules that account for the observed data. However, few researchers would insist that their grammars are the actual rules children use when speaking or understanding speech.

> *Theoretical adequacy,* the last and most ambitious level, is achieved when a finite set of principles is discovered that not only accounts for all the language behaviors observed but also is the actual set of mechanisms used by language-learning children.

In our view, a theory of language acquisition must explain not only why children say what they do, but also why they eventually speak like adults. This developmental perspective obviously presents researchers with additional concerns. In other words, we can neither aim our theoretical arrow not knowing the adult target, nor can we hit a known adult language target without a mechanism to get the arrow into it.

Distinguishing Features of Theoretical Approaches

Language acquisition research and speculation may be grouped into several general theoretical approaches to the problem. The rest of this chapter attempts to outline these competing approaches and compares them on several dimensions relevant to their explanations of both steady-state language behavior and language development. These features include distinctions of (1) structuralism versus functionalism, (2) competence versus performance, and (3) nativism versus empiricism.

The methods and relevant data for each approach are also considered. It is important to note that some distinctions described are, in a sense, artificially bipolar. As will be apparent, some of the extreme positions are complementary rather than truly opposite (see Zimmerman & Whitehurst, 1979 for a discussion of structuralism versus functionalism). However, the use of contrasts should facilitate recognition of critical similarities and differences between various approaches.

Structuralism versus Functionalism

A structural description of behavior attempts to discover invariant processes or mechanisms underlying observable data. Chomsky's rules of grammar and Watson's stimulus–response bonds are examples of such structures. Functional accounts of behavior seek to establish predictive relationships between environmental or situational variables and language. The aim of a functional account of language is the prediction and control of verbal behavior in different contexts and individuals.

The structural–functional distinction may be illustrated by the following example. If a child said, "I want milk," structuralists would analyze the form of the utterance, finding it to be composed of a subject *(I)*, a main verb *(want)*, and an object *(milk)*. They might then take this sentence as evidence that the child knows the English word-order rule governing active, declarative (i.e., subject–verb–object) sentences. This rule should enable the child to create an unlimited number of similar sentences from it. Functionalists would examine the situation in which the utterance "I want milk" occurred. They might determine that this particular utterance, if said in the presence of the mother, is frequently followed by a glass of milk. The occurrence of the utterance, then, is jointly determined by the context (presence of mother and hunger or thirst) and its consequences (receiving a glass of milk). The exact form of the utterance is considered unimportant. Notice that in this case, structuralists and functionalists are describing different aspects of language behavior, the former accounting for syntax and the latter focusing on the pragmatic, social use of language. These perspectives are complementary, and both are necessary to fully explain the child's language behavior.

Competence versus Performance

Competence refers to the individual's knowledge of language, or the underlying rules that may be deduced from language behavior. *Performance* refers to actual instances of language use. In other words, competence and performance distinguish the individual's abstract linguistic knowledge and the use of this knowledge. For example, a mature speaker of English might say, "She will be home yesterday," although they know, upon reflection, that such an utterance is ill-formed. Mistakes of this type are typically attributed to performance problems such as lapses of attention or memory rather than a basic ignorance of the rules of English grammar. This distinction is important because of the concept of competence. For example, one must be very careful that the utterances used for determining grammatical rules are not cluttered with performance mistakes. For this reason, historically, many researchers have used judgments of grammaticality rather than language use to discover a speaker's linguistic competence (e.g., Gleitman, Gleitman, & Shipley, 1972). In addition, notice that only structuralists are typically concerned with competence, whereas functionalists are more concerned with performance.

Nativism versus Empiricism

The third dimension concerns the emphasis placed upon either the child or the environment in the process of language acquisition. This is another example of the old nature–nurture issue. On one side, nativists insist that language is too complex and is acquired too rapidly to have been learned through any known methods (e.g., imitation), so some critical aspects of the language system must be innate. In contrast, empiricists focus on the influence of the environment and the nature of the interactive language contexts within which the child is immersed.

Language researchers typically do not adhere strictly to either extreme on the nativistic–empiricistic continuum. Few will disagree that language acquisition is determined both by the child's innate capacities and linguistic experiences. The course of early development is too invariant across many languages and contexts not to have some innate component. Similarly, very restricted linguistic experience yields little or no language. In a classic study, hearing children of deaf parents, who did not sign to them, largely failed to learn to speak or sign (Sachs, Bard, & Johnson, 1981). The recognition of the necessity of both factors has not inhibited theorists from stressing the role of one factor at the expense of the other. Rarely are the two factors given equal credit.

Evaluating Research Methods

The major approaches to language acquisition may also be compared with respect to the methods frequently used and the data that each theory attempts to explain. The approach followed by researchers usually determines the data and methods they consider relevant. Unfortunately, this sometimes leads to a complete separation of research efforts, with one group pursuing longitudinal observations of the changing grammars of a small number of children and other investigators performing experiments on sizable groups of children to change the frequency of particular verbal behaviors. The developmental perspective and the subjects chosen for study are also dependent upon the researchers' theoretical views. For example, those who argue that language is uniquely human, largely maturational, and composed of syntactic structures might observe maturing grammars in human children. For them, studies of adults or nonhuman animals would be considered largely irrelevant, and experimentation fruitless. In contrast, those who believe that language differs little from other motor activities and is learned in much the same way might try to reinforce communicative behavior in chimpanzees.

At first glance, it may appear that the approaches outlined in this chapter are so different that they don't even attempt to answer the same questions. Is agreement possible when the theoretical approaches differ so drastically? In any scientific endeavor, diversification of research methods and strategies should lead ultimately to convergent validity. That is, the more one examines a problem from different angles, the more likely it is that a solution will be discovered. Moreover, the broad range of language behavior needing explanation (phonetics, semantics, etc.) may require just as much diversity to answer all the important questions.

In the sections that follow, some of the competing approaches are outlined. They are organized into two main groups: the classic and interactionist approaches. The classic approaches are, historically, the first opposing set of theories: the behavioral and the linguistic. Although neither has survived intact over the past fifty years of empirical work, their principles are the foundations of modern theories and models. The interactionist position is further subdivided into the cognitive approach, the social approach, and the usage/gestural approach. Each area is outlined according to the distinctions previously delineated (e.g., structural–functional). Finally, a brief evaluation of all the approaches is presented in order to highlight the strengths and weaknesses of each.

Classic Behavioral Approaches

General Assumptions

All behavioral theories share a common focus on the observable and measurable aspects of language behavior. Whenever possible, behaviorists avoid mentalistic explanations of language behavior that rely on such constructs as intentions or "implicit knowledge" of grammatical rules. Because these mental processes are not easily defined or directly measurable, behaviorists search for observable environmental conditions (stimuli) that co-occur and predict specific verbal behaviors (responses). This is not to say that behaviorists deny the existence of internal mechanisms. They recognize that overt behavior has a base in the brain and that research into these neurological processes is necessary for a better understanding of behavior. What behaviorists reject are internal structures or processes with no specific physical correlate such as grammars (Zimmerman & Whitehurst, 1979).

Clearly, behaviorists emphasize performance over competence. In fact, few would even acknowledge the existence of competence or any knowledge that is separated from observable behavior. Skinner (1957) argued that behavioral scientists should not accept traditional categorizations of linguistic units (e.g., words and sentences), but should examine language as they would any other behavior. They should search for the functional units as they occur and the relationships that predict their occurrence.

Behaviorists also focus on learning because they regard language as a skill, not essentially different from any other behavior. For example, Watson (1924) stated, "Language as we ordinarily understand it, in spite of its complexities, is in the beginning a very simple type of behavior. It is really a manipulative habit." Skinner (1957) argued that language is a special case of behavior only because it is behavior that is reinforced exclusively by other people. Apart from the effect that language has on someone else, verbal behavior does not produce any reinforcement in and of itself.

The emphasis on learning places behaviorists squarely at the empirical end of the nativism–empiricism continuum. Although they admit that humans have specialized physiological structures (e.g., fine motor control of the lips, tongue, and larynx) that allow them to speak, speaking is assumed to be learned through the same principles as rats learn to run mazes. Speaking (and understanding speech) must be brought under the control of stimuli in the environment by reinforcement, imitation, and successive approximations to mature performance (known as shaping). The child is typically viewed as a passive recipient of environmental pressures, much as a malleable piece of clay is molded into new shapes. Behaviorists rarely acknowledge that children, in turn, may affect their environment. In fact, Skinner (1957) stated that a speaker should be considered as merely an "interested bystander," having no active role in the process of language behavior or development.

Behavioral Language Learning

One of the simplest ways of explaining changes in behavior is through the connection or association of stimuli in the environment and certain responses of the organism. The process of forming such associations is known as **classical conditioning**. The associations formed between arbitrary verbal stimuli and internal responses are often cited as the source of word meanings (Staats, 1971). For example, a child may learn the word *hot* in the following manner: A hotplate (unconditioned stimulus, UCS) touched by a curious infant results in physiological pain (unconditioned response, UCR). When the infant's mother cries out, "Hot!" prior to touching, this word (conditioned stimulus, CS) becomes associated with the primary stimulus of heat and gradually acquires the power to elicit a response (conditioned response, CR) in the child that is similar to the response to the heat itself.

Once a CS (a word) has come to elicit a CR, it can then be used as a UCS to modify the response to another CS. For example, if a new CS, such as the word *fire,* frequently occurs with the word *hot,* it may come to elicit a CR similar to the response to *hot.* The associations formed between several stimuli (CSs) and a single response lead to the formation of associations between the stimuli themselves. Thus, not only may arbitrary verbal CSs be associated with specific internal meanings (CRs), the words themselves may be connected by stimulus–stimulus associations. In this way, classical conditioning is used to account for the interrelationship of words and word meanings.

Whereas behaviorists use the principles of classical conditioning to account for the child's development of receptive vocabulary, additional learning principles must be applied to explain productive speech. Operant conditioning is the form of learning most often used to fill this role (Moerk, 1983; Osgood, 1953). Operant conditioning concerns the changes in voluntary, non-reflexive behavior that arise because of environmental consequences contingent upon that behavior. Simply put, behaviors that most frequently result in rewards tend to be repeated, whereas behaviors that result in punishment do not tend to recur. All behavioral accounts of language acquisition assume that children's productive speech is shaped by differential reinforcers and punishments supplied by environmental agents (e.g., parents). Behaviorists assume that children's speech that more closely approximates adult speech will be rewarded, whereas meaningless or inappropriate speech will be ignored or punished. Parents gradually change their reinforcement practices, eventually restricting rewards to only those utterances that are meaningful and adult-like.

Throughout development, behaviorists assume that children's caretakers industriously train children to perform verbal behaviors, usually after the parent has provided an example: "Say bye-bye. Bye-bye." In this way, the adult provides the child with both mature speech exemplars and training in imitation of adult speech. When children successfully imitate what the adult just pronounced, the children are rewarded. In addition, the word *dog* is provided in the presence of dogs, *boy* in the presence of boys, and so on. Thus, the acquisition of both receptive and productive vocabulary begins to accelerate as all the types of learning—classical, operant, and imitative—converge to direct and control the child's language behavior. Behaviorists assume that the course of language development is determined largely by the course of training, not maturation.

Children's word combinations are assumed to be acquired in much the same fashion as single words. Parents train simple word combinations through shaping and imitation training, rewarding successive approximations to adult-like word strings. Some behaviorists explain these word combinations as response chains, with the first word and current context serving as a stimulus for the second word, which with the context serves as a stimulus for the next word, and so forth. These word chains are also known as **Markov sentence models** (Mowrer, 1960). Clearly, the child need not have heard every possible chain or string of words in order to produce and understand them. It is only necessary for the child to have associations between pairs of words, between individual words and the environmental context, and between words and possible internal mediating stimuli.

Behaviorist interpretations assume increasing complexity in the response unit. Just as sounds were shaped into words in infancy, such that words become the functional response unit, combinations of words come to serve as new, larger response units. Whitehurst (1982) argued that some word patterns (e.g., "the boy's shoe," "the boy's bike," "the boy's dog") become grammatical frames ("the boy's X"), where insertion of novel lexical items with similar properties is allowed ("the boy's toothbrush"). It should be noted, however, that most behaviorists do not view such grammatical frames as true grammatical rules. A "rule," according to Skinner (1957), is a special verbal behavior that allows extensive responding without direct exposure to established contingencies. The fact that children eventually come to speak in accordance with formal linguistic rules did not imply to Skinner that children's early speech is indeed rule-governed. Because young children cannot verbalize or make explicit the rules (e.g., "You add *-ed* to the verb stem to create past tense"), Skinner assumed that children's speech is not rule-governed, but is shaped directly by the contingencies alone.

The basic processes of learning (i.e., classical and operant conditioning) are assumed to direct and control the increasing complexity of children's verbal behavior. Although all these processes continue to function into adulthood, the accelerated rate of learning during childhood seems to require additional learning principles, which facilitate the rapid acquisition of complex behaviors. Thus, behaviorists rely on imitation as an especially important factor in language learning, because it allows a shortcut to mature behavior without laborious shaping of each and every verbal response. Imitation may be an exact copy of observed behavior, but it is not limited to exact copies (Bandura & Walters, 1963). Children may perform behaviors through imitation that only partially resemble the modeled behavior. Whitehurst and Vasta (1975) suggest that children can acquire grammatical frames through imitation, substituting their own words appropriate to the new context in which the utterance occurs. Neither is imitation limited to behaviors that follow modeled behavior closely in time; imitations may occur after a considerable delay. When children successfully imitate new words and forms, behaviorists assume that reinforcement occurs, either from adults or from the children themselves. The fact that the process of imitating in itself becomes reinforcing suggests that children will use imitation more frequently over time. Thus, imitation serves as a relatively flexible and frequently used learning strategy that enables rapid learning of complex language behaviors.

In summary, behaviorists focus on the simple mechanisms involved in learning. Language development is considered to be a problem of linking various stimuli in the environment to internal responses, and these internal responses to overt verbal behavior. Language development is viewed as a progression from random verbalizations to mature communication through the simultaneous application of classical and operant conditioning and imitation. The time it takes children to acquire language is seen as a limitation of the training techniques of the parents rather than maturation of the child. Moreover, behaviorists typically do not credit the child with knowledge of rules, with intentions or meaning, or with the ability to abstract important properties from the language environment. Rather, certain environmental stimuli evoke and strengthen certain responses in the child. The sequence of language acquisition, then, is determined primarily by which environmental stimuli are most salient at any point in time, and by the child's past experience with those stimuli. The learning principle of reinforcement, according to the behavioral approach, plays the major role in the process of language acquisition.

Evaluation of the Behavioral Approaches

Supporting Evidence.   Most accounts of word meaning have shown that networks of associations of varying qualities and strength are involved in semantics (Smith, 1978). How are these associations learned initially, and are word meanings actually acquired through these associations?

Through the careful application of behavior modification techniques such as shaping and reinforcement, many children with very limited speech skills have made considerable progress in learning to speak or use language, especially children with autism (many following procedures first developed by Lovaas, 1977; see Ospina et al., 2008, and Chapter 9). Thus, regardless of the role of behavioral training in typical language development, it has been shown to be extremely useful in fostering language skills in children with certain language learning disorders.

The effects of imitation have also been studied extensively by behaviorists (for a review, see Speidel & Nelson, 1984). These studies usually involve an adult model who uses particular grammatical forms in differing sentential contexts. Unfortunately, the simple provision of novel grammatical exemplars by adult models has not yielded convincing evidence that typically developing children will always learn the modeled form. Whitehurst and Novak (1973) demonstrated new grammatical forms to children under two conditions. In the first condition, an adult simply modeled the target rule for the child. The second condition involved "imitation training," which encouraged the child to try to reproduce the form if imitation had not occurred spontaneously. Such "imitation training" was much more effective in getting the children to use the targeted linguistic rule in novel sentences.

Some of the modern usage-based approaches discussed later in this chapter are reflections of earlier behavioral suggestions of syntactic frames. Both Tomasello (2003) and Mintz (2003) have categorized mothers' child-directed speech into several syntactic types (e.g., *wh*-questions, imperatives). Tomasello further taxonomized the syntactic types into the initial words that framed the utterance (e.g., "Are you _____," "Let's _____," "What did _____"). He found that over half of all maternal speech addressed to their children began with one of the fifty-two initial word frames, and 45 percent of the mothers' speech began with just seventeen of the items. The frequency with which parents use such "frames" has been shown to relate to children's pace of language development in English (St. Clair, Monaghan, & Christiansen, 2010) and other languages (Weisleder & Waxman, 2010). There is also support for the behaviorist view that an environment that is responsive to young children's utterances may foster these children's language development. By responding contingently to their infants' babbling, mothers evidently encourage their young children to babble more using the phonemes of their language (Goldstein & Schwade, 2008). Moreover, a pattern of maternal responsiveness to their children's early expressive output is often associated with the children's attainment of a range of language development milestones (Tamis-LeMonda, Bornstein, & Baumwell, 2001). That is, mothers who are more responsive to their children's vocal behavior typically have children who show more rapid language growth.

Contrary Evidence.   The problem with much of the above research concerns a very important distinction between changing levels of performance versus acquiring new behaviors. Clearly, to increase adults' use of known grammatical structures is quite a different proposition than teaching children new grammatical rules. In other words, the behaviorists must test their assumptions and relationships in experiments on the subjects about whom they theorize, namely, children. Further, behaviorists must search for evidence of their critical factors (e.g., shaping, reinforcement) in children's natural home environments.

If a learning factor that is effective in the lab does not occur in the child's natural environment, then that factor cannot explain language acquisition. Many researchers (Morgan, Bonamo, & Travis, 1995; Pinker, 1994; Wexler & Culicover, 1980) have argued that children are not carefully shaped and tutored in the home, regardless of the effectiveness of these techniques in the lab. McNeill (1966) cited the following example reflecting the importance of maturation:

Child:	Nobody don't like me.
Mother:	No. Say, "Nobody likes me."
Child:	Nobody don't like me.
	—eight repetitions of the above—
Mother:	Now listen carefully. Say, "Nobody likes me."
Child:	Oh! Nobody don't likes me.

The failure of careful, patient tutoring is clear in this anecdote. Further studies (Brown & Hanlon, 1970; Hirsh-Pasek, Treiman, & Schneiderman, 1984; Penner, 1987) found that parents do not explicitly reward or praise their children for producing grammatically correct utterances, nor do they punish them for producing ungrammatical statements. Instead, parents were more likely to respond with praise, such as "Right" or "Good" when the semantic relationships were true, regardless of whether the utterance was syntactically appropriate.

There are also data that question the *directionality* of imitation in child language; recent studies have shown that maternal imitation of the child's vocalizations is as common as children imitating adult models (Pelaez, Virues-Ortega, & Gewirtz, 2011). Moreover, adult imitation of the child's early language attempts is also associated with language growth, complicating classical accounts of behavioral shaping.

The assumption that language is "just another behavior" is also unlikely. There are simply too much data that suggest that humans are uniquely constructed to detect and process language information differently from other information. As Chapter 2 reports, infants display a number of speech perception skills very early in infancy that are unlikely to be learned.

In summary, the behavioral approach has not fulfilled its original promise of prediction and control of language behavior in normally functioning individuals. Although language performance can be shaped in the lab, researchers are hard pressed to (1) find clear instances of similar tutelage in the home and (2) prove that children's language gains are manipulated via reinforcement. In spite of the major failures of the behavioral approach, it should be remembered that language acquisition is a form of behavioral change over time. As such, the study of language acquisition must incorporate some aspects of general learning mechanisms, which the behaviorist approach has studied extensively. To totally neglect the learning approach would be tantamount to "throwing the baby out with the bathwater."

Linguistic Approaches

General Assumptions

Linguistic approaches typically assume that language has a structure or grammar that is somewhat independent of language use. This independent rule system determines the sentences that are "grammatical" or permissible in any particular language. Grammars consist of a finite set of rules, shared by all the speakers of that language, that allow the generation of an infinite set of mutually comprehensible sentences. The rules of grammar are not unlike the rules that govern mathematics (e.g., associativity, commutativity), which allow the solution of an infinite number of problems with a finite set of theorems. Chomsky (1957) argued that an adequate grammar must be generative or creative in order to account for the myriad of sentences that native speakers of a language can produce and understand. Adult speakers of any language can produce and understand sentences they have never said or heard before, simply by using a single grammatical rule and inserting various lexical items. Chomsky (1957) argued that a true grammar should describe the speaker's knowledge of all permissible utterances (competence) rather than just the utterances actually produced (performance).

Over the years, Chomsky has revised or discarded many of his original ideas. For example, he jettisoned such distinctions as deep structure and surface structure as basically misguided. Chomsky's approach to language that had become known as government and binding theory in the 1980s (see Chapter 5) was superseded by an approach known as the minimalist program (Chomsky, 1995).

In Chomsky's approach, the component of the brain devoted to language is referred to as the **language faculty**. This faculty in its initial state is genetically determined and similar across the human species, with the exception of those individuals with serious pathology (Chomsky & Place, 2000). The theory accounting for this initial state is known as **universal grammar**. Universal grammar contains the system of grammatical rules and categories common to all the world's languages. Chomsky described the initial state of the faculty of language as similar to a fixed network connected to a switch box. The network contains the principles and properties of the language faculty in the form of a finite array of switches that are set by experience. If the switches become set in one particular way, then the outcome will be French; set in another way, the outcome will be Maori. Each human language in this approach is the product of a specific setting of switches—a setting of parameters.

Although the structure of the language faculty has yet to be discovered, Chomsky (1995) speculated on its likely properties and principles. The language faculty must have at least two components: a cognitive system involved in information storage and performance systems that access this information and make use of it in different ways. Chomsky, furthermore, assumed that the cognitive system interacts with two performance systems, the articulatory-perceptual and the conceptual-intentional. At the interface (known as **phonetic form**) with the articulatory-perceptual system, the cognitive system of the language faculty connects to the pronunciation system. At the interface (known as **logical form**) with the conceptual-intentional system, the cognitive system of the language faculty connects with the conceptual system. According to Chomsky (1995, p. 2), "This 'double interface' property is one way to express the traditional description of language as sound with a meaning, traceable at least back to Aristotle."

Most of the systems Chomsky (1957, 1965, 1982) devised to account for language share some common elements. All show separate semantic, syntactic, and phonological subsystems, as well as a discontinuity between what a speaker wishes to say (intentions or concepts) and the form the utterance eventually takes to convey that meaning (spoken form). All include a flexible syntactic system whereby the same intention can be encoded several ways, for example, "She hit me" and "I was hit by her." Conversely, a spoken surface form, such as "She was killed by the river" may be interpreted (or produced from) two different concepts (i.e., "The river killed her" or "Someone killed her near the river"). Thus, one of the most important tasks confronting the language-learning child is how to map meaningful concepts on to the ambiguous spoken exemplars provided by the language environment (Pinker, 1994). Chomsky (1980) also advanced the view that children could not acquire language through their experiences in these environments because he believed that there was not sufficient useful language-related input available to children. This argument became known as the **poverty of stimulus** argument. If the language environments of children were as limited and degenerate as Chomsky claimed, then much of the children's language acquisition must rest on innate abilities or structures.

Theorists who follow the linguistic approach argue that language is innate in humans. This position has been a source of healthy controversy over the years. Helping to fuel the debate is the problem that investigators differ in what they mean when they contend that a behavior is innate. Some consider innateness to be a set of constraints on the course of development, given a set of expected experiences (Elman, 1999). Chomsky (1988) and many others take a more radical view. They argue that humans have a genetically determined language capacity. This capacity evolved into a grammar that is different from and independent of other forms of cognition (e.g., general learning or memory). The fact that children learn different languages very quickly has resulted in the position that "children must therefore have built into their brains a universal grammar, a plan shared by the grammars of all languages" (Kandel, Schwartz, & Jessel, 1995, p. 639). Once a language parameter is set in development, it will restrict the set of forms allowed in that language.

These assumptions about the nature of language and the learning situation confronting children have profound implications. First, there is a "formal chasm between the input and output of language learning" (Pinker, 1987). In general, this means that what the child hears in speech is only indirectly related to the formal parameter settings that are assumed to be the end product of language learning. If language learning consists of children forming a succession of hypotheses about these principles and parameters, there is simply too much ambiguity between different meanings and the spoken sentence for language to be learned by a naive learner. The fact that children do, in fact, master their native tongues across the world in spite of the indecipherable nature of language has come to be called the **learnability problem**. Second (and contrary to the behaviorists), linguists assume that children are never told which sentences are correct and incorrect, neither in the speech they hear nor through correction of their own productive errors (Morgan et al., 1995; Pinker, 1994; and many others).

LAD and Development

The innate language component has been traditionally labeled a **language acquisition device** or **LAD** (Chomsky, 1965; Lenneberg, 1967) that bestows upon the child a host of information about grammatical classes and possible transformations (McNeill, 1970). The LAD operates on the raw linguistic data in children's language to produce the particular abstract grammar of the children's native tongue. The LAD is assumed to be a physiological part of the brain that is a specialized language processor. Just as wings allow birds to fly, the LAD allows children enough innate knowledge of language to speak (Pinker, 1994). The innate knowledge must consist of aspects of language that are universal to all languages. Because children initially have the capacity to learn any language, the properties of the LAD cannot be specific to any one tongue such as English. The exact nature of the LAD and its attendant mechanisms is a matter of great debate (see Morgan, 1990).

In an early formulation, McNeill (1970) argued that children are innately endowed with "strong linguistic universals" such as the concepts of "sentence" and grammatical classes, and some aspects of phonology, all of which are necessary for the proper development of a grammar. Since then, others have confined the innate linguistic capacities to some inherent constraints and biases to treat the language environment in special ways (Wexler, 1999). Children are regarded as "little cryptographers," who must employ their inherent knowledge of languages to decipher their mother tongue. As children are exposed to their native language, a series of linguistic "parameters" are set. For example, a child hearing English would over time be "set" to use word order to signal relations between words, whereas someone hearing Italian might be "set" to use inflections.

Obviously, the linguistic approach is biased toward the structural and nativist ends of the continuum. Linguists search for commonalities across children, cultures, and languages to discover the inherent organization that can be deduced from features that are universal to all languages. As Pinker (1994) put it, "differences between individuals are so boring!" It should be noted that the linguistic approach recognizes the need for experience with the language environment. However, this approach insists that the environment merely triggers the maturation of a physiologically based language system (LAD), or sets certain parameters, but does not shape or train verbal behavior. In addition, the linguistic approach favors competence over performance, although both concepts are considered acceptable topics of research. Competence is emphasized because it reflects the formal organization of grammar, whereas children's performance is too susceptible to errors that are irrelevant to the structure of language.

The child's task of acquiring a language, within this view, is considerably simpler when certain critical aspects of the task are assumed to be present at birth. Newborns immediately begin to detect the sounds in the environment that are linguistically significant. As they mature, they begin to produce only those sounds that have been present in their linguistic environment. This process may be facilitated by some innate imitative tendencies, through which the child automatically reproduces facial motor movements (lip and tongue configurations that correlate with different sounds) seen in adults (see review by Nagy, 2006). As their phonological skills mature, children are simultaneously forming primitive, unlabeled concepts for referents in their environment, such as *milk* (K. Nelson, 1981). At some point, the child may hear an adult say, "Do you want some milk?" and conclude that *milk* is the label that refers to the primitive concept of milk, even though this word was not taught specifically. The reason that the child chose the word *milk* to represent the concept, rather than the other words in the string, is that the child possesses mechanisms for categorizing words into appropriate grammatical classes. In other words, children can, almost automatically, differentiate nouns from verbs by their differing patterns of usage in adult speech.

Many have speculated that children are particularly sensitive to commonalities in usage and meaning. For example, nouns usually refer to things, verbs to actions or relations. Moreover, these classes of words, things versus acts, tend to occur in predictable combinations with other words. Thus, *snurt* used in the medial position in the sentence "He snurt himself" conveys considerable information about the permissible uses of the word in other sentences such as "Can I snurt the bread?" or "I snurted until my brains fell out." These critical combinatorial cues may also derive from examples of how the word combines with grammatical morphemes, such as *-ed,* usually meaning that the root is a verb (Lidz, Gleitman, & Gleitman, 2003). Children move rapidly from the acquisition of their first word to the realization that "everything has a name" (Bates, Bretherton, & Snyder, 1988), which leads to great increases in vocabulary size. In spite of the fact that children now know many words, they use only one word per utterance during this stage. Although each word occurs in isolation, the linguistic approach typically assumes that grammatical relations govern each word. That is, each word constitutes a sentence and is assumed to be a direct expression of children's intentions. The child does not string more words together in this stage only because of performance limitations, such as memory or attentional factors. The child's notion of a hierarchically organized sentence structure is further differentiated over time into noun phrases, verb phrases, and so on. Thus, children move from the one-word stage to two words at a time to multiword utterances by testing their own evolving grammars against the data provided by the environment. Some have called this process **hypothesis testing** to highlight the child's active role in the acquisition of syntactic rules (Ninio, 2011).

Evaluation of the Linguistic Approaches

Supporting Evidence. Research supporting the linguistic approaches has followed several lines. One supports the concept of grammar as the link between what is meant and what is said. This would support Chomsky's (1965) distinction between underlying intentions and the overt sentences. Besides the intuition that differing underlying concepts are necessary to account for ambiguous sentences, some empirical data have been sought to confirm the existence of grammar-specific processing.

Several studies showed that if subjects heard a "click" while processing a sentence, they perceived the sound as having occurred at the nearest constituent boundary, regardless of when it actually occurred (Garret, Bever, & Fodor, 1966). Thus perception of sentences is determined by the principles of syntactic organization (parsing into constituents) that linguists have described. Further, subjects can be primed to use specific sentence structures in preference to other forms (Bock, 1989). Thus, research suggests that comprehending a sentence consists of actively processing the hierarchical sentence structure to determine the meaning.

Evidence of the emergence of linguistic rules was also sought in children's spontaneous speech, primarily using longitudinal, in-depth observations of small numbers of children. (For a classic review of these studies, see Brown, 1973.) Many focused on the phenomenon of overregularization, defined as the inappropriate application of a grammatical rule. For example, a child might say, "I eated a cookie." This utterance may be taken as evidence that the child knows the rule for the formation of past tense for regular verbs (add *-ed* to the root) and has overapplied this rule to irregular forms. Brown and Bellugi (1964) concluded that children must be inducing the latent structure of language, since they could never have heard these errors in adult speech. Moreover, many studies have found evidence of similar rule use in children from a wide range of languages and cultures, including Finnish (Bowerman, 1973), Turkish (Slobin, 1982), Russian (Slobin, 1966), and Japanese (Hakuta, 1977).

The cross-cultural or cross-linguistic perspective also has proven to be a rich source of data concerning the biological basis of language (Slobin, 1986). Because the LAD is assumed to function in all children, it must allow the acquisition of any language, so similar patterns of development across several languages are taken as evidence of the LAD's operation. Slobin has found that young children use subject–object word order, regardless of the order used by mature speakers of their native language; thus it may be a universal. McNeill (1966) argues that the LAD also allows children to presuppose the existence of grammatical classes, such as nouns, verbs, and so on, because these classes are common to all languages and are acquired relatively early in development.

The surprising speech perception abilities of infants may also bolster the maturational view of language development. Many studies (see Chapter 2) document categorical perception of consonants and vowels within months of birth. Molfese, Molfese, and Molfese (2007) even found that infants' brains responded asymmetrically to language sounds versus non-language sounds. Thus, children seem to be especially sensitive to the sounds of human language and quickly achieve adult-like sound-discrimination abilities. Moreover, the early patterns of babbling in infancy are remarkably similar over many languages and situations (Levitt & Uttman, 1992).

Some of the evidence that children are endowed with a capacity to generate symbols and to organize communicative expressions systematically has come from longitudinal investigations of ten deaf children of hearing parents who elected not to sign with their children (Goldin-Meadow, Özyürek, Sancar, & Mylander, 2009). Rather, these parents worked diligently to develop spoken language skills in their children. These efforts, however, proved unsuccessful. Thus, the children were reared in loving environments that did not provide them with a useful language model.

Early in their development, all ten of the children were observed producing several different types of gestures, called "home signs" (Goldin-Meadow & Feldman, 1977; Goldin-Meadow & Mylander, 1984, 1990). Deictic gestures were used by the children to indicate specific objects, persons, and locations in their immediate environment. In most instances, these gestures consisted of points. A second group, characterizing gestures, were stylized pantomimes. These mimetic gestures clearly resembled the actions or objects to which the children were referring. The third group of gestures, known as markers, were quite similar to gestures used by most American speakers. Examples of markers included nodding the head for an affirmation or extending a finger to signify "Wait." By combining their gestures, children were able to convey a wide range of semantic relations.

One of the ten original children, David, has been the focus of continuing investigation. Systematic analyses of David's gestural production have shown that his gestural communication became more language-like as he grew older. David learned to refer to absent objects (Butcher, Mylander, & Goldin-Meadow, 1991) and to adapt his characterizing gestures depending upon whether the gestures served a noun or verb role (Goldin-Meadow, Butcher, Mylander, & Dodge, 1994). Finally, many of David's gestures began to structurally resemble signs from formal sign languages used by deaf persons. That is, many of his signs were made using the same locations and the same movements as signs from sign languages (Singleton, Morford, & Goldin-Meadow, 1993). Thus, David, with very little if any useful input, appears to have created a communication system with a number of properties in common with languages. Children who receive limited linguistic input have a capacity to create an effective communication system that is similar in a number of ways to the language of normally developing children (Goldin-Meadow, 2003). This avenue of research has been expanded to a number of communities around the world (such as China, Turkey, and Nicaragua) where deaf children have been observed to develop home sign systems that contain major properties of established languages (Goldin-Meadow, 2011; Goldin-Meadow et al., 2009).

Further support for the nativist position comes from three additional sources. First, deaf individuals who are not exposed to sign language during the critical period for language development display worse adult sign language ability than that of learners who acquire sign language as a second language (Mayberry, 2010). Second, the study of non-native speakers immersed in a second language suggests that there may be a critical period, after which acquisition becomes difficult or impossible (Johnson & Newport, 1989). Also, studies of Genie, who was almost totally deprived of linguistic input until age 13, show that she still did not acquire syntax after years of intensive training, even though her semantic (and cognitive) development had advanced more normally (Curtiss, 1981; see discussion in Chapter 1). Those concerned with the species specificity of language have determined that only humans have the ability to create and understand potentially infinite combinations of linguistic symbols (Terrace & Bever, 1976). Finally, studies have confirmed that human infants can learn much more complex "grammar-like" sequences than can non-human primates, even after extensive training (Saffran, Hauser, Seibel, Kapfhamer, Tsao, & Cushman, 2008).

In the early 1990s, Gopnik (1990; Gopnik & Crago, 1991) reported a family in England with a grammatical deficit called **feature-blind aphasia** that appears to follow Mendelian dominant inheritance patterns. Specifically, Gopnik (1990) reported that afflicted family members had trouble with grammatical morphemes such as *-ed* to denote past tense. It looked as if they were incapable of normal grammatical generalization and had to learn each verb's past tense individually. (See additional discussion of this family in Chapter 9.) Using this as evidence for a genetic basis for learning syntactic regularities, Pinker (1991) suggested theoretically dissociating regular from irregular forms. He argued that an innate basis for syntactic capacity had been unequivocally supported, although he doubted that only one gene controlled all syntactic forms. Researchers (Enard et al., 2002) have identified the culprit gene (named FOXP2). The gene seems to code for a protein that binds to other genes to activate them. Mutations in FOXP2 and other genes have now been identified in a variety of human communication disorders (see Vargha-Khadem, Gadian, Copp, & Mishkin, 2005 and Chapter 9 for further discussion of the genetic bases of childhood speech and language disorders).

Some linguists have tried to test the formal learnability of certain grammars, much as mathematicians test the adequacy of a set of axioms in proving a theorem. Learnability theorists (Pinker, 1984; Wexler & Culicover, 1980) reason that if languages are acquired by learning syntactic rules, then those rules must be learnable or, in some sense, discoverable from the raw linguistic data provided by the environment. Their basic assumption is that the sample strings of words that children hear are all positive exemplars or "true" instances of permissible sentences, and they are given no **negative evidence**, that is, information about unacceptable strings (as we noted in the behavioral section). This type of learning situation is called **text presentation**. Without any information concerning their errors, children would never arrive at the correct rules, so some rules must be innate, or some alternatives must be ruled out *a priori* (Grimshaw & Pinker, 1989). Morgan and colleagues (1995) investigated the possible effects of one kind of negative evidence on children's developing language. Using Brown's Adam, Eve, and Sarah data, Morgan and colleagues (1995) applied sophisticated time-series regression analysis to detect the effects of error correction on children's syntax gains over time. They reported significant *negative* correlations between parental corrections and children's later use of correct forms. They concluded that adult corrections, called **recasts**, actually impeded language development. The general conclusion was that grammar is unlearnable through any known principles and must be largely innately programmed.

Contrary Evidence.   Ironically, the same assumptions thought to be the strong points of the linguistic approach in the 1960s have attracted serious criticism. Some linguists focus too exclusively on language competence, discarding much of the data from adults and children as irrelevant to linguistic theory. Many now agree that these grammars are untestable as psychological theories (see Morgan, 1990). A similar problem exists with formal tests of the "learnability" of grammars (e.g., Chomsky, 1957). After Wexler (1982; Wexler & Culicover, 1980) showed that an early grammar was "unlearnable," Chomsky (1982) replaced it with a revised system, reasoning that the tested grammar was not descriptively accurate.

These oft-changed adult grammars have made it more difficult for other investigators to examine developmental mechanisms systematically. This is akin to an archer trying to strike a target when the target is constantly moving. Moreover, concluding that grammar is not learned through any known principles is not equivalent to concluding that it is innate. Pinker (1984) calls this the **poverty of imagination** postulate, meaning that just because someone cannot imagine how a particular behavior might have been learned, it does not necessarily follow that it was not learned (is innate).

Pinker's postulate is a play on another major argument by nativist theorists: that the language input that children hear is not sufficiently broad or uniformly well-formed to permit full language learning; this is called the **poverty of the stimulus** argument. This seemed to be a reasonable assumption when researchers examined natural adult conversations: It is indeed full of false starts, elliptical (incomplete) utterances, and even occasional errors. However, in recent years, researchers have used actual transcripts of parent–child interactions as input to computer learning algorithms with surprising success, suggesting that the input addressed to language learning children may be quite sufficient to guide their acquisition of syntax (Xuân-Nga Cao, Stoyneshka, Tornyova, Fodor, & Sakas, 2008).

Probably the most vulnerable point to the linguistic approach concerns the assumption of text learning or the lack of negative evidence (Pinker, 1984, 1989). The no-negative-evidence postulate is so central to learnability theory that it may be the "smoking gun" (Moerk, 1991b). If children are provided any information at all about the acceptability of sentences in their language, then the elaborate arguments of "learnability" fall apart (see Bohannon, MacWhinney, & Snow, 1990; Valian, 1999). Indeed, there is an emerging consensus that parents respond differentially to children's grammatical and ungrammatical utterances. Although parents rarely provide overt signals of approval or disapproval of the child's grammar, they may provide the negative evidence needed by children to facilitate their grammatical development. Bohannon and Stanowicz (1988) examined both parents and other adults conversing with children. They found that more than 90 percent of adult exact imitations followed children's well-formed speech, whereas more than 70 percent of adults' recasted or expanded imitations followed children's language errors. In this study, parents and nonparents rarely reproduced children's language errors. Instead, the children's language errors were immediately *changed* into alternative forms that were correct grammatically. Similar proportions of adult use of grammatically correct alternative forms have been observed in French (Chouinard & Clark, 2003). Chouinard and Clark surmised that a child intuits that an adult utterance is corrective feedback when the apparent intended meaning of the adult's utterance is the same as that of the child's utterance, but the grammatical form is different.

The use of recasted responses by adults evidently has an effect on children's language use and development. Once children hear a recasted response that shows correct grammatical usage, they are three to eight times more likely to attempt to repeat the correction than at any other time in conversation (Farrar, 1992). Several studies (e.g., Proctor-Williams & Fey, 2007; Saxton, 2000; Saxton, Backley, & Gallaway, 2003) have examined the effects of corrective recasts on typically developing children's subsequent grammatical development. There were immediate and long-term improvements in children's grammatical usage when adults used corrective recasts, with particularly striking results when the recasts followed children's errors. These findings led Saxton, Houston-Price, and Dawson (2005) to propose that it is the direct contrast of an adult's corrective recast and the child's ungrammatical utterance that often facilitates grammatical development.

How should these findings about the effects of corrective recasts on children's language development be interpreted? Critically, the central assumption of the linguistic approach about the absence of negative evidence available to language-learning children is wrong. Adults respond differentially to children's speech errors with recasts, and children are quite sensitive to such feedback. What has not yet been determined, however, is whether this negative evidence is *necessary* for the children's successful grammatical development.

Similarly, Gopnik's (1990) discovery of a "grammar gene" may have been premature. We now know that the inherited genetic disability was not limited to grammar but impaired most aspects of speech as well as language use in this family. The report by Morgan and colleagues (1995) on the inhibitory effects of recasts also has turned out to have equivocal results. Bohannon, Padgett, Nelson, and Mark (1996) employed a formal modeling procedure to test the adequacy of Morgan's statistical procedures. They found that Morgan's time-series analyses could not discriminate between the data generated by models in which (1) recasts totally determined grammatical learning, (2) recasts supplemented other learning, (3) recasts inhibited learning, or (4) recasts had nothing to do with grammatical learning whatsoever.

Some of the other evidence supporting the linguistic approach is also open to criticism. Language does not develop as rapidly as had been supposed, as the acquisition of complex rules (e.g., relative clauses) and the subtleties of syntax continue well past age 4 and possibly through adulthood (Chomsky, 1969; Nippold, 2006), as many of the chapters in this textbook discuss. The linguistic approach has also generally minimized the effects of differing language environments. Taken to its extreme (e.g., Pinker, 1994), this view suggests that the LAD could construct a grammar from any kind of linguistic textual presentation, no matter how abstract, complex, or error-filled. However, children exposed to language only through the medium of television do not learn a language. In a classic case study, Sachs and colleagues (1981) reported on a family in which both parents were deaf but both children had normal hearing. The parents elected not to sign to their children in order to stress spoken speech. The children had little contact with normal hearing/speaking adults and were exposed to spoken English by watching television. At age 4, when entering preschool, the oldest child had little productive speech, severe articulation problems, and no syntax, although he did combine words. With exposure to typically developing English speakers and school and speech therapy, the boy soon improved to within the normal range. This example suggests that simple exposure to language is insufficient to fuel normal language learning.

Chomsky's views on the fundamental nature of language have continued to evolve. In 2002, Hauser, Chomsky, and Fitch proposed that the quintessential feature of all language is recursion. This capacity of recursion is the ability of speakers to insert or embed phrases inside one another. Such a capacity, they claim, enables human beings to generate complex utterances with widely varying meanings. This depiction of recursion as the cornerstone of language, however, has not gone unchallenged. One criticism has been that recursion is more of a cognitive ability than a linguistic capacity. Another serious challenge to Chomsky's view is the claim by Everett (2005) that recursion is absent from the Pirzhã language (in northwestern Brazil). If the Pirzhã language is indeed without recursion, then the claim about the universality and essential nature of recursion will need to be revisited and rejected. However as Ninio (2011) suggests, ignoring the potential linguistic models, whatever they may turn out to be, is like aiming your language arrow at no target at all.

Interactionist Approaches

General Assumptions

If the classic behavioral and linguistic approaches are radical complements on the ends of each theoretical continuum, then the interactionist approach might be considered a moderate compromise. This approach recognizes and often accepts the more powerful arguments from both camps. Interactionists, as the name implies, assume that many factors (e.g., social, linguistic, maturational/biological, cognitive) affect the course of development, and that these factors are mutually dependent upon, interact with, and modify one another. Not only may cognitive or social factors modify language acquisition, but language acquisition will in turn modify the development of cognitive and social skills (Vygotsky, 1962). Thus, not only are these variables interactive, the causal relationships among them are reciprocal.

There are three basic types of interactive approaches: cognitive, social, and usage-based gestural. In the cognitive approach, we discuss the theory of Jean Piaget and its implications for the development of language. Next, the growth of knowledge about human cognition (perception, problem solving, memory) has encouraged scholars to apply the information processing paradigm to language behavior. We will focus on the **competition model** (Bates & MacWhinney, 1987). The second interactive approach focuses on children's socialization. Language acquisition emerges from and develops within social interaction. This approach demands that social factors be explored as causal candidates in language development. Finally, in a version of Haekel's Law where development retraces evolution, the **usage and gestural approach** emerged from accounts of the evolution of language in primitive communicative systems in prehistory (Rizzolatti & Arbib, 1998). This approach recognizes that symbols developed from their natural iconicity in gesture and that words emerge from such gestures (Tomasello, 2008).

Cognitive Approaches: Piaget's Theory and Information-Processing Models

The cognitive theory of Jean Piaget shares many important features with the traditional linguistic account of language acquisition. Both emphasize internal structures as the ultimate determinants of behavior and find support in the invariant order of acquisition across languages and environments. They also agree upon the basic nature of language as a symbolic system for the expression of intention. The distinctions between competence and performance, and between underlying intentions and spoken sentences, are typically retained by cognitive researchers. In spite of these similarities, there are also some major theoretical differences between the two. Most important is Piaget's assumption that language *per se* is not a separate innate characteristic, but is rather only one of several abilities that result from cognitive development. According to Piaget (1954), language is structured or constrained by reason; basic linguistic developments must be based upon or derived from even more basic, general changes in cognition (Bates & Snyder, 1987). The sequence of cognitive development, then, largely determines the sequence of language development.

In 1975, Piaget and Chomsky met and debated the issue of nativism in language, with Chomsky asserting that the general mechanisms of cognitive development cannot account for the abstract, complex, and language-specific structures of language. Moreover, he reiterated the belief that the linguistic environment is unable to account for the structures that appear in children's language. Therefore, language, or at least aspects of linguistic rules and structure, must be innate. Piaget, on the other hand, insisted that the complex structures of language were neither innate nor learned. Instead, these structures emerge as a result of the continuing interaction between the child's current level of cognitive functioning and his or her current linguistic, and nonlinguistic, environment. This interactive approach is known as **constructivism** as opposed to strict nativism or empiricism. Bates and Snyder (1987) explained that the resulting structure in language may not resemble either the structure of external reality or the structure of the simple, innate cognitive schemas with which the child began exploring his or her environment. Instead, the structure is:

> an inevitable emergent solution to a series of interactions. Because that structure is inevitable, it does not have to be innate. There is no reason for nature to waste perfectly good genes on an outcome that is going to happen anyway. Applied to language, this approach suggests that the semantic and grammatical structures of language are the inevitable set of solutions to the problem of mapping certain non-linguistic, cognitive meanings and social intentions onto the highly constrained linguistic channel, and vice-versa. (Bates & Snyder, 1987, p. 172)

Traditional linguistic and cognitive interactionist approaches disagree on the data that each regards as relevant to the explanation of child language acquisition. Whereas both approaches preserve a distinction between competence and performance, typically linguists insist that only competence is important to theories of grammar and that performance factors are simply annoying complications. To Piagetians, on the other hand, performance "limitations" provide some of the most useful data. The child's cognitive capacities are assumed to be qualitatively, as well as quantitatively, different from those of adults. Thus, the different way in which the child reasons about the world will affect the way in which she approaches the language acquisition task. Children's linguistic performance, including their errors, may reveal not only their knowledge of the structure of language but also the structure of their knowledge. The cognitive constraints and abilities that determine linguistic performance are assumed to be the same ones that underlie the child's language competence.

To illustrate the relation between cognitive development and language development, we will examine the earliest stage in Piaget's (1954) account of the development of intelligence. The period of development from birth to approximately 18 to 24 months of age is described as the period of sensorimotor intelligence. According to Piaget (1945/1962, 1936/1963), the child needs to complete, or nearly complete, the sensorimotor period before using language. This period of development is depicted as prelinguistic since the child has not yet acquired the mental representational skills that are necessary for symbol usage. Words, because they can represent or stand for objects, events, and properties, constitute the quintessential symbol. In Piaget's account, children in the sensorimotor period understand the world only through direct sensation of it (sensory) and the activities they perform upon it (motor). Children do not yet recognize the separate and continued existence of objects apart from their own direct experience of them. Objects that are out of sight are also out of mind, ceasing to exist as soon as they are not in the child's immediate perceptual environment.

During the second year of life, children establish the concept of object permanence, understanding that objects have permanence and an identity apart from their own perception. The acquisition of this concept often is measured by evaluating children's performance on an object-permanence task. If young children search accurately for an object after hidden displacements, then such behavior is interpreted by Piaget as indicating that the children have formed a mental image or representation of the hidden object. Symbolic play in children also is seen by Piaget as utilizing mental representational skills and thus is related to language development as well.

Sinclair-de Zwart (1969) argued that a child in the sensorimotor period has no need for symbols to represent objects in the environment since the objects are either present, hence serving as their own referents, or they are totally absent and nonexistent for the child. Once object permanence is achieved, the child may begin to use symbols to represent objects that are no longer present, and these symbols become the child's first true words. In this view, object permanence is a necessary precursor for language.

Similarly, other cognitive developments are assumed to occur before they are reflected in the child's linguistic skills. For example, children's first word combinations have been posited to be dependent upon the child's perception of semantic relations among objects and people in the world (Bowerman, 1982). With the realization that animate beings typically act upon inanimate things, the child then combines the symbols for these concepts in a similar fashion. Thus, the child's first grammar is composed of semantic classes, with animate actors (subject) followed by actions (verb), and inanimate acted-upons (object). It is only later in the course of development that the more abstract grammatical classes of subjects, predicates, noun phrases, verb phrases, and so on, are formed through the reorganization of the more primitive semantic categories. This linguistic reorganization is assumed to reflect an underlying restructuring of cognitive schemas.

In summary, the Piagetian approach views language as only one expression of a more general set of human cognitive activities. Proper development of the cognitive system is considered a necessary precursor of linguistic expression. The major task facing the cognitive interactionist, then, is to identify the sequence of cognitive maturation and to explain how these cognitive developments are reflected in language acquisition.

Evaluation of Piaget's Theory

Supporting Evidence. Piaget's model of language acquisition depicts language as emerging from or intimately tied to advances in children's cognitive development. Researchers who have examined this model have sought evidence that the attainment of certain basic cognitive abilities precedes or co-occurs with children's expressive language. A number of studies have shown that the achievement of various early language milestones often coincides or correlates with many nonlinguistic attainments, such as symbolic play with objects, imitation of gestures and sounds, and tool use (for reviews, see Bates, Benigni, Bretherton, Camaioni, & Volterra, 1979; Corrigan, 1978). Bates (1976) found that children's first words typically occurred after the realization that other people may serve as agents. Furthermore, in many children, there is a precipitous increase in vocabulary and volubility (often called the vocabulary spurt) that takes place in the latter half of the second year (Bloom, Lifter, & Broughton, 1985; Nelson, 1973; but see Ganger & Brent, 2004). This dramatic increase in vocabulary size, moreover, coincides in most children with their attainment of the last stage of sensorimotor development.

Nonlinguistic accomplishments related to other aspects of language acquisition also have been demonstrated. Corrigan (1978) discovered that the appearance of two-word combinations was related to Piaget's final stage of sensorimotor intelligence. Other investigators (e.g., Branigan, 1979; Fenson & Ramsey, 1980) reported that children begin joining two or more words into a single intonational contour, or two or more gestures into single, planned motor units, around 20 months of age. Further, Bates and her colleagues found significant correlations between the appearance of multiword speech and multi-schema gestures. Taken together, these results indicate that the transition from one-word to multiword speech is part of the more general shift toward "chunking" and the planning of higher-order motor schemas (Bates, Beeghley-Smith, Bretherton, & McNew, 1983).

The work of Slobin (1979) and others (e.g., Block & Kessel, 1980) further suggests that the acquisition of a particular productive morpheme (e.g., tense or plural markers) follows the child's understanding of the semantic properties that the morpheme encodes. In other words, children do not grammatically mark relationships in their spontaneous productive speech until they know the concept that the marker denotes. On this basis, Slobin (1982) suggested that new functions are first expressed in old forms and new forms first express old functions. For example, children must first grasp the primitive concept of past before they will talk about past events using old forms (e.g., "The other day" to refer to a displacement in time), and after this they may use the new form (e.g., past-tense markers on the main verb). A related argument (Bowerman, 1982; Sinclair-de Zwart, 1973) suggests that cognitive-semantic categories of agent, action, and patient more adequately describe early sentences than the abstract syntactic forms of subject, verb, and object. Bates and her colleagues (1983) concluded that children use cognitively based meanings to decipher the grammatical code in their language. Indeed, early grammars based upon cognitive-semantic categories seem to be the strongest asset of the cognitive-interactionist approach. Additionally, children with Specific Language Impairment (see Chapter 9) also show delays in attainment of some Piagetian skills, such as conservation (Mainela-Arnold, Evans, & Alibali, 2006), although the directionality of the relationship is not yet clear—it may be that earlier language ability fosters measurable cognitive skills, or the opposite—that one requires a given level of cognition to attain linguistic proficiency.

Contrary Evidence. The cognitive approach suggests that language in and of itself is not innate, but that perhaps nonlinguistic, cognitive precursors of language are. However, there are several criticisms that may be leveled at the Piagetian cognitive view. Many of the studies relating cognitive and language development implicitly assume that abilities that emerge at the same point in development (e.g., the acquisition of object permanence and the onset of the vocabulary spurt) share underlying cognitive mechanisms. In addition, positive correlations between cognitive and linguistic achievements often are taken as reflections of causal relationships. As Curtiss (1981) and others (Newport, Gleitman, & Gleitman, 1977) noted many years ago, age-related correlations and co-developments occur frequently, such as first molar teeth appearing around the time of first words, yet such similar co-occurrences are rarely assumed to be causally related.

A better method of sorting out these relations is to identify cognitive achievements that always precede particular linguistic attainments. Then, if any child develops the linguistic skill without also displaying the supposedly prerequisite cognitive skill, the hypothesis would be clearly disproved. Unfortunately, as Bates and Snyder (1987) pointed out, such clear instances are very difficult to find. But there are sufficient instances to seriously call into question Piaget's claim that completion, or near completion, of the sensorimotor period is a prerequisite for language use. Children learning to sign from their deaf parents often demonstrate symbolic sign usage and combine signs long before they attain full object permanence or complete the sensorimotor period (Bonvillian, Orlansky, Novack, & Folven, 1983). Similarly, a small percentage of children are quite precocious in their spoken language development while their cognitive development proceeds at a normal rate (Ingram, 1981). In light of these findings, it appears necessary to considerably revise Piaget's model of language emergence. Perhaps the cognitive skills that children need to master before using language are the abilities to recognize and identify objects and to recognize that objects continue to exist when they are no longer in view. The ability to identify objects and to conduct elementary searches for nonpresent objects emerges in children months before children attain the full range of sensorimotor skills.

As noted previously, Sinclair-de Zwart (1973) suggested that development of the object concept should precede the child's first true words. This does not appear to be the case in some instances. There is, however, a growing body of evidence that more specific cognitive attainments *do* correlate with particular linguistic milestones (Corrigan, 1978; Gopnik, 1984; Gopnik & Meltzoff, 1987). For example, the development of "disappearance" words (e.g., *all gone*) is related to object-permanence acquisition; "success and failure" terms (e.g., *There! Uh-oh*) appear around the same time as means–ends understanding (solving problems through insight rather than trial and error); and certain ways of categorizing or grouping objects, which develop around 18 months of age, coincide with the vocabulary spurt in children. Gopnik and Meltzoff (1987), in their *specificity hypothesis,* avoid some of the pitfalls present in assessing causal connections between cognition and language by asserting that children learn *specific* words related to the very specific cognitive problems that interest them at a given time. They do not attempt to answer the chicken-and-egg question, "Which came first?"—but focus on the fact that certain cognitive and linguistic events do coincide.

Finally, the work of Curtiss (1981) and others has identified situations in which language and cognitive skills may be separable. Children with Turner's syndrome score quite poorly on cognitive tasks yet exhibit normal language skills. The case study of Genie, a child reared in severe isolation, suggests that semantic and cognitive development are parallel (both proceeded normally with training), but syntax and morphology are quite different (these were delayed). In other cases, syntax and morphology are normal or even advanced, whereas semantic development lags, apparently owing to cognitive disabilities. Thus, Curtiss (1981) argued that the acquisition of syntax and morphology must be somewhat independent of other cognitive developments. Williams syndrome (discussed in Chapter 9) provides another example of what appears to be a dissociation between cognitive ability (impaired in WS) and language (relatively spared). Bates (1993) and others (e.g., Newport, 1976) have suggested that during infancy and early childhood, cognitive and linguistic development proceed more or less in tandem, but then they begin to take different paths. Although these case studies of atypical language development cannot provide compelling counterevidence, they should caution us against making sweeping statements about the cognitive bases of language acquisition.

In summary, the broad assertion by Piaget that cognitive development determines language development has been seriously questioned by a number of researchers. Moreover, despite an abundance of correlation evidence in this area, methodological problems prevent a clear causal interpretation of much of the data. However, the studies so far indicate that continued research aimed at specific relations between cognition and language should prove more rewarding.

Information-Processing Approach

One of the more recent cognitive approaches to language learning is derived from the information-processing paradigm. This paradigm is common in experiments on human memory, perception, and problem solving. In essence, the human information processing system is a mechanism that encodes stimuli from the environment, interprets those stimuli, stores stimulus representations and results of operations on them in memory, and allows information retrieval. As we noted previously, one way of approaching language acquisition is to begin with mature language use and then consider how such a system might develop (Gleitman & Wanner, 1982). There is considerable evidence about the nature of adult language processing and memory, and this approach views children, however naive and primitive they may be, as qualitatively similar to adults. Simply put, children are information processors in transition from novice to skilled status.

Although there are several information processing approaches to language, we will focus on one of these, known as the *competition model* (Bates & MacWhinney, 1989; MacWhinney, 1989, 1999). This model emphasizes both structure and function in learning language, but in a novel way. Specifically, the functions involved are communicative functions, such as establishing topicality and requesting and identifying a location. The structures are language mechanisms that produce strings of spoken words that encode those communicative functions. As Bates and MacWhinney (1987) argued, the structure emerges from the communicative function that the structure serves: "The idea that grammars routinely spawn forms that play no role in facilitating communication is foreign to the position" (p. 160). Information processing models such as the competition model are meant to address language performance rather than competence, but it is their position that the structures that produce language performance at any time, even during development, are the same structures that allow linguists to make grammatical judgments (competence). Thus, although this approach explicitly models language performance, it may also account for the nature of linguistic competence.

Before elaborating the details of the competition model, it will be necessary to distinguish between two basic types of information processing. In **serial processing**, operations are performed one at a time, sequentially, whereas in **parallel processing**, multiple operations occur simultaneously. The linguistic approach discussed previously relies largely on serial processing, in that intentions are formulated first, before application of grammatical realization functions (e.g., passives, questions), which are also performed in serial order. Moreover, current conceptions of the linguistic approach suggest that innate linguistic parameters such as word order are set sequentially through exposure.

More recent cognitive approaches assume that language comprehension as well as production involve parallel processing. In parallel processing, networks of processors are connected such that multiple operations or decisions proceed concurrently. Such networks have come to be called **parallel-distributed processors** or **PDPs** (Rummelhart & McClelland, 1987). (An example of a PDP network is shown in Figure 7.1.) PDP models

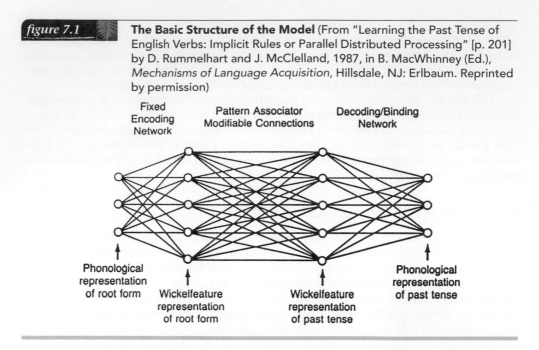

figure 7.1   **The Basic Structure of the Model** (From "Learning the Past Tense of English Verbs: Implicit Rules or Parallel Distributed Processing" [p. 201] by D. Rummelhart and J. McClelland, 1987, in B. MacWhinney (Ed.), *Mechanisms of Language Acquisition*, Hillsdale, NJ: Erlbaum. Reprinted by permission)

consist of a series of processing units called **activation nodes**. These are meant to resemble or model individual neurons or assemblies of neurons in the brain. Each node is connected to other nodes by pathways that vary in the strengths of their connections. (Hence, these models are sometimes called **connectionist models**.) The pathways are meant to model the dendrites and axons that connect neurons in the brain. Activation nodes, like neurons, are decision mechanisms. They receive input from other nodes across pathways of varying strength, weigh the input, then "decide" whether to "fire" and send information to subsequent levels. For example, a series of phonetic features that make up the word *bat* would be fed to the earliest input level of the network (far left in Figure 7.1). The resulting pattern of activation (decisions of each node) is passed to the initial level of a pattern associator network. The initial word features are further modified and then passed to the second level of the pattern associator. The output connections, known as a decoding network, take these modified word features and generate another pattern of activation that represents the output pattern of sound sequences (see far right portion of Figure 7.1). The place where all learning occurs is in the middle set of nodes called the pattern associator.

The way the system "learns" new patterns, such as the formation of plurals, is through changing the way input patterns are transferred from the encoding to the output level. Depending upon whether the output pattern generated by the system successfully matches a criterion, the relative strengths of the connections between the associator nodes are adjusted. For example, the system might try to generate the plural of *house*. The phonetic representation of house is fed into the associator network as a pattern of activation strengths. The associator network sends another pattern of activation to the decoding network. The criterion plural, *houses,* is then compared with the output. If the system, in fact, generates the match, *houses,* then the connections in the pattern associator responsible for that guess are left alone. If, on the other hand, the system generates a mismatch (e.g., when presented the word *mouse,* it generates the response *mouses,* which does not match the criterion plural *mice*), this results in a backwards adjustment of the connections in the pattern associator. If an output node should have been activated but was not, the connections are strengthened by some small incremental amount. If the output node was activated but should not have been, then the strength of the prior connections is decreased by the same small amount. With sufficient presentations of root word forms, such as *mouse, house, horse, moose,* and so on, and their corresponding correct plural forms, the system will eventually converge, through these incremental adjustments, on the correct plural representation for each root item. Note that the system will also proceed through an error stage, since similar-sounding words will lead to overgeneralization errors. In the example above, a PDP network, after being presented with *house* and *houses,* is likely to respond with *mouses* when presented with *mouse,* because the activation patterns are similar.

Using PDP models as a base, Bates and MacWhinney (1989) proposed their competition model. They argued that PDP networks may be thought of as allowing all known syntactic forms, words, and phonetic patterns to compete simultaneously to represent any particular meaning and communicative function. For example, *mice* and *mouses* are both present as possible activation patterns. Which of these is ultimately used depends upon the current levels of activation of each. Over the course of development, the patterns that most successfully match adult speech are more likely to occur again (are strengthened), and erroneous, primitive patterns will eventually disappear. This critical matching function takes place when children's responses are matched against the criteria of adult speech the children hear. Thus, PDP models in general, and the competition model specifically, are empirical and not nativistic. Children learn speech from the exemplars provided to them. No innate biases or constraints are necessary for them to learn eventually to process language like adults.

Very specific predictions about the course of language development may be derived from the competition model. Learning occurs dependent upon the probability of form–function matches. Therefore, those forms most frequently addressed to children will be learned before rarer forms. This is known as cue availability and accounts for both the fact that children from English-speaking homes learn English forms and not Spanish, and less obviously, that children learn highly frequent verb forms (*is, was, were*) before less frequent forms. Children learning English acquire word-order forms early compared with Italian-speaking children, because word order in Italian is not a good indicator of the word's role in a sentence.

In summary, the competition model of language performance is a specific adaptation of a PDP information processing system. The language-learning mechanism within this model employs cognitive structures that are radically different from any previously proposed. They are not behaviorist stimulus–response associations, nor are they interrelated rule systems as suggested by linguists. Rather, they consist of multilayered networks of connections that function to interpret linguistic input and generate speech. The way PDP networks function allows predictions to be made concerning the course of language development. According to the competition model, the rate at which a particular linguistic form is mastered is determined by the nature of the form–function relations in that language system and the way these relations are presented to children. Language learning within this system is therefore empirical—the only innate structure required is a powerful PDP learning mechanism.

Evaluation of the Information-Processing Approach

Supporting Evidence.   PDP processes are frequently implicated in adult cognition. Semantic memory may be organized as networks of varying semantic strengths (Smith, 1978). When words are presented, they activate or prime related words. In classic examples, after hearing the word *nurse,* people quickly recognize semantically related words such as *woman* and *doctor* (Meyer & Schwaneveldt, 1971), as well as phonologically related words such as *purse* and *hearse* (Rubin, 1975). Thus, prior processing causes some spreading activation throughout the system or network of information related to the **priming** stimulus. This phenomenon can be easily demonstrated. Have a friend say the word *silk* out loud five times, then quickly answer this question: "What do cows drink?" Most people readily respond with "milk," although upon reflection they realize that cows rarely drink what they produce. The word *milk* was doubly primed, first with the similar sounds in *silk* and then with semantic association to *drink* and *cows*. This priming subtly changes the current state of the language network, such that one particular response *(milk)* becomes more likely than any other response. Cortical representation of a broadly disseminated semantic network has been shown through fMRI imaging studies (Binder, Desai, Graves, & Conant, 2009). Syntactic priming has been demonstrated as well (Bock, 1989). Prior exposure to passive sentences makes subsequent passive use more likely, even when topics and lexical items change.

The PDP model has been tested in a computerized simulation of the acquisition of past-tense forms. Rummelhart and McClelland (1987) presented a PDP simulation with over 400 different verbs and their past-tense forms. The frequency of presentation was matched to what a child might be exposed to, namely, irregular verbs like *take/took* were presented more frequently and prior to the presentation of regular verbs like *walk/walked*. Although the simulation never learned any rules *per se* (e.g., "add *-ed* to form the past tense"), the pattern of learning was remarkably similar to that found in children by Pinker (1991). The simulation initially used every verb correctly and then passed to an overregularization stage, ultimately regularizing only regular verbs and correctly producing exceptions. Any completely novel verbs were regularized. Moreover, the child's tendency to overregularize varies with verb class, making *blowed* for *blew* more common than *singed* for *sang* (Bybee & Slobin, 1982), and the PDP simulation displayed similar patterns. General PDP nets can also be "damaged" after acquiring aspects of language, and they show performance deficits strikingly similar to those of brain-damaged human patients (Marchman, 1993). One of the strengths of the PDP model is these very specific predictions, in contrast to the often vague predictions of linguistic theory, such as "overregularizations will occur and eventually disappear" (Elman et al., 1996).

One of the last impediments to the PDP approach was the hierarchical organization of sentences. Connectionist networks, like children, must extract phrase structure organization (which is hierarchical, see Chapter 5) from sentences, despite the fact that the sentences are presented one word at a time. Elman (1993) devised a network with a transitory memory structure. This network contained a separate loop of *neural nodes* that were mostly influenced by recent input and whose activity decayed rapidly in time. The system was set up to "guess" the next word in sentential sequences. The point was to present this system with sentences like "The dog who bit the cows *was large*." The critical bit was to show that the system could "guess" that the main verb should match the real sentence subject *dog* and not the closest sequential noun *cows*. It is remarkable that the network Elman (1993) devised could eventually perform this task. However, there was more to the story. If the network was presented adult-like sentences containing the embedded clauses it was meant to process, then it failed to successfully learn the hierarchical structures. Only if the network initially received simple, short sentences or the memory loop in the learning net started off with a very limited capacity would the system proceed to extract appropriate clausal information from more complex sentences.

A subsequent paper (Rohde & Plaut, 1999) showed that Elman's (1993) network could still learn clausal information correctly without restricting the network's memory or simplifying the input. They devised a simple grammar that allowed relative clauses. Unlike Elman's (1993) demonstration, which was free of semantic relations, Rohde and Plaut (1999) devised a lexicon with realistic semantic restrictions (e.g., proper nouns cannot act on themselves, as in "Mary chased Mary"). They found that the system learned under both restricted and unlimited input, but learned relative clauses better under unrestricted input. They also found that Elman's system could learn clausal structure without a memory restriction if training was extended to 240,000 sentences. Their point was that learning a syntactic system was not as difficult a problem as either the linguistic approach or Elman (1993) believed.

The strongest support of the information processing approach comes from its application in the competition model. Within the competition model, the statistical properties (availability and reliability) of syntactic forms determine their rate of acquisition, so that cues that consistently signal particular meanings should be learned first. An extensive review of several candidate cues (case marking, word order, semantics) across a number of different languages (French, English, Italian, Turkish, and Hungarian) supports this prediction, virtually without exception (Bates & MacWhinney, 1989; MacWhinney, 1987). This was true even when predictions were contrary to supposed "universals." For example, Pinker (1984) proposed that all children rely on word order as an initial cue to sentence meaning over other cues, such as case markings; however, Turkish children, whose language has an extremely reliable case marking system, master case marking considerably sooner than word order (Slobin & Bever, 1982). The competition model also accounts for many behaviors observed in bilinguals and second language learners (Ping, 2009). As one example, Dutch speakers acquiring English initially use valid Dutch cues to interpret English, but gradually shift to appropriate English cues with increasing exposure (MacDonald, 1987).

Contrary Evidence. To the extent that this model shares assumptions with the linguistic position, it is susceptible to the same criticisms. For example, the competition model also assumes *text presentation* (no corrective feedback of language errors). Thus, the child must be endowed with extremely powerful learning mechanisms. Given the evidence that corrective feedback does occur regularly, these learning mechanisms may be more powerful than is necessary. According to the principle of **parsimony**, theorists should use the simplest of all available alternative explanations, if they all describe the data equally well. Whenever information in the environment can account for children's behavior, it may be inefficient or redundant to credit them with internal processes designed to achieve identical goals. Although the competition model is based on language cues actually available to children, it is, as yet, woefully underspecified with respect to the conversational social context in which those cues are embedded.

Indeed, Rohde and Plaut (1999) admitted that the power of their model might have relied on being context-free. In other words, their system learned syntax in a simplified world without having to (1) decipher the ongoing social situation, (2) decide whom to address, (3) decide how to achieve a particular real-world goal, and (4) simultaneously learn syntax. It may be that the extra-linguistic context, which language is supposed to describe and socially manipulate, places demands on the learner that require simplified input for learning in all tasks to proceed. Thus, learning patterns from powerful PDP models may not generalize to how real children learn language.

One of the factors that make PDP networks so appealing may ultimately prove to be misleading. PDP models seductively resemble the organization of neurons in the brain. Thus, we may be tempted to adopt this model because of its superficial resemblance to the biological system, when in fact closer inspection of the operation of neurons and PDP nodes reveals vast differences, as researchers noted soon after the model was advanced (Grossberg & Stone, 1986). Finally, Fodor and Pylyshyn (1988) attacked the PDP approach on theoretical grounds. They argued that PDP networks were the mere mechanism whereby linguistic rules were expressed. Although the PDP networks contain no linguistic rules, sets of universal parameters or principles, they behave as if they did. Therefore, the PDP systems are simply uninteresting methods of linguistic expression in the same way that computer chips implement calculations of elegant mathematical equations. Further, PDP models handle problems well that can be presented all at once, such as pictures or graphics. What they handle only with difficulty are problems that are presented sequentially, and natural language is just such a problem. Indeed, the more powerful PDP models (described above) succeed only if their total task is to guess the next word in a sentence, which seems an unlikely simulation of what children do when learning their mother tongue. Finally, the PDP competition model is a simple sentence processor requiring only text presentation for success (Rohde & Plaut, 1999). Just as pure linguistic models fare poorly without specifying how social interaction drives language learning, PDP is similarly handicapped. As stated above, language does not seem to be learned in the absence of social interaction.

Social Interaction Approach

The social interaction approach also combines many aspects of both the traditional behavioral and linguistic positions. For example, social interactionists typically agree with linguists who stress that language has a structure and follows certain rules that make it quite different from other behaviors. However, this approach shares with the behaviorists an emphasis on the role of the environment in producing such structure. Specifically, social interactionists believe that the structure of human language may have arisen out of the social-communicative functions that language plays in human relations (Bates & MacWhinney, 1982; Ninio & Snow, 1999). Conversely, a more mature linguistic structure allows more varied and sophisticated ways of socially relating to others. In Figure 7.2, the directions of possible causal relations emphasized by the behavioral, linguistic, and social interactionist positions are outlined.

The behavioral approach views children as passive beneficiaries of the language training techniques employed by their parents. In this view, children's language development from one time to another (arrow *c* in Figure 7.2) is considered to be the exclusive result of parental action (arrow *a* in Figure 7.2). The linguistic approach sees children as active and specialized language processors, whose maturing neural systems guide development. Linguistic approaches acknowledge that although children may affect what their parents say (arrow *b* in Figure 7.2) at any one time, whatever the parents provide children in the way of language experience only triggers the maturation of children's innate tendencies. In contrast to these views, social interactionists argue that children cue their parents (arrow *b*) into supplying the appropriate language experience (arrow *a*) that the children require for language advancement (arrow *c*). Interactionists see children and their language environment as a dynamic system, both requiring the other for (1) efficient social communication at any point in development and (2) improving the child's linguistic skill.

Social interactionists agree that children must acquire grammatical skills much as the linguists have suggested. They, too, search for common forms across children, cultures, and languages (Bohannon & Warren-Leubecker, 1988). On the other hand, these skills may have developed from much simpler rote associations and imitations learned within the social context (Moerk, 1991a). Therefore, although this approach tries to explain language structure, it is simply less committed to the form of the structure and to the time of its development than the linguistic approach.

Simultaneously, the functions of language in social communication are considered to be central throughout development. The linguistic approach attempts to abstract children's language development away from the day-to-day functions emphasized by behaviorists. Yet the intricate grammatical structures described by linguists are useless to a child (and probably would not occur) unless they have a practical function, such as understanding and making oneself understood. Humans are such social organisms that it would be odd indeed if there were no relationship between language and social skills in the acquisition of a communicative system. The social

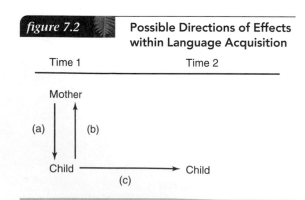

figure 7.2 **Possible Directions of Effects within Language Acquisition**

Time 1   Time 2

Mother

(a)   (b)

Child ⟶ Child
(c)

interactionist approach might be taken as an attempt to account for children's changing linguistic abstractions by examining how those abstractions might be derived from functioning social communication (Berko Gleason, 1977; Tomasello, 2003).

The competence–performance issue is considered more moderately by this approach in contrast to the behavioral or linguistic approaches. Since interactionists acknowledge grammatical structure, they also pursue explanations of the child's language competence. In contrast, what children actually know about language (competence) can only be measured through what they say and understand (performance) within the context of social conversation. For example, interactionists realize that children's parents usually bear the burden of communication, phonetically emphasizing important content words, slowing the rate of their speech, frequently repeating themselves, and supplying critical nonverbal cues such as pointing, in order to aid communication (Berko Gleason, 1977; Snow, 1972, 1999). Some say that parents supply a *scaffold* or supportive communicative structure (Bruner, 1978) that allows efficient communication despite the young child's primitive linguistic system. Thus, children often look much more linguistically sophisticated than they actually are. Many years ago, Vygotsky (1962) argued that for the young child, language is at first only a tool for social interaction. Gradually, the child begins to use language in his own private interactions with the environment, by talking aloud during play, or verbalizing intended actions. As a result, language eventually becomes the source for structure of the child's actions, governing or directing thought. Thus, the role of language changes over the course of development from a social tool to a private tool, as the child internalizes linguistic forms.

Tomasello's (2003) social usage–based theory of language acquisition differs substantially from Chomsky's universal grammar theory. Whereas universal grammar assumes that there is an innate language-acquisition device that requires relatively minimal input for the child's successful development of grammar, Tomasello (2003) advances the view that language acquisition is the product of more general cognitive and social processes. In social interaction theory, grammar is seen as emerging in the child largely through such cognitive skills as pattern finding and by the child's repeated interactions with adult caregivers. Rather than emphasizing the presence of innate linguistic rules and categories as in universal grammar, Tomasello (2003) argued that only a small number of general cognitive and social processes are necessary to account for children's language acquisition.

The social interactionist argues that innate linguistic mechanisms alone cannot explain children's mastery of language and, moreover, that linguistic competence goes beyond conditioning and imitation to include nonlinguistic aspects of interaction: turn-taking, mutual gaze, joint attention, context, and cultural conventions (see Ninio & Snow, 1999). Many social interactionists point to the special nature of the speech directed to children (sometimes known as *motherese* or **child-** or **infant-directed speech [CDS/IDS]**) as an important experience, which may simply facilitate, or even be required for, normal language development. Again, the innate linguistic predispositions must interact with the environment in order to mature.

Social Interactive Language Learning.   The caregiver's role in providing the child with appropriate language experience is emphasized by the interactive approach. Adults' unusual vocal behavior (motherese or CDS) is viewed as equally important as the child's innate linguistic discriminations in explaining children's eventual ability to segment the sound stream appropriately. Mothers also spend a great deal of time in face-to-face social interaction with their infants, performing the vocal behaviors described above. Social interactionists believe that children's maturing ability to control their vocal apparatus is assisted by watching adults produce the exaggerated sounds characteristic of baby talk (Field et al., 1982). Moreover, the nurturing patterns of social play interaction between mothers and infants is believed to be the basis of later conversational patterns, such as conversational turn-taking (Stern, Beebe, Jaffe, & Bennett, 1977; see Chapter 2).

Interactionists believe that language has an underlying structure and that children express intentions in their speech. But how do children map their intentions onto the linguistic code? Many have observed that children's caretakers (usually the mother) impute intentions and meaning to the child's speech, regardless of what the child says. Even when a child is simply babbling, mothers attempt to interpret their vocalizations as if they were quite meaningful. As parents continue in their attempts to decipher these vocalizations, critical events begin to occur. These events, which Golinkoff (1983) called *conversational bouts,* consist of meaning negotiations between the child and the parent. For example, a child might babble "glub" while hungry. The mother interprets "glub" through the present context and her knowledge of the child's past history, and offers the child milk. If the child continues to fuss because milk is not the object of the child's intention, the mother will continue to offer different food items until the child stops fussing; she may then conclude that the child's utterance "glub" was a request for the item that terminated the conversational bout. Thereafter, the mother will treat the utterance "glub" as a request for the food item that terminated the prior bout. Thus, underlying structure mapping is not innate, but negotiated or conventionalized through social interaction.

Zukow-Goldring (2001) emphasized the importance of gesture in early communication. One behavior of children that strongly predicts the onset of first words in infancy is pointing. The related caregiver behaviors that draw the child's attention to a word's referent are *offers* when the focus is a noun (holding up a ball to the infant and saying *ball*) and *demonstrations* when the focus is a verb. When CDS users gesture, their gestures are often synchronous with the spoken word, assisting infants in deducing which verbal code corresponds to the referent (Zukow-Goldring, 1996). The importance of gesture is further shown during conversational bouts in which communication breaks down. After failed negotiations of meaning, gesture takes a more central role, directing children's attention to alternative meanings.

The social interaction approach also suggests that some early language may be taught by the parents and learned through rote or imitation by the children. Despite some obvious failures to teach grammatical forms (e.g., McNeill, 1970), parents insist on teaching children social conventions such as *bye-bye* and politeness routines (Berko Gleason & Weintraub, 1976). It is not known yet whether such deliberate instruction is critical for the rest of language development, but it is believed that social use of language is assisted by such teaching. Moreover, the success of teaching social routines suggests that instruction in other forms of language might be of equal benefit.

The role of the child's language environment is stressed throughout development. It is assumed that the child's maturation and current level of grammatical skill interact with the language data provided to the child to determine the further course of development (see Hirsh-Pasek & Golinkoff, 1996). Assuming that children deduce grammatical rules from the consistencies in their linguistic environment (e.g., subjects come before verbs, plurals are signaled with a terminal -*s*), the child's task is made easier by pacing the complexity of the data or problem to be solved with the child's language level. That is, caregivers try to provide grammatically simpler input (CDS) to children who are linguistically naive. As the child grows older and increases in language skill, the data provided by the environment also increase in complexity. This is probably not because of any conscious effort on the part of parents to give specific language instruction, but simply an effort to facilitate communication. When children fail to comprehend a parental utterance, the statement is usually simplified and repeated. Since the complexity of the speech addressed to the children is determined largely by cues from the children

Social interactionists stress the role of parental input language in children's language development.

themselves (Bohannon & Marquis, 1977), one might think of language acquisition in this view as a self-paced lesson.

The parent also may have an effect upon the child independent of the interactive conversational system described above. The interactive view of language acquisition suggests that there may be some instances when the parents provide language exemplars that are particularly salient to the child. Snow (1999) argued that the process of mapping meaning onto the language code is assisted when the code provided by the parent closely parallels the young child's attention. Not only must parents talk about things in the child's immediate environment, they must also focus their comments upon the objects to which their children are attending. It is thought that the mapping of meaning, for example, between a ball and the word *ball,* is enhanced when the word is used frequently while the child is holding or playing with a ball. It is possible that the extensive occurrence of this phenomenon in infancy through early childhood is necessary for the normal development of children's vocabulary and early syntax.

In a similar fashion, children might notice the difference between their own immature sentences and more mature versions if the two closely co-occur. Nelson (1977, 1981) insisted that parental recasts of their children's utterances are particularly powerful events that children use to modify their grammars into more mature versions. He argues that children's attention is focused upon the relevant aspects of the environment and their own intentions, which together result in an utterance. For example, a child may feel thirsty, see Mom open the refrigerator, want a glass of milk, and utter, "Want milk." The mother expands and recasts the child's utterance immediately in several forms, "Oh, do you want a glass of milk? Please, may I have some milk?" It is thought that the contrast between the mature and primitive forms may highlight syntactic differences for the child at a time when there is a close correspondence among the environmental context, the child's intentions, and the linguistic form, which encodes those intentions and referents.

The interactive approach also recognizes the possibility that simple imitation may have important functions in language development. Although it may not be as important as the behaviorist approach insists, children may test linguistic hypotheses gained through the imitation of forms (Snow, 1978; Stine & Bohannon, 1983). Children are most likely to imitate forms that they only partially understand (Bloom, Hood, & Lightbown, 1974; Clark, 1977). This may be an interaction between the process of acquiring the form and the social-conversational role that imitation plays. Stine and Bohannon (1983) argued that partially understood forms (e.g., dependent clauses) are imitated as a possible test of the grammatical rule that generates that form. At the same time, imitation is a conversational signal of partial comprehension that usually results in a recast of the full original sentence. For example, an adult tells a child, "The man who opened the door was your uncle." The child imitates, "Man who opened the door?" The parent then responds, "Yes, your uncle opened the door." It is possible that such conversational interactions, involving imitation, hypothesis testing, and recasts combine to demonstrate new forms and their equivalent transformations.

In summary, the social interactive approach assumes that language development is primarily the result of acquiring grammatical skill. The child is also assumed to bring a number of innate predispositions to the language-learning situation that constrain children in their search for linguistically relevant principles. On the other hand, the environment is believed to be almost as constrained as the children, in order to supply children with the types of language experience necessary for development. Language development is viewed as an orderly interactive process in which social interaction assists language acquisition, and the acquisition of language allows more mature social interaction.

Evaluation of Social Interaction Theory

Supporting Evidence.   One of the strengths of the social interactionist approach is its eclectic nature. Because the interactionist believes that language emerges from the interplay between children's linguistic and cognitive capacities and their social language environment, this position borrows from the methods and strengths of the other areas. Therefore, much of the supporting evidence for this approach has been presented previously. The point of departure of this position pivots around the role played by the language addressed to children (motherese or CDS). In contrast to other positions, the social interactive approach has sought evidence from mother–child conversations that the simplified and "fine-tuned" nature of CDS assists the process of acquisition.

The adult's tendency to use a special form of language apparently begins within minutes of the child's birth. Despite the infant's ability to respond differentially to speech and nonspeech stimuli (Vouloumanos, Hauser, Werker, & Martin, 2010), child-directed speech simplifies and highlights (through differential prosodic stress) important linguistic distinctions (Soderstrom, 2007). CDS has been observed in virtually all languages, and it is used by all adult speakers (including fathers) when addressing children (Berko Gleason & Weintraub, 1978). The role of CDS becomes even more important in light of research that shows that children prefer to listen to this type of speech from birth (Fernald & Kuhl, 1987), throughout infancy, and childhood (Rileigh, 1973). Moreover, DeCasper and Fifer (1980) found that infants prefer to hear their own mothers' CDS over other mothers' CDS. Clearly, infants prefer this type of speech, and if given a choice, will seek the voices of their mothers within hours of birth. Aspects of CDS, particularly speech clarity and slower rate, appear to facilitate infants' ability to associate words with their referents (Song, Demuth, & Morgan, 2010).

Several questions emerge from the data on CDS. First, what variables control the linguistic modifications observed in CDS? The answer seems to be both obvious and intuitive: Simplified and exaggerated speech is a more effective approach when communicating with someone who is less linguistically sophisticated. The exact amount of simplification required for more efficient communication seems to be determined by feedback from the listener, informing the speaker of the adequacy of the listener's comprehension of prior statements. Berko Gleason (1977) argued that children rarely offer the little nods and "uh-huhs" that periodically punctuate adult conversations and mark successful communication. The lack of these listener's signals may cue a speaker to simplify. We do know that infant-directed speech varies as a function of feedback from the child (Smith & Trainor, 2008).

Bohannon and his colleagues (Bohannon & Marquis, 1977; Bohannon, Stine, & Ritzenberg, 1982; Warren-Leubecker & Bohannon, 1982, 1983) also insisted that listeners played a very active role in controlling the speech they hear. They found comprehension feedback to be a powerful signal that elicits simplified speech from both adults and children as young as 3 years. Simply put, children are less likely to signal comprehension of longer, more complex sentences, and when children signal such failures ("What?" "Huh?"), adults tend to shorten and simplify their next utterances. This pattern of conversational interaction also has been observed in adults in both English and Spanish (Bohannon, 1989). This process works equally well when the listener is a foreigner and understands little of the native language. The summary effect of this system seems to be a fine-tuning of the syntactic and conceptual complexity of the speech addressed to any child. Moreover, because children control the speech addressed to them, most speakers should use similar CDS, thus avoiding possible confusing variability in the linguistic environment. As children grow in their ability to comprehend more complex sentences, their success is signaled and their linguistic environment keeps pace.

An example of this process was reported by Sachs (1983), who observed her daughter, Naomi, acquiring past-tense markers. Before Naomi's spontaneous use of the past tense, Sachs found little evidence of her own use of the form when addressing her daughter. But just before the first appearance of -*ed*-marked verbs in Naomi's speech, Sachs found that her own use of that form increased markedly. Was this a random event in which a mother suddenly and inexplicably chose to use the past tense when addressing her child? Obviously, it was not. The interactionist explanation suggests that Naomi's signals of noncomprehension limited the use of the form by her mother until Naomi began to struggle with a primitive concept of *displacement in time* (see earlier discussion of the cognitive approach). As Naomi began to signal comprehension of the few past-tense tokens used by her mother, the mother's use of the form increased. This possibly provided Naomi with the linguistic data on the past tense, within characteristically simple sentences of CDS that were required to master the form.

Another question involves the possible benefits of CDS to the developing child. The benefits of CDS may assist with the "meaning mapping" problem addressed earlier by the linguistic approach (e.g., Gleitman & Wanner, 1982). One characteristic of CDS is that the topic of discussion is usually something concrete and the object of children's transitory attention (Tomasello & Farrar, 1986). Adults use both the direction of children's gaze and the topics of their speech to determine conversational content. In their review of the literature, Tomasello and Farrar (1986) concluded that those mothers who spend more time talking about the object of the child's visual gaze patterns had babies who (1) used their first words earlier and (2) had larger initial vocabularies. Since the majority of semantic forms are provided when the child's attention is focused on the meaning of that form, maybe *meaning mapping* is not as mysterious as some have suggested.

A number of studies have delineated some of the features of CDS that may be important for child language acquisition (e.g., Barnes, Gutfreund, Satterly, & Wells, 1983; Cross, 1977; Newport et al., 1977). One early study (Bonvillian, Raeburn, & Horan, 1979) found that young children were more successful in imitating novel sentences when the sentences were shorter in length and adults spoke to them more slowly and with intonation. A second study (Furrow, Nelson, & Benedict, 1979) examined six 18-month-olds and their mothers over the course of nine months. They found that the mothers who used longer and more complex speech when speaking to their children had children who showed the least language gains at the end of the study. In other words, the more the mothers used CDS, the more rapidly their children acquired language. Imitation plus expansions and extensions (Barnes et al., 1983; Newport et al., 1977) are positively associated with language development, as are simple recasts (Nelson, 1991). As mentioned previously, these types of adult responses also tend to follow children's language errors (Bohannon & Stanowicz, 1989; Farrar, 1992). It is possible that adult recasts may be essential in assisting children to converge on the correct form of their native language.

Although it is unethical to deliberately delay children's language learning by experimentally manipulating the environment, there are some parents who, tragically for their children, do so of their own volition. In cases of neglect, the person who is responsible for the child generally fails to provide minimally adequate support for the child's emerging physical, emotional, and intellectual capacities. The overall rate of mother–child interaction for neglectful mothers, in comparison with control-group mothers, has been shown to be much lower, with the level of maternal verbal instructional interaction particularly depressed. Thus, mother–child verbal interaction has been targeted as an important aspect of intervention in cases of child neglect or maltreatment (Thomas & Zimmer-Gembeck, 2011). In addition to reduced rate of interaction, neglectful mothers have been found to produce many fewer words and grammatical utterances in their speech to their young children than do adequately rearing mothers (Christopoulos, Bonvillian, & Crittenden, 1988).

Are there developmental consequences associated with this impoverished environment? Fox, Long, and Langlois (1988) found that severely **neglected children** scored much lower on measures of language comprehension than other maltreated children or control-group children. In a second study (Culp et al., 1991), both the receptive and expressive language skills of neglected children were found to be delayed by six to nine months. Children identified as abused and neglected were four to eight months delayed; and children who had been abused but not neglected were zero to two months delayed. Unlike their language skills, the levels of cognitive development of the three groups of maltreated children did not differ. In light of their findings, the investigators concluded, "language development is particularly vulnerable in an environment devoid of parent–child social language exchange" (Culp et al., 1991, p. 377). The most compelling recent example of the effects of verbal neglect on child development has emerged from studies of Romanian orphans left basically unattended in poor-quality orphanages (Johnson et al., 2010).

Contrary Evidence. One problem with the social interactionist position is its broad scope. It embraces children's emerging cognitive and linguistic capacities while stressing the central role of social interaction. This tendency to welcome elements from all other approaches makes it difficult to assess its explanatory utility. As with Piaget's cognitive and the information processing approaches, social interaction theory has outstripped data collection "to a startling degree" (Bates et al., 1983). Thus many of its explanations rest on untested intuitions and assumptions. Because the details of this approach have yet to be specified, true counterevidence may be difficult to find. On the other hand, some of the basic assumptions about CDS have been addressed.

Findings from two different research areas raise questions about aspects of social interaction theory. In one, the deaf children of non-signing, hearing parents evidently played the dominant role in the development of their signing communication systems; these systems had many language-like properties (Goldin-Meadow, 2003; Goldin-Meadow & Mylander, 1990). (This research is discussed as supportive of the innatist, linguistic approach earlier this chapter.) The children in this study showed the ability to generate their own gestural, linguistic symbols and to combine them in systematic ways consistent with the innatist view. Although these findings are used to bolster the contribution of innate skills to language development, important aspects of social interaction cannot be ignored; it is important to note that the children were not developing their home signs in a communicative vacuum. In caring for their children and teaching them speech skills, the parents interacted frequently with their children. This interaction would have involved the establishment of joint attention and probably the parents' use of a range of facial expressions and nonsign, deictic gestures (e.g., pointing, showing) to convey their intentions. Moreover, once the children began producing their own sign gestures, the parents played a supportive role by both responding to and using the children's sign gestures. This pattern of responding to and using the children's sign gestures by the parents may have helped these gestural communication systems become firmly established.

Several studies (e.g., Hoff-Ginsburg, 1986) have investigated the necessity of simplified speech using correlation methods. They found that the complexity of maternal speech addressed to the children was unrelated to the children's language gains. Despite the fact that these children were, on average, older than those of Furrow and his colleagues (1979), this suggests that the simplifications within CDS may not predict children's language growth in the simple, linear fashion suggested by the Furrow study. (For a review of this research, see Bohannon & Hirsh-Pasek, 1984; Bohannon & Warren-Leubecker, 1988.)

Although researchers consistently have documented certain features in CDS that differ from adult–adult speech patterns, the mere presence of these differences does not, in itself, suggest that CDS is necessary or even helpful to the language-learning child. Instead, correlation studies relating the relative prevalence of CDS features in mothers' speech with their children's language growth provide only hints of the effects of specific input features. Moreover, Baker and Nelson (1984) argue that it is impossible based upon simple correlation studies to determine "who is leading whom" in language development. Only experimental studies that manipulate the frequency of CDS features and examine the effects on child language acquisition can circumvent these problems. The experimental studies of recasts by Nelson and his colleagues represent a solution to this dilemma (see Nelson, Welsh, Camarata, & Butkovsky, 1995). These authors have shown that recasts can facilitate the acquisition of previously unused syntactic forms. Unfortunately, other features of CDS have not been examined experimentally, so conclusions regarding their effects are premature.

Another problem with CDS relates to the great variety of features that differentiate CDS from other speech registers (see Chapter 10). Even if the language-learning child requires CDS, it is entirely possible that only a few features are really critical in this function. Most

CDS studies have focused on global measures, such as mean length of utterance or frequency of usage of particular grammatical types, and similarly general measures of child language growth. Although the sheer amount of language stimulation provided by the mother is significantly correlated with children's language growth, Bates and colleagues (1983) justifiably argued that these quantitative relationships do not prove the hypothesis that CDS "teaches" the child language structure. In order to test these claims, one must examine very specific types of linguistic input and relate them to specific measures of child language output. Once we have narrowed our focus in this way, we may find that some aspects of child language are quite malleable and sensitive to linguistic input, whereas others are relatively immune (e.g., Gleitman, Newport, & Gleitman, 1984; Goldin-Meadow, 1982).

The correlation studies reported here are also problematic in the statistical assumption of linear relations, which has been addressed by many critics (e.g., Bates et al., 1983; Bohannon & Hirsh-Pasek, 1984). One conceptual implication of the linearity assumption is that "if some maternal input is good, then more is better" (Bates et al., 1983, p. 43). This may be true up to a point, in that a minimal or threshold value of linguistic input is required, but additional input is irrelevant. Second, when the age range of the children studied is broad, it is inappropriate to assume that the oldest children should benefit from more CDS in the same way that the youngest children would. For example, the greatest simplification in MLU would dictate that mothers use single-word speech. Whereas this may be the best level of complexity to use for maximal benefit to a 1-year-old (Furrow et al., 1979), it would certainly hinder further language acquisition in a 4-year-old (Bohannon & Hirsh-Pasek, 1984).

In summary, despite the methodological problems involved in testing its fundamental assertion, the social interactionist approach seems to hold a great deal of promise. It employs the empirical perspective of the behaviorists by acknowledging the importance of environmental sources of language data. It also recognizes children as specialized language processors who must not only acquire the language code, but, in turn, must teach it to their own children later through conversation.

Gestural and Usage-Based Approach

In the gestural and usage-based approach, the roots of language are depicted as consisting primarily of communicative pointing and iconic or pantomimic gestures. This focus on gestural communication as comprising the roots of human language may be seen as suggesting that early human communication was not that far removed from the gestural communication present in non-human primates. Human language, with its roots in gestural communication, most likely appeared first as a manual-visual sign communication system. Spoken language, in this view, emerged only relatively recently in human history, and was based on long-standing neural mechanisms shaped by gestural and sign communication (Corballis, 2010; Stokoe, 2001). The development of spoken language skills, moreover, is seen as largely socially and cognitively later developments both in evolution and in development. (Tomasello, 2003, 2008).

Gestural and Sign Origins

When most scholars have discussed the nature of language and studied how children acquire their first language, the focus has been on spoken language and its development. Only in recent decades have scholars expanded the focus to include the signed languages used by members of deaf communities. Systematic investigations of sign language, such as American Sign Language, have shown that they are full and genuine languages (Klima & Bellugi, 1979). With the recognition of signed languages as full languages, some linguists and neurolinguists advanced the view that human language most likely emerged as a visual-gestural means of communication (Armstrong, 2008; Armstrong, Stokoe, & Wilcox,

1995; Corballis, 2002; Stokoe, 2001). That is, our human ancestors probably communicated primarily through visual-motor signs and gestures, and spoken language did not appear until much later in the course of human evolution. According to this approach, the relatively rapid and recent emergence of spoken language as the dominant form of communication for most persons took place because it was based on an already well-established neural architecture shaped by many millennia of effective gestural communication.

One hypothesis advanced to account for why visual-gestural communication preceded the emergence of speech in early humans is that early gestural (or visual and motor) communication likely rested on a neural mechanism already present in our prehominid ancestors: **mirror neurons** (Arbib, 2005; Rizzolatti & Sinigaglia, 2008). Mirror neurons are active not only when one produces a specific action, but also when one observes the same (or similar) action produced by others. Mirror neurons thus may enable an individual who views another person perform motor actions understand those actions if that individual has the capacity to produce those same actions (Corballis, 2010; Rizzolatti & Sinigaglia, 2008). The mirror neuron system appears to be located near those areas in the brain responsible for both manual control and the syntactic aspects of human language production (Binkofski & Buccino, 2004). The presence of these different mechanisms in the same region of the brain has led some investigators to propose that the mirror neuron system played a critically important role in humankind's development of, first, a gestural communication system, and subsequently, the emergence of language (Ferrari, Gallese, Rizzolatti, & Fogassi, 2003).

If one adopts the view that human language emerged from gestural and sign communication, then that change in perspective may lead one to question long-held notions about the nature of language. Among those defining characteristics that should be reexamined are those of the arbitrary or symbolic relationship between a word and its underlying concept, the preeminence of syntax in language, and the views that language abilities are genetically determined and solely the province of human beings (see Chapter 1).

Linguistics traditionally has emphasized the symbolic or arbitrary relationships between words and their underlying concepts as a critical defining characteristic of language. If, however, one examines signs from different signed languages, one will see that many signs have a clear tie to the concepts they represent. That is, a characteristic that differentiates many signs from nearly all vocal words is that signs can be formed so that they resemble objects, actions, or properties. This pantomime-like characteristic of signs is known as iconicity. The representational aspect of many signs and gestures, moreover, is largely equivalent to the semantic component of languages. Highly iconic signs also have a communication advantage, as they likely would have been relatively easily understood by others because of their resemblance to the actions, objects, or properties for which they stand. While likely being an effective way for early humans to communicate, iconic signs and gestures may also have served as a bridge to more arbitrary vocal utterances when these signs and gestures were produced together with vocalizations.

After Chomsky revolutionized the field of linguistics in the 1950s and 1960s, syntax (the rules of word combination) became the foremost attribute or defining characteristic of language for many scholars. Claims of similarity in the structure of the world's languages were presented as evidence of a special trait for language that was genetically determined. A special human symbol-manipulating neural mechanism was seen as underlying all of the world's languages (Pinker, 1994). This view of language, however, emerged from the study of spoken languages, with many of the analyses conducted on only a relatively small portion of all the world's languages, Indo-European languages. But if one examines how signed languages convey information, then the presence of basic syntactic components, such as a distinct subject and predicate in an utterance, becomes much less evident.

Another characteristic of visual-manual signs that differentiates them from spoken words is that signs can incorporate movement into their production. That is, by making a sign move, one can convey action, a property of verbs. This movement can also indicate the location or direction of the action depending on where the action is produced.

Moreover, if the context for sign production has been established, then the location and direction of a sign's movement might also specify who was the agent of the action as well as the recipient or object of the action. Signers may also modify how they form signs (e.g., slow down, speed up) to convey additional information without having to increase the number of signs in a particular sign utterance. Indeed, Stokoe (2001) argued that a single iconic gesture or sign, incorporating the movement aspects mentioned above, can convey the same information as that of a complete spoken sentence without requiring the mastery of distinct syntactic rules. In light of these characteristics of signs and gestures, then it should be apparent that they had the capacity to serve as quite efficient and effective vehicles of communication for early humans.

If one adopts the view that language developed from its roots in gestural and sign communication, then the claim that language abilities are solely the province of human beings becomes considerably less apparent. Studies of gestural and sign communication in non-human primates (e.g., Gardner & Gardner, 1969; Gardner, Gardner, & van Cantfort, 1989; Patterson & Cohn, 1990; Patterson & Linden, 1981) have shown that non-human primates are capable of acquiring substantial sign vocabularies and of combining signs into short utterances when taught to sign by human caregivers. Less well known is the finding that studies of ape gestural behavior have shown that apes are capable of generating their own communicative gestures without human instruction, and that some of these gestures have an iconic component (Tanner & Byrne, 1999). Taken together, these studies suggest that humans and non-human primates, with ancestors in common, share various language-related abilities. Moreover, the transition from ape gestural and sign communication to the communication and language of early humans may be much closer than traditionally depicted.

Chomsky (1965) also advanced the view that the capacity to produce and understand language was primarily the result of a hard-wired organ in humans rather than the product of more general cognitive abilities and social interaction. The study of gestural communication in infants, however, suggests that social interaction plays an important role in early communicative and language development. Prior to producing referential spoken words, infants typically produce an array of communicative gestures. These gestures often include extending one's arms to be picked up, showing and giving an object to a caregiver, and communicative pointing (Bates et al., 1979). These gestures may not only communicate the infant's desires, but they also indicate the infant's growing awareness that the caregiver is a sentient being worthy of interaction. Of the different communicative gestures produced by infants, the act of communicative pointing may play a particularly important role (Tomasello, 2008). Such points serve to indicate or specify a particular object or event in the immediate environment. Points also have a vital communicative function as they can effectively direct others' attention to some nearby thing or event. A communicative point, for example, might convey to another that a particular object or activity was desired or of interest, or it might serve to draw attention to a looming danger. Communicative pointing thus appears to be of special importance in establishing a clear reference in early communication. Both for contemporary human infants and for early humankind, the act of communicative pointing sets the stage for more language-like exchanges.

Tomasello (2008) argued that the roots of language are in communicative gestures, especially communicative pointing. This is the case both for the origins of language in early human beings, where communication most likely consisted largely of pointing and iconic or pantomimic gestures, and for infants today, where communicative acts set the stage for subsequent language production and understanding.

Usage-Based Theory

Tomasello's (2003) usage-based theory of language acquisition also differs substantially from Chomsky's theory of universal grammar. Tomasello (2003) argued that language acquisition is primarily the product of more general cognitive and social processes. In usage-based theory, grammar is seen as emerging in the child largely through such cognitive skills as pattern finding and by the child's repeated interactions with adult caregivers. Rather than emphasizing the presence of innate linguistic rules and categories as in the universal grammar approach, Tomasello asserted that only a small number of general cognitive and social processes are necessary to account for a child's acquisition of language.

Language is seen more as a social phenomenon, as a child learns language within the context of social interaction. In this approach, the acquisition of language rests on the more fundamental skills of establishing joint attention, learning to read others' intentions, and acquiring the ability to act on objects in ways similar to that of adults (or imitative learning). In this social interaction and learning framework, the initial common ground between adult caregiver and young child is that of joint attention. An infant, toward the end of the first year, begins to look where an adult is looking or pointing. This joint attention frame helps the young child and the adult caregiver discern what objects and actions are the focus of each other's attention. Infants in their first year also typically learn to establish eye contact with others and to initiate various communicative actions such as showing or giving objects. These behaviors show that the infant is coming to understand that the adult caregiver is a perceiving, knowledgeable being with particular communicative intentions. This joint attention frame, moreover, helps the child recognize the object or action to which the caregiver is referring. This, in turn, facilitates the child's learning of the names or labels of these objects or actions. As a young child learns to imitate an adult's intentional actions, the child better understands the nature of these actions and how they might be varied or modified. Also, when the child produces these actions in an interactive exchange with an adult, this helps the child to learn another's perspective on these actions. The young child's ability to discern the intentions of others extends to the language domain as well, as when the young child struggles to comprehend the utterances of others.

An important early step in the child's acquisition of language is the development of the ability to understand and use linguistic symbols or words. Such linguistic symbols not only represent concepts in the cognitive domain, but they have important social components as well. The particular names or labels given to concepts are the products of social conventions within a linguistic community. Moreover, these linguistic symbols are used when interacting with others, often when trying to direct another individual's attention to particular objects or actions present in the environment.

For Tomasello (2003), pattern-finding ability is an important cognitive or perceptual skill that facilitates the young child's language acquisition. This early-emerging ability is essential to language development in several ways. In the acquisition of linguistic symbols, the ability to recognize distinct patterns across similar objects or actions is important in the formation of different conceptual categories. For example, objects similar in shape are likely to be called by the same name. The recognition of similarities in sensorimotor actions also helps in the child's learning of object categories and types of action. That is, objects or actions that are similar in function are likely to be represented by the same name or linguistic symbol. Tomasello also points out that very young children are adept at recognizing patterns in sequentially presented auditory input. This ability to discern patterns in the linguistic utterances that the child hears in turn assists the child in constructing utterances.

After they acquire the ability to produce linguistic symbols, young children begin combining these symbols into two- and three-word combinations. Tomasello observes that this ability to combine items is not limited to the domain of language. Infants often combine actions to produce purposeful sequential sensorimotor behaviors, with the mental combination of actions underlying the children's overt physical production of these actions. Young children's development and use of early word combinations, moreover, is greatly facilitated both by hearing a vast number of utterances from others in their environments and by their production of an increasing number of words and word combinations. Many of the large number of utterances that children hear from their adult caregivers are especially tailored to the children's immediate frames of attention and thus may make them more readily understood.

In usage-based theory, as word combinations are processed and produced more frequently and readily by young children over time, the children begin to perceive similarities in structure across these utterances. This emerging ability to create structural mappings across utterances is an important step in the development of grammar. It is this ability to discern patterns and similarities across utterances that enables children to realize the more abstract nature of language structure.

When children repeatedly hear and produce certain grammatical structures involving particular words, these constructions are said by Tomasello to become entrenched. That is, linguistic behaviors that are frequently repeated become routinized or automatized over time. Moreover, once these constructions are habitual, they become difficult to change. As certain forms of usage are becoming firmly established, Tomasello also observes that children are becoming less likely to use these forms or constructions in novel ways that they have not heard before. Instead, children are likely to learn alternative forms or constructions for use in these new contexts. More complex forms only emerge after considerable time and usage. In this way, usage theory holds that language rules are **epigenetic** and emerge only after the patterns in simpler constructions are detected and tentatively employed.

In summary, Tomasello (2003, 2008) has effectively integrated a wide range of findings and ideas from different areas of psychology, linguistics, anthropology, and philosophy in his approach to language acquisition. He begins by adopting the view that the roots of language are in communicative gestures. Of these gestures, he underlines the critical importance of communicative pointing; communicative pointing is essential in the establishment of reference and of joint attention between the child and caregiver. From there, Tomasello relies on findings from studies of cognitive and perceptual processing in his discussion of the learning of linguistic symbols, and of emerging pattern-recognition abilities in the learning of linguistic structures. Throughout these processes, children typically are deeply involved in social interactions that facilitate their language acquisition.

Evaluation of Usage-Based Theory

An important limitation of the gestural origins of human language is that gestures, and speech for that matter, leave no trail of artifacts for paleolinguists to mark a date when it was used. Until a time machine is invented, the earliest language systems are not observable. Misguided pharaonic "experiments" that attempted to address language origins by rearing children in isolation from established, spoken language failed to detect evidence of "ontogeny recapitulating phylogeny" (see Chapter 1). Moreover, even if some reliable patterns emerged in isolated modern children, the results could not be generalized to genetically different children from hundreds of thousands or even millions of years prior (Bonvillian, Garber, & Dell, 1997).

Although it is impossible to recreate the conditions of language emergence and the primitive hominids who first communicated, it is informative to investigate how both humans and their close relatives process signs, gestures, and actions. Our growing understanding of how infants and nonhuman primates view their social world may lead to important future breakthroughs by analogy (see Egan, Bloom, & Santos, 2010). Both infants and monkeys display solid understanding of human intentions and stare longer at scenes where blindfolded humans behave as if they had seen critical visual information to which they should not have been privy (Flombaum & Santos, 2006). Another area that holds potential clues is the effects of gestures on spoken language acquisition in both normal and atypical children.

Usage-based theory focuses on joint attention for early acquisition in typical children (Tomasello, 2008). However, high-functioning children with Autism Spectrum Disorder and those with Asperger's syndrome may pose some difficulty with this assertion. These children typically master the phonology and syntax of their caregivers' language, albeit at slower rates. Yet these children rarely use gestures communicatively and have considerable difficulty mastering normal eye-gaze patterns, specifically establishing joint attention (see Chapter 9). Furthermore, children with autistic spectrum disabilities are distinguished by their inability to appreciate others' feelings and intentions. Although they acquire the formal use of language, up to and including syntax, they continue to have life-long trouble with its appropriate social usage (Loveland & Tunali, 1993). These problems emerge early and are obvious to all. Children with autism frequently talk interminably in monologues with little interest in their listeners. They often interrupt other speakers and interject information unrelated to ongoing topics. Clearly, these children are mastering elements of language without most of the social support deemed central by usage-based theory.

Perhaps the formal language system and the social use of language follow different developmental paths. For typically developing children, these bicameral aspects of language use go hand in hand. The social situation normally aids children in the acquisition of the formal constructs of spoken language, whereas children with autism must deduce the formal rules of speech with only minimal input from the social situation. However, this would suggest that establishing joint attention, using communicative gestures and appreciating others' points of view and intentions is only critical for the acquisition of social speech usage and not the formal rules of language. We doubt usage-based theorists would agree, insisting on the centrality of the social interaction as critical to all aspects of language development (see Ninio, 2011).

Because Tomasello's theory is relatively new, it has not been around long enough to have its precise predictions adequately tested. Do children master first the forms most used by their caretakers (Ninio, 2011)? Does mastery of the initial forms predict the emergence of more complex constructions as predicted by the pattern of initial mastery (Tomasello, 2008)? Only time and further investigation will provide the answers to these questions.

SUMMARY

Admittedly, no developmental psycholinguist seriously believes that magic is at the root of language acquisition, despite our frustrated attempts to identify the actual processes involved. One of the reasons that we have failed to discover simple and easily observable processes in language learning may be that they do not exist, owing to the importance of the phenomenon to the developing child. In other words, there is simply so much pressure placed on children to communicate successfully that there are probably many routes to the goal, and within each route, a great deal of variability may be tolerated (see Chapter 8).

The behaviorist approach probably has suffered most from an overreliance on presumably simple principles to explain language development. Although reinforcement may explain food searching in rats, it has failed to explain the average human child's search for communicative competence. If the child's parents and peers do industriously shape verbal behavior, then we must have overlooked it somehow, or it must be much more subtle and indirect than the laborious tutelage performed in laboratory settings. On the other hand, some of the behaviorist mechanisms, such as imitation in the modern guise of mirror neurons, continue to show promise as an integral part of the language-learning process.

From left to right. Interactionists: Elizabeth Bates (1947–2003) and Brian Mac-Whinney (Carnegie Mellon University). Nativist: Steven Pinker (Harvard University).

There is unacknowledged agreement among the competing camps. The more articulated model of imitation (Bandura & Walters, 1963) includes a process called general disinhibition, wherein the observing learner is more likely to perform a behavior in the general class of behavior as that observed in the model. This suggests that the learner had access to the behavior all along and imitation merely disinhibited it, allowing the behavior to be performed. Imitation, thus, seems to play a "releasing" function to innate language parameters, which seems remarkably similar to the most recent innatist position (Pinker, 1994) and to the "priming" effects used to support PDP models. Clearly, researchers from either camp might be perturbed at the liberties of comparison we have taken. Yet the point to be made here is far from frivolous. The behaviorist approach offers much to the concerned developmental psycholinguist. Just as Piaget argued that cognitive development is epigenetic (complex cognitive processes arise from simpler functions), it is probable that language learning at least partially depends on simpler skills such as those described by behaviorists (Moerk, 1992). Indeed, when examined closely, some of these basic principles are featured in most of the theoretical approaches. For example, Nelson's (1977) recasts could be considered a special form of imitation or modeling that comes into play as feedback to children when they make language errors (Bohannon & Stanowicz, 1988; Farrar, 1992).

The linguistic approach also currently suffers several maladies. The first concerns the nativism–empiricism issue and the **nominalist fallacy**. Researchers fall into this fallacy when they think that giving a phenomenon a special name sufficiently explains the phenomenon. When an observer is at a loss to explain the origin of a form in children's speech, it would behoove them to realize that simply labeling it as innate neither helps us determine its relation to other forms nor to predict when it should appear in the developmental progression (Pinker, 1994). On the other hand, employing information theory to determine the formal learnability of a particular grammar seems promising if the nominalist fallacy can be avoided. The work of Wexler and Culicover (1980) and Pinker (1984) has attempted to model the minimal necessary principles for the acquisition of grammar. They found grammar unlearnable unless the children were given information either that some sentences are impermissible or that some aspects of grammar are innate. If this approach is utilized to test new grammars and other assumptions, then some of the possible combinations of psychological processes and competing grammars may be excluded *a priori*.

Many psycholinguists have been reluctant to accept the arguments for the presence of an innate language acquisition device that enables young children to acquire complex grammars rapidly and without formal instruction. An important reason behind many scholars' reluctance is that the emergence of such a device or structure appeared to be at odds with findings from studies of evolution and from what is known about the onset of human language. The vocal structures and their corresponding cerebral controls necessary for autonomous speech emerged relatively recently in human evolution, probably between 100,000 and 170,000 years ago (Corballis, 2002). This suggested time frame for the onset of spoken language would make oral language a very recent event in the course of human evolution. For a language acquisition device, wired for grammar, also to have emerged recently and nearly simultaneously with that of human vocal structures, struck many scholars as not being in accord with the gradual and incremental steps typically seen in evolution.

The transition to modern grammatical speech may be more plausible if one accepts the proposition that spoken language was built on a scaffolding of manual communication. There are important similarities in the production of spoken and signed languages; both involve the relatively rapid production of sequential movements and are under the control of the left hemisphere in most individuals. Scholars (e.g., Corballis, 2010; Stokoe, 2001) have advanced the view that communicative gestures and manual signs preceded the emergence of speech in the evolution of human language. Their position is supported from studies of signing and gesture production in nonhuman primates, lateral dominance in its relation to speech and sign, and the integration of gesture and speech seen in human communication today.

Before students of developmental psycholinguistics reject the linguistic approach outright, they should reflect upon the logical nature of grammar (Ninio, 2011). The internal structure of language that produces and decodes speech will probably be discovered within the linguistic approach. As long as linguists allow children's performance data to bear upon conclusions concerning the child's language competence, then a coherent explanation that achieves Chomsky's (1965) third level of theoretical adequacy (psychological reality) will be achieved. Without such a system describing the organized nature of adult language or the progression of emerging grammars in children, any explanation of language or its acquisition will remain as a disorganized heap of data.

The obvious solution to the controversy between the behaviorist and linguistic approaches lies in the contribution of the various interactional approaches, each of which provides important foci for research. The cognitive approach stresses that language is only one of many complex cognitive skills that children acquire. Moreover, the structure of language and the processes involved in its learning are constrained by the nature of the child's thought at the time of acquisition. The information processing theorists emphasize the cognitive processing demands of language learning. They look to the availability and reliability of linguistic cues that signal important communicative functions. It is their position that the nature of the information to be processed determines the course of development. The social interactionist approach highlights the social context in which language is learned, without which language learning seems impossible and perhaps unnecessary. This approach seeks the critical aspects of social interaction that allow normal language learning to proceed. Finally, the usage and gestural approach imbeds itself in both emerging cognition and social interaction. Children, like early hominids, start out by using referential pointing and using iconic gestures in social interaction. The gestural communication framework sets the stage for subsequent communication using either manual or vocal signs. More flexible complex language forms only emerge later after the simpler forms are automatized.

These three interactional approaches seem to hold the most promise for the future, perhaps because of their eclectic natures. Recognizing the strengths of the historically earlier theoretical camps, the interactionist borrows freely from each. By avoiding a strict insistence on simple associations or strong innate mechanisms, interactionists may circumvent the more obvious pitfalls. Until language theories incorporate a general learning model that accurately specifies both the psychologically valid language faculty and the environmental variables required for children to develop language in natural settings, the language-acquisition process will continue to be opaque.

SUGGESTED PROJECTS

1. Read Skinner's *Verbal Behavior* (1957). Write a synopsis of his position on the problem of language description and acquisition. Compare Skinner's terms, such as *tact, mand,* and *autoclitic,* with traditional grammatical categories devised by linguists.

2. Select some friends to play the following games, one subject at a time. Using Figure 7.3, see if they can solve the puzzles you present. The figure provides a simple concept-formation problem, with the top set of stimuli serving as "maternal exemplars" and the bottom sets of stimuli serving as opportunities for "child responses." Note that each stimulus has several features, including size (large, medium, and small), shape (circle, triangle, and square), pattern (open, vertical stripes, and horizontal stripes), and position (left, middle, and right). You begin the game by selecting one of the twelve stimulus features as "correct," without telling the "child" subject. For example, if "left" is going to be the correct "linguistic" rule, you should now point to the leftmost stimulus in the top "maternal" array. The subject should then try to guess the correct form

in the numbered arrays below. Various forms of language-learning assumptions can be tested:

A. *No-negative-evidence assumption.* Regardless of what the subjects choose, act totally delighted that they chose anything at all and record their choices. Never correct the subject for a wrong stimulus choice. Offer to call Grandma to tell her the "baby" has uttered his or her first word. After several subjects, compare the resultant patterns of responses to see if they converged on the same solution (e.g., "left").

B. *Implicit negative evidence.* Proceed as above; however, whenever subjects make a correct choice, point to the choice they have made and say, "That one." When the subject makes an error (e.g., any choice other than the left stimulus), point to the left stimulus and say, "That one." Never tell the subjects that they are right or wrong and act delighted that they are "speaking" (i.e., playing the game). After several subjects, compare the pattern of their choices. Did they converge on the rule you selected? How did they do this if you never told them they were right or wrong?

Compare your data to the theoretical positions of formal language-learning theorists such as Pinker or Wexler. Read Farrar (1992) and briefly discuss the negative-evidence issue in comparison to your data.

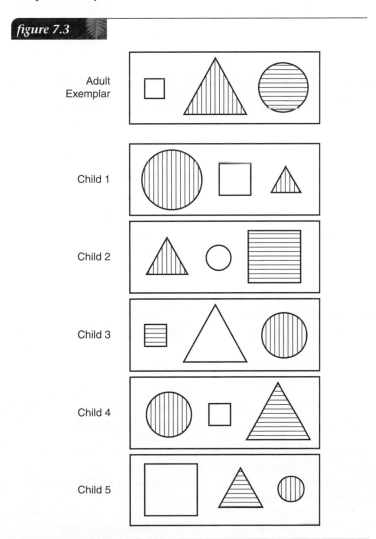

figure 7.3

3. Record a child in normal conversation. Observe and describe as completely as possible the contextual situation in which the conversation occurred (if videotaping is possible, even better). Select at least thirty utterances by the child and analyze them according to the various theoretical perspectives: behaviorist, linguistic, cognitive, and social interactionist. Try to account for the data that each position would consider important.

4. Come up with your own demonstration of semantic and phonetic priming. Select priming words and questions that target a wrong answer to a question, for example, say "folk" five times then answer the question, "What is the white part of an egg called?" Most people will answer "yolk." Try a demonstration in which your prime is spelled out loud (instead of pronounced) five times. Does it work as well? Discuss the differences in your results in light of the various major theories.

5. Create a set of iconic signs or gestures for common objects or actions. When creating each manual sign consider which hand-shape will be used, what movements are involved with the hand-shape, and under what conditions the sign should appear. When ten to fifteen signs are so described, use them in front of class or in front of a friend and have them write down what they thought the sign meant. Order the signs by percent agreement. What do the most easily understood signs have in common? What do the least understood signs share?

SUGGESTED READINGS

Behaviorism

MacCorquodale, K. (1970). On Chomsky's review of Skinner's verbal behavior. *Journal of the Experimental Analysis of Behavior, 13*, 83–99.

Skinner, B. F. (1957). *Verbal behavior.* Englewood Cliffs, NJ: Prentice-Hall.

Linguistic

Chomsky, N. (1995). *The minimalist program.* Cambridge, MA: MIT Press.

Pinker, S. (1994). *The language instinct: How the mind creates language.* New York: William Morrow.

Cognitive

Elman, J., Bates, E., Johnson, M., Karmiloff-Smith, A., Parisi, D., & Plunkett, K. (1996). *Rethinking innateness: A connectionist perspective on development.* Cambridge, MA: MIT/Bradford.

MacWhinney, B. (1987). The competition model. In B. MacWhinney (Ed.), *Mechanisms of language acquisition* (pp. 249–308). Hillsdale, NJ: Erlbaum.

Piaget, J. (1926). *The language and thought of the child.* New York: Harcourt Brace Jovanovich.

Pinker, S., & Prince, A. (1988). On language and connectionism: Analysis of a parallel distributed processing model of language acquisition. *Cognition, 28*, 73–193.

Social

Bohannon, J., & Warren-Leubecker, A. (1988). Recent developments in child-directed speech: You've come a long way, Baby-Talk. *Language Science, 10*(1), 89–110.

Hirsh-Pasek, K., & Golinkoff, R. (1996). *The origins of grammar: Evidence from early language comprehension.* Cambridge, MA: MIT Press.

Usage and Gestural

Tomasello, M. (2008). *Origins of human communication.* Cambridge, MA: Bradford Book, MIT Press.

KEY WORDS

activation nodes
child-directed speech (CDS)
classical conditioning
communicative pointing
competition model
connectionist models
constructivism
epigenetic
feature-blind aphasia
joint attention
language acquisition device
    (LAD)

language faculty
learnability problem
logical form
Markov sentence models
mirror neurons
negative evidence
neglected children
nominalist fallacy
parallel-distributed proces-
    sors (PDPs)
parallel processing
parsimony

phonetic form
poverty of imagination
poverty of the stimulus
priming
recasts
serial processing
signs
text presentation
universal grammar

REFERENCES

Arbib, M. (2005). The mirror system hypothesis: How did protolanguage evolve? In M. Tallerman (Ed .), *Language origins: Perspectives on evolution* (pp. 21–47). New York: Oxford University Press.

Armstrong, D. F. (2008). The gestural theory of language origins. *Sign Language Studies, 8,* 289–314.

Armstrong, D. F., Stokoe, W. C., & Wilcox, S. E. (1995). *Gesture and the nature of language.* Cambridge, UK: Cambridge University Press.

Baker, N., & Nelson, K. (1984). Recasting and related conversational techniques for triggering syntactic advances by young children. *First Language, 5,* 3–22.

Bandura, A., & Walters, R. (1963). *Social learning and personality development.* New York: Holt, Rinehart, & Winston.

Barnes, S., Gutfreund, M., Satterly, D., & Wells, G. (1983). Characteristics of adult speech which predict children's language development. *Journal of Child Language, 10,* 65–84.

Bates, E. (1976). *Language and context: Studies in the acquisition of pragmatics.* New York: Academic Press.

Bates, E. (1993). Comprehension and production in early language development: Comments on Savage-Rumbaugh et al. *Monographs of the Society for Research in Child Development, 58* (3–4)(Serial No. 233), 222–242.

Bates, E., Beeghley-Smith, M., Bretherton, I., & McNew, S. (1983). Social basis of language development: A reassessment. In H. Reese & L. Lipsett (Eds.), *Advances in child development and behavior* (Vol. 16, pp. 8–75). New York: Academic Press.

Bates, E., Benigni, L., Bretherton, I., Camaioni, L., & Volterra, V. (1979). *The emergence of symbols: Cognition and communication in infancy.* New York: Academic Press.

Bates, E., Bretherton, I., & Snyder, L. (1988). *From first words to grammar: Individual differences and dissociable mechanisms.* Cambridge, UK: Cambridge University Press.

Bates, E., & MacWhinney, B. (1982). Functionalist approach to grammar. In E. Wanner & L. Gleitman (Eds.), *Language acquisition: The state of the art* (pp. 173–218). New York: Cambridge University Press.

Bates, E., & MacWhinney, B. (1987). Competition, variation, and language learning. In B. MacWhinney (Ed.), *Mechanisms of language acquisition* (pp. 157–194). Hillsdale, NJ: Erlbaum.

Bates, E., & MacWhinney, B. (1989). Functionalism and the competition model. In B. MacWhinney & E. Bates (Eds.), *The crosslinguistic study of sentence processing* (pp. 3–76). Cambridge, UK: Cambridge University Press.

Bates, E., & Snyder, L. (1987). The cognitive hypothesis in language development. In I. Uzgiris & J. McV. Hunt (Eds.), *Research with scales of psychological development in infancy* (pp. 168–206). Champaign-Urbana: University of Illinois Press.

Berko Gleason, J. (1977). Talking to children: Some notes on feedback. In C. Snow & C. Ferguson (Eds.), *Talking to children: Language input and acquisition* (pp. 199–205). Cambridge, UK: Cambridge University Press.

Berko Gleason, J., & Weintraub, S. (1976). The acquisition of routines in child language. *Language in Society, 5,* 129–136.

Berko Gleason, J., & Weintraub, S. (1978). Input language and the acquisition of communicative competence. In K. Nelson (Ed.), *Children's language* (Vol. 1, pp. 177–202). New York: Gardner Press.

Binder, J. R., Desai, R. H., Graves, W. W., & Conant, L. L. (2009). Where is the semantic system? A critical review and meta-analysis of 120 functional neuro-imaging studies. *Cerebral Cortex*, 19(12), 2767–2796.

Binkofski, F., & Buccino, G. (2004). Motor functions of the Broca's region. *Brain and Language, 89*, 362–369.

Block, E., & Kessel, F. (1980). Determinants of the acquisition order of grammatical morphemes: A reanalysis and reinterpretation. *Journal of Child Language, 7,* 181–189.

Bloom, L., Hood, P., & Lightbown, P. (1974). Imitation in language development: If, when, and why? *Cognitive Psychology, 6,* 380–420.

Bloom, L., Lifter, K., & Broughton, J. (1985). The convergence of early cognition and language in the second year of life: Problems in conceptualization and measurement. In M. Barrett (Ed.), *Children's single-word speech.* Chichester, UK: Wiley.

Bock, K. (1989). Syntactic persistence in language production. *Cognitive Psychology, 18,* 128–149.

Bohannon, J. (1989). Control of adult speech in Spanish. *Acta Paedologica, 2*(1), 48–60.

Bohannon, J., & Hirsh-Pasek, K. (1984). Do children say as they're told? A new perspective on *motherese*. In L. Feagans, C. Garvey, & R. Golinkoff (Eds.), *The origins and growth of communication* (pp. 176–195). Norwood, NJ: Ablex.

Bohannon, J., & Marquis, A. (1977). Children's control of adult speech. *Child Development, 48,* 1002–1008.

Bohannon, J., & Stanowicz, L. (1988). Adult responses to children's language errors: The issue of negative evidence. *Developmental Psychology, 24,* 684–689.

Bohannon, J., & Stanowicz, L. (1989). Bidirectional effects of imitation: A synthesis within a cognitive model. In K. E. Nelson & G. Speidel (Eds.), *A new look at imitation in language acquisition* (pp. 122–150). Norwood, NJ: Ablex.

Bohannon, J., Stine, E. L., & Ritzenberg, D. (1982). The effects of experience and feedback on motherese. *The Bulletin of the Psychonomic Society, 19,* 201–204.

Bohannon, J., & Warren-Leubecker, A. (1988). Recent developments in child-directed speech: You've come a long way, Baby-Talk. *Language Science, 10*(1), 89–110.

Bohannon, J. N., MacWhinney, B., & Snow, C. E. (1990). Negative evidence revisited: Beyond learnability or who has to prove what to whom? *Developmental Psychology, 26,* 221–226.

Bohannon, J. N., Padgett, R., Nelson, K. E., & Mark, M. (1996). Useful evidence on negative evidence. *Developmental Psychology, 32,* 551–555.

Bonvillian, J. D., Garber, A. M., & Dell, S. B. (1997). Language origin accounts: Was the gesture in the beginning? *First Language, 17,* 219–239.

Bonvillian, J. D., Orlansky, M. D., Novack, L. L., & Folven, R. J. (1983). Early sign language and cognitive development. In D. Rogers & J. A. Sloboda (Eds.), *The acquisition of symbolic skills* (pp. 207–214). New York: Plenum Press.

Bonvillian, J. D., Raeburn, V. P., & Horan, E. A. (1979). Talking to children: The effects of rate, intonation, and length on children's sentence imitation. *Journal of Child Language, 6,* 459–467.

Bowerman, M. (1973). Structural relationships in children's utterances: Syntactic or semantic? In T. Moore (Ed.), *Cognitive development and the acquisition of language* (pp. 197–215). New York: Academic Press.

Bowerman, M. (1982). Reorganizational processes in lexical and syntactic development. In E. Wanner & L. Gleitman (Eds.), *Language acquisition: The state of the art* (pp. 319–346). Cambridge, UK: Cambridge University Press.

Branigan, G. (1979). Some reasons why some successive single word utterances are not. *Journal of Child Language, 6,* 411–421.

Brown, R. (1973). *A first language: The early stages.* Cambridge, MA: Harvard University Press.

Brown, R., & Bellugi, U. (1964). Three processes in the child's acquisition of syntax. *Harvard Educational Review, 34,* 133–151.

Brown, R., & Hanlon, C. (1970). Derivational complexity and the order of acquisition in child speech. In J. R. Hayes (Ed.), *Cognition and the development of language* (pp. 11–53). New York: Wiley.

Bruner, J. (1978). The role of dialogue in language acquisition. In A. Sinclair, R. Jarvella, & W. Levelt (Eds.), *The child's conception of language* (pp. 241–256). New York: Springer-Verlag.

Butcher, C., Mylander, C., & Goldin-Meadow, S. (1991). Displaced communication in a self-styled gesture system: Pointing at the nonpresent. *Cognitive Development, 6,* 315–342.

Bybee, J., & Slobin, D. (1982). Rules and schemas in the development and use of the English past tense. *Language, 58,* 265–289.

Chomsky, C. (1969). *The acquisition of syntax in children from 5 to 10.* Cambridge, MA: MIT Press.

Chomsky, N. (1957). *Syntactic structures.* The Hague: Mouton.

Chomsky, N. (1965). *Aspects of the theory of syntax.* Cambridge, MA: MIT Press.

Chomsky, N. (1980). *Rules and representations.* Oxford, UK: Blackwell.

Chomsky, N. (1982). *Lectures on government and binding.* New York: Foris.

Chomsky, N. (1988). *Language and problems of knowledge.* Cambridge, MA: MIT Press.

Chomsky, N. (1995). *The minimalist program.* Cambridge, MA: MIT Press.

Chomsky, N., & Place, U. T. (2000). The Chomsky-Place correspondence 1993–1994. In T. Schoneberger (Ed.), *The analysis of verbal behavior, 17,* 7–38.

Chouinard, M. M., & Clark, E. V. (2003). Adult reformulations of child errors as negative evidence. *Journal of Child Language, 30,* 637–669.

Christopoulos, C., Bonvillian, J. D., & Crittenden, P. M. (1988). Maternal language input and child maltreatment. *Infant Mental Health Journal, 9,* 272–286.

Clark, E. (1977). Strategies and the mapping problem in first language acquisition. In J. Macnamara (Ed.), *Language learning and thought* (pp. 147–168). New York: Academic Press.

Corballis, M. C. (2002) *From hand to mouth: The origins of language.* Princeton, NJ: Princeton University Press.

Corballis, M. C. (2010). Mirror neurons and the evolution of language. *Brain and Language, 112,* 25–35.

Corrigan, R. (1978). Language development as related to stage six object permanence development. *Journal of Child Language, 5,* 173–190.

Cross, T. (1977). Mother's speech and its association with rate of linguistic development in young children. In N. Waterson & C. Snow (Eds.), *The development of communication* (pp. 199–216). New York: Wiley.

Culp, R. E., Watkins, R. V., Lawrence, H., Letts, D., Kelly, D. J., & Rice, M. L. (1991). Maltreated children's language and speech development: Abused, neglected, and abused and neglected. *First Language, 11,* 377–389.

Curtiss, S. (1981). Dissociations between language and cognition: Cases and implications. *Journal of Autism and Developmental Disorders, 11,* 15–30.

DeCasper, A., & Fifer, W. (1980). Of human bonding. *Science, 208,* 1174–1176.

Egan, L., Bloom, P. & Santos, L. R. (2010). Choice-induced preferences in the absence of choice: Evidence from a blind two choice paradigm with young children and capuchin monkeys. *Journal of Experimental Social Psychology, 46,* 204–207.

Elman, J. (1993). Learning and development in neural networks: The importance of starting small. *Cognition, 48*(1), 71–99.

Elman, J., Bates, E., Johnson, M., Karmiloff-Smith, A., Parisi, D., & Plunkett, K. (1996). *Rethinking innateness: A connectionist perspective on development.* Cambridge, MA: MIT/Bradford.

Elman, J. L. (1999). The emergence of language: A conspiracy theory. In B. MacWhinney (Ed.), *The emergence of language* (pp. 1–27). Mahwah, NJ: Erlbaum.

Enard, W., Przeworski, M., Fisher, S., Lai, C., Wiebe, V., Kitano, T., Monaco, A., & Pääbo, S. (2002). Molecular evolution of FOXP2, a gene involved in speech and language. *Nature, 418,* 869–872.

Everett, D. L. (2005). Cultural constraints on grammar and cognition in Pirzhã. *Current Anthropology, 46,* 621–646.

Farrar, J. (1992). Negative evidence and grammatical morpheme acquisition. *Developmental Psychology, 28,* 90–98.

Fenson, L., & Ramsey, D. (1980). Decentration and integration of the child's play in the second year. *Child Development, 51,* 171–178.

Fernald, A., & Kuhl, P. (1987). Acoustic determinants of infant preference for motherese speech. *Infant Behavior and Development, 10,* 279–293.

Ferrari, P. F., Gallese, V. Rizzolatti, G., & Fogassi, L. (2003). Mirror neurons responding to the observation of ingestive and communicative mouth actions in the monkey ventral premotor cortex. *European Journal of Neuroscience, 17,* 1703–1714.

Field, T., Woodson, R., Greenberg, R., & Cohen, D. (1982). Discrimination and imitation of facial expressions by neonates. *Science, 218,* 179–181.

Flombaum, J. & Santos, L. (2006). Rhesus monkeys attribute perceptions of others. *Current Biology, 15,* 447–452.

Fodor, J., & Pylyshyn, Z. (1988). Connectionism and cognitive architecture: A critical analysis. *Cognition, 28,* 3–71.

Fox, L., Long, S., & Langlois, A. (1988). Patterns of language comprehension deficit in abused and neglected children. *Journal of Speech and Hearing Disorders, 53,* 239–244.

Furrow, D., Nelson, K., & Benedict, H. (1979). Mothers' speech to children and syntactic development: Some simple relationships. *Journal of Child Language, 6,* 423–442.

Ganger, J., & Brent, M. R. (2004). Reexamining the vocabulary spurt. *Developmental Psychology, 40*(4), 621–632.

Gardner, R. A., & Gardner, B. T. (1969). Teaching sign language to a chimpanzee. *Science, 165,* 664–672.

Gardner, R. A., Gardner, B. T, & van Cantfort, T. E. (Eds.) (1989). *Teaching sign language to chimpanzees.* Albany: State University of New York Press.

Garrett, M., Bever, T., & Fodor, J. (1966). The active use of grammar in speech perception. *Perception and Psychophysics, 1,* 30–32.

Gleitman, L., Gleitman, H., & Shipley, E. (1972). The emergence of the child as grammarian. *Cognition, 1,* 137–164.

Gleitman, L., Newport, E., & Gleitman, H. (1984). The current status of the motherese hypothesis. *Journal of Child Language, 11,* pp. 43–79.

Gleitman, L., & Wanner, E. (1982). Language acquisition: The state of the state of the art. In E. Wanner & L. Gleitman (Eds.), *Language acquisition: The state of the art* (pp. 3–48). Cambridge, UK: Cambridge University Press.

Goldin-Meadow, S. (1982). The resilience of recursion: A study of a communication system developed without a conventional language model. In E. Wanner & L. Gleitman (Eds.), *Language acquisition: The state of the art* (pp. 51–77). Cambridge, UK: Cambridge University Press.

Goldin-Meadow, S. (2003). *The resilience of language: What gesture creation in deaf children can tell us about how all children learn language.* New York: Psychology Press.

Goldin-Meadow, S. (2011). Widening the lens on language learning: Language creation in deaf children and adults in Nicaragua: Commentary on Senghas. *Human Development, 53*(5), 303–311.

Goldin-Meadow, S., Butcher, C., Mylander, C., & Dodge, M. (1994). Nouns and verbs in a self-styled gesture system: What's in a name? *Cognitive Psychology, 27,* 259–319.

Goldin-Meadow, S., & Feldman, H. (1977). The development of language-like communication without a language model. *Science, 197,* 401–403.

Goldin-Meadow, S., & Mylander, C. (1984). Gestural communications in deaf children: The effects and non-effects of parental input on language development. *Monographs of the Society for Research in Child Development, 49* (3–4) (Serial No. 207).

Goldin-Meadow, S., & Mylander, C. (1990). Beyond the input given: The child's role in the acquisition of language. *Language, 66,* 323–355.

Goldin-Meadow, S., Özyürek, A., Sancar, B., & Mylander, C. (2009). Making language around the globe: A crosslinguistic study of homesign in the United States, China, and Turkey. In J. Guo, E. Lieven, N. Budwig, S. Ervin-Tripp, K. Nakamura, & Ş. Özçalişkan, (Eds.) , *Crosslinguistic approaches to the psychology of language: Research in the tradition of Dan Isaac Slobin* (pp. 27–39). New York: Psychology Press.

Goldstein, M. H., & Schwade, J. A. (2008). Social feedback to infants' babbling facilitates rapid phonological learning. *Psychological Science,* 19(5), 515–523.

Golinkoff, R. (1983). The preverbal negotiation of failed messages: Insights into the transition period. In R. Golinkoff (Ed.), *The transition from preverbal to verbal communication.* Hillsdale, NJ: Erlbaum.

Gopnik, A. (1984). The acquisition of "gone" and the development of the object concept. *Journal of Child Language, 11,* 273–292.

Gopnik, A., & Meltzoff, A. (1987). The development of categorization in the second year and its relation to other cognitive and linguistic developments. *Child Development, 58,* 1523–1531.

Gopnik, M. (1990). Feature-blind grammar and dysphasia. *Nature, 334,* 715.

Gopnik, M., & Crago, M. D. (1991). Familial aggregation of a developmental language disorder. *Cognition, 39,* 1–50.

Grimshaw, J., & Pinker, S. (1989). Positive and negative evidence in language acquisition. *Behavioral and Brain Sciences, 12,* 341–342.

Grossberg, S., & Stone, G. (1986). Neural dynamics of word recognition and recall: Attentional priming, learning, and resonance. *Psychological Review, 93,* 46–74.

Hakuta, K. (1977). Word order and particles in the acquisition of Japanese. *Papers and Reports on Child Language Development* (Stanford University), *(13),* 110–117.

Hauser, M. D., Chomsky, N., & Fitch, W. T. (2002). The faculty of language: What is it, who has it, and how did it evolve? *Science, 298,* 1569–1579.

Hirsh-Pasek, K., & Golinkoff, R. (1996). *The origins of grammar.* Cambridge, MA: MIT Press.

Hirsh-Pasek, K., Treiman, R., & Schneiderman, M. (1984). Brown and Hanlon revisited: Mother's sensitivity to ungrammatical forms. *Journal of Child Language, 11,* 81–88.

Hoff-Ginsburg, E. (1986). Function and structure in maternal speech: Their relation to the child's development of syntax. *Developmental Psychology, 22,* 155–163.

Ingram, D. (1981). The transition from early symbols to syntax. In R. Schiefelbusch & D. D. Bricker (Eds.), *Early language: Acquisition and intervention.* Baltimore: University Park Press.

Johnson, D., Guthrie, D., Smyke, A., Koga, S., Fox, N., Zeanah, C., & Nelson, C. (2010). Growth and associations between auxology, caregiving environment, and cognition in socially deprived Romanian children randomized to foster vs ongoing institutional care. *Archives of Pediatrics & Adolescent Medicine,* 164(6), 507–516.

Johnson, J., & Newport, E. (1989). Critical period effects in second language learning: The influence of maturational state on the acquisition of English as a second language. *Cognitive Psychology, 21,* 60–99.

Kandel, E., Schwartz, J., & Jessell, T. (Eds.). (1995). *Essentials of neural science and behavior*. Norwalk, CT: Appleton & Lange.

Klima, E. S., & Bellugi, U. (1979). *The signs of language*. Cambridge, MA: Harvard University Press.

Lenneberg, E. (1967). *Biological foundations of language*. New York: Wiley.

Levitt, A., & Uttman, J. (1992). From babbling towards the sound system of English and French: A longitudinal two-case study. *Journal of Child Language, 19,* 19–49.

Lidz, J., Gleitman, H., & Gleitman, L. (2003). Understanding how input matters: Verb learning and the footprint of universal grammar. *Cognition*, 87(3), 151–178.

Lovaas, O. I. (1977). *The autistic child: Language development through behavior modification*. New York: Irvington.

Loveland, K., & Tunali, B. (1993). Narrative language in autism and the theory of mind hypothesis: A wider perspective. In S. Baron-Cohen, H. Tager-Flusberg, & D. J. Cohen (Eds.), *Understanding other minds: Perspectives from autism*. Oxford: Oxford University Press.

MacDonald, J. (1987). Sentence interpretation in bilingual speakers of English and Dutch. *Applied Psycholinguistics, 8,* 379–414.

MacWhinney, B. (Ed.). (1987). *Mechanisms of language acquisition*. Hillsdale, NJ: Erlbaum.

MacWhinney, B. (1989). Competition and teachability. In M. Rice & R. Schiefelbusch (Eds.), *The teachability of language* (pp. 63–104). Baltimore: Paul H. Brookes.

MacWhinney, B. (Ed.). (1999). *The emergence of language*. Mahwah, NJ: Erlbaum.

Mainela-Arnold, E., Evans, J. L., & Alibali, M. W. (2006). Understanding conservation delays in children with Specific Language Impairment: Task representations revealed in speech and gesture. *Journal of Speech, Language, and Hearing Research*, 49(6), 1267–1279.

Marchman, V. (1993). Constraints on plasticity in a connectionist model of the English past tense. *Journal of Cognitive Neuroscience*, 5(2), 215–234.

Mayberry, R. I. (2010). Early language acquisition and adult language ability: What sign language reveals about the critical period for language. In M. Marshark, & P. Spencer (Eds.), *The Oxford handbook of deaf studies, language, and education, Vol. 2* (pp. 281–291). New York: Oxford University Press.

McNeill, D. (1966). Developmental psycholinguistics. In F. Smith & G. Miller (Eds.), *The genesis of language* (pp. 15–84). Cambridge, MA: MIT Press.

McNeill, D. (1970). *The acquisition of language: The study of developmental psycholinguistics*. New York: Harper & Row.

Meyer, D., & Schwaneveldt, R. (1971). Facilitation in recognizing pairs of words: Evidence of a dependence between retrieval operations. *Psychological Review, 90,* 227–234.

Mintz, T. (2003). Frequent frames as a cue for grammatical categories in child directed speech. *Cognition*, 90(1), 91–117.

Moerk, E. (1983). *The mother of Eve—As a first language teacher*. Norwood, NJ: Ablex.

Moerk, E. L. (1991a). *Language training and learning: Processes and products*. Baltimore: Paul H. Brookes.

Moerk, E. L. (1991b). Positive evidence on negative evidence. *First Language, 11,* 219–251.

Moerk, E. L. (1992). *A first language taught and learned*. Baltimore: Paul H. Brookes.

Molfese, D., Molfese, V., & Molfese, P. (2007). Relation between early measures of brain responses to language stimuli and childhood performance on behavioral language tasks. In D. Coch, G. Dawson, & K. Fischer (Eds). *Human behavior and the developing brain, Vol. 2.: Atypical development* (pp. 191–211). New York: Guilford.

Morgan, J. (1990). Input, innateness, and induction in language acquisition. *Developmental Psychobiology, 23,* 661–678.

Morgan, J., Bonamo, K. M., & Travis, L. L. (1995). Negative evidence on negative evidence. *Developmental Psychology, 31,* 180–197.

Mowrer, O. H. (1960). *Learning theory and the symbolic processes*. New York: Wiley.

Nagy, E. (2006). From imitation to conversation: the first dialogues with human neonates. *Infant & Child Development, 15*(3), 223–232.

Nelson, K. (1973). Structure and strategy in learning to talk. *Monographs of the Society for Research in Child Development, 38*(1–2) (Serial No. 149).

Nelson, K. (1981). Acquisition of words by first-language learners. In H. Winitz (Ed.), *Annals of the New York Academy of Sciences, 379,* 148–160.

Nelson, K. E. (1977). Facilitating children's acquisition of syntax. *Developmental Psychology, 13,* 101–107.

Nelson, K. E. (1981). Toward a rare-event cognitive comparison theory of syntax acquisition. In P. Dale & D. Ingram (Eds.), *Child language: An international perspective* (pp. 229–240). Baltimore: University Park Press.

Nelson, K. E. (1991). On differentiated language learning models and differentiated interventions. In N. A. Krasnegor (Ed.), *Biological and behavioral determinants of language development.* Hillsdale, NJ: Erlbaum.

Nelson, K. E., Welsh, J., Camarata, S., & Butkovsky, L. (1995). Available input for language-impaired children and younger children of matched language levels. *First Language, 15,* 1–17.

Newport, E. (1976). Motherese: The speech of mothers to young children. In N. Castellan, D. Pisoni, & G. Potts (Eds.), *Cognitive theory* (Vol. 2). Hillsdale, NJ: Erlbaum.

Newport, E., Gleitman, L., & Gleitman, H. (1977). Mother, I'd rather do it myself: Some effects and non-effects of motherese. In C. Snow & C. Ferguson (Eds.), *Talking to children: Language input and acquisition* (pp. 109–149). Cambridge, UK: Cambridge University Press.

Ninio, A. (2011). *Syntactic development, its input and output.* New York: Oxford University Press.

Ninio, A., & Snow, C. (1999). The development of pragmatics: Learning to use language appropriately. In W. Ritchie & T. Bhatia (Eds.), *Handbook of child language acquisition* (pp. 347–386). New York: Academic Press.

Nippold, M. (2006). *Later language development: School-age children, adolescents and young adults (3rd ed.).* Austin, TX: Pro-Ed.

Osgood, C. (1953). *Method and theory in experimental psychology.* New York: Oxford University Press.

Ospina, M., Krebs Seida, J., Clark, B., Karkhaneh, M., Hartling, L., Tjosvold, L., Vandermeer, B., & Smith, V. (2008). Behavioural and developmental interventions for autism spectrum disorder: A clinical systematic review. *PloS One, 3*(11), e3755.

Patterson, F., & Cohn, R. H. (1990). Language acquisition by a lowland gorilla: Koko's first ten years of vocabulary development. *Word, 41,* 97–143.

Patterson, F., & Linden, E. (1981). *The education of Koko.* New York: Holt, Rinehart and Winston.

Pelaez, M., Virues-Ortega, J., & Gewirtz, J. L. (2011). Reinforcement of vocalizations through contingent vocal imitation. *Journal of Applied Behavior Analysis, 44*(1), 33–40.

Penner, S. (1987). Parental responses to grammatical and ungrammatical child utterances. *Child Development, 58,* 376–384.

Piaget, J. (1954). *The origins of intelligence.* New York: Basic Books.

Piaget, J. (1962). *Play, dreams, and imitation in childhood.* New York: Norton. (Original work published 1945.)

Piaget, J. (1963). *The origins of intelligence in children.* New York: Norton. (Original work published 1936.)

Ping, L. (2009). Lexical organization and competition in first and second languages: Computational and neural mechanisms. *Cognitive Science, 33*(4), 629–664.

Pinker, S. (1984). *Language learnability and language development.* Cambridge, MA: Harvard University Press.

Pinker, S. (1987). The bootstrapping problem in language acquisition. In B. MacWhinney (Ed.), *Mechanisms of language acquisition.* Hillsdale, NJ: Erlbaum.

Pinker, S. (1989). *Learnability and cognition.* Cambridge, MA: MIT Press.

Pinker, S. (1991). Rules of language. *Science, 253,* 530–535.

Pinker, S. (1994). *The language instinct: How the mind creates language.* New York: Morrow.

Proctor-Williams, K., & Fey, M. E. (2007). Recast density and acquisition of novel irregular past tense verbs. *Journal of Speech, Language, and Hearing Research,* 50(4), 1029–1047.

Rileigh, K. (1973). Children's selective listening to stories: Familiarity effects involving vocabulary, syntax, and intonation. *Psychological Reports, 33,* 255–266.

Rizzolatti, G., & Arbib, M. A. (1998). Language within our grasp. *Trends in Neuroscience, 21,* 188–194.

Rizzolatti, G., & Sinigaglia, C. (2008). *Mirrors in the brain—How our minds share actions and emotions.* (F. Anderson, Trans.) Oxford, UK: Oxford University Press.

Rohde, D. L. T., & Plaut, D. C. (1999). Language acquisition in the absence of explicit negative evidence: How important is starting small? *Cognition, 72,* 67–109.

Rubin, D. (1975). Within word structure in the tip-of-the-tongue phenomenon. *Journal of Verbal Learning and Verbal Behavior, 13,* 392–397.

Rummelhart, D., & McClelland, J. (1987). Learning the past tense of English verbs: Implicit rules or parallel distributed processing. In B. MacWhinney (Ed.), *Mechanisms of language acquisition* (pp. 195–248). Hillsdale, NJ: Erlbaum.

Sachs, J. (1983). Talking about there and then: The emergence of displaced reference in parent–child discourse. In K. Nelson (Ed.), *Children's language, Vol. 4* (pp. 1–28). Hillsdale, NJ: Erlbaum.

Sachs, J., Bard, B., & Johnson, M. L. (1981). Language learning with restricted input: Case studies of two hearing children of deaf parents. *Applied Psycholinguistics, 2*(1), 33–54.

Saffran, J., Hauser, M., Seibel, R., Kapfhamer, J., Tsao, F., & Cushman, F. (2008). Grammatical pattern learning by human infants and cotton-top tamarin monkeys. *Cognition,* 107(2), 479–500.

Saxton, M. (2000). Negative evidence and negative feedback: Immediate effects on the grammaticality of child speech. *First Language, 20,* 221–252.

Saxton, M., Backley, P., & Gallaway, C. (2003). Negative input for grammatical errors: Effects after a lag of 12 weeks. *Journal of Child Language, 32,* 643–672.

Saxton, M., Houston-Price, C., & Dawson, N. (2005). The prompts hypothesis: Clarification requests as corrective input for grammatical errors. *Applied Psycholinguistics, 26,* 393–414.

Sinclair-de Zwart, H. (1969). Developmental psycholinguistics. In D. Elkind & J. Flavell (Eds.), *Studies in cognitive development: Essays in honor of Jean Piaget* (pp. 315–336). New York: Oxford University Press.

Sinclair-de Zwart, H. (1973). Language acquisition and cognitive development. In T. Moore (Ed.), *Cognitive development and the acquisition of language* (pp. 9–25). New York: Academic Press.

Singleton, J. L., Morford, J. P., & Goldin-Meadow, S. (1993). Once is not enough: Standards of well-formedness in manual communication created over three timespans. *Language, 69,* 638–715.

Skinner, B. F. (1957). *Verbal behavior.* Englewood Cliffs, NJ: Prentice-Hall.

Slobin, D. (1966). The acquisition of Russian as a native language. In F. Smith & G. A. Miller (Eds.), *The genesis of language: A psycholinguistic approach* (pp. 129–148). Cambridge, MA: MIT Press.

Slobin, D. (1979). *Psycholinguistics* (2nd ed.). Glenview, IL: Scott Foresman.

Slobin, D. (1982). Universal and particular in the acquisition of language. In E. Wanner & L. Gleitman (Eds.), *Language acquisition: The state of the art* (pp. 128–170). Cambridge, UK: Cambridge University Press.

Slobin, D. (1986). Crosslinguistic evidence for the language-making capacity. In D. Slobin (Ed.), *The crosslinguistic study of language acquisition* (Vol. 2, pp. 1157–1256). Hillsdale, NJ: Erlbaum.

Slobin, D., & Bever, T. (1982). Children use cannonical sentence schemas: A crosslinguistic study of word order and inflections. *Cognition, 12,* 229–265.

Smith, E. (1978). Theories of semantic memory. In W. K. Estes (Ed.), *Handbook of learning and cognitive processes* (Vol. 6). Hillsdale, NJ: Erlbaum.

Smith, N. A., & Trainor, L. J. (2008). Infant-directed speech is modulated by infant feedback. *Infancy*, 13(4), 410–420.

Snow, C. (1972). Mother's speech to children learning language. *Child Development, 43,* 549–565.

Snow, C. (1978). The conversational context of language acquisition. In R. Campbell & P. Smith (Eds.), *Recent advances in the psychology of language* (Vol. 4a). New York: Plenum Press.

Snow, C. E. (1999). Social prespectives on the emergence of language. In B. MacWhinney (Ed.), *The emergence of language* (pp. 257–276). Mahwah, NJ: Erlbaum.

Soderstrom, M. (2007). Beyond babytalk: Re-evaluating the nature and content of speech input to preverbal infants. *Developmental Review*, 27(4), 501–532.

Song, J., Demuth, K., & Morgan, J. (2010). Effects of the acoustic properties of infant-directed speech on infant word recognition. *Journal of the Acoustical Society of America*, 128(1), 389–400.

Speidel, G. E., & Nelson, K. E. (Eds.). (1984). *The many faces of imitation in language learning.* New York: Springer-Verlag.

St. Clair, M. C., Monaghan, P., & Christiansen, M. H. (2010). Learning grammatical categories from distributional cues: Flexible frames for language acquisition. *Cognition*, 116(3), 341–360.

Staats, A. (1971). Linguistic-mentalistic theory versus an explanatory S-R learning theory of language development. In D. Slobin (Ed.), *The ontogenesis of grammar* (pp. 103–150). New York: Academic Press.

Stern, D., Beebe, B., Jaffe, J., & Bennett, S. (1977). The infant's stimulus world during social interaction: A study of caregiver behaviors with particular reference to repetition and timing. In H. Schaffer (Ed.), *Studies in mother–infant interaction* (pp. 177–202). London: Academic Press.

Stine, E. L., & Bohannon, J. N. (1983). Imitation, interactions and acquisition. *Journal of Child Language, 10,* 589–604.

Stokoe, W. (2001). *Language in hand: Why sign came before speech.* Washington, DC: Gallaudet University Press.

Tamis-LeMonda, C., Bornstein, M., & Baumwell, L. (2001). Maternal responsiveness and children's achievement of language milestones. *Child Development, 72,* 748–768.

Tanner, J. E., & Byrne, R.W. (1999). The development of spontaneous gestural communication in a group of zoo-living gorillas. In S. T. Parker, R. W. Mitchell, & H. L. Miles (Eds.). *The mentalities of gorillas and orangutans: Comparative perspectives* (pp. 211–239). Cambridge, UK: Cambridge University Press.

Terrace, H., & Bever, T. (1976). What may be learned from studying language in the chimpanzee? *Annals of the New York Academy of Sciences, 280,* 579–588.

Thomas, R., & Zimmer-Gembeck, M. J. (2011). Accumulating evidence for parent–child interaction therapy in the prevention of child maltreatment. *Child Development,* 82(1), 177–192.

Tomasello, M. (2003). *Constructing a language: A usage-based theory of language acquisition.* Cambridge, MA: Harvard University Press.

Tomasello, M. (2008). *Origins of human communication.* Cambridge, MA: Bradford Book, MIT Press.

Tomasello, M., & Farrar, J. (1986). Joint attention and early language. *Child Development, 57,* 1454–1463.

Valian, V. (1999). Input and language acquisition. In W. Ritchie & T. Bhatia (Eds.), *Handbook of child language acquisition* (pp. 497–530). New York: Academic Press.

Vargha-Khadem, F., Gadian, D. G., Copp, A., & Mishkin, M. (2005). FOXP2 and the neuroanatomy of speech and language. *Nature Reviews Neuroscience*, 6(2), 131–138.

Vouloumanos, A., Hauser, M. D., Werker, J. F., & Martin, A. (2010). The tuning of human neonates' preference for speech. *Child Development*, 81(2), 517–527.

Vygotsky, L. S. (1962). *Thought and language.* Cambridge, MA: MIT Press.

Warren-Leubecker, A., & Bohannon, J. (1982). The effects of expectation and feedback on speech to foreigners. *Journal of Psycholinguistic Research, 11,* 207–215.

Warren-Leubecker, A., & Bohannon, J. (1983). The effects of verbal feedback and listener type on the speech of preschool children. *Journal of Experimental Child Psychology, 35,* 540–548.

Watson, J. (1924). *Behaviorism.* Chicago: University of Chicago Press.

Weisleder, A., & Waxman, S. (2010). What's in the input? Frequent frames in child-directed speech offer distributional cues to grammatical categories in Spanish and English. *Journal of Child Language, 37*(5), 1089–1108.

Wexler, K. (1982). A principle theory for language acquisition. In E. Wanner & L. Gleitman (Eds.), *Language acquisition: The state of the art* (pp. 288–315). Cambridge, UK: Cambridge University Press.

Wexler, K. (1999). Maturation and growth of grammar. In W. Ritchie & T. Bhatia (Eds.), *Handbook of child language acquisition* (pp. 55–110). New York: Academic Press.

Wexler, K., & Culicover, P. (1980). *Formal principles of language acquisition.* Cambridge, MA: MIT Press.

Whitehurst, G. (1982). Language development. In B. Wolman (Ed.), *Handbook of developmental psychology.* Englewood Cliffs, NJ: Prentice-Hall.

Whitehurst, G., & Novak, G. (1973). Modeling, imitation training, and the acquisition of sentence phrases. *Journal of Experimental Child Psychology, 16,* 332–335.

Whitehurst, G., & Vasta, R. (1975). Is language acquired through imitation? *Journal of Psycholinguistic Research, 4,* 37–59.

Xuân-Nga Cao, K., Stoyneshka, I., Tornyova, L., Fodor, J. D., & Sakas, W. G. (2008). Bigrams and the richness of the stimulus. *Cognitive Science, 32*(4), 771–787.

Zimmerman, B., & Whitehurst, G. (1979). Structure and function: A comparison of two views of the development of language and cognition. In G. Whitehurst & B. Zimmerman (Eds.), *The functions of language and cognition.* New York: Academic Press.

Zukow-Goldring, P. (1996). Sensitive caregiving fosters the comprehension of speech: When gestures speak louder than words. *Early Development and Parenting, 5*(4), 195–211.

Zukow-Goldring, P. (2001). Perceiving referring actions: Latino and Euro-American infants and caregivers comprehending speech. In K. Nelson, A. Aksu-Koç, & C. Johnson (Eds.), *Children's language* (Vol. 11, pp. 140–163). Mahwah, NJ: Erlbaum.

Variation in Language Development

Implications for Research and Theory

Beverly A. Goldfield
Rhode Island College

Catherine E. Snow
Harvard Graduate School of Education

Ingrid A. Willenberg
Macquarie University

Both psychologists and linguists who study language development have typically looked for commonalities across young language learners in babbled sounds, first words and early sentences, and the eventual elaborations of syntax. Their interest in language *universals* has been largely motivated by the undeniable fact that the ability to learn language is shared by all normally developing human infants. However, the words and sentences of children learning to talk within and across language communities reveal interesting differences as well as overlapping milestones. Consider these two English language learners. At 18 months, Johanna has a substantial vocabulary of single words that label important objects and entities in her world. She can talk about food (*banana, apple, cheese*), clothing (*sock, shoes, hat*), animals (*birdie, cat*), household items (*keys, light*), and toys (*dolly, ball*). Non-nominals are fewer: *hi, bye-bye, up, down, no.* Many of her words are learned and used in the course of naming games that she plays with her parents. Bath time elicits *nose, teeth, eyes, ears, face, hair, belly.* Picture books are also enjoyed as opportunities for displaying Johanna's word knowledge.

Eighteen-month-old Caitlin also has words for things to eat, wear, and play with. However, her lexicon includes many non-nominals (e.g., *there, pretty, nice, yuck, ouch, no, bye-bye, uh-oh, down, up*) and quite a few phrases (e.g., *let's go, bless you, sit down, hey you guys, lemme see*), some of which may be attributed to the presence and influence of an older sibling. Caitlin produces these phrases with appropriate melodic (e.g., "Where are you?") or emphatic ("Don't touch!") intonation. Like Johanna, she enjoys picture books, but this context elicits more "conversation" than labeling. On one such occasion, Caitlin sat with Mom and a familiar book, turned to a favorite page, and delivered a prosodically varied but

241

Picture books elicit labels from some children and animated conversation from others.

unintelligible 27-second discourse, embellished with the pauses, gesticulations, and gathering momentum of a narrative.

Johanna and Caitlin have each made considerable progress since first words appeared at about 12 months of age. They talk about familiar entities and events and they have some words in common. However, there is considerable variation in these early lexicons, and researchers have noted variability in the early words and sentences of other language learners. These studies have grappled with the problem of how best to describe such differences. Are Johanna and Caitlin attending to different aspects of their environment, using language for different purposes, or segmenting the speech they hear in different ways? Are there differences in the language their caregivers use? Or perhaps broader socio-economic factors, including the social settings in which parents and children interact and their purposes for engaging in conversation, are influencing the variation we see.

For the most part these issues have been explored for children learning English. We will need further evidence from other languages to sort out the problems that varied languages present and the array of solutions that individuals bring to the task of learning to talk, including data from children learning more than one language. These solutions, moreover, carry with them implications for a number of recent theoretical proposals, such as how early lexical development is related to grammar, whether distinct modules or general learning mechanisms support acquisition, and the extent to which nouns and the learning principles that apply to object labels are the most prominent features of first words.

This chapter begins by tracing the history of research into language variation, then examines variation at different levels of language learning, and finally considers how these data may inform current theoretical debates.

The History of Variation in Child Language Research

The topic of language variation has not always been of interest to child language researchers and early textbooks would hardly have devoted an entire chapter to its discussion. This change can best be understood by considering the history of child language research. Interest in language variation followed almost two decades of research committed to documenting universal patterns of acquisition. Even though researchers during this period typically reported (and dismissed as unimportant) variations in the *rate* of language development, they placed greater emphasis on *similarities* among children in the sequence of development. At one level, the emphasis on commonalities grew out of a practical need for basic information about the nature and sequence of development. Another contributing factor, however, was the influence of linguistic theory on child language research. Chomsky's (1957) theory of **transformational syntax** offered a new and coherent way of accounting for structural principles of adult linguistic competence that cut across inter- and intralinguistic diversity. The kinds of questions asked and the methods used to study child language were direct outcomes of applying the new theory to problems of acquisition. Child language research focused on questions of *structure*, with the intent of documenting the *rules* governing children's early sentences.

The focus on linguistic universals during this period carried with it certain assumptions about the methods that could be used to investigate child language. For instance, since all normally developing children were thought to construct similar rule systems, longitudinal study of a single child or a few children was a typical research paradigm (e.g., Braine, 1963; Brown, 1973). Many studies looked cross-linguistically for common structures and stages of acquisition (e.g., Slobin, 1968). Although this paradigm guided much research and outlined the major dimensions of language development, it also biased us toward seeing shared patterns in the data. Children in some studies were selected for inclusion because of the ease with which the researcher could understand and record their speech. Children with less clear articulation or "messy," jargon-like strings in their early speech were less likely to be included. Similarly, utterances that appeared to be advanced, imitative, or non-rule-generated in an otherwise predictable corpus of child speech were often relegated to the anomalous or miscellaneous category and were excluded from further study.

Several factors are responsible for the paradigm change represented by an interest in language variation. First, linguistic theory grew more attentive to *semantic* and *pragmatic aspects* of adult language, and child language research also began to shift away from an exclusive emphasis on syntax. In the 1970s investigators became interested in the *meaning* and *function* of early words and sentences. As the scope of child language research broadened in the 1980s, departures from a universal acquisition sequence began to be noticed and accorded some significance. Using larger samples of children to study the *meaning* and *function* as well as the *form* of early language, investigators have since observed that children vary along all three dimensions.

Another factor contributing to increased reports of variation is the attention now paid to children and child utterances previously excluded. Children with poor articulation and early jargon-like sentences have been studied (Adamson & Tomasello, 1984; Peters, 1977, 1983). Some investigators study children without a priori decisions about the representativeness of their language or language environment. Small sample longitudinal studies based on monthly one-hour recording sessions have given way to dense sampling techniques with as much as 30 hours of recording in a six-week period (e.g., Lieven, Salomo, & Tomasello, 2009) and explicit cross-language comparisons (e.g., Stoll, Abbott-Smith, & Lieven, 2009). We also have the benefit of studies of children from *diverse language communities* (e.g., Slobin, 1985, 1992, 1997) and larger samples selected to reflect *varied cultural* and *socioeconomic groups* (e.g., Heath, 1983; Hoff-Ginsberg, 1991, 1998; Lieven, Pine, & Barnes, 1992; Rowe & Goldin-Meadow, 2009). We will examine variation related to language community, bilingual acquisition, and socioeconomic status later in this chapter.

The research on language variation has explored one or more of the following questions: (1) In what *ways* does language-learning vary? (2) What *factors* contribute to variation? and (3) What are the *implications* of language variation for understanding the process of acquisition, for devising an adequate theory of language development, and for clarifying the complex interdependence of cognitive, social, and linguistic factors in development?

Variation in Early Words

Nelson's (1973; see also follow-up work in Hampson & Nelson, 1993) study of early lexical development was the first to draw attention to variability among young language learners. Nelson collected diary data on the productive vocabularies of eighteen children (seven boys and eleven girls). The first fifty words of each child were assigned to form classes (nominals, action words, modifiers, personal-social items, function words) based on content or the child's first use of a word. Nelson found that all of the children acquired words for familiar people, animals, food, toys, vehicles, and household objects. The children varied, however, in the proportion of nominals in their vocabulary. Ten **referential** children had early lexicons that were dominated by words for *objects*. These children moved predictably from single words to a two-word stage. A sudden spurt of new words near the fifty-word level often preceded the appearance of word combinations. An early preference for object labels was positively related to talk about objects and negatively related to talk about self in a follow-up speech sample at 24 months of age.

Eight **expressive** children followed a different route. They had fewer object labels but more pronouns and function words than the first group. They also acquired more personal-social expressions, which were usually longer than a single word. From early on, these children used phrases such as "go away," "stop it," "don't do it," and "I want it." Their transition into syntactic combinations was less clear and not marked by a rapid increase in new vocabulary.

Although there was no difference in the age at which the two groups acquired fifty words, children in the referential group included both early and late talkers who tended to learn words at a faster rate than children in the expressive group, who evidenced a slower, steadier rate of acquisition.

Nelson argued that these differences reflected the children's differing hypotheses about how language is used. Children with referential language were learning to talk about and categorize the objects in their environment. Children with expressive speech were more socially oriented and were acquiring the means to talk about themselves and others.

Although Nelson introduced an important new approach to the study of language development, subsequent research has pointed out a number of problems with the original referential–expressive distinction. The first concerns parent-reported data. Parental reports have been a valuable source of child language data for as long as linguists and psychologists have observed and recorded development. Parents are with their children in varied contexts in and out of the home and are typically the child's earliest and most consistent conversational partners. However, research comparing recorded observations of speech with parental diary records finds that parents report more nouns and fewer verbs than children actually use (e.g., Bates, Bretherton, & Snyder, 1988; Benedict, 1979; Pine, 1992b; Tardif, Gelman, & Xu, 1999). This discrepancy may be due to parental bias to notice and report words for objects. On the other hand, children may know a number of labels that they use only in specific contexts. Words such as *lion, moon*, and *peas* may be elicited during book reading, bedtime, and dinner, respectively, but are less likely to occur in a recorded play session. In any case, the extent to which a child's lexicon is judged to be "referential" or "expressive" can be expected to vary with how the researcher obtains information on the child's vocabulary.

A second problem concerns how frequently children actually use the various words that they know. Even in cases where nouns account for about half of children's reported vocabulary, they may be used less often than other words (Pine, 1992b). Thus, word tokens may suggest a different pattern than the distribution of word types in the child's lexicon.

Finally, Nelson's original classification scheme is a mixture of formal and functional characteristics. The word "door," for example, could be classified as a nominal if the child used the word when simply touching it, or as an action word if the child appeared to want to go outside. This confounding of formal and functional criteria has led to some confusion in how to interpret the referential and expressive distinction. Without independent observational evidence of how children are actually using their words, we cannot confirm Nelson's suggestion that the referential–expressive distinction reflects children's differing hypotheses about the functions of language.

Subsequent research has looked directly at functional differences in children's early speech. Pine (1992a) collected diary data on the first 100 words of seven children and coded audiotaped speech samples for various functions, including attention, labeling, description, demand, and protest. Although children varied considerably in the proportion of common nouns in their lexicon (a range of 28 to 54 percent at fifty words, and 35 to 67 percent at 100 words), there was no relationship between referential vocabulary and any functional category at either vocabulary level.

Thus, although children may vary in the kinds of words they acquire, there is no consistent support for the notion that children with relatively more nouns use language in more naming and fewer social contexts. Many, if not most, early words serve a variety of functions, and the *distribution, function*, and *frequency* of word usage are related but separable aspects of early lexical development.

A number of studies have subsequently confirmed some version of the referential–expressive distinction in children's first words. Some children acquire relatively more common nouns or words that label and describe the properties of objects, whereas other children acquire many words to describe their own actions and states and use more phrases

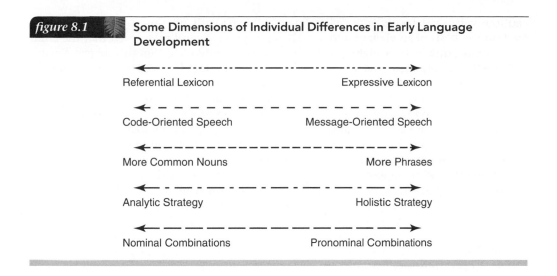

figure 8.1 **Some Dimensions of Individual Differences in Early Language Development**

Referential Lexicon — Expressive Lexicon

Code-Oriented Speech — Message-Oriented Speech

More Common Nouns — More Phrases

Analytic Strategy — Holistic Strategy

Nominal Combinations — Pronominal Combinations

(e.g., Bretherton, McNew, Snyder, & Bates, 1983; Goldfield, 1987; Lieven et al., 1992; Pine & Lieven, 1990). It is important to note, however, that the referential–expressive dimension is not a dichotomy, but rather a continuum along which individual children vary. Most children appear to acquire a relative balance of referential and expressive language; only a few children acquire a distribution extreme enough to be called a distinct style or strategy. A close examination of the extremes, however, should help us to disentangle the possible mechanisms and processes that contribute to early lexical development for all children (see Figure 8.1).

Segmenting the Speech Stream

The difficulties inherent in describing children's early speech in terms of formal and/or functional characteristics have led researchers to alternative ways of conceptualizing variation. The tendency of some children to acquire longer, phrase-like utterances during the single-word stage suggests that children may differ with respect to the length of the linguistic units that they segment from adult speech. A sample of such phrasal speech can be found in our introductory illustration of Caitlin's early language. Note that Caitlin's phrases are two and three words in length, but the individual words do not occur alone, suggesting that the entire "package" has been learned as a whole. Moreover, she produces these phrases with adult-like intonation.

Although segmentation may be facilitated by the shorter utterances, exaggerated intonation, pauses, repetitions, and stress patterns of child-directed talk, children must build their lexicons from the raw material of connected speech. The units that they select may thus be single words or longer phrases. A number of studies report children who orient to syllables and segments and others who attend to prosodic tunes that unify larger sequences of speech (Echols, 1993; Peters, 1977, 1983). Seth and Daniel represent these differing strategies:

> [F]ormulaic children, like Seth, pay attention to "horizontal" information such as the number of syllables, stress, intonation patterns . . . word-oriented children, like Daniel, pay more attention to the vertical segmental information contained in single (usually stressed) syllables focusing on the details of consonants and vowels. (Peters & Menn, 1993, p. 745)

A distinction that may be related to these differing segmentation strategies occurs in children's early *phonological* systems as well. Ferguson (1979), for example, has described cautious versus risk-taking approaches. Some children's early utterances seem to be generated on the basis of an elegant and orderly set of phonological rules, such that the child form of any adult word is highly predictable. These children (e.g., Smith's subject Amahl, 1973) either apply their rule system consistently to imitated as well as to spontaneous forms or else resist imitating words that would constitute violations of the restrictions on their output. Other children, in contrast, operate with fairly sloppy phonological systems, showing alternation among several ways of producing most words and applying their phonological rules optionally. Typically, the children with sloppy phonological systems incorporate imitated (and thus progressive) forms into their lexicon quite easily and may be more likely to show improvement in production as a result of direct modeling.

Plunkett (1993) suggests that articulatory fluency and articulatory precision are inversely related in early speech. Phrasal speech represents segmentation that overshoots a target adult word. Such expressions tend to be produced fluently but with less precise articulation of the individual phonetic segments. Articulatory precision is the outcome of an alternate strategy that undershoots the adult target word by focusing on accurate production of sublexical units. Variation in perceptual acuity, in verbal memory, and/or in characteristics of the input may influence the kinds of linguistic units that are perceptually salient and likely to be used. The sounds learners attend to may be the sounds that they hear often and know they can produce, resulting in a kind of articulatory filter that may be unique to each child (Vihman, 1993).

Lieven and colleagues (1992) have coined the term *frozen phrases* for phrasal speech that appears before true word combinations. They defined frozen phrases as utterances containing two or more words that had not previously occurred as single units in the child's speech. They examined the number of common nouns, personal-social words, and frozen phrases in a sample of twelve children who were observed longitudinally. They found that personal-social words declined as vocabulary increased, suggesting that such words may not be a stable defining characteristic of expressive style. On the other hand, the proportion of common nouns and frozen phrases in children's lexicons remained stable when the first fifty words were compared to the second fifty, and the two measures were negatively correlated at both vocabulary levels. This pattern of results suggests that frozen phrases and common nouns may more precisely define two approaches to early lexical development. Moreover, there was no significant correlation between either measure and age at which fifty and 100 words were acquired, suggesting that neither strategy affords an advantage at this level of development.

Peters (1977, 1983) describes how the child she observed acquired both phrasal speech and more clearly articulated single words. She termed these two kinds of speech *gestalt* and *analytic,* respectively. However, as Pine and Lieven (1993) point out, the segmentation of phrases from adult speech is also an analytic process. What differs is the length of the unit that children extract from the speech that they hear. The occurrence of phrasal units in children's early speech raises a number of questions about the relationship between the lexicon and syntax. We will return to this topic after first reviewing the evidence for variation in early syntactic development.

Variation in Early Sentences

Two years after Nelson's study of variability in early words, Bloom, Lightbown, and Hood (1975) reported that children also differ in the early stages of multiword speech. They found that the sentences of the four children they observed had similar content (they talked about a common set of semantic categories such as recurrence, negation, actions, and states) that emerged in a similar order. However, the form of their early sentences differed.

All four children used a *pivot strategy* to encode negation and nonexistence *(no + X, no more + X)* and recurrence *(more + X, 'nother + X)*. This strategy consisted of combining one of a small class of *function words* and any one of a larger, varying set of *content words*. Eric and Peter used this same approach to express action, location, and possession by combining all-purpose pronouns with content words. They produced utterances such as *I finish, play it, sit here*, and *my truck*. During this same period Kathryn and Gia expressed the same semantic relations by combining content words, as in *Gia push, touch milk, sweater chair*, and *Kathryn sock*.

Bloom and colleagues (1975) claim that the children were using two different combinatorial strategies. The pronominal approach used by the two boys allowed them to begin encoding relationships between objects and events without relying on specific lexical items. Because they used a varied lexicon in single-word utterances and in sentences with *no* and *more*, their strategy could not be attributed to simply not knowing enough labels. The two girls, on the other hand, preferred to talk about the same meanings using specific nouns. When mean length of utterance (MLU) approached 2.5, the two systems began to overlap. Children using a **pronominal strategy** began to combine content words, whereas the **nominal strategy** children started using pronouns in their utterances.

A number of researchers argue that children's earliest sentences reflect specific lexical combinations rather than instantiations of more abstract semantic roles or syntactic rules (e.g., Childers & Tomasello, 2001; Lieven, Pine, & Baldwin, 1997; Theakston, Lieven, Pine, & Rowland, 2002; Tomasello, 1992). If this is the case, we would expect considerable variation in early grammatical development, with children differing in the words and patterns used to express their sentential meanings. An early pronominal style, for example, may begin with a few rote phrases (e.g., *my bottle; I do it*) that eventually evolve into productive patterns (*my ball, my cookie, my mommy; I found it, I get it, I see it*).

These data also suggest that a global measure such as MLU may obscure differences in how children lengthen their utterances. Some children may put together sentences that emphasize semantic content, whereas others focus on grammatical morphology (Rollins, Snow, & Willett, 1996). Children who are *language matched* using MLU may thus exhibit profoundly different knowledge of the grammatical system.

We will present more evidence for varied approaches to early syntax in the next section, which reviews research on children who have been observed from early words to first sentences.

Stability of Style across Words and Sentences

The variation we have seen in strategies children use for segmenting the speech they hear, for expressing early meanings, and for introducing structure into their language may simply represent different entry points into the language system, or they may be early signs of differences that persist across development. To what extent is this variation stable?

There is some evidence that children's early *lexical preferences* are reflected in the form of their first word combinations. Nelson (1975) followed the later language development of her original referential–expressive sample and found that referential speakers began with a high proportion of nouns in early sentences. With increasing MLU, the use of pronouns increased while nouns decreased for these children. Children from the original expressive group began with a balance of noun and pronoun use. Pronoun use changed very little for this group, but nouns increased with advanced MLU.

Lieven (1980) reports that early sentences of the three children she observed appeared to derive from characteristics of their single-word speech. For one child, both single words and early constructions (e.g., *there, mommy, there Julian*, and *there mommy*) were used to gain adult attention rather than to convey reference. The other two children were more likely to describe attributes and actions of people and things in both their single- and multiple-word utterances.

As we saw earlier, some children, such as Caitlin, acquire a number of phrases in the early stages of learning to talk. Nelson's expressive speakers produced *go away, stop it, don't do it, I want it*. Such phrases are the result of segmenting larger units from adult speech. It is not clear, however, how these early units are related to later grammatical development. Some research suggests that early phrasal speech is unrelated to later analyzed productions. Bates and colleagues (1988) followed children from first words to early sentences. Observations and parent interviews were used to assess language at 10, 13, 20, and 28 months of age. Bates and colleagues report that an **analytic style,** which included high levels of comprehension and flexible noun production at 13 months, predicted advanced grammatical development at 28 months. Variables that suggested an early **rote** or **holistic style,** on the other hand, were unrelated to later grammatical progress.

Pine and Lieven (1990, 1993), however, argue that cross-sectional, age-related measures confound strategy differences with variation due to developmental level. Because the proportion of nouns increases as vocabulary totals rise, children assessed at the same age but different vocabulary levels will differ in the number of nouns in their lexicon, regardless of their particular style or strategy. Thus, assessments of variation should be based on comparable vocabulary totals (as was the case for Nelson's original study).

However, using controlled vocabulary levels, Bates and colleagues (1993) continue to find evidence that early phrasal speech is unrelated to later grammatical development, whereas Pine and Lieven (1993) argue that early frozen phrases predict later productive word combinations. The apparent discrepancy may be due, in part, to differences in age and the measures used to assess style differences and grammatical progress. Bates and colleagues (1993) found no relationship between the number of closed-class words (prepositions, articles, auxiliary verbs, question words, pronouns, quantifiers, and connectives) that children used at 20 months and the extent to which children's sentences included words and inflections that indicate grammatical complexity (prepositions, articles, auxiliary verbs, copulas, modals, possessives, plurals, and tense markers) at 26 months using data from parent surveys. Using both parent report and audio recordings of children at 11 and 20 months, Pine and Lieven (1993) report that the proportion of frozen phrases was positively related to number of productive word combinations whereas proportion of common nouns was unrelated to sentence production. Thus, the two studies are concerned with somewhat different aspects of grammar at two different periods of development.

Children's acquisition of frozen phrases has led researchers to reconsider the processes that underlie early syntactic development. Phrasal speech allows some children to derive combinatorial patterns by segmenting phrases into frames with slots that can then be filled with other lexical items (Pine & Lieven, 1993). Peters (1977, 1983) also suggests that phrasal utterances may be stored, retrieved, and used as single lexical items that are later analyzed and broken down into productive components. She suggests the term *fission* for the eventual breakdown of phrasal speech, as distinguished from the complementary process of building sentences by combining units, which she calls *fusion.* Individual children may favor one or the other approach as their entry into syntax. Detailed longitudinal analyses reveal that children formulate many of their early sentences by building up distributional patterns around specific lexical items (e.g., *want x, there's a x, what's x doing*). As we mentioned earlier, specific patterns may more accurately characterize early grammatical development than more general semantic (e.g., agent + action) or syntactic (e.g., verb + object) relations. That is, children first isolate individual segments and look for patterns in what comes before or after. Children differ, however, in the size of the items (words, formulae, or partially analyzed phrases) that they isolate and combine.

The tendency to imitate adult speech is another dimension of variation that predicts some stability across language levels. Children who have a strong tendency to imitate prosodic patterns may, as a result, acquire phrasal units as well as single words during the one-word stage, produce more high-frequency items of low semantic value (such as pronouns) during the early sentence stage, and have messier phonological systems all along. Relationships between imitativeness and the tendency to be expressive, to produce longer utterances, and to show high levels of unintelligibility have been reported (Bloom et al., 1975; Ferguson & Farwell, 1975; Nelson, 1973), but other studies have found that children with referential language imitate more and suggest that these differences lie more in what children imitate than in how much. Whereas children with expressive speech imitate large units and social expressions, children with referential language tend to imitate object labels, particularly those they do not already know (Leonard, Schwartz, Folger, Newhoff, & Wilcox, 1979; Nelson, Baker, Denninger, Bonvillian, & Kaplan, 1985).

The evidence that variations in strategy or style are somewhat stable over the toddler period raises the possibility that more extended longitudinal studies would find even more substantial stability. For example, do children show the same preferences when faced with language-related tasks such as learning to read? Bussis, Chittenden, Amarel, and Klausner (1984) found that early readers seemed to split into two groups. Some children used more meaning-driven reading strategies, often previewing texts and studying illustrations to get a sense of the content before reading, skipping easily over passages they couldn't read, and sometimes making up substitute passages for bits they could not decode. Other beginning readers were highly faithful to the text, sounding out unknown words carefully, and building for themselves highly sequenced text representations. Long-term longitudinal studies may help us sort out whether the young language learners who prefer conservative, data-gathering, analytic strategies persist in these for reading, while their more risk-taking holistic peers maintain their preferred strategies across age as well.

Sources of Variation

Given that the variation we have described above exists and is robust, the question that arises is what might explain it. Does variability reflect child factors—for example, degree of sociability, disparities in perceptual processing mechanisms, or cognitive style? Does it perhaps reflect differences in how caregivers interact with or talk to children? Does this variation anticipate differences that characterize the range of different languages within the human community? In other words, is the learner of English who concentrates on single words revealing an expectation that her language will be one like Chinese, with little morphology, whereas the more holistic learner who includes syllabic slots where adults produce affixes is expecting a language more like Turkish or Polish?

Child Factors

Perhaps the most obvious difference among child language learners is in rate of learning. Some children begin talking close to their first birthday, whereas others wait another six months or more before words appear. As the lexicon nears fifty words, many children exhibit a "vocabulary spurt" that signals a period in which rate of word learning accelerates dramatically (Goldfield & Reznick, 1990). By 18 months, the average child has a vocabulary of about seventy-five words, although perfectly normal 2-year-olds may have far fewer (Fenson et al., 1994).

The kinds of style or strategy differences that we have described, however, are not simply the result of observing children with differing rates of development. Children with relatively more referential or expressive speech achieve language milestones at the same age and there appears to be no clear advantage for either style when correlated with later vocabulary or grammatical measures (Bates et al., 1993; Hampson & Nelson, 1993; Pine & Lieven, 1990).

As we noted earlier, children may be differentially sensitive to the prosodic tunes that unify whole phrases or to the syllables and segments that make up single words. The source of these differences may be found in developmental asymmetries in the multiple mechanisms that support language acquisition. That is, differences in the rate at which attention, perception, and memory mature and are available to parse, store, and analyze the input stream may affect the size and form of the linguistic units children produce. Bates and colleagues (1993) and others have noted that younger learners must approach the problem of language acquisition with less memory capacity and fewer analytic skills than older learners, often producing forms they do not fully understand. On the other hand, there is the possibility that some children are more cautious about making mistakes, and disinclined to talk—in short, shy. Shy children have been shown to talk less and less complexly in a way that remains stable through kindergarten and first grade (Evans, 1993). Horgan (1981) also suggests that differences between younger and older language learners may be a function of their tendency to be cautious or to take risks. Fifteen pairs of children were matched on MLU but differed in age by at least six months. The faster (younger) learners tended to use more nouns and more complex noun phrases and made more grammatical errors. The slower (older) learners used fewer and less elaborate noun phrases but more complex verb phrases and were more advanced on comprehension tasks.

Horgan suggests that the slower children were more cautious language learners, with good receptive abilities but a more guarded approach to displaying their verbal skills. They may also have attended more to the details of language structure, as evidenced by their use of more auxiliaries and more kinds of constructions. The faster children, with their more frequent errors, were risk takers, especially with the finer points of grammatical structure. Similar differences in the tendency to take risks with new syntactic forms versus to proceed cautiously until mastery is achieved have been found for children observed by Kuczaj and Maratsos (1983).

We do not yet have the longitudinal data that would provide the basis for claiming that slow starters at language acquisition turn out to be the children called shy, but it is clear that such shy children are likely to be slower second-language learners (Fillmore, 1979), as well as less obviously competent communicators in their first language.

Other child factors to consider include Nelson's (1973) proposal that some babies organize their world around objects, whereas others focus on people. Children's differing hypotheses about what language is for (to organize and categorize objects or to talk about self and others) derive from these differing organizations of experience. Mothers of referential children more often reported that their children favored manipulative toys, supporting the notion that preexistent cognitive differences may influence children's speech style.

Studies of children's language and play provide some support for linguistic differences that map onto object and social preferences. On the one hand, children who acquire more referential speech are more attentive to toys (Rosenblatt, 1977) and excel at object manipulation and spatial constructions (Wolf & Gardner, 1979). Similarly, children with more noun + noun combinations have higher levels of performance on object categorization tasks (Shore, Dixon, & Bauer, 1995). Children with more expressive speech orient more toward adults (Rosenblatt, 1977) and engage in more social-symbolic play (e.g., puppets and toy telephones) (Wolf & Gardner, 1979).

Goldfield (1987), however, suggests that episodes of *shared attention* to objects may contribute more to the acquisition of referential language than the sheer quantity of object or social behavior. Children who acquired relatively more nominals did not differ from their less referential peers on measures of time in toy play or frequency of social behaviors. Children with more nominals, however, more often initiated episodes of joint attention to objects by showing, giving, or bringing toys to their mother. Children with more expressive speech were not less interested in objects nor more sociable than their peers. However, they were more likely to interrupt or leave their toy play to seek social attention, rather than to share or show a toy. Differences in the use of objects to mediate social interaction may, in turn, influence the language parents address to children. Child pointing typically elicits a maternal label (Masur, 1982), and children who more frequently point to objects acquire more nouns (Goldfield, 1990).

Input Factors

Children learn to talk in the course of their interactions with any number of conversational partners, including parents, day care providers, siblings, and peers. Each social contact provides a unique source of language variance. It is likely that Crystal learned some phrasal speech from her older brother (e.g., *lemme see, you know what*), and other researchers have noted that laterborns tend to acquire more phrasal speech (Nelson et al., 1985; Pine, 1995). Day care offers even more varied language models.

Although adult speech to children shares many features, there are also clear differences in how parents talk to children and encourage their children to talk. Stable differences have been noted in maternal conversational style, including mothers' preferred use of language to direct behavior, elicit conversation, or instruct their children (Olsen-Fulero, 1982). Moreover, at least some aspects of maternal style are related to variation in child speech.

Fewer nouns, more social expressions, and more verbs are related to maternal speech that refers to persons or that directs the child's behavior in some way (Della Corte, Benedict, & Klein, 1983; Furrow & Nelson, 1984; Goldfield, 1987; Nelson, 1973; Pine, 1994). More nouns, on the other hand, are associated with maternal utterances that refer to and describe objects and that request and reinforce names for things (Della Corte et al., 1983; Furrow & Nelson, 1984; Goldfield, 1987; Hampson, 1988). Although the simple frequency of nouns in maternal talk is unrelated to children's speech style (Furrow & Nelson, 1984; Nelson, 1973), maternal descriptions that include nouns are related to the proportion of nouns in the first fifty words (Pine, 1994). It is important, then, to consider specific linguistic forms, such as nouns, in relation to the pragmatic focus (what parents talk about and for what purpose) of parental speech.

Correlations, of course, cannot tell us the extent to which parental speech affects child language, or vice versa. They do suggest, though, that parents and children may be seeking out different opportunities for interaction and conversation. A good deal of children's referential language, for example, may originate in certain *routinized naming games*, such as pointing to and naming animals in a book or touching and naming facial features.

Nelson (1973) observed that 28 percent of the first fifty words acquired by referential children referred to body parts—almost surely learned in this kind of routine—whereas none of the expressive children had acquired labels for parts of the body. Expressive children, on the other hand, learn many conventional social expressions (e.g., *hi, bye, please, thank you, let's go*, and *oh dear*) that typically mark arrivals, departures, and social exchanges. Mothers of children with more expressive speech tend to use many such stereotypical utterances (Nelson, 1973; Plunkett, 1993).

The extent to which characteristics of the input language influence the course of acquisition has received mixed empirical support and continues to provoke theoretical debate. Hampson and Nelson (1993) demonstrated a relationship between maternal language at 13 months and child grammar at 20 months when children were grouped on the basis of their language style. They found a significant, positive relationship between nouns in maternal speech and child MLU only for those children with more than 40 percent nouns in their spontaneous speech. No such relationship was found for children with more expressive speech (40 percent or fewer nouns). The two groups had similar numbers of early and late talkers at 13 months and did not differ on MLU at 20 months. Thus, children with differing approaches to learning to talk may make differential use of selected aspects of the input. This suggests that it is crucial to consider variation, and the extent to which child strategy and caregiver speech style overlap, in studies that examine the efficacy of the input for acquisition.

Socioeconomic Status (SES)

Some of the input differences we have described have also been noted to vary along with family socioeconomic status (SES), especially when SES is indexed by level of maternal education. That is, parents from high-SES families tend to talk to their children using more object labels and fewer directives than parents from low-SES families (Hoff-Ginsberg, 1991, 1998;

Different contexts provide varied opportunities for language learning.

Lawrence & Shipley, 1996). The most consistent finding, however, is the relationship between SES and rate of vocabulary development. In a landmark study, Hart and Risley (1995) found that children from upper-middle-class families, on average, had produced about 1,200 different words by age 3, whereas children from socially isolated, single-parent, welfare-dependent families had produced only about 600 different words. Hart and Risley traced these differences back to one simple factor: the amount of language the children had heard. Extrapolating from monthly hour-long recordings, Hart and Risley estimated that the children from the upper-middle-class families had heard 30 million words by the age of three, whereas the children in welfare families had heard only 10 million.

The Hart and Risley findings foreshadowed a large array of subsequent studies, in pointing out three important and now robustly demonstrated facts. First, children from low-SES households, on average, learn language more slowly than children from higher-SES households, achieving lower levels of vocabulary in particular and meeting many milestones at a later age (e.g., Arriaga, Fenson, Cronan & Pethick, 1998; Farkas & Beron, 2004; Hoff-Ginsberg, 1998). Second, parents with more education and higher incomes, on average, talk more to their children, are more responsive to their children's language, and encourage children to talk more, than parents with low levels of education, with low incomes, and/or experiencing high levels of life stress (e.g., Hoff, Loursen, & Tardiff, 2002; Lawrence & Shipley, 1996; Rowe, 2008). Third, differences in children's language development, in particular speed of vocabulary acquisition, are strongly related to amount of parental language input (e.g., Hoff, 2003; Huttenlocher, Haight, Bryk, Seltzer, & Lyons, 1991; Pan, Rowe, Singer, & Snow, 2005).

Two additional points from the Hart and Risley report have been less widely noted, but are equally important in understanding and thinking about the consequences of SES variability in language skills. First, variation in amount of parental input could be quite large within any of the three groups Hart and Risley distinguished, and this variation predicted child language accomplishments within social class groups. In other words, the relation between SES and amount of language is not deterministic, and children of any social class who hear little talk will have fewer opportunities to learn language (e.g., Huttenlocher, Vasilyeva, Waterfall, Vevea, & Hedges, 2007; Pan et al., 2005; Pungello, Iruka, Dotterer, Mills-Koonce, & Reznick, 2009). Second, quantity of talk is strongly related to quality of talk. In other words, mothers who talk more also use more different words, talk about a wider variety of topics, and engage children more in fantasy play, narratives, and explanations (Beals & Tabors, 1995; Weizman & Snow, 2001). Furthermore, more talkative mothers are also likely to be more responsive to children, to talk about the child's focus of attention, and to model for children what they want to say (Carpenter, Nagell, & Tomasello, 1998; Tamis-LeMonda, Bornstein, Baumwell, & Damast, 1996). It is thus difficult to determine whether the positive effects of exposure to a lot of talk reflect quantity alone, or the rich, elaborated, and responsive talk that is associated with high quantity.

One way to dig deeper into the question of quality versus quantity is to think about a very common activity in households with young children: parents and children reading books together. We know that middle-class families on average own more children's books and read them more often. Indeed, programs such as Reach Out and Read and Reading Is Fundamental are designed precisely to provide books to children in low-income families. Book reading is a highly propitious context for "high-quality" interactions, because the books provide interesting topics, novel vocabulary words, attractive pictures, and opportunities for repetition and questioning. Experience with picture books is a strong predictor of child language outcomes (Senechal, LeFevre, Hudson, & Lawson, 1996), also among children in low-income families (Raikes, Pan, Tamis-LeMonda, Brooks-Gunn, & Constantine, 2006). Although low-SES mothers might be less naturally inclined to read books with their children than more highly educated mothers, they do respond well to instruction in how to read in ways that are more productive—asking open-ended questions, encouraging the child to take over the responsibility for telling the story, and using books as a context for engaging, elaborated conversations (Whitehurst, Falco, Lonigan, & Fischel, 1988). Such interactions are referred to as "dialogic reading," and there is strong evidence that they contribute to language outcomes (Mol, Bus, De Jong, & Smeets, 2008). Furthermore, while there are social class differences in the likelihood that parents will engage extensively in book reading with their children, differences in styles of interaction between middle-class and working-class families are less pronounced during book-reading than during other kinds of interactions (Snow et al., 1976).

The explanations for social class differences in interaction style and in child language outcomes are multiple and complicated. One explanation is that we raise our children as we were raised, and thus social class differences replicate themselves. Another is that families living under conditions of poverty, stress, and crowding do not have the emotional resources to be as attentive and responsive to young children as families with more educational, social, and financial resources. Another is that small differences early in life become larger with age, as children who start to talk early elicit more responsiveness and more language whereas later or less active talkers reduce their own access to input, particularly in lower SES families (Farran & Haskins, 1980). Another possible explanation is cultural—that ethnic groups overrepresented among low-income families may prefer less talkative, more obedient children. Whatever the explanation, it is clear that variation in language outcomes due to social class is large and is related to patterns of parent-child interaction. Because of the robust relationship between child language skills and ease of learning to read (Snow, Burns, & Griffin, 1998), these differences can have important consequences for children's readiness for school and literacy.

Linguistic Factors

Children may start learning language with their own preferences and tendencies, and caregivers may emphasize certain aspects of language or provide richer input about some domains than others. In addition, languages differ from one another in the problems they pose to the learner. These differences may interact with learner and input factors to exaggerate variation.

Each language can be seen as exploiting in its own particular way the capacities for elaboration, generalization, and rule learning that human beings possess. Both prosodic tune and segmentation into words are relatively accessible to English language learners. Slavic languages such as Polish, however, challenge speakers to learn several dozen noun endings, including markings for six cases that in singular have distinct forms for masculine, feminine, and neuter (Smoczynska, 1985). This patterning is made more complex by its **synthetic** character; for example, a particular suffix that reflects the synthesis of masculine, singular, and genitive might have no phonetic relation to the feminine singular genitive or the masculine singular dative. Since nouns in Slavic are never produced without suffixed case and gender markings, it may be almost inevitable that children choose a risk-taking strategy that leads to many errors, since they cannot learn the entire paradigm instantly. Turkish, on the other hand, also is characterized by many suffixes, but they are **agglutinated** rather than synthetic; that is, added on in a predictable sequence. Turkish learners may benefit from a tendency to use a prosodic strategy that incorporates dummy syllables for the affixes not yet learned, as that strategy creates precisely the slots into which the to-be-learned material must fit. Thus, the use of fillers and dummy syllables may be more common in learners of some languages than others, as well as varying across learners of the same language (Peters, 2001).

Unfortunately, the data on acquisition of languages other than English are relatively sparse, lacking in the large-sample studies that make examining variation feasible. Both word and tune babies have been observed for Danish (Plunkett, 1993), German (Stern & Stern, 1928), and Norwegian (Simonsen, 1990, data available at the CHILDES Archive: http://childes.psy.cmu.edu/data-xml/Germanic/Norwegian.zip). Holistic, prosodic learners are also found in Hebrew (Berman, 1985), Hungarian (MacWhinney, 1985),

French (Clark, 1985), Italian (Bottari, Cirpriani, & Chilosi, 1994), and Portugese (Scarpa, 1990). As was the case for Peters's (1977) subject, Minh, the German tune baby observed by Elsen (1996) used some referential speech during naming routines and when looking at picture books. The tendency of some children learning English to seize upon whole words rather than on morphological modifications of words raises the question of what such children would do if they were learning Inuktitut or Hebrew, where "words" as such can hardly be identified through the massive morphological changes that every shift in meaning imposes. Cross-linguistic analyses have also yielded more diversified patterns than those identified for English speakers. Three patterns (emphasizing nouns versus phrases and fillers versus verbs, adjectives, and grammatical words) have been observed for French language learners at 20 months of age (Bassano, Maillochon, & Eme, 1998).

Languages also differ in the ease with which children may extract specific parts of speech such as nouns or verbs. In English, nouns may be more salient than verbs because children hear them at the beginning and end of subject–verb–object (SVO) sentences and nouns occur with fewer grammatical inflections than verbs; pragmatic factors also favor nouns over verbs in production (Goldfield, 1993, 2000). Japanese, Korean, and Mandarin Chinese, on the other hand, are languages that highlight verbs by frequently deleting nominal referents and positioning verbs at the ends of sentences (Clancy, 1985; Rispoli, 1989; Tanouye, 1979; Tardif, 1996). These interlinguistic differences appear to have consequences for language learners. As we have seen, children learning English differ in their emphasis on nouns in the first fifty words; nevertheless, noun learning is a prominent aspect of vocabulary acquisition, and the proportion of nouns typically increases between fifty and 200 words (Bates et al., 1993). In contrast, Japanese, Korean, and Mandarin learners typically start with more verbs and fewer nouns than English learners (Choi, 2000; Gopnik & Choi, 1991, 1995; Kim, McGregor, & Thompson, 2000); thus, highly referential children acquiring these languages may have absolute levels of nouns much lower than relatively expressive children learning English. Italian shares some characteristics of pro-drop languages that highlight verbs, but Italian verbs are more morphologically complex and variable, and, unlike Mandarin, Italian is not a null-object language. Italian-speaking mothers use more verb types and tokens than noun types and tokens (Camaioni & Longobardi, 2001). Overall, the input to Italian children is more like English than Mandarin, and as for English learners, children learning Italian produce more nouns but fewer verbs than Mandarin speakers (Bassano, 2000; Tardif, Shatz, & Naigles, 1997).

Bilingual Language Learners

Bilingual first language acquisition (BFLA)—exposure to two or more languages within the first three to four years of life (De Houwer, 1995)—introduces variations in the development of each of those languages in comparison with monolingual children. Although there is consensus that the language development of bilingual children proceeds along the same broad stages as for monlinguals, namely babbling, single words, two-word combinations, multiword combinations, and multi-clause combinations (De Houwer, 1995; Genesee, Paradis, & Crago, 2004), there is evidence for qualitative and quantitative variation due to cross-linguistic interactions that occur between the child's two languages. Researchers have explored these variations by examining bilingual children's productions of target-deviant utterances; namely, utterances that deviate from adult grammatical forms (Genesee et al., 2004) and are therefore not likely to be due to input factors.

The existing findings show that the extent to which bilingual children's target-deviant forms resemble those of monolinguals is language-specific. In some cases, the target-deviant forms produced by bilingual children have been similar to those of monolinguals; in other cases differences have been either quantitative (similar but occurring with greater frequency) or qualitative (completely different deviant forms). For example, Genesee and colleagues (2004) studied negative verb forms (e.g., *She can't play; He is not going to school*) in French-English bilinguals and found that negative verbs were acquired earlier in French than in English and that acquisition in each of these languages corresponded to the stages observed in monolingual English and French children. They also found that bilingual children used similar target-deviant forms to monolinguals. In contrast, Yip and Matthews (2000) found that in their production of relative clauses, English-Cantonese bilingual children used target-deviant structures that do not occur in the productions of either monolingual English or Cantonese-speaking children. Dopke (1998) reports that in their acquisition of word order in German verb phrases, German-English bilingual children used target-deviant structures more frequently than monolinguals and that the target-deviant structures used reflected the word order rules of English.

While there is much research examining the patterns of language development in bilingual children, there is less research studying the rate of development. Insufficient research and methodological problems make it difficult to find a conclusive answer to the question of whether bilingual children develop their languages at rates similar to monolinguals (Genesee et al., 2004). Nicoladis and Genesee (1996) report that bilingual children tend to have smaller vocabularies than their same-age monolingual peers. However, there is evidence that the conceptual vocabularies (total number of semantic concepts expressed in either of the child's languages) of bilingual children are similar in size to those of monolinguals (Junker & Stockman, 2002). David and Wei (2008) found that bilingual children produced similar proportions of nouns and verbs to monolinguals, but showed considerable variation in overall vocabulary size and proportion of translation equivalents (semantic concepts represented in both languages).

Studies of input differences in the two languages of bilingual children have confirmed the findings of research with monolinguals that the quantity and quality of linguistic input are key factors in language acquisition (David & Wei, 2008), demonstrating that differences in amount of exposure to each of their languages are associated with differences in grammatical (e.g., Blom, 2010) and semantic (e.g., Pearson, Fernandez, Lewedeg, & Oller, 1997) development. When parental input consists of more complex and lexically diverse utterances, bilingual children tend to produce longer utterances with more diverse vocabulary in the corresponding language (David & Wei, 2008). Further variations in language input may be introduced by sociocultural differences in linguistic interactions with children. Studies have shown, for example, that in English caregiver–child interactions, there is a large emphasis on naming objects, whereas in Asian cultures, these interactions tend to center around appropriate behavior and kinship ties, and that these differences are reflected in children's vocabularies (Chan & Nicoladis, 2010).

Context: The Interaction of Child, Caregiver, and Language

As we have seen, both child and caregiver factors predict differences in children's approach to the problems that varied languages present to them. The challenge for research is to understand how available learning mechanisms interact with environmental supports. One approach is to consider that language is learned and used in a myriad of contexts that make up the daily life of children and their conversational partners. Nelson (1981) observed that the context in which language is used will determine the form and function of the input. As we noted earlier, book reading may be a particularly effective context for acquiring object labels at all levels of SES. Other situations in the child's life—eating, dressing, playing with siblings and peers, playing with toys, rough-and-tumble play, nursery rhymes and songs—provide quite different contexts for input and acquisition. Each context provides a unique opportunity to learn some aspect of language: whole words or phrases, object labels or words for actions and states, describing or demanding, prosodic or segmental accuracy. Thus, as the range of contexts varies, opportunities for language learning will vary (see Figure 8.2). For children learning two languages, contexts for language learning may also vary within and across languages.

figure 8.2   Sources of Variation in Child Language Development

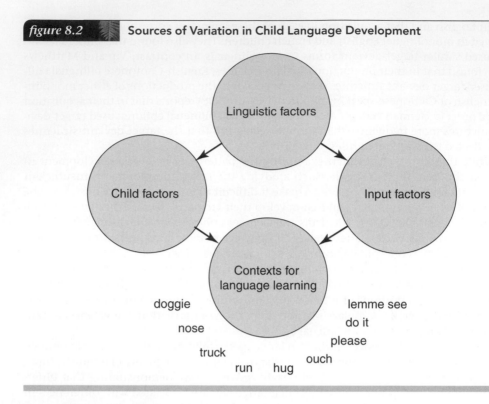

The interests of both child and caregiver, moreover, will influence the kinds of contexts that make up the daily events and routines of a particular parent–child pair. Goldfield (1987) found that lexical variation was best predicted by a combination of child and caregiver variables. Johanna was the most referential child in this sample. She gave clear evidence that shared attention to objects was a familiar and enjoyable interactive context. Almost half (48 percent) of her attempts to engage her mother involved showing or giving a toy. Moreover, her mother's speech clearly and consistently supported the extraction and acquisition of single words that named objects. Talk about toys was the largest category of maternal speech (41 percent) and she highlighted names for things during all types of play, from book reading ("egg in the hole book," "Look! See the tree?") to ball games ("Ayy it's a ball") and pretend play ("Here's a woman—you can put the woman in the truck"). Nouns made up 76 percent of Johanna's first fifty words, and only one of these was a phrase (*get you*).

Other children may experience relatively more contexts in which the focus is on the child's behavior, performance, or social play. Caitlin, the child with highly expressive speech, included a toy in only 18 percent of her social initiations. She was more likely to pause in her play to look and smile at her mother. Caitlin's mother, moreover, often engaged her baby in social play, using conversational formulae and routines more than any other mother in the sample. Almost half (48 percent) of her utterances were questions and directives used to prompt her daughter's performance and to engage her participation in shared play. Sixty-one percent of Caitlin's first fifty words consisted of socially expressive speech, and many of these, as we pointed out earlier, were phrases.

Most children, however, are likely to learn a more balanced mix of nouns, phrases, and socially expressive speech, acquired through participation in a range of contexts. Peters (1983) observed that Minh's use of analytic and gestalt language was often tied to specific contexts. One-word utterances were likely in situations such as naming pictures in a book, whereas gestalt language was often copied from songs and storybook rhymes.

Implications of Variation for Theories of Language Acquisition

The fact of variation in language acquisition has implications for theories and methods in the study of language development. Early studies in the modern era of language research assumed that universal aspects of acquisition were the proper object of study and that phenomena that varied across languages and children were trivial. Thus, small-sample studies were the norm, and no attempt was made to select children who represented the range of possible approaches to acquisition. We see now that variation can tell us about the processes by which children extract information from the linguistic interactions in which they participate. Assessing the extent and type of variation helps us to construct a theory of how children learn, rather than just a description of what they know. Moreover, emphasis on the study of English learners has limited the data we report and the theories we construct. English is a language with relatively impoverished morphology and little opportunity to exploit word-order variation in simple sentences. Thus, the range of normal variation in approaches to language may be limited by the characteristics of English, and we are in danger of thinking that characteristics of English learners (e.g., a tendency to start with nouns) are in fact universal for all language learners.

Children such as Johanna, whose early language consists of clearly articulated single words that are predominantly nouns, are well represented in the bulk of language development research. Cross-linguistic studies, however, reveal that non-nominals figure more prominently in the early speech of children learning languages other than English. Italian children appear to learn fewer nouns than their English-speaking peers (Camaioni & Longobardi, 1995), and Japanese, Mandarin, and Korean speakers are precocious verb learners (Clancy, 1985; Gopnik & Choi, 1991, 1995; Tardif, 1996). Because English speakers (including parents and researchers) value nouns, much of our research efforts have been limited to understanding the principles that govern the acquisition of object labels. The emphasis on nouns may be misleading. For example, unlike nouns, nonostensive rather than ostensive contexts appear to be more conducive to the acquisition of verbs (Tomasello & Kruger, 1992). By limiting our explanations of word learning to nouns, we may be missing many of the cognitive and linguistic resources that children bring to the task of learning to talk.

Expressive speakers such as Caitlin, who acquire numerous phrases, appear less frequently in the literature. However, the early use of phrasal utterances may be more common than has been previously acknowledged. Longer, expressive phrases occur throughout the one-word period and appear to be more common in samples of children from varied social backgrounds (e.g., Lieven et al., 1992). Attention to phrasal speech has resulted in improved methodologies and criteria for determining the length and productivity of children's linguistic units (Lieven et al., 1997; Plunkett, 1993). Connectionist models have also revealed neural networks that segment units larger than single words from connected "speech." These models demonstrate how dramatic differences in output may emerge from small differences in the learner (i.e., network) and/or in the input (Elman, 1990; Redington & Chater, 1998). Connectionist models also offer a potentially valuable methodological tool for exploring the extent to which a single learning mechanism can account for the kinds of variability we have described within and across domains (e.g., the lexicon versus syntax) that have been characterized as distinct language modules. The fact of variation in semantics, morphology, and syntax and the continuity observed from first words to early sentences argue against a strictly modular explanation of language development.

Interest in children's use of phrasal speech is especially important in view of the fact that a significant proportion of everyday adult speech may consist of phrases stored and retrieved as a whole. These formulae consist of idioms (e.g., *kick the bucket*), collocations (e.g., *sheer/pure coincidence*), adjuncts (e.g., *by and large*), sentence frames (e.g., *please pass the x*), and standard situational utterances (e.g., *can I help you?*) (Nattinger & DeCarrico, 1992; Pawley & Snyder, 1983). Wray (1998) argues that formulae perform important sociolinguistic functions that ease the burden of constructing utterances from scratch each time we have something to say, especially in the course of communicatively predictable situations. Although syntactic theory has focused largely on rule-generated constructions, more recent theoretical formulations (e.g., Cullicover & Jackendoff, 2006) have begun to address the storage and retrieval of complex structures with their associated meanings. The next step is to discover the processes by which children acquire, store, and produce the full range of communicatively effective utterances.

Methods for collecting data on language acquisition have been developed on the assumption that all children go about it much the same way. Thus, many analyses of children's spontaneous speech are based on utterances elicited in the context of play with toys, usually a set of novel toys provided by the experimenter. Children who rely on imitation and routine contexts as sources of their utterances may be relatively disadvantaged in this novel situation and need to be observed during more familiar daily events. Similarly, phrasal speech may be more consistently elicited during interactions with an older sibling.

It is also important to note that different cultures vary in the degree to which they encourage and support various child tendencies. The highly referential child is appropriate and rewarding to a middle-class American mother, who sees naming as a sensible and intelligent way to use language, but not to a Kaluli mother, who would view naming as "talking to no purpose" (Schieffelin, 1986). The skill of imitation may be relatively little valued by American mothers, but it is crucial for children whose caregivers instruct them to repeat modeled utterances as a way both to learn and to function socially, as do Kaluli (Schieffelin, 1986), Kwara'ae (Watson-Gegeo & Gegeo, 1986), and Basotho (Demuth, 1986) mothers. The existence of cultural variation in the language-learning environment has been proposed by many as an argument against a strong environmental influence on language acquisition; we see variation instead as a fact that must be understood, in the light of information from relevant research, as evidence that children have many mechanisms available for the acquisition of language that are differentially exploited in different cultural and linguistic contexts.

SUMMARY

It is important to reiterate that even though variation in styles or strategies for language acquisition is striking, the differences observed may reflect preferences or tendencies rather than dichotomies. Children who are classified as highly *imitative* produce many nonimitated utterances. *Pronominal* children produce some nominal word combinations. *Referential* children are not incapable of socially *expressive* speech. Language acquisition is a remarkably buffered process with a high rate of success; clearly, most children control many different strategies and mechanisms that contribute to language development.

We are left with the question of where the differences originate. It has been suggested that children's varying approaches to language and other cognitive problem areas reflect basic *temperamental* differences—for example, in risk-taking tendencies—or in asymmetries in how information is processed. Such hypotheses await further, more interdisciplinary investigations to test them adequately. Hardy-Brown (1983), for example, suggests that we employ research designs from the field of behavioral genetics to disentangle the effects of heredity and environment on variation in rate and style of acquisition. These methodologies would include adoption studies, which assess the cognitive and linguistic abilities of both birth and adoptive parents and compare these measures to the child's developing linguistic skills. Meanwhile, the fact of variation has implications not only for *theory*, but for *research* and *educational practice* as well. We can apply what we know about variation to amend and improve our methods of *collecting* language data, *teaching* reading and foreign languages, and *intervening* with children at risk for language delay or deviance.

The recognition that there are many ways to learn a language and that normally developing children may differ from one another in how they accomplish the task should help us to think more creatively about *therapy, intervention*, and *education*. A single therapeutic or educational method is unlikely to work for all children, and the failure of one method does not imply that success is impossible. The child who is language-delayed or language-impaired, like the normally developing child, may exploit or avoid imitation, may search cautiously for rules or recklessly try out utterances, may be more easily involved in social games, or may demand a referential vocabulary. All of these preferences are compatible with successful language acquisition, and all can be utilized by parents, teachers, and therapists.

SUGGESTED PROJECTS

1. To examine the influence of context, record the speech of one child at the single-word stage with a parent in a variety of situations: book reading, bathing, outdoor play, play with toys, dinner time. Analyze the words the child produces in each context in terms of Nelson's (1973) referential/expressive distinction.

2. Record the interactions of three different caregiver–child pairs (children should be about the same age and/or vocabulary level). Code parental speech for its communicative intent (e.g., descriptions versus behavioral directives as used by Pine, 1994). Do the parents differ on these dimensions?

3. Ask the parents of two first-born and two later-born children to keep a record of all unique speech productions over the course of one week. Do the children, especially the later born, produce phrasal speech?

SUGGESTED READINGS

Bates, E., Bretherton, I., & Snyder, L. (1988). *From first words to grammar: Individual differences and dissociable mechanisms.* Cambridge, UK: Cambridge University Press.

Lieven, E. V. M. (1996). Variation in a crosslinguistic context. In D. Slobin (Ed.), *The crosslinguistic study of language acquisition, Volume 5: Expanding the contexts.* Hillsdale, NJ: Erlbaum.

Nelson, K. (1981). Individual differences in language development: Implications for development and language. *Developmental Psychology, 17,* 170–187.

Peters, A. (1983). *The units of language acquisition.* Cambridge, UK: Cambridge University Press.

Shore, C. M. (1995). *Individual differences in language development.* Thousand Oaks, CA: Sage.

KEY WORDS

agglutinated
analytic style
expressive

nominal strategy
pronominal strategy
referential

rote/holistic style
synthetic
transformational syntax

REFERENCES

Adamson, L. B., & Tomasello, M. (1984). An "expressive" child's language development. *Infant Behavior and Development, 7,* 467–478.

Arriaga, R. I., Fenson, L., Cronan, T., & Pethick, S. J. (1998). Scores on the MacArthur Communicative Development Inventory of children from low- and middle-income families. *Applied Psycholinguistics, 12,* 209–223.

Bassano, D. (2000). Early development of nouns and verbs in French: Exploring the interface between lexicon and grammar. *Journal of Child Language, 27,* 521–559.

Bassano, D., Maillochon, I., & Eme, E. (1998). Developmental changes and variability in the early lexicon: A study of French children's naturalistic productions. *Journal of Child Language, 25,* 493–531.

Bates, E., Bretherton, I., & Snyder, L. (1988). *From first words to grammar: Individual differences and dissociable mechanisms.* Cambridge, UK: Cambridge University Press.

Bates, E., Marchman, V., Thal, D., Fenson, L., Dale, P., Reznick, J. S., Reilly, J., & Hartung, J. (1993). Developmental and stylistic variation in the composition of early vocabulary. *Journal of Child Language, 21,* 85–123.

Beals, D., & Tabors, P. (1995). Arboretum, bureaucratic, and carbohydrates: Preschoolers' exposure to rare vocabulary at home. *First Language, 15,* 57–76

Benedict, H. (1979). Early lexical development: Comprehension and production. *Journal of Child Language, 6,* 183–200.

Berman, R. A. (1985). The acquisition of Hebrew. In D. I. Slobin (Ed.), *The cross-linguistic study of language acquisition, Vol. 1: The data* (pp. 225–271). Hillsdale, NJ: Erlbaum.

Blom, E. (2010). Effects of input on the early grammatical development of bilingual children. *International Journal of Bilingualism, 14*(4), 422–446.

Bloom, L., Lightbown, P., & Hood, L. (1975). Structure and variation in child language. *Monographs of the Society for Research in Child Development, 40.*

Bottari, P., Cipriani, P. & Chilosi, A. (1994). Protosyntactic devices in the acquisition of Italian free morphology. *Language Acquisition, 3,* 327–369.

Braine, M. D. S. (1963). The ontogeny of English phrase structure: The first phase. *Language, 39,* 1–13.

Bretherton, I., McNew, S., Snyder, L., & Bates, E. (1983). Individual differences at 20 months: Analytic and holistic strategies in language acquisition. *Journal of Child Language, 10,* 293–320.

Brown, R. (1973). *A first language.* Cambridge, MA: Harvard University Press.

Bussis, A. M., Chittenden, E. A., Amarel, M., & Klausner, E. (1984).

Inquiry into meaning: An investigation of learning to read. Hillsdale, NJ: Erlbaum.

Camaioni, L., & Longobardi, E. (1995). Nature and stability of individual differences in early lexical development of Italian speaking children. *First Language, 15,* 203–218.

Camaioni, L., & Longobardi, E. (2001). Noun versus verb emphasis in Italian mother-to-child speech. *Journal of Child Language, 28,* 773–785.

Carpenter, M., Nagell, K., & Tomasello, M. (1998). Social cognition, joint attention, and communicative competence from 9 to 15 months of age. *Monographs of the Society for Research in Child Development, 63(4), Serial No. 255.*

Chan, W. H., & Nicoladis, E. (2010). Predicting two Mandarin-English bilingual childrens' first 50 words: Effects of frequency and relative exposure in the input. *International Journal of Bilingualism, 14*(2), 237–270.

Childers, J. B., & Tomasello, M. (2001). The role of pronouns in young children's acquisition of the English transitive construction. *Developmental Psychology, 37,* 739–748.

Choi, S. (2000). Caregiver input in English and Korean: Use of nouns and verbs in book-reading and toy-play contexts. *Journal of Child Language, 27,* 69–96.

Chomsky, N. (1957). *Syntactic structures.* The Hague: Mouton.

Clancy, P. M. (1985). The acquisition of Japanese. In D. I. Slobin (Ed.), *The cross-linguistic study of language acquisition, Vol. 1: The data* (pp. 373–524). Hillsdale, NJ: Erlbaum.

Clark, E. V. (1985). The acquisition of Romance, with special reference to French. In D. J. Slobin (Ed.), *The crosslinguistic study of language acquisition, Vol. 1: The data* (pp. 687–782). Hillsdale, NJ: Erlbaum.

Cullicover, P. W., & Jackendoff, R. (2006). The simpler syntax hypothesis. *Trends in Cognitive Sciences, 10*(9), 413–418.

David, A., & Wei, L. (2008). Individual differences in the lexical development of French-English bilingual children. *International Journal of Bilingual Education and Bilingualism, 11*(5), 598–618.

De Houwer, A. (1995). Bilingual language acquisition. In P. Fletcher &

B. MacWhinney (Eds.), *The handbook of child language* (pp. 219–250). Cambridge, MA: Blackwell.

Della Corte, M., Benedict, H., & Klein, D. (1983). The relationship of pragmatic dimensions of mothers' speech to the referential–expressive distinction. *Journal of Child Language, 10*, 35–44.

Demuth, K. (1986). Prompting routines in the language socialization of Basotho children. In B. Schieffelin & E. Ochs (Eds.), *Language socialization across cultures* (pp. 51–79). New York: Cambridge University Press.

Dopke, S. (1998). Competing language structures: The acquisition of verb placement by billingual German-English children. *Journal of Child Language, 25*, 555–584.

Echols, C. H. (1993). A perceptually based model of children's earliest productions. *Cognition, 46*, 245–296.

Elman, J. L. (1990). Finding structure in time. *Cognitive Science, 14*, 179–211.

Elsen, H. (1996). Two routes to language: Stylistic variation in one child. *First Language, 16*, 141–158.

Evans, M. A. (1993). Communicative competence as a dimension of shyness. In K. H. Rubin &J. B. Asendorpf (Eds.), *Social withdrawal, inhibition, and shyness in childhood* (pp. 189–212). Hillsdale, NJ: Erlbaum.

Farkas, G., & Beron, K. (2004). The detailed age trajectory of oral vocabulary knowledge: Differences by class and race. *Social Science Research, 33*, 464–497.

Farran, D. C., & Haskins, R. (1980). Reciprocal influence in the social interactions of mothers and three-year-old children from different socioeconomic backgrounds. *Child Development, 51*, 780–791.

Fenson, L., Dale, P., Reznick, J. S., Bates, E., Thal, D., & Pethick, S. (1994). Variability in early communicative development. *Monographs of the Society for Research in Child Development, 59*.

Ferguson, C. A. (1979). Phonology as an individual access system: Some data from language acquisition. In C. J. Fillmore, D. Kempler, & W. S.-Y. Wang (Eds.), *Individual differences in language ability and language behavior.* New York: Academic Press.

Ferguson, C. A., & Farwell, C. (1975). Words and sounds in early language acquisition. *Language, 51*, 419–439.

Fillmore, L. W. (1979). Individual differences in second language acquisition. In C. J. Fillmore, D. Kempler, & W. S.-Y. Wang (Eds.), *Individual differences in language ability and language behavior.* New York: Academic Press.

Furrow, D., & Nelson, K. (1984). Environmental correlates of individual differences in language acquisition. *Journal of Child Language, 11*, 523–534.

Genesee, R., Paradis, J., & Crago, M. B. (2004). Dual language development and disorders: A handbook on billingualism and second language learning. Baltimore: Paul H. Brookes.

Goldfield, B. (1987). The contributions of child and caregiver to referential and expressive language. *Applied Psycholinguistics, 8*, 267–280.

Goldfield, B. A. (1990). Pointing, naming, and talk about objects: Referential behavior in children and mothers. *First Language, 10*, 231–242.

Goldfield, B. A. (1993). Noun bias in maternal speech to one-year-olds. *Journal of Child Language, 20*, 85–99.

Goldfield, B. A. (2000). Nouns before verbs in comprehension vs. production: The view from pragmatics. *Journal of Child Language, 27*, 501–520.

Goldfield, B. A., & Reznick, J. S. (1990). Early lexical acquisition: Rate, content, and the vocabulary spurt. *Journal of Child Language, 17*, 171–183.

Gopnik, A., & Choi, S. (1991). Do linguistic differences lead to cognitive differences? A cross-linguistic study of semantic and cognitive development. *First Language, 11*, 199–215.

Gopnik, A., & Choi, S. (1995). Names, relational words, and cognitive development in English and Korean speakers: Nouns are not always learned before verbs. In M. Tomasello & W. E. Merriman (Eds.), *Beyond names for things* (pp. 63–80). Hillsdale, NJ: Erlbaum.

Hampson, J. (1988). Individual differences in style of language acquisition in relation to social networks. In S. Salzinger, J. Antrobus, & M. Hammer (Eds.), *Social networks of children, adolescents, and college students*. Hillsdale, NJ: Erlbaum.

Hampson, J., & Nelson, K. (1993). The relation of maternal language to variation in rate and style of language acquisition. *Journal of Child Language, 20*, 313–342.

Hardy-Brown, K. (1983). Universals and individual differences: Disentangling two approaches to the study of language acquisition. *Developmental Psychology, 19*, 610–624.

Hart, B., & Risley, T. (1995). *Meaningful differences in the everyday experience of young American children*. Baltimore: Paul H. Brookes.

Heath, S. B. (1983). *Ways with words: Language, life, and work in communities and classrooms*. Cambridge, UK: Cambridge University Press.

Hoff, E. (2003). The specificity of environmental influence: Socioeconomic status affects early vocabulary development via maternal speech. *Child Development, 74*, 1368–1378.

Hoff, E., Loursen, B., & Tardiff, T. (2002). Socioeconomic status and parenting. In M. H. Bornstein (Ed.), *Handbook of parenting. Ecology and biology of parenting* (Vol II, pp 161–188). Mahwah, NJ: Erlbaum.

Hoff-Ginsberg, E. (1991). Mother–child conversation in different social classes and communicative settings. *Child Development, 62*, 782–796.

Hoff-Ginsberg, E. (1998). The relation of birth order and socioeconomic status to children's language experience and language development. *Applied Psycholinguistics, 19*, 603–629.

Horgan, D. (1981). Rate of language acquisition and noun emphasis. *Journal of Psycholinguistic Research, 10*, 629–640.

Huttenlocher, J., Haight, W., Bryk, A., Seltzer, M. & Lyons, T. (1991). Early vocabulary growth: Relation to language input and gender. *Developmental Psychology 27*, 236–48.

Huttenlocher, J., Vasilyeva, M., Waterfall, H. R., Vevea, J. L., & Hedges, L. V. (2007). The varieties of speech to young children. *Developmental Psychology, 43* (5), 1062–1083.

Junker, D. A., & Stockman, I. J. (2002). Expressive vocabulary of German-English bilingual toddlers. *American Journal of Speech-Language Pathology, 11*, 381–394.

Kim, M., McGregor, K. K., & Thompson, C. K. (2000). Early lexical development in English and Korean-speaking children: Language-general and language-specific patterns. *Journal of Child Language, 27*, 225–254.

Kuczaj, S. A., & Maratsos, M. P. (1983). The initial verbs of yes-no questions: A different kind of general grammatical category. *Developmental Psychology, 19*, 440–443.

Lawrence, V. W., & Shipley, E. F. (1996). Parental speech to middle and working class children from two racial groups in three settings. *Applied Psycholinguistics, 17*, 233–255.

Leonard, L., Schwartz, R., Folger, M., Newhoff, M., & Wilcox, M. (1979). Children's imitations of lexical items. *Child Development, 59*, 19–27.

Lieven, E. V. M. (1980). *Language development in young children*. Unpublished doctoral dissertation, Cambridge University.

Lieven, E. V. M., Pine, J. M., & Baldwin, G. (1997). Lexically based learning and early grammatical development. *Journal of Child Language, 24*, 187–219.

Lieven, E. V. M., Pine, J. M., & Barnes, H. D. (1992). Individual differences in early vocabulary development: Redefining the referential-expressive distinction. *Journal of Child Language, 19*, 287–310.

Lieven, E., Salomo, D., & Tomasello, M. (2009). Two-year-old children's production of multiword utterances: A usage-based analysis. *Cognitive Linguistics, 20* (3), 481–507.

MacWhinney, B. (1985). Hungarian language acquisition as an exemplification of a general model of language development. In D. I. Slobin (Ed.), *The crosslinguistic study of language acquisition, Vol. 2: Theoretical issues* (pp. 1069–1155). Hillsdale, NJ: Erlbaum.

Masur, E. F. (1982). Mothers' responses to infants' object-related gestures: Influences on lexical development. *Journal of Child Language, 9*, 23–30.

Mol, S., Bus, A., De Jong, M., & Smeets, D. (2008). Added value of dialogic parent-child book readings: A meta-analysis. *Early Education and Development, 19*, 7–26.

Nattinger, J. R., & DeCarrico, J. S. (1992). *Lexical phrases and language teaching.* Oxford: Oxford University Press.

Nelson, K. (1973). Structure and strategy in learning to talk. *Monographs of the Society for Research in Child Development, 38.*

Nelson, K. (1975). The nominal shift in semantic-syntactic development. *Cognitive Psychology, 7,* 461–479.

Nelson, K. (1981). Individual differences in language development: Implications for development and language. *Developmental Psychology, 17,* 170–187.

Nelson, K. E., Baker, N., Denninger, M., Bonvillian, J., & Kaplan, B. (1985). Cookie versus do-it-again: Imitative-referential and personal-social-syntactic-initiating language styles in young children. *Linguistics, 23,* 433–454.

Nicoladis, E., & Genesee, F. (1996). A longitudinal study of pragmatic differentiation in young bilingual children. *Language Learning, 46,* 439–464.

Olsen-Fulero, L. (1982). Style and stability in mother conversational behavior: A study of individual differences. *Journal of Child Language, 9,* 543–564.

Pan, B. A., Rowe, M. L., Singer, J. D., & Snow, C. E. (2005). Maternal correlates of growth in toddler vocabulary production in low-income families. *Child Development, 76*(4), 763–782.

Pawley, A., & Snyder, F. H. (1983). Two puzzles for linguistic theory: Nativelike selection and nativelike fluency. In J. C. Richards & R. W. Schmidt (Eds.), *Language and communication.* New York: Longman.

Pearson, B. Z., Fernandez, S., Lewedag, V., & Oller, D. K. (1997). Input factors in lexical learning in bilingual infants (ages 10 to 30 months). *Applied Psycholinguistics, 18,* 41–58.

Peters, A. M. (1977). Language learning strategies: Does the whole equal the sum of the parts? *Language, 53,* 560–573.

Peters, A. M. (1983). *The units of language acquisition.* Cambridge, UK: Cambridge University Press.

Peters, A. M. (2001). Filler syllables: What is their status in emerging grammar? *Journal of Child Language, 28,* 229–242.

Peters, A. M., & Menn, L. (1993). False starts and filler syllables: Ways to learn grammatical morphemes. *Language, 69,* 742–777.

Pine, J. M. (1992a). The functional basis of referentiality: Evidence from children's spontaneous speech. *First Language, 12,* 39–55.

Pine, J. M. (1992b). How referential are "referential" children? Relationships between maternal-report and observational measures of vocabulary composition and usage. *Journal of Child Language, 19,* 75–86.

Pine, J. M. (1994). Environmental correlates of variation in lexical style: Interactional style and the structure of the input. *Applied Psycholinguistics, 15,* 355–370.

Pine, J. M. (1995). Variation in vocabulary development as a function of birth order. *Child Development, 66,* 272–281.

Pine, J. M., & Lieven, E. V. M. (1990). Referential style at thirteen months: Why age-defined cross-sectional measures are inappropriate for the study of strategy differences in early language development. *Journal of Child Language, 17,* 625–631.

Pine, J. M., & Lieven, E. V. M. (1993). Reanalyzing rote-learned phrases: Individual differences in the transition to multi-word speech. *Journal of Child Language, 20,* 551–571.

Plunkett, K. (1993). Lexical segmentation and vocabulary growth in early language acquisition. *Journal of Child Language, 20,* 43–60.

Pungello, E. P., Iruka, I. U., Dotterer, A. M., Mills-Koonce, R., & Reznick, J. S. (2009). The effects of socioeconomic status, race, and parenting on language development in early childhood. *Developmental Psychology, 45,* 544–557.

Raikes, H., Pan, B., Tamis-LeMonda, C. S., Brooks-Gunn, J., & Constantine, J. (2006). Mother-child bookreading in low-income families: Correlates and outcomes during the first three years of life. *Child Development, 77,* 924–953.

Redington, M., & Chater, N. (1998). Connectionist and statistical approaches to language acquisition: A distributional perspective. *Language and Cognitive Processes, 13,* 129–191.

Rispoli, M. (1989). Encounters with Japanese verbs: Caregiver sentences and the categorization of transitive and intransitive action verbs. *First Language, 9,* 57–80.

Rollins, P. R., Snow, C. E., & Willett, J. B. (1996). Predictors of MLU: Semantic and morphological developments. *First Language, 16,* 243–259.

Rosenblatt, D. (1977). Developmental trends in infant play. In B. Tizard & D. Harvey (Eds.), *Biology of play.* London: William Heinemann Medical Books.

Rowe, M. L. (2008). Child-directed speech: Relation to socioeconomic status, knowledge of child development, and child vocabulary skill. *Journal of Child Language, 35,* 185–205.

Rowe, M. L., & Goldin-Meadow, S. (2009). Differences in early gesture explalin SES disparities in child vocabulary size at school entry. *Science, 323,* 951–953.

Scarpa, E. (1990). Intonation and dialogue processes in early speech. In G. Conti-Ramsden & C. Snow (Eds.) *Children's language, Volume 7.* New York: Psychology Press.

Schieffelin, B. (1986). *How Kaluli children learn what to say, what to do, and how to feel.* New York: Cambridge University Press.

Senechal, L., LeFevre, I. A., Hudson, E., & Lawson, P. (1996). Knowledge of storybooks as a predictor of young children's vocabulary. *Journal of Educational Psychology, 88,* 520–536.

Shore, C., Dixon, W., & Bauer, P. (1995). Measures of linguistic and non-linguistic knowledge of objects in the second year. *First Language, 15,* 189–202.

Simonsen, H. G. (1990). *Child phonology: System and variation in three Norwegian children and one Samoan child.* Doctoral dissertation, Department of Linguistics and Philosophy, University of Oslo. (Data available at http://childes.psy. cmu.edu: Germanic–Norwegian.

Slobin, D. I. (1968). *Early grammatical development in several languages, with special attention to Soviet research* (Working Paper No. 11). Berkeley: University of California, Language-Behavior Research Laboratory.

Slobin, D. I. (1985). *The cross-linguistic study of language acquisition, Vol. 1.* Hillsdale, NJ: Erlbaum.

Slobin, D. I. (1992). *The crosslinguistic study of language acquisition, Vol. 3.* Hillsdale, NJ: Erlbaum.

Slobin, D. I. (1997). *The crosslinguistic study of language acquisition, Vol. 5: Expanding the contexts.* Hillsdale, NJ: Erlbaum.

Smith, N. (1973). *The acquisition of phonology: A case study.* London: Cambridge University Press.

Smoczynska, M. (1985). The acquisition of Polish. In D. I. Slobin (Ed.), *The cross-linguistic study of language acquisition, Volume 1* (pp. 595–686). Hillsdale, NJ: Erlbaum.

Snow, C. E., Arlman-Rupp, A., Hassing, Y., Jobse, J., Joosten, J. & Vorster, J. (1976). Mothers' speech in three social classes. *Journal of Psycholinguistic Research, 5,* 1–20.

Snow, C. E., Burns, M. S., & Griffin, P. (1998). *Preventing reading difficulties in young children.* Washington, DC: National Academy Press.

Stern, C., & Stern, W. (1928). *Die kindersprache.* Leipzig, Germany.

Stoll, S., Abbot-Smith, K., & Lieven, E. (2009). Lexically restricted utterances in Russian, German, and English-directed speech. *Cognitive Science, 33,* 75–103.

Tamis-LeMonda, C. S., Bornstein, M. H., Baumwell, L., & Damast, A. M. (1996). Responsive parenting in the second year: Specific influences on children's language and play. *Early Development and Parenting 5,* 173–183.

Tanouye, E. K. (1979). The acquisition of verbs in Japanese children. *Papers and Reports on Child Language Development, 17* (Department of Linguistics, Stanford University), 49–56.

Tardif, T. (1996). Nouns are not always learned before verbs: Evidence from Mandarin speakers' early vocabularies. *Developmental Psychology, 32,* 492–504.

Tardif, T., Gelman, S. A., & Xu, F. (1999). Putting the "noun bias" in context: A comparison of English and Mandarin. *Child Development, 70,* 620–635.

Tardif, T., Shatz, M., & Naigles, L. (1997). Caregiver speech and children's use of nouns versus verbs: A comparison of English, Italian, and Mandarin. *Journal of Child Language, 24,* 535–565.

Theakston, A. L., Lieven, E. M., Pine, J. M., & Rowland, C. F. (2002). Going, going, gone: The acquisition of the verb "go." *Journal of Child Language, 29*, 783–811.

Tomasello, M. (1992). *First verbs: A case study of early grammatical development.* Cambridge, UK: Cambridge University Press.

Tomasello, M., & Kruger, A. C. (1992). Joint attention on actions: Acquiring verbs in ostensive and nonostensive contexts. *Journal of Child Language, 19*, 311–333.

Vihman, M. M. (1993). Variable paths to early word production. *Journal of Phonetics, 21*, 61–82.

Watson-Gegeo, K., & Gegeo, D. (1986). Calling-out and repeating routines in Kwara'ae children's language socialization. In B. Schieffelin & E. Ochs (Eds.), *Language socialization across cultures.* New York: Cambridge University Press.

Weizman, Z. O., & Snow, C. E. (2001). Lexical input as related to children's vocabulary acquisition: Effects of sophisticated exposure and support for meaning. *Developmental Psychology, 37*(2), 265-279.

Whitehurst, G., Falco, F., Lonigan, C., & Fischel, J. E. (1988). Accelerating language development through picture book reading. *Developmental Psychology, 24*, 552–559.

Wolf, D., & Gardner, H. (1979). Style and sequence in symbolic play. In M. Franklin & N. Smith (Eds.), *Early symbolization.* Hillsdale, NJ: Erlbaum.

Wray, A. (1998). Protolanguage as a holistic system for social interaction. *Language and Communication, 18*, 47–67.

Yip, V. & Matthews, S. (2000). Syntactic transfer in a Cantonese-English bilingual child. *Bilingualism: Language and Cognition, 3*, 193–208.

Atypical Language Development

Nan Bernstein Ratner
University of Maryland, College Park

As Chapter 7 noted, most children acquire the complexities of language so quickly and easily that it is difficult to construct a fully adequate theory to account for this remarkable achievement. Unfortunately, not all children acquire language easily and well. In this chapter we examine some major causes and patterns of language delay and disorder. The study of childhood language disorders is important for a number of reasons.

First, the case of individuals who fail to learn language normally allows us to evaluate claims that have been made about possible prerequisites for the normal acquisition process. As Marcus and Rabagliati (2006) note, "Human developmental disorders . . . offer special insight into the genetic, neural and behavioral basis of language because they provide a way to study naturalistically what cannot be controlled in the lab."

For instance, when a child with intellectual disability does not learn to use language rapidly or appropriately, we may test hypotheses about the possible role that cognitive development plays in language development. Conversely, cases in which cognition is grossly impaired but language appears relatively spared may cause us to question the relationship between cognition and language. The role of sufficient access to adult input in fostering language learning is highlighted when we examine patterns of language difficulty experienced by children who are deaf or hearing impaired. Children who fail to master grammatical rules in the absence of deficits in other areas of functioning invite us to consider whether language is a discrete "module" of human ability. Thus, theories of normal language acquisition must be able to predict how the process might be disrupted to produce a variety of child language-learning disorders (Leonard, 1998).

Second, the study of language disorders in children represents one attempt to apply findings about the typical language acquisition process to a practical problem: What can be done to aid children who experience difficulty in acquiring language? By examining the specific patterns of delay and disorder that certain children encounter during language development and by reviewing what we already know about the sequence and nature of typical language development, we can more effectively target our attempts to remediate their difficulties.

Without treatment, delayed or disordered language development may lead to depressed reading ability, poor oral and writing skills, and even problematic social behavior and psychosocial adjustment (U.S. Preventive Services Task Force, 2006). Children with histories of language impairment show depressed educational and vocational outcomes, although these can be modified and mediated by effective intervention and social support networks (Johnson, Beitchman, & Brownlee, 2010). As we learn more about the factors that hinder children's language development, we hope to discover that certain disorders are preventable or respond best if intervention occurs very early in the child's life (Bailey, Bruer, Symons, & Lichtman, 2001). In other words, if we can identify environmental or physical factors that predispose children to communicative disorder, we may be able to intervene and reduce the number of children who develop long-term difficulty with language skills.

The U.S. Preventive Services Task Force (2006) estimates that speech and language delay affects from 5 to 8 percent of pre-school-aged children. In this chapter we describe some major patterns of language disturbance. In each case, we review what is known about affected children's development, how current theory attempts to explain the nature of their communicative difficulty, and what can be done to aid such children in improving their language skills. These major syndromes of language disorder involve children with *hearing impairment, intellectual disabilities, autism spectrum disorder, pervasive developmental disorder,* and *specific language impairment.* Although the chapter discusses them separately, it is worth noting that many of the behaviors of concern, and many of the approaches to treatment, cross the boundaries between these categories of disorder. In fact, in recent years it has become evident that there is great overlap in symptoms among disorders such as pervasive developmental disorder, intellectual impairment, and specific language impairment. At the end of this chapter we will note some conditions that lead to difficulty in producing speech as opposed to language. Such *speech disorders* include delayed or disordered articulation and stuttering.

The emphasis on **evidence-based practice (EBP)** in both speech language pathology and education has increased attention to the validation of effective interventions through careful study and data collection. Although there is still a relative scarcity of information on "best practices" in language intervention, particularly with regard to treatment of diverse types of communication disorders and the conditions that accompany them, there has been a rapid growth in the publication of therapy-outcome studies that can guide more effective intervention. Additionally, we will discuss how **response to intervention (RTI)** models have been developed to identify children making inadequate academic progress in language and literacy related skill areas and to assess what level of intervention is most appropriate to bring the child to a grade-appropriate level of function.

Communicative Development and Severe Hearing Impairment

The Nature and Effects of Differing Types of Hearing Loss

We know that it is necessary to be exposed to a language to learn one: We learn only the language or languages we hear spoken around us, rather than any possible human language. We know, too, that if certain conditions limit linguistic exposure, language development may be severely hindered. Such is the case with significant **hearing impairment.** Roughly one in every 1,000 American infants is born with some form of hearing impairment, although rates vary by region and are affected by numerous risk factors (Mehra, Eavey, & Keamy, 2009). Hearing loss can also occur over childhood and later, due to many factors. By age 6, six out of 1,000 children will have some degree of permanent hearing loss, although it may not be functionally handicapping (Choo & Meinzen-Derr, 2010).

There has been a decline in the incidence of profound early-childhood hearing loss over the past decades. The current prevalence of profound hearing loss at 1.1 percent of school-aged children now appears somewhat stabilized (Mitchell & Karchmer, 2006). The majority of children with hearing impairment are considered **prelingually deaf**

(Mehra, Eavey, & Keamy, 2009), which means that their hearing loss was present at birth or happened before they began to talk.

Children who are born with hearing impairment that limits their perception of sounds to those exceeding 60 **decibels (dB),** or about the intensity level of a baby's cry, generally will not be able to develop spontaneous oral language that approximates that of normal children. Children born with profound losses exceeding 90 dB are considered functionally deaf and will not develop speech and language skills spontaneously without educational and therapeutic intervention. Just as important, such children will eventually demonstrate language comprehension difficulties, even when the mode of language presentation (e.g., writing) bypasses their problems of auditory reception.

Hearing losses vary in severity and type. Generally, the extent to which a child is handicapped by hearing loss depends upon the severity of the loss, the conditions causing the loss, the utility of assistive devices in restoring some hearing ability, and the age at which the hearing loss occurred (Scheetz, 2012). Although hearing aids (HAs) and **cochlear implants** (CIs) may provide the child with the ability to hear some otherwise inaudible sounds, they cannot restore normal hearing function, especially in cases of severe and profound loss. A conventional hearing aid amplifies the sound signal conveyed to the inner ear's residual hearing ability, while a cochlear implant stimulates the auditory nerve directly. A concise comparison of the two types of devices can be found at the National Institute on Deafness and Other Communication Disorders (NIDCD) site: **www. nidcd.nih.gov/health/hearing/coch.asp**. Numerous simulations of how hearing impairment affects speech perception, as well as simulations of what speech sounds like when processed through a CI are available on the Internet.

In 2000, fewer than 2,000 students were identified as having cochlear implants in a survey of students with hearing impairments served by special education services in the United States (Mitchell, 2004). In contrast, by 2005, the U.S. Food and Drug Administration estimated that approximately 15,000 U.S. children had received such implants (**www.nidcd. nih.gov**). Scheetz (2012) estimates that between 90 and 95 percent of children born deaf in the developed world now receive implants. Similarly, the number of children receiving implants prior to one year of age (Cosetti & Roland, 2010) has risen dramatically. In fact, there is growing expectation that some children with implants can achieve communication skills virtually identical to those of normally hearing children. However, this level of achievement is not uniform, and it rests on a number of factors discussed later in this chapter.

An important predictor of educational outcome of children who are hearing impaired is the age at which the hearing loss is identified (Yoshinaga-Itano, 2003). Fewer than half of all children eventually identified as deaf have obvious risk factors or behavioral symptoms (Samson-Fang, Simons-McCandless, & Shelton, 2000). Thus, there is great need for universal screening of all newborns to ascertain hearing status. Recent mandates for newborn infant screening have made it much more likely that severe hearing loss will be detected early and enable rapid intervention. In 2005, over 90 percent of infants born in the United States received newborn hearing screenings (Centers for Disease Control, 2005). Prior to such mandates, the average age at which U.S. children with significant hearing impairment were identified was 2 years of age or older (Schirmer, 2001). Now, most children are identified well before 6 months of age; research suggests that identification and appropriate intervention prior to six months, well before children

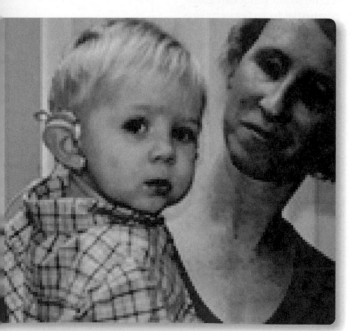

If implanted early enough, cochlear implants enable many children with profound hearing loss to achieve age-appropriate speech and language skills.

would be expected to produce their first words, significantly improves language outcomes (Meinzen-Derr, Wiley, & Choo, 2011).

How does one identify a hearing loss in an infant? The majority of neonatal screenings carried out in newborn nurseries throughout the United States and other developed countries employ technologies such as otoacoustic emissions (OAEs) and/or auditory brainstem responses (ABR) (Choo & Meinzen-Derr, 2010), both of which rely on reflexive responses to auditory stimuli and do not require the listener to provide a behavioral response (such as you may have done in a hearing test at some point in your life, by raising your hand or pressing a button).

Losses that are **congenital** (present at birth) or that occur prelingually (before the child has learned language skills, the period when the majority of significant hearing losses in children occur) are much more disruptive of the language-acquisition process than are losses acquired later in life (see Schirmer, 2012, for a discussion of hearing measurement and impairment). Children who have had access to the ambient language, even for a short while, demonstrate a higher level of linguistic achievement than those who have not had such exposure. Additionally, there is some suggestion that the **etiology** (cause) of the hearing loss may affect a child's linguistic progress. Approximately 30–40 percent of children with significant hearing loss have other concomitant disabilities that also greatly may affect their ability to master speech and language skills (Meinzen-Derr, Wiley, Grether, & Choo, 2011).

It is important to understand how severe hearing impairment limits the child's access to linguistic input. Not all conversations occur face to face, and children who are deaf miss those that take place out of their line of sight. We probably underestimate the degree to which we gain important linguistic insight from language interchanges that occur around us. Thus, even if the child with profound deafness can focus on a speaker's face during conversation, **lipreading** (also called **speechreading**) does not automatically guarantee successful interpretation of the conversation. The notion that lipreading is an easy answer to hearing loss is but one of many myths about deafness discussed by Scheetz (2012). Many sounds, such as velars and liquids, are made in the back of the mouth and are not easily visible on the lips. Additionally, there are many sounds in English and in other languages that resemble one another on the lips but are acoustically distinct, such as /p/, /b/, and /m/.

More than 95 percent of children who are considered deaf are born to hearing parents (Kushalnager et al., 2010), which means that the parents and their young child do not share a mutually intelligible communication system in the crucial early years of language development. Children who are deaf born to deaf parents who use sign language as a preferred method of communication—and thus can include the children in their language system from birth—provide an interesting comparison situation that we address later. Children born deaf and raised in nonsigning households who develop their own rudimentary sign languages (Goldin-Meadow, 2007) are rare and are more relevant to discussion of theories of the innate component of language acquisition (see Chapter 7) than to this section, since such children do not achieve mastery of any extant human language.

As we survey the historical impairments associated with profound hearing loss, even when children are fitted with **amplification** (hearing aids) and provided with extensive **aural rehabilitation,** we note that cochlear implants (CIs) appear to have made the most difference in affecting outcomes among children with significant hearing impairment. Geers, Brenner, and Tobey (2011) followed a cohort of children for more than ten years following implantation; they found that more than 75 percent of them were fully **mainstreamed** (in full regular classroom inclusion) by high school. Spencer, Barker, and Tomblin (2003) report that many children with implants are using language and reading at grade level, something rarely achieved by children with conventional aids. The same group (Tomblin, Barker, Spencer, Zhang, & Gantz, 2005) found advantages in expressive language ability for children implanted closer to 12 months of age, when contrasted with later in development.

Despite the advantages that they may provide over conventional hearing aids, CIs still require extensive educational support to yield positive outcomes in speech, language, and literacy (Teagle & Moore, 2002), and the language proficiency outcomes of children who receive CIs vary substantially, for reasons that are still not well understood (Geers, Spehar, & Sedey, 2002) but clearly include both socioeconomic factors as well as whether the child has additional co-occurring disabilities (Hyde & Power, 2006).

Phonological Development

To an observer, the articulation of children with significant hearing loss may be the most evident manifestation of their disability. Historically, even in developed countries, the speech of many children with hearing impairment has been rated as quite unintelligible despite years of speech training. In developing countries, where hearing loss may not be identified or remediated early or well enough, both speech and language skills may be significantly impaired. Certain classes of sounds (especially high-frequency sibilents and less visible phonemes) are likely to be omitted or misarticulated. Sounds at the ends of words and those embedded in consonant clusters are also likely to be missed by the hearing-impaired child. The speech of children who are deaf or hearing impaired is also characterized by distinctive patterns of prosody that distinguish it from the speech of those with normal hearing; it lacks the fluid coarticulation patterns that are seen in normal conversational speech. Recent research suggests that many young children who use CIs achieve greater intelligibility than children using conventional hearing aids but may still demonstrate noticeably impaired articulation (Flipsen & Parker, 2008). Speech-production training may remedy some of these problems and has been associated with additional vocabulary growth as well as improved speech perception scores and reading performance, perhaps because children may be exposed to new words in the course of their speech therapy (Paatsch, Blamey, Sarant, & Bow, 2006).

Currently available CIs do not do well in conveying the acoustical information that signals intonation/prosody, or tone. (This is a major weakness for the use of CIs in remediating the language deficits of children learning tone languages, such as Chinese.) A recent approach to this problem has been **bimodal** fitting, in which the child receives a CI in one ear, and a conventional hearing aid in the other. This appears to improve children's perception of intonation contours (Straatman, Rietveld, Beijen, Mylanus, & Mens, 2010). Bimodal fitting may also benefit children's language development (discussed in more detail in the next sections) more than bilateral cochlear implantation (Nittrouer & Chapman, 2009).

Language Development

Problems in acquiring syntax and semantics and in using these skills to develop proficiency in reading and writing are much more significant factors in the ability of children with hearing loss to succeed educationally and vocationally than is their typical articulation disability. Historically, the reading abilities of older children and adults who are deaf found that their reading ability never surpassed that of third-grade hearing children (Scheetz, 2012). Almost 1,000 high school students with hearing impairments recently completed the reading comprehension subtest of the Stanford Achievement Test; their median performance was equivalent to that of a typical fourth-grade student (Kaderavek & Pakulski, 2007).

It is important to note, however, that individual children with profound hearing impairment, even prior to the advent of cochlear implants, have achieved good reading proficiency (Kaderavek & Pakulski, 2007). Chapter 10 reminds us that mastery of reading and writing is inextricably linked to knowledge of the oral language system, a system to which the child with hearing impairment has impeded access. On a positive note, children using implants have recently been shown to demonstrate a higher level of reading achievement than children using conventional hearing aids, particularly if they are implanted within the first two years of life.

Lexical Development

Some of the problems that children who are deaf experience with both oral and written language are due to depressed vocabulary skills. Classroom instruction is simply unable to provide students who are deaf with the roughly 3,000 words per year that a hearing child acquires by merely overhearing or reading new words in context. Historically, adults who are deaf (those who would have grown up without the benefits of CIs) tend to have lexical abilities more typical of a fourth-grade student with normal hearing (Paul, 2009). In younger individuals, Sarant, Holt, Dowell, Rickards, and Blamey (2009) found that almost 70 percent of the children they tracked, whether they used CIs or conventional hearing aids, were functioning below age level. When children are implanted before 1 year of age, their progress in acquiring first words and two-word combinations may still lag behind that of peers with normal hearing, but proceeds in roughly the same way (Nott, Cowan, Brown, & Wigglesworth, 2009).

Grammatical Development

A description of the types of syntactic structures that pose particular problems for English-speaking students who are deaf was made possible by a historic series of studies carried out by Quigley and his co-workers (for details, see Quigley & Paul, 1987). In general, students who are deaf have trouble comprehending many of the same structures that are troublesome for normally developing children: constructions that violate typical subject–verb–object (S–V–O) patterns in English, such as passives, embedded clauses, and questions (Friedmann & Szterman, 2011). Students who are deaf, however, also have particular problems with modals, verb auxiliaries, infinitives, and gerunds. Even with cochlear implantation and intensive auditory-oral education, grammatical skills in children who are deaf appear to grow more slowly than vocabulary skills (Geers, Moog, Biedenstein, Brenner, & Hayes, 2009). This may be because some aspects of English morphosyntax (such as function words and grammatical endings on words) are still difficult to hear and/or produce, even with a cochlear implant. Additionally, the mastery of sentence-level syntactic structure may rely on good auditory memory skills; hearing impairment is thought to depress children's auditory memory skill development (Pisoni & Cleary, 2003). The combined effects of such difficulties can be observed in the following typical writing samples, taken from Scheetz (2012, pages 178–180):

> My pet. I have dog name is Rickey and my sisters with Rickey. Play green ball fun Rickey. I want playground. Than Rickey bath finish next ready Rickey favorite feed eat all and water. Than and Rickey little bed soft sleep (*writing sample from a 5th-grade child who is deaf*)

> My brother ask my family talk about buy new kitten. My brother said "please buy pet kitten" then my family said "fine." My brother was happy. My family and brother in car. They go to animal store. My brother favorite black kitten. My brother was buy kitten. My brother want name kitten is Lucky. (*writing sample from a 10th-grade student who is deaf*)

> Anyway, life is not always perfect. I wish I can rewind my whole life and do it the right way without break somebody's heart. Not only that, it can be relate to school, family, friend and yourself. Like, while you in school, you got one big fat F on your test. That grade pull everything down, and you want to retake it. Some teacher don't approve it, but if you got it retake then you're lucky. If not, then it is hard to keep up with a good work. (*writing sample from 11th-grade student who is deaf*)

The repetitive style and overuse of simple sentence types that characterize these writing samples may reflect dependence on classroom drills for the development of syntactic proficiency. This instruction typically focuses on simple sentences. There has been some concern that overemphasis on grammar sacrifices larger concerns, such as the use of language to communicate effectively (McAnally, Rose, & Quigley, 2007). Emphasis on simple sentence structures may also affect both reading and writing ability. The writing of older students who are hearing impaired often lacks the more sophisticated elements found in secondary school efforts (Yoshinaga-Itano, Snyder, & Mayberry, 1996). This pattern in complicated by the fact that almost a quarter of all students who are deaf come from non-English-speaking households and are learning English as a second language (Gallaudet Research Institute, 2008).

It is most tempting to tackle the kinds of writing errors seen above by emphasizing appropriate use of articles, helping verbs, and so on. However, Schirmer (2000, 2001) notes the very age-appropriate text-construction abilities that children who are deaf can show when they are taught that writing involves more than use of grammatically correct sentences. The following passage provides a strong contrast to the writing deficiencies exemplified in the previous examples:

> Being born into a family of hearing people, my exposure to the Deaf community was minimal. . . . One summer, I made the decision to go to Youth Leadership Camp for Deaf high school students. At first, I had some aversion to going to the camp because it was outside the safe circle of my friends. . . . But I learned very much about friends, teamwork, and unity. When I returned to school, I felt more involved and closer to many deaf people. We were all the same, deaf. We were a minority in America, so we had to stick together for support and unity. I realized that this is what Deaf community means. The unity of the deaf people, a group of people together, knowing each other, and having a connection despite any distance. (*Schirmer, 2001, p. 82*)

Reading and Writing Skills

We have used writing samples to illustrate some of the specific types of linguistic errors made by children who are deaf. Many can be tracked back to either depressed vocabulary skill or difficulties in mastering grammatical rules. However, additional factors can impact the literacy outcomes for children who are deaf. In an alphabetic language, such as English, phonological awareness ability is critical to decoding the individual letter strings to identify target words. Early cochlear implantation appears to aid children with development of phonological awareness skills (Johnson & Goswami, 2010). Additionally, children who are deaf show diminished ability to perform morphological segmentation and definition, a useful skill in decoding newly encountered vocabulary items (Gaustad, Kelly, Payne, & Lylak, 2002).

Pragmatic Skills

Fewer studies been done to examine pragmatic development in children who are hearing-impaired or deaf. However, it seems likely that diminished access to language input impacts pragmatic development, and some research confirms this problem. Pragmatic skills were impaired in one cohort of children with hearing impairment, regardless of whether the child had a CI or a conventional hearing aid (Thagard, Hilsmier, & Easterbrooks, 2011). Critically, the level of pragmatic skill predicted the children's academic progress in mainstreamed classes. Thus, it is important that children be helped with the broader pragmatic aspects of language use that may be missed in hearing impairment.

Educational Approaches to the Development of Language in Children Who Are Deaf

The dramatic portrayal of students attending a school for the deaf seen in the Oscar-winning movie *Children of a Lesser God* (1986) is not the typical educational environment for most students with profound hearing impairment today. Now, approximately three-quarters of children who are deaf or severely hearing impaired attend local public schools (Antia, Reed, & Kreimeyer, 2005). Additionally, most children who are deaf or profoundly hearing impaired are born into hearing families and thus are not exposed to **American Sign Language (ASL)** early in life.

There are three primary communication methods used in deaf education: **oral/aural, total communication,** and **bilingual/bicultural (bi-bi).** Each has undergone relative waves of popularity (Scheetz, 2012). In the United States, the oral/aural approach is historically the oldest (Easterbrooks & Baker, 2002). Proponents of an oralist approach to deaf education have believed that children who are deaf are best served by instruction in lipreading, in maximum use of residual hearing (through amplification and auditory training), and in articulation to improve their speech. This approach is now typically associated with the label **auditory verbal therapy**, which has emerging documentation of efficacy, particularly in the education of children who receive cochlear implants (Rhoades, 2006).

Some educators became dismayed in the 1960s and 1970s by the relatively poor academic achievement of graduates of older, orally focused programs and developed approaches to support oral language input with manual sign systems; this combination is called **total communication**. A number of sign systems were developed to convey manual representations of English sentence structure along with spoken language (and alternative systems were developed for speakers of other languages). These systems translate words and grammatical morphemes used in spoken English into easily visible hand configurations and gestures. An overview of the most commonly used sign systems is provided by Scheetz (2012). Most of the American systems share some common features: They generally adapt some American Sign Language (or Ameslan) signs for vocabulary, invent new signs to convey grammatical concepts not expressed by discrete signs in ASL (such as articles, auxiliary verbs, and inflectional morphology), and produce sentences that duplicate the syntactic structure of English. The result tends to resemble what might occur if one attempted to speak a foreign oral language, such as French, simply by placing French lexical items into an English grammatical framework (e.g., "mon frère's voiture" for the phrase "my brother's car" rather than the correct form: "la voiture de mon frère"). For example, the sentence "*The* boy *is* eat*ing*" contains a number of elements not found in ASL (those in italics). Sign systems typically have invented new signs for those elements and would sign the phrase as written, but the ASL version would more closely resemble "Boy eat-eat-eat" in English; reduplicated movement in ASL signals the progressive aspect, and the article is not necessary.

Signed communication continues to play an important role even in the everyday lives of children who have received cochlear implants. A recent study (Hyde & Punch, 2011) found that up to 20 percent of parents and 30 percent of teachers continued to use signed communication with children who have CIs. Multiple reasons for using combined input were given, ranging from the pragmatic (e.g., a need to communicate with the child when the CI was not functioning or available [they must be removed for swimming, bathing, etc.]), to the educational (more input was thought to foster better language development) to the social (use of sign was thought to aid the child in maintaining a Deaf identity).

One manual system is distinct in its orientation and is more closely associated with oralist approaches to deaf education: **Cued speech,** used by relatively fewer children who are deaf and their teachers/parents, uses hand shapes near the mouth to disambiguate lipreading. Like other signed systems, it is also being used in some settings to augment the benefits provided by cochlear implants (Leybaert & LaSasso, 2010).

Although TC was the most popular approach to deaf education throughout the last part of the past century (Scheetz, 2012), there are some difficulties associated with its implementation. Parents are often encouraged to use sign systems at home to increase the language input to the child. However, both parents and teachers often find it difficult to communicate fluently in what is, to them, a foreign language, and many adults fail to include important grammatical features of English in their signed input, thus limiting the child's exposure to the language (Easterbrooks & Baker, 2002).

A movement that gathered strength some time after total communication approaches emerged is **bilingual-bicultural (bi-bi) deaf education** (Easterbrooks & Baker, 2002). Bi-bi programs are modeled after English as a Second Language (ESL) and foreign-language immersion programs, and they emphasize the positive aspects of Deaf culture. (We capitalize Deaf when it is used to describe the community and culture of individuals who are deaf or hearing impaired.) There is some evidence to suggest that knowing ASL as a first language may aid children who are deaf to develop better skills with the English language, in much the same way that knowing a first language provides a basis for learning others. Many years ago, Strong and Prinz (1997) correlated students' abilities to use ASL with improved literacy levels, regardless of whether ASL had been learned from deaf parents. These data suggest that acquisition of ASL, a natural language, supports second language skills in English more strongly than does an artificial system modeled on English. Thus, in bi-bi education ASL is used as the primary language of instruction in order to instill it as the child's first language, and Deaf culture is an important component in the curriculum. English language skills are taught after competence in ASL is reached. In a survey conducted over the past decade, slightly over 40 percent of students in U.S. residential and day-school deaf education programs were using some form of bi-bi programming, while a large portion of the remainder were using manually coded English/total communication (LaSasso & Lollis, 2003).

While historical debates have concentrated more on the types of approaches used in deaf education, more current discussion addresses its timing. Increasingly large amounts of data suggest that early identification, amplification, or implantation before a year of age and early toddler language stimulation programs are associated with the best language outcomes for children with severe to profound permanent hearing loss (Moog & Geers, 2010).

Any communicative system that maximizes the opportunity for fully developed language interaction between children who are deaf and those around them is likely to improve their progress in mastering language. Parental socioeconomic status and involvement in the child's educational programming also correlate with the development of language proficiency. Connor and Zwolan (2004) found socioeconomic status to be a more potent predictor of literacy outcomes in children who eventually received cochlear implants than method of communication, although children who were using total communication prior to implantation had higher vocabularies before surgical intervention. Children from poorer households tend to have less good literacy outcomes, for a number of reasons, including parental support for language and literacy interventions and monitoring of implant or hearing-aid function. Racial and economic disparities have emerged in other studies tracking outcomes of hearing impairment in childhood as well, both in the United States and elsewhere (Barton, Stacey, Fortnum, & Summerfield, 2006; Hyde & Power, 2006).

Neither ASL nor any particular manual systems have emerged as the most efficacious vehicle for supporting acquisition of English skills in children who are deaf. Additionally, White (2007) notes an increasing tendency for parents to opt for their children to be placed in programs with an oral/aural focus, rather than in sign language–based educational options, which were much more popular in earlier years.

Kaderavek and Pakulski (2007) conclude that both sign language–educated and oral/aurally educated students can have excellent literacy outcomes; they believe that the difference between successful and unsuccessful achievement lies in the strategies used to support children's later literacy development, rather than in the modality used to teach literacy skills.

Acquisition of ASL as a First Language

Many of the relatively few U.S. children who are deaf and who are born to deaf parents grow up learning ASL as their first language. American Sign Language is a distinct language within the scope of the world's languages, with its own syntactic, semantic, and configurational rules. For excellent coverage of the linguistic and psycholinguistic properties of ASL, see Emmorey and Lane (2000), and Easterbrooks and Baker (2002). ASL is not based on English grammar and has rules for expressing S–V–O relationships, tense, pluralization, and so on, that are different from the rules for these concepts in English. American Sign Language, like other sign languages of the world, is not transparently meaningful to speakers of English or users of other sign languages. That is, one cannot easily follow an ASL conversation without knowing the specific rules of ASL.

The acquisition of ASL by children learning ASL from birth (and by some children with normal hearing exposed to both oral and signed language by one parent having normal hearing and one parent who is deaf [Prinz & Prinz, 1981]) essentially confirms that the language disabilities of hearing-impaired children stem from deficient input rather than other possible causes. That is, children learning ASL as a first language generally develop their first signed words at approximately the same age as children who are acquiring oral language. There are marked similarities in the courses of ASL and oral language development (Holowka, Brosseau-Lapré, & Pettito, 2002). The two-word stage in early ASL usage is characterized by semantic relations similar to those seen in early spoken language productions. Overregularizations of grammatical features and overextensions of vocabulary meaning have been noted. Moreover, accelerated use of vocabulary and combinatorial language has been observed when ASL-using infants are compared to oral-language learning infants of similar ages (Bonvillian, Orlansky, & Novack, 1983). A concise review of studies that have examined acquisition of sign language as a first language is provided by Barnes (2010).

Over the past decade, the emerging technology of cochlear implantation was seen by some as endangering the future of both sign languages and Deaf culture. This debate has not been resolved (Sparrow, 2010; Pray & Jordon, 2010). However, this debate now occurs within a changing demographic context. Most children born deaf are not born to deaf/ Deaf parents, and an increasingly large number of American children who are deaf come from an increasingly diverse set of linguistic and cultural backgrounds. Thus, the future of Deaf culture may be determined by many factors that go beyond the impacts of cochlear implant technology. A recent survey suggests that many adults who are deaf see themselves and coming generations as bicultural and bilingual, bridging the perspectives of the hearing and Deaf cultures, and their respective languages (Gale, 2011).

Teaching Sign Language to Typically Developing Babies with Normal Hearing

There has been increased interest in using sign language to advance the early language development of typically developing, hearing toddlers. In part, this has been based on research suggesting that babies may be capable of using manual languages before they have developed the skills necessary to produce differentiated speech sounds and thus may profit from deliberate efforts by parents to provide them with an "easier" form of early communication. Preliminary reports of the effectiveness of teaching sign to typically developed babies was conducted by Acredolo and Goodwyn (2002), which was translated into a number of popular products, such as BabySigns©. A recent review by Barnes (2010) concludes that the long-term language development gains promised by such products probably do not exceed those provided by simply creating more opportunities for infants and their parents to engage in the typical range communicative interactions that foster later language and literacy skills.

Sign Language and the Brain

Chapter 1 surveyed the neurological substrates that underlie oral language development and use. What happens when a child learns a visual rather than an auditory language? When visual input has linguistic significance, as do signs for a native deaf signer, this input is processed by areas of the brain typically used for processing spoken language, in the dominant (normally left) hemisphere, even though the nondominant hemisphere is normally activated during visuospatial tasks (Sakai, Tatsuno, Suzuki, Kimura, & Ichida, 2005). However, because a language such as ASL does require some visuospatial processing that is not required by oral languages, native deaf signers appear to recruit both the left and right hemisphere during sentence processing (Newman, Bavelier, Corina, Jezzard, & Neville, 2001). Neuroimaging studies have also shown strong parallels in language processing patterns by people who learn either an oral or signed language as their first language, during the critical period, and those who learn either later in life, and do not achieve native-like proficiency (Malaia & Wilbur, 2010). Brain damage also affects linguistic processing in sign language users in ways predicted from study of hearing individuals (for review, see Peperkamp & Mehler, 1999).

Are *You* at Risk for Hearing Impairment?

Before leaving this section, we would like to note that there is one segment of the population in most Western societies in which the incidence of hearing loss is *increasing* over recent years: the age range between adolescence and young adulthood (Shargorodsky, Curhan, Curhan, & Eavey, 2010). As many as one in five adolescents may now have some measurable hearing loss. This increase appears attributable to noise exposure, caused primarily by listening to music played at too high a volume. Public awareness campaigns, such as Listen to your Buds (**www. asha.org**) are growing to educate children and teens about the damaging long-term effects of listening to overamplified music, whether through earbuds or in social contexts.

Intellectual Disability and Communicative Development

Cognitive Disability and the Language-Acquisition Process

About 1 percent of children can be classified as having an intellectual disability by performance on standardized cognitive tests. Despite increasing dissatisfaction with the use of intelligence quotients (IQ) to measure mental development, they continue to be used to define and describe this population. Previously referred to by the term *mental retardation,* the term **intellectual disability** is now preferred in most circles (Schalock et al., 2007). The American Association on Intellectual and Developmental Disabilities (AAIDD), previously the American Association on Mental Retardation, defines intellectual disability using criteria that combine evidence of depressed general intellectual functioning with limitations in adaptive behaviors in areas such as "communication, self-care, home living, social skills, community use, self-direction, health and safety, functional academics, leisure, and work" (Luckasson et al., 2002). Traditionally, mild intellectual disability may be indicated by IQ performance falling between 50 and 70; moderate degrees of disability by IQ scores of approximately 35 to 50; severe intellectual disability by IQ scores between 20 and 35; and profound intellectual impairment by scores falling below IQ 20 to 25; most individuals with intellectual disabilities are classified as mildly impaired (Owens, 2010). The majority of children with IQs below 50 have severe language problems, and children with higher IQs may still experience language disability.

Intellectual disability (ID) may result from a number of discrete etiologies. Understanding how intellectual disability affects language development specifically is made more difficult by the high prevalence of concomitant disorders. Children diagnosed with ID may also have conditions such as cerebral palsy, seizures, hearing and vision loss, and attention-deficit/hyperactivity disorder (ADHD). The subgroups of children with ID whose distinct profiles have been analyzed most intensively have been those with **Down syndrome (DS), Williams syndrome (WS),** and **fragile X (fra X) syndrome**. DS, the most common genetic cause of intellectual impairment, is characterized by relatively weaker linguistic performance than might be expected from mental age, whereas fragile X, a common inherited form of retardation, results in fewer problems with language (relative to mental age), at the expense of impaired articulation and fluency (Barnes et al., 2009). Most major syndromes of ID appear to be characterized by a variety of neuroanatomical abnormalities in the cerebral cortex, hippocampus, or other brain regions, as well as impaired neuronal connectivity (Dierssen & Ramakers, 2006).

Clinicians and theorists interested in the relation between generalized cognition and language are often intrigued by children with Williams syndrome, a rare condition in which cognition, especially visuospatial skill, is impaired but language may appear intact or even precocious (a recent summary of research on Williams syndrome is provided by Martens, Wilson, & Reutens, 2008). Over the past twenty years, this apparent dissociation between cognitive and linguistic skills has prompted some to suggest that language is a modular skill that does not rely on general intelligence. Other rare cases of supposed dissociations between cognition and language in individuals with intellectual disability have been reported (Smith & Tsimpli, 1995), but Williams syndrome appears to be the best-known condition for which this claim has been made.

The following examples from Bellugi, Mills, Jernigan, Hickok, and Galaburda (1999) contrast a child with Williams syndrome, age 17, with an IQ of 50 (sample 1), with a child having Down syndrome, age 18, with a similar IQ of 55 (sample 2):

1. Once upon a time when it was dark at night . . . the boy had a frog. The boy was looking at the frog . . . sitting on the chair, on the table, and the dog was looking through . . . looking up to the frog in a jar. That night, she sleeped and slept for a long time, the dog did. But the frog was not gonna go to sleep. The frog went out from the jar. And when the frog went out . . . the boy and the dog were still sleeping. Next morning it was beautiful in the morning. It was bright and the sun was nice and warm. Then suddenly when he opened his eyes . . . he looked at the jar and suddenly the frog was not there. The jar was empty. There was no frog to be found.

2. The frog is in the jar. The jar is on the floor. The jar is on the floor. That's it. The stool is broke. The clothes is laying there.

However, many researchers argue that, although morphosyntax is less impaired in WS than in other etiologies of ID, it is still quite impaired (see Brock, 2007; Mervis & Becerra, 2007). Children with WS are often viewed as having exceptionally sophisticated vocabulary for their mental ages, certainly more so than children with Down syndrome, but still lower than for children who are typically achieving. Children with WS are much better at mastering concrete vocabulary than words that refer to relative concepts (time, size, quantity) (Mervis & John, 2008). Other areas of language development, such as prelinguistic speech-perception skills, profiles of early vocabulary accumulation, and early pragmatic skills, show signs of delay. Children with WS are more impaired than children with DS, for example, in following nonverbal pragmatic cues, such as eye gaze (John & Mervis, 2010). Grammatical abilities, while somewhat stronger (e.g., the ability to make novel compounds) (Zukowski, 2005), still appear consistent with cognitive abilities in most cases (Mervis & Becerra, 2007), although stronger than those of Down syndrome children (Brock, 2007). Close examination reveals impairment in using specific grammatical forms, such as the passive (Perovic & Wexler, 2010). Such evidence of depressed language capacity in WS children weakens the argument for a dissociation between cognition and language, or modularity of the language faculty (see Chapter 7). Moreover, Mervis and Becerra (2007) noted strong associations between the scores that individuals with WS attain on tests of cognitive function and their language test scores. They observe that the majority of children with WS could profit from language therapy, particularly with complex vocabulary, figurative language, and pragmatics, but that most do not receive therapy unless they are making frequent grammatical errors. Brock (2007) concludes that "many of the claims [previously] made concerning language [selective preservation of] language abilities in Williams syndrome have been somewhat overstated" (p. 121).

As in other cases of ID, there has been recent interest in tracking how well individuals with WS do as they reach adulthood. While there appear to be continuing improvements in adaptive skills, language growth appears to plateau and shows relatively little growth

(Howlin, Elison, Udwin, & Stinton, 2010), unlike that seen in typical adults, who achieve steady growth in vocabulary over the lifespan, given the normal range of life experiences.

Owens (2010) has proposed a multifaceted model of the language deficit in other ID conditions. In this model, he notes that while children with ID appear to have adequate attentional capacity, they have more trouble than typical peers in attending to relevant stimuli in the immediate environment. In addition, even from infancy, children with ID appear to have difficulty processing auditory stimuli and up to 25 percent of those with Down syndrome may present with some form of auditory processing difficulty (Rondal, 2009).

Further, as input stimuli are processed, the child with ID is less able to use efficient organizational strategies to aid in storage and retrieval of linguistic information. Examples of such strategies include the creation of associations in order to help remember items and the categorization of concepts to facilitate retrieval. Applying stored knowledge to new situations requires transfer, or generalization, an area that is particularly weak in most individuals with ID. Finally, children with ID have depressed short-term and long-term memory abilities (Owens, 2010). Phonological working memory, so critical to processing spoken and written language, is also impaired (Schuchardt, Maehler, & Hasselhorn, 2011). There is evidence that auditory information is less well remembered than visual information, and that nonlinguistic input is remembered better than that containing linguistic information (see discussion in Fidler, 2005). Visual, verbal, and auditory working memory skills appear to predict individual variation in language growth for children having Down syndrome in particular (Jarrold, Baddeley, & Phillips, 2002), while gross measures of nonverbal IQ do not appear particularly informative in estimating language or speech skills (Cleland, Wood, Hardcastle, Wishart, & Timmons, 2010). Similar to typically developing toddlers, use of spontaneous manual gestures appears to predict and serve as a bridge to acquisition of early vocabulary, although the process is more protracted than seen in children without ID (Zampini & D'Odorico, 2009).

The slow rate of language development in children with ID, particularly those with Down syndrome, may leave such children with minimal language skills as the sensitive period for language acquisition draws to a close and the capacity for first-language learning diminishes (see Chapters 7 and 11). Thus, it is not surprising that early intervention, within the first three years of life, can be important in establishing necessary skills (van der Schuit, Segers, van Balkom, & Verhoeven, 2011a, b), but it must be continued in order to maintain progress. Recent support has been found for responsivity education/prelinguistic milieu teaching, which trains the toddler's use of gestures, vocalizations, and joint eye gaze during interactions with parents (Fey et al., 2006). A similar program, which emphasized use of augmentative communication strategies, such as manual signs, produced good results, particularly when the cohort of children with ID receiving the language intervention was compared to a cohort of children not receiving intensive language stimulation (van der Schuit et al., 2011a, b).

Most investigations find that children with ID seem to follow a path of linguistic development that is similar to that of typically developing children below a mental age of 10 years, whereas patterns of language ability become qualitatively different from that seen in typical development after this level has been reached. However, Chapman and colleagues (Chapman, 1999; Thordardottir, Chapman, & Wagner, 2002) have documented continued development of language abilities in adolescents with

With appropriate support such as that provided by IDEA, children with Down syndrome can achieve at levels unimaginable only a few years ago. Here, Jenny Friedman celebrates her graduation from Palatine High School with her best friend Danielle Burns. Photo courtesy of the Jenny Friedman Foundation (**www.jennyfriedmanfoundation.org**), which works to help people with special needs.

Down syndrome, partial evidence against the critical period hypothesis; thus, they argue strongly that expressive language skills should be a continued focus of intervention for adolescents and young adults with DS. In fact, many mainstreamed adolescents with ID are successfully integrated into classes through the high school years, an achievement never envisioned in prior generations.

Language Development

Children with intellectual disability typically demonstrate depressed language ability when compared with typically developing children of the same chronological age. However, researchers are more concerned with discovering the specific patterns of language production and comprehension that characterize this population and identifying possible factors that predict mastery of certain linguistic skills. Both questions have important implications for aiding the development of linguistic ability in individuals with ID.

Examination of patterns of linguistic development has yielded increasing evidence that children with diagnoses of intellectual disability demonstrate language skills best described as delayed rather than deviant. That is, their patterns of language production and comprehension closely resemble those seen in younger, typically developing children. In general, **mental ages (MAs)** are a fairly good predictor of language abilities in children with ID; however, differences may be seen between children with and without intellectual disability having identical MAs and even between cognitively impaired children matched for MA in their global language profiles (Miller, 1999). Additionally, there are some indications that this population experiences relatively disproportionate difficulty with morphosyntactic skills, at least in English (Chapman, 1999), and less relative difficulty with pragmatic linguistic abilities than would be expected from general estimates of their linguistic development.

Some specific patterns have been noted for children with Down syndrome, about 10 to 12 percent of whom may also be diagnosed with autism spectrum disorder, covered later in this chapter (see a recent review by Rondal, 2009). The average child with DS may lag behind age-matched typically developing peers by 20 months by age 3, and by more than 2 years by age 4 (Berglund, Eriksson, & Johansson, 2001). Rondal (2009) estimates that it may take many children with Down syndrome four to five years to achieve a mental age (MA) of 18 months, and fifteen years to achieve an MA of 6 years. However, individual children with Down syndrome are capable of a higher level of functioning, given appropriate stimulation and intervention.

From the earliest stages of language development, there is tremendous heterogeneity in the early vocabulary development of children with DS; over one two-year study, some children acquired fewer than fifty words, while others acquired more than 400 (Vandereet, Maes, Lembrechts, & Zink, 2010). However, the slow rate of vocabulary development overall becomes more evident if contrasted with the rate of vocabulary development in typical children that was described in Chapter 4. One of the specific child word learning principles mentioned in Chapter 4 appears severely compromised in DS: the new name/nameless category principle that allows typically developing children to quickly assume that any newly heard word should be linked to any new and unnamed concept being observed or illustrated in an interaction (Rondal, 2009). Vocabulary growth may be aided when children are provided with bimodal (oral plus manual gesture or signs) input and support (Vandereet, Maes, Lembrechts, & Zink, 2010). A recent study contrasted the interactions of children with DS and children with ASD (autism spectrum disorders) and their mothers. Children with DS had no problems interacting with their mothers over activities and objects of joint attention (as opposed to children with ASD), but children with DS did not appear to be able to track symbolic references (either labels or pronouns) during play very well (such as responding appropriately to the mother's request to "turn it around" in reference to a toy they were playing with) (Adamson, Bakeman, Deckner, & Romski, 2009).

Studies of later vocabulary development have produced varied results, with some studies showing vocabulary either higher, lower, or commensurate with nonverbal cognitive skills (Roberts et al., 2007). Children with Down syndrome also show delays in expressive syntactic development that exceed their delays in lexical acquisition (Finestack & Abbeduto, 2010). They are particularly likely to omit function words and verbs when compared to typically developing children who have similar mean length of utterance (MLU) profiles (Chapman, 1999).

Children with Down syndrome tend to show poorer linguistic ability overall than children with similar mental ages but with differing etiologies of intellectual disability. Additionally, expressive language skills lag behind comprehension and nonverbal cognitive skills (Chapman et al., 2002). Berglund and colleagues (2001) commented, "Children with Down syndrome in general need a somewhat larger vocabulary than children in the (typically developing) group to reach a corresponding level of grammar" (p. 190). Syntactic comprehension ability predicts the narrative performance of children with DS, suggesting that they attempt to construct more ambitious stories than MLU-matched, younger comparison children (Miles & Chapman, 2002).

By the time they are older, children with Down syndrome construct more sophisticated narratives than might be predicted by their language ages (Boudreau & Chapman, 2000) and create written narratives appropriate to peers matched by ability to read single words on standardized batteries (Kay-Raining Bird, Cleave, White, Pike, & Helmkay, 2008). In addition, in some cases, relatively strong receptive vocabulary skills are observed in adolescents with Down syndrome, as they acquire a broader array of life experiences (Roberts et al., 2007), although increasing deficits may be observed in grammatical comprehension, verbal working memory skills, and unsupported narrative tasks (Chapman, 2006). Some language skills may decline with age, when many individuals with Down syndrome develop Alzheimer's disease, a form of dementia that impairs linguistic function, described in Chapter 11 (Rondal, 2009).

Conversely, over the span of development, pragmatic skills tend to remain a relative strength for most children with Down syndrome, although, as noted, a minority of them are concurrently diagnosed with autism, which is characterized by great weakness in pragmatic function (Roberts et al., 2007). Some aspects of pragmatic function, such as appreciating humor, remain somewhat depressed; since most humor requires linguistic sophistication, it is not surprising that many individuals with ID find it easier to appreciate humor when it is non-verbal in nature (physical, visually supported humor (Degabriele & Walsh, 2010)). With appropriate intervention and academic support, many children with Down syndrome can achieve very well in typical school settings. Additionally, emerging data suggest that children with Down syndrome can perform as well in bilingual contexts, if appropriately supported at home and in school, as those who are reared in monolingual environments. Thus, there appears to be no reason to limit a child with DS to use of only one language to maximize language outcomes (Feltmate & Kay-Raining Bird, 2008; Edgin, Kumar, Spanó, & Nadel, 2011).

Phonological development is also atypical in individuals with Down syndrome, for multiple reasons. A few are mentioned here: In some children, the relatively enlarged tongue (macroglossia) in DS makes accurate place of articulation for speech sounds more difficult. Oral-motor abilities are also weaker than in typically developing children. The rate of hearing loss as well as auditory processing difficulties complicates representation of speech sounds, while depressed auditory memory makes storage of phonological representations more difficult (Rondal, 2009).

Fragile X syndrome, as noted, has its own distinctive but variable pattern of communicative deficit. It is the most frequent inherited cause of intellectual disability in boys; girls are affected less often and are typically less impaired in function and appearance. Affected males have characteristic physical features that become more apparent in late childhood and adolescence. At younger ages, children with fragile X may have delayed onset and development of lexical and grammatical abilities, accompanied by evidence of oral-motor impairment (poor sucking and feeding skills and developmental articulation errors). Spiridigliozzi, Lachiewicz, Mirrett, and McConkie-Rosell (2001) provide an overview of the communicative profiles commonly seen in children with fragile X. Some of its symptoms resemble those in autism spectrum disorder (ASD, see following section), such as social withdrawal. In fact, up to 25 percent of individuals with fragile X are also diagnosed with autism (Price, Roberts, Vandergrift, & Martin, 2007). At young ages (Roberts, Mirrett, Anderson, Burchinal, & Neebe, 2002), the social interaction of children with fragile X does not appear as delayed or deviant as that of children with autism. However, a more recent study found that more than half of a large sample of young children with fragile X were nonverbal and were learning to communicate using augmentative communication strategies (Brady, Skinner, Roberts, & Hennon, 2006).

In addition to lexical and syntactic delays that seem relatively well correlated with nonverbal cognitive skills, boys with fragile X also have speech rate and articulation patterns that may limit their intelligibility and often demonstrate **perseveration** (repetition) of topics and phrases in conversation with others (Murphy & Abbeduto, 2007). In comparisons among groups of boys with fragile X, Down syndrome, and typical development, Price and colleagues (2007) observed depression in a number of linguistic domains, including vocabulary, grammatical morphology, and sentence construction, as well as in language comprehension for boys with fragile X, both with and without concomitant autism. The children with fragile X slightly outperformed those with Down syndrome, but all clearly warranted intervention based on each child's specific profile of strengths and weaknesses. Weaknesses in grammatical ability continue through adolescence (Finestack & Abbeduto, 2010); teens with fragile X continue to outperform peers with Down syndrome, but both groups have significantly impaired language skills when compared to those of typical same-age peers.

Teaching Language to Children with Intellectual Disability

The different types of ID conditions covered in this section each come with a fairly distinctive profile of difficulties, although there are some overlapping areas of weakness. One question that has not yet been answered is whether different subtypes of ID respond differently to different language therapy approaches (Fidler, Philofsky, & Hepburn, 2007). Evidence suggests that language intervention results are maximized when treatment begins as early as possible, even shortly after birth, if a syndrome such as Down is identified (Fey et al., 2006). Owens (2010) summarizes some of the relevant considerations and approaches to language intervention with children who have intellectual disability.

A recent intervention study suggests that accumulation of a basic vocabulary of at least 50 words, often followed by a vocabulary "spurt" such as seen in many typically developing children (see Chapter 4), appears to "bootstrap" the development of multiword utterances and grammar (van der Schuit, Segers, van Balkom, & Verhoeven, 2011a, b).

Generalization of language skills outside the clinical setting to spontaneous everyday usage is particularly troublesome for this group of children, whether the generalization requires either minimal or substantial differences between known instances and novel circumstances. Therapy will be most effective with this group, as with other groups of language-handicapped children, if it is pragmatic in orientation, emphasizing functional communication as a primary goal. In other words, careful attention should be paid to selecting vocabulary and syntax needed to communicate in the daily environment. Some efficacy has been shown for use of the Hanen program ("It Takes Two to Talk") (Girolametto & Weitzman, 2006) with young children who have Down syndrome; this program also emphasizes functional contexts for parent–child interaction that can stimulate language growth.

In severe cases of communicative impairment, the use of **augmentative or alternative communication (AAC)** systems or devices may be suggested (for reviews of considerations in such a therapeutic approach, see Beukelman & Mirenda, 2005; Romski, Sevcik, Cheslock, & Barton, 2006). Examples of such alternatives to oral communication are the use of communication boards, which allow children to select symbols or pictures to communicate with others, and the use of sign systems, discussed previously. Although they are not symbolically or cognitively less complex than spoken language, sign systems may provide somewhat of a "teachability" advantage; that is, the child's hands may be shaped and his or her production reinforced more easily than attempts at intelligible vocalizations. Many children supported in early intervention through nonverbal systems later progress to oral communication, despite some professional and family concerns that use of augmentative systems will depress the initiative to acquire oral skills. In fact, a recent meta-analysis of studies that examined the impact of AAC on concomitant development of speaking ability found that almost 90 percent of cases demonstrated gains in speech after intervention that included AAC (Millar, Light, & Schlosser, 2006).

Parent counseling may facilitate language gains, as in other disorders. For instance, Down syndrome is typically diagnosed early, unlike some other etiologies of ID. This permits early intervention that focuses on facilitative parent–child interactions. Other chapters in this text have emphasized the contributions of parental interaction style to children's language development, as well as the role that children themselves play in eliciting patterns of conversation with their parents. Because of this bidirectional set of influences, parents of children with ID, as well as parents of other children with delayed or disordered language development, may use a greater number of imperatives and ask fewer questions than do parents of children who are developing more typically. This is presumably because the children respond better to these types of utterances. However, such styles can be linked to slower progress in language even in typical populations; hence, findings from such studies can help to counsel parents in using input styles that are more helpful to children's continued language growth (de Falco, Venuti, Esposito, & Bornstein, 2011).

Autism Spectrum Disorder/Pervasive Developmental Disorder

General Characteristics

Of the conditions discussed in this chapter, perhaps none has seen such an explosion of research publications over the last few years than autism, with literally thousands of new peer-reviewed articles appearing since the last edition. A person seeking to amalgamate even small topics within the study of ASD will quickly become familiar with the somewhat dispiriting analogy of digging out a beach with a spoon. In the sections that follow, we will endeavor to summarize the major recent findings in ASD, with particular attention to language, the subject of this text.

The **autism spectrum disorders (ASDs),** sometimes called **pervasive developmental disorders (PDDs),** include a number of conditions that have both distinguishing and overlapping characteristics. All PDDs are characterized by impairments in social reciprocity and communication, and by behavioral rigidity. ASD/PDD includes **autism, Asperger syndrome, Rett syndrome,** and **pervasive developmental disorder— not otherwise specified (PDD-NOS),** as well as disintegrative disorder (Landa, 2007). Current diagnostic criteria for autism revolve around four major sets of communicative features: (1) either significantly delayed onset of spoken language or its total absence; (2) impaired patterns of conversational initiation and response; (3) stereotypical and repetitive use of any language skills that the child has; and (4) lack of imaginative or socially imitative play that would be appropriate to the child's developmental level (Landa, 2007). Play with toys is also usually impaired (Toth, Dawson, Meltzoff, Greenson, & Fein, 2007). Additional social impairments revolve around what are generally perceived to be pragmatic aspects of language and nonverbal behavior, such as appropriate use of nonverbal gaze, particularly joint attention with others to aspects of the contexts surrounding interactions, facial expression, and so on, as well as an inability to share interests or enjoyment with others. These features are often described under the rubric of "lack of social or emotional reciprocity" by the *Diagnostic and Statistical Manual-IV* (DSM-IV; American Psychiatric Association, 2000).[0]

Until relatively recently, an additional criterion for the diagnosis of autism was onset of symptoms prior to 30 months of age. However, this criterion has been eliminated, as evidence of a wider age of onset has become apparent (Leonard et al., 2010). Most parents become concerned by their children's behaviors before age 2, usually on the basis of both language delay and abnormal interpersonal behaviors (Jonsdottir, Saemundsen, Antonsdottir, Sigurdardottir, & Olason, 2011), although firm diagnosis is still not made in the majority of cases until age 3 to 4 (Mandell, Novak, & Zubritsky, 2006). Children with more obvious language impairment and aberrant motor behaviors such as hand flapping or toe walking may be identified up to a year earlier (Mandell et al., 2006), while children with milder symptoms may be identified later (Jonsdottir et al., 2011).

However, studies are now identifying clear prelinguistic markers of later ASD diagnosis to which parents may be responding, including the child's lack of responsivity to his or her name and aberrant eye-gaze behaviors during retrospective analyses of videos of first birthday celebrations (Nadig et al., 2007; Sullivan et al., 2007). By 18 to 24 months, patterns of gazing, gesturing, and communicating distinguish children with ASD from typically developing children and those with other types of developmental delay (Wetherby, Watt, Morgan, & Shumway, 2007). For this reason, the American Academy of Pediatrics is now recommending that pediatricians screen for autism at 18 and 24 month well-baby visits, using one of the assessment tools being developed to assess the communicative and social behaviors that are usually compromised in ASD (Gupta et al., 2007; Zwaigenbaum et al., 2009).

As we will discuss further in a later section, there is growing evidence of a genetic basis for autism, and younger siblings of children already diagnosed with ASD are at elevated risk to be identified with autism as well. This has permitted a growing number of prospective studies in which such children are followed to identify a range of precursor or associated behaviors (the so-called "broad autism phenotype," or BAP) that might permit earlier identification of ASD, as well as contribute to a better understanding of the nature of the disorder (Zwaigenbaum et al., 2007). These studies have identified a number of early characteristics of autism, including delays in fine and gross motor development as well as receptive and expressive language delays (Landa & Garrett-Mayer, 2006). Some studies of siblings of children with ASD have also tracked older siblings to identify BAP characteristics that may inform the nature of autism and how its component symptoms are genetically transmitted (Ben-Yizhak, Yirmiya, Seidman, Alon, Lord, & Sigman, 2011).

Some children with autism appear to develop language normally, but then regress in communicative ability; Jones and Campbell (2010) report estimates that up to one-half of children with ASD are reported by parents to have shown regression, which may occur in other disorders that sometimes share overlapping features with autism, such as acquired epileptic aphasia (also called Landau-Kleffner syndrome); regression may in fact be due to other forms of epilepsy (seizure disorder) that emerge over time in many children first diagnosed with ASD. Jones and Campbell's study found regression in roughly 30 percent of the cohort that they followed, but was not able to identify firm predictors of regression. Later

---

[0]The DSM-V is currently being readied for release in 2013. As currently proposed, it will contain some changes relevant to the discussion of autism in this chapter. In particular, two diagnoses will be removed, that of Asperger Syndrome and PDD-NOS. There is disagreement about some of these changes (see, for example, Wing, Gould, & Gillberg, 2011). In particular, changes in how Asperger's syndrome is diagnosed concern some professionals and families with children with ASD (Kaland, 2011; Mattila et al., 2011).

language prognosis may be less favorable for children who have experienced regression (Bernabei, Cerquiglini, Cortesi, & D'Ardia, 2007).

Rett syndrome is also characterized by autistic behaviors, intellectual disability, and sudden regression in communicative abilities in early childhood (see Bartolotta, Zipp, Simpkins, & Glazewski, 2011; Van Acker, Loncola, & Van Acker, 2005). The disorder affects girls and is caused by a specific gene mutation. In infancy, symptoms also include motor delay and sleep dysfunction, and progress over early childhood to include motor rigidity and loss of hand control, seizures, and scoliosis (deformation of the spine). Unfortunately, girls affected with Rett syndrome often die in adolescence or early adulthood. When compared to the literature on ASD in general, there currently are limited data to inform language intervention for girls with Rett syndrome (Sigafoos et al., 2009).

A differential diagnosis of autism must distinguish it from intellectual disability and the other PDD disorders, such as Asperger syndrome (AS). These distinctions are often subtle. Children with AS demonstrate similar but much milder patterns of social and pragmatic indifference than those seen in autism, restricted and repetitive interest patterns, and do not have as obvious a delay in very early stages of language or cognitive development (Klin, McPartland, & Volkmar, 2005). Thus, AS is particularly difficult to distinguish from cases of high-functioning autism (HFA; Noterdaeme, Wriedt, & Höhne, 2010) and may lie along a continuum of symptom severity rather than representing a distinct disorder (this is why a current proposal for the revision of the DSM would remove AS as a separate diagnostic category). However, distinguishing among the possible subtypes of the ASDs/PDDs is of little value unless it leads us to a better understanding of how these conditions arise, how they are best treated, and how we can best estimate treatment outcomes.

Causation

When it was first described years ago, autism was presumed by many to have its origins in a disturbance of the parent–child relationship; since then, there has been growing agreement that the disorder in fact has an organic (physical) basis. Both autism and PDD appear to be highly heritable genetic disorders, and work to identify the actual gene or genes responsible for autism has been facilitated by the Autism Genome Project Consortium (Szatmari et al., 2007), which has already identified a large number of candidate genes (Betancur, 2011; see also Yang & Gill, 2007). The heterogeneity of individual profiles in ASD and PDD makes it likely that it is *not* a single, unitary disorder, with one single cause.

In addition to the high number of siblings of children with ASD who also develop ASD themselves, a number of studies note that there is a disproportionate incidence of other childhood language disorders in the families of children with autism (Constantino, Zhang, Frazier, Abbacchi, & Law, 2010). Constantino and colleagues found that approximately 11 percent of siblings could be classified with ASD using traditional criteria, while an additional 20 percent had language delays, some of which displayed ASD-like characteristics. However, research to identify a gene that would link specific language impairment (SLI; see following section) and autism has not yet yielded a likely candidate (Bishop, 2010). Some research components of classic genetic studies are limited by the particulars of autism: Few autistic people marry and have children of their own, and adoption studies are rare. Nonetheless, ongoing research has identified candidate regions for the genetic deficit in autism, although it is possible that the array of features that characterize ASDs may be caused by multiple different genes.

The precise nature of the underlying neuropsychological deficit in ASD is still a matter of great dispute. A variety of cerebral cortical differences have also been found across studies comparing individuals with autism to peers without ASD. A major finding has been evidence of accelerated brain growth during the time period in which symptoms are first identified (Courchesne, Campbell, & Solso, 2011). Advances in brain imaging continue to improve investigation of the potential neural substrates in ASD. To date, anatomical findings include atypicalities in brain weight and size, particularly in regions such as the corpus callosum, cerebellum, superior temporal gyrus, and hippocampus. Atypical growth trajectories in brain areas, such as an early overgrowth in frontal cortex, as well as later degeneration of brain regions in cortex and amygdala have been identified (Courchesne, Campbell, & Solso, 2011). Researchers have also found evidence of potential reduction in connectivity among brain regions that may be compatible with excessively rapid early brain growth (Minshew & Keller, 2010; Wass, 2011).

The subtle neurological differences that have been reported do not readily predict why children with autism demonstrate the particular behaviors that they do. Some electrophysiological studies have detected abnormalities in the processing of language and nonverbal auditory signals, as well as face recognition by children with ASD (Corbett et al., 2009). It has been difficult to carry out functional processing and imaging studies with children who have ASD, because of rather obvious behavioral limitations that often limits study to rather high-functioning individuals with ASD and the fact that certain well-developed neuroimaging techniques for examining language processing are not typically approved for use with children. Thus, at this point, it is difficult to locate the neurological substrates that produce the specific social, linguistic, and cognitive symptoms that so classically describe autism.

Even as we examine the neurological bases for autism spectrum disorders, it is still unclear how such deficits arise. Because epidemiological surveys suggest a growing number of children diagnosed with ASD/PDD syndromes, concerns have been voiced about the possible role of immunizations and vaccinations in triggering autistic syndrome onset. In prior editions of this text, we have repeatedly provided evidence to support the professional consensus that PDD is *not* caused by reactions to infant immunizations (such as measles-mumps-rubella—MMR) nor any of the components in their preparation; this evidence continues to grow, while the data supporting the initial hypothesis have now been discredited and retracted for a number of reasons (Child Health Alert, 2010). An unfortunate consequence of this unfounded hypothesis was a decline in the number of infants receiving immunization against dangerous and potentially fatal or handicapping childhood diseases. Moreover, there appears to have been a long-term trend in the improved differential diagnosis of PDDs from other conditions, particularly intellectual disability; as the apparent prevalence rates for autism rise, those for ID appear to be falling at an equivalent rate (Fombonne, 2005).

Specific Social and Communicative Weaknesses in Autism Spectrum Disorder

A unique constellation of weaknesses appears to underlie most cases of autism spectrum disorder: failure to acquire and use joint attentional skills, symbol use, and **theory of mind**.

Joint Attention.   Deficits in joint attention are seen when a child has difficulty in orienting to or attending to a social partner, flexibly shifting eye gaze between people and objects in the environment, following the gaze or pointing behavior of others, or getting the attention of others to initiate interaction (Mundy & Burnette, 2005). In the first study that examined possible prelinguistic precursors of ASD diagnosis, Osterling and Dawson (1994) analyzed first-birthday videotapes of children later diagnosed with the disorder. Even at this young age, the children showed a noticeable lack of pointing and showing activity and did not look at the faces of others or respond as frequently when people called their names when compared to typically developing children. Continued study of such retrospective sources of information, studies of young children with ASD, as well as experimental study of younger siblings at risk for ASD have shown early impairment in these crucial skills (Meindl & Cannella-Malone, 2011). Ability to respond to bids for joint attention is strongly linked to language development in young children with ASD (Murray, Creaghead, Manning-Courtney, Shear, Bean, & Prendeville, 2008).

Symbol Use.   As Chapter 1 noted, language is an inherently symbolic behavior. Children with ASD/PDD appear to have particular difficulty in learning both verbal labels for concepts as well as conventionalized gestures, such as waving and pointing. Strikingly, what differentiates these children from those with very specific expressive language disorders (SLI, next section) is that they do not compensate for a lack of verbal ability by substituting communicative gestures, such as pointing. They also demonstrate a lack of the symbolic play that typically emerges just prior to the normal acquisition of first words (Woods & Wetherby, 2003).

Theory of Mind.   Walenski and colleagues (2006) note that many of the behaviors seen in autism can be attributed to the rather unique failure of children with ASD to develop what is called a *theory of mind* (TOM): understanding the intentions and mental states of others in their environment. People may be seen merely as a "means for meeting a behavioral goal," a concept illustrated when a child with autism uses an adult's arm as a tool to reach things beyond his or her own grasp, rather than requesting help. Normal toddlers map the meanings of novel words in conversation partially by following the eye gaze of the speaker to determine reference. However, using eye gaze to track others' intentions is particularly impaired in children with ASD (Vivanti et al., 2011).

The TOM account of the cognitive deficit in autism contrasts with two alternative accounts, that of impairment in **executive function** and that of **weak central coherence** (Rajendran & Mitchell, 2007). Executive functions include those involved in attention, memory, planning, self-perception, and impulse control, among others. Some researchers argue that results of TOM tasks involving children with autism reflect a more general set of deficits in these areas rather than something specific to social perception. Happé & Booth (2008), alternatively, suggest that individuals with autism process information in a fragmented, piecemeal way, rather than searching for and extracting overall meaning, global gestalt, or conceptual coherence.

Language

Landa (2007) and Eigsti, de Marchena, Schuh, and Kelley (2011) present excellent surveys of the communicative deficit in autism. Both reviews note that approximately 20 to 25 percent of children with autism do not achieve more than a five-word spoken vocabulary, and two-thirds of those who do achieve this minimum level have substantial deficits in both expressive and receptive language skills. The remaining third of the population appears to have good abilities in the structural aspects of language, but difficulty with its pragmatic aspects. Thus, there is a wide variety of language profiles in autism. Researchers have examined the language of those children who do acquire some language skills in detail in an attempt to ascertain whether their communicative difficulties stem from impairment of isolated linguistic skills, developmental "scatter" across skill areas (Eigsti et al., 2011), or from more global patterns of either linguistic or cognitive deficiency. Phonological skills (articulation) in autism appear to be stronger than other areas of language knowledge and use (however, Shriberg and colleagues [2001] found a high rate of articulation errors in the speech of older children with HFA and Asperger syndrome; similar results were obtained by Rapin, Dunn, Allen, Stevens, and Fein [2009]). Whether age-appropriate or not, use of segmental features of phonology contrasts with much more widely observed problems with the suprasegmental aspects of language (e.g., prosody: intonation and stress) seen in most children with autism, including those with HFA (Grossman, Bemis, Skwerer, & Tager-Flusberg, 2010).

The lexicon appears to be relatively well developed in autism (Walenski et al., 2006), although mental state verbs requiring the child to understand abstract mental processes may be absent. Additionally, some of the well-known biases that govern infant and toddler word-learning in the typical population (see Chapter 4), such as the tendency to link novel objects with novel words, or mutual exclusivity, appear to be delayed in ASD (see discussion in Eigsti et al., 2011).

There is a limited literature on morphological development in children with ASD (Eigsti et al., 2011). Syntactic development is delayed, but normal in patterning, showing a reliance on a relatively narrow range of grammatical constructions and reduced use of forms that initiate social interaction, such as questions. Children with ASD show less complex syntax than do mental-age-matched peers (Eigsti, Bennetto, & Dadlani, 2007), and relatively poorer ability to judge the grammaticality of sentences (Eigsti & Bennetto, 2009). Reversal of personal pronouns (e.g., using *you* rather than *I*) may reflect the difficulty that the child with autism has in conceptualizing roles and perspectives in conversation (Tager-Flusberg et al., 2009).

Strikingly, despite the prevalence of **echolalia** (immediate or delayed repetition of the speech of others) in this population, Kjelgaard and Tager-Flusberg (2001) found children with autism to be relatively impaired on tasks requiring nonsense-word repetition, a classic marker of specific language impairment (SLI; discussed in a later section of this chapter). There may in fact be subgroups of children with ASD who show relatively slight language impairment, while others are more significantly impaired or delayed (Lindgren, Folstein, Tomblin, & Tager-Flusberg, 2009).

As noted, most observers have viewed the language deficits in autism as lying primarily in the pragmatic or social domains. Pragmatic abnormalities in communicative development precede the appearance of oral language and may persist even after children make enough progress in communication development to no longer meet strict criteria for a diagnosis of ASD (Kelley, Paul, Fein, & Naigles, 2006). As noted earlier, children with autism apparently do not engage in prelinguistic conversations with their caretakers (using body movement, facial expression, or babbling) as typically developing children do. However, since the disorder is usually diagnosed after the first year of life, early linguistic development of children with ASD is not well understood; this is why retrospective and prospective studies are very informative. Children who are more responsive to mothers' attempts to establish joint attention have a more positive prognosis for the establishment of expressive language (Meindl & Cannella-Malone, 2011). However, even the most linguistically adept individuals with autism have extreme difficulty in using language to establish or maintain joint interaction. Classic autistic behaviors illustrate a form–function dissociation: Language development is not spurred by the drive to socialize, and emerging forms are not used in the service of social interaction.

Echolalia

The echolalic behavior of children with autism is particularly fascinating. About 75 percent of children with autism are reported to exhibit echolalia at some point (Loveland & Tunali-Kotoski, 2005). Echolalia is the act of repeating language heard in the speech of others. It may take a number of forms. *Immediate echolalia* occurs relatively soon after the model has been presented. Many typically developing children may repeat a caretaker's utterance before responding, perhaps as a review of what they have just heard. *Delayed echolalia,* on the other hand, is the repetition of utterances or phrases hours, days, or even weeks after the model was first heard. It is particularly common in the speech of echolalic children with autism. Additionally, one can also speak of echolalia as being either exact or *mitigated* in nature; mitigated repetitions contain minor changes in structure from the original model.

Researchers have noted that a great deal of autistic echolalia is somewhat mitigated. Since children's abilities to repeat adult models have often been viewed as an estimate of their own grammatical capacity (Bernstein Ratner, 2000), it can be argued that changes that children with autism make in their echolalic renditions of utterances may provide some insight into the degree to which language input is being processed rather than simply stored for playback as unanalyzed wholes.

When viewed in this way, there is some evidence that echolalia may be a communicative strategy that the child with autism uses to participate in conversational interactions and that its frequency is likely to diminish as he or she develops more spontaneous communicative speech (Loveland & Tunali-Kotosk, 2005). Tager-Flusberg and Calkins (1990) suggested that some children with autism may imitate to maintain a conversational role, rather than to foster their grammatical development. They found no evidence that imitated utterances were appreciably longer or more advanced than spontaneous speech produced by children with ASD. Echolalia may be a "stepping stone" by which some children with ASD gradually break down large verbal units into smaller, meaningful linguistic gambits.

Treatment

Knowing whether a treatment improves the communication abilities of a child with ASD is more than an academic question for most readers of this text; virtually everyone now seems to know someone in their family or social circle who has ASD. However, determining whether an intervention is effective is a complex issue. We first need to distinguish between individual reports that may or may not have been of sufficient quality to reach publication in a professional journal, as well as those that do get published but involve small numbers of people, or fairly preliminary results. In ASD as well as other major conditions that can devastate quality of life for the individual and his or her family, there are large numbers of relatively unfounded intervention recommendations that range from simply inadequate from a scientific viewpoint to those that frankly seek only to take financial advantage of desperate parents (Shute, 2010). A number of organizations provide some guidance in interpreting the quality of therapy recommendations, using checklists of features that distinguish more and less valid reports (see **www.asha.org/slp/evaluate.htm** for a brief list of some questions you or others may want to ask when considering a communication intervention).

Hurth, Shaw, Izemon, Whaley, and Rogers (1999) listed some agreed-upon practices for diminishing the impact of ASD on the child's development, and none of these appear to have changed over the past editions of this text:

1. Intervention should be provided as early as possible.
2. Intervention should be intensive in scope and frequency; children may require up to twenty-five hours per week of guided instruction to achieve gains in functioning (National Research Council, 2001).
3. Parents and family members should be integrally involved in any treatment approach that is selected.
4. Treatment must include and focus on social and pragmatic aspects of communication.
5. Instruction should be systematic, but customized to the profile of the individual child's strengths and weaknesses.
6. Emphasis should be placed on teaching for generalization (helping the child to expand responses beyond the teaching exemplars).

Moreover, Tager-Flusberg and colleagues (2009) have issued joint recommendations for both assessment procedures and benchmark measures to be used in ascertaining whether an intervention has been effective. The working group emphasized the primacy of spontaneous language sampling and parental report over standardized test scores. One reason for this is that, at the earliest ages at which ASD is suspected (ages 1–3 years), the few available standardized language tests are not very reliable. The working group also emphasized the utility of expressing outcomes in terms of benchmark achievements seen in typical language development (and covered in prior chapters in this text). The proposed benchmarks are defined in detail in Tager-Flusberg et al. (2009) and include criteria for attainment of first words, word combinations, sentence production, including appropriate use of pragmatics.

Rogers and Ozonoff (2006) present excellent overviews of the approaches that have been used to address the functional and communicative needs of children with PDD/ASD, and more detailed descriptions and evaluations of many specific programs may be found in Howlin (2005) in Volkmer, Paul, Klin, and Cohen (2005). It is possible to place most major treatment paradigms on a continuum that positions **behavioral interventions** on one end, and what may be termed "developmental social-pragmatic approaches" at the other end, with additional treatment recommendations lying between these perspectives. Kane, Connell, and Pellecchia (2010) contrast basically the same concepts using the terms *naturalistic* versus *contrived*.

Behavioral approaches are most often associated with the late Ivar Lovaas (1987, 1996), who showed that some children with ASD were responsive to operant paradigms using discrete trial learning. In traditional behavioral approaches, a target skill is identified, a teacher instruction or prompt is given, the child responds, the response is consequated (with praise or some form of reinforcement if it is correct, verbal feedback if incorrect), and some attempt is made to guide the child to the actual desired response. **Applied behavior analysis (ABA)** was designed to increase the probability of generalization of skills learned in these more traditional models. Over the years, a major refinement from earlier models is that the child's interests should guide the selection of targets and activities in treatment. A recent meta-analysis of ABA-designed programs showed them to produce measurable gains in children's language skills (Virués-Ortega, 2010); results of programs modeled closely after Lovaas' original program have been among the best in producing measurable improvements in IQ and behavior (Eldevik, Hastings, Hughes, Jahr, Eikeseth, & Cross, 2009). A review by Brunner and Seung (2009) concurred with this assessment, while another was less convinced of their effectiveness (Spreckley & Boyd, 2009). Reichow and Wolery (2009) and Makrygianni and Reed (2010) found that outcomes appear to be moderated by the training of the provider, time in treatment and total number of therapy hours. This is of potential concern, because, as programs have become more popular, there has been a rapid growth in parent-administered therapy programs that use volunteer therapists, rather than professionally directed clinic programs. In contrast to teaching new skills, there is general agreement that ABA can reduce problematic or self-injurious behavior in individuals with autism; a meta-analysis of a large number of "small N" published studies appears to confirm its utility (Campbell, 2003), and individual case reports continue to suggest its value.

Among treatment models that base their intervention strategies on findings from beneficial behaviors seen in typical parent–child language learning interactions are Incidental Language Teaching (Hart, 1985), **pivotal response training (PRT)** (Koegel & Frea, 1993), and milieu training (Kaiser, Yoder, & Keetz, 1992). Brunner and Seung (2009) note that milieu teaching and PRT have "empirically demonstrated efficacy" and can improve children's communicative and adaptive skills (Baker, Ericzén, Stahmer, & Burns, 2007). One recent meta-analysis (Kane, Connell, & Pellecchia, 2010) specifically compared more naturalistic and more "contrived" (therapist-led) language interventions. They found some surprising trends that will need to be pursued in future studies; naturalistic interventions appear best at fostering initial acquisition of a given language target, while generalization of the skill may require more "contrived" drill to more firmly instate the skill.

Over the years, the conceptual concerns raised in Chapter 7 regarding the underlying bases of successful communication development led other researchers to attempt more socially and pragmatically based programs. Prizant, Wetherby, and Rydell (2000) offered a developmental pragmatics model **(SCERTS: Social Communication, Emotional Regulation, and Transactional Support)** that emphasizes the establishment of child-focus-led preverbal communicative "bids" prior to more formal linguistic responses and endorses multiple modalities of response (speech, gesture, AAC) and manipulation of functional, everyday contexts for learning. A multifaceted approach, **TEACCH (Treatment and Education of Autistic and related Communication-Handicapped Children)** (Campbell, Schopler, Cueva, & Hallin, 1996), includes changes in the physical features of the teaching environment, predictability in daily scheduling, individual goal-directed workstations, and cues that aid the child in task completion, among other components. A recent review (Brunner & Seung, 2009) found the current evidence for the effectiveness of TEACCH surprisingly "limited and exploratory," given its widespread use. TEACCH and ABA currently are the two most parent-requested intervention approaches for children with ASD in the United States. While often positioned as philosophical contrasts in orientation, some researchers find that they share a number of common premises, some of which were listed earlier in this section (Callahan, Shukla-Mehta, Magee, & Wie, 2010). Despite differences across interventions, the National Research Council (2001) recommends naturalistic and developmental approaches to teaching language to children with ASD, in order to maximize their communicative abilities and the potential for skill generalization. An additional overarching prerequisite for successful response to treatment is fostering attention to adult caretakers or teachers in children with ASD; Patten and Watson (2011) review common features across a number of intervention approaches that appear to improve children's ability to attend to therapeutic interactions.

Most studies that report therapy outcomes in autism treatment, as in other child or adult language disorders, involve small numbers of participants, and it often becomes difficult for researchers or parents to determine whether something that appears to have "worked" to improve communication in a very small sample of children will generalize meaningfully to larger numbers. A growing approach to consolidating multiple small intervention studies in language intervention as well as other fields, such as medicine, psychology or social work, is to conduct what is called a **meta-analysis**. In meta-analyses, the findings from large numbers of small studies are combined across common elements to ascertain larger effects (or non-effects) of a treatment. We discuss the results of selected meta-analyses of treatment approaches in this chapter. A meta-analysis has the ability, given sufficient design and detail, to sort through the bramble of large numbers of small reports to identify trends that suggest effective, as opposed to ineffective interventions.

Most meta-analyses also identified gaps in the designs of many studies that they reviewed, as well as across investigations; there are virtually no examples of "head-to-head" comparisons of two or more different therapies to see which might lead to different amounts or types of improvement.

For nonverbal children with autism, just as in some approaches with children having ID, some treatments make use of augmentative and alternative communication (AAC), in which signs and visual symbol systems augment or replace verbal communication strategies (see Mirenda, 2003, for a survey of such approaches). Ganz and colleagues (2011) aggregated the results of many small single-subject reports to suggest that use of AAC produces modest gains in communication, particularly when children are younger, and do not have additional complicating conditions beyond the primary diagnosis of ASD. Some outcome data have supported the use of the Picture Exchange Communication System (PECS), in which the nonverbal child with autism is trained to initiate requests using pictures of desired items. A meta-analysis of responses to PECS suggests that while communication ability showed modest gains across studies, suggesting that PECS holds "promise" as an effective therapy approach, speech gains made by children with ASD receiving PECS therapy were negligible or even negative (Flippin, Reszka, & Watson, 2010). A separate meta-analysis of PECS by Hart and Banda (2010) basically concurs in this assessment, but found some more positive speech outcomes. PECS is one of the few ASD treatments to have been contrasted with an alternative therapy. In two equal groups of eighteen children, PECS was found to be superior to milieu teaching in increasing interaction with examiners using pictorial cues (Yoder & Lieberman, 2010).

In less impaired children, despite favorable single-subject reports, non-intensive school-based therapies designed to foster social skills per se do not appear to yield large gains, regardless of specific approach employed, according to a meta-analysis conducted by Bellini, Peters, Benner, and Hopf (2007). The authors concluded that interventions probably need to be of greater intensity and better tailored to individual children's specific needs to maximize gains. A second meta-analysis by Bellini and Akullian (2007) did find that video modeling and self-modeling (in which the child with ASD is exposed to video of himself performing a desired behavior) did produce some measurable gains in social-communication and functional skills in higher-functioning children with ASD. Brunner and Seung (2009) summarize the available literature on self-modeling and concur that it can be effective in working with children with ASD.

The NRC (2001) concluded that when children with ASD are taught how to communicate more effectively, their use of aggressive or socially inappropriate behaviors may diminish. Thus, language use is not only a symptom of the autistic syndrome, but an important tool in its management. In this regard, functional analysis can be extremely helpful. In **functional analysis** (Koegel, Koegel, Frea, & Smith, 1995), children's inappropriate behaviors are scrutinized for potential motivation or function and replaced with more appropriate responses. For example, one nonverbal, nonlinguistic child with PDD often aggressively scratched others when he appeared upset. This response was gradually shaped into a sign for "angry," which alerted adults before he acted out his frustrations.

In contrast to an emphasis on therapy approaches, some recent meta-analyses of effective therapy in ASD have focused on the targets of therapy, such as joint attention or symbolic play. White and colleagues (2011) provide evidence that therapy can improve joint attention skills that generalize, particularly when embedded in naturalistic environments. Kasari, Paparella, Freeman, and Jahromi (2008) found language outcome benefits when toddlers were assigned to conditions that emphasized development of either symbolic play or joint attention skills. Conversely, although Theory of Mind (TOM) impairments are thought to be a partial basis for the symptoms of autism, treatments that improve TOM do not appear to ameliorate the other social and linguistic symptoms of ASD (Begeer et al., 2011).

Despite the relatively small evidence base for effective treatments, there are indications that some intervention approaches are *not* likely to produce communicative gains. Evidence of what does *not* seem to work is important, given the understandable desire of families to pursue all possibly effective treatments. For example, auditory integration therapy (AIT) did *not* show measurable benefits in a meta-analysis of published studies that was conducted by Sinha, Silove, Wheeler, and Williams (2006). The American Speech-Language-Hearing Association (ASHA, 2004) has also questioned whether AIT has shown evidence of effectiveness in the treatment of autism as well as other communication disorders.

Whatever approach is taken, language outcomes appear to be strongly related to the age of diagnosis, initial cognitive and language profile, and amount of speech-language intervention that the child receives (Turner, Stone, Pozdol, & Coonrod, 2006). Thus, early identification of the ASD and intensive early intervention are critical. Many recent studies specifically assess interventions provided to very young children who display symptoms of ASD. Landa, Holman, O'Neill, and Stuart (2011) found promising gains in social engagement of toddlers with ASD when a conventional intensive communication intervention was augmented with specific targets to teach joint attention and socially engaged vocal imitation.

To date, the long-term prognosis for children diagnosed with autism has not been promising, and the rate of cognitive and linguistic development appears to slow after mid-childhood, although some improvements continue to be seen in social and adaptive behaviors (Sigman & McGovern, 2005). The optimism that we find in this edition from more numerous and consolidated reports of effective therapies for ASD do not temper our concern that the overall impacts of ASD on linguistic, social, intellectual, and functional long-term outcomes are still very sobering.

There is a significant amount of variability in later outcomes for children with ASDs; those with relatively high IQ and successful language acquisition (and a subset of relatively high-functioning children diagnosed with Asperger syndrome) appear to have the highest likelihood of achieving functional independence later in life (Howlin, 2005). Howlin notes that it is clear that outcomes will depend on degree of therapeutic support not only early in life, but throughout the school years and even into the adult years.

🖎Specific Language Impairment

General Identity and Prevalence

The largest proportion of children who demonstrate language delay or disorder do not have hearing impairment, cognitive impairment, or autism. Moreover, they show no gross signs of brain dysfunction, although minor brain dysfunction may be suspected or probable. Such children demonstrate language impairment as their single obvious developmental disability. For this reason, they are often given the diagnosis of **specific language impairment (SLI).** As Leonard (1998) points out, the diagnosis of SLI is one of exclusion; that is, alternative explanations for the child's failure to learn language have been sought and not found. A large-scale study found that, of over 6,000 5-year-old children, over 7 percent could be considered specifically language impaired, based on actual linguistic and nonlinguistic test performance (Tomblin et al., 1997). Most of these children were still functioning below age expectations for language skills four years later (Tomblin, Zhang, Buckwalter, & O'Brien, 2003). A very concise overview of the past twenty-five years of research into SLI is provided by Leonard (2009).

Not all studies that have examined children with SLI have used the same criteria to identify the disorder. This fact has confounded interpretation of the many studies that have examined such children's functioning. Currently, the conventional criteria for identification of SLI include the following (Leonard, 1998): language test scores falling below 1.25 standard deviations from the mean, a performance IQ of at least 85, normal hearing as assessed by screening at conventional levels, a negative recent history of **otitis media** (middle ear infections), no evidence of obvious neurological dysfunction, intact oral-motor structure and function, and grossly normal patterns of social interaction. Many researchers and clinicians also use descriptive measures to define SLI (Leonard, 2003): deficits in finite verb morphology (use of the past tense, third-person-singular marker, and copular and auxiliary verb forms), nonword repetition, and phoneme discrimination tasks. These added features are proposed not so much to define the disorder in order to qualify children for services as to ensure that researchers are studying the same groups of children.

Language Profiles of Children with Specific Language Impairment

From "Late Talker" to Language Impaired: The Early Course of SLI. In general, studies of the language abilities of children with SLI suggest that their linguistic development is best characterized as *delayed* in quality rather than deviant, although this characterization is still disputable. Most appear to begin life as "late talkers," a diagnosis now made by about age 2 (Rescorla & Lee, 2001). Many "late talkers" do in fact make good language progress in the years from 2 to 4, which is why SLI is not a recommended diagnosis until age 4 (Paul, 2007). However, although many such children catch up to their peers, up to 40 percent of children whose communicative development is delayed at age 2 continue to experience immature patterns of speech and language use, demonstrate additional language problems, and are at risk for later educational failure (Rescorla, 2005).

There is also mounting concern that late-talking toddlers need to be distinguished from children with ASD, discussed in the section above. A number of features seem to differentiate toddlers with specific problems in learning to talk from those with ASD. Ellis Weismer and colleagues (2011) note that even toddlers with milder forms of ASD (in that they are verbal) show much slower language development than mental-aged matched late talkers.

Even when late talking is not a sign of the other conditions discussed in this chapter, the evidence increasingly suggests that the language-delayed preschooler of today may well become a future student with *learning disabilities*. Researchers estimate that a large number of such children eventually show depressed reading achievement (Snowling, Bishop, & Stothard, 2000). Law, Tomblin, and Xuyang (2008) found a declining rate of growth in receptive language skills among children with SLI enrolled in a major American study of child language development over the school years. Such relative disadvantage has important ramifications for general educational progress as well as reading skill development. Major longitudinal studies of late-talking children, such as that carried out by Leslie Rescorla (2009), have shown that while many late talkers achieve linguistic skills within the normal range as they progress through school, their measured scores by the end of high school are persistently and significantly below those achieved by the typically developing children that they were paired with for long-term study. Thus, SLI is a disorder that presents with changing symptoms over the lifespan, with more obvious problems early in childhood and more subtle deficits in the later school years and beyond.

Lexicon

Early Vocabulary Patterns. It sometimes appears that children with SLI perform less well at all language tasks than their peers with more typical language skills (see Figure 9.1). Some studies suggest that their language development is delayed from the outset, with emergence of a core single-word vocabulary trailing behind expectations by almost a full year. Norming studies of parental vocabulary report have specifically targeted a subpopulation of toddlers (about 10 to 15 percent of all young children) who show relatively good comprehension but poor expressive vocabulary and lack of combinatorial speech at age 2 (Rescorla & Alley, 2001). A fairly high proportion of such **early language delay (ELD)** or "late-talking" children continue to demonstrate language and articulation delays as they mature, although some "late bloomers" catch up to their peers in language performance (Paul, 2007). As noted earlier, Leonard's (1998) comprehensive review of the available data suggests that from one-quarter to one-half of children who are late to talk may progress to a diagnosis of SLI by school age. Children with familial histories of speech and language delay are more likely to show persistent problems than children without such family histories who are late to talk, but the researchers (Dale, Price, Bishop, & Plomin, 2003) could not identify additional probable risk factors that might allow professionals to predict which late talkers were most likely to need future intervention and which might spontaneously catch up with their peers.

Later Vocabulary Patterns. It is estimated that approximately 25 percent of children with language impairments have some difficulty with lexical retrieval (Messser & Dockrell, 2006). Older children with SLI continue to be slow at *word mapping,* and possible reasons for this problem are not clear (Alt & Plante, 2006). Such children may require almost twice as many presentations of novel words to learn them under experimental conditions (Gray, 2003) and rely on a smaller expressive lexicon and a higher proportion of *general all-purpose (GAP)* nouns and verbs, such as *thing* or *do,* than their non-impaired peers. Other researchers find children with SLI to be generally slower and less accurate when faced with naming tasks (Messer & Dockrell, 2006) and to have sparser lexical representations, such that their word definitions lack the detail provided by their peers (Mainella-Arnold, Evans, & Coady, 2010). A subset of children with SLI are said to exhibit word-finding problems or **anomia;** that is, they experience marked difficulty in retrieving words for common concepts that they seem to comprehend (Newman & German, 2002). This may be due to shallow semantic or phonological coding that allows the child only partial access to concepts or word forms during the typical pacing of conversational interaction (Li & McGregor, 2010). Conceivably, it would be this type of shallow mapping that would result in some "near misses" of vocabulary choices, as in, "That boy is the same *old [age] as me, and he has the same *strong [strength]," and "We can't *stove [cook] that food." This **confrontation naming,** or word-retrieval, problem may result in speech characterized by **circumlocutions,** or efforts to get around the blockage. A mother of one child with SLI reported that her son requested "something round and English" *(an English muffin)* for his breakfast; another child with SLI labeled pictures on an articulation test in the following manner: "on my brother's pants" *(zipper)* and "you eat breakfast with it" *(spoon).* Still other children do not readily process ambiguous words, or metaphorical uses of language. For example, a common language test asks children to provide multiple definitions of targeted words in phrases, such as "The noise of the *fans* disturbed the boy." A 12-year-old with SLI, while frustrated and aware of the nature of the task, could not provide both meanings of this simple sentence. A more risqué anecdotal report had an American child contemplating his friend's visit to a European "topless beach," wondering aloud how a beach could lack a cover.

Finally, when children with SLI obtain one meaning for a word, it may block further meanings, leading to problems in disambiguation or inappropriate word usage. In an example provided by a colleague that is both comical and telling, a 4-year-old child quite seriously labeled a test photograph of a fried egg as *brain* (in all likelihood as a response to the then-current public service announcements against drug abuse that warned "this is your brain on drugs" while showing a similar picture), despite everyday evidence to the contrary.

Children with SLI also appear less able to derive the meanings of novel words from syntactic context. Shulman and Guberman (2007) found that children with SLI performed even more poorly than high-functioning children with autism in learning the appropriate nature of a novel (nonsense) verb (e.g., whether it was transitive or intransitive: "The dog is *zirping* the cat" versus "The dog and cat are *zirping*") from its surrounding syntactic cues.

Morphosyntax

The vast majority of children with SLI are not identified on the basis of lexical performance; rather, they are identified by their failure to achieve normal syntactic production with or without accompanying deficits in comprehension. Their abilities to use grammatical morphemes and to utilize a wide array of simple and complex sentence structures are particularly depressed when compared to those of normal peers. In children learning English, this morphological deficit is quite striking. Specific structures that children with SLI have difficulty mastering include plurals, possessives, tense and agreement markers, articles, auxiliary verbs, the copula (verb *to be*), prepositions, and complementizers *(to)* in structures such as "I need *to go* now." (For an extremely thorough review, see Leonard, 1998.)

Such difficulties are apparent even when children with SLI are matched to children of similar **language age (LA)** as measured by mean length of utterance (MLU), which is a measure of length of utterance in morphemes (see Chapter 5). Thus, even at matched utterance lengths, children with SLI include fewer grammatical inflections than their typically developing peers. Further, verb and noun morphology are much more poorly developed than one would predict given the size of the child's lexicon (Leonard, Miller, & Gerber, 1999).

Children with SLI are more likely to omit grammatical morphemes (in English) than to misuse them or misplace them. Among the inflections listed above that show the most significant impairment are verb inflections and agreement in the use of the copula and auxiliary *be,* tense markers (Leonard, Camarata, Pawlowska, Brown, & Camarata, 2006), and the auxiliary verb *do.* Confusion of case in the use of pronouns (e.g., *me* for *I*) is also common. Figure 9.1 provides language samples from some children with SLI that show these patterns.

As children with SLI grow, their morphological deficits may become less obvious, while problems in the use of advanced sentence structures and narrative coherence become more apparent, as the third sample in Figure 9.1 illustrates. It is at this point that specific language impairment begins to affect school achievement significantly, as deficits in language abilities affect the child's ability to master text reading, writing assignments, and discourse.

Pragmatics

One might expect that a child who has problems with expressive language and who may also have subtle comprehension deficits will experience difficulty in many social situations. Thus, it is not surprising that many children with SLI experience difficulty with a range of pragmatic functions (Brinton & Fujiki, 2005), although pragmatic deficits in these children are less pervasively seen across studies than those involving morphosyntax. Rather,

---

figure 9.1	Some Examples of Conversation from Children with SLI

Mother:	Do you know how to drive a truck?
Child (age 3):	No way!
Mother:	No way?
Child:	Oh me get big me grow up me mailman?
Mother:	When you grow up and get big, can you be a mailman? . . . would you bring me the mail? How many letters?
Child:	Lots.
Child:	Me take some my big big big bag.
Mother:	You're gonna bring them in your big big big bag?
Child:	Yes. Me bring my truck. . . . Me bring soda truck.
Mother:	You'll drive in a soda truck? You know, dogs bark at mailmen. What will you do when dogs bark at you?
Child:	No me come in.
Mother:	You won't come in?
Child:	No.

(SLI child at age 2;11 [Gleason, 1998, p. 101]).

Troy:	This the fireperson. This the bell (indicating the fire alarm).
Mother:	Does the bell ring in an emergency?
Troy:	No. The bell, it has . . . the car come out.
Mother:	The cars come out when the bell rings?
Troy:	(Nods) The telephone do that, too!

(SLI child at age 4;7 [Plante & Beeson, 1999])

"So a circus was there and they had these other hands. He had these other people in it/so he first got in a train/and so he didn't get in the train cause he could fly/so he/Mr. Tyler. He was happy/he didn't care if the train was broke down/and so this little guy, Timothy, a little mouse, he gets on and they found a boat/so they sailed on the boat/and so hippopotomus/no/the elephant had to go up in a tiny bed/so the bed broke down and they try to (unintelligible) hippopotomus up there . . ."

(A 9-year-old with SLI, retelling the story of Dumbo [Nelson, 1998])

---

pragmatic deficits seem to directly reflect impairments in language knowledge and use, making children with SLI functionally more like younger children, a significant social handicap for them (Katsos, Roqueta, Estevan, & Cummins, 2011). In studies, children with SLI produce less appropriate requests, respond less appropriately to the requests of others, or display less sensitivity to their conversational partners' needs for information or clarification. Children with SLI are less adept at entering or guiding conversations (Liiva & Cleave, 2005), and display depressed narrative abilities (Wetherell, Botting, & Conti-Ramsden, 2007).

Some children with SLI additionally demonstrate a tendency to interpret language very literally, a pattern with pragmatic consequences. One child with SLI responded to the subtle indirect request for sharing implied by "Your snack looks good" by responding, "Yes, and it tastes good, too!" Such a tendency toward literal interpretation will lead a child to ignore the intent behind many conversational gambits. Further, children with shallow knowledge of word meaning may alienate peers unintentionally. For example, Brinton and Fujiki (1995) report one child who used the term *liar* to refer to anyone who said something inaccurate, regardless of intent to deceive.

Because pragmatic deficits appear to be exacerbated when children are in a group setting, it is not surprising that the classroom peers of children with SLI are less likely to pick them as preferred classmates (Gertner, Rice, & Hadley, 1994). A logical result is that many children with SLI have noticeably lowered self-esteem (Jerome, Fujiki, Brinton, & James, 2002). It is unclear whether pragmatic and syntactic deficits arise separately in such children, whether their pragmatic deficits may be attributable to subtle linguistic deficiencies, or whether pragmatic deficiency actually constrains the development or display of certain syntactic skills. For example, in a recent study, children with SLI were less able than typically developing peers to provide an emotional interpretation of how a character might feel in a particular situation. This problem was related to language ability, but it may or may not stem entirely from poorer language skills (Ford & Milosky, 2003). Thus, evidence exists to support each position in part, and different SLI children may demonstrate different patterns of relative pragmatic–syntactic disorder.

Profiles of depressed social competence can be seen in children with SLI as early as the preschool years (McCabe, 2005). Children who reach school age with residual language problems carry an increased risk of psychosocial maladjustment when followed into adolescence. Risk appears to be elevated when children are diagnosed with a concomitant problem that can affect social interaction, such as attention-deficit/hyperactivity disorder (ADHD) (Snowling, Bishop, Stothard, Chipcase, & Kaplan, 2006). Such findings emphasize the importance of early diagnosis and intervention for language delay, as well as the potential need for monitoring and support that goes beyond speech-language therapy in helping children with SLI to avoid social impairment.

Concomitant Problems

A number of children with SLI also demonstrate articulation disorders along with their language difficulties. From an opposite perspective, a high proportion of children referred for articulation problems demonstrate concurrent language disorder (Shriberg, Tomblin, & McSweeny, 1999). This is not surprising, given the delayed profiles of phonological development seen in many toddlers with early language delay (Rescorla & Bernstein Ratner, 1996). Some children with SLI are also very disfluent in conversation and narrative; some repeat sounds and words often enough to be erroneously labeled as stuttering (Boscolo, Bernstein Ratner, & Rescorla, 2002; Finneran, Leonard, & Miller, 2009) (see next section for more information on stuttering).

As noted earlier, many children with specific language impairment continue to have difficulties with aspects of language as they mature into adolescence and adulthood (Rescorla, 2005; Wetherell et al., 2007). At these later points in development, their problems are less obvious. Adolescents and adults with language problems may use and be able to process less sophisticated syntax, rather than making obvious grammatical errors. They may have difficulty with ambiguous words and sentences, figurative and metaphorical language, and following the essential gist of stories or lectures. Thus they are at great risk for reading failure or dyslexia, particularly problems in reading connected text, in addition to decoding isolated words. **Dyslexia** is a distinct impairment that can co-occur with SLI as well as present by itself (Catts, Adlof, Hogan, & Weismer, 2005); in many cases, the presumed underlying problem in reading is, in fact, a more central disorder of auditory and/or linguistic processing. For instance, readers with dyslexia have difficulty in assigning a cartoon avatar to passages spoken by native English speakers or speakers of an unfamiliar language, such as Mandarin (Perrachione, Del Tufo, & Gabrieli, 2011). Because of the elevated risk of later reading problems in children with SLI, they should be carefully monitored during reading instruction. Some recent preschool programs for children with SLI have begun to employ interventions designed to prevent later reading failure; many of these train **phonological awareness**, or how sounds of the language match to letters in alphabetic reading/writing systems (Roth, Troia, Worthington, & Handy, 2006; Snowling & Hulme, 2011).

As with other chapters in this text, we are concerned with language disorder across the lifespan. Specific language impairment continues to have an impact that lasts throughout the adult years. However, until recently, tests of adult language ability were primarily designed to assess the consequences of stroke or the major neurological conditions that affect language discussed in Chapter 11. These kinds of tests are not appropriate in assessing more subtle impairment in language knowledge and use. Thus, there is a need for more sensitive measures of impairment in adults that may be impacting educational, occupational or social function; such measures are currently under development (Fidler, Plante, & Vance, 2011).

Finally, many chapters in this text emphasize the benefits that accrue to researchers when data in language development and disorder are shared across research sites. In addition to the well-known CHILDES Project (discussed elsewhere in this text), which has a section devoted to children with atypical language development, database sharing specific to the large-scale study of children with SLI is also under development (EpiSLI: Tomblin, 2010).

Causative Explanations

A few researchers have proposed that children with SLI merely represent the low end of the normal distribution of language talents in children. However, there is a broader consensus, given recent research, that SLI reflects underlying brain dysfunction at some level, even though it is not grossly manifest. If we assume that language impairment arises from brain dysfunction, it follows that such children would display varied patterns of linguistic and nonlinguistic performance, depending on the extent and location of this hypothetical cerebral damage.

In many cases, there is evidence of a familial, genetic component to SLI (Barry, Yasin, & Bishop, 2007). The now well-studied "KE" family, which has an extremely high level of transmission of a complex profile of SLI (accompanied by other speech problems) was thought to provide clues to the genetic transmission of the disorder (see Chapter 7). However, the identified mutation of the gene, called FOXP2, once mistakenly thought to be the "language gene," has not been found in large samples of children who have more typical profiles of SLI (Meaburn, Dale, Craig, & Plomin, 2002). No one has yet identified "the gene for language" or explained how a single genetic dysfunction could disrupt the normal acquisition and use of linguistic abilities. Currently, other candidate genes in the vicinity of FOXP2 look promising but will require much additional work to verify. Emerging data suggest that the two most common features of SLI, impairment in phonological working memory and deficits in the use of grammatical morphology, are linked to two different genetic loci (chromosomes 16q and 19q; Falcaro et al., 2008). There is also accumulating evidence of some common linkage between ASD (see the previous section) and SLI (Whitehouse, Bishop, Ang, Pennell, & Fisher, 2011), as well as identification of another gene, CNTNAP2, that appears to be a stronger predictor of overall language ability than FOXP2.

Despite the likelihood that we will identify genetic markers for many cases of SLI, it is already apparent that many children diagnosed with SLI come from families with no obvious history of the condition. Thus it is likely that in most cases, the basis of SLI is complex, may involve multiple genes, and may interact with environmental risk factors (Bishop, 2006).

Models of SLI

Understanding what mechanism(s) underlie the behavioral profiles seen in SLI has great importance. If we can determine what causes the child to have difficulty learning language, we can develop more specific methods of early identification and effective treatment. Further, understanding why some children find language learning so difficult can inform models that attempt to explain normal language acquisition, since a model that predicts successful acquisition should also be able to predict conditions under which less than optimal development will occur.

There are a large number of candidate models to explain SLI. Among the most influential are the following:

- Children with SLI suffer from underlying *deficits in the temporal processing of auditory signals*. In a series of studies, Tallal and her co-workers (see Tallal, 2003, for a summary of this line of research) demonstrated that children with SLI have difficulty processing rapid acoustic events, and this difficulty can be seen in late infancy, even before expressive language problems become evident (Benasich & Tallal, 2002; Choudhury, Leppanen, Leevers, & Benasich, 2007). Additionally, they extended their findings to a treatment protocol that has produced impressive (and controversial) results (Tallal et al., 1996). Children in treatment studies were given practice with speech stimuli that were selectively lengthened and amplified, with gradual fading to normal values. Many children participating in this intervention protocol (now available commercially, as Fast ForWord®) were reported to make large gains on standardized measures of language administered pre- and post-treatment, although functional gains were not as well documented. However, a series of replication studies have been unable to document the level of improvement reported by the program's authors for either language or reading skills, when the program is used alone, or in conjunction with traditional language therapy (Fey, Finestack, Gajewski, Popescu, & Lewine, 2010; Strong, Torgerson, Torgerson, & Hulm, 2011). In a large-scale study, Gillam and colleagues (2008) found that progress made by children using the program did not exceed progress made while using commercially available language-enrichment computer programs or traditional language therapy.

  However, the debate over possible auditory processing deficits in children with SLI continues. Some studies show little evidence of atypical auditory processing (Bishop, Adams, Nation, & Rosen, 2005), whereas others show evident patterns of depressed performance on auditory processing tasks, even those that extend beyond processing of brief acoustic cues (Corriveau, Pasquini, & Goswami, 2007). For example, Weber-Fox, Leonard, Wray, and Tomblin (2010) found atypical processing of rapid auditory stimuli that accompanied both behavioral and ERP responses to morphological errors in adolescents with SLI. Still others suggest that children with SLI do more poorly on experimental nonsense stimuli than on meaningful acoustic stimuli, which may reflect poor task-demand or attentional skills rather than primary perceptual deficits (Coady, Evans, Mainela-Arnold, & Kluender, 2007). Auditory processing deficits may explain why children with SLI who speak Chinese as a first language have difficulty differentiating among words that differ only in contrasting tones (Wong, Chiocca, & Sun, 2009).

- Children with SLI have *difficulty processing grammatical morphology with low phonetic substance, or salience* (the **"surface hypothesis"**; Leonard, 1998). In comparing data from English-, Italian-, and Hebrew-speaking children with SLI, Leonard observed some common patterns of language formulation that suggest that children with specific language impairment are limited in their ability to process low-phonetic-substance (short, unstressed) or sparsely represented (infrequent) morphemes in all three languages. Usage of such morphemes may be additionally conditioned by their perceived contributions to meaning. For instance, children with SLI often have difficulty using morphological markers that are short and unstressed and carry little phonetic substance, whereas similarly low-substance forms that do not carry morphological information are not as troublesome. Thus, a child may use and perceive the [s] that is the last sound in *box* more effectively than the [s] that is used to mark the plural in *rocks*. However, in comparing the performance of children with SLI and children with mild hearing impairment on production of verb morphology, Norbury, Bishop, and Briscoe (2001) found differences in error patterns that did not strongly support a pure perceptual salience account. Some authors also question whether SLI reflects true deficits in linguistic knowledge or is the result of competing linguistic stresses on a somewhat fragile and limited language system. Leonard and his colleagues observe that many children with SLI can spontaneously produce difficult forms in some limited contexts, but not in others. They suggest that, when it is overloaded, the child's system cannot fully meet all demands, and some aspects of communication are executed imperfectly. When one aspect of a linguistic task is very stressful (e.g., the required syntax is complex), other aspects of the child's production are more likely to contain errors (in phonology or fluency, for instance). Montgomery and Leonard (2006) attempted to facilitate the processing of low-substance morphological inflections in children with SLI by acoustically enhancing them in an experimental task, but performance was not significantly improved.

- Children with SLI have *immature/incomplete grammatical knowledge.* Views of SLI as the product of diminished or fluctuating capacity contrasts with the hypothesis that children with SLI have different underlying grammatical rule systems, in which certain features of the grammar are missing or undeveloped. Such accounts seem most appealing when a child's difficulty with apparently diverse linguistic forms can be accounted for by positing that a single concept affecting many structures is missing from the child's grammar. One specific proposal, the **extended optional infinitive** account (Rice, Wexler, Marquis, & Hershberger, 2000), suggests that children with SLI remain "stalled" in a normal developmental phase during which children learning English appear to believe that marking of tense and agreement in main clauses is optional (see Chapter 5). Such an approach to the grammar would result in both deficient use of verb morphology and inappropriate assignment of case to pronouns, both of which are distinguishing characteristics of SLI. There are some concerns about the extended optional infinitive account: Some children use forms that are not present at all in the input language, some common errors may not resemble the native language infinitival form, children with disorders other than SLI often produce errors similar to those seen in SLI, and errors in some language communities do not involve verb tense morphology.

- Children with SLI have *generally slowed processing ability,* which leads to difficulties that include, but transcend, language. The so-called **generalized slowing hypothesis** (Miller et al., 2006) follows work suggesting that children with SLI need about one-third more time to execute a range of perceptual and motor functions, and that they display general motor skill deficits (Zelaznik & Goffman, 2010). Such slowing might contribute to, or interact with, other proposals that suggest that SLI is the outcome of limited processing capacity in some children. The underlying limit may be one of slowed capacity, as advanced above, or of limits on processing "space," or vulnerability to competing demands on the system.

A related hypothesis is that SLI is at least partially due to deficits in memory, specifically phonological working memory (see Gathercole, 2006, and related commentary in the same journal issue). Evidence for working-memory deficits comes from work by Montgomery and others (see an updated review by Montgomery, Magimairaj, & Finney, 2010). A recent meta-analysis of a growing body of experimental data (Estes, Evans, & Else-Quest, 2007) shows a large disadvantage for children with SLI on **nonword repetition (NWR)** tasks that vary in stimulus length, thus taxing phonological memory capacity. However, even short nonwords may be more difficult for children with SLI to repeat than for children with more typical language development. Slowed rate of processing may interact to impair phonological short-term memory abilities (Montgomery & Windsor, 2007). These abilities may be inherited to some extent: Nonword-repetition weaknesses have even been observed in parents of children diagnosed with SLI and distinguish families that have SLI-affected members from unaffected families (Barry et al., 2007).

Is SLI Universal?

Yet another approach to evaluating theories of SLI is to examine how well they predict language impairment in differing languages. Although it is obvious that children learning any language can show specific language impairment, growing interest has been expressed in comparing patterns of language disability in children with SLI from different language communities. Leonard (1998) summarizes data from Italian, Spanish, German, Hebrew, Dutch, Swedish, Croatian, Hungarian, Japanese, Greek, and Inuktitut (an Eskimo-Aleut language). SLI in additional language communities is described each year. Recent examples include closer examination of French (Thordadottir & Namazi, 2007), Cantonese (Wong, Klee, Stokes, Fletcher, & Leonard, 2010), and British Sign Language (Mason et al., 2010).

One immediate outcome of such studies is an understanding that, although SLI manifests itself most obviously in English as a failure in the use of inflectional morphology, it looks quite different in other languages, particularly those in which inflectional endings on verbs are pervasive and do not permit the child to hypothesize that a bare verb stem is an acceptable word of the language. That is, a child learning English knows that *walk* is a word, just as *walks* and *walked* are words. A child learning Spanish would never presume that the root of the verb *to walk (caminar)* could be legitimately used in conversation. One can say *camino, caminamos, camina,* and so on, but one cannot, under any circumstances, say *camin-*. Thus, the nature of the language to be learned will create different problem spaces for children with SLI in different language communities of the world.

The actual mechanisms responsible for deficient language development in children with SLI have yet to be discovered, but work has begun to identify certain factors that place children at risk for language delay and disorder. Current research suggests that a variety of factors, some of which are amenable to preventive measures, predispose certain children to language and learning disability. As noted earlier, there is increased understanding of genetic risk factors. Other factors are sociolinguistic and socioeconomic and tend to emphasize the need for early identification and early identification of language delay and disorder (Hayiou-Thomas, 2008). Finally, we are now positioned to identify prelinguistic risk factors or markers for children with SLI and other developmental language disorders, both genetic and behavioral. For instance, younger siblings of children with SLI show atypical responses to prelinguistic perceptual tasks (see Chapter 2; Benasich & Tallal, 2002), and when viewed retrospectively, children with delayed spoken language development themselves perform less poorly in such laboratory experiments (Newman, Bernstein Ratner, Jusczyk, Jusczyk, & Dow, 2006).

Language Intervention with Children Who Are Specifically Language Impaired

Many principles of language intervention that apply to working with the children we have discussed in previous sections are used with children who have SLI as well. Excellent surveys of general treatment principles, and examples of techniques are provided by Kaderavek (2011) and Nelson (2010).

A meta-analysis by Cable and Dornsch (2011) suggests that a wide number of therapy approaches appear to facilitate linguistic development in late-talking toddlers. One meta-analysis suggests that expressive vocabulary problems respond best to therapy, with mixed evidence for the effectiveness of therapy for expressive grammatical problems, and few studies available to document the effectiveness of therapy for receptive language impairment (Law, Garrett, & Nye, 2004). General language stimulation is not as effective as therapy that focuses on the specific linguistic skills that the child needs to master (Leonard, Camarata, Pawloswka, Brown, & Camarata, 2008). Distributed intervention sessions, rather than massed practice of individual grammatical targets, appears to be most effective (Proctor-Williams, 2009).

Imitation, **recasting** (Camerata & Nelson, 2006), modeling, and **expansion** all appear to be effective approaches to language intervention in this population. Proctor-Williams (2009) defines and illustrates a broad array of approaches used in language therapy, and summarizes other factors that appear to influence the effectiveness of therapy, including how much time is spent in the intervention setting. Figure 9.2 provides some examples of these techniques used in treating grammatical impairment in SLI (as well as in the other disorders discussed in this chapter). Most of these procedures are adapted in some way from patterns that have been shown to influence language growth in typically developing children, such as joint book reading (Cole, Maddox, & Lim, 2006) and

figure 9.2	**Some Approaches to Treatment of Language Impairment.** In each of the following cases, we will assume that the target form to be learned by the child is either a copular or an auxiliary be form. Setting: The child and the therapist are engaged in play with clay. (Adapted from Bernstein & Tiegerman-Farber, 2002, Leonard, 1998, and Proctor-Williams, 2009.) In these examples, the targets are italicized to help the reader locate the desired response; in therapy, these might sometimes be emphasized, but such emphasis would need to be faded for language to sound natural

Approach	**Explanation**	**Example**
Imitation/mand	Child is asked to repeat model presented by therapist.	Clinician: I *am* rolling the clay. You are, too. Say, "I *am* rolling." Child: I *am* rolling.
Imitation/feedback	Gradually, the request for imitation may be faded to include only a question prompt.	Clinician: I *am* rolling the clay. I *am* rolling. What are you doing? Child: I *am* rolling.
Imitation of child's correct form, or corrected imitation of error	The adult may imitate the child's correct utterance to reinforce it, or make a small change to provide the contrast form.	Child: The clay *is* sticky! Adult: Yes! The clay *is* sticky! Child: The clay sticky. Adult: Yes, the clay *is* sticky!
Modeling	Adult models a target form; child takes turns creating utterances having the target form.	Clinician: I *am* rolling the clay. I *am* pounding the clay. I *am* stretching the clay. What *are* you doing? Child: I *am* smushing clay.
Focused stimulation	Child is exposed to a large number of exemplars of the target form or word; the child may then be asked questions requiring use of the target form or word.	Clinician: Here *is* green clay. Let's make vegetables. Lettuce *is* green. Cabbage *is* green. A pea *is* green. A green bean *is* green. Cucumber *is* green. Here, you make a tomato (hands child green clay). Child: No. Tomato *is* red. Clinician: That's right. Tomato *is* red. (hands child red clay)
Conversational recasting	The adult responds to the child's spontaneous language by rephrasing to include the target form.	Child: This green clay. Clinician: That's right. This *is* green clay. It *is* green.
Expansion	The adult responds to the child's spontaneous language by including additional information.	(Similar to recasting, but a broader set of targets are used; the child's utterances are expanded to include new elements.) Child: This clay no good. Clinician: This clay *isn't* any good. It *isn't*. It *is* too dry.

(Continued)

figure 9.2	(Continued)

Approach	Explanation	Example
Time delay or slowed presentation	Slowing the pace of conversation and waiting for the child to supply a required form.	Adult: All these cans of clay *are mine*! (pulls the materials toward her and waits) Child: No, these *are mine*!
Scaffolding	The adult provides structure for the child's attempts. Gradually, this structure is faded to allow the child to produce the target on his own.	Clinician: Look at these snakes I made. This one *is* very big. This one *is* very small. And this one *is*. . . Child: Skinny! Clinician: Right. This one *is* skinny. And this one . . . Child: *is* fat.
Direct instruction	The rule is explicitly provided. This works better for older, second-language learners than for young children with language delay or disorder, who typically lack the metalinguistic awareness to talk about language rules.	Adult: We are going to work on how to talk about one thing and more than one thing. Here *is* some clay. Here *are* some cans of clay. We say *is* for one thing and *are* for more than one thing.

focused stimulation (Ellis Weismer & Robertson, 2006), in addition to imitation, recasting, and expansion, noted above. However, in a treatment setting (rather than in typical interactions during the child's day), nearly one recast per minute may be required to change a child's use of incorrect expressive language forms (Leonard et al., 2006). Thus, most researchers agree that children with SLI need more exposure to language targets than their nonimpaired peers to learn them.

A key problem facing children with SLI as well as children with other forms of language impairment is generalization. Children who are typically developing find it very easy to create new sentences by analogy to the large variety of grammatical examples they have heard; most children with language disorders do not. This is the crux of the challenge for language teachers—to teach children to be able to create utterances they have not specifically been taught to say. Even explicit explanation of a grammatical rule does not help some children with SLI acquire and use a new language structure. Numerous specific procedures and discussion about approaches to language remediation with children may be found in Owens (2010), McCauley and Fey (2006), and Paul (2007), among others. Fey, Long, and Finestak (2003) provide some guiding principles for structuring and implementing language therapy, as seen in Figure 9.3.

Nelson (2010) discusses classroom-based intervention for school-aged children and adolescents with SLI, whereas Ukrainetz (2006) discusses approaches that scaffold the transition to successful literacy and discourse abilities in children with SLI.

Not all effective interventions require the child interact only with an SLP; especially in very young children with SLI or other forms of language impairment, specialist-guided parental intervention is very effective (Roberts & Kaiser, 2011). Additionally, most of us probably think of school-based "speech-language therapy" in the form of what is called the "pullout" model: the speech-language pathologist and the student with SLI meet outside the classroom to work on targets in the SLP's office. However, some research has begun to suggest that this model is not as effective as those in which the SLP comes into the classroom to work on skills within the context of the curriculum (Stephenson, 2008).

figure 9.3	**Ten Principles to Guide Language Instruction for Children with SLI**
	(Adapted from Fey, Long, & Finestack, 2003)

1. The primary goal of intervention should be to improve understanding and use of syntax and grammar in order to improve conversation, narrative and expository abilities, and other educationally required uses of language, both written and oral.

2. Grammar should rarely, if ever, be the sole target of language intervention.

3. Do not teach to master a form or ability in a single step; select intermediate goals that will help the child to use language functionally and stimulate further communicative development.

4. The child must be "ready" (developmentally) to acquire targeted forms and have a communicative need for them.

5. Clinicians and teachers should manipulate the child's social, physical, and language environment to provide opportunities to use targeted forms.

6. As appropriate, clinicians and teachers should extend oral language targets by using reading and writing environments that call on such forms. For example, the past tense may be used more in narratives (stories) than in conversation.

7. Clinicians and teachers should manipulate discourse so that it is easier for the child to identify targeted forms, through stress or ellipsis. For example, an argument over whether the child WILL or WON'T do something provides a strong and salient contrast between modals for the child.

8. Recast children's errors into more mature, adultlike forms to help the child compare his errors with more advanced productions.

9. Always present the child with full, grammatical models, rather than telegraphic speech.

10. Use elicited imitation to provide the child with practice on contrasting forms, but in combination with the other strategies listed above, not as a sole teaching strategy.

An ever-increasing number of children with SLI are bilingual and face language-learning challenges in two or more languages. Kohnert & Ebert (2010) summarize the many challenges in understanding and working with this population, as well as the potential benefits we will gain in understanding SLI and its many manifestations when we compare how SLI affects a child's performance across languages.

While it used to be conventional for children to be identified and served for special needs services after showing significant distress in the academic environment, most American schools have now adopted what is called the **Response to Intervention (RTI)** approach to adjusting classroom instruction for children who are either at risk for academic failure, or who seem to be having problems meeting curricular expectations. RTI acknowledges that not all children who are not performing well in school have an actual disability. Rather, poor performance on large-scale screening measures, or teacher observation of difficulty, can trigger adjustments made in instruction for that child, or for a whole class of children. Children who do not respond to such more limited approaches, or whose difficulties appear to stem from special needs may then be referred for services under IDEA. A summary of RTI principles and applications to early childhood education is provided by Greenwood, Bradfield, Karminski, Linas, Carta, and Nylander (2011).

Atypical Speech Development

We have described in some detail four major forms of language disorders. There are, in addition, many conditions that lead to atypical speech development. Speech disorders constitute another field of inquiry altogether, and we mention them here only briefly. As in the case of disordered language development, disordered speech development may evolve both from known organic causes and syndromes and from unknown etiology. For instance, significant hearing impairment in children typically results in poor articulation ability;

motor disorders in children, such as **cerebral palsy,** often affect the ability to articulate normally. Children with cerebral palsy often demonstrate problems with respiratory support for speech and difficulty producing or controlling the rapid movements of the larynx, jaw, tongue, and lips necessary for the normal rapid rate of conversational speech (Workinger, 2005). It is important to point out that in many cases of cerebral palsy, receptive language ability and intellectual functioning are unimpaired, although recent trends in the survival rate for at-risk infants have increased both the rate of cerebral palsy and the rate of concomitant disorders (Hayes, 2010).

Cleft palate is a condition in which various facial structures, particularly the hard and soft palates, fail to develop properly during the first trimester of gestation. A typical result is the inability to control the intra-oral air pressure necessary for normal speech development. Air leaks cut through the palatal defect and the nostrils, producing a nasal speech quality and an inability to produce certain classes of phonemes, such as sibilants and high-pressure stops and fricatives (e.g., /p/, /b/, /f/, /v/). (See Chapter 3 and review Figure 3.1 to understand why this happens.) Like the child with cerebral palsy, the child with cleft-palate speech often mistakenly elicits listener perceptions of linguistic or cognitive deficiency. The vast majority of children with cleft palate, however, possess normal linguistic and intellectual ability. Cleft-palate speech can usually be substantially improved by a combination of surgical and speech therapy intervention (Kuehn & Henne, 2003).

A large proportion of speech disorders in children have traditionally been termed *functional* articulation disorders (i.e., their etiology is unknown, just as in the case of SLI). Children with functional articulation disorders appear to have normal perceptual and motor skills but do not progress in learning speech sound production as well as their peers (Bernthal, Bankson, & Flipsen, 2008).

In general, children whose articulation development is perceived to be either slow or defective demonstrate phonological patterns similar to those exhibited by younger, typically developing children (see Chapter 3 to review these typical patterns). Thus, phonemes that emerge late in typical child phonology may be missing or misarticulated in the speech of children with articulation impairments. Additionally, phonological processes that are common in very young children's word productions—such as consonant-cluster reduction, final-consonant deletion or devoicing, stopping of continuant sounds, or gliding of liquids (see Chapter 3)—may persist in the speech of older children with disordered speech, as may other residual speech errors (Bauman-Waengler, 2012). Additionally, syntax and phonology may interact to create varying degrees of difficulty with both articulation and grammar for individual children (Haskill & Tyler, 2007).

Therapy can be effective in remediating phonological/articulation disorders of unknown etiology (Gierut & Hulse, 2010). Some children are aided by a *semantic* approach; for example, they would be made aware that failure to include final consonants results in inability to distinguish among words in the language (e.g., *bead, beat, beach, beak*). Other children are helped by direct instructions regarding placement of the articulators for the correct production of problematic sounds. For instance, an /s/ can be produced if the child is told to say /t/, then gradually slide the tongue back. Other approaches exist as well. Overviews of the major issues involved in assessing and remediating children's articulation disorders are provided by Bernthal, Bankson, and Flipsen (2008), and Bauman-Waengler (2012).

Therapy helps children with speech and hearing impairments overcome problems with phonology, grammar, and word knowledge.

Childhood Stuttering

A small percentage of children fail to develop normal fluency skills. As with language and articulation ability, fluent speech evolves over the course of child development. Thus, even typically developing children demonstrate a tendency to hesitate, to repeat or prolong sounds, syllables, and words, or to insert fillers in their utterances such as *um* and *well* between words. This behavior is most obvious during the period of most rapid progress in language acquisition, usually between the ages of 2 and 4 years; because such disfluency is normal, it is called **developmental disfluency** and is not considered to be a problem.

However, some children's fluency appears to differ both quantitatively and qualitatively from that seen in normal development; children may demonstrate greater degrees of disfluency, such as more than ten repeated words, syllables, or sounds per 100 words (Bloodstein & Bernstein Ratner, 2008). More of their disfluencies are part-word repetitions than one would expect in typical child speech, and there are likely to be more repetitions of a repeated segment than in normal speech. Most children occasionally repeat a syllable or word once, such as "but-but I don't want to," while the stuttering child may produce "b-b-b-but I don't want to." Prolonged segments are of excessive duration, and the quality of the prolongation appears tense. Finally, as the child continues to experience difficulty in producing fluent utterances, he or she may begin to demonstrate signs of self-awareness and frustration. Such symptoms of clinical **stuttering** most typically emerge just prior to 3 years of age (Yairi & Ambrose, 2005).

As with many of the disorders surveyed in this chapter, the cause of stuttering is presently not known. Developmental stuttering is a puzzling disorder when viewed against others covered in this chapter, because stuttering emerges after the child has experienced successful speech and language development. Moreover, the extreme discomfort and struggle seen when very young stuttering children experience disfluency is incompatible with levels of self-monitoring for speech that are characteristic of children this age and distinctly different from the relative unconcern demonstrated by other groups of children with deficient speech and language skills (Bloodstein & Bernstein Ratner, 2008).

There is a genetic predisposition to develop stuttering (Yairi & Ambrose, 2005). Additionally, a growing body of research concludes that stutterers show atypical brain activation patterns when either listening to or producing speech; see a representative study by Chang, Kenney, Loucks, and Ludlow (2009) and summary of both anatomical and neurophysiological differences between people who stutter and typical fluent speakers in Bloodstein and Bernstein Ratner (2008). Some investigators have posited that stuttering may result from problems in motor planning or coordination (see Olander, Smith, & Zelasnik, 2010). Because of known linguistic influences on the frequency and location of stuttering in children's speech (Bloodstein & Bernstein Ratner, 2008), other researchers have either posited an underlying linguistic basis for stuttering or suggested that stuttering reflects an inability of the child's system to deal with simultaneous language formulation and motor speech production demands (Smith & Kelly, 1997).

More than half of all children who stutter as preschoolers recover before the age of 7, most within a relatively short time (12 to 18 months) after onset of symptoms (Bloodstein & Bernstein Ratner, 2008). Boys tend to recover less often, as do children with positive family histories of persistent stuttering, and those with poorer language skills, to name some prognostic indicators (Yairi & Ambrose, 2005). For those children who continue to experience difficulty in producing fluent speech, therapy can be most helpful when it both teaches more fluent speech style (so-called *fluency shaping*) and also helps the child to learn how to move through stuttering moments more easily, as well as avoid the development of counterproductive responses to the fear of stuttering, such as speaking fears and distracting ancillary behaviors (*stuttering modification* therapy). Bloodstein and Bernstein Ratner (2008) and Manning (2009) provide guidelines for the diagnosis and treatment of fluency disorders in children.

Evaluation of Suspected Speech and Language Disorders in Children

Parents are usually the first to suspect that a child is not developing language skills normally. The child may not have begun to use understandable words by 18 months of age, although other children they know began to acquire language as early as 9 months or 1 year of age. Or the child may not appear to hear well. Or she may appear to use sentence structures that seem too immature for her age. Some specific warning signs have been identified that should prompt parents to seek professional guidance; they include the following potential indicators of delayed or deviant communicative development (see the National Institutes of Health; **www.nidcd.nih.gov/health/voice/speechandlanguage.html** for further information):

- Failure to babble by 12 months of age.
- Lack of conventionalized gestures such as pointing, waving, or blowing kisses by 1 year of age.
- No spoken words by 18 months of age.
- Fewer than 50 single words and no two-word combinations by 24 months of age.
- Any evidence of speech or language regression, regardless of age.

How does one determine whether a child's communicative development appears normal or disturbed? What is the difference between individual variation (Chapter 8) and atypical variation that places the child at a communicative disadvantage? Evaluation of the communicative competence of children with suspected language disorders is the task of **speech-language pathologists.** Before appraising the child's language skills, hearing acuity is usually evaluated by an **audiologist** to ensure that the child will be able to comply with assessment demands and to rule out hearing impairment as the possible basis for the suspected speech-language delay.

A variety of assessment devices and procedures can aid in the identification of children who will need therapeutic intervention to develop adequate communication skills. A number of articulation tests (see Bernthal, Bankson, & Flipsen, 2008) compare both the number and pattern of a child's articulation errors against expected performance for her age. The measurement of a child's language skills may be both theoretically and practically more difficult, however (Nelson, 2010; Paul, 2007). It is difficult to appraise the full range of morphological, syntactic, and pragmatic skills needed to be an effective and age-appropriate communicator in the limited time of a diagnostic session.

Because language skills encompass such a large and varied domain, tests of language ability in children are extremely numerous and diverse, and we cannot easily describe them in this chapter. Paul (2007) and Nelson (2010) provide extensive overview descriptions of many of the commonly used tests of child language ability. We will note that many tests of language performance can be faulted for limited **content validity**—they are able to sample only a small range of possible language skills and usually do so in ways that do not duplicate real-world communicative situations. Additionally, most standardized language tests are not designed to evaluate the performance of children younger than 3 years. There has been increased interest in the use of parental report measures, which can reliably identify language-delayed and normal children as young as 20 to 24 months; among these are the *MacArthur-Bates CDI* and the *Language Development Survey* (Rescorla, Bernstein Ratner, Jusczyk, & Jusczyk, 2005), which have now been translated into numerous languages around the world. Such measures utilize parental estimates of specific vocabulary, grammatical morphemes, and sentence patterns used by the child, rather than actual samples of the child's speech.

It is widely acknowledged that structured tests of language comprehension and production should be supplemented by structural and pragmatic analysis of spontaneous language samples. Nelson (2010) and Owens (2010) provide guidelines for syntactic evaluation of spontaneous language. These are more time-consuming appraisal techniques that yield a more complete and representative picture of a child's expressive grammatical ability.

The growing number of non-English-speaking and bilingual children who require assessment for suspected language delay or disorder has placed large challenges on the development of adequate measures of development for learners of other languages, as well as the particular needs of bilingual speakers, whose two languages must be considered both separately to appraise ability to function in each, as well as together, to observe the child's overall linguistic skills. Few tests are currently available to meet these two large needs (Dollaghan & Horner, 2011).

Finally, it is critical that speech and language assessment be linguistically unbiased; for example, some features of SLI, such as agreement marking, overlap with nonmainstream dialects of American English and must be accounted for in order to avoid misdiagnosis of normal nonmainstream dialect users or minority-population English language learners as language impaired (Roseberry-McKibbin, 2007). There has been recent emphasis on the use of standardized assessment measures that specifically target the differential diagnosis of language variation from language disorder (Seymour & Pearson, 2004).

We close this section on treatment by noting the growing emphasis on treatment of children with communication disorders of all types in the most inclusive and least restrictive environments, as required by the **Individuals with Disabilities Education Act (IDEA).** Over the years, a major effect of this legislation has been to increase the inclusion of children with language and other disabilities into the general curriculum and classroom. McCormick, Loeb, and Shieffelbusch (2003) survey the positive and growing effect that the IDEA has had on assessment and treatment of children with communicative disorders. As noted earlier, a move to RTI will also presumably lead to earlier and more effective identification of children who require help to succeed academically.

SUMMARY

Some common themes appear when reviewing recent research on children with many types of developmental communication disorders. One is that of genetics; tremendous strides have been made in the last ten years to isolate genetic markers for autism, deafness, intellectual disability, and SLI. There has been rapid recent progress in the search to identify genes associated with autism as well as language learning and reading disabilities. It is likely that many of these disabilities are influenced by multiple genes. Although such discoveries are not likely to have an immediate effect on the management of these disorders, they do have the eventual potential to isolate treatments that reduce particular symptoms and that facilitate earlier identification and intervention with developmental disorders of communication. In some areas, such as autism and stuttering, genetic findings have had a major effect on older theories of etiology that put childrearing practices or experience at the basis of the disorder and provided grist for unwarranted parental guilt over the child's problem. At the same time, one's genotype (genetics) or phenotype (presenting symptoms) are not destiny: In the theoretical debate between nativists, social interactionists, and emergentist positions, it is quite relevant to note that appropriate intervention (nurture) has the documented ability to affect language outcomes in children who present with communication disorders. For special educators, speech-language pathologists, parents, and others, the debate over the relative contributions of nature and nurture to language outcomes that are covered in Chapter 7 is not an academic exercise. It is an everyday empirical challenge, whose successes and failures inform theory but greatly affect individual children.

A second theme involves distinction, as well as overlap, among the various disorders we have surveyed. Many old defining characteristics of language disorders appear to be softening. For example, some classic views of the differences between autism and SLI now seem to require revision; as noted earlier, there is substantial overlap in many of their symptoms as well as their genetic histories.

Increasingly, in order to understand what aspects of language impairment are unique to various childhood disorders, researchers now compare multiple groups of children. Whereas prior studies might have compared children with SLI and typically developing children, for example, recent studies utilize multiple comparison groups, such as typically developing children, children with Down syndrome, and children with SLI (Eadie, Fey, Douglas, & Parsons, 2002). This study did not find major differences between children with SLI and Down syndrome when the children were matched for MLU on similar tasks. However informative it is to compare multiple groups of children to isolate the specific bases of particular language profiles, this method is not simple. How should groups be matched? On language ability, nonverbal language ability, IQ? None has proven to be quite satisfactory. Such gross measures do not adequately capture the behavioral "essence" of each child's disability, nor what methods will work best for helping any individual child to communicate better. Grouping children by their primary diagnosis, as we have done in this chapter, misses the very individual and unique profiles that they demonstrate; for case studies of individual children who face challenges learning language because of the conditions discussed in this chapter, see Tiegerman-Farber and Radziewicz (2008).

Finally, there have been changes in the treatment of many types of communicative disorders over the past few years. Some changes have been brought about by technological advances, such as cochlear implants and computer-assisted speech processing programs. Others have been more philosophical or programmatic, such as the increased emphasis on early detection of communicative impairment in very young children, and more naturalistic and inclusive teaching/learning environments for the remediation of communicative impairments.

In summary, although the vast majority of children master language skills easily, other children may be comparatively slow language learners and, in some cases, fail to acquire normal adultlike language abilities. Four major conditions adversely affect both the speed and success of language learning and can lead to life-long functional impacts on quality of life. Hearing impairment limits the child's exposure to a sufficiently large and intelligible language model. Intellectual disability is usually accompanied by a slower rate of language development and less proficient final language ability, although it is not clear whether children's problems with language stem directly from specific cognitive skill deficiencies or from other, more global patterns of behavior.

Children with ASD demonstrate language profiles that are usually described as severely deviant in quality, demonstrating a lack of pragmatic appropriateness as well as structural deficiencies. The nature of the underlying deficit in autism has yet to be determined; however, analysis of the striking language patterns seen in children with autism may help to answer questions about the origins of the aberrant behaviors of this syndrome.

The largest proportion of children with delayed or impaired language development have weak or delayed language skills when compared to their peers, but they do not suffer from obvious neurological, cognitive, or perceptual impairment. These children with specific language impairment are thought to demonstrate poor ability to abstract and learn language rules and skills. Many children who show such a pattern of depressed language functioning during early development apparently also go on to experience difficulty with academic skills during their school years and beyond.

Language impairment—which affects the child's ability to use the lexicon, syntax, and pragmatic systems of language—needs to be differentiated from speech impairment, which affects the child's ability to articulate the phonological component of language. Some speech impairment is due to defects in oral structure (such as cleft palate); other forms may be due to problems in motor coordination of the structures necessary for speech production (as in the case of cerebral palsy). Still other children misarticulate because they do not hear language models correctly (in the case of hearing impairment). However, many children demonstrate delayed patterns of articulation development that are not easily explained by these considerations.

Finally, although all children are occasionally disfluent during the language learning years, some children demonstrate patterns of sound and syllable repetition, prolongation of sounds, and tense pauses between sounds and words in utterances that lead them to be perceived as children who stutter. The cause of stuttering is, like so many of the disorders we have considered in this chapter, basically unknown, although motor planning and linguistic encoding difficulty are two of the more commonly considered current approaches to its understanding and treatment.

Treatment of children with communicative handicaps is most effective when it considers the normal sequence of language development and attempts to integrate current beliefs about environmentally facilitating factors in normal language acquisition into the therapeutic process. That is why the other chapters in this text are important in guiding future professionals. Success in speech and language teaching appears to be guided in large part by knowledge of when children are ready to learn certain skills, given what they already seem to know. Additionally, the degree to which the language skills being taught can be made pragmatically relevant to everyday communicative needs is extremely important. Finally, the manner in which linguistic skills are introduced and reinforced also appears to be extremely important, although current research does not indicate a single most effective way to teach language skills to children. When all is said and done, we are still better able to identify language disability in children than to rectify it. Continued research into the bases of impairment in the differing populations of children who have communication disorders is crucial to the improvement of methods for overcoming their linguistic handicaps.

SUGGESTED PROJECTS

1. View the evening news or another television program with the sound off. Attempt to transcribe what the speakers are saying and to summarize the content of the news stories or program plot. How successful are you? Write a paper that discusses the degree to which a lack of auditory information makes following spoken conversation difficult.

2. Arrange a discussion of the relative merits of cochlear implants, even if they endanger the viability of the sign languages used around the world. *Media tip:* Make arrangements to view the award-winning film *Sound and Fury* (2001); commentary and PBS view times are available at **www.pbs.org/wnet/soundandfury/film/index.html**; the film can also be purchased for a very minimal fee or rented. Should all children with profound hearing losses be outfitted with cochlear implants? A sequel to this movie was made in 2006; see **www.soundandfuryfilm.com/sixyears/index.php?section=aronson**. Does seeing this movie change any of your original opinions? View the commentary that has emerged on numerous social networking sites. Do any of the contributors change your initial impressions? If so, which ones? If not, why?

3. Try to arrange a visit to a school or class that has children who are hearing impaired, cognitively impaired, autistic, or language delayed. Write up and share your observations with others in your class. Be sure to address the children's patterns of communicative ability, as well as the techniques that are being used to remediate and augment their language skills. *Media tip:* The text *Exploring Communication Disorders: A 21st Century Introduction through Literature and Media* (Tanner, 2003) provides examples of written and video portrayals of children with a variety of communication disorders. To what extent does your observation match the text description provided in this

chapter? To what extent does it match the media portrayal? Compare both your observations and media descriptions to a collection of case studies in actual communication disorders provided by Tanner (2003).

4. If you can, arrange to observe a speech-language pathologist's therapeutic interaction with a communicatively impaired child. (Many universities operate speech-language and hearing clinics, as do many hospitals and schools. Additionally, some pathologists work in individual practices.) In a short report, summarize your impressions of the child's communicative problem. Then discuss and analyze the techniques used by the pathologist to teach a particular language skill. To what extent do they resemble approaches covered in this chapter? If they involve other approaches, work with the therapist to understand the evidence base for their use.

5. If you are able to gain appropriate institutional approval to carry out and record a conversation with an individual who has one of the communication disorders covered in this chapter, compare his or her apparent language understanding and use with that of a typical age- or developmentally matched peer. If you analyze across areas of linguistic skill (phonology, grammar, semantics, pragmatics, etc.), in what areas do you see differences between the profiles? What aspects would seem most crucial to remediate, in your opinion? Do you have any thoughts about a preferred approach, given the therapies surveyed in this chapter?

SUGGESTED READINGS

McCauley, R., & Fey, M. (Eds.). (2006). *Treating language disorders in children.* Baltimore: Brookes. (Contains video examples of a variety of intervention approaches discussed in this chapter.)

Owens, R. (2010). *Language disorders: A functional approach to assessment and intervention* (5th ed.). Boston: Allyn & Bacon.

Paul, R. (2007). *Language disorders in children* (3rd ed.). New York: Mosby. (Contains video samples of children with atypical language, and examples of assessment and intervention.)

KEY WORDS

American Sign Language (ASL)
amplification
anomia
applied behavior analysis (ABA)
Asperger syndrome
audiologist
auditory verbal therapy
augmentative or alternative communication (AAC)
aural rehabilitation
autism
autism spectrum disorder (ASD)
behavioral intervention
bilingual/bicultural (bi-bi) approach to deaf education

bimodal fitting of cochlear implants
cerebral palsy
circumlocution
cleft palate
cochlear implants
confrontation naming
congenital
content validity
cued speech
decibel (dB)
developmental disfluency
Down syndrome (DS)
dyslexia
early language delay (ELD)
echolalia
etiology
evidence-based practice (EBP)

executive function
expansion
extended optional infinitive
fragile X (fra X) syndrome
functional analysis
generalization
generalized slowing hypothesis
hearing impairment
imitation
Individuals with Disabilities Education Act (IDEA)
intellectual disability
language age (LA)
lipreading (also known as speech reading)
mainstreaming
mental age (MA)
meta-analysis

modeling
nonword repetition (NWR)
oral/aural approach to deaf
  education
otitis media
perseveration
pervasive developmental
  disorder (PDD)
pervasive developmental
  disorder—not otherwise
  specified (PDD-NOS)
phonological awareness
pivotal response training
  (PRT)

prelingually deaf
recasting
response to intervention
  (RTI)
Rett syndrome
SCERTS (Social
  Communication,
  Emotional Regulation,
  and Transactional
  Support)
specific language impair-
  ment (SLI)
speech-language patholo-
  gist

speechreading
stuttering
surface hypothesis
TEACCH (Treatment and
  Education of Autistic and
  related Communication-
  Handicapped Children)
theory of mind
total communication
universal newborn screen-
  ing
weak central coherence
Williams syndrome (WS)

REFERENCES

Acredolo, L. & Goodwyn, S. (2002). *Baby signs: How to talk with your baby before your baby can talk.* New York: McGraw-Hill.

Adamson, L., Bakeman, R., Deckner, D., & Romski, M. (2009). Joint engagement and the emergence of language in children with autism and Down syndrome. *Journal of Autism & Developmental Disorders, 39*(1), 84–96.

Alt, M., & Plante, E. (2006). Factors that influence lexical and semantic fast mapping of young children with specific language impairment. *Journal of Speech, Language and Hearing Research, 49,* 941–954.

American Psychiatric Association. (2000). *Diagnostic and statistical manual of mental disorders* (4th ed., text revision). Washington, DC: Author.

American Speech-Language-Hearing Association. (2004). *Auditory integration training* [Position statement]. Available from www.asha.org/policy

Antia, S. D., Reed, S., & Kreimeyer, K. H. (2005). Written language of deaf and hard-of-hearing students in public schools. *Journal of Deaf Studies and Deaf Education, 10,* 243–255.

Bailey, D., Bruer, J., Symons, F., & Lichtman, J. (2001). *Critical thinking about critical periods.* Baltimore: Paul H. Brookes.

Baker-Ericzén, M. J., Stahmer, A. C., & Burns, A. (2007). Child demograph-
ics associated with outcomes in a community-based Pivotal Response Training program. *Journal of Positive Behavior Interventions, 9,* 52–60.

Barnes, S. (2010). Sign language with babies: what difference does it make? *Dimensions of Early Childhood, 38*(1), 21–30.

Barnes, E., Roberts, J., Long, S., Martin, G., Berni, M., Mandulak, K., & Sideris, J. (2009). Phonological accuracy and intelligibility in connected speech of boys with fragile X syndrome or Down syndrome. *Journal of Speech, Language & Hearing Research, 52*(4), 1048–1061.

Barry, J. G., Yasin, I., & Bishop, D. V. M. (2007). Heritable risk factors associated with language impairments. *Genes, Brain & Behavior, 6,* 66–76.

Bartolotta, T., Zipp, G., Simpkins, S., & Glazewski, B. (2011). Communication skills in girls with Rett syndrome. *Focus on Autism & Other Developmental Disabilities, 26*(1), 15–24.

Barton, G. R., Stacey, P. C., Fortnum, H. M., & Summerfield, A. Q. (2006). Hearing-impaired children in the United Kingdom, IV: Cost-effectiveness of pediatric cochlear implantation. *Ear and Hearing, 27,* 575–588.

Bauman-Waengler, J. (2012). *Articulatory and phonological impairments: A clinical focus* (4th ed.). Boston: Allyn & Bacon.

Begeer, S., Gevers, C., Clifford, P., Verhoeve, M., Kat, K., Hoddenbach, E., & Boer,

F. (2011). Theory of Mind training in children with autism: A randomized controlled trial. *Journal of Autism & Developmental Disorders, 41*(8), 997–1006.

Bellini, S., & Akullian, J. (2007). A meta-analysis of video modeling and video self-modeling interventions for children and adolescents with autism spectrum disorders. *Exceptional Children, 73,* 264–287.

Bellini, S., Peters, J. K., Benner, L., & Hopf, A. (2007). A meta-analysis of school-based social skills interventions for children with autism spectrum disorders. *Remedial and Special Education, 28,* 153–162.

Bellugi, U., Mills, R., Jernigan, T., Hickok, G., & Galaburda, A. M. (1999). Linking cognition, brain structure and brain function in Williams syndrome. In H. Tager-Flusberg (Ed.), *Neurodevelopmental disorders* (pp. 111–136). Cambridge, MA: MIT Press.

Benasich, A., & Tallal, P. (2002). Infant discrimination of rapid auditory cues predicts later language impairment. *Behavioral Brain Research, 136,* 31–50.

Ben-Yizhak, N., Yirmiya, N., Seidman, I., Alon, R., Lord, C., & Sigman, M. (2011). Pragmatic language and school related linguistic abilities in siblings of children with autism. *Journal of Autism and Developmental Disorders, 41*(6), 750–760.

Berglund, E., Eriksson, M., & Johansson, I. (2001). Parental reports of spoken language skills in children with Down syndrome. *Journal of Speech, Language and Hearing Research, 44,* 179–191.

Bernabei, P., Cerquiglini, A., Cortesi, F., & D'Ardia, C. (2007). Regression versus no regression in the autistic disorder: Developmental trajectories. *Journal of Autism and Developmental Disorders, 37,* 580–588.

Bernstein Ratner, N. (2000). Elicited imitation and other methods for the analysis of trade-offs between speech and language skills in children. In L. Menn & N. Bernstein Ratner (Eds.), *Methods for studying language production* (pp. 291–312). Mahwah, NJ: Erlbaum.

Bernthal, J., Bankson, N., & Flipsen, P. (2008). *Articulation and phonological disorders* (6th ed.). Boston: Allyn & Bacon.

Betancur, C. (2011). Etiological heterogeneity in autism spectrum disorders: More than 100 genetic and genomic disorders and still counting. *Brain Research,* 138042–138077.

Beukelman, D., & Mirenda, P. (2005). *Augmentative and alternative communication: Supporting children and adults with complex communication needs* (3rd ed.). Baltimore: Paul H. Brookes.

Bishop, D. (2006). What causes specific language impairment in children? *Current Directions in Psychological Science, 15,* 217–221.

Bishop, D. (2010). Overlaps between autism and language impairment: Phenomimicry or shared etiology? *Behavior Genetics, 40*(5), 618–629.

Bishop, D., Adams, C. V., Nation, K., & Rosen, S. (2005). Perception of transient nonspeech stimuli is normal in specific language impairment: Evidence from glide discrimination. *Applied Psycholinguistics, 26,* 175–194.

Bloodstein, O., & Bernstein Ratner, N. (2008). *A handbook on stuttering* (6th ed.). Clifton Park, NY: Cengage.

Bonvillian, J., Orlansky, M., & Novack, L. (1983). Developmental milestones: Sign language acquisition and motor development. *Child Development, 54,* 1435–1445.

Boscolo, B., Bernstein Ratner, N., & Rescorla, L. (2002). Fluency characteristics of children with a history of Specific Expressive Language Impairment (SLI-E). *American Journal of Speech-Language Pathology, 11,* 41–49.

Boudreau, D., & Chapman, R., (2000). The relationship between event representation and linguistic skill in narratives of children and adolescents with Down syndrome. *Journal of Speech, Language and Hearing Research, 43,* 1146–1159.

Brady, N., Skinner, D., Roberts, J., & Hennon, E. (2006). Communication in young children with fragile X syndrome: A qualitative study of mothers' perspectives. *American Journal of Speech-Language Pathology, 15,* 353–364.

Brinton, B., & Fujiki, M. (2005). Social competence in children with language impairment: Making connections. *Seminars in Speech and Language, 26,* 151–159.

Brock, J. (2007). Language abilities in Williams syndrome: A critical review. *Development and Psychopathology, 19,* 97–127.

Brunner, D., & Seung, H. (2009). Evaluation of the efficacy of communication-based treatments for Autism Spectrum Disorders: A literature review. *Communication Disorders Quarterly, 31,* 15–41.

Cable, A., & Domsch, C. (2011). Systematic review of the literature on the treatment of children with late language emergence. *International Journal of Language & Communication Disorders, 46*(2), 138–154.

Callahan, K., Shukla-Mehta, S., Magee, S., & Wie, M. (2010). ABA versus TEACCH: The case for defining and validating comprehensive treatment models in autism. *Journal of Autism & Developmental Disorders, 40*(1), 74–88.

Camerata, S., & Nelson, K. (2006). Conversational recast intervention with preschool and older children. In R. McCauley & M. Fey (Eds.), *Treating language disorders in children* (pp. 237–266). Baltimore: Paul H. Brookes.

Campbell, J. (2003). Efficacy of behavioral interventions for reducing problem behavior in persons with autism: A quantitative synthesis of single-subject research. *Research in Developmental Disabilities, 24,* 120–138.

Campbell, M., Schopler, E., Cueva, J., & Hallin, A. (1996). Treatment of autistic disorder. *Journal of the American Academy of Child Adolescent Psychiatry, 35,* 134–143.

Catts, H. W., Adlof, S. M., Hogan, T. P., & Weismer, S. E. (2005). Are specific language impairment and dyslexia distinct disorders? *Journal of Speech, Language & Hearing Research, 48,* 1378–1396.

Centers for Disease Control (CDC). (2005). 2005 Preliminary hearing screening summary. Retrieved at www.cdc.gov/ncbddd/ehdi/documents/Screen_Summ_05_B.pdf

Chang, S., Kenney, M., Loucks, T. J., & Ludlow, C. L. (2009). Brain activation abnormalities during speech and non-speech in stuttering speakers. *NeuroImage, 46*(1), 201–212.

Chapman, R. (1999). Language development in children and adolescents with Down syndrome. In J. Miller, M. Leddy, & L. Leavitt (Eds.), *Improving the communication of people with Down syndrome* (pp. 41–60). Baltimore: Paul H. Brookes.

Chapman, R. (2006). Language learning in Down syndrome: The speech and language profile compared to adolescents with cognitive impairment of unknown origin. *Down Syndrome Research and Practice, 10,* 61–66.

Chapman, R., Hesketh, L., & Kistler, D. (2002). Predicting longitudinal change in language production and comprehension in individuals with Down syndrome: Hierarchical linear modeling. *Journal of Speech, Language and Hearing Research, 45,* 902–915.

Child Health Alert. (2010) …And the "Final Word" on the role of vaccines as a cause of autism. *Child Health Alert, 282–283.*

Choo, D., & Meinzen-Derr, J. (2010). Universal newborn hearing screening in 2010. *Current Opinion in Otolaryngology & Head and Neck Surgery, 18,* 399–404.

Choudhury, N., Leppanen, P. H. T., Leevers, H. J., & Benasich, A. A. (2007). Infant information processing and family history of specific language impairment: Converging evidence for RAP deficits from two paradigms. *Developmental Science, 10,* 213–236.

Cleland, J., Wood, S., Hardcastle, W., Wishart, J., & Timmins, C. (2010). Relationship between speech, oromotor, language and cognitive abilities in children with Down's syndrome. *International Journal of Language & Communication Disorders, 45*(1), 83–95.

Coady, J. A., Evans, J. L., Mainela-Arnold, E., & Kluender, K. R. (2007). Children with specific language impairments perceive speech most categorically when tokens are natural and meaningful. *Journal of Speech, Language and Hearing Research, 50,* 41–57.

Cole, K., Maddox, M., & Lim, Y. (2006). Language is the key: Constructive interactions around books and play. In R. McCauley & M. Fey (Eds.), *Treating language disorders in children* (pp. 149–174). Baltimore: Paul H. Brookes.

Connor, C. M., & Zwolan, T. A. (2004). Examining multiple sources of influence on the reading comprehension skills of children who use cochlear implants. *Journal of Speech, Language and Hearing Research, 47,* 509–526.

Constantino, J., Zhang, Y., Frazier, T., Abbacchi, A., & Law, P. (2010). Sibling recurrence and the genetic epidemiology of autism. *The American Journal of Psychiatry, 167*(11), 1349–1356.

Corbett, B., Carmean, V., Ravizza, S., Wendelken, C., Henry, M., Carter, C., & Rivera, S. (2009). A functional and structural study of emotion and face processing in children with autism. *Psychiatry Research, 173*(3), 196–205.

Corriveau, K., Pasquini, E., & Goswami, U. (2007). Basic auditory processing skills and specific language impairment: A new look at an old hypothesis. *Journal of Speech, Language and Hearing Research, 50,* 647–666.

Cosetti, M. & Roland, J. (2010). Cochlear implantation in the very young child: issues unique to the under-1 population. *Trends in Amplification, 14*(1), 46–57.

Courchesne, E., Campbell, K., & Solso, S. (2011). Brain growth across the life span in autism: Age-specific changes in anatomical pathology. *Brain Research,* 1380138–1380145.

Dale, P., Price, T., Bishop, D., & Plomin, R. (2003). Outcomes of early language delay, I: Predicting persistent and transient language difficulties at 3 and 4 years. *Journal of Speech, Language and Hearing Research, 46,* 544–560.

de Falco, S., Venuti, P., Esposito, G., & Bornstein, M. H. (2011). Maternal and paternal pragmatic speech directed to young children with Down syndrome and typical development. *Infant Behavior & Development, 34,* 161–169.

Degabriele, J., & Walsh, I. (2010). Humour appreciation and comprehension in children with intellectual disability. *Journal of Intellectual Disability Research, 54*(6), 525–537.

Dierssen, M. M., & Ramakers, G. A. (2006). Dendritic pathology in mental retardation: From molecular genetics to neurobiology. *Genes, Brain & Behavior, 5*(Suppl2), 48–60.

Dollaghan, C., & Horner, E. (2011). Bilingual language assessment: A meta-analysis of diagnostic accuracy. *Journal of Speech, Language and Hearing Research, 54,* 1077–1088.

Eadie, P., Fey, M., Douglas, J., & Parsons, C. (2002). Profiles of grammatical morphology and sentence imitation in children with specific language impairment and Down syndrome. *Journal of Speech, Language and Hearing Research, 45,* 720–732.

Easterbrooks, S., & Baker, S. (2002). *Language learning in children who are deaf and hard of hearing: Multiple pathways.* Boston: Allyn & Bacon.

Edgin, J. O., Kumar, A. A., Spanò, G. G., & Nadel, L. L. (2011). Neuropsychological effects of second language exposure in Down syndrome. *Journal of Intellectual Disability Research, 55*(3), 351–356.

Eigsti, I., & Bennetto, L. (2009). Grammaticality judgments in autism: Deviance or delay. *Journal of Child Language, 36*(5), 999–1021.

Eigsti, I., Bennetto, L., & Dadlani, M. (2007). Beyond pragmatics: morphosyntactic development in autism. *Journal of Autism & Developmental Disorders, 37*(6), 1007–1023.

Eigsti, I., de Marchena, A. B., Schuh, J. M., & Kelley, E. (2011). Language acquisition in autism spectrum disorders: A developmental review. *Research in Autism Spectrum Disorders, 5*(2), 681–691.

Eldevik, S., Hastings, R. P., Hughes, J., Jahr, E., Eikeseth, S., & Cross, S. (2009). Meta-analysis of early intensive behavioral intervention for children with autism. *Journal of Clinical Child and Adolescent Psychology, 38*(3), 439–450.

Ellis Weismer, S., Gernsbacher, M., Stronach, S., Karasinski, C., Eernisse, E., Venker, C., & Sindberg, H. (2011). Lexical and grammatical skills in toddlers on the autism spectrum compared to late talking toddlers. *Journal of Autism & Developmental Disorders, 41*(8), 1065–1075.

Ellis Weismer, S., & Robertson, S. (2006). Focused stimulation approach to language intervention. In R. McCauley & M. Fey (Eds.), *Treating language disorders in children* (pp. 175–202). Baltimore: Paul H. Brookes.

Emmorey, K., & Lane, H. (2000). *The signs of language revisited.* Mahwah, NJ: Erlbaum.

Estes, K. G., Evans, J. L., & Else-Quest, N. M. (2007). Differences in the nonword repetition performance of children with and without specific language impairment: A meta-analysis. *Journal of Speech, Language and Hearing Research, 50,* 177–195.

Falcaro, M. M., Pickles, A. A., Newbury, D. F., Addis, L. L., Banfield, E. E., Fisher, S. E., & ... Conti-Ramsden, G. G. (2008). Genetic and phenotypic effects of phonological short-term memory and grammatical morphology in specific language impairment. *Genes, Brain & Behavior, 7*(4), 393–402.

Feltmate, K., & Kay-Raining Bird, E. (2008). Language learning in four bilingual children with Down syndrome. A detailed analysis of vocabulary and morphosyntax. *Canadian Journal of Speech-Language Pathology and Audiology, 32*(1), 6–20.

Fey, M., Finestack, L., Gajewski, B., Popescu, M., & Lewine, J. (2010). A preliminary evaluation of Fast ForWord-Language as an adjuvant treatment in language intervention. *Journal of Speech, Language & Hearing Research, 53*(2), 430–449.

Fey, M., Long, S., & Finestack, L. (2003). Ten principles of grammar facilitation for children with specific language impairments. *American Journal of Speech-Language Pathology, 12,* 3–15.

Fey, M., Warren, S., Brady, N., Finestack, L., Bredin-Oja, S., Fairchild, M., et al. (2006). Early effects of prelinguistic milieu teaching and responsivity education for children with developmental delays and their parents. *Journal of Speech, Language and Hearing Research, 49,* 526–547.

Fidler, D. (2005). The emerging Down syndrome behavioral phenotype in early childhood. *Infants and Young Children, 18,* 86–103.

Fidler, D. J., Philofsky, A., & Hepburn, S. L. (2007). Language phenotypes and intervention planning: Bridging research and practice. *Mental Retardation and Developmental Disabilities Research Reviews, 13,* 47–57.

Fidler, L. J., Plante, E., & Vance, R. (2011). Identification of adults with developmental language impairments. *American Journal of Speech-Language Pathology, 20*(1), 2–13.

Finestack, L., & Abbeduto, L. (2010). Expressive language profiles of verbally expressive adolescents and young adults with Down syndrome or fragile X syndrome. *Journal of Speech, Language, and Hearing Research, 53*(5), 1334–1348.

Finneran, D. A., Leonard, L. B., & Miller, C. A. (2009). Speech disruptions in the sentence formulation of school-age children with specific language impairment. *International Journal of Language & Communication Disorders, 44*(3), 271–286.

Flippin, M., Reszka, S., & Watson, L. (2010). Effectiveness of the picture exchange communication system (PECS) on communication and speech for children with autism spectrum disorders: a meta-analysis. *American Journal of Speech-Language Pathology, 19*(2), 178–195.

Flipsen, P., & Parker, R. G. (2008). Phonological patterns in the conversational speech of children with cochlear implants. *Journal of Communication Disorders, 41*(4), 337–357.

Fombonne, E. (2005). The changing epidemiology of autism. *Journal of Applied Research in Intellectual Disabilities, 18,* 281–294.

Ford, J., & Milosky, L. (2003). Inferring social reactions in social situations: Differences in children with language impairment. *Journal of Speech, Language and Hearing Research, 46,* 21–30.

Friedmann, N., & Szterman, R. (2011). The comprehension and production of Wh-questions in deaf and hard-of-hearing children. *Journal of Deaf Studies and Deaf Education, 16*(2), 212–235.

Gale, E. (2011). Exploring perspectives on cochlear implants and language acquisition within the Deaf community. *Journal of Deaf Studies & Deaf Education, 16*(1), 121–139.

Gallaudet Research Institute. (2008). *Regional and national summary report of data from the 2007–2008 annual survey of deaf and hard of hearing children and youth.* Washington, DC: Gallaudet University.

Ganz, J. B., Earles-Vollrath, T. L., Mason, R. A., Rispoli, M. J., Heath, A. K., & Parker, R. I. (2011). An aggregate study of single-case research involving aided AAC: Participant characteristics of individuals with Autism Spectrum Disorders. *Research in Autism Spectrum Disorders, 5*(4), 1500–1509.

Gathercole, S. (2006). Nonword repetition and word learning: The nature of the relationship. *Applied Psycholinguistics, 27*, 513–543.

Gaustad, M., Kelly, R., Payne, J.-A., & Lylak, E. (2002). Deaf and hearing students' morphological knowledge applied to printed English. *American Annals of the Deaf, 147*, 5–19.

Geers, A. E., Brenner, C. A., & Tobey, E. A. (2011). Long-term outcomes of cochlear implantation in early childhood: sample characteristics and data collection methods. *Ear & Hearing, 32*(1), 2S–12s.

Geers, A. E., Moog, J. S., Biedenstein, J., Brenner, C., & Hayes, H. (2009). Spoken language scores of children using cochlear implants compared to hearing age-mates at school entry. *Journal of Deaf Studies & Deaf Education, 14*(3), 371–385.

Geers, A., Spehar, B., & Sedey, A. (2002). Use of speech by children from Total Communication programs who wear cochlear implants. *American Journal of Speech-Language Pathology, 11*, 50–58.

Gertner, B., Rice, M., & Hadley, P. (1994). The influence of communicative competence on peer preferences in a preschool classroom. *Journal of Speech and Hearing Research, 37*, 913–923.

Gierut, J. A., & Hulse, L. E. (2010). Evidence-based practice: A matrix for predicting phonological generalization. *Clinical Linguistics & Phonetics, 24*(4–5), 323–334.

Gillam, R., Loeb, D., Hoffman, L., Bohman, T., Champlin, C., Thibodeau, L., & ... Friel-Patti, S. (2008). The efficacy of Fast ForWord language intervention in school-age children with language impairment: A randomized controlled trial. *Journal of Speech, Language & Hearing Research, 51*(1), 97–119.

Girolametto, L., & Weitzman, E. (2006). It takes two to talk—The Hanen program for parents. In R. McCauley & M. Fey (Eds.), *Treating language disorders in children* (pp. 77–104). Baltimore: Paul H. Brookes.

Gleason, P. (1998). *Psycholinguistics: Instructor's manual* (2nd ed.). Fort Worth, TX: Harcourt Brace Jovanovich.

Goldin-Meadow, S. (2007). The challenge: Some properties of language can be learned without linguistic input. *Linguistic Review, 24*(4), 417–421.

Gray, S. (2003). Word-learning by preschoolers with specific language impairment: What predicts success? *Journal of Speech, Language and Hearing Research, 46*, 56–67.

Greenwood, C. R., Bradfield, T., Kaminski, R., Linas, M., Carta, J. J., & Nylander, D. (2011). The Response to Intervention (RTI) approach in early childhood. *Focus on Exceptional Children, 43*, 1–22.

Grossman, R. B., Bemis, R. H., Skwerer, D., & Tager-Flusberg, H. (2010). Lexical and affective prosody in children with high-functioning autism. *Journal of Speech, Language & Hearing Research, 53*(3), 778–793.

Gupta, V. B., Hyman, S. L., Johnson, C. P., Bryant, J., Byers, B., Kallen, R., et al. (2007). Identifying children with autism early? *Pediatrics, 119*, 152–153.

Happé, F., & Booth, R. (2008). The power of the positive: revisiting weak coherence in autism spectrum disorders. *Quarterly Journal Of Experimental Psychology, 61*(1), 50–63.

Hart, B. (1985). Naturalistic language training techniques. In S. Warren & A. Rogers-Warren (Eds.), *Training functional language* (pp. 63–88). Baltimore: University Park Press.

Hart, S. L., & Banda, D. R. (2010). Picture Exchange Communication System with individuals with developmental disabilities: A meta-analysis of single subject studies. *Remedial & Special Education, 31*, 476–488.

Haskill, A., & Tyler, A. (2007). A comparison of linguistic profiles in subgroups of children with specific language impairment. *American Journal of Speech Language Pathology, 16*, 209–221.

Hayes, C. (2010). Cerebral palsy: classification, diagnosis and challenges of care. *British Journal of Nursing, 19*(6), 368–373.

Hayiou-Thomas, M. (2008). Genetic and environmental influences on early speech, language and literacy development. *Journal Of Communication Disorders, 41*(5), 397–408.

Holowka, S., Brosseau-Lapré, F., & Pettito, L. (2002). Semantic and conceptual knowledge underlying bilingual babies' first signs and words. *Language Learning, 52*, 205–262.

Howlin, P. (2005). Outcomes in autism spectrum disorders. In F. Volkmer, R. Paul, A. Klin, & D. Cohen (Eds.), *Handbook of autism and pervasive developmental disorders, Volume 1* (3rd ed., pp. 201–220). Hoboken, NJ: Wiley.

Howlin, P., Elison, S., Udwin, O., & Stinton, C. (2010). Cognitive, linguistic and adaptive functioning in Williams syndrome: Trajectories from early to middle adulthood. *Journal of Applied Research in Intellectual Disabilities, 23*(4), 322–336.

Hurth, J., Shaw, E., Izeman, S., Whaley, K., & Rogers, S. (1999). Areas of agreement about effective practices among programs serving young children with autism spectrum disorders. *Infants and Young Children, 12*, 17–26.

Hyde, M., & Power, D. (2006). Some ethical dimensions of cochlear implantation for deaf children and their families. *Journal of Deaf Studies and Deaf Education, 11*, 102–111.

Hyde, M., & Punch, R. (2011). The modes of communication used by children with cochlear implants and the role of sign in their lives. *American Annals of the Deaf, 155*(5), 535–549.

Jarrold, C., Baddeley, A., & Phillips, C. (2002). Verbal short-term memory in Down syndrome: A problem or memory, audition or speech? *Journal of Speech, Language and Hearing Research, 45*, 531–544.

Jerome, A., Fujiki, M., Brinton, B., & James, S. (2002). Self-esteem in children with specific language impairment. *Journal of Speech, Language and Hearing Research, 45*, 700–715.

John, A. E., & Mervis, C. B. (2010). Comprehension of the communicative intent behind pointing and gazing gestures by young children with Williams Syndrome or Down Syndrome. *Journal of Speech, Language & Hearing Research, 53*(4), 950–960.

Johnson, C. J., Beitchman, J. H., & Brownlie, E. B. (2010). Twenty-year follow-up of children with and without speech-language impairments: Family, educational, occupational, and quality of life outcomes. *American Journal of Speech-Language Pathology, 19*(1), 51–65.

Johnson, C. & Goswami, U. (2010). Phonological awareness, vocabulary and reading in deaf children with cochlear implants. *Journal of Speech, Language and Hearing Research, 53*, 237–261.

Jones, L., & Campbell, J. (2010). Clinical characteristics associated with language regression for children with autism spectrum disorders. *Journal of Autism and Developmental Disorders, 40*(1), 54–62.

Jonsdottir, S., Saemundsen, E., Antonsdottir, I., Sigurdardottir, S., & Olason, D. (2011). Children diagnosed with Autism Spectrum Disorder before or after the age of 6 years. *Research in Autism Spectrum Disorders, 5*(1), 175–184.

Kaderavek, J. (2011). *Language disorders in children: Fundamental concepts of assessment and intervention.* Boston: Allyn & Bacon.

Kaderavek, J., & Pakulski, L. (2007). Facilitating literacy development in young children with hearing loss. *Seminars in Speech and Language, 28*, 69–78.

Kaiser, A., Yoder, P., & Keetz, A. (1992). Evaluating milieu teaching. In S. Warren & J. Reichle (Eds.), *Causes and effects in communication and language intervention* (pp. 9–48). Baltimore: Paul H. Brookes.

Kaland, N. (2011). Brief report: Should Asperger Syndrome be excluded from the forthcoming DSM-V?. *Research in Autism Spectrum Disorders, 5* (3), 984–989.

Kane, M., Connell, J. E., & Pellecchia, M. (2010). A quantitative analysis of language interventions for children with autism. *Behavior Analyst Today, 11*(2), 128–144.

Kasari, C., Paparella, T., Freeman, S., & Jahromi, L. B. (2008). Language outcome in autism: Randomized comparison of joint attention and play interventions. *Journal of Consulting and Clinical Psychology, 76*(1), 125–137.

Katsos, N., Roqueta, C., Estevan, R., & Cummins, C. (2011). Are children with Specific Language Impairment competent with the pragmatics and logic of quantification? *Cognition, 119*(1), 43–57.

Kay-Raining Bird, E., Cleave, P., White, D., Pike, H., & Helmkay, A. (2008). Written and oral narratives of children and adolescents with Down syndrome. *Journal of Speech, Language & Hearing Research, 51*(2), 436–450.

Kelley, E., Paul, J., Fein, D., & Naigles, L. (2006). Residual language deficits in optimal outcome children with a history of autism. *Journal of Autism and Developmental Disorders, 36*(6), 807–828.

Kjelgaard, M., & Tager-Flusberg, H. (2001). An investigation of language impairment in autism: Implications for genetic subgroups. *Language and Cognitive Processes, 16,* 287–308.

Klin, A., McPartland, J., & Volkmar, F. (2005). Asperger syndrome. In F. Volkmar, R. Paul, A. Klin, & D. Cohen (Eds.), *Handbook of autism and pervasive developmental disorders, Volume 1* (3rd ed., pp. 88–125). Hoboken, NJ: Wiley.

Koegel, R., & Frea, W. (1993). Treatment of social behavior in autism through the modification of pivotal social skills. *Journal of Applied Behavior Analysis, 26,* 369–377.

Koegel, R., Koegel, L., Frea, W., & Smith, A. (1995). Emerging interventions for children with autism: Longitudinal and lifestyle implications. In R. Koegel & L. Koegel (Eds.), *Teaching children with autism: Strategies for initiating positive interactions and improving learning opportunities.* Baltimore: Paul H. Brookes.

Kohnert, K., & Ebert, K. (2010). Beyond morphosyntax in developing bilinguals and "Specific" Language Impairment. *Applied Psycholinguistics, 31*(2), 303–310.

Kuehn, D., & Henne, L. (2003). Speech evaluation and treatment for patients with cleft palate. *American Journal of Speech-Language Pathology, 12,* 103–120.

Kushalnagar, P., Mathur, G., Moreland, C., Napoli, D., Osterling, W., Padden, C., & Rathmann, C. (2010). Infants and children with hearing loss need early language access. *The Journal of Clinical Ethics, 21*(2), 143–154.

Landa, R. (2007). Early communication development and intervention for children with autism. *Mental Retardation and Developmental Disabilities Research Reviews, 13,* 16–25.

Landa, R. J., Holman, K. C., O'Neill, A. H., & Stuart, E. A. (2011). Intervention targeting development of socially synchronous engagement in toddlers with autism spectrum disorder: a randomized controlled trial. *Journal of Child Psychology & Psychiatry, 52*(1), 13–21.

Landa, R., & Garrett-Mayer, E. (2006). Development in infants with autism spectrum disorders: A prospective study. *Journal of Child Psychology and Psychiatry, 47,* 629–638.

LaSasso, C., & Lollis, J. (2003). Survey of residential and day schools for deaf students in the United States that identify themselves as bilingual-bicultural. *Journal of Deaf Studies and Deaf Education, 8,* 79–91.

Law, J., Garrett, Z., & Nye, C. (2004). The efficacy of treatment for children with developmental speech and language delay/disorder: A meta-analysis. *Journal of Speech, Language, and Hearing Research, 47,* 924–943.

Law, J., Tomblin, J., & Xuyang, Z. (2008). Characterizing the growth trajectories of language-impaired children between 7 and 11 years of age. *Journal of Speech, Language & Hearing Research, 51*(3), 739–749.

Leonard, H., Dixon, G., Whitehouse, A. O., Bourke, J., Aiberti, K., Nassar, N., & ... Glasson, E. J. (2010). Unpacking the complex nature of the autism epidemic. *Research in Autism Spectrum Disorders, 4*(4), 548–554.

Leonard, L. (1998). *Children with specific language impairment.* Cambridge, MA: MIT Press.

Leonard, L. (2003). Specific language impairment: Characterizing the deficits.

In Y. Levy & J. Schaeffer (Eds.), *Language competence across populations: Toward a definition of specific language impairment.* Mahwah, NJ: Erlbaum.

Leonard, L. (2009). Some reflections on the study of children with Specific Language Impairment. *Child Language Teaching and Therapy, 25*(2), 169–171.

Leonard, L., Camarata, S. M., Pawlowska, M., Brown, B., & Camarata, M. N. (2006). Tense and agreement morphemes in the speech of children with specific language impairment during intervention: Phase 2. *Journal of Speech, Language and Hearing Research, 49,* 749–770.

Leonard, L., Camarata, S., Pawlowska, M., Brown, B., & Camarata, M. (2008). The acquisition of tense and agreement morphemes by children with specific language impairment during intervention: phase 3. *Journal of Speech, Language, and Hearing Research, 51*(1), 120–125.

Leonard, L., Miller, C., & Gerber, E. (1999). Grammatical morphology and the lexicon in children with specific language impairment. *Journal of Speech, Language and Hearing Research, 42,* 678–689.

Leybaert, J., & LaSasso, C. (2010). Cued speech for enhancing speech perception and first language development of children with cochlear implants. *Trends In Amplification, 14*(2), 96–112.

Li, S., & McGregor, K. K. (2010). Lexical-semantic organization in children with Specific Language Impairment. *Journal of Speech, Language & Hearing Research, 53*(1), 146–159.

Liiva, C., & Cleave, P. (2005). Role of initiation and responsiveness in access and participation for children with Specific Language Impairment. *Journal of Speech, Language and Hearing Research, 48,* 868–883.

Lindgren, K. A., Folstein, S. E., Tomblin, J., & Tager-Flusberg, H. (2009). Language and reading abilities of children with autism spectrum disorders and specific language impairment and their first-degree relatives. *Autism Research, 2,* 22–38.

Lovaas, O. (1987). Behavioral treatment and normal educational and intellectual functioning in young autistic children.

Journal of Consulting and Clinical Psychology, 55, 3–9.

Lovaas, O. (1996). The UCLA young autism model of service delivery. In C. Maurice, G. Green, & S. Luce (Eds.), *Behavioral intervention for young children with autism: A manual for parents and professionals* (pp. 241–248). Austin, TX: Pro-Ed.

Loveland, K., & Tunali-Kotoski, B. (2005). The school-aged child with an autistic spectrum disorder. In F. Volkmer, R. Paul, A. Klin, & D. Cohen (Eds.), *Handbook of autism and pervasive developmental disorders, Volume 1* (3rd ed., pp. 247–287). Hoboken, NJ: Wiley.

Luckasson, R., Borthwick-Duffy, S., Butinx, W., Coulter, D., Craig, E., Reeve, A., Schalock, R., Snell, M., Spitalnik, D., Spreat, S., & Tassé, M. (2002). *Mental retardation: Definition, classification and systems of supports* (10th ed.). Washington, DC: American Association on Mental Retardation (now the American Association on Intellectual and Developmental Disabilities).

Mainela-Arnold, E., Evans, J., & Coady, J (2010). Explaining lexical-semantic deficits in specific language impairment: The role of phonological similarity, phonological working memory, and lexical competition. *Journal of Speech, Language & Hearing Research, 53*(6), 1742–1756.

Makrygianni, M. K., & Reed, P. (2010). A meta-analytic review of the effectiveness of behavioural early intervention programs for children with Autistic Spectrum Disorders. *Research in Autism Spectrum Disorders, 4*(4), 577–593.

Malaia, E., & Wilbur, R. B. (2010). Early acquisition of sign language: What neuroimaging data tell us. *Sign Language & Linguistics, 13*(2), 183–199.

Mandell, D. S., Novak, M. M., & Zubritsky, C. D. (2006). Factors associated with age of diagnosis among children with autism spectrum disorders. *Journal of the American Academy of Child and Adolescent Psychiatry, 45,* 657–657.

Manning, W. (2009). *Clinical decision making in fluency disorders* (3rd ed.). Clifton Park, NY: Delmar/Cengage.

Marcus, G., & Rabagliati, H. (2006). What developmental disorders can tell us about the nature and origins of language. *Nature Neuroscience, 9,* 1226–1229.

Martens, M., Wilson, S., & Reutens, D. (2008). Research Review: Williams syndrome: A critical review of the cognitive, behavioral, and neuroanatomical phenotype. *Journal of Child Psychology and Psychiatry, and Allied Disciplines, 49*(6), 576–608.

Mason, K., Rowley, K., Marshall, C. R., Atkinson, J. R., Herman, R., Woll, B., & Morgan, G. (2010). Identifying Specific Language Impairment in deaf children acquiring British Sign Language: Implications for theory and practice. *British Journal of Developmental Psychology, 28*(1), 33–49.

Mattila, M., Kielinen, M., Linna, S., Jussila, K., Ebeling, H., Bloigu, R., & ... Moilanen, I. (2011). Autism Spectrum Disorders according to DSM-IV-TR and comparison with DSM-5 draft criteria: An epidemiological study. *Journal of the American Academy of Child and Adolescent Psychiatry, 50*(6), 583–592.

McAnally, P., Rose, S., & Quigley, S. (2007). *Reading practices with deaf children* (2nd ed.). Austin, TX: Pro-Ed.

McCabe, P. C. (2005). Social and behavioral correlates of preschoolers with specific language impairment. *Psychology in the Schools, 42,* 373–387.

McCauley, R., & Fey, M. (Eds.). (2006). *Treating language disorders in children.* Baltimore: Paul H. Brookes.

McCormick, L., Loeb, D. F., & Schieffelbusch, R. (Eds.). (2003). *Supporting children with communication difficulties in inclusive settings.* Boston: Allyn & Bacon.

Meaburn, E., Dale, P., Craig, I., & Plomin, R. (2002). Language-impaired children: No sign of the FOXP2 mutation. *Neuroreport, 13,* 1075–1077.

Mehra, S. S., Eavey, R. D., & Keamy, D. (2009). The epidemiology of hearing impairment in the United States: newborns, children, and adolescents. *Otolaryngology— Head and Neck Surgery, 140*(4), 461–472.

Meindl, J. N., & Cannella-Malone, H. I. (2011). Initiating and responding to joint attention bids in children with autism: A review of the literature. *Research in Developmental Disabilities, 32*(5), 1441–1454

Meinzen-Derr, J., Wiley, S., & Choo, D. I. (2011). Impact of early intervention on expressive and receptive language development among young children with permanent hearing loss. *American Annals of the Deaf, 155*(5), 580–591.

Meinzen-Derr, J., Wiley, S., Grether, S., & Choo, D. I. (2011). Children with cochlear implants and developmental disabilities: A language skills study with developmentally matched hearing peers. *Research in Developmental Disabilities: A Multidisciplinary Journal, 32*(2), 757–767.

Mervis, C., & Becerra, A. (2007). Language and communicative development in Williams syndrome. *Mental Retardation and Developmental Disabilities Research Reviews, 13,* 3–15.

Mervis, C., & John, A. (2008). Vocabulary abilities of children with Williams syndrome: Strengths, weaknesses, and relation to visuospatial construction ability. *Journal of Speech, Language & Hearing Research, 51*(4), 967–982.

Messer, D., & Dockrell, J. E. (2006). Children's naming and word-finding difficulties: Descriptions and explanations. *Journal of Speech, Language and Hearing Research, 49,* 309–324.

Miles, S., & Chapman, R. (2002). Narrative content as described by individuals with Down Syndrome and typically developing children. *Journal of Speech, Language and Hearing Research, 45,* 175–189.

Millar, D., Light, J., & Schlosser, R. (2006). The impact of augmentative and alternative communication intervention on the speech production of individuals with developmental disabilities: A research review. *Journal of Speech, Language and Hearing Research, 49,* 248–264.

Miller, C. A., Leonard, L. B., Kail, R. V., Xuyang, Z., Tomblin, J. B., & Francis, D. J. (2006). Response time in 14-year-olds with language impairment. *Journal of Speech, Language and Hearing Research, 49,* 712–728.

Miller, J. (1999). Profiles of language development in children with Down syndrome. In J. Miller, M. Leddy, & L. Leavitt (Eds.), *Improving the communication of people with Down syndrome* (pp. 11–40). Baltimore: Paul H. Brookes.

Minshew, N., & Keller, T. (2010). The nature of brain dysfunction in autism: Functional brain imaging studies. *Current Opinion in Neurology, 23*(2), 124–130.

Mirenda, P. (2003). Toward functional augmentative and alternative communication for students with autism: Manual signs, graphic symbols and voice output communication aids. *Language, Speech and Hearing Services in Schools, 34,* 203–216.

Mitchell, R. (2004). National profile of deaf and hard of hearing students in special education from weighted survey results. *American Annals of the Deaf, 149,* 337–350.

Mitchell, R. E., & Karchmer, M. A. (2006). Demographics of deaf education: More students in more places. *American Annals of the Deaf, 151,* 95–104.

Montgomery, J., Magimairaj, B., & Finney, M. (2010). Working memory and specific language impairment: an update on the relation and perspectives on assessment and treatment. *American Journal of Speech-Language Pathology, 19*(1), 78–94.

Montgomery, J. W., & Leonard, L. B. (2006). Effects of acoustic manipulation on the real-time inflectional processing of children with specific language impairment. *Journal of Speech, Language, and Hearing Research, 49,* 1238–1256.

Montgomery, J. W., & Windsor, J. (2007). Examining the language performances of children with and without specific language impairment: Contributions of phonological short-term memory and speed of processing. *Journal of Speech, Language and Hearing Research, 50,* 778–797.

Moog, J., & Geers, A. (2010). Early educational placement and later language outcomes for children with cochlear implants. *Otology & Neurotology, 31*(8), 1315–1319.

Mundy, P., & Burnette, C. (2005). Joint attention and neurodevelopmental models of autism. In F. Volkmer, R. Paul, A. Klin, & D. Cohen (Eds.), *Handbook of autism and pervasive developmental disorders, Volume 1* (3rd ed., pp. 650–681). Hoboken, NJ: Wiley.

Murphy, M. M., & Abbeduto, L. (2007). Gender differences in repetitive language in fragile X syndrome. *Journal of Intellectual Disability Research, 51,* 387–400.

Murray, D. S., Creaghead, N. A., Manning-Courtney, P., Shear, P. K., Bean, J., & Prendeville, J. (2008). The relationship between joint attention and language in children with autism spectrum disorders. *Focus on Autism & Other Developmental Disabilities, 23*(1), 5–14.

Nadig, A. S., Ozonoff, S., Young, G. S., Rozga, A., Sigman, M., & Rogers, S. J. (2007). A prospective study of response to name in infants at risk for autism. *Archives of Pediatrics and Adolescent Medicine, 161,* 378–383.

National Institute on Deafness and Other Communication Disorders. (1995). *National strategic plan for language and language disorders* (NIH publication 97–3217). Bethesda, MD: NIH.

National Research Council. (2001). *Educating children with autism.* Committee on Educational Interventions for Children with Autism. Washington, DC: National Academy Press.

Nelson, N. W. (2010). *Language and literacy disorders: Infancy through adolescence.* Boston: Allyn & Bacon.

Newman, A., Bavelier, D., Corina, D., Jezzard, P., & Neville, H. (2001). A critical period for right hemisphere recruitment in American Sign Language processing. *Nature Neuroscience, 5,* 76–81.

Newman, R., Bernstein Ratner, N. B., Jusczyk, A. M., Jusczyk, P. W., & Dow, K. A. (2006). Infants' early ability to segment the conversational speech signal predicts later language development: A retrospective analysis. *Developmental Psychology, 42,* 643–655.

Newman, R. S., & German, D. J. (2002). Effects of lexical factors on lexical access among typical language-learning children and children with word-finding difficulties. *Language and Speech, 45,* 285–316.

Nittrouer, S., & Chapman, C. (2009). The effects of bilateral electric and bimodal electric–acoustic stimulation on language development. *Trends in Amplification, 13*(3), 190–205.

Norbury, C., Bishop, D., & Briscoe, J. (2001). Production of English finite verb morphology: A comparison of SLI and mild-moderate hearing impairment. *Journal of Speech, Language and Hearing Research, 44,* 165–178.

Noterdaeme, M., Wriedt, E., & Hohne, C. (2010). Asperger's syndrome and high-functioning autism: language, motor and cognitive profiles. *European Child & Adolescent Psychiatry, 19*(6), 475–481.

Nott, P., Cowan, R., Brown, P., & Wigglesworth, G. (2009). Early language development in children with profound hearing loss fitted with a device at a young age: Part I--the time period taken to acquire first words and first word combinations. *Ear & Hearing, 30*(5), 526–540.

Olander, L., Smith, A., & Zelaznik, H. (2010). Evidence that a motor timing deficit is a factor in the development of stuttering. *Journal of Speech, Language & Hearing Research, 53*(4), 876–886.

Osterling, J., & Dawson, G. (1994). Early recognition of children with autism: A study of first birthday home videotapes. *Journal of Autism and Developmental Disorders, 24,* 247–257.

Owens, R. (2010). *Language disorders: A functional approach to assessment and intervention* (5th ed.). Boston: Allyn & Bacon.

Paatsch, L. E., Blamey, P. J., Sarant, J. Z., & Bow, C. P. (2006). The effects of speech production and vocabulary training on different components of spoken language performance. *Journal of Deaf Studies and Deaf Education, 11,* 39–55.

Patten, E., & Watson, L. R. (2011). Interventions targeting attention in young children with autism. *American Journal of Speech-Language Pathology, 20*(1), 60–69.

Paul, P. (2009). *Language and deafness* (4th ed.). Boston: Jones and Bartlett Publishers.

Paul, R. (2007). *Language disorders from infancy through adolescence* (3rd ed.). New York: Mosby.

Peperkamp, S., & Mehler, J. (1999). Signed and spoken language: A unique underlying system? *Language and Speech, 42,* 333–346.

Perovic, A., & Wexler, K. (2010). Development of verbal passive in Williams syndrome. *Journal of Speech, Language, and Hearing Research, 53*(5), 1294–1306.

Perrachione, T., Del Tufo, S., & Gabrieli, J. (2011). Human voice recognition depends on language ability. *Science, 333,* 595–596.

Pisoni, D., & Cleary, M. (2003). Measures of working memory span and verbal rehearsal speed in deaf children after cochlear implantation. *Ear and Hearing, 24,* 106S–120S.

Pray, J., & Jordon, I. K. (2010). The Deaf community and culture at a crossroads: Issues and challenges. *Journal of Social Work in Disability & Rehabilitation, 9,* 168–193.

Price, J., Roberts, J., Vandergrift, N., & Martin, G. (2007). Language comprehension in boys with fragile X syndrome and boys with Down syndrome. *Journal of Intellectual Disability Research, 51,* 318–326.

Prinz, R., & Prinz, E. (1981). Acquisition of ASL and spoken English by a hearing child of a deaf mother and a hearing father, Phase II: Early combinatorial patterns. *Sign Language Studies, 30,* 78–88.

Prizant, B., Wetherby, A., & Rydell, P. (2000). Communication intervention issues for young children with Autism Spectrum Disorders. In A. Wetherby & B. Prizant (Eds.), *Autism Spectrum Disorders: A transactional developmental perspective.* Baltimore: Paul H. Brookes.

Proctor-Williams, K. (2009). Dosage and distribution in morphosyntax intervention: Current evidence and future needs. *Topics in Language Disorders, 29*(4), 294–311.

Quigley, S., & Paul, P. (1987). Deafness and language development. In S. Rosenberg (Ed.), *Advances in applied psycholinguistics, Vol. 1: Disorders of first language development.* Cambridge, UK: Cambridge University Press.

Rajendran, G., & Mitchell, P. (2007). Cognitive theories of autism. *Developmental Review, 27,* 224–260.

Rapin, I., Dunn, M., Allen, D., Stevens, M., & Fein, D. (2009). Subtypes of language disorders in school-age children with autism. *Developmental Neuropsychology, 34*(1), 66–84.

Reichow, B., & Wolery, M. (2009). Comprehensive synthesis of early intensive behavioral interventions for young children with autism based on the UCLA Young Autism Project Model. *Journal of Autism & Developmental Disorders, 39*(1), 23–41.

Rescorla, L. (2005). Age 13 language and reading outcomes in late-talking toddlers. *Journal of Speech, Language and Hearing Research, 48*, 459–472.

Rescorla, L. (2009). Age 17 language and reading outcomes in late-talking toddlers: Support for a dimensional perspective on language delay. *Journal of Speech, Language, and Hearing Research, 52*(1), 16–30.

Rescorla, L., & Alley, A. (2001). Validation of the Language Development Survey (LDS): A parent report tool for identifying language delay in toddlers. *Journal of Speech, Language and Hearing Research, 44*, 434–445.

Rescorla, L., & Bernstein Ratner, N. (1996). Phonetic profiles of toddlers with Specific Expressive Language Impairment (SLI-E). *Journal of Speech and Hearing Research, 39*, 153–165.

Rescorla, L., Bernstein Ratner, N., Jusczyk, P., & Jusczyk, A. (2005). Concurrent validity of the Language Development Survey: Associations with the MacArthur-Bates Communicative Development Inventories: Words and Sentences. *American Journal of Speech-Language Pathology, 14*(2), 156–163.

Rescorla, L., & Lee, E. (2001). Language impairment in young children. In T. Layton, E. Crais, & L. Watson (Eds.), *Handbook of early language impairment in children: Nature* (pp. 1–55). Albany, NY: Delmar.

Rhoades, E. (2006). Research outcomes of Auditory-Verbal intervention: Is the approach justified? *Deafness and Education International, 8*, 125–143.

Rice, M. L., Wexler, K., Marquis, J., & Hershberger, S. (2000). Acquisition of irregular past tense by children with specific language impairment. *Journal of Speech, Language and Hearing Research, 43*, 1126–1145.

Roberts, M., & Kaiser, A. (2011). The effectiveness of parent-implemented language interventions: a meta-analysis. *American Journal of Speech-Language Pathology, 20*, 180–199.

Roberts, J., Mirrett, P., Anderson, K., Burchinal, M., & Neebe, E. (2002). Early communication, symbolic behavior and social profiles of young males with fragile X syndrome. *American Journal of Speech-Language Pathology, 11*, 295–304.

Roberts, J., Price, J., & Malkin, C. (2007). Language and communication development in Down syndrome. *Mental Retardation and Developmental Disabilities Research Reviews, 13*, 26–35.

Rogers, S., & Ozonoff, S. (2006). Behavioral, educational and developmental treatments for autism. In S. Moldin & J. Rubenstein (Eds.), *Understanding autism: From basic neuroscience to treatment* (pp. 443–473). Boca Raton, FL: Taylor & Francis.

Romski, M., Sevcik, R., Cheslock, M., & Barton, A. (2006). The system for augmenting language. In R. McCauley & M. Fey (Eds.), *Treating language disorders in children* (pp. 123–147). Baltimore: Paul H. Brookes.

Rondal, J. A. (2009). Spoken language in persons with Down syndrome: A lifespan perspective. *International Journal of Early Childhood Special Education, 1*(2), 138–163.

Roseberry-McKibbin, C. (2007). *Language disorders in children: A multicultural and case perspective.* Boston: Allyn & Bacon.

Roth, F. P., Troia, G. A., Worthington, C. K., & Handy, D. (2006). Promoting awareness of sounds in speech (PASS): The effects of intervention and stimulus characteristics on the blending performance of preschool children with communication impairments. *Learning Disability Quarterly, 29*, 67–88.

Sakai, K. L., Tatsuno, Y., Suzuki, K., Kimura, H., & Ichida, Y. (2005). Sign and speech: A modal commonality in left hemisphere dominance for comprehension of sentences. *Brain, 128*, 1407–1417.

Samson-Fang, L., Simons-McCandless, M., & Shelton, C. (2000). Controversies in the field of hearing impairment: Early identification, educational method and cochlear implants. *Infants and Young Children, 12*, 77–88.

Sarant, J., Holt, C., Dowell, R., Rickards, F. & Blamey, P. (2009). Spoken language development in oral preschool children with permanent childhood deafness. *Journal of Deaf Studies and Deaf Education, 14*, 205–216.

Schalock, R. L., Luckasson, R. A., Shogren, K. A., Borthwick-Duffy, S., Bradley, V., Buntinx, W. H. E., Coulter, D., Craig, E., Gomez, S., Lachappelle, Y., & Reeve, A., et al. (2007). The renaming of mental retardation: Understanding the change to the term intellectual disability. *Intellectual and Developmental Disabilities, 45*, 116–124.

Scheetz, N. (2012). *Deaf education in the 21st century: Topics and trends*. Boston: Allyn & Bacon.

Schirmer, B. (2000). *Language and literacy development in children who are deaf* (2nd ed.). Boston: Allyn & Bacon.

Schirmer, B. (2001). *Psychological, social and educational dimensions of deafness*. Boston: Allyn & Bacon.

Schuchardt, K., Maehler, C., & Hasselhorn, M. (2011). Functional deficits in phonological working memory in children with intellectual disabilities. *Research in Developmental Disabilities, 32*(5), 1934–1940.

Seymour, H., & Pearson, B. Z. (2004). The diagnostic evaluation of language variation: Differentiating dialect, development and disorder. *Seminars in Speech and Language, 25*, 1.

Shargorodsky, J., Curhan, S., Curhan, G., & Eavey, R. (2010). Change in prevalence of hearing loss in US adolescents. *The Journal of the American Medical Association, 304*(7), 772–778.

Shriberg, L., Paul, R., McSweeny, J., Klin, A., Cohen, D., & Volkmar, F. (2001). Speech and prosody characteristics of adolescents and adults with high-functioning autism and Asperger syndrome. *Journal of Speech, Language and Hearing Research, 44*, 1097–1115.

Shriberg, L. D., Tomblin, J. B., & McSweeny, J. L. (1999). Prevalence of speech delay in 6-year-old children and comorbidity with language impairment. *Journal of Speech, Language and Hearing Research, 42*, 1461–1481.

Shulman, C., & Guberman, A. (2007). Acquisition of verb meaning through syntactic cues: A comparison of children with autism, children with specific language impairment (SLI) and children with typical language development (TLD). *Journal of Child Language, 34*, 411–423.

Shute, N. (2010). Desperate for an autism cure. *Scientific American, 303*(4), 80–85.

Sigafoos, J., Green, V. A., Schlosser, R., O'Reilly, M. F., Lancioni, G. E., Rispoli, M., & Lang, R. (2009). Communication intervention in Rett syndrome: A systematic review. *Research in Autism Spectrum Disorders, 3*(2), 304–318.

Sigman, M., & McGovern, C. (2005). Improvement in cognitive and language skills from preschool to adolescence in autism. *Journal of Autism and Developmental Disorders, 35*, 15–23.

Sinha, Y., Silove, N., Wheeler, D., & Williams, K. (2006). Auditory integration training and other sound therapies for autism spectrum disorders: A systematic review. *Archives of Disease in Childhood, 91*, 1018–1022.

Smith, A., & Kelly, E. (1997). Stuttering: A dynamic, multifactorial model. In R. Curlee & G. Siegel (Eds.), *Nature and treatment of stuttering: New directions* (2nd ed.). Boston: Allyn & Bacon.

Smith, N., & Tsimpli, I.-M. (1995). *The mind of a savant: Language learning and modularity*. Oxford: Blackwell.

Snowling, M., Bishop, D., & Stothard, S. (2000). Is preschool language impairment a risk factor for dyslexia in adolescence? *Journal of Speech, Language and Hearing Research, 41*, 587–600.

Snowling, M. J., Bishop, D. V. M., Stothard, S. E., Chipchase, B., & Kaplan, C. (2006). Psychosocial outcomes at 15 years of children with a preschool history of speech-language impairment. *Journal of Child Psychology and Psychiatry, 47*, 759–765.

Snowling, M., & Hulme, C. (2011). Evidence-based interventions for reading and language difficulties: Creating a virtuous circle. *British Journal of Educational Psychology, 81*, 1–23.

Sparrow, R. (2010). Implants and ethnocide: learning from the cochlear implant controversy. *Disability & Society, 25*, 455–466.

Spencer, L., Barker, B., & Tomblin, J. (2003). Exploring the language and literacy outcomes of pediatric cochlear implant users. *Ear and Hearing, 24*, 236–247.

Spiridigliozzi, G., Lachiewicz, A., Mirrett, S., & McConkie-Rosell, A. (2001). Fragile X syndrome in young children. In T. Layton, E. Crais, & L. Watson (Eds.), *Handbook of early language impairment in children: Nature*. Albany, NY: Delmar.

Spreckley, M., & Boyd, R. (2009). Efficacy of applied behavioral intervention in preschool children with autism for improving cognitive, language, and adaptive behavior: a systematic review and meta-analysis. *Journal of Pediatrics, 154*(3), 338–344.

Stephenson, J. (2008). Classroom-based interventions may be more effective than pull-out programs for speech-language pathology interventions for young children with specific language impairment. *Evidence-Based Communication Assessment & Intervention, 2*(2), 70–72.

Straatman, L., Rietveld, A., Beijen, J., Mylanus, E., & Mens, L. (2010). Advantage of bimodal fitting in prosody perception for children using a cochlear implant and a hearing aid. *The Journal of the Acoustical Society of America, 128*(4), 1884–1895.

Strong, M., & Prinz, P. (1997). A study of the relationship between American Sign Language and English literacy. *Journal of Deaf Studies and Deaf Education, 2*, 37–46.

Strong, G. K., Torgerson, C. J., Torgerson, D., & Hulm, C. (2011). A systematic meta-analytic review of evidence for the effectiveness of the 'Fast ForWord' language intervention program. *Journal of Child Psychology & Psychiatry, 52*(3), 224–235.

Sullivan, M., Finelli, J., Marvin, A., Garrett-Mayer, E., Bauman, M., & Landa, R.

(2007). Response to joint attention in toddlers at risk for autism spectrum disorder: A prospective study. *Journal of Autism and Developmental Disorders, 37*, 37–48.

Szatmari, P., Paterson, A. D., Zwaigenbaum, L., Roberts, W., Brian, J., Xiao-Qing, L., et al. (2007). Mapping autism risk loci using genetic linkage and chromosomal rearrangements. *Nature Genetics, 39*, 319–328.

Tager-Flusberg, H., & Calkins, S. (1990). Does imitation facilitate the acquisition of grammar? Evidence from a study of autistic, Down's syndrome and normal children. *Journal of Child Language, 17*, 591–606.

Tager-Flusberg, H., Rogers, S., Cooper, J., Landa, R., Lord, C., Paul, R., & ... Yoder, P. (2009). Defining spoken language benchmarks and selecting measures of expressive language development for young children with autism spectrum disorders. *Journal of Speech, Language, and Hearing Research, 52*(3), 643–652.

Tallal, P. (2003). Language learning disabilities: Integrating research approaches. *Current Directions in Psychological Science, 12*, 206–211.

Tallal, P., Miller, S., Bedi, G., Byma, G., Wang, X., Nagarajan, S., et al. (1996). Language comprehension in language-learning impaired children improved with acoustically modified speech. *Science, 271*, 81–84.

Tanner, D. (2003). *Exploring communication disorder: A 21st century introduction through literature and media*. Boston: Allyn & Bacon.

Teagle, H., & Moore, J. (2002). School-based services for children with cochlear implants. *Language, Speech and Hearing Services in Schools, 33*, 162–171.

Thagard, E., Hilsmier, A., & Easterbrooks, S. (2011). Pragmatic language in deaf and hard of hearing students: Correlation with success in general education. *American Annals of the Deaf, 155*(5), 526–534.

Thordardottir, E., Chapman, R., & Wagner, L. (2002). Complex sentence production by adolescents with Down syndrome. *Applied Psycholinguistics, 23*, 163–183.

Thordardottir, E. T., & Namazi, M. (2007). Specific language impairment in French-speaking children: Beyond grammatical morphology. *Journal of Speech, Language and Hearing Research, 50,* 698–715.

Tiegerman-Farber, E., & Radziewicz, C. (2008). *Language disorders in children: Real families, real issues, and real interventions.* Boston: Allyn & Bacon.

Tomblin, J. B. (2010). The EpiSLI Database: A publicly available database on speech and language. *Language, Speech & Hearing Services in Schools, 41*(1), 108–117.

Tomblin, J. B., Barker, B. A., Spencer, L. J., Zhang, X., & Gantz, B. J. (2005). The effect of age at cochlear implant initial stimulation on expressive language growth in infants and toddlers. *Journal of Speech, Language, and Hearing Research, 48,* 853–867.

Tomblin, J. B., Records, N. L., Buckwalter, P., Zhang, X., Smith, E., & O'Brien, M. (1997). Prevalence of specific language impairment in kindergarten children. *Journal of Speech, Language and Hearing Research, 40,* 1245–1261.

Tomblin, J. B., Zhang, X., Buckwalter, P., & O'Brien, M. (2003). The stability of primary language disorders: Four years after kindergarten diagnosis. *Journal of Speech, Language and Hearing Research, 46,* 1283–1296.

Toth, K., Dawson, G., Meltzoff, A., Greenson, J., & Fein, D. (2007). Early social, imitation, play, and language abilities of young non-autistic siblings of children with autism. *Journal of Autism and Developmental Disorders, 37,* 145–157.

Turner, L. M., Stone, W. L., Pozdol, S. L., & Coonrod, E. E. (2006). Follow-up of children with autism spectrum disorders from age 2 to age 9. *Autism, 10,* 243–265.

Ukrainetz, T. (Ed.). (2006). *Contextualized language intervention: Scaffolding PreK–12 literacy achievement.* Eau Claire, WI: Thinking Publications.

U.S. Preventive Services Task Force. (2006). Screening for speech and language delay in preschool children: Recommendation statement. *American Family Physician, 73,* 1605–1610.

Van Acker, R., Loncola, J., & Van Acker, E. (2005). Rett syndrome: A pervasive developmental disorder. In F. Volkmer, R. Paul, A. Klin, & D. Cohen (Eds.), *Handbook of autism and pervasive developmental disorders, Volume 1* (3rd ed., pp. 126–164) Hoboken, NJ: John Wiley & Sons.

Vandereet, J., Maes, B., Lembrechts, D., & Zink, I. (2010). Predicting expressive vocabulary acquisition in children with intellectual disabilities: A 2-year longitudinal study. *Journal of Speech, Language & Hearing Research, 53*(6), 1673–1686.

van der Schuit, M., Segers, E., van Balkom, H., & Verhoeven, L. (2011a). Early language intervention for children with intellectual disabilities: A neurocognitive perspective. *Research in Developmental Disabilities, 32*(2), 705–712.

van der Schuit, M., Segers, E., van Balkom, H., & Verhoeven, L. (2011b). How cognitive factors affect language development in children with intellectual disabilities. *Research in Developmental Disabilities, 32*(5), 1884–1894.

Virués-Ortega, J. (2010). Applied behavior analytic intervention for autism in early childhood: Meta-analysis, meta-regression and dose–response meta-analysis of multiple outcomes. *Clinical Psychology Review, 30*(4), 387–399.

Vivanti, G., McCormick, C., Young, G. S., Abucayan, F., Hatt, N., Nadig, A., & … Rogers, S. J. (2011). Intact and impaired mechanisms of action understanding in autism. *Developmental Psychology, 47*(3), 841–856.

Walenski, M., Tager-Flusberg, H., & Ullman, M. (2006). Language in autism. In S. Moldin & J. Rubenstein (Eds.), *Understanding autism: From basic neuroscience to treatment* (pp. 175–204). Boca Raton, FL: Taylor & Francis.

Wass, S. (2011). Distortions and disconnections: Disrupted brain connectivity in autism. *Brain & Cognition, 75*(1), 18–28.

Weber-Fox, C., Leonard, L. B., Wray, A., & Tomblin, J. (2010). Electrophysiological correlates of rapid auditory and linguistic processing in adolescents with Specific Language Impairment. *Brain and Language, 115*(3), 162–181.

Wetherby, A. M., Watt, N., Morgan, L., & Shumway, S. (2007). Social communication profiles of children with autism spectrum disorders late in the second year of life. *Journal of Autism and Developmental Disorders, 37*, 960–975.

Wetherell, D., Botting, N., & Conti-Ramsden, G. (2007). Narrative skills in adolescents with a history of SLI in relation to non-verbal IQ scores. *Child Language Teaching and Therapy, 23*, 95–113.

White, K. R. (2007). Early intervention for children with permanent hearing loss: Finishing the EHDI revolution. *Volta Review, 106*, 237–258.

White, P. J., O'Reilly, M., Streusand, W., Levine, A., Sigafoos, J., Lancioni, G., & … Aguilar, J. (2011). Best practices for teaching joint attention: A systematic review of the intervention literature. *Research in Autism Spectrum Disorders, 5*(1), 1283–1295.

Whitehouse, A. O., Bishop, D. M., Ang, Q. W., Pennell, C. E., & Fisher, S. E. (2011). CNTNAP2 variants affect early language development in the general population. *Genes, Brain & Behavior, 10*(4), 451–456.

Wing, L., Gould, J., & Gillberg, C. (2011). Autism Spectrum Disorders in the DSM-V: Better or worse than the DSM-IV? *Research in Developmental Disabilities, 32*(2), 768–773.

Wong, A., Ciocca, V., & Sun, Y. (2009). The perception of lexical tone contrasts in Cantonese children with and without Specific Language Impairment (SLI). *Journal of Speech, Language & Hearing Research, 52*(6), 1493–1509.

Wong, A. Y., Klee, T., Stokes, S. F., Fletcher, P., & Leonard, L. B. (2010). Differentiating Cantonese-speaking preschool children with and without SLI using MLU and lexical diversity (D). *Journal of Speech, Language & Hearing Research, 53*(3), 794–799.

Woods, J., & Wetherby, A. (2003). Early identification of and intervention for infants and toddlers who are at risk for autism spectrum disorder. *Language, Speech and Hearing Services in Schools, 34*, 180–193.

Workinger, M. (2005). *Cerebral palsy resource guide for speech-language pathologists.* Clifton Park, NY: Thomson/Delmar.

Yairi, E., & Ambrose, N. (2005). *Early childhood stuttering: For clinicians by clinicians.* Austin, TX: Pro-Ed.

Yang, M. S., & Gill, M. (2007). A review of gene linkage, association and expression studies in autism and an assessment of convergent evidence. *International Journal of Developmental Neuroscience, 25*, 69–85.

Yoder, P., & Lieberman, R. (2010). Brief Report: Randomized test of the efficacy of picture exchange communication system on highly generalized picture exchanges in children with ASD. *Journal of Autism and Developmental Disorders, 40*(5), 629–632.

Yoshinaga-Itano, C. (2003). From screening to early identification and intervention: Discovering predictors to successful outcomes for children with hearing loss. *Journal of Deaf Studies and Deaf Education, 8*, 11–30.

Yoshinaga-Itano, C., Snyder, L., & Mayberry, R. (1996). How deaf and normally hearing students convey meaning within and between written sentences. *Volta Review, 98*, 9–38.

Zampini, L., & D'Odorico, L. (2009). Communicative gestures and vocabulary development in 36-month-old children with Down's Syndrome. *International Journal of Language & Communication Disorders, 44*(6), 1063–1073.

Zelaznik, H. N., & Goffman, L. (2010). Generalized motor abilities and timing behavior in children with Specific Language Impairment. *Journal of Speech, Language & Hearing Research, 53*(2), 383–393.

Zukowski, A. (2005). Knowledge of constraints on compounding in children and adolescents with Williams syndrome. *Journal of Speech, Language, and Hearing Research, 48*, 79–92.

Zwaigenbaum, L., Bryson, S., Lord, C., Rogers, S., Carter, A., Carver, L., & ... Yirmiya, N. (2009). Clinical assessment and management of toddlers with suspected autism spectrum disorder: insights from studies of high-risk infants. *Pediatrics*, *123*(5), 1383–1391.

Zwaigenbaum, L., Thurm, A., Stone, W., Baranek, G., Bryson, S., Iverson, J., et al. (2007). Studying the emergence of autism spectrum disorders in high-risk infants: Methodological and practical issues. *Journal of Autism and Developmental Disorders, 37*, 466–480.

Language and Literacy in the School Years

Gigliana Melzi
New York University

Adina R. Schick
New York University

In the first few years of life, children master the rudiments of their native language. This remarkable achievement appears to require little conscious effort, and it occurs in a wide variety of contexts. By their third birthday, children have acquired a large and varied vocabulary. They string together multiword utterances, participate appropriately in conversations, and make simple jokes. They even begin to talk about objects and events that are not present in their immediate context. By the time children enter kindergarten, usually around age 5, they have acquired a relatively sophisticated command of language, an accomplishment that has sometimes led researchers to believe that language development is essentially complete. However, major tasks still await the child, and developments that are as dramatic as those of the early years are yet to come.

This chapter describes changes that occur during the school years as children interact with printed text. Before discussing the process of learning to read and write, we turn our attention to two trends in oral language development that are qualitatively different from earlier developments. The first is children's growing ability to produce connected multi-utterance language, as seen, for example, in their autobiographical and fictional narratives. The second is children's evolving knowledge of the language system itself, reflected in their expanding metalinguistic awareness and in their acquisition of literacy.

Our focus on extended discourse and metalinguistic awareness is not meant to imply that development in other domains has abated. Quite the contrary, children continue to acquire greater expertise in the phonological (Hua & Dodd, 2006), semantic, syntactic (Tomasello, 2003), and pragmatic (Ninio & Snow, 1996) domains of language, as has been described in earlier chapters. Taking semantic development as an example, children's vocabulary continues to grow at a rapid rate during the school years (Nagy & Scott, 2000), with approximately 3,000 new words added to their lexicon each year (Graves, 2009). Parental input continues to be an important factor in children's vocabulary growth, with the density and context of sophisticated or rare words like *vehicle, cholesterol,* and *tusks* being a robust predictor of future vocabulary growth (Snow, Porsche, Tabors, & Harris, 2007). A significant portion of new words also comes from reading (National Reading

Panel, 2000), a finding that illustrates the importance of literacy, as well as the manner in which literacy interacts with ongoing language development.

Lexical development is also related to world knowledge, knowledge that in most children develops rapidly throughout the school years. Children who know more about a wide range of topics acquire new words more easily than children whose knowledge of the world is more limited. With the acquisition of new words, the breadth and depth of semantic knowledge also increases (Landauer & Dumais, 1997). Bringing the process full circle, the addition of new words to the child's vocabulary is facilitated by the presence of an already rich lexicon (Nagy & Scott, 2000). The dramatic lexical growth throughout the school years should make it clear that the progress that was made in the early years continues. This progress serves as an important foundation for further growth and, in most instances, allows the child to acquire qualitatively new skills like reading and writing.

The chapter is organized topically. We look first at children's use of a form of language termed **academic language**, or talk that focuses on phenomena that are not immediately present (Dickinson & Tabors, 2001; Snow et al., 2007). Examples of academic language in extended oral discourse include narratives and explanations. Next, we consider metalinguistic knowledge or the awareness of the language system itself. Children's awareness of the rule-governed nature of the language system evolves rapidly during the school years, especially as they begin to interact with text, and we will describe some of the developments of this period. Linguistic awareness is an important component of literacy, our next topic. Literacy implies fluent mastery of reading and writing. We will describe how children acquire these important skills and what happens when they find reading difficult. Throughout our discussion, we pay close attention to the major skills children develop within each area as well as linguistic or cultural variations in the developmental process. Given the increase in immigration and globalization, in this revision we consider throughout all sections, the case of **dual-language learning** (DLL) or bilingual children.

In the United States, dual-language learners, young children learning two or more languages, are most often from immigrant families. These children typically enter school speaking a language other than English and often begin acquiring English during the preschool years. Current statistical trends, for instance, demonstrate that from 1995 to 2005, the number of dual-language learning children enrolled in U.S. schools increased by 57 percent (Maxwell, 2009). The great majority of dual-language learners in the United States (about 72 percent) are Spanish-speaking children from Latino backgrounds (NCES, 2009). By contrast, many monolingual English-speaking children encounter a second language exclusively in school settings, especially in the high school years. Although there is controversy as to when it is best to begin formal instruction, many high school and college students are required to complete several years of a "foreign language." Learning a second language is often viewed as drudgery, and many adolescents have little opportunity to use the languages they are studying outside the classroom. Thus, most native English-speaking adolescents enter adulthood as functionally monolingual, whereas adults in the rest of the world are often bilingual or multilingual, at least to some extent. In fact, across the world, multilingualism is becoming normative, with English—and in particular American English—considered a lingua franca, or the language needed to participate in a globalized international community (Dörnyei & Csizer, 2002).

These contexts have implications for the process of learning a second language. When a speaker gains a second language while retaining a first language, as is the case of people acquiring English to participate in a globalized society, the process is called **additive bilingualism**. Often, the acquisition of the second language is seen as an asset, as a way to enhance the prestige and social and economic prowess of the speaker (Tabors & Snow, 2002). Thus, a teenager living in Shanghai might take classes outside of school to acquire English in order to attend college in the United States, while still remaining fluent in her native language. In contrast to additive bilingualism, **subtractive bilingualism** refers to the loss of fluency in one's native language that occurs when acquiring a second language. Subtractive bilingualism is seen mostly in children of immigrants. The language of their parents, the language of the old country, is gradually replaced by the dominant language of the new country, as the children interact and speak more and more with peers and other adults who are not speakers of their native language. In some settings, the language of the old country is even stigmatized; thus, a 9-year-old Latino immigrant might shy away from speaking Spanish at home, preferring instead the language of his new schoolmates.

The notion that language development is a life-span process is a guiding principle of this book. Children's early experiences with language usually occur with adults, most likely their primary caregivers. In the first years of life, the child has the advantage of interacting with helpful and knowledgeable speakers. As we will see, where the child's linguistic skill is weak or incomplete, the parent can fill in, or *scaffold* (Bruner, 1983). However, as children mature, they are more likely to find themselves in the company of other children, where they must fend for themselves. Peer interactions represent true testing grounds for children's evolving communicative competence (Blum-Kulka & Snow 2004; Nicolopoulou, 2002). In time, peer interactions can become more important than parent–child interactions (Cazden & Beck, 2003; Harris, 2009; Pellegrini, Mulhuish, Jones, Trojanowska, & Gilden, 2002). As children begin to enter the larger world, their language skills play a very important role in their social and cognitive development. This chapter will bring us to the threshold of adolescence, connecting the early years of language development described in the preceding chapters to the changes that occur during adolescence and adulthood, some of which are described in Chapter 11.

Extended Oral Discourse

Throughout the school years, children continue to acquire new words at a rapid rate. They learn to master ever more complex syntactic structures (Nippold, 2000) and begin to use a variety of genres of **extended discourse**. Much of children's earliest speech is embedded in the immediate conversational context; it revolves around the child's needs and wants. Conversation for the sake of conversation is uncommon, as is talk about people, objects, and events that are not part of the current context. However, as children get older, they increasingly find themselves in situations in which they are speaking to conversational partners (e.g., peers, teachers) who might lack shared knowledge. In these settings, children need to learn to talk about themselves and their experiences in ways that are comprehensible and meaningful to others. In school settings, children are asked to describe phenomena that are not immediately present, like what they did while on vacation or why birds migrate. In sharing narratives about their personal experience and in providing explanations, children are using extended discourse, a form of academic language. This is language that refers to people, events, and experiences that move beyond the immediate context (Snow et al., 2001).

Extended discourse can express two quite distinct modes of thought, the **paradigmatic mode** and the **narrative mode** (Bruner, 1986). The paradigmatic mode is scientific and logical, and the language of paradigmatic thought is consistent and non-contradictory. Many upper-grade classroom assignments, such as presentations in science courses, require children to think and write paradigmatically. In contrast, the narrative mode of thought focuses on human intentions. The language of narrative thought can be more varied, reflecting both the content of the story and the style of the storyteller. Although the level of mastery across both modes of thought varies according to children's individual and cultural experiences, in general, children develop some level of mastery across both modes of thought.

Autobiographical and Fictional Narratives

Narratives are a discourse genre that represent experiences—real or imagined—in story form. At a minimum, a narrative must contain at least two sequential independent clauses about a single experience (Labov, 1972). Autobiographical or personal narratives are stories about firsthand events, often experienced by the storyteller. Fictional narratives, by comparison, are comprised of imaginary events and can be told from various points of view. Through the telling and sharing of stories, narrators (children and adults alike) make sense of their lived experiences and explore a range of possible worlds.

The following example is part of a longer narrative told by a boy, almost 4 years old. He had been prompted by his mother to describe a recent visit to a fire station. Although the initial focus of the narrative was on what he saw (fire tools, a steering wheel), the key point of the narrative describes what the storyteller identified as a "mistake."

> But you know what I didn't . . . that was not, that I, that I think was a mistake for him to do. He let me wear the big heavy fire hat. But that was a mistake. Because when we got home I was, I was crying. And my eyes were starting to hurt. And actually my head hurt. And my, actually my hand and arm and elbow hurt. I was so sick when I got home.

In this narrative, the child has given linguistic expression to past events. He cites the wearing of a heavy fire hat as the cause of his illness and does so as part of a story. Following his narrative, his mother provided a paradigmatic explanation for what "really" happened. In her explanation, she used the word "associated" in its logical and scientific sense, to make clear that one event (wearing the fire hat) was temporally but not causally connected to another (the child's illness).

Interest in the development of children's narrative skills has grown in recent years (Berman & Slobin, 1994; Fivush, Haden, & Reese, 2006; Melzi & Caspe, 2007; Strömqvist & Verhoeven, 2004). During the school years most children master the ability to tell coherent narratives. Development proceeds from single-utterance narratives produced by children as young as age 2 to novella-length personal stories shared between adolescents. This developmental progression is initially fostered during daily interactions with parents, caregivers and important others. During these early conversations, the adults take the lead in the production of the story through the use of closed-ended questions with yes/no answers. By the end of the preschool years, as children acquire greater linguistic proficiency, the adults shift to use more open-ended "wh" questions that help scaffold children's independent contributions to the story (Farrant & Reese, 2000). With time, children become less reliant on adult scaffolding and become more adept at selecting and weaving information to construct and tell stories.

As children get older and have more opportunities to engage in storytelling, they learn to organize their narratives in more conventional ways. The ways in which children's narratives are structured has been analyzed from a variety of perspectives, including story grammar (which focuses on the structural elements and problem-solving aspects of stories; Stein & Albro, 1997), stanza analysis (which uses the notion of lines and groups of lines, or stanzas; Gee, 1986; Hymes, 2004), and high-point analysis (Labov, 1972; Peterson & McCabe, 1983). In high-point analysis, the classic story builds up to a climactic point that is then resolved. In addition to describing what happened (a process termed *reference* by Labov), classic high-point narratives include *evaluation,* the narrator's attitude toward what happened.

Using high-point analysis, Peterson and McCabe (1983) described the developmental trajectory of the structure used in children's personal narratives from ages of four to nine. The youngest children told *leapfrog narratives,* in which the child unsystematically jumps from one event to another, often leaving out important points, as well as causal and temporal connections. The most mature form of narrative is the *classic narrative,* in which events build to a high point or climactic event, are briefly suspended and evaluated, and then are resolved. Classic narratives were relatively uncommon in 4-year-olds, but made up about 60 percent of the narratives of 8- and 9-year-olds. The following is a classic narrative from a 7½-year-old girl (the high point is in bold type):

I had a bird for a really long time and I took him out to play a little. But then [when] I was playing with him, all of the sudden, he flew so high I couldn't even catch him. So he flew so high, and I was screaming, "*Jaja!*" His name was Jaja. So I was screaming, "*Jaja, Jaja!*" And he wasn't coming back, **so he flew away**. I was soo sad. I was crying and crying. Then my mother was like, "*Oh, don't cry cause we're gonna get another pet.*" Then I went to school the next day and I got so tired and everyone was like, "*What happened? What happened?*" And I was crying and crying. And then like maybe we're gonna get another pet.

By the time children reach middle childhood, they are able to organize their personal stories in more conventional ways.

Evaluation is a critical feature of high-point analysis, as it marks the climactic or key event of the story. Evaluation describes how the narrator feels about the events being depicted and can be expressed in a number of ways, including, internal state terms (*soo sad, crying, tired*), repetitions (*crying and crying*), and negatives, such as events that did not happen (*I couldn't even catch him; he wasn't coming back*). With age, children expand the types of evaluations they include (Peterson & Biggs, 2001; Peterson & McCabe, 1983); a continued emphasis on evaluation also marks the development of narratives through adolescence. In comparing narratives from preadolescent, adolescent, and adult African Americans, Labov's (1972) seminal work showed that evaluations increased threefold from preadolescents to adults.

As children interact with others, they share autobiographical narratives as a way to establish and maintain social relationships. Even though autobiographical narratives are the story type most frequently shared in everyday conversations, children also engage in fantasy narration (Preece, 1987). Like autobiographical narratives, fictional and fantasy narratives, too, develop in the context of everyday interactions with caregivers, not only through the sharing of oral narratives, but also during play routines and book reading interactions. By the time children are 5 years old, they have acquired an elementary narrative scheme for fictional narratives with basic narrative components (Hudson & Shapiro, 1991; Price, Roberts, & Jackson, 2006). The following is an example of a story told by a 6½-year-old girl to her mother.

There was once a Grr family. And this Grr family was a monster. And there was a lot of other Grr people. And none of the town's folks liked them. So, they, they, they just stayed in their forest. And then there was a little girl named Lucy. And she came on picking the berries. And she was really scared cause she met the Grr family! And they said, "Do you wanna go home and do you wanna play with us?" And she decided to play with them so they played a couple games. And then they returned her home safely. And the townspeople said, "We like Lucy but we don't like the Grr family. So let's not let the Grr family come back here." And they got Lucy and they brought her to a tower guarded by a dragon. That dragon would not let her go out of the castle only to get a drink or some food. But he would watch her, so she couldn't run away. And Mrs. Grr, and boy and girl Grr helped Mr. Grr find Lucy. Even frog Grr helped them. They all looked and looked and then they found the tower. They looked and saw the dragon. And they looked and saw Lucy. They had to decide which to get, which to do. Get Lucy or just avoid the dragon. They wanted to just get Lucy. They got all the people that were willing to help. Some of them died from the dragon. But not all of them. Most of them didn't. But the dragon died fully. And they went over and got Lucy and lived happily ever after. The end.

The structure of fictional narratives, such as the one shared above, is similar to that of autobiographical narratives in that both contain orienting and supporting details (introducing main characters such as Lucy and the Grr family), a series of events related to the actions of a protagonist (playing with the Grr family, being locked up in a tower), and evaluative information (really scared) (Uccelli, Hemphill, Pan, & Snow, 1999). However, the two forms of narratives follow different developmental trajectories (Allen, Kertoy, Sherblom, & Petit, 1994). Children's personal narratives, for example, tend to be more cohesive than their fictional narratives (Hadley, 1998). However, their fictional narratives are typically longer and more detailed than their personal narratives as children are creating imaginary worlds instead of representing lived events (Allen et al., 1994). Children, in fact, enjoy stories that depart from actual experiences and include that which is unexpected, in particular those stories with happy outcomes and morals (Toolan, 2001). This characteristic is seen in the Grr family narrative where at the end the main protagonists (the Grr family and Lucy) triumph and, in the child's own words, *lived happily ever after.*

The fictional narratives shared in the home are influenced by those told in school settings. As part of the classroom literacy curriculum, for instance, children are frequently exposed to the fiction genre and are encouraged to read, write, and share stories that fit a particular model. Although children continue to be exposed to and share fantastical stories, most of the fictional stories they are exposed to, while not true, are grounded in truth— or at least in plausible situations. Thus, imagination still plays a large role in terms of the content, but the events depicted could happen, and the narratives include the basic story elements children are exposed to in the elementary and middle school years, such as plot, characters, setting, theme, and point of view. The example below is a fictional story told by an 8½-year-old about a girl who wanted the lead role in a play. Although the story was shared orally with her mother, the story below, as compared to the younger child's narrative, contains many of the characteristics typical of a creative writing assignment that places emphasis on the development of the plot, main characters, and a main theme.

Once there was a girl name Lila who loved to act. She and her sister made up plays and performed to her parents. On her eighth birthday, she figured out that there was an acting class, and she joined. After acting a little bit in that class, she found out that she was gonna do a play called *The Wizard of Oz*. She had her heart set on Dorothy. She practiced and practiced and practiced. And finally the day of the audition came, but she was so nervous. Her body didn't move the right way. Her voice squeaked. And she was so disappointed after she'd only gotten the part of a munchkin. She came home crying to her sister. And her sister said, *"It's okay. Just do your best. There's no small part, only small actors. You're a big actor."* And Lila promised to do her best. So she learned her lines, and she learned everybody else's lines and songs too. She also liked her part. She was a goofy and good munchkin. And finally the day of the show came! And she skipped into the theater to see the director, and all the other kids [were] surrounding him. The director was saying he might want to cancel the show. Dorothy had laryngitis. *"Wait, does anyone know her part?"* The girls looked around at each other, and finally Lila shyly rose her hand. *"Okay,"* said the director, *"Try it."* But Lila started to protest, *"Wait! What about my Munchkin part!"* *"We really need a Dorothy,"* said the director. So Lila took some deep breaths and did it. She felt so proud of herself at the end, even though she made some mistakes. It went great. Her sister was also proud of her too. The End.

Unlike the fictional story told about Lucy and the Grr family, this story is more realistic, describing a plausible scenario an 8-year-old might experience. The story is more cohesive and the narrator develops at greater depth the setting, plot, and main character. In addition, the theme of the story is more complex than *good triumphs over evil*, as with the Grr family narrative. In this story, Lila is rewarded for loving what she does and for making the best of a situation she initially disliked.

In summary, children first learn to tell stories in the context of conversations they have with their primary caregivers. Over the childhood years, children engage in various forms of narrative interactions and become more proficient at constructing and sharing different types of stories. It is important to note that the discourse used with children during these formative narrative conversations is both reflective of and dictated by cultural markers, leading to culturally preferred styles of narration.

Cultural and Linguistic Variations in Narrative Development

Early ethnographic work on narrative use has highlighted differences across cultural communities in the frequency with which stories are shared, the functions narratives serve, and the roles adults and children play in the co-construction of stories (Heath, 1983; Miller, 1982). Recent work has focused on the uses and patterns of narrative discourse in the primary context of narrative development, namely, parent–

Like autobiographical narratives, fantasy narratives also develop in the context of everyday conversations with family members.

child conversations (Leichtman, Wang, & Pillemer; 2003; Melzi, 2000; Miller, Cho, & Bracey, 2005; Minami, 2002). Findings from this growing line of inquiry show cultural variations in the topics that parents and children talk about and the ways in which parents guide their children's narrative production. Researchers conclude that cultural values and ideological orientations (e.g., highlighting the self or others), communicative patterns in the specific communities (e.g., communicating in subtle ways or direct ways), and expecta tions about what constitutes a good story lead to differences in the ways parents support children's developing narrative abilities, and thus in the ways children construct their narratives in the future (Fivush & Haden, 2003; McCabe, Bailey, & Melzi, 2008).

One aspect of parent narrative support that has been greatly investigated is elaborativeness. Elaboration is a discourse feature through which parents either provide or request from their child new information that sustains the storyline. Although all parents use elaborative language during narrative interactions with their children, they differ in the extent to and the manner in which they do so (Fivush et al., 2006; Schick & Melzi, 2010). Specifically, some mothers are highly elaborative and engage their children in lengthy conversations, providing much of the structure and supplying rich, descriptive detailed information. These mothers encourage their children to co-construct the narrative as they ask open-ended questions and expand on their children's utterances. By contrast, less elaborative mothers typically engage their children in shorter conversations, supplying little detail and asking fewer questions; the questions they do ask are repetitive, requesting the same type of information and seeking specific answers while providing little new information (Fivush et al., 2006). Maternal elaborativeness is reflective of the socialization goals adopted by a particular sociocultural group (Wang & Fivush, 2005). Thus, because in the United States children are typically imbued with a sense of individualism and a feeling of autonomy and independence, European American mothers often adopt a high-elaborative style as they engage their children in conversations about the self. In comparison to U.S. American mothers, the styles used by mothers from other cultures (mostly Asian) seem to involve less elaboration (Wang, 2004; Wang & Fivush, 2005). The extent to which parents provide or request new information (i.e., elaboration) during narrative interactions is predictive of children's vocabulary, print knowledge, narrative, and memory skills (Fivush et al., 2006; Reese, 1995).

Current work has also begun to uncover the diverse ways in which children from different speech and cultural communities structure their independent narratives, that is, narratives told to an unrelated adult or shared with peers (McCabe & Bliss; 2003; Nicolopoulou, 2002). Not only do cultural communities value different ways of organizing and telling stories, but also different languages offer distinct linguistic resources for constructing well-organized narratives. For example, languages differ in the number of verb tenses and ways of marking aspect, as well as in the number and variety of adjectives and adverbs available to narrators. These linguistic differences influence the structure and content of children's narratives (Berman & Slobin, 1994; Gutiérrez-Clellen, 2002; Minami, 2008). Spanish-speaking Peruvian Andean children, for instance, convey evaluation not by suspending the narrative as described by Labovian frameworks, but by *departing* from the order of events, such as introducing a different but related experience at the high point of the narrative (Uccelli, 2008). Japanese children, as another example, connect temporally distinct events thematically, often using a structure that reflects *haiku,* a culturally valued literary form (Minami, 2002). Similarly, one of the many structures valued in African American communities is a *topic-associating style*, which links several episodes thematically and involves several principal characters, as well as shifts in time and setting (Champion, 2003; Michaels, 1991).

Given the cultural and linguistic differences in narrative development, recent research has begun to investigate the narratives told by bilingual children (Fiestas & Peña, 2004; Pearson, 2002; Uccelli & Paéz, 2007). Although this work is quite limited, the focus has been on comparing the narratives children use across their two (or more) languages. Overall findings suggest that some narrative strategies are transferred across languages, such as overall narrative structure complexity and elaborativeness. Moreover, recent research suggests that children's narrative skills in their dominant language might act as a bootstrap for the narrative skills in the weaker language (Anstatt, 2008).

Extended Discourse in the Classroom

The ability to narrate well and to use other forms of extended discourse is an important precursor to literacy (Snow et al., 2001) and continues to be linked to literacy achievement throughout the school years. In elementary school classrooms, for example, teachers tell children engaging fictional stories in the form of book reading and often encourage children to share their stories with their peers during *sharing time* (Cazden, 2001). As they share stories in the classroom, children learn to weave together their experiences in a way that makes them meaningful not only for their peers but also for the teacher. Teachers serve as a unique form of audience; their role in not simply to listen to the story, but to also use sharing time as a teaching event by commenting on, interpreting, questioning, and critiquing both the content and structure of the narrative. Providing the necessary support and input in the classroom context is challenging for teachers, not only because they might be unaware of the children's personal experiences, but also because children might use a culturally preferred narrative style unfamiliar to the teacher.

Sara Michaels (1991) has documented what can happen in school when teachers are not familiar with children's culturally influenced ways of organizing their stories. A first-grade African American girl who constructed a thematically linked narrative was told by her teacher that she should talk "about things that are really, really very important," and "to stick with one thing" (Michaels, 1991, pp. 316, 320). The way this girl usually made sense of her world through her personal narratives was devalued and explicitly discouraged. Instead, she was urged to adopt a narrative style that conformed to the dominant discourse of the classroom (a single-experience narrative). Although there is nothing intrinsically wrong with teaching students to use different ways of organizing stories, a teacher's implicit devaluation of the narrative style of a child's cultural community might have negative consequences (Champion, Katz, Muldrow, & Dail, 1999; Mainess, Champion, & McCabe, 2002). In a follow-up interview one year later, the African American child angrily portrayed her first-grade teacher as uninterested in what she had to say. Because this experience occurred early in her educational experience, the influence on her attitude toward teachers, school, and literacy was potentially profound (Ogbu, 1990). Thus, there is a need for educators to address these potential conflicts and to provide educational environments that nurture cultural and linguistic diversity as well as foster academic achievement of all children.

In addition to narratives, other forms of extended discourse skills, such as definitions and explanatory talk, are important part of classroom discourse (Lehrer, 1994). As with narratives, children's initial experiences with definitions and explanatory talk are likely to occur in the home, where caregivers use explanations as a way of conveying knowledge about language and the world. In the following example, an aunt introduces and defines a new word to her 6-year-old nephew, who is watching a baseball game. At the end of the interaction, the child grasps the meaning of the word and uses it productively to convey his feelings about his team.

Child:	Look! Look! It was a foul pitch! A foul pitch. Oh man! That makes me so upset. I'm so angry and upset. Now, how are they gonna win?
Aunt:	You're upset about the foul pitch? Is it depressing?
Child:	Pressing? What's that? What does that mean, pressing?
Aunt:	Depressing. Depressing is like when something happens that makes you feel sad and upset.
Child:	Pressing, it's called? Huh? Pressing?
Aunt:	Depressing. Things that are depressing make you so sad or upset that you kind of feel like giving up hope.
Child:	Oh yeah, that's what this is. It's depressing. These METS, they make me so upset. How are they gonna win? They are so depressing!

Teachers are often very explicit in their encouragement of these types of extended discourse. In first-grade classrooms, teachers have been noted to provide definitions about words children encounter and elicit explanations about objects (e.g., candles, board games) children had brought to sharing time by saying, "Pretend we don't know a thing about candles," or "Tell us how to play. Pretend we're all blind and can't see the game" (Michaels, 1991). Exposure to extended discourse in both home and preschool settings predicts competence in a number of skills that are important to the acquisition of literacy (Dickinson & Tabors, 2001).

Metalinguistic Development in the School Years

The rapid unfolding of **metalinguistic awareness** is an especially notable characteristic of language development during the school years. As we saw in Chapter 4, metalinguistic awareness is knowledge about language itself. In using language, children need not have conscious awareness of its complex rule-governed nature. In time, however, some aspects of the system gain saliency as a result of the child's active exploration of the system through language play (Kuczaj, 1982). In addition, ongoing cognitive development and exposure to literacy influences children's understanding of the linguistic system (Doherty, 2000).

At the most basic level, a precursor of metalinguistic awareness is seen in children's corrections of their own speech (Clark, 1978). However, the awareness that underlies self-correction does not necessarily include a conscious understanding of the language system; self-correction shows only that the child recognizes ideal models or rules and notes implicitly a discrepancy between her linguistic behavior and the model or rule. True metalinguistic awareness, by contrast, requires *explicit* knowledge of the language system.

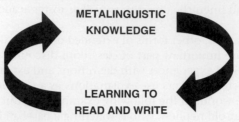

figure 10.1 **Metalinguistic Knowledge Develops in the Preschool Years as Children Grow Cognitively and Gain Greater Control of Language.** However, Literacy Instruction and Development Fosters Attainment of More Sophisticated Metalinguistic Skills.

Metalinguistic awareness is considered a critical skill for success in school, and has been linked to reading comprehension and academic language.

Research shows that there is a bidirectional relation between metalinguistic awareness and literacy instruction (see Figure 10.1). That is, although the awareness of language as a system is necessary for literacy development, exposure to reading and writing fosters greater awareness of language per se. Nevertheless, as with narratives, metalinguistic awareness begins to develop before children can read and write, in the context of everyday interactions with family and friends.

Language Play and Verbal Humor

One aspect of language use that is particularly salient in children is the propensity to play with language (Dunn, 1988). In the early school years, play with language represents a sizable portion of children's language. In one study, approximately one-quarter of all utterances produced by kindergarten children contained some form of language play (Ely & McCabe, 1994). Children treat language as they would any other object, as a rich source of material that can be playfully exploited (Garvey, 1977). All components of language are subject to manipulations, and spontaneous word play and rhyming sometimes lead to the invention of new, often nonsense words. In the following example, a 5-year-old child who clearly did not like bananas used repetition and partial rhyming to amplify her feelings of disgust:

> Yuck I hate bananas.
>
> They're icky.
>
> They're slimy.
>
> They're gooey. (Ely & McCabe, 1994, p. 26)

The almost poetic quality of this spontaneous utterance is echoed in children's more explicit attempts at creating poetry. Ann Dowker (1989) asked young children to generate poems in response to pictures. One boy, aged 5½, produced the following lines in response to a picture of a snowy day:

> It's a latta with a peed,
>
> A plappa plotty pleed.
>
> And there's a wop,
>
> A weep,

A stop.

And yes. No.

Sledge.

Fledge. (Dowker, 1989, p. 192)

These excerpts show that children have a propensity to play with the phonological features of language. This early verbal play sharpens children's linguistic skills and leads to greater awareness of the phonological properties of language. For example, children's early exposure to certain playful forms of language like nursery rhymes correlates positively with their later development of literacy (Bryant, Bradley, Maclean, & Crossland, 1989). Classroom instructional practices take advantage of children's naturally playful disposition by incorporating games as a way of teaching phonemic awareness (Adams, Foorman, Lundberg, & Beeler, 1997).

"... They're icky. They're slimy. They're gooey."
Children may employ poetic devices to express their feelings of disgust.

School-age children also display a great interest in riddles and other interactive language play. **Riddles** are word games (usually structured as questions) that are dependent on phonological, morphological, lexical, or syntactic ambiguity (Pepicello & Weisberg, 1983). To solve a riddle correctly, children must have some insight into the ways that words can be ambiguous. In the following examples of riddles, the first plays primarily on morphological ambiguity, the second on syntactic ambiguity (phrase structure):

Question: Where did the king hide his armies?
Answer: In his sleevies.
Question: How is a duck like an icicle?
Answer: They both grow down.

Between the ages of 6 and 8, children display a heightened interest in riddles (McDowell, 1979). Children's ability to solve riddles varies with their knowledge of the genre itself and also with their metalinguistic development. Skill in solving riddles is also positively correlated with children's reading ability (Ely & McCabe, 1994). Thus, language play is a marker of children's developing mastery of the language system and also a possible means of acquiring linguistic knowledge.

Verbal humor represents another form of language play. Humor is a universal feature of language across culture (Apte, 1985). To become full participants in the discourse of their community, children must become familiar with its basic forms of humor. Children's ability to both produce and appreciate verbal humor develops over time and is closely associated with their growing mastery of all aspects of language. Younger children, who have a limited appreciation of the social and situational aspects of language, are more likely than are older children to find simple scatological utterances like "poo-poo head" humorous. Older children are less amused by such simple pragmatic violations and are more likely to focus on the semantic and syntactic manipulations found in conventional jokes and puns. At a later stage, adolescents are similar to adults in their comprehension and production of verbal humor, including the use of irony and sarcasm (Dews et al., 1996), as described in Chapter 4.

Teasing is another type of complex verbal play that occurs across cultural communities and serves multiple socializing functions (Schieffelin & Ochs, 1986; Tholander, 2002). For example, in Mexicano families, teasing with or around children serves not only as a form of verbal play but also as a means of social control and of creating intimate bonds (Eisenberg, 1986). Among British Bangladeshi working-class adolescent girls, as another example, teasing serves to establish and maintain intimacy, to express toughness and release tension, as well as to negotiate their intersecting cultural identities (Pichler, 2006). Some forms of teasing are highly structured, ritualistic, and require metalinguistic sophistication. *Sounding, playing the dozens, snapping,* or *woofing* is an activity that is found in African American communities, predominantly among adolescent males (Labov, 1972; Morgan, 2002), although it has also been documented in female and mixed-sex groupings among adults (Goodwin, 1990). This ritualistic verbal game has many rules that must be followed to ensure its playful nature. Sounding involves placing figures who are highly significant (e.g., the mother) in implausible contexts (Fox, cited in Morgan, 2002, p. 58; Labov, 1972, pp. 312, 319), as in the following examples:

> That's why your mother is so dumb: She was filling out a job application and it said "Sign here." And she put "Aquarius."
>
> Your mother so skinny, she do the hula hoop in a Applejack.
>
> Your mother play dice with the midnight mice.

Sounding builds upon preceding utterances, with the goal being to outwit one's interlocutor by generating a statement that cannot be topped; it is a way in which verbal skill is performed and practiced in the presence of an audience. One study of elementary school children found that frequent engagement in sounding was associated with better comprehension of figurative language, such as metaphors (Ortony, Turner, & Larson-Shapiro, 1985).

Thus verbal play and humor facilitate the explicit understanding of language as a system, and yet sophisticated verbal play and humor require metalinguistic skills. We now turn to the different types of metalinguistic awareness that have been related to children's development of reading and writing.

Phonological Awareness

As mentioned in Chapter 4, one particular area that has received much attention in recent years is children's awareness and manipulation of the sound system of language, referred to as *phonological awareness*. Specifically, phonological awareness is defined as the understanding that words are made up of sound units, including larger units (syllables) and smaller units (phonemes). For example, we know that the word *cat* is composed of one syllable and three different phonemes, /k/, /æ/, and /t/. Phonological awareness develops mostly between the ages of 3 and 8. Children's verbal play in the preschool years, such as rhyming and using nonsense words, is the first indicator of their developing awareness of the phonological properties of language. Later milestones include identification of the first sounds of words, comparison of the sounds of one word to those of another word, correct **segmentation** (or breaking up) of words into smaller units, blending individual sounds to form a word, and using the sound patterns for decoding and spelling (Snow, 2006). As children grow older and interact more with both oral and written language (e.g., learn more words, learn the letters of the alphabet), their phonological awareness skills become more refined and diverse. For instance, whereas most 5-year-olds are able to identify correctly that *hat* rhymes with *cat* and that the initial sounds of the two words differ, they will need three more years to understand that *giant* and *jail* are spelled with two different letters despite starting with the same sound, /j/.

Researchers agree that phonological awareness is strongly linked to children's ability to read and write. Most research shows that phonological awareness fosters the development of literacy *and* is fostered by literacy instruction (Castle & Colheart, 2004; Chow, McBride-Chang, & Burgess, 2005). Although phonological awareness continues to develop throughout the lifespan, the most dramatic growth in phonological awareness occurs in the early school years as a result of literacy instruction that emphasizes sound–symbol correspondence. The robust association between phonological awareness and reading seems to hold true regardless of type of language (alphabetic or not), especially in the early stages of reading. Its significance for later literacy acquisition is not yet well documented and seems to depend on various factors, such as the structure, orthography, and script of the language, as well as the instructional experiences of the child (McBride-Chang, 2004). In alphabetic languages, such as English and Spanish, phonemic awareness facilitates reading and spelling. By contrast, in nonalphabetic languages such as Chinese, syllabic awareness plays a more significant role since written characters map onto syllables, not phonemes (McBride-Chang, Bialystok, Chong, & Li, 2004).

Semantic and Syntactic Awareness

Semantic awareness or metasemantic knowledge evolves slowly over the school years. Children come to understand that words are basic units of the language system and that the relationship between the phonological constituents of words and their referents are arbitrary (Homer & Olson, 1999). By age 10, children have acquired a clear understanding of the use of the term *word*. At this same age, children are able to provide formal definitions of words through the use of the copula and a superordinate relative clause (e.g., "A bird is a kind of animal that likes to fly") (Kurland & Snow, 1997; Snow, 1990) and come to understand nonliteral language forms, such as idioms, similes, and metaphors. Defining words in this manner is a regular part of classroom discourse, and skill in producing formal definitions is positively correlated with vocabulary growth (Nagy & Scott, 2000) and reading acquisition (Roth, Speece, & Cooper, 2002).

   Syntactic awareness or metasyntactic knowledge is sometimes assumed to underlie children's ability to correct syntactic errors. Five year old children can correct ungrammatical sentences, but often their corrections reflect their propensity to correct the deviant *semantic meaning* created by the syntactic errors. When young children are asked to correct the syntax, but not the semantic meaning, of sentences that are both syntactically *and* semantically deviant (e.g., "The baby eated the typewriter"), their rates of failure are relatively high (Bialystok, 1986).

   Syntactic awareness also includes an understanding of syntactic structure. Ferreira and Morrison (1994) studied children's developing knowledge of sentence structure. They found that even before formal schooling, 5-year-olds can identify the subject of a sentence like "The mailman delivered a shiny package" about 80 percent of the time. In general, schooling may be the single most important source of explicit knowledge about syntax, since talk about terms like *subject* and *verb* is extremely rare outside of educational settings. In reviewing the evidence on metasyntactic development, including a classic cross-cultural study by Scribner and Cole (1981), Gombert (1992) argued that explicit syntactic awareness comes only through formal education in literacy skills. Syntactic awareness has been found to be associated with successful use of word definitions (Scott & Nagy, 1997) and improved reading comprehension (Nagy, 2007; Nation & Snowling, 2000).

Pragmatic Awareness

Pragmatic awareness or metapragmatic knowledge includes an awareness of the relationship between language and the social context in which it is being used (Ninio & Snow, 1996). Common examples of pragmatic awareness include the ability to judge referential adequacy, the ability to determine comprehensibility, and the ability to describe *explicitly* the social rules (e.g., politeness rules) governing language use.

   In judging referentially inadequate messages, children aged 5 and under often blame the listener, *who should have listened better,* not the speaker, for communicative failure. After age 8, children are able to identify the speaker as the source of the problem (Robinson, 1981). Similar age trends were found in a study by Hughes and Grieve (1980), in which children were asked bizarre questions such as, "Is red heavier than yellow?" or "Is milk bigger than water?" Beyond metaphorical interpretations, these questions require clarification of the speaker's intended meaning. Yet very few 5-year-old children asked for clarification. Instead, they attempted to answer the question in a straightforward manner. By contrast, most 7-year-olds gave responses that reflected their uncertainty about the speaker's intended meaning (e.g., "Milk is bigger, isn't it?").

Pragmatic awareness requires more than knowing how to use language in culturally appropriate ways. Children must be able to articulate the rules explicitly. In spite of the observation that younger children frequently fail to follow the social norms of language use, for example, by being verbally polite (Berko Gleason, 1973), there are some anecdotal accounts of young children's awareness of these same rules. In one such example, a kindergarten girl chastises her classmate for nagging (Ely & Berko Gleason, 1995, p. 267):

Mark:	Can I pick up the turtle, John?
Teacher:	Not right now.
Mark:	Please, John.
Allison:	No nagging. When, when he [Mark] keep telling him [the teacher] and telling him, that's nagging.

By late childhood and early adolescence, most children have a fairly solid understanding of the rules governing language use in everyday social contexts (Berko Gleason, Hay, & Cain, 1988). It is unclear what role metapragmatic knowledge plays in literacy acquisition. There are some studies that show that greater pragmatic awareness as a result of dialect shifting might lead increased literacy achievement.

Metalinguistic Awareness in Two Languages

Given the rise in globalization, current research on metalinguistic awareness development has reintroduced the question of whether bilingualism fosters the development of metalinguistic skills and places children at an advantage for literacy acquisition. Most of the work has compared bilingual and monolingual children's performance on specific metalinguistic tasks (Bialystok, 2004). Overall this work shows that being bilingual fosters children's ability to think about language per se, leading to increased metalinguistic skills. This is particularly true for the word awareness skills of bilingual children, who are exposed to two labels for the same referent. For example, a bilingual Creole- and English-speaking Haitian child learning that the same food on her plate can be called duri or rice will learn about the arbitrary relation between words and their referents at an earlier age than a child learning only English.

However, the relation between bilingualism and other forms of metalinguistic knowledge is more complex and depends on various factors, including child's level of competency in both languages, as well as literacy instruction. For example, only fully balanced bilingual children appear to outperform their monolingual counterparts in particular syntactic awareness skills, such as in detecting and correcting syntax-based errors in sentences that contain distracting information (Bialystok, 2004). By contrast, children's proficiency in other areas of syntactic awareness, including the ability to explain grammatical errors, is related to oral proficiency in the target language, rather than their bilingualism. Moreover, although some research studies report that bilingual children are at an advantage in terms of their phonological awareness, such as their ability to detect the number of phonemes at the beginning or end of a word (e.g., Eviater & Ibrahim, 2000), others show no relation, or even show a disadvantage for bilingual children. It appears that the bilingual advantage in phonological awareness is mediated by a number of variables, such as the child's age and formal literacy instruction in the classroom, as well as the orthography of the language pairs (e.g., Spanish-English versus Chinese-English) (Bialystok, 2007; Cheung, Chen, Lai, Wong, & Hills, 2001).

Given the bidirectional relation between metalinguistic awareness and literacy in mono-lingual children, one interesting question regarding bilingual children concerns the association between metalinguistic awareness in one language and literacy development in the other. Research, for the most part, has yet to offer a conclusive answer to this question, especially as it pertains to the later school years. However, there are some studies that suggest a transfer across languages, especially with regard to phonological and word awareness, leading researchers to conclude that metalinguistic awareness in one language does facilitate reading ability in the second (Bialystok, 2002; Genesee, Geva, Dressler, & Kamil, 2008).

Thus far, our discussion has focused on two oral language skills that prepare children for literacy acquisition. We now turn our attention to literacy development per se, beginning with early exposure to print.

Early Literacy: Exposure to Print

Children growing up in literate societies are exposed, in varying degrees, to literacy in their homes and in their communities, and this exposure is an important introduction to formal literacy instruction. Children's earliest awareness of the function and form of literacy has been termed **emergent literacy** (Teale & Sulzby, 1986; Whitehurst & Lonigan, 2002). Young children are able to recognize **environmental print** on road signs (e.g., STOP) and in familiar commercial logos (e.g., Coca-Cola and McDonald's). They also acquire some of the conventions of print, including, for example, that in written English reading proceeds from left to right, and from top to bottom, and that printed words are separated from one another by spaces.

While children are learning about the forms of literacy, they are also being exposed to some of the functions literacy serves. Although form is relatively standard across communities of English speakers (reading always proceeds from left to right), there is variation in the functions of literacy. For example, in some homes, literacy might be emphasized across various contexts and serve a wide range of practical and leisure functions. Children growing up in homes like these might frequently encounter their parents and older siblings engaged in reading and writing for work or recreation, and they themselves might be read to extensively. Children growing up in homes where literacy serves exclusively instrumental functions (e.g., reading bills and school notices; writing checks and grocery lists) might develop very different notions about its uses and worth (Dickinson & Tabors, 2001; Gee, 2002; Heath, 1983).

In addition, parents vary in the degree to which they actively encourage the development of emergent literacy (e.g., Hammer, 2001; Sénéchal & Le Fevre, 2002). Parents who frequently engage their children in literacy-related activities (alphabet games, book reading) prepare them well for school-based literacy. This kind of focus on literacy also communicates that competence in reading, writing, and extended discourse is socially and culturally valued. Children from households where there is much continuity between the focus on extended discourse at home and the dominant and valued academic language of the classroom are at a distinct advantage upon entering school (Gee, 2002; Heath, 1983).

Children from economically disadvantaged homes are at a greater risk for failing to acquire basic literacy skills (Snow et al., 2007). These differences have been attributed to the early literacy environments in the home, including children's exposure to shared book reading. Children from low-income families typically experience a fraction of the number of hours of shared book reading that middle-class children experience (Hart & Risley, 1995). Although the difference in the frequency of exposure to book reading might explain a portion of the observed socioeconomic status

Shared book reading between parents and children is an important introductory step to literacy.

differences in the acquisition of literacy skills, other risk factors, such as residing in urban areas where poverty is concentrated also play a role.

The degree to which home environments support literacy is of great interest from both a theoretical and a practical perspective (Dickinson & Tabors, 2001; Whitehurst & Lonigan, 1998). For example, shared book reading between parents and children is a very important introductory step to literacy and can foster positive attitudes toward literacy (Bus, 2002). Shared book reading is not only an opportunity to gain knowledge about the conventions of print; it is also an opportunity for extended discourse that is stimulated by the material being read, and a source of introduction to novel words.

Different styles of book sharing interactions are associated with particular long-term effects, with the best outcomes across a variety of measures being associated with an inter-active, dyadic, or collaborative approach in which the child's verbal participation is encouraged (Haden, Reese, & Fivush, 1996; Reese & Cox, 1999; Sénéchal, 1997; Whitehurst, Arnold, Epstein, & Angell, 1994). Using an experimental design, Reese and Cox (1999) assessed three different styles of book reading: a *describer style,* in which the parent provides description and encourages labeling; a *comprehender style,* in which meaning, inferences, and predictions are stressed; and a *performance style,* in which the story is read in its entirety, although it is preceded by comments and followed by prompts regarding inferences and evaluations. Overall, the describer style produced the greatest gains in vocabulary and print skills, but outcomes were dependent on children's initial skill levels. For example, children with initially strong vocabularies benefited more from the performance style.

Building on this work, reading interventions programs, such as dialogic reading, have been developed that encourage mothers to elicit information from their children and to foster children's participation (Whitehurst & Lonigan, 1998). Nonetheless, although this book-sharing style is common among middle-class European American families, it might not be aligned with the literacy practices of all communities, and thus, not as effective for all children. For example, in a recent meta-analysis investigating the effectiveness of interactive (i.e., dialogic) reading on vocabulary development, Mol, Bus, De Jong, and Smeets (2008) showed that although dialogic reading is beneficial for middle-class families, it is not as effective for everyone, such as mother–child dyads from low-income, culturally diverse backgrounds.

Recent work on book sharing among culturally diverse groups sheds further light on this topic showing that an interactive style, such as the one used by English-speaking European American mothers, might not be the preferred storytelling style in other groups. In a study conducted with middle-class Peruvian and European American mothers in their home countries, Melzi and Caspe (2005) found that when sharing a wordless children's picture storybook, Peruvian mothers adopted a *storytelling style* in which they acted as the sole narrator of an engaging story with minimal child participation. European American mothers, by comparison, preferred to adopt a *storybuilding style,* a more interactive style in which they co-constructed the story with their children. In an extension of that study, Caspe (2009) examined the book-sharing styles of low-income, Spanish-speaking Dominican and Mexican immigrant families living in New York City. The majority of the mothers (68 percent) in Caspe's study preferred to act as the sole narrator (i.e., they adopted a storytelling style, rather than a more interactive style). Interestingly, after controlling for years of maternal education and children's initial developmental level, the storytelling style was most beneficial for children's print-related literacy scores at the end of the school year. Similar findings about the narrator-audience distinction as an important dimension of maternal scaffolding during mother–child book sharing interactions have been noted among other cultural groups, including East Indian mothers (Harkins & Ray, 2004), Brazilian mothers (Zilles, Melzi, Knecht, & Lopes, 2008), and Spanish-speaking Puerto Rican mothers (Caspe & Melzi, 2008). Melzi, Schick, and Kennedy (2011) suggest that this narrator-audience distinction is indicative of a new narrative dimension which they labeled narrative participation.

Snow and her colleagues (2007; Dickinson & Tabors, 2001) have been examining the relationship between the early literacy environment and children's acquisition of literacy skills in a longitudinal study of ethnically diverse low-income families. They find that the amount of extended discourse at home, the density of rare or sophisticated words in home conversations, and parental support for literacy activities (e.g., book reading) at age 4 predicted to varying degrees a number of kindergarten language and literacy skills, including narrative production, emergent literacy (e.g., knowledge of the conventions of literacy, letter names), and receptive vocabulary, even when controlling for important demographic variables (family income, mother's education) (Dickinson & Tabors, 2001). Moreover, the quality of the parent–child relationship is predictive of the child's writing ability, with good relationships being positively associated with children's ability to write well.

However, preschool environments (including extended teacher discourse, classroom curriculum, and classroom exposure to rare words) were even better predictors of many of these same skills (Dickinson & Tabors, 2001). Reading comprehension, for example, appears to be relatively unrelated to any of the home measures; instead, it is more strongly associated with school factors such as practice with structured materials like workbooks. One of the more compelling findings was that children who were exposed to optimal language and literacy experiences at home but had poor preschool experiences performed below average on the kindergarten language and literacy measures. In other words, the better-than-average home environment was not enough to buffer the adverse effects of a poor preschool environment. However, children who came from homes in which language and literacy experiences were below average, but had optimal preschool experiences, performed above average on the kindergarten measures (narrative production, emergent literacy, and receptive vocabulary). These findings emphasize the important role that preschools can play in ameliorating later academic outcomes, especially for children from low-income households (Dickinson & Tabors, 2001, p. 330).

Reading

Components of Reading

Reading is a complex process. It involves a number of components that in the skilled reader work together in a seamless fashion, so much so that written text appears to convey meaning almost automatically. Table 10.1 lists some of the major components that underlie skilled reading.

table 10.1 Stages in Solving Riddles
Target riddle: What dog keeps the best time? Answer: A watch dog.

Level 0
Absent or minimal response: "I don't know."

Level 1
Illogical or negative attempt at explication: "Because dogs don't really have watches."

Level 2
Explanation focuses on the situation to which the language referred, not the language itself: "Because a watch dog is a kind of dog and also it keeps time."

Level 3
Incongruity is clearly attributed to the language itself: "Because, well, watch dogs are really dogs to watch and see if anybody comes in but watch dogs . . . It's a joke 'cause it's also another *word* for telling time."

Source: From Ely & McCabe (1994).

Most 6-year-olds are at Level 1; most 8- and 9-year-olds perform at Level 3.

figure 10.2 **Letter Detection Requires Recognizing Many Different Graphic Forms.** Some forms of the letter A.

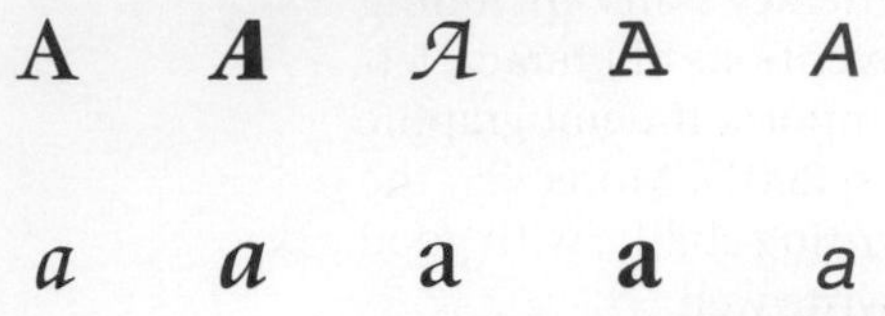

A   *A*   𝒜   A   A

a   *a*   a   **a**   a

Letter Recognition. The first component involves detection of the features of the letters of the alphabet, leading to **letter recognition.** Texts come in a variety of different forms, from highly regular and readable print to highly variable and barely legible handwritten script. Even standard print takes a variety of forms, so that dramatically different typefaces or fonts produce different graphic patterns. In order to identify a letter correctly, the reader must be able to extract its defining features. For example, the letter *A* can appear in many forms (see Figure 10.2). It is important to stress that even in skilled readers, each letter of a word is recognized, although processing is very rapid (Rayner, Foorman, Perfetti, Pesetsky, & Seidenberg, 2001).

Grapheme–Phoneme Correspondence Rules. An understanding of the **alphabetic principle** and knowledge of **grapheme–phoneme correspondence rules** are critical components in reading a language like English. According to the alphabetic principle, letters of the alphabet represent the sounds of oral language. **Graphemes** are the actual graphic forms or elements of the writing system, the letters of the alphabet, for example. As noted in Chapter 3, phonemes are the basic sounds of a language. Thus grapheme–phoneme correspondence rules define the relationship between a letter, or combination of letters, and the sound they represent.

In a perfect alphabetic system, grapheme–phoneme correspondence rules would have three characteristics:

1. They would be simple: There would be a one-to-one correspondence between each symbol and each sound.
2. They would be transparent: The name of a grapheme and the sound it represents would be identical.
3. They would be completely regular: There would be no exceptions to the two features listed above.

Orthographic systems with nearly perfect one-to-one grapheme–phoneme relationships are termed **shallow orthographies.** Italian represents an example of a shallow orthography, and readers of Italian can use spelling as a reliable guide to pronunciation and pronunciation as a reliable guide to spelling (Perfetti, 1997). In contrast, English is considered a **deep orthography**, in that the relationships between graphemes and phonemes are more variable. For example, the letter *i* sometime sounds like itself, as in the pronoun *I*. However, it can also represent many other sounds, including the /I/ of *bit,* the /iy/ of *radio,* and so on. Furthermore, graphemes represent abstract forms, phonemes, whose actual phonetic form varies according to the other speech sounds (phonemes) with which it is combined.

To achieve fluency in reading English, the child must master these and other irregularities of the grapheme–phoneme correspondence rules (Bryne & Fielding-Barnsley, 1998). This task is particularly difficult because segmenting words into their constituent phonemes is not a straightforward or intrinsically intuitive skill. Although some children gain awareness of segmenting through informal instruction and exposure to texts like nursery rhymes, many children require formal instruction before acquiring explicit knowledge of phonemic segmentation.

Word Recognition. The recognition of letter strings as representing conventional words in the orthography of the language defines the next component of reading, **word recognition.** Many laboratory studies of word recognition compare subjects' response time in recognizing different classes of words or letter combinations. True words (e.g., *king*) are words that follow the orthographic conventions of the language and are part of the language. Nonsense words are words that do not exist in the language (e.g., *gink*), although they are possible words because they follow conventional orthographic rules. False words are words that violate the orthographic rules (e.g., *nkgi*) and would be unlikely to be found in the language. In these *lexical decision tasks,* true words are recognized more rapidly than nonsense words or false words.

Semantic Knowledge.   Most of the time, the word that is read is a word that is known to the reader. Its recognition stimulates a number of possible meanings based on the reader's **semantic knowledge.** Semantic knowledge refers to all the information about a word, its possible meanings, and its relations to other words and to real-world referents. (See the discussion of semantic networks in Chapter 4.) Incomplete semantic knowledge impedes comprehension of written text. A colleague of ours recalled the time when as a young reader he encountered a story about a boy who lived in Washington and whose father worked in the *Cabinet.* His semantic knowledge of the word *cabinet* was limited to its meaning *cupboard.* How could a grown man fit in a cabinet? What kind of work would he do inside a cabinet? As a child, our colleague had a great deal of difficulty understanding an important aspect of the story, so much so that more than forty years later he still remembered how puzzled he was!

Comprehension and Interpretation.   The final component of the reading process encompasses the ability to comprehend and interpret texts. Successful comprehension and interpretation depend on a number of developing skills and knowledge, including the **automaticity** of word recognition, vocabulary size, the capacity of working memory, and world knowledge (National Reading Panel, 2000). In order to accommodate children's developing abilities, books for young readers are age-graded, that is, designed specifically for children's evolving skill levels and knowledge bases.

Reading Development

Because reading is a complex skill, expertise in reading evolves slowly. In addition, purposes for reading change with age. Although there are a number of different models of reading development (Ehri, 1991; Frith, 1985; Harm & Seidenberg, 1999; Perfetti, 1992), we will focus on the model Jean Chall (1996) has formulated, a model that describes the stages through which children pass. Chall's model (see Table 10.2) begins with prereaders, young children in the preschool years (stage 0), and ends with college-aged readers (stage 5).

The prereader pretends to read, although she may have acquired some important concepts about the conventions of printed texts and may possess some elementary reading skills (e.g., recognizing her own name). In this stage, the child is primarily using top-down processes in making hypotheses about what reading is all about (Chall, 1996). According to **top-down models** of reading, reading is a *psycholinguistic guessing game* that consists of generating and testing hypotheses (Goodman, 2005; Smith, 2004). With the onset of formal instruction (stage 1), bottom-up processes become important. **Bottom-up models** of reading hold that reading is largely dependent upon accurate perception of the letter strings that make up words (Gough, 1972). Stages 1 and 2 have been characterized as "learning to read." The emphasis is on mastering decoding skills, on recognizing and sounding out words. In order to facilitate this decoding process, many of the texts children read during these stages are relatively simple and contain little knowledge that is truly new.

In Chall's model, a major shift occurs between stages 2 and 3, which normally occurs after the third grade. Where stages 1 and 2 were characterized as "learning to read," stages 3 through 5 have been characterized as "reading to learn." Here the focus is on extracting meaning from texts, and many of the materials children read contain new knowledge,

table 10.2	Components of Skilled Reading
1	Detection of visual features of letters leading to letter recognition
2	Knowledge of the grapheme–phoneme correspondence rules
3	Word recognition
4	Semantic knowledge
5	Comprehension, interpretation

including new words or phrases for a variety of never-before-encountered concepts. During stages 3 through 5, reading is best characterized as interactive, with the child drawing on both bottom-up and top-down processes. Children move from reading texts with a single focus to reading from an array of texts that present more diverse perspectives. At the highest level (stage 5), the mechanics of decoding are highly **automatized,** so that reading is rapid and efficient. More important, the goals of reading are more intellectually sophisticated than at previous stages. Now reading is a process through which readers seek to broaden their knowledge. Snow (1993, p. 12) has defined sophisticated college-level literacy as involving "the ability to read in ways adjusted to one's purpose (to enjoy light fiction, to memorize factual material, to analyze literature, to learn facts and discover ideas in texts, to judge the writer's point of view, and to incorporate information and perspectives from texts into one's own thinking but also to question and disagree with information and opinions expressed)." Clearly, such high-level reading involves both the ability to comprehend accurately the literal meaning of text, as well as the ability to reflect on the broader meaning of the text itself (Grigg et al., 2003; Snow et al., 1998).

Approaches to Reading Instruction

Models of the stages through which skilled reading is attained have implications for reading instruction. How best to teach young children to read (and write) has been a source of controversy (Adams, Treiman, & Pressley, 1998; National Reading Panel, 2000; Rayner et al., 2001). The controversy reflects differences in theories of child development and learning, as well as the concern that some teaching methods may be associated with higher frequencies of reading failure (Flesch, 1985). Nevertheless, proponents of varying viewpoints share the same goal: They all want children to acquire a solid mastery of the basic skills of reading and writing.

There have been a number of approaches to the teaching of reading. The belief that reading is primarily a perceptual process involving vision has been largely discredited, although it was a dominant force in instruction for the early part of the last century. More recent approaches treat reading as a language-based activity (Wolf, Vellutino, & Berko Gleason, 1998). Within this conceptualization, two different aspects of reading are stressed: reading for meaning and reading as decoding. According to proponents of **reading for meaning**, children should be encouraged to treat texts as sources of meaning. The function, rather than the form, of written language is stressed. Reading familiar texts (e.g., basal readers) and fostering the development of a large sight vocabulary are common features of the reading-for-meaning approach. Formal instruction often involves a look–say approach, in which whole words and sentences are presented to children, who are encouraged to say them aloud. Within the reading-for-meaning approach, when children encounter unfamiliar words, they are encouraged to use their knowledge of context (including pictures that accompany the text) to make a best guess. Thus, this approach presumes that children will use top-down processes extensively.

A currently popular variant of the reading-for-meaning approach is termed the **whole language** or **literature-based** approach (Goodman, 2005; Martinez & McGee, 2000).

Presented more as a philosophy of learning than a specific instructional method (Rayner et al., 2001), whole language models are based on a conceptualization of the child as an active learner who seeks to construct meaning from interactions with texts. According to this view, the texts that children encounter must contain complete ("whole") meaningful language. Attention to the mechanics of decoding is usually secondary to the goal of obtaining meaning from any given text.

In contrast to whole language approaches to reading instruction, **reading as decoding,** or **phonics**, methods emphasize bottom-up skills (Adams, 2002). These methods explicitly teach decoding, particularly grapheme–phoneme correspondence rules. Instruction focuses on acquiring fluency in naming the letters of the alphabet, segmenting and blending phonemes, and learning the grapheme–phoneme rules. Reading for comprehension and meaning are felt to be dependent on successful, rapid, and automatic decoding. Within a decoding approach, when children encounter unfamiliar words, they are encouraged to sound them out, letter by letter. Children with strong decoding skills can employ **phonological recoding**, the process wherein letter strings are transformed into a pronunciation that is then recognized as a word (Ehri, 1998).

Which approach is best? Historically, this has been a controversial question. More recently, several influential analyses of the vast literature on the effects of different reading programs point to the importance of presenting most children with some formal instruction in phonics (National Reading Panel, 2000; Snow et al., 1998). This is especially true of children whose home literacy experiences have been limited. For example, in a study of at-risk children, explicit decoding instruction was compared to less explicit code instruction (Foorman, Francis, Fletcher, Schatsschneider, & Mehta, 1998). Children who had received explicit code instruction were later able to read more quickly and recognize more words than children who had experienced less explicit code instruction.

Based on a thorough review of the extensive literature on reading instruction, the National Reading Panel (2000) assessed the effectiveness of a number of methodological practices, including instruction in alphabetics (phonemic awareness, phonics), fluency, and comprehension (vocabulary, text). The findings support the explicit teaching of phonemic awareness and phonics, the encouragement of guided oral reading (reading aloud under the supervision of a parent or teacher), and age-appropriate vocabulary instruction. The teaching of a number of comprehension strategies (comprehension monitoring, question answering, and summarizing texts) was also endorsed.

Thus, although some children acquire decoding skills through informal exposure to reading (Thompson, Cottrell, & Fletcher-Flinn, 1996), reading itself is not a natural process (Liberman, 1999). For most children, becoming a skilled reader requires some explicit instruction in decoding skills. Obviously, reading instruction can combine some of the positive features of the whole language approach (meaningful texts) with formal instruction in decoding (Fitzgerald & Noblit, 2000; Snow et al., 1998).

Learning to Read in a Second Language

As mentioned in the introduction, dual-language learners are entering schools in the United States at a higher rate than ever before (Hammer, 2009). These children are acquiring English as a second language in a society in which English is the dominant language. Because their first language is rarely supported in school, they often face the challenge of acquiring literacy in a language in which they are not fully proficient (August & Hakuta, 1997; Oller & Eilers, 2002; Snow et al., 1998). Current national statistics show that dual-language learners in the United States, on average, achieve much lower levels of literacy than their English-only counterparts (Snow & Kang, 2006). However, in a recent longitudinal study with heterogeneous groups of dual-language learning children, Lesaux, Rupp, and Siegel (2007) found that although there are differences in reading comprehension and word reading during the kindergarten years between monolingual and DLL children, by fourth grade, these differences become negligible.

It is important to remember that national statistics might be confounded with various other at-risk factors associated with lower academic performance, such as residing in urban centers where poverty is concentrated and where social problems associated with poverty are more prevalent. In a recent study, for instance, Mancilla-Martínez and Lesaux (2010) followed a group of low-income Spanish-English DLL children from preschool to the end of fifth grade. Although their results showed the children's overall reading comprehension was three years behind grade-level at the end of the study, the authors carefully note that most of children were struggling readers at the start of the study who would have benefited from being taught in their own language first.

Educators of dual-language learners face the challenge of determining whether it is better to begin literacy instruction in the child's native language or to move directly toward promoting literacy in the second language. For dual-language learners, oral language ability in the language of instruction—including phonological skills, a solid vocabulary base, morphological and syntactic knowledge, as well as pragmatic and discourse skills—is integral to the acquisition of reading (Lesaux & Geva, 2008). In other words, a child will not be successful at learning to read in English if she does not have oral language skills in English. Moreover, there are data (reviewed in Snow et al., 1998; Tabors & Snow, 2002) suggesting that if children begin to master literacy in their native language, they are able to transfer literacy skills to the second language in major areas, such as phonological awareness, reading decoding, and reading comprehension. Therefore, it might be more beneficial for immigrant children who enter the U.S. school system with limited English proficiency to be taught to read in their native language.

When Learning to Read Is Difficult

Not all children learn to read easily. Causes of reading failure that are beyond the individual child include attending inadequate schools and living in poor neighborhoods (Snow et al., 1998). These factors reflect exposure to environments in which resources and expectations regarding literacy may be less than optimal. Risk factors specific to individual children include cognitive deficits, language-specific problems, reduced preliteracy experiences, and a family history of reading problems (Snow et al., 1998). (See Chapter 9 for a discussion of atypical language development.)

One group of children that experiences much difficulty in learning to read (and write) is of particular concern to educators, researchers, and parents. These children are of average or above-average intelligence; they have no significant social-emotional or cognitive deficits; and they have received adequate instructional support. Despite these resources, they fail to achieve age-appropriate mastery of the fundamental aspects of written language and are often diagnosed as dyslexic (Shaywitz, 1996). **Dyslexia and developmental dyslexia** are terms used to describe reading failure in children (and adults) who are otherwise unimpaired.

Historically, dyslexia was thought to be caused by deficits in visual-perceptual processing, with spontaneous letter reversals being a classic example (e.g., treating a *b* as a *d* and a *w* as an *m*). Currently, however, visual-perceptual deficits are felt to play only a minor role in dyslexia (Fletcher, Foorman, Shaywitz, & Shaywitz, 1999); the dominant view is that dyslexia is a language-specific disorder, characterized by marked deficits in linguistic processing (Morrison, 1993; Shankweiler, 1999; Stanovich, 1993, 2000). Although there is no consensus as to whether dyslexia is a single disorder or a cluster of related disorders (dyslexias), it is clear that dyslexic children have significantly more problems in phonological processing than children of average reading abilities. For example, children with dyslexia perform poorly in segmenting words, in naming, and in phonological short-term memory tasks (Stanovich, 1993). The incidence of dyslexia is reported to be between 3 and 10 percent of the population; however, rates vary according to the age of the population studied and the diagnostic criteria employed (Catts, 1996; Shaywitz, Escobar, Shaywitz, Fletcher, & Makuch, 1992; Shaywitz, Shaywitz, Fletcher, & Escobar, 1990). Histories of reading difficulties are significantly higher than average in parents of dyslexic children (Scarborough, 1998), and there are data that suggest that dyslexia might be in part a genetic disorder (DeFries & Alarcon, 1996; Grigorenko et al., 1997). Finally, based on brain-imaging studies, children with dyslexia manifest disruption in underlying neurological processes that are believed to be related to reading (Shaywitz et al., 2002).

Writing

In this chapter we have presented reading before writing, as is conventional. However, writing and reading are inextricably linked, and both influence and are influenced by the child's ongoing language development and metalinguistic knowledge (Adams et al., 1998). The traditional approach held that children could only learn writing through formal instruction. Writing should follow the elementary mastery of reading, because through reading children would acquire the grapheme–phoneme correspondence rules and would learn the conventions of print. Within this traditional approach, early instruction in writing often involved having children practice forming the letters of the alphabet and copying texts.

Garton and Pratt (1989) have questioned the logic of this approach. They believe that children, as active learners, acquire much information about writing even before they receive formal instruction in reading. They cite four benefits to encouraging prereading children to experiment with writing. First, children who spontaneously make writing marks on a page are actively involved in the writing process (versus passively copying letters and texts). Second, in making efforts to write what they themselves say, children begin to become aware of the relation between spoken and written language. Third, children who, on their own, write single letters and letter strings to represent words are beginning to discover the alphabetic principle. Fourth, and finally, as children read back what they have written, however inaccurately, they are being exposed to the association between writing and reading.

Development of Spelling

DOT MAK NOYS

Don't make noise.

B CYIYIT

Be quiet. (Read, 1980)

In many instances, children write in order to communicate (Bissex, 1980). They want to say something *in writing* to themselves or to others. In children's earliest writing, there may be little relation between the letter strings they write and what they intend "to say" (Bialystok, 1995). Eventually, they will be confronted with the task of mastering the conventions of standard spelling. The grapheme–phoneme correspondence rules that must be learned in order to read are the same rules that must be learned in order to spell conventionally. Children must come to recognize that the vowel sound /uw/ can take many different orthographic forms, as in the words *do, food, group, blue, knew, super,* and *fruit* (Treiman, 1993). In addition, *the letter names themselves* can be a source of confusion to beginning spellers (Treiman, Weatherston, & Berch, 1994), and children need to be able to distinguish letter names from letter sounds (McBride-Chang, 1999; Treiman, Tincoff, Rodríguez, Mouzaki, & Francis, 1998). The confusion between letter names and letter sounds explains why kindergarten children are more likely to spell the phoneme /w/ with a *y,* because the name of y (/wai/) begins with /w/.

Children often rely on creative or invented spelling (Read, 1986; Richgels, 2002; Treiman, 1993) in their early writing. **Invented spelling** is systematic rule-governed spelling that is created (invented) by developing writers. In its early stages it is in large part phonetic, as the invented spellings children use are generally not modeled by adults or found in printed texts (Read, 1986). Children's early attempts at encoding language orthographically reveal that they are active learners who seek rational solutions to mapping the sounds of their oral language (Adams et al., 1998). For example, Read found that many young children deleted the nasals /m/, /n/, and /nj/, particularly when the nasal precedes a true consonant. As in the example above, *don't* is spelled DOT. Other examples of this strategy include spelling *monster* as MOSTR, and *New England* as NOOIGLID (Read, 1986). It appears as if children are analyzing the speech stream in a way that is qualitatively different from that of adults, often treating nasals as part of the preceding vowel instead of perceiving nasals as distinct phonemes (Treiman, Zukowski, & Richmond-Welty, 1995).

Gentry and Gillet (1993) have formulated a stage theory of spelling. Children start at a precommunicative level in which they write random letters that have little correspondence to what may be intended. They then pass through several phonetic stages (HMT DPD for Humpty Dumpty and DASY DEC for Daisy Duck) before finally arriving at a conventional stage (p. 25). Underlying the pattern of development is a progression of strategies that children employ. They begin by using phonetics, then they look to regularities in orthographic patterns, and finally they utilize their knowledge of the origins of word roots.

Development of Writing and Genres of Writing

Children master spelling in order to write—to say something in writing—and they are able to do so in ever more sophisticated ways as their writing develops. Part of learning to write entails mastering the concept of genres. The term **genre** refers to discourse that is specific to particular contexts and functions, similar to the differences we discussed earlier between autobiographical and fantasy narratives. Genres are characterized by consistencies in form and content. A science report, a fictional short story, and a lyric poem are likely to take different forms, focus on very different contents, and are often produced for very different occasions. In order to become fully literate, competent writers, children must learn the conventions of a variety of genres over the course of their schooling (Hicks, 1997; Pappas, 1998; Shiro, 2003).

One genre of writing that is common in the early school years is **expressive style** (Britton, 1990). Expressive writing is informal personal writing, sometimes characterized as thinking out loud, and includes diary entries and letters to friends. Above all, expressive writing is characterized by the writer's close awareness of self and close relationship with the reader. Because it often fulfills a personal need, children need little prompting to engage in expressive writing.

A third-grader's final science project (see below) contains elements of expressive writing, seen particularly in his adoption of a first-person voice, although, as we will see, the general form of the essay is more expository than expressive:

> Hi I Perry, the pituitary gland. I control other endocrine glands, growth, mother's milk production and I also control the amount of water the kidneys remove from the blood. I also tell other endocrine glands to produce their own hormones. You can come visit me at the base of the brain. Sometimes when I really get mad I give very little growth hormones. But doctors always give injections of growth hormones. I produce the hormone which controls growth. I tell the ovaries to produce a hormone called progesterone. I've heard a pituitary made a person over nine feet. Some pepole call me master gland. I'm reddish-gray. There's this relly cool feedback mechanism of mine. This makes sure that enough of each hormone circulates in the body. I also have three lobes. I forgot to tell you but I connect to the hypothalamus by a stalk. Oh and I'm the size of a pea. Bye.

Overall, the writing is coherent. The style is marked by a mixture of formal and informal prose, reflecting the influence of ongoing exposure to written genres of language, including science texts, as well as the child's longstanding experience with oral language. His essay also includes some fairly sophisticated technical terms *(feedback mechanism)* and rare vocabulary words (e.g., *injection* versus *shot*) that were copied down in the course of doing his research. Although *progesterone* is spelled correctly, there are several inventive spelling errors of relatively common words (e.g., *pepole, relly*). In addition, there are a number of errors of syntax, primarily omissions of function words. Nevertheless, the essay achieves what the author intended; it successfully conveys information about the pituitary gland to the reader, and does so in an engaging and, at times, humorous manner.

Despite the informal tone of the text, its overall form can be characterized as expository. **Expository writing** is organized hierarchically and is closely associated with Bruner's paradigmatic mode of thought, discussed earlier. Good expository writing requires organization, with key points and arguments presented clearly, concisely, and logically. Young children find expository writing especially difficult. Early attempts at expository writing often represent *knowledge telling* or *knowledge dumping,* in which children

Expository writing is organized logically and hierarchically. Narrative writing follows a chronological time line.

list ideas as they come to mind, with no clearly marked beginnings or endings and little overall organization (Bereiter & Scardamalia, 1987). Over time, and with instruction, children may learn to revise their written work (Beal, 1990). The best writers plan what they are going to write while keeping the potential reader in mind. They are also able to put their plan into action and are able to revise successfully what they have written (Flowers & Hayes, 1980).

In contrast to the logical and hierarchical basis of expository writing, **narrative writing** is organized chronologically and uses a time line as its organizational basis. Written personal and fantasy narratives follow a chronological order. The developmental course of narrative writing is varied, in part because it is generally neglected in high school and in college, where most writing assignments require an expository style. Outside of creative writing courses, few older students have extensive experience in narrative writing.

Although much of children's writing takes place in school settings under the direction of teachers, writing is a social process. Writing is often shared with peers, and writing projects are sometimes set up to be collaborative (Dyson, 2003). The social aspects of writing are not just restricted to school. As was noted in our discussion of the home-school study by Snow and her colleagues, writing was associated with positive parent–child interactions. Children who have generally positive relationships with their parents may develop confidence that they have something to say in their writing. Thus, some of the origins of good writing may begin very early in a child's life.

Skill in writing develops slowly in most children and adolescents and reaches maturity only in adulthood, and then only in some writers (Applebee, Langer, Mullis, & Jenkins, 1990). Currently, there is concern regarding children's ability to write well. A recent national study summarized its findings by calling writing the "neglected R" (National Commission on Writing, 2003). Although many students in grades four through twelve can master the basics of writing, far fewer—only about 25 percent—can write proficiently. Basic writing is characterized as being "acceptable in the fundamentals of form, content, and language . . . [with] . . . grammar, spelling, and punctuation [that] *are not an utter disaster*" (emphasis added). In contrast, proficient writing comprises "first-rate organization, convincing and elaborated responses to the tasks assigned, and the use of rich, evocative, and compelling language" (pp. 16–17). In order to improve children's writing, the commission recommends that the time devoted to writing in school be doubled; it also urges that writing be a component in all subject matters. The underlying premise behind the emphasis on writing is the claim that good writing is not just sophisticated knowledge dumping. Rather, good writing is learning; it is a way of using language to understand the world (p. 13).

Learning to Write in a Second Language

Most of the research on dual language learners' literacy development during the school years focuses on the reading process. Although less is known about the writing process, similar to reading acquisition, dual-language learners with solid oral language skills in the second language, particularly listening comprehension and vocabulary, have better writing skills in that language. Other oral language abilities that play a role in writing development include semantic and syntactic knowledge, as well as a strong foundation in academic language (Leseaux & Geva, 2008). The one area where dual-language learners seem to have a slight advantage is in spelling. Not only is the development of spelling skills among dual-language learners similar to that of monolingual children, but DLL children are as proficient in their spelling as are native speakers of the target language (Leseaux & Geva, 2008). Interestingly, dual-language learners who are poor readers have been found to have stronger spelling skills as compared to monolingual speakers who are poor readers (D'Angiulli, Siegel, & Serra, 2001).

As with reading acquisition, writing research on DLL children suggests that there is some cross-linguistic transfer in second language writing (Davis, Carlisle, Beeman, 1999). Bilingual children seem to use code-switching as a strategy to scaffold their writing. For example, they might include certain words in the other language as a way to bring their point across. In addition to lexical code-switching, children also use conceptual code-switching as a way to express their thoughts in an authentic manner. That is, DLL children code-switch based on the language of the "world" in which they have experienced the event they are writing about (Escamilla, 2007). Finally, during the early elementary school years, children use phonetic code-switching to facilitate the spelling process, especially when learning a second language with a deep orthographic system, such as English. Despite this interdependence between languages, even in the first grade, children do recognize that some writing conventions are language specific—such as accents in Spanish or apostrophes in English (Gort, 2006)—and some are universal.

SUMMARY

During the school years, children's language development becomes increasingly individual. It is easier to describe the language of the typical 2-year-old than it is to describe the language of the typical 12-year-old. In this chapter we have seen how language undergoes change and growth during the school years. For many children, these developments are positive. Ideally, they are built on extensive early experiences with oral language, including many conversations with parents and other adults, especially conversations in which academic language was encouraged and supported.

Children following a positive trajectory learn to joke and tease comfortably with other children. When confronted with formal instruction in reading and writing, they may already have a basic grasp of many of the important concepts. They might already read, having inferred the alphabetic principle and the basic grapheme–phoneme correspondence rules from their many encounters with books read to them by parents. Throughout the middle school years, their ability to read and write improves rapidly. They read to learn, and through school assignments and extracurricular activities, they acquire strong foundations in the literate knowledge base of their culture.

Not all children follow this pattern. Many do not have extensive emergent literacy experiences at home. Many are in poor schools where reading and writing instruction is inadequate, where literate materials like books are scarce, and where rates of reading failure are high. Dual-language learners often face the added challenge of developing literacy skills in their second language, and might feel pressured to suppress their native language in favor of the dominant language, and even children who do learn to read and write well may have few opportunities to use their literacy skills in meaningful and satisfying ways.

Thus, in its extreme forms, language development in the school years can follow two opposite courses. One course represents arrested development and lost opportunities, with the progress of the early years overshadowed by stagnation, particularly in the failure to acquire a solid grasp of literate language. This developmental trajectory makes the transition to adolescent and adult years problematic. The other course represents a continuation of the dramatic developments the child experienced in the first five to six years of life. Building on these strong foundations, children following this route achieve even greater mastery of oral language and develop a strong and sophisticated command of written language as well. These developments in turn enhance the transition into adolescence and adulthood, preparing the child for eventual mastery of the rich variety of complex modes of oral and written language he or she will continue to encounter.

SUGGESTED PROJECTS

1. Peterson and McCabe (1983) developed a technique for eliciting narratives from children. When talking to their subjects, they included prompts about specific events, for example: "The other day I had to go to the doctor and got a shot. Has anything like that ever happened to you?" Using this approach, gather a small sample of narratives from a younger and an older child. What kinds of differences do you see in the structures of the two types of stories? How are the stories older children tell different from those shared by younger children?

2. Ask younger (around age 6) and older (around age 8) children to share with you the best made-up story they can think of or have heard. Compare the development of plot, theme, and characters from the story told by the younger and older child. Does schooling seem to influence the way in which older children construct their stories?

3. Find three children between the ages of 5 and 7: one who does not read, one who is just learning to read, and one who reads relatively well. Using an interesting children's book, ask each child about the conventions of print (Where do you begin reading? What are the spaces between the words for? What are punctuation marks for?). Ask each child what it means to read and how you learn to read. How do the children's notions about reading compare with what we know about reading?

4. Find an interesting object (an egg beater, an animal skull) and ask children of different ages to "write anything you want" about the object for 5 minutes. Compare the children's performances, paying attention to their writing form. Look also for invented spelling in younger children's writing. What developmental trends do you notice?

SUGGESTED READINGS

August, D., & Shanahan, T. (2008). *Developing reading and writing in second-language learners: Lessons from the report of the National Literacy Panel on language-minority children and youth.* New York: Routledge.

Bialystok, E. (2001). *Bilingualism in development: Language, literacy, and cognition.* New York: Cambridge University Press.

Fivush, R., & Haden, C. A. (2003). *Autobiographical memory and the construction of a narrative self:* *Developmental and cultural perspectives.* Mahwah, NJ: Erlbaum.

Hulme, C., & Joshi, R. M. (Eds.). (1998). *Reading and spelling: Development and disorders.* Mahwah, NJ: Erlbaum.

Neuman, S. B., & Dickinson, D. K. (Eds.). (2002). *Handbook of early literacy research.* New York: Guilford Press.

Rayner, K., Foorman, B. R., Perfetti, C. A., Pesetsky, D., & Seidenberg, M. S. (2001). How psychological science informs the teaching of reading. *Psychological Science in the Public Interest, 2,* 31–74.

Snow, C. E., Burns, M. S., & Griffin, P. (Eds.). (1998). *Preventing reading difficulties in young children.* Washington: National Academy Press.

Snow, C. E., & Kang, Y. K. (2006). Becoming bilingual, biliterate, bicultural. In K. A. Renninger & I. E. Sigel (Eds.), *Handbook of child psychology, Volume 4: Child psychology in practice* (6th ed.). Hoboken, NJ: Wiley.

KEY WORDS

academic language
additive bilingualism
alphabetic principle
automaticity (automatized)
bottom-up model
deep orthographies
dual-language learners
dyslexia (developmental dyslexia)
emergent literacy
environmental print
expository writing
expressive style

extended discourse
genre
grapheme
grapheme–phoneme correspondence rules
invented spelling
letter recognition
metalinguistic awareness
narrative mode
narratives
narrative writing
paradigmatic mode
phonological recoding

reading as decoding (phonics)
reading for meaning
riddles
segmentation
semantic knowledge
shallow orthographies
subtractive bilingualism
top-down model
verbal humor
whole language (literature based)
word recognition

REFERENCES

Adams, M. J. (2002). Alphabetic anxiety and explicit, systemic phonics instruction. In S. B. Neuman & D. K. Dickinson (Eds.), *Handbook of early literacy research* (pp. 66–80). New York: Guilford Press.

Adams, M. J., Foorman, B. R., Lundberg, I., & Beeler, T. (1997). *Phonemic awareness in young children: A classroom curriculum.* Baltimore: Paul H. Brookes.

Adams, M. J., Treiman, R., & Pressley, M. (1998). Reading, writing, and literacy. In I. E. Sigel & K. A. Renninger (Eds.), *Handbook of child psychology,* (Vol. 4, 5th ed., pp. 275–355). New York: Wiley.

Allen, M. S., Kertoy, M. K., Sherblom, J. C., & Petit, J. M. (1994). Children's narrative productions: A comparison of personal event and fictional stories. *Applied Psycholinguistics, 15,* 149–176.

Anstatt, T. (2008). Aspect and tense in storytelling by Russian, German and bilingual children. *Russian Linguistics, 32,* 1–26.

Applebee, A., Langer, J., Mullis, I., & Jenkins, L. (1990). *The writing report card, 1984–88. Findings from the nation's report card.* The National Assessment of Education Progress. Princeton, NJ: Educational Testing Service.

Apte, M. L. (1985). *Humor and laughter: An anthropological approach.* Ithaca, NY: Cornell University Press.

August, D., & Hakuta, K. (Eds.). (1997). *Improving schooling for language-minority children: A research agenda.* National Research Council and Institute of Medicine. Washington, DC: National Academy Press.

Beal, C. R. (1990). The development of text evaluation and revision skills. *Child Development, 61,* 247–258.

Bereiter, C., & Scardamalia, M. (1987). *The psychology of written communication.* Hillsdale, NJ: Erlbaum.

Berko Gleason, J. (1973). Code switching in children's language. In T. E. Moore (Ed.), *Cognitive development and the acquisition of language* (pp. 159–167). New York: Academic Press.

Berko Gleason, J., Hay, D., & Cain, L. (1988). Social and affective determinants of language acquisition. In M. L. Rice & R. L. Schiefelbusch (Eds.), *The teachability of language* (pp. 171–186). Baltimore: Paul H. Brookes.

Berman, R. A., & Slobin, D. I. (1994). *Relating events in narrative: A cross-linguistic developmental study.* Hillsdale, NJ: Erlbaum.

Bialystok, E. (1986). Factors in the growth of linguistic awareness. *Child Development, 57,* 498–510.

Bialystok, E. (1995). Making concepts of print symbolic: Understanding how writing represents language. *First Language, 15,* 317–338.

Bialystok, E. (2002). Acquisition of literacy in bilingual children: A framework for research. *Language Learning, 52,* 159–199.

Bialystok, E. (2004). Impact of bilingualism on language and literacy development. In T. K. Bhatia & W. C. Ritchie (Eds.), *Handbook of bilingualism* (pp. 577–601). Oxford: Blackwell.

Bialystok, E. (2007). Cognitive effects of bilingualism. *The International Journal of Bilingual Education and Bilingualism, 10*(3), 210–223.

Bissex, G. (1980). *GNYS AT WORK: A child learns to read and write.* Cambridge, MA: Harvard University Press.

Blum-Kulka, S., & Snow, C. E. (2004). The potential of peer talk [special issue]. *Discourse Studies, 6*(3).

Britton, J. (1990). Talking to learning. In D. Barnes, J. Britton, & M. Torbe (Eds.), *Language, the learner and the school* (4th ed., pp. 89–130). Portsmouth, NH: Heinemann.

Bruner, J. (1986). *Actual minds, possible worlds.* Cambridge, MA: Harvard University Press.

Bruner, J. S. (1983). *Child's talk: Learning to use language.* New York: W. W. Norton.

Bryant, P. E., Bradley, L., Maclean, M., & Crossland, J. (1989). Nursery rhymes, phonological skills and reading. *Journal of Child Language, 16,* 407–428.

Bryne, B., & Fielding-Barnsley, R. (1998). Phonemic awareness and letter knowledge in the child's acquisitions of the alphabetic principle. *Journal of Educational Psychology, 81,* 313–321.

Bus, A. G. (2002). Joint caregiver–child storybook reading: A route to literacy development. In S. B. Neuman & D. K. Dickinson (Eds.), *Handbook of early literacy research* (pp. 179–191). New York: Guilford Press.

Caspe, M. (2009). Low-income Latino mothers' book sharing styles and children's emergent literacy development. *Early Childhood Quarterly, 24,* 306–324.

Caspe, M. & Melzi, G. (2008). Spanish-speaking Latin American mother-child narrative discourse. In A. McCabe, A. L. Bailey, & G. Melzi (Eds.), *Spanish-language narration and literacy: Culture, cognition, and emotion* (pp. 6–33). New York: Cambridge University Press.

Castle, A., & Colheart, M. (2004). Is there a causal link from phonological awareness to success in learning to read? *Cognition, 91*(1), 77–111.

Catts, H. W. (1996). Defining dyslexia as a developmental language disorder: An expanded view. *Topics in Language Disorders, 16,* 14–29.

Cazden, C. B. (2001). *Classroom discourse: The language of teaching and learning* (2nd ed.). Westport, CT: Heinemann.

Cazden, C. B., & Beck, S. W. (2003). Classroom discourse. In A. C. Graesser, A. M. Gernsbacher, & S. R. Goldman (Eds.), *Handbook of discourse processes* (pp. 165–197). Mahwah, NJ: Erlbaum.

Chall, J. S. (1983). *Stages of reading development.* New York: McGraw-Hill.

Chall, J. S. (1996). *Stages of reading development* (2nd ed.). New York: McGraw-Hill.

Champion, T. B. (2003). *Understanding storytelling among African American children: A journey from Africa to America.* Mahwah, NJ: Erlbaum.

Champion, T. B., Katz, L., Muldrow, R., & Dail, R. (1999). Storytelling and story-making in an urban classroom: Building bridges from home to school culture. *Topics in Language Disorders, 19,* 52–67.

Cheung, H., Chen, H.-C., Lai, C. Y., Wong, O. C., & Hills, M. (2001). *The development of phonological awareness: Effects of spoken language experience and orthography. Cognition, 81,* 227–241.

Chow, B. W., McBride-Chang, C., & Burgess, S. (2005). Phonological processing skills and early reading abilities in Hong Kong Chinese kindergarteners learning to read

English as a second language. *Journal of Educational Psychology, 97*(1), 81–87.

Clark, E. V. (1978). Awareness of language: Some evidence from what children say and do. In A. Sinclair, R. J. Jarvella, & W. J. Levelt (Eds.), *The child's conception of language* (pp. 17–43). New York: Springer-Verlag.

D'Angiulli, A., Siegel., L. S., & Serra, E. (2001). The development of reading in English and Italian in bilingual children. *Applied Psycholinguistics, 22*, 479–507.

Davis, L. H., Carlisle, J. F., & Beeman, M. (1999). Hispanic children's writing in English and Spanish when English is the language of instruction. *Yearbook of the National Reading Conference, 48*, 238–248.

DeFries, J. C., & Alarcon, M. (1996). Genetics of specific reading disability. *Mental Retardation and Developmental Disabilities Research Reviews, 2*, 39–47.

Dews, S., Winner, E., Kaplan, J., Rosenblatt, E., Hunt, M., Lim, K., et al. (1996). Children's understanding of the meaning and functions of verbal irony. *Child Development, 67*, 3071–3085.

Dickinson, D. K., & Tabors, P. O. (Eds.). (2001). *Beginning literacy with language: Young children learning at home and school.* Baltimore: Paul H. Brookes.

Doherty, M. J. (2000). Children's understanding of homonymy: Metalinguistic awareness and false belief. *Journal of Child Language, 27*, 367–392.

Dörnyei, Z., & Csizer, K., (2002). Some dynamics of language attitudes and motivation: Results of a longitudinal nationwide survey. *Applied Linguistics 23*, 421–426.

Dowker, A. (1989). Rhyme and alliteration in poems elicited from young children. *Journal of Child Language, 16*, 181–202.

Dunn, J. (1988). *The beginnings of social understanding.* Cambridge, MA: Harvard University Press.

Dyson, A. H. (2003). "Welcome to the jam": Popular culture, school literacy, and the making of childhoods. *Harvard Educational Review, 73*, 328–361.

Ehri, L. C. (1991). Learning to read and spell words. In L. Rabin & C. A. Perfetti (Eds.), *Learning to read: Basic research and its implications* (pp. 57–73). Hillsdale, NJ: Erlbaum.

Ehri, L. C. (1998). Word reading by sight and by analogy in beginning readers. In C. Hulme & R. M. Joshi (Eds.), *Reading and spelling: Development and disorders* (pp. 87–111). Mahwah, NJ: Erlbaum.

Eisenberg, A. R. (1986). Teasing: Verbal play in two Mexicano homes. In B. B. Schieffelin & E. Ochs (Eds.), *Language socialization across cultures* (pp. 182–198). New York: Cambridge University Press.

Ely, R., & Berko Gleason, J. (1995). Socialization across contexts. In P. Fletcher & B. MacWhinney (Eds.), *Handbook of child language* (pp. 251–270). Oxford: Blackwell.

Ely, R., & McCabe, A. (1994). The language play of kindergarten children. *First Language, 14*, 19–35.

Escamilla, K. (2007). The role of code-switching in the written expression of early elementary simultaneous bilingual. *American Educational Research Association.* Boulder: University of Colorado-Boulder.

Eviatar, Z., & Ibrahim, R. (2000). Bilingual is as bilingual does: Metalinguistic abilities of Arabic-speaking children. *Applied Psycholinguistics, 21*(4), 451–471.

Farrant, K., & Reese, E. (2000). Maternal style and children's participation in reminiscing: Stepping stones in children's autobiographical memory development. *Journal of Cognition and Development, 1*(2), 193–225.

Ferreira, F., & Morrison, F. J. (1994). Children's metalinguistic knowledge of syntactic constituents: Effects of age and schooling. *Developmental Psychology, 30*, 663–678.

Fiestas, C. E., & Peña, E. D. (2004). Narrative discourse in bilingual children: Language and task effects. *Language, Speech, and Hearing Services in Schools, 35*(2), 155–168.

Fitzgerald, J., & Noblit, G. (2000). Balance in the making: Learning to read in an ethnically diverse first-grade classroom. *Journal of Educational Psychology, 92*, 3–22.

Fivush, R., & Haden, C. A. (2003). *Autobiographical memory and the* construction of a narrative self: *Developmental and cultural perspectives*. Mahwah, NJ: Erlbaum.

Fivush, R., Haden, C. A., & Reese, E. (2006). Elaborating on elaborations: Role of maternal reminiscing style in cognitive and socio-emotional development. *Child Development, 77*(6), 1568–1588.

Flesch, R. (1985). *Why Johnny can't read* (2nd ed.). New York: Harper & Row.

Fletcher, J. M., Foorman, B. R., Shaywitz, S. E., & Shaywitz, B. A. (1999). Conceptual and methodological issues in dyslexia research: A lesson for developmental disorders. In H. Tager-Flusberg (Ed.), *Neurodevelopmental disorders* (pp. 271–306). Cambridge, MA: MIT Press.

Flowers, L. S., & Hayes, J. R. (1980). The dynamics of composing: Making plans and juggling constraints. In L. Gregg & E. Steinberg (Eds.), *Cognitive processes in writing* (pp. 31–50). Hillsdale, NJ: Erlbaum.

Foorman, B. R., Francis, D. J., Fletcher, J. M., Schatschneider, C., & Mehta, P. (1998). The role of instruction in learning to read: Preventing reading failure in at-risk children. *Journal of Educational Psychology, 90,* 37–55.

Frith, U. (1985). Beneath the surface of dyslexia. In K. Patterson, J. Marshall, & M. Coltheart (Eds.), *Surface dyslexia* (pp. 301–330). London: Erlbaum.

Garton, A., & Pratt, C. (1989). *Learning to be literate: The development of spoken and written language.* New York: Blackwell.

Garvey, C. (1977). Play with language and speech. In S. Ervin & C. Mitchell-Kernan (Eds.), *Child discourse* (pp. 27–47). New York: Academic Press.

Gee, J. P. (1986). Units in the production of narrative discourse. *Discourse Processes, 9,* 391–422.

Gee, J. P. (2002). A sociocultural perspective on early literacy development. In S. B. Neuman & D. K. Dickinson (Eds.), *Handbook of early literacy research* (pp. 30–42). New York: Guilford Press.

Genesee, F., Geva, E., Dressler, C., & Kamil, M. L. (2006). Synthesis: Cross-linguistic relationships. In D. August & T. Shanahan (Eds.), *Developing literacy in second-language learners: A report of the national literacy panel on minority-language children and youth* (pp. 153–174). Mahwah, NJ: Erlbaum.

Gentry, J. R., & Gillet, J. W. (1993). *Teaching kids to spell.* Portsmouth, NH: Heinemann.

Gombert, J. E. (1992). *Metalinguistic development.* Chicago: University of Chicago Press.

Goodman, K. S. (2005). *What's whole in whole language.* Berkeley, CA: RDR Books.

Goodwin, M. H. (1990). *He-said-she-said: Talk as a social organization among Black children.* Bloomington: Indiana University Press.

Gort, M. (2006). Strategic code-switching, interliteracy, and other phenomena of emergent bilingual writing: Lessons from first grade dual language classrooms. *Journal of Early Childhood Literacy, 6*(3), 323–354.

Gough, P. B. (1972). One second of reading. In J. F. Kavanagh & I. G. Mattingly (Eds.), *Language by eye and ear* (pp. 331–358). Cambridge, MA: MIT Press.

Graves, F. M. (2009). *Essential readings on vocabulary Instruction.* Newark, DE: International Reading Association.

Grigg, W. S., Daane, M. C., Uin, Y., & Campbell, J. R. (2003). *The Nation's Report Card: Reading 2002* (NCES 2003-521). Washington, DC: U.S. Department of Education, Institute of Education Sciences, National Center for Education Statistics.

Grigorenko, E. L., Wood, F. B., Meyer, M. S., Hart, L. A., Speed, W. C., Shuster, B. S., & Pauls, D. L. (1997). Susceptibility loci for distinct components of developmental dyslexia on chromosomes 6 and 16. *American Journal of Human Genetics, 60,* 27–39.

Gutiérrez-Clellen, V. F. (2002). Narratives in two languages: Assessing performance of bilingual children. *Linguistics in Education, 13*(2), 175–197.

Haden, C. A., Reese, E., & Fivush, R. (1996). Mothers' extratextual comments during storybook reading: Stylistic differences over time and across texts. *Discourse Processes, 21,* 135–169.

Hadley, P. A. (1998). Language sampling protocols for eliciting text-level discourse. *Language, Speech, and Hearing Services in Schools, 29,* 132–147.

Hammer, C. S. (2001). "Come sit down and let mama read": Book reading interactions between African American mothers and their infants. In J. L. Harris, A. G. Kamhi, & K. E. Pollock (Eds.), *Literacy in African American communities* (pp. 21–43). Mahwah, NJ: Erlbaum.

Hammer, C. S. (2009). *Dual language learners' early language development and academic outcomes.* Retrieved April 28, 2011, from www7.nationalacademies .org/cfe/Paper_Carol_Hammer.pdf

Harkins, D. A., & Ray, S. (2004). An exploratory study of mother-child storytelling in East India and Northeast United States. *Narrative Inquiry, 14*(2), 347–367.

Harm, M. W., & Seidenberg, M. S. (1999). Phonology, reading acquisition, and dyslexia: Insights from connectionist models. *Psychological Review, 106,* 491–528.

Harris, J. R. (2009). *The nurture assumption: Why children turn out the way they do.* New York: Free Press.

Hart, B., & Risley, T. R. (1995). *Meaningful differences in the everyday experience of young American children.* Baltimore, MD: Paul H. Brookes.

Heath, S. B. (1983). *Ways with words.* New York: Cambridge University Press.

Hicks, D. (1997). Working through discourse genres in school. *Research in the Teaching of English, 31,* 459–485.

Homer, B. D., & Olson, D. R. (1999). Literacy and children's conception of words. *Written Language and Literacy, 2,* 113–140.

Hua, Z., & Dodd, B. (2006). *Phonological development and disorders in children: A multilingual perspective.* Clevedon, UK: Multilingual Matters.

Hudson, J. A., & Shapiro, L. R. (1991). From knowing to telling: The development of children's scripts, stories, and personal narratives. In A. McCabe, & C. Peterson (Eds.), *Developing narrative structure* (pp. 89-136). Hillsdale, NJ: Erlbaum.

Hughes, M., & Grieve, R. (1980). On asking children bizarre questions. *First Language, 1,* 149–160.

Hymes, D. (2004). *In vain I tried to tell you": Essays in Native American ethnopoetics*

(2nd ed.) Lincoln: University of Nebraska Press.

Kuczaj, S. A. (1982). Language play and language acquisition. In H. Reese (Ed.), *Advances in child development and behavior* (pp. 197–232). New York: Academic Press.

Kurland, B. F., & Snow, C. E. (1997). Longitudinal measurement of growth in definitional skill. *Journal of Child Language, 24,* 603–625.

Labov, W. (1972). *Language in the inner city: Studies in the Black English vernacular.* Philadelphia: University of Pennsylvania Press.

Landauer, T. K., & Dumais, S. T. (1997). A solution to Plato's problem: The latent semantic analysis theory of acquisition, induction, and representation of knowledge. *Psychological Review, 104,* 211–240.

Lehrer, A. (1994). Understanding lectures. *Discourse Processes, 17,* 259–281.

Leichtman, M. D., Wang, Q., & Pillemer, D. B. (2003). Cultural variations in interdependence and autobiographical memory: Lessons from Korea, China, India, and the United States. In R. Fivush & C. A. Haden (Eds.), *Autobiographical memory and the construction of a narrative self: Developmental and cultural perspectives* (pp. 73–97). Mahwah, NJ: Erlbaum.

Lesaux, N. K., & Geva, E. (2008). Synthesis: Development of literacy in second-language learners In D. L. August & T. Shanahan (Eds.), *Developing reading and writing in a second-language learners* (pp. 27–59). New York: Routledge.

Lesaux, N. K., Rupp, A. A., & Siegel, L. S. (2007). Growth in reading skills of children from diverse linguistic backgrounds: Findings from a 5-year longitudinal study. *Journal of Educational Psychology, 99,* 821–834.

Liberman, A. (1999). The reading researcher and the reading teacher need the right theory of speech. *Scientific Studies of Reading, 3,* 95–112.

Mainess, K. J., Champion, T. B., & McCabe, A. (2002). Telling the unknown story: Complex and explicit narration by African American preadolescents— Preliminary examination of gender and socioeconomic issues. *Linguistics and Education, 13,* 151–173.

Mancilla-Martínez, J., & Lesaux, N. K. (2010). Predictors of reading comprehension for struggling readers: The case of Spanish-speaking language minority learners. *Journal of Educational Psychology, 102,* 701–711.

Martinez, M. G., & McGee, L. M. (2000). Children's literature and reading instruction: Past, present, and future. *Reading Research Quarterly, 35,* 154–169.

Maxwell, L. A. (2009). Shifting landscapes: Immigration transforms communities. *Education Week, 28*(17), 1–8.

McBride-Chang, C. (1999). The ABCs of the ABCs: The development of letter-name and letter-sound knowledge. *Merrill-Palmer Quarterly, 45,* 285–308.

McBride-Chang, C. (2004). *Children's literacy development.* New York: Oxford University Press.

McBride-Chang, C., Bialystok, E., Chong, K., & Li, Y. (2004). Levels of phonological awareness in three cultures. *Journal of Experimental Child Psychology, 89,* 93–11.

McCabe, A., Bailey, A. L., & Melzi, G. (2008). *Spanish-language narration and literacy: Culture, cognition, and emotion.* Cambridge, UK: Cambridge University Press.

McCabe, A., & Bliss, L. S. (2003). *Pattern of narrative discourse: A multicultural, lifespan approach.* Boston: Allyn & Bacon.

McDowell, J. H. (1979). *Children's riddling.* Bloomington: Indiana University Press.

Melzi, G. (2000). Cultural variations in the construction of personal narratives: Central American and European American mothers' elicitation discourse. *Discourse Processes, 30*(2), 153–177.

Melzi, G., & Caspe, M. (2005). Variations in maternal narrative styles during book reading interactions. *Narrative Inquiry, 15*(1), 101–125.

Melzi, G., & Caspe, M. (2007). Research approaches to narrative, literacy, and education. In N. Hornberger & K. A. King (Eds.), *Encyclopedia of language and education: Vol. 10. Research methods in language and education* (2nd ed., pp. 151–164). New York: Springer.

Melzi, G., Schick, A., & Kennedy, J. (2011). Narrative participation and elaboration: Two dimensions of maternal elicitation style. *Child Development.*

DOI: 10.1111/j.1467–8624.2011.01600.x [in press]

Michaels, S. (1991). The dismantling of narrative. In A. McCabe & C. Peterson (Eds.), *Developing narrative structure* (pp. 303–351). Hillsdale, NJ: Erlbaum.

Miller, P. J. (1982). *Amy, Wendy, and Beth: Learning language in South Baltimore.* Austin: University of Texas Press.

Miller, P. J., Cho, G. E., & Bracey, J. R. (2005). Working-class children's experiences through the prism of storytelling. *Human Development, 48,* 115–135.

Minami, M. (2002). *Culture-specific language styles: The development of oral narrative and literacy.* Clevedon, UK: Multilingual Matters.

Minami, M. (2008). Telling good stories in different languages: Bilingual children's styles of story construction and their linguistic and educational implications. *Narrative Inquiry, 18*(1), 83–110.

Mol, S. E., Bus, A. G., de Jong, M. T., & Smeets, D. J. H. (2008). Added value of dialogic parent child book readings: A meta-analysis. *Early Education and Development. Special Issue: Parent-Child Interaction and Early Literacy Development, 19*(1), 7–26.

Morgan, M. H. (2002). *Language, discourse, and power in African American culture.* New York: Cambridge University Press.

Morrison, F. J. (1993). Phonological processes in reading acquisition: Toward a unified conceptualization. *Developmental Review, 13,* 279–285.

Nagy, W. (2007). Metalinguistic awareness and the vocabulary-comprehension connection. In R. K. Wagner, A. Muse, & K. Tannenbaum (Eds.), *Vocabulary acquisition and its implications for reading comprehension* (pp. 52–77). New York: Guilford.

Nagy, W. E., & Scott, J. A. (2000). Vocabulary processes. In M. L. Kamil, P. B. Mosenthal, P. D. Pearson, & R. Barr (Eds.), *Handbook of reading research* (pp. 269–284). Mahwah, NJ: Erlbaum.

Nation, K., & Snowling, M. J. (2000). Factors influencing syntactic awareness skills in normal readers and poor comprehenders. *Applied Psycholinguistics, 21,* 229–241.

National Commission on Writing in America's Schools and Colleges. (2003). *The neglected "R": The need for a writing revolution.* New York: College Board.

National Reading Panel. (2000). *Teaching children to read: An evidence-based assessment of the scientific research literature on reading and its implications for reading instruction* (NIH Pub. No. 00-4769). Washington, DC: National Institute of Health.

NCES. (2009). *The condition of education.* Washington, DC: U.S. Government Printing Office.

Nicolopoulou, A. (2002). Peer-group culture and narrative development. In S. Blum-Kulka & C. E. Snow (Eds.), *Talking to adults.* Mahwah, NJ: Erlbaum.

Ninio, A., & Snow, C. E. (1996). *Pragmatic development.* Boulder, CO: Westview Press.

Nippold, M. A. (2000). Language development during the adolescent years: Aspects of pragmatics, syntax, and semantics. *Topics in Language Disorders, 20,* 15–28.

Ogbu, J. V. (1990). Cultural model, identity, and literacy. In J. W. Stigler, R. A. Shweder, & G. Herdt (Eds.), *Cultural psychology: Essays on comparative human development* (pp. 520–541). New York: Cambridge University Press.

Oller, D. K., & Eilers, R. E. (Eds.). (2002). *Language and literacy in bilingual children.* Clevedon, UK: Multilingual Matters.

Ortony, A., Turner, T. J., & Larson-Shapiro, N. (1985). Cultural and instructional influences on figurative language comprehension by inner city children. *Research in the Teaching of English, 19,* 25–36.

Pappas, C. C. (1998). The role of genre in the psycholinguistic game of reading. *Language Arts, 75,* 36–44.

Pearson, B. Z. (2002). Narrative competence among monolingual and bilingual school children in Miami. In D. K. Oller & R. E. Eilers (Eds.), *Language and literacy in bilingual children* (pp. 135–174). Clevedon, UK: Multilingual Matters Ltd.

Pellegrini, A. D., Mulhuish, E., Jones, I., Trojanowska, L., & Gilden, R. (2002). Social contexts of learning literate language: The role of varied, familiar

and close peer relationships. *Learning and Individual Differences, 12,* 375–389.

Pepicello, W. J., & Weisberg, R. W. (1983). Linguistics and humor. In P. E. McGhee & J. H. Goldstein (Eds.), *Handbook of humor research.* New York: Springer-Verlag.

Perfetti, C. A. (1992). The representation problem in reading acquisition. In P. B. Gough, L. C. Ehri, & R. Treiman (Eds.), *Reading acquisition* (pp. 145–174). Hillsdale, NJ: Erlbaum.

Perfetti, C. A. (1997). The psycholinguistics of spelling and reading. In C. A. Perfetti, L. Rieben, & M. Fayol, *Learning to spell: Research, theory, and practice across languages* (pp. 21–38). Mahwah, NJ: Erlbaum.

Peterson, C., & Biggs, M. (2001). "I was really, really, really mad!" Children's use of evaluative devices in narrative about emotional events. *Sex Roles, 45,* 801–825.

Peterson, C., & McCabe, A. (1983). *Developmental psycholinguistics: Three ways of looking at a child's narrative.* New York: Plenum Press.

Pichler, P. (2006). Multifunctional teasing as a resource for identity construction in the talk of British Bangladeshi girls. *Journal of Sociolinguistics, 10*(2), 225–249.

Preece, A. (1987). The range of narrative forms conversationally produced by young children. *Journal of Child Language, 14,* 273–295.

Price, J. R., Roberts, J. E. & Jackson, S. C. (2006). Structural development of the fictional narratives of African American preschoolers. *Language, Speech, and Hearing Services in the Schools, 37,* 178–190.

Rayner, K., Foorman, B. R., Perfetti, C. A., Pesetsky, D., & Seidenberg, M. S. (2001). How psychological science informs the teaching of reading. *Psychological Science in the Public Interest, 2,* 31–74.

Read, C. (1980). Creative spelling by young children. In T. Shopen & J. M. Williams (Eds.), *Standards and dialects in English.* Cambridge, MA: Winthrop Publishers.

Read, C. (1986). *Children's creative spelling.* London: Routledge & Kegan Paul.

Reese, E. (1995). Predicting children's literacy from mother-child conversations. *Cognitive Development, 10*(3), 381–405.

Reese, E., & Cox, A. (1999). Quality of adult book reading affects children's emergent literacy. *Developmental Psychology, 35,* 20–28.

Richgels, D. J. (2002). Invented spelling, phonemic awareness, and reading and writing instruction. In S. B. Neuman & D. K. Dickinson (Eds.), *Handbook of early literacy research* (pp. 142–158). New York: Guilford Press.

Robinson, E. J. (1981). The child's understanding of inadequate messages and communication failures: A problem of ignorance or egocentrism? In W. P. Dickson (Ed.), *Children's oral communication skills* (pp. 167–188). New York: Academic Press.

Roth, F. P., Speece, D. L., & Cooper, D. H. (2002). A longitudinal analysis of the connection between oral language and early reading. *Journal of Educational Research, 95,*259–272.

Scarborough, H. S. (1998). Early identification of children at risk for reading disabilities: Phonological awareness and some other promising predictors. In B. K. Shapiro, P. J. Accardo, & A. J. Capute (Eds.), *Specific reading disability: A view of the spectrum* (pp. 77–121). Timonium, MD: York Press.

Schick, A., & Melzi, G. (2010). Children's oral narrative development across contexts. *Early Education & Development, 21(3),* 293–317.

Schieffelin, B. B., & Ochs, E. (1986). *Language socialization across cultures.* New York: Cambridge University Press.

Scott, J. A., & Nagy, W. E. (1997). Understanding the definitions of unfamiliar verbs. *Reading Research Quarterly, 32,* 184–200.

Scribner, S., & Cole, M. (1981). *The psychology of literacy.* Cambridge, MA: Harvard University Press.

Sénéchal, M. (1997). The differential effect of storybook reading on preschoolers' acquisition of expressive and receptive vocabulary. *Journal of Child Language, 24,* 123–138.

Sénéchal, M., & Le Fevre, J.-A. (2002). Parental involvement in the development of children's reading skill: A five-year longitudinal study. *Child Development, 73,* 445–460.

Shankweiler, D. (1999). Words to meaning. *Scientific Studies of Reading, 3,* 113–127.

Shaywitz, B. A., Shaywitz, S. E., Pugh, K. R., Mencl, W. E., Fulbright, R. K., Skudlarski, P., et al. (2002). Disruption of posterior brain systems for reading in children with developmental dyslexia. *Biological Psychiatry, 52,* 101–110.

Shaywitz, S. E. (1996, May). Dyslexia. *Scientific American, 275,* 98–104.

Shaywitz, S. E., Escobar, M. D., Shaywitz, B. A., Fletcher, J. M., & Makuch, R. (1992). Evidence that dyslexia may represent the lower tail of a normal distribution of reading ability. *New England Journal of Medicine, 326,* 145–150.

Shaywitz, S. E., Shaywitz, B. A., Fletcher, J. M., & Escobar, M. D. (1990). Prevalence of reading disability in boys and girls. *Journal of the American Medical Association, 264,* 998–1002.

Shiro, M. (2003). Genre and evaluation in narrative development. *Journal of Child Language, 30,* 165–195.

Smith, F. (2004). *Understanding reading: A psycholinguistic analysis of reading and learning to read* (6th ed.). Mahwah, NJ: Erlbaum.

Snow, C. E. (1990). The development of definitional skill. *Journal of Child Language, 17,* 697–710.

Snow, C. E. (1993). Families as social contexts for literacy development. In C. Daiute (Ed.), *The development of literacy through social interaction* (pp. 11–24). New Directions for Child Development, No. 61. San Francisco: Jossey-Bass.

Snow, C. E. (2006). What counts as literacy in early childhood. In K. McCartney & D. Phillips (Eds.), *Blackwell handbook of early childhood development* (pp. 274–294). Malden, MA: Blackwell.

Snow, C. E., Burns, M. S., & Griffin, P. (Eds.). (1998). *Preventing reading difficulties in young children.* Washington, DC: National Academy Press.

Snow, C.E., Tabors, P. O., & Dickinson, D. K. (2001). Language development in the preschool years. In D. K. Dickinson & P. O. Tabors (Eds.), *Beginning literacy with language: Young children learning at home and school* (pp. 1-25). Baltimore: Paul H. Brookes.

Snow, C. E., & Kang, Y. K. (2006). Becoming bilingual, biliterate, bicultural. In K. A. Renninger & I. E. Sigel (Eds.), *Handbook of child psychology, Volume 4: Child psychology in practice* (6th ed., pp. 75–102). Hoboken, NJ: Wiley.

Snow, C. E., Porche, M. V., Tabors, P. O., & Harris, S. R. (2007). *Is literacy enough? Pathways to academic success for adolescents.* Baltimore, MD: Brookes Publishing.

Stanovich, K. E. (1993). A model for studies of reading disability. *Developmental Review, 13,* 225–245.

Stanovich, K. E. (2000). *Progress in understanding reading: Scientific foundations and new frontiers.* New York: Guilford Press.

Stein, N. L., & Albro, E. R. (1997). Building complexity and coherence: Children's use of goal-structured knowledge in telling stories. In M. Bamberg (Ed.), *Narrative development: Six approaches* (pp. 5–44). Mahwah, NJ: Erlbaum.

Strömqvist, S., & Verhoeven, L. (2004). *Relating events in narrative: A cross-linguistic developmental study* (Vol. 2). Mahwah, NJ: Erlbaum.

Tabors, P. O., & Snow, C. E. (2002). Young bilingual children and early literacy development. In S. B. Neuman & D. K. Dickinson (Eds.), *Handbook of early literacy research* (pp. 159–178). New York: Guilford Press.

Teale, W. H., & Sulzby, E. (Eds.). (1986). *Emergent literacy: Writing and reading.* Norwood, NJ: Ablex.

Tholander, M. (2002). Cross-gender teasing as a socializing practice. *Discourse Processes, 34*(3), 311–383.

Thompson, G. B., Cottrell, D. S., & Fletcher-Flinn, C. M. (1996). Sublexical orthographic-phonological relations early in the acquisition of reading: The knowledge sources account. *Journal of Experimental Child Psychology, 62,* 190–222.

Tomasello, M. (2003). *Constructing a language: A usage-based theory of language acquisition.* Cambridge, MA: Harvard University Press.

Toolan, M. (2001). *Narrative: A critical linguistic introduction.* New York: Routledge.

Treiman, R. (1993). *Beginning to spell: A study of first grade children.* New York: Oxford University Press.

Treiman, R., Tincoff, R., Rodríguez, K., Mouzaki, A., & Francis, D. J. (1998). The foundations of literacy: Learning the sounds of letters. *Child Development, 69,* 1524–1540.

Treiman, R., Weatherston, S., & Berch, D. (1994). The role of letter names in children's learning of phoneme-grapheme relations. *Applied Psycholinguistics, 15,* 97–122.

Treiman, R., Zukowski, A., & Richmond-Welty, E. D. (1995). What happened to the "n" of sink? Children's spelling of final consonant clusters. *Cognition, 55,* 1–38.

Uccelli, P. (2008). Beyond chronicity: Evaluation and temporality in Spanish-speaking children's personal narratives. In A. McCabe, A. Bailey, & G. Melzi (Eds.), *Culture, cognition, and emotion: Spanish-speaking children's narratives* (pp. 175–212). New York: Cambridge University Press.

Uccelli, P., Hemphill, L., Pan, A. P., & Snow, C. (1999). Telling two kinds of stories: Sources of narrative skill. In L. Balter, & C. S. Tamis-Lemonda (Eds.), *Child psychology: A handbook of contemporary issues* (pp. 215–236). Philadelphia: Psychology Press.

Uccelli, P., & Páez, M. M. (2007). Narrative and vocabulary development of bilingual children from kindergarten to first grade. *Language, Speech, and Hearing Services in Schools, 38,* 225–236.

Wang, Q. (2004). The emergence of cultural self-construct: Autobiographical memory and self-description in American and Chinese children. *Developmental Psychology, 40,* 3–15.

Wang, Q., & Fivush, R. (2005). Mother-child conversations of emotionally salient events: Exploring the functions of emotional reminiscing in European-American and Chinese families. *Social Development, 14*(3), 473–495.

Whitehurst, G. J., Arnold, D. S., Epstein, J. N., & Angell, A. L. (1994). A picture book reading intervention in day care and home for children from low-income families. *Developmental Psychology, 30,* 679–689.

Whitehurst, G. J., & Lonigan, C. J. (1998). Child development and emergent literacy. *Child Development, 68,* 848–872.

Whitehurst, G. J., & Lonigan, C. J. (2002). Emergent literacy: Development from prereaders to readers. In S. B. Neuman & D. K. Dickinson (Eds.), *Handbook of early literacy research* (pp. 11–29). New York: Guilford Press.

Wolf, M., Vellutino, F., & Berko Gleason, J. (1998). A psycholinguistic account of reading. In J. Berko Gleason & N. Bernstein Ratner (Eds.), *Psycholinguistics* (2nd ed., pp. 409–451). Fort Worth: Harcourt Brace Jovanovich.

Zilles, A., Melzi, G., Knecht, F., & Lopes, G. (2008, July). *Linguistic and cultural variations in mother-child narratives.* Paper presentation at the International Association for the Study of Child Language, Edinburgh, Scotland.

Developments in the Adult Years

Loraine K. Obler
City University of New York Graduate Center

We might think that language learning stops at some point, but adults learn new vocabulary as the need and opportunity arise. My son recently used a word that I'm pretty sure I'd never heard before: *incentivize*. I could understand the word because I know the meanings of its component morphemes: *incentive* and *-ize*, and the meaning I derived made sense in the context of our conversation. This turns out to be a useful word in my academic world as well: I've now used it myself, when talking with fellow faculty members about how we could encourage our students to do more of the types of academic activities that we find useful in their education. However, it's not only new lexical items that we learn throughout life; we also learn new ways to use language. Picking precisely the best search words to Google specific information is a skill that has become quite useful in recent years, for example.

Of course, in addition to picking up new words in conversation or in searching the Internet, there are more formal ways that we continue to learn language in adulthood: We can study foreign languages in classes or via software, learn new software applications, study technical writing, public speaking, and even more effective listening. For bilinguals and **polyglots**, there are programs to teach simultaneous translation. Medical schools teach doctors-in-training how to communicate effectively with their patients (Arnold et al., 2009), particularly those from an earlier generation (McFarland, Rhoades, Roberts, & Eleazer, 2006). In any job, profession, or hobby, we pick up new and relevant terminology that we did not know earlier and that others outside our circle might not know. Although we do not usually consider all these post-childhood language skills aspects of language acquisition, they are part of the development process.

In order to produce new language items, some practice is usually necessary. Many adolescents, as well as adults, practice what they might say in an expected situation or review what they *did* say in a recent situation and could have said differently. There are even organizations that provide media training to help individuals prepare for interviews and public appearances, such as learning to produce sound bites on television or the Internet. Additionally, adolescents' and adults' ability to criticize themselves, to observe variation in others' usage, and to select among possible styles contributes to their ability to use a variety of *registers* (see Chapter 6) with confidence. For instance, the ability to leave a complete, concise voice-mail message is now considered a valuable life skill (children learn it, too). Today, because even phone calls are often considered intrusive, what we need to learn, instead, is how to put a useful subject line on our email messages. (For example, research suggests that students would rather email their professors than call them or go to office hours [Kelly, Keaten, & Finch, 2004]; Readers: Do you agree?)

Not only do our modes of communication change with advances in technology; in addition, over time, language itself changes, and adults must adjust to these changes. New vocabulary items enter the language (e.g., *truthiness*); certain lexical items become stigmatized (e.g., "*oriental*," now replaced by *Asian* or *Asian American* when referring to people); others become de-stigmatized (e.g., the verb *to suck*, meaning to be bad), although there are often generational differences in reaction to such words; new intonation uses develop (e.g., the exaggerated one that accompanies "duh," which we translate as "Well, that's obvious!"). Some linguists do not consider these post-childhood language changes to be part of language acquisition, but we challenge that view, appreciating that the language changes of adulthood are a part of the developmental continuum.

One might argue that the special language registers and skills of adolescence and adulthood are different from the core language learned in childhood in that they are relatively optional. Only the people who need such registers and find themselves exposed to them have a chance to acquire them. This is not essentially different from what happens in childhood, however: Children in highly educated families tend to acquire larger vocabularies than do children from families without such advantages; children who learn to read early, easily, and well tend to acquire more vocabulary from their reading than do those for whom reading is a chore. Children exposed to only one language are limited to learning just that one language unlike children in bilingual environments where being bilingual is valued. In adulthood, as well, language acquisition results from speakers' needs to communicate, very much as happens in earlier stages of the life span.

In this chapter we first consider registers acquired in adulthood that we employ in social situations and at work; these are compared with the more explicit learning of second or foreign languages. When we next turn to the language developments of advanced age, it is useful to see the way separate language subsystems differentiate. Finally, we focus on language patterns that result from brain damage, in order to distinguish changes resulting from disease from the changes typical of healthy aging.

The Language of Peer and Social Groups

Special registers are mastered starting in childhood and in adolescence and are refined in adulthood for social and professional activities and for many aspects of interpersonal relationships. One of the primary divisions in our society, of course, is that between females and males. Early gender differences are discussed in Chapters 6 and 10. The acquisition of gender-appropriate speech styles (sometimes called genderlects) continues into adulthood. In the popular press, Tannen (1990) and others (Hannah & Murachver, 2007) have described how women and men differ in their styles of language use. According to Tannen, women, as a rule, use language more for rapport, whereas men use it more for competition. Such language mechanisms as interruption and holding the floor have been studied in the past to see how they indicate differences in power (Edelsky, 1981). In some societies, males may interrupt females more often than females interrupt males (Shaw, 2000). But broad assertions about differences are often stereotypical; the claims that men, in general, interrupt more than women do and that women talk more than men have been examined extensively, and major reviews of this literature (James & Clarke, 1993; James & Drakich, 1993) come to conclusions that disagree with the models embodied in the popular stereotypes. Many of the older claims about gender differences in language have not been supported by recent research. For example, there is no evidence that women speak more than men, and, in fact, about 16,000 words a day appears to be the norm for both genders (Cameron, 2007). Role and situation undoubtedly account for many differences that have been observed and we might expect to see gender-marked registers in situations in which males and females fulfill traditional sex roles, such as when they are fathers or mothers. Gender differences in language continue to be an active topic of linguistic research (Cameron, 2010), but recent studies of the differences between male and female conversational style have concentrated more on word choice preferences of men and women (and how they can be exploited in advertising, among other concepts; Motschenbacher, 2007).

Bonding language serves not only to identify members within a group but also to distinguish members from outsiders. An experimental method that demonstrates this is the **matched-guise model**. Lambert (1972) used it first with French–English bilinguals in Canada, but it has since been used in many other situations. In this paradigm, the same speaker is recorded twice, speaking in two separate languages. Listeners are not told that they are hearing the same speaker more than once; they are simply asked to listen to each recording and to comment on various characteristics of the speaker. Thus, their responses betray the stereotypes they have about the subgroups with which the speakers can be identified. For example, in the 1972 study, Canadian bilinguals judged a male to be taller, more intelligent, and more handsome when he was speaking English than when he was speaking French. A lecturer with upper-class pronunciation was deemed more intelligent than the same lecturer using a lower-class accent. This matched-guise approach was used by Dixon, Mahoney, and Cocks (2002) to study listeners' attributions of how guilty a young man sounded in an interview with a standard-accent police inspector. The same speaker saying the same words was rated as more likely to be guilty when he spoke with a working-class accent instead of a standard accent.

As Chapter 2 demonstrates, even infants show a preference for their own dialects or their own infant-directed register, indicating a very sophisticated understanding of nuances in language use. Romaine (1984), Andersen (1996), and others have demonstrated that even very young children are aware of social differences in language use, and in adolescence, they become more sophisticated in identifying their features and sometimes in switching between different varieties or dialects for different purposes.

Special registers are also used to create bonds among members of larger subgroups of society. In many subcultures, such as sports communities, gay male communities, biker communities, or religious communities, one can indicate membership in the community by means of specific lexical items, conventionalized phrases, and intonation patterns. The use of registers appropriate to different contexts begins early in life and continues across the life span. Wagner, Greene-Havas, and Gillespie (2010) are among the many researchers who have studied the development of children's ability to appreciate the use of register.

Intimate conversations are structured differently from conversations with acquaintances or strangers, as the classic study by Hornstein (1985) observed. Hornstein recorded sixty telephone conversations, one-third between close friends, one-third between strangers, and one-third between acquaintances. Even in telephone conversations, the procedures used for opening a conversation and for negotiating its conclusion are distinctly different for close friends. In particular, with close friends, some people feel no need to identify themselves when they call. Conversations or chats between friends can be less goal-oriented or structured; sometimes they are simply for keeping in touch. Between strangers or even acquaintances, a phone conversation needs to have a more practical purpose, and often, these days, such calls are scheduled in advance; rather than miss people when making a phone call, many people in our culture now resort to email.

Formal social relations are maintained by a highly refined set of skills called *manners*. Through experience we learn what to say and what not to say in specific adult situations. One learns the appropriate way to congratulate someone or to express condolence. In her *Miss Manners* book and syndicated columns, etiquette instructor Judith Martin (2005) has asked readers to think about their listeners' perspectives in creating polite responses, rather than being totally spontaneous. In response to an announced pregnancy she advises, "Oh, how wonderful! When is it to be?" and not "Was this planned?" or "Aren't you concerned about population growth?" Over time, the rules on appropriate usage may change, and cause changes in both social and professional guidelines. In one case that was covered by the news media in 2003, the City Council of Bristol, England, debated whether staff in the city administrative buildings should continue the friendly but inappropriately informal practice of calling strangers who come for public services *dear* and *love* rather than *ma'am* and *sir* (Lyall, 2003).

Language at Work

In Chapter 10, we discussed some of the language developments of adolescence. Entering the workforce in young adulthood requires a new set of language skills. Consider the catalog of special language skills that much adult work requires. For many people, work involves special telephone, emailing, and tweeting skills, all of which require an estimation of another person's behavior even though one cannot see nonverbal responses. Use of emoticons and acronyms like "lol" (for our elder readers, "laughing out loud") and its more intensive form, "rotfl" ("rolling on the floor laughing"), only partially compensates for this lack of opportunity to use prosody and emphasis. Other jobs require the ability to produce forms of scientific writing that should be communicative but non-emotional. The conventions of high-tech messaging must be used differently for business compared to personal communications—for example, one may permit oneself to send unedited messages to friends but not to one's professors. Figuring out what to place in the subject line to make the readers' job easier requires high-level theory-of-mind calculations that take the reader's perspective.

Next, consider the special jobs that involve skills in more than one natural language. For example, there are those who prepare translations for a living. Some translate scientific texts and need a particular set of skills; others translate literary texts and need another, overlapping set of skills. There are also *simultaneous interpreters*—people who provide immediate translations at official events where listeners speak (or sign) different languages from those in which a given speaker is speaking. In order to perform this work, one must have mastered at least two languages and must have the ability to listen and speak at practically the same time. In courtrooms and health-care situations, where people must listen carefully to English translations, sequential translators listen to one- or two-sentence units of speech, then the speaker pauses and the translator translates. Thus, it is not surprising that working memory skills play a large role in predicting who will be a good simultaneous interpreter (Christoffels, de Groot, & Kroll, 2006).

Therapists also require specialized language abilities, both in speaking and in listening. Counselors and therapists listen to their clients and patients; sometimes they must decode a message that says one thing on the surface but means another. Therapists must also learn to respond in ways that will help effect change in the client, so-called "therapeutic listening" (Fitzgerald & Leudar, 2010). In theater performance, special language skills are required of the actors—in particular, the ability to speak memorized lines as if they were spontaneous and to use a louder-than-usual voice as if it were natural. Many members of the clergy employ a special rhythm and voice modulations in delivering their sermons, as well as special use of terminology, specific to their congregants' background and expectations (see Wharry, 2003, for an example).

Then there are professional editors, who do not necessarily create written language themselves, but who take the efforts of others and mold them into effective written pieces. Good editing requires an ability to impose logical and artistic structure on someone else's thoughts. Finally, there are the creative writers in our society, from journalists to novelists and poets. Even though many of us thought we had, or were thought to have, precocious language skills at an early age, writers develop their talents through hard work. Creative writers often attend workshops and seminars to discuss their work and improve their skills; their style may evolve over many years. The novelist Henry James developed a more elaborate or convoluted writing style during his adult years, perhaps due in part to the invention of the typewriter, which permitted him to shift to dictating his works (Edel, 1969). Dictation, as often seen these days with software speech recognition programs, requires certain additional skills, such as the ability to articulate clearly (and often unnaturally) and concentrate on what one is saying to limit word choice to options less likely to confuse the program. This still happens frequently, as most of us know from unsatisfying conversations with automated telephone answering services as well; see Meddeb and Frenz-Belkin (2010), who aptly title their article: "What? I didn't say THAT!!!"

Even in work realms that do not focus on language, there is a certain amount of **jargon** to be acquired. Among the best studied are the special registers used in health care, the legal field, and the political arena. Medical jargon is used to enable health-care workers to communicate effectively with one another; it may also be used to ensure their sense of expertise and power in relation to the clients who come to them without knowledge of this jargon (Landro, 2010). For example, what the lay person calls *senility,* the health-care worker may call DAT (*Dementia of the Alzheimer's Type).* Ideally, the health-care worker should be able to use the appropriate jargon with colleagues but converse in lay terms with clients; recent research suggests, however, that this does not always happen and that patients may not fully comprehend what their doctors are saying to them (Castro et al., 2007).

Similar phenomena exist in the legal community, with initiates becoming quite fluent in the lexicon, syntax, and idioms of legal language, while lay people flounder unless translations are provided. The now-classic finding that many jurors do not understand their instructions (Charrow, 1982) has resulted in greater awareness that jury instructions need to be phrased in lay language that avoids legal jargon (Miles & Cottle, 2011). In addition to these particular professions, most other work or recreational situations have their own special linguistic terminology. This may range from a few specialized lexical items that refer to elements of the job to ways of creating new terms. There is special syntax that must be mastered in many jargons—such as using "pull" as a noun and "sky" as a verb when discussing the game Ultimate Frisbee.

Listener characteristics matter as well in effective use of register. Being a university lecturer requires a style of discourse that demands sensitivity to the audience, their apparent level of understanding, and the redundancy/repetition that would be inappropriate if the same material were written. Today, the skills needed for lecturing also include the ability to support presentations visually. Learning how best to convey (or comprehend) information in slides that are visible during a lecture is a skill that many presenters need to acquire, as most students can appreciate—some instructors are definitely better than others (Clark, 2008)! The ability of college professors to appreciate whether students understand the lecture, even if they are looking at a screen rather than at the lecturer, using their facial expressions, also requires sophisticated theory of mind.

Second-Language Acquisition in Adulthood

Lenneberg (1967) argued that, after puberty, acquiring a new language is quite difficult. Although there may be maturational factors involved, most researchers agree that motivation to learn a second language becomes more crucial with age; the child is motivated to learn in order to communicate, but for the adult, "motivation" is more complex and can range from social to economic factors. Other researchers, such as Snow (1998), argue that the child has more time to devote to acquiring a language, whereas the adult is never able to focus solely on acquisition. Snow found the speed of language acquisition in younger children was actually slower than that of older children and adults when syntactic abilities were compared. Clearly, there are larger social factors involved as well; in some cultures—such as that of French Canada, where there is great financial advantage to speaking French like a native speaker—a substantially greater percentage of native speakers of English can sound like native speakers of French despite acquiring the second language after puberty. Actually, the further we explore the many factors at play in second-language acquisition success, the more complicated the picture becomes, since specific abilities underlying language acquisition play a role too (Sparks, Patton, Ganschow, & Humbach, 2009).

Some have argued that earlier is not necessarily better with respect to all aspects of learning a second language. That is, they claim that learning a second language after the first has been mastered is more useful than learning two at the same time. Some have argued that learning to read in a second language is best mastered after learning to read in the first; others have argued that acquiring a second language some years after the first prevents interlanguage interference (Bahrick, Hall, Goggin, Bahrick, & Berger, 1994).

Sometimes we learn important lessons from exceptionally talented (or untalented) second-language learners. One early study of an excellent post-pubertal learner, a left-hander, who may have had unusual brain organization (non-standard lateralization of language functions, something that two-thirds of left-handers possess, relative to right-handers) was conducted by Novoa, Fein, and Obler (1988). Lamm and Epstein (1999), in contrast, found that left-handedness, especially in boys, is linked to poorer performance in adolescent second-language acquisition. Perhaps left-handers' greater right-hemisphere dominance or bilateral organization for language results in differential extremes of second-language learning ability, although this concept requires further research. Clearly people with unusual neurological function may do a good job of language learning: Smith, Tsimpli, Morgan, and Woll (2011) report on the abilities of Christopher, a well-known and publicized savant with particularly good skills for learning new languages, despite the fact that he also has severe Autism Spectrum Disorder (ASD) (see Chapter 9)

We conclude that there appear to be sensitive periods for certain aspects of language acquisition. In order to learn a first language like a native speaker, it is often the case that acquisition must start early in life. Certain individuals—perhaps those with greater bilateral organization for language—may acquire a second language with a native-like accent and abilities well into adulthood—these may be called near-native speakers (Hyltenstam & Abrahamsson, 2003). Another subset, in contrast, will have difficulty learning two languages in any post-childhood situation.

Language Developments with Advanced Age

In most Western societies, an increasingly larger segment of the population is older adults. For example, in 2009, it was estimated that roughly 13 percent of the U.S. population was over 65 (U.S. Census Bureau, Population Estimates Program, 2009). There are many stereotypes of language use by older speakers: It is thought that they have diminished lexical abilities and increased trouble remembering the names of things and of other people, that their comprehension is impaired, and that their discourse tends to ramble. In fact, these stereotypes are too simplistic to explain the diversity of language behaviors associated with advanced age. From research, we learn that there are language changes that result both from direct changes in language areas of the brain and also from strategies to compensate for memory or attentional decline associated with aging. These changes have been reported across many languages (e.g., Juncos-Rabadan & Iglesias, 1994).

Lexicon

Difficulty finding the word they are looking for is the primary language complaint of older people. When given certain sorts of lexical tasks, in particular **confrontation-naming** tasks, there is no question that some 70-year-olds perform substantially worse than younger adults. In confrontation-naming tasks, participants are shown a picture

Intellectual curiosity and an openness to new ideas characterize successful aging.

(or an object) and are asked to say its name. In a series of studies from our laboratory (e.g., Nicholas, Obler, Albert, & Goodglass, 1985; Goral, Spiro, Albert, Obler, & Connor, 2007) we required participants to name pictures. For both common nouns and verbs, there was a slight decline for 60-year-olds as a group and a significant decline among 70-year-olds as a group. Longitudinal study of the same subjects (Au et al., 1995; Barth Ramsey, Nicholas, Au, Obler, & Albert, 1999) indicates that scores decline several points for subject groups aged 50 and older over the course of seven years. Proper nouns—the names of people—especially well-known names, can be particularly hard to retrieve with advancing age (Cohen & Burke, 1993; Juncos-Rabadan, Facal, Rodriguez, & Pereiro, 2010).

Even using idiomatic expressions (such as "skating on thin ice") is harder in older adults (although comprehending familiar ones is not [Conner et al., 2011; Rapp & Wild, 2011]). We use such terms all the time, and they are critical to everyday success in language comprehension, whether in conversation or reading.

Studies of passive access to the lexicon, however, seem to show no decrement with aging. That is, if older adults are not asked to produce the label for a concept, but rather to recognize that label or name, they perform just as well or better than younger adults. Indeed, those who are less well-educated actually show improvement in vocabulary scores with advancing age into the highest ages studied, their ninth decade of life (Goral et al., 2007).

A number of factors appear to moderate the word retrieval abilities of older adults. For example, Newman and German (2005) found that older adults had more trouble retrieving words learned more recently (later age-of-acquisition) and words judged to be less familiar. In contrast, such effects did not influence younger adults' naming patterns.

As noted earlier, the use of specific vocabulary terms changes over time and over generations of speakers. Because of this, older individuals may use archaic terms (like calling the refrigerator an *ice box*), and some of them may fail to name some pictures correctly on instruments like the Boston Naming Test because they use a word that is no longer common, such as calling a bicycle a *wheel,* a usage that was once quite common.

Older adults do not appear to have different strategies on naming tasks from those of younger adults. Nicholas and her colleagues (1985) looked at whether older adults made different types of errors. Although the older adults did use relatively more circumlocutions in their correct responses ("moving on his hands and knees, crawling" for crawling) and did tend to comment on the task more (perhaps as a way to delay responding, or to buy time), it was clear that the most common naming errors for all participants were semantically related words or words that were both semantically and phonologically related (e.g., *elevator* for *escalator*). Thus, the authors concluded that the different styles were related not to different response strategies, but to the greater difficulty of the task for older people, whether they were trying to name verbs, common nouns, or proper nouns.

However, individual differences on naming tasks may be explained by one's experiences in using language. Barresi, Obler, Au, and Albert (1999) have demonstrated that older adults who are more socially active and have more opportunities to engage in conversation perform somewhat better on a naming test, whereas those who watch television more perform significantly worse.

Some authors have argued (e.g., Goulet, Ska, & Kahn, 1994) that we do not know for certain that naming ability declines with age, because no studies have considered all the necessary factors that may interact with naming abilities, such as the medications that subjects are taking or their general health status. If older adults are in good physical health, they might name as well as younger adults. Indeed, Albert et al. (2009) have demonstrated that older adults with hypertension perform worse than those without it on naming tests. Not all health conditions are linked to naming abilities; however, diabetes, which is linked to comprehension deficits in aging, did not appear to affect naming in one study of older adults (Albert et al., 2009). The impacts of drugs used to lower cholesterol levels are under increasing scrutiny, with some studies finding that verbal memory is improved by treatment, others finding cases of individual word retrieval problems that improve after the drugs are discontinued, and others reporting no major patterns of cognitive or memory change (Benito-León, Louis, Vega, & Bermejo-Pareja, 2010).

Differences in brain structure can be seen between better and poorer namers among older individuals. Obler et al. (2010) demonstrated that the better namers among people aged 55–85 showed more robust preservation of areas in both hemispheres of the brain; these areas may be used to compensate for problems with naming.

In sum, it appears that the mental lexicon itself does not change with advanced age, although large numbers of new words can be acquired over the life span. Access for production will become more difficult for many, however, and there may be a bit of semantic degradation (Barresi, Nicholas, Connor, Obler, & Albert, 2000). It is possible that the ability to learn new words decreases in advanced age, but it is quite clear that naming words, rather than recognizing them, becomes harder for many older speakers.

Comprehension

In "advanced" societies, virtually all people are exposed to so much noise over their lifetimes that their hearing deteriorates with age. Recent studies (Vogel et al., 2010) also suggest that the increased use of personal music players at loud volume by many younger people will lead to even greater degrees of hearing loss in later life than their parents and grandparents have experienced (Shargorodsky et al., 2010). Relatively good hearing is required for comprehension of spoken language. Thus, if hearing is not checked before testing the ability to repeat individual words or the ability to understand sentences and paragraphs, older subjects could perform worse than healthy younger subjects. The questions of interest to the linguist, however, focus primarily on any change in the brain substrates for comprehension with advanced age, as well as comprehension strategies that older listeners use to deal with hearing loss.

Obler, Nicholas, Albert, and Woodward (1985) hypothesized that older adults rely more heavily on lipreading and face reading than younger people and also that they rely more on semantics (guessing what someone is saying, given the context). Neither of these hypotheses proved to be true, because it turns out that listeners of all ages rely on face reading when that cue is available. In one condition, 120 healthy adults (ages 30–79) saw a speaker on a TV screen at the same time that they heard comprehension questions such as, "The lion was killed by the tiger; who died?" In the second, they heard the same sorts of questions over the same earphones, but could not see the speaker's face. The same advantage between the first and second conditions was found for all four age groups tested, suggesting that all listeners rely equally heavily on face reading when they can, regardless of their age.

By contrast, noise level can impair older adults' comprehension. A number of studies seem to suggest that elder adults are very susceptible to the complicating effects of noise (which is hard to escape in most current social environments) on speech perception (e.g., Larsby, Hällgren, & Lyxell, 2008). Others (e.g., Gordon-Salant, 2005) find that subtle temporal processing deficits in aging listeners will degrade their speech perception skills.

Regardless of whether their hearing is impaired, Obler, Fein, Nicholas, and Albert (1991) demonstrated that older adults do rely more heavily than younger adults on plausibility; that is, responding to complex sentences such as, "The doctor who helped the patient who was sick was healthy; was the doctor healthy?" was easier than "The guide who drove the tourist who was bored was excited; was the guide bored?" Ability to comprehend complex syntactic structures is also progressively difficult with advancing age from the 30s to the 70s. Kemper (1987) found that left-branching structures, in which modifiers pile up before the structures that they modify (e.g., the *tall, skinny, greedy* aristocrat) caused the greatest difficulty, compared to right-branching structures (e.g., the aristocrat *who was tall, skinny, and greedy*). This suggests that syntactic structure interacts with memory load in rendering comprehension progressively more difficult with increasing age. Another way that elders successfully comprehend difficult language structures was tested by Kahn and Till (1991). Story materials that conformed to semantic and pragmatic expectations permitted older adults to interpret pronouns markedly better than when pronoun use did not conform to expectations.

Speech rate also affects elders' comprehension. Bergman (1980) reported that older adults do worse than younger adults when listening to either slowed-down or sped-up synthesized speech (the kind of speech we sometimes encounter in automatic phone handling systems). This kind of information can be useful in programming materials for older listeners, especially because many speakers seem to think that slowing speech rate down always makes it easier for older listeners to follow.

On tasks that require sentence and paragraph processing, older adults often perform worse than younger subjects in numbers of items, concepts, or themes retrieved (Cohen, 1979; Kemtes & Kemper, 1997), suggesting that memory load is important in comprehending materials that are longer than a single sentence in length. Older adults who used an elaborative rehearsal strategy on a verbal working-memory task were able to compensate for this, and also showed better reading comprehension (Harris & Qualls, 2000).

Executive functions—those abilities that our brain has to prioritize information to maximize attention, problem solving, and similar abilities—also influence language processing. Executive function abilities tend to decline in groups of older adults relative to younger adults (e.g., Mahoney, Verghese, Goldin, Libton, & Holtzer, 2010). Such declines can be linked to poorer comprehension. Goral et al. (2011) found a correlation between older adults' performance on executive functions measures and comprehension of sentences with the most complex structures (e.g., "The reporter that the senator attacked admitted the error," "Because the ceiling light is not off, the room is not dark"). Similar findings were seen via ERP (evoked response potentials) to typical and less-typical phrases by Federmeier, Kutas, and Schul (2010).

Discourse

There are a variety of popular beliefs in Western culture about the discourse of older people: Older people tend to run on or to go off on tangents; older people tend to tell stories over and over again without realizing it; bilingual elders can no longer limit themselves to the language appropriate to the listener. But research shows that these popular beliefs tend to be true only for patients with **dementia**, a disease-induced loss of intellectual function. In healthy adults, language may even become more elaborate with age. Hints of this have occurred in studies referred to earlier; for example, older people are more likely than 30-year-olds to give definitions consisting of more than one word, and older people are more likely to give comments and circumlocutions on naming tasks.

In contrast, some research on oral discourse does show deficits with advancing age. Bromley (1991) analyzed self-descriptions written by 240 adults, ranging in age from 20 to 86. When such variables as education and socioeconomic status were controlled, age-related effects were still seen for sentence complexity and length. Although subjects had as long as they wanted to write their descriptions, sentence complexity correlated with sentence length, and both decreased with age.

In another study of discourse, Kynette and Kemper (1986) found less varied syntactic use in older subjects (in their 70s and 80s) when they analyzed their spontaneous speech during a 20-minute interview. The older subjects also made more grammatical errors than did those in their 50s and 60s in the use of morphological markers such as past tense and subject–verb agreement. Ulatowska, Cannito, Hayashi, and Fleming (1985) found pronoun use to be more ambiguous by speakers over the age of 76, as compared to middle-aged and "young-old" groups (subjects between the ages of 60 and 75). Similarly, when Kemper, Rash, Kynette, and Norman (1990) collected story narratives from adults aged 60 to 90, with increasing age, the stories showed less syntactic complexity within sentences and had fewer cohesive links (such as use of pronouns and conjunctions) to signal connections among sentences. Using longitudinal data, Kemper, Thompson, and Marquis (2001) demonstrated that the decline in syntactic complexity started for individuals in their sixties, became marked in their seventies, and then tended to plateau at the lowest level in their eighties.

Not all aspects of discourse appear to decline with age; rather, more elaborate structures may be used for certain tasks. For example, Bates, Marchman, Harris, Wulfeck, and Kritchevsky (1995) showed animated film scenarios of both simple and complex activities to a wide range of participants and found that older adults (aged 67 to 100) used the same range of syntactic structures as adults aged 50 to 66, who in turn tended to use more complex structures than college students in describing the film clips. Likewise, in cultures that value tale telling, it is the older storytellers who are considered the most skilled performers. In my own research (Obler, 1980) in Beit Safafa, a Palestinian village that is now part of Jerusalem, those considered to be the best tale tellers were all in their sixties and older. It is precisely the ability to use elaborate speech that makes a tale effective entertainment. This elaboration includes not only details and connections between sentences and larger units, but also personalization and an ability to create rhythm.

Speech

Not only does voice quality change with age (we are actually quite accurate in judging people's age from listening to their voices), older adults' speech is also slower than that of younger adults, by 20 to 25 percent (Smith, Wasowicz, & Preston, 1987). Older speakers have also been reported to produce more **disfluencies**, such as stuttering, word repetitions, and sentence fragments (Ehrlich, Obler, Clark, & Gerstman, 1995) in speech, but they are able to repair speech errors as well as younger adults (McNamara, Obler, Au, & Albert, 1992). Recent work suggests that patients with dementia differ from normally aging speakers in the use of more frequent hesitations that appear to reflect their greater difficulty in formulating language (Gayraud, Lee, & Barkat-Defradas, 2011).

Nonlinguistic Cognitive Factors Influencing Performance

Four non-language cognitive abilities have been reported to have substantial influence on language. One is **speed of processing**, the second is **inhibition**, the third is **working memory,** and the fourth is **attention.** Collectively, these are often considered **executive functions**, since they are the brain's way of governing its own behaviors. Speed of processing was referred to earlier in this chapter. Speech is produced at slower rates by older speakers (Smith et al., 1987), and the ability to process and repeat speeded speech declines with aging (Wingfield, Prentice, Koh, & Little, 2000; Janse, 2009). Even the ability to generate lists of words based on their starting with a certain letter, or *not* including a certain letter (known as verbal fluency), is linked to basic measures of speed of processing (Bryan, Luszcz, & Crawford, 1997). While verbal fluency declines as we age (Auriacombe et al., 2006), this decline can be modified by amount of prior education, and strength of working memory. We also appear to be staying mentally healthy longer: Llewellyn & Matthews (2009) found that older adults actually perform better on verbal fluency tasks now than when such tasks were first normed in the 1990s. However, speed of reading for comprehension clearly declines with age, according to research (Harris, Rogers, & Qualls, 1998).

Inhibition, in the cognitive-psychology sense, means the ability to ignore irrelevant stimuli. It seems to become more difficult with advancing age (Burke, 1997). When written discourse is prepared with extraneous words written in italics, for example, and participants are instructed to ignore the words in italics, it is harder for older adults than younger ones to skip over the italicized words when reading aloud (Dywan & Murphy, 1996). However, bilingual adults have an edge over monolinguals when it comes to ignoring distracting responses (Bialystok, Craik, Klein, & Viswanathan, 2004). This is probably because they have superior attention strategies that have evolved over time to keep their two or more languages separated for production and comprehension purposes. In fact, there is emerging evidence that this type of "cognitive exercise" in bilingualism may delay the onset of dementia symptoms in this group of speakers (e.g., Bialystok, Craik, & Freedman, 2007).

Working memory—the ability to keep information in mind while processing—declines with age, and this decline has been linked to sentence-comprehension problems. However, Wingfield and colleagues (2000) remind us that the ability to process language with advancing age is remarkably spared in light of the marked declines in the underlying processes that support it, such as speed of processing, working memory, and actual cellular interconnections. We must assume, then, that older adults are aware of their diminished abilities and use conscious and unconscious strategies to compensate for them.

Attentional abilities also change over the life span. Recent research suggests that older adults are not more likely than younger ones to be distracted; however, if a deliberate distraction is introduced during language processing tasks, brain scans show that older adults find it more difficult to resume their train of thought and refocus on the original task (Clapp, Rubens, Sabharwal, & Gazzaley, 2011).

Language Strategies with Aging

The behavioral psychologist B. F. Skinner wrote about the ways he used language for "intellectual self-management" (Skinner, 1983). For example, when he needed to remember the name of someone, he found it helpful to recall his original use of the name and then go through the alphabet, trying each letter as the initial letter of the name. He and his wife also developed some pragmatic routines that made it possible for him to avoid having to remember names socially. For example, when he had to introduce his wife to someone whose name he had forgotten and there was a chance that the two had met previously, Skinner said to his wife, "Of course you remember?" and she quickly interrupted, "Yes, of course. How are you?" The Skinners assumed that acquaintances may or may not have remembered meeting Mrs. Skinner but probably did not trust their own memories, either.

Skinner also developed numerous uses of written language to facilitate diminished memory and attention: "In place of memories, memoranda" was his motto. Thus, he carried around a notepad so that he would jot down thoughts as they occurred to him and ensure that they would not be lost. He also used detailed outlines to plan papers in advance and kept a written index of what he had said so that he would not repeat himself or go off on a tangent. His general strategy was that one can do nothing about the actual accessibility of language, but one can enhance the conditions under which verbal behavior must occur. Not all of us can be as creative as Skinner and his wife were in dealing with memory loss by using our own self-developed strategies, but large numbers of studies are showing that programs to help older people develop and use mnemonic or memory improvement strategies can be quite effective (Rebok, Carlson, & Langbaum, 2007).

Auditory verbal abilities can also be deliberately supported. One way of tracking what one has said or thought is to record them and listen to the recordings later. Bergman

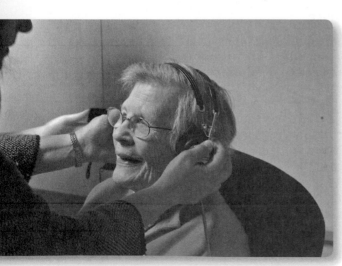

Hearing loss can isolate as we grow older; here, a woman celebrates her 100th birthday by being fitted for a new set of hearing aids.

(2002) wrote about his strategies for dealing with increasing hearing problems as he got older. When working with colleagues on research data that required listening to digits in order to record them, he chose to work only in his second language, Hebrew, because the words for the digits are more distinctive from each other in that language than in his first language, English.

Adult Language and Brain Damage

Damage to the adult brain brings about several different sorts of language and communication disturbances. In particular, we consider *aphasia*, essentially, language disturbances from dominant-hemisphere (usually left-hemisphere) damage, language disturbance from nondominant-hemisphere (usually right-hemisphere) damage, and the language disturbance of the dementias.

Aphasia

Aphasia is language disturbance resulting from localized or delimited impairment of the language areas of the brain (see Figure 1.1 in Chapter 1). For most individuals, these areas are primarily in the cortex, the exterior part of the brain, and in the central area of the left hemisphere. Traditionally, aphasia has been divided into several major types, which are not age-related, but which refer to the type of language disturbance a patient shows (see Table 11.1). Thus, in **Broca's aphasia**, the patient produces speech with effort and telegrammatically, but comprehension is relatively good. One patient with agrammatic Broca's aphasia, when asked what had happened to him, replied, in full, "*Stroke. Two years ago and et months, eight months.*" A second, who had been a mechanical engineer, replied, in full, "*Five months ago, I, I, here and here and here* (pointing to his leg, his arm, and his mouth). *Seven o'clock; it's, gone.*"

In **Wernicke's aphasia**, by contrast, production of speech is quite fluent, but comprehension is very poor. The classic Wernicke's aphasic patient will make paragrammatic errors, as in this example from a 70-year-old patient, studied by Elmera Goldberg: "*I have liked to watch the doctor works on the robot.*" In writing, as in speech, word substitutions contribute to, but do not fully account for, the empty content. Consider the following segment of a three-paragraph essay written for Dr. Joyce West by a 56-year-old plumber who had completed eight years of education. He wrote this nearly two and a half years after his stroke:

> It was not too long before that call came over me. I had to go the hospital. I was not too long to wait for my cause. They discoursed my cause for being there. They finally discovered that I had a strock But they discouted the streant of the strock. Well they finally got that selthed.

table 11.1	Adult Aphasia Types and Symptoms	
	Comprehension	Speech
Broca's aphasia	Good	Effortful, nonfluent, telegrammatic
Wernicke's aphasia	Poor	Fluent, empty
Global aphasia	Poor	Virtually none
Conduction aphasia	Good	Only poor for repetition
Anomic aphasia	Good	Many circumlocutions

In **global aphasia**, both comprehension and production are impaired; in **conduction aphasia**, spontaneous production and comprehension are relatively good as well, but the ability to repeat is impaired. In **anomic aphasia**, only the ability to name items is lost.

Aphasia may occur suddenly in childhood as a result of either stroke or accident (as in **childhood aphasia**); children with *specific language impairment,* who have had difficulty acquiring language from its earliest stages (see Chapter 9) may have difficulties learning language, with no evident brain damage. Aphasia can be seen in young adults who have suffered traumatic injuries from vehicle accidents or war wounds. However, the primary population of aphasic individuals in the Western world today is found among older adults who have suffered strokes. Many of these individuals are bilingual, because half the world population speaks more than one language. In bilingual aphasia, usually the languages are impaired similarly, and the language that was the better-known language before the aphasia remains the better-known one after the aphasia. Sometimes unusual patterns are seen, however (see Lorenzen & Murray, 2008), and in older individuals with aphasia, as compared to younger ones, one cannot predict that the most proficient language around the time that the aphasia started will be the one that will return first (Obler & Albert, 1977) or will respond best to therapy.

The classic aphasia types are shown in Table 11.1. In these, aphasia onset is generally quite sudden and is often due to stroke. Another additional class of aphasia has been documented in recent decades, in which there is a slow progression of language symptoms: **primary progressive aphasia (PPA)**. In PPA, there is no obvious physical reason for the progressive decline in abilities. These types of aphasia may be of a relatively fluent variety, with primary problems in word retrieval and knowing the meanings of low-frequency words that were previously understood. PPA may also be of a nonfluent variety, with little ability to initiate speech, and production of grammatically reduced sentences such as those seen in agrammatism. While primary progressive aphasia may lead to dementia, it does not necessarily do so, even though the fluent subtype is often called Semantic Dementia (Gorno-Tempini et al., 2011; Kertesz et al., 2010).

There are several additional points to be made about how the language disturbances of aphasia relate to age. First, the ability to recover from aphasia varies substantially across the life span. In young children, perhaps up until the age of puberty, the recovery from even severe aphasia is likely to be nearly complete. Only the most sophisticated testing can detect language deficits in these patients (Dennis & Whitaker, 1976; Devlin et al., 2003). After brain damage in young adulthood, there is often substantial recovery as well. A notable relatively recent case is that of network newscaster Bob Woodruff, who was injured by a roadside bomb in Iraq in 2006, and who recovered from expressive aphasia well enough to resume his TV reporting career. Although there are also older adults who recover from aphasia, recovery is much less frequent in this population, and it is hard to predict which aphasic patients will recover. Patients with certain types of aphasia in the early stages after brain injury or stroke are much more likely than others to recover. As in many communication disorders, individuals from low socioeconomic status groups tend to show greater impairment initially and achieve lower end-point abilities as well (Connor, Obler, & Tocco, 2001).

Over the years, certain types of aphasia therapy have proven helpful for individuals with aphasia. Melodic Intonation Therapy (MIT) helps some individuals who have nonfluent aphasias. As its name implies, this therapy encourages the use of exaggerated intonation and rhythm in retraining language skills (see original reports by Sparks, Helm, & Albert, 1974). In addition to functional gains made by patients, some research suggests that MIT normalizes cortical activity during language production (Belin et al., 1996).

Semantic-feature therapy has proven useful for patients with trouble with lexical retrieval (Boyle & Coelho, 1995; Kiran & Bassetto, 2008). In this type of therapy, patients are cued with semantic information for concepts they are having trouble producing. Antonucci (2009) provides a detailed example of how this therapy was used to help a group of patients with aphasia.

A third type of therapy that has emerged more recently is constraint-induced therapy. This type of language therapy is based on an approach to physical therapy for people who have difficulty using their dominant hand and arm due to stroke. Such individuals often deliberately build up the abilities of their nondominant hand to compensate and do not exercise the dominant one at all. We now know that if the nondominant hand is restrained, the dominant one can often reacquire substantial function with intense practice. Similarly, for language, in constraint-induced aphasia therapy, nonfluent patients are required to use language rather than gesturing and are given intense schedules of treatment. A growing number of studies report substantial and lasting improvement for patients receiving this type of intervention (see Cherney, Patterson, Raymer, Frymark, & Schooling [2008] for a review).

Right-Hemisphere Damage and Language

Until the middle of the twentieth century, it was assumed that the left hemisphere was dominant for language and the right hemisphere had little if anything to do with language. Although basic language skills like phonology and the lexicon and syntax are not impaired when patients suffer right-hemisphere damage, the ability to use language appropriately in broader, pragmatic senses is affected. For example, Brownell, Michel, Powelston, and Gardner (1983) discovered that the ability to appreciate humor is impaired in patients with right-hemisphere damage. Others (e.g., Bloom, Borod, Obler, and Gerstman, 1992; Sherratt, 2007) demonstrated that discourse involving emotional content is particularly impaired in such patients.

Pragmatic aspects of discourse production are particularly impaired, such as its coherence (Bloom, Borod, Obler, & Gerstman, 1993). When we see a picture of a man and a boy standing by a dirty car and the man says to the boy, "That car certainly does look dirty," we understand that the man is not only commenting on the way the car looks, but he may be indirectly requesting that the boy clean it. Although patients with left-hemisphere damage are likely to appropriately select the underlying meaning, those with right-hemisphere damage may be unable to appreciate such underlying pragmatic meanings.

Prosodic aspects of speech production are also impaired in right-brain-damaged patients (Ross & Monnot, 2008). Intonation, for example, may be flat, conveying little emotion. The ability to appreciate prosody in the speech of others is also impaired (Brownell, Gardner, Prather, & Martino, 1995). (See Table 11.2 for a comparison of the language and communication problems associated with left- and right-hemisphere damage.)

There is evidence that processing emotional language may involve more right-hemisphere involvement than processing nonemotional language. One set of "words" that convey emotional prosody and implications are called vocal emblems. These are items like

table 11.2	Language and Communication Problems Associated with Left- and Right-Hemisphere Damage
Left-Hemisphere Damage	**Right-Hemisphere Damage**
• Naming problems	• Tangential speech
• Effortful speech	• Inference problems
• Phonemic and phonetic distortions	• Humor impaired
• Speech devoid of meaning	• Appreciation and production of emotion impaired
• Speech with few functors	
• Word substitutions	• Prosody impaired
• Little speech initiated	
• Comprehension problems for words and/or sentences	

"Pee-uw" and "Wow!" that are word-like in that they convey a meaning "That stinks" and "Amazing!," but generally occur in isolation, unlike regular words. Patients with right-brain damage perform only a bit worse than normal age-matched controls on such items, however, while patients with left-brain damage perform significantly worse than both groups, suggesting that these items are processed more like words than like emotion.

Language in the Dementias

The onset of aphasia is usually sudden, particularly in the case of aphasia resulting from stroke or accident. In the case of a tumor, there is a progressive onset of aphasia, but the lesion, or area of damage, is still relatively limited. With **dementing diseases** such as Alzheimer's, by contrast, there is more widespread damage to the brain. This damage may be subtle enough in any individual location that it is not revealed by our current brain imaging technology. Nevertheless, after death, postmortem study of the brain shows changes at the cellular level that have been reflected in the progressive deterioration of cognitive abilities. These abilities include memory, problem solving, and learning, as well as language comprehension and production.

There are a number of diseases that include dementia. As people in many societies live longer, the incidence of dementing diseases—particularly **Alzheimer's disease (AD)**— increases, since it is relatively rare before age 70 (0.6 percent) but markedly more common in individuals over age 84 (8.4 percent in the United States) (Hubert et al., 1995). Other disorders that are also increasing in prevalence, such as diabetes, also continue to increase the number of individuals who develop AD and other dementias (Ahtiluoto et al., 2010). We must first distinguish among the various sorts of dementia, then we can describe the language behaviors associated with them.

One basic distinction in the dementias involves whether the brain damage is primarily *cortical* (on the surface of the brain) or *subcortical* (beneath the surface of the brain). In diseases such as **Parkinson's disease** and *progressive supranuclear palsy,* it is predominantly subcortical structures that are impaired, whereas in diseases such as Alzheimer's, it is predominantly cortical structures that are impaired. Thus, it is not surprising that the language disturbance in Alzheimer's disease may mimic that seen in the aphasias (see Table 11.3). Specifically, the language disturbance of early Alzheimer's disease looks like anomic aphasia, in which the primary deficit is in the ability to name things. (Alzheimer himself reported a patient who, when shown coins and asked "What are these?" said (in German), *"That is…that is…we have them…there…there."* (Alzheimer, 1911; translation by Pamela Mathews, personal communication). By the mid to late stage, the language disturbance in AD looks like Wernicke's aphasia: Patients produce fluent, poorly monitored speech with syntactically correct usage of some words and occasional *jargon* items (nonsense words). Like many people with aphasia, patients with Alzheimer's disease also have difficulty in comprehension of language and in repeating sentences that are quite long or quite improbable. Overviews of the language disturbances seen in AD and other forms of dementia are provided by Reilly and colleagues (2010) and Croot (2009).

By the late stages of AD, most patients produce little language and are sometimes thought to be mute. Other patients may talk when no one is around and/or not talk when people are present. The language produced at this stage is almost entirely stereotypic, with no content. Thus, in the late stage, patients with DAT (Dementia of the Alzheimer's Type, another commonly used term for the disorder) may look like patients with global aphasia, who produce and comprehend very little language. Even in the late stages, however, some pragmatic competence remains. Patients may still maintain eye contact appropriately or respond to formulaic questions such as, "How are you today?" (Causino, Obler, Knoefel, & Albert, 1994).

In the early stages of DAT, the ability to read may actually be better for patients with Alzheimer's disease than the ability to understand spoken language, because spoken language requires more consistent attention. However, the ability to write deteriorates fairly

table 11.3	The Stages of Language Decline in Alzheimer's Disease

Early Stage

Primarily naming problems
Some discourse problems
Mild comprehension problems for complex materials
Problems with repetition of long complex sentences only
Reading aloud spared; some problems with writing

Mid-Stage

Fluent, empty discourse
Word substitutions
Occasional jargon nonwords
Poor repetition of sentences
Impaired comprehension
Reading aloud relatively spared
Writing impaired in parallel to oral production
Bilingual subjects impaired in language choice

Late Stage

Little language produced
No comprehension testable
No repetition ability
One or two low-level pragmatic abilities spared

rapidly. In the early stages, problems in writing are simply misspellings and an occasional omission or inappropriate addition of an inflectional suffix. By early to mid stages, however, the ability to read aloud is markedly better spared than the ability to read for comprehension. Patterson, Graham, and Hodges (1994) have demonstrated that the ability to read irregularly spelled words such as *placebo* aloud is impaired even in the early stages. As the disease progresses, words learned earlier in life are recognized better than those learned later (Cuetos, Herrera, & Ellis, 2010). By the later stages of DAT, patients produce nonsense words and incomplete sentences and eventually refuse to write altogether. An overview of the general patterns of reading and writing typically seen in DAT is provided by Harnish and Neils-Strunjas (2008).

In those dementias that co-occur with subcortical disease, in particular Parkinson's disease, the speech abilities are more obviously impaired rather than underlying language abilities. Patients tend to speak very softly, and their speech is inarticulate, speeding up to a mumble after the first several words. When one asks these patients to write, however, or listens carefully to their oral language production, language deficits can be observed (see Murray, 2008, for a review). For example, one can note certain mild errors of syntax, particularly the deletion of morphemes or the inappropriate addition of morphemes. For instance, the patient may write, *"The grandchildren comes around."*

In subcortical as in cortical impairment, the incorrect use of grammatical forms may also occur. For example, in telling us the story of Little Red Riding Hood, one patient said, "The wolf took a liking *toward* the basket," instead of "The wolf took a liking *to* the basket." Another, in concluding his description of the Cookie Theft Picture from the Boston Diagnostic Aphasia Examination, said *"Oh, what else is there's to it?"* (MacNamara, Obler, Au, Durso, & Albert, 1992). Such examples suggest a certain lack of self-monitoring on the part of the patients.

Mistakes in the use of idioms are of interest to the theoretician because they suggest that idioms are not necessarily represented in unitary fashion in the brain, but may be broken up. Kempler and Van Lancker (1988) showed that for patients with Alzheimer's disease, comprehension is impaired for high-frequency idioms whose meaning is not transparent (e.g., a *blue mood*). Papagno, Lucchelli, Muggia, and Rizzo (2003) suggest that for patients with DAT, the major problem in understanding idioms is their inability to suppress literal interpretations of idiomatic phrases.

Specific studies of naming, sentence comprehension, and discourse abilities in Alzheimer's disease have been undertaken. Adults with AD or semantic dementia often experience difficulty naming items or pictures (anomia) or make naming errors (Reilly, Peelle, Antonucci, & Grossman, 2011). Researchers have asked if naming is impaired because the lexicon itself is losing its internal structure, or is it rather that access to the lexicon is difficult? Hough (2004) found that, while typically functioning older adults show impaired lexical access, those with DAT make errors that suggest that they have deficits in the earlier conceptual (semantic) stages of word retrieval in addition to access difficulties. Participants with DAT especially had difficulty with category naming and did not appear to be helped by facilitative contexts, while typical aging adults improved when asked to name items shown in contextual vignettes. This implies that the internal structure of the lexicon is degrading, as well as access routes. However, in our own studies, when we measured the semantic distance between patients' errors and their targets on a naming task, we saw that the distance was no greater for patients with Alzheimer's disease than it was for typical age-matched individuals (Nicholas, Obler, Au, & Albert, 1996).

Comprehension of syntax is also impaired, as many studies show (e.g., Bickel et al., 2000). However, Rochon, Waters, and Caplan (2000) demonstrated that, even in the early stages of dementia of the Alzheimer's type, certain syntactic structures—primarily those that encode more propositions—are particularly difficult for patients. They concluded that comprehension was actually more affected by the number of semantic propositions in an utterance than the syntax per se. As working memory declines, patients with DAT experience growing problems with complex sentences.

Aspects of pragmatic abilities also break down over the course of Alzheimer's dementia. Murray (2010) notes that the amount of information that patients with AD conveyed in narrative discourse was significantly less than that provided by typical aging adults, or aging adults with depression. This has the effect of making discourse produced by patients with AD seem relatively incoherent (St-Pierre, Ska, & Beland, 2005). In a longitudinal study, Tomeda and Bayles (1993) studied the development of discourse over five years in three patients from the early-mid to mid-late stages of the disease. The total words used during a picture-description task declined with the progression of the disease to the late stages. Not surprisingly, the amount of information conveyed decreased across the five years of testing. In the early stages studied, conciseness was impaired, but by the later stages it became a meaningless measure.

Written discourse breaks down relatively early in dementia; oral discourse breaks down more subtly and over a longer course in Alzheimer's disease. Ehrlich and colleagues (1995) studied the characteristics of picture-description narratives in patients with probable Alzheimer's disease; with increased information load and information complexity, the discourse of the patients with Alzheimer's disease became both emptier and briefer. Bates and her colleagues (1995) demonstrated that patients with Alzheimer's dementia use less complex syntax—fewer passives overall, for example, and relatively more passives that employ the word *get* (e.g., "The vase got broken")—than did age-matched peers. However, preference for less complex syntax does not fully account for the generalized diminishment of discourse content. Presumably, decreased working memory (and long-term memory when required) as well as diminished self-monitoring functions all contribute to the impairments in discourse for patients with DAT.

A relatively well-publicized series of studies has revealed that writing samples from adults produced many years prior to diagnosis of AD (for instance, nuns' diaries, or physicians' medical school application essays) show subtle "precursors" of later difficulty (Engelman, Agree, Meoni, & Klag, 2010). In recent years, there have even been numerous analyses of the earlier writings of many well-known historical or literary figures (see an example using the author Iris Murdoch by Garrard, Maloney, Hodges, & Patterson, 2005). Although we do not yet have any clinical use for this type of finding, it does illustrate the rather gradual decline in cognitive and language skills that characterizes DAT in its fully developed form. Some researchers are working to develop clinically useful measures of early detection using language tasks, such as picture description (Forbes-McKay & Venneri, 2005).

Bilingual patients with Alzheimer's disease can lose the ability to choose the right language to address their listener. They may also mistakenly code-switch between their two or more languages when their listener speaks only one (De Santi, Obler, Sabo-Abramson, & Goldberger, 1989; Hyltenstam & Stroud, 1989).

Since aphasia is the most studied of the language and communication disturbances resulting from brain damage, it is understandable that therapies have been developed primarily for aphasia. However, because the incidence of dementia is increasing as people live longer, researchers and clinicians have been working to develop therapies to improve or at least forestall communication deficits in patients who have both language disturbances and learning difficulties. Conversation groups may be helpful in slowing decline. Training caregivers to speak more slowly, to use simple syntax, and to ask more focused questions can also help patients continue to engage in conversation. Some examples of such approaches are provided by Bryan and Maxim (2006).

Additionally, as anyone who watches television advertising knows, drugs are under development that show promise in slowing the progress of dementia. However, at the time of this writing, none appear able to remediate or substantially delay eventual symptoms; this is why both behavioral and pharmacological solutions to this growing and major health condition are the subject of widespread research investigations (Saddichha & Pandey, 2008).

Two factors have been linked to lower likelihood of developing dementia. One is education, and the second is bilingualism or multilingualism. People with more years of education are less likely to show signs of dementia at any age than those with less education (Ngandu et al., 2007). It is unclear whether education actually provides **cognitive reserve** that delays the onset of dementia or whether it permits individuals to compensate for decline and thus avoid being noticed. (Either way, it might be a good reason to continue your education!) Studies of bilinguals and multilinguals suggest there may be a delay in the onset of dementia by about five years compared to monolinguals (Craik, Bialystok, & Freedman, 2010; Kavé et al., 2008). This advantage may be conveyed by the need for bilinguals to use extra cognitive resources in order to keep their languages separated during talking and listening.

Of the numerous ways to conceptualize both the language changes that take place over the healthy life span as well as how adult language is impaired by brain damage, there is an interesting model that links to the other chapters of this text: the **regression hypothesis**. Roman Jakobson (1941) suggested that the language deficits of aphasia appear in the reverse order of the process of development of language in childhood (that is, those skills learned latest by children are those most likely to be lost in aphasia. While it might seem intuitively appealing, Jakobson's hypothesis has not held up to close scrutiny (see Berko Gleason, 1978, and Menn & Obler, 1990). Patients who lose the ability to produce plurals and past tenses do not have the same morphological systems as children who are just acquiring those inflections. For instance, a person with Broca's aphasia may be able to make an /-Iz/ plural like *nurses* but not the more common /-z/ plural seen in *gloves*. This is a pattern that is not seen in children, who acquire the /-z/ form of the plural before the /-Iz/ form (see Chapter 5). So acquisition of language, when studied in detail, is not the reverse of language loss in aphasia or dementia. In part, this is evident from the fact that there is a wide variety of language among people with aphasias and dementias, but much less variability in the stages of language acquisition in children.

A number of authors have suggested that dementia be considered a more appropriate field for looking at the regression hypothesis, since in dementia one sees a progressive deterioration that is more strictly a reversal of language and cognitive development than the sudden impairment of aphasia. Moreover, as with the child in whom language development is closely linked to other cognitive development, in the patient suffering from dementia, the progress of language deficits is closely linked to the progression of non-language cognitive deficits. However, even in dementia there are more differences to be seen among patients than similarities. In particular, specific automatic abilities, which are late skills for children, may remain intact until a very late stage in patients with dementia. Patients with advanced dementia may retain only swear words or politeness routines acquired in later childhood. Children at the one- or two-word stage are quite different from older people at these stages.

SUMMARY

Language development after childhood can be relatively subtle, and any changes one might see each year between the ages of 20 to 70 might be far harder to observe than those between the ages of 1 and 8 years of age. Older children continue to acquire expertise in pragmatic linguistic behaviors, such as those pertaining to gender and social class, along with the new language skills they learn as they participate in activities with their peers and at school. (See Chapters 6 and 10.) As adolescents and adults join different subcultures, they acquire language registers appropriate to those subcultures. Many work situations require distinctive language use as well, in order for adults to be successful in their chosen careers or occupations.

Learning a second language may occur at any age. It appears, however, that after early school-age there is some decline in abilities, and after around puberty it is more difficult for most people to acquire native-like phonological proficiency in a new language without strong motivations to do so.

In very late adulthood, certain language changes are obvious, while other areas of language ability remain unchanged for the most part. Access to the lexicon becomes problematic for many older individuals—even those without aphasia or dementia—who may obviously search for a specific word or idiom. We can deduce, however, that the lexicon itself remains unchanged for the most part, since when they are given a word to define, older individuals can do this with the proficiency of any young adult. Learning new words continues throughout the life span, but it is possible that it becomes somewhat more difficult in older adulthood.

Studies of comprehension in retirement-age language users suggest that, in addition to the obvious difficulties brought on in advanced societies by peripheral hearing loss, there are changes in the ability to comprehend complex materials. Whether these are strictly due to the brain's ability to process linguistic features or whether they are secondary to memory and attentional changes remains unclear. Moreover, many aging adults develop successful strategies to get around these problems.

The data on possible changes in discourse production with aging continue to emerge. Some studies have reported increased elaborateness, whereas others have reported less varied and less complex syntax. These discrepancies often seem linked to different task requirements. In any event, in typically aging adults, discourse production does not appear to suffer the same degree of decline that lexical access and comprehension manifest.

Two forms of brain damage are likely to affect the aging population in advanced cultures; these result in aphasia and dementia. Fluent aphasias (such as Wernicke's aphasia) are more likely to occur in older people than in younger ones. There is debate as to whether recovery from aphasia becomes more difficult with advancing age, although successful recovery can be seen in younger patients.

Specific language disorders associated with dementing diseases such as Alzheimer's disease (also known as DAT) have been described. Overall, the language and communication behavior looks similar to what is seen in the fluent aphasias: Anomia is seen in the early stages, and Wernicke's aphasia-like symptoms predominate in mid to late stages. Subcortical dementias (such as seen in advanced Parkinson's disease), by contrast, primarily produce speech, rather than language problems. Although it was once popular to imagine that the course of language decline in aging was the mirror image of language acquisition (Roman Jakobson's regression hypothesis), language changes in Alzheimer's disease and in many cases of aphasia are not a reversal of the process of language development in childhood.

SUGGESTED PROJECTS

The ideal projects to be suggested from a study of life-span development of language are longitudinal studies. In a semester or even a year, it is simply not possible to see natural language change in adults, except in language learners and in a limited number of patients with dementia or aphasia. The following projects can give some sense of language change with time by using a cross-sectional approach or a post-hoc longitudinal approach.

1. Find an older friend who agrees that he or she forgets the names of things more than previously. Gather pictures of people who were famous in his or her childhood and young adulthood and see what sort of strategies the person uses when he or she cannot remember specific names.

2. Look up some words using Google's Ngram (Michel et al., 2011) to see words that were more common when an older acquaintance was younger (e.g., "atom"). Discuss with him or her the things he or she has noticed that are called something different today from what they were called when the person was young. See whether you can find instances of idiomatic speech that you use that he or she is not be familiar with, or would not use, then ask him or her to recall idiomatic speech he or she used that his or her parents did not use.

3. Find someone who wrote journals at the age of 20 and continued writing them through the age of 60 or 70 and who is prepared to share the journals with you. Note how the language changes over the years, not only in terms of content, but also in the vocabulary and idioms used and in the form of sentences and paragraphs. A similar project would be to compare the writing styles of a poet or novelist who has produced very different works in early and late career (e.g., W. B. Yeats, W. H. Auden, Colette, Shakespeare, Racine, Plato, Drabble).

4. Spend a day with someone who has several children of different ages. Observe how the adult has developed different language registers appropriate to the age of each child. Detail what the differences are.

5. List the special language skills you have learned in college or graduate school. Consider what you have been taught and also what you have learned about constructing a composition, using speech appropriately in different classes, and acquiring the jargon of your major field.

6. In thinking about question 5, have a friend who is not in your field read one of your term papers. Ask that person to circle the names of terms or phrases he or she doesn't understand. How many of them are there? Compare this to a popular news or web-based article on a similar topic. Are there fewer jargon terms? Are those that are used defined as the reader encounters them?

SUGGESTED READINGS

Goral, M., Spiro, A., Albert, M. L., Obler, L. K., & Connor, L. (2007). Changes in lexical retrieval ability during adulthood, *Mental Lexicon, 2,* 215–238.

Kemper, S., Rash, S., Kynette, D., & Norman, S. (1990). Telling stories: The structure of adults' narratives. *European Journal of Cognitive Psychology, 2,* 205–228.

Obler, L. K., & Pekkala, S. (2008). Language and communication in aging. In B. Stemmer & H. Whitaker (Eds.), *Handbook of neurolinguistics*. Oxford: Elsevier.

Wingfield, A., & Stine-Morrow, E. A. L. (2000). Language and speech. In F. I. M. Craik & T. Salthouse (Eds.), *The handbook of aging and cognition* (2nd ed., pp. 155–219). Mahwah, NJ: Erlbaum.

KEY WORDS

Alzheimer's disease (also, DAT, Dementia of the Alzheimer's Type)
anomic aphasia
Broca's aphasia
confrontation naming
dementia

Dementia of the Alzheimer's Type (DAT)
dementing diseases
disfluencies
executive functions
global aphasia
inhibition
jargon

matched guise model
Parkinson's disease
polyglot
regression hypothesis
speed of processing
Wernicke's aphasia
working memory

REFERENCES

Albert, M. L., Spiro, A. R., Sayers, K., Cohen, J., Brady, C., Goral, M., & Obler, L. K. (2009). Effects of health status on word finding in aging. *Journal of the American Geriatrics Society*, 57, 2300–2305.

Ahtiluoto, S., Polvikoski, T., Peltonen, M., Solomon, A., Tuomilehto, J., Winblad, B., & Kivipelto, M. (2010). Diabetes, Alzheimer disease, and vascular dementia: A population-based neuropathologic study. *Neurology*, 75(13), 1195–1202.

Alzheimer, A. (1911). Über eigenartige Krankheitsfälle des späteren Alters. *Zbl Ges Neurol Psych*, 4, 356–385 (Translated and with an introduction by H. Förstl and R. Levy, 1991).

Andersen, E. S. (1996). A cross-cultural study of children's register knowledge. In D. Slobin, J. Gerhardt, A. Kyratzis, J. Guo, D. Slobin, J. Gerhardt, & . . . J. Guo (Eds.) , *Social interaction, social context, and language: Essays in honor of Susan Ervin-Tripp* (pp. 125–142). Hillsdale, NJ: Erlbaum.

Antonucci, S. (2009). Use of semantic feature analysis in group aphasia treatment. *Aphasiology*, 23(7–8), 854–866.

Arnold, R. W., Losh, D. P., Mauksch, L. B., Maresca, T. M., Storck, M. G., Wenrich, M. D., & Goldstein, E. A. (2009). Lexicon creation to promote faculty development in medical communica-tion. *Patient Education and Counseling*, 74, 179–83.

Au, R., Joung, P., Nicholas, M., Obler, L., Kass, R., & Albert, M. (1995). Naming ability across the adult life span. *Aging and Cognition, 2*, 300–311.

Auriacombe, S., Lechevallier, N., Amieva, H., Harston, S., Raoux, N., & Dartigues, J. (2006). A longitudinal study of quantitative and qualitative features of category verbal fluency in incident Alzheimer's disease subjects: Results from the PAQUID study. *Dementia and Geriatric Cognitive Disorders*, 21(4), 260–266.

Bahrick, H., Hall, L., Goggin, J., Bahrick, L., & Berger, S. (1994). Fifty years of language maintenance and language dominance in bilingual Hispanic immi-grants. *Journal of Experimental Psychology, General, 123*, 264–283.

Barresi, B., Nicholas, M., Connor, L., Obler, L. K., & Albert, M. L. (2000). Semantic degradation and lexical access in age-related naming failures. *Aging, Neuropsychology and Cognition, 7*, 169–178.

Barresi, B., Obler, L. K., Au, R., & Albert, M. L. (1999). Language related factors influencing naming in adulthood. In H. Hamilton (Ed.), *Old age and language: Multidisciplinary perspectives*. New York: Garland.

Barth Ramsey, C., Nicholas, M., Au, R., Obler, L. K., & Albert, M. L. (1999). Verb naming in normal aging. *Applied Neuropsychology, 6*(2), 57–67.

Bates, E., Marchman, V., Harris, C., Wulfeck, B., & Kritchevsky, M. (1995). Production of complex syntax in normal aging and Alzheimer's disease. *Language and Cognitive Processes, 10,* 487–539.

Belin, P., Van Eeckhout, P., Zilbovicius, M., Remy, P., François, C., Guillaume, S., & . . . Samson, Y. (1996). Recovery from non-fluent aphasia after melodic intonation therapy: A PET study. *Neurology, 47*(6), 1504–1511.

Benito-León, J., Louis, E., Vega, S., & Bermejo-Pareja, F. (2010). Statins and cognitive functioning in the elderly: a population-based study. *Journal of Alzheimer's Disease, 21*(1), 95–102.

Bergman, M. (1980). *Aging and the perception of speech.* Baltimore: University Park Press.

Bergman, M. (2002). An audiologist's hearing: Personal reflections. *Audiology Today, 11, 33–35.*

Berko Gleason, J. (1978). The acquisition and dissolution of the English inflectional system. In A. Caramazza & E. Zurif (Eds.), *Language acquisition and language breakdown.* Baltimore: Johns Hopkins University Press.

Bialystock, E., Craik, F., Klein, R., & Viswanathan, M. (2004). Bilingualism, aging and cognitive control: Evidence from the Simon task. *Psychology and Aging, 19,* 290–303.

Bialystok, E., Craik, F. M., & Freedman, M. (2007). Bilingualism as a protection against the onset of symptoms of dementia. *Neuropsychologia, 45*(2), 459–464.

Bickel, C., Pantel, J., Eysenbach, K., & Schroder, J. (2000). Syntactic comprehension deficits in Alzheimer's disease. *Brain and Language, 71*(1), 432–448.

Bloom, R., Borod, J., Obler, L. K., & Gerstman, L. (1992). Impact of emotional content on discourse production in patients with unilateral brain damage. *Brain and Language, 42,* 153–164.

Bloom, R., Borod, J., Obler, L. K., & Gerstman, L. (1993). Suppression and facilitation of pragmatic performance. *Journal of Speech and Hearing Research, 36,* 1227–1235.

Boyle, M., & Coelho, C. A. (1995). Application of Semantic Feature Analysis as a treatment for aphasic dysnomia. *American Journal of Speech-Language Pathology, 4,* 94–98.

Bromley, D. B. (1991). Aspects of written language production over adult life. *Psychology and Aging, 6,* 296–308.

Brownell, H., Gardner, H. J., Prather, P., & Martino, G. (1995). Language, communication, and the right hemisphere. In H. S. Kirshner (Ed.), *Handbook of neurological speech and language disorders* (pp. 325–349). New York: Marcel Dekker.

Brownell, H., Michel, D., Powelston, J., & Gardner, H. (1983). Surprise but not coherence: Sensitivity to verbal humor in right hemisphere patients. *Brain and Language, 18,* 20–27.

Bryan, J., Luszcz, M., & Crawford, J. (1997). Verbal knowledge and speed of information processing as mediators of age differences in verbal fluency performance among older adults. *Psychology and Aging, 12,* 473–478.

Bryan, K. (Ed.), & Maxim, J. (Ed.). (2006). *Communication disability in the dementias.* London, England: Whurr.

Burke, D. (1997). Language, aging, and inhibitory deficits: Evaluation of a theory. *Journal of Gerontology: Psychological Sciences, 52B,* 254–264.

Cameron, D. (2010). Sex/Gender, language and the new biologism. *Applied Linguistics, 31*(2), 173–192.

Cameron, D. (2007). *The myth of Mars and Venus: Do men and women really speak different languages?* Oxford: Oxford University Press.

Castro, C. M., Wilson, C., Wang, F., & Schillinger, D. (2007). Babel babble: Physicians' use of unclarified medical jargon with patients. *American Journal of Health Behavior,* 31S85–S95.

Causino, M., Obler, L., Knoefel, J., & Albert, M. (1994). Spared pragmatic abilities in late-stage Alzheimer's disease. In L. K. Obler, R. Bloom, S. De Santi, & J. Ehrlich (Eds.), *Discourse in clinical populations.* Hillsdale, NJ: Erlbaum.

Charrow, V. (1982). Linguistic theory and the study of legal and bureaucratic language. In L. Obler & L. Menn (Eds.), *Exceptional language and linguistics*. New York: Academic Press.

Cherney, L. R., Patterson, J. P., Raymer, A., Frymark, T., & Schooling, T. (2008). Evidence-based systematic review: Effects of intensity of treatment and constraint-induced language therapy for individuals with stroke-induced aphasia. *Journal of Speech, Language & Hearing Research, 51*(5), 1282–1299.

Christoffels, I. K., de Groot, A. B., & Kroll, J. F. (2006). Memory and language skills in simultaneous interpreters: The role of expertise and language proficiency. *Journal of Memory and Language, 54*(3), 324–345.

Clapp, W., Rubens, M., Sabharwal, J. & Gazzaley, A. (2011). Deficit in switching between functional brain networks underlies the impact of multitasking on working memory in older adults. *Proceedings of the National Academy of Sciences, 108*(15).

Clark, J. (2008). Powerpoint and pedagogy: Maintaining student interest in university lectures. *College Teaching, 56*, 39–45.

Cohen, G. (1979). Language comprehension in old age. *Cognitive Psychology, 11*, 412–429.

Cohen, G., & Burke, D. (1993). Memory for proper names: A review. *Memory, 1*, 249–263.

Conner, P. S., Hyun, J., O'Connor, B., Anema, I., Goral, M., Monereau-Merry, M., Rubino, D., Kuckuk, R., & Obler, L. K. (2011). Age-related differences in idiom production in adulthood. *Clinical Linguistics and Phonetics, 25*, 89–91.

Connor, L. T., Obler, L. K., & Tocco, M. (2001). Effect of socioeconomic status on aphasia severity and recovery, *Brain and Language, 78*, 254–257.

Craik, F., Bialystok, E., & Freedman, M. (2010). Delaying the onset of Alzheimer disease: Bilingualism as a form of cognitive reserve. *Neurology, 75*(19), 1726–1729.

Croot, K. (2009). Progressive language impairments: Definitions, diagnoses, and prognoses. *Aphasiology, 23*(2), 302–326.

Cuetos, F., Herrera, E., & Ellis, A. (2010). Impaired word recognition in

Alzheimer's disease: The role of age of acquisition. *Neuropsychologia, 48*(11), 3329–3334.

Dennis, M., & Whitaker, H. (1976). Language acquisition following hemi-decortication: Linguistic superiority of the left over the right hemisphere. *Brain and Language, 3*, 404–433.

De Santi, S., Obler, L., Sabo-Abramson, H., & Goldberger, J. (1989). Discourse abilities and deficits in multilingual dementia. In Y. Joanette & H. Brownell (Eds.), *Discourse abilities in brain damage: Theoretical and empirical perspectives*. New York: Springer.

Devlin, A. M., Cross, J. H., Harkness, W. W., Chong, W. K., Harding, B. B., Vargha-Khadem, F. F., & Neville, B. R. (2003). Clinical outcomes of hemispherectomy for epilepsy in childhood and adolescence. *Brain, 126*(3), 556–566.

Dixon, J. A., Mahoney, B., & Cocks, R. (2002). Accents of guilt?: Effects of regional accent, race, and crime type on attributions of guilt. *Journal of Language and Social Psychology, 21*, 162–168.

Dywan, J., & Murphy, W. (1996). Aging and inhibitory control in text comprehension. *Psychology and Aging, 11*, 199–206.

Edel, L. (1969). *Henry James: The treacherous years: 1895–1901*. New York: J. B. Lippincott.

Edelsky, C. (1981). Who's got the floor? *Language in Society, 10*, 383–421.

Ehrlich, J., Obler, L., Clark, L., & Gerstman, L. (1995). Influence of structure on narrative production in adults with dementia of the Alzheimer's type. *Journal of Communication Disorders, 19*, 79–100.

Engelman, M., Agree, E., Meoni, L., & Klag, M. (2010). Propositional density and cognitive function in later life: Findings from the Precursors Study. *Journals of Gerontology. Series B, Psychological Sciences and Social Sciences, 65*(6), 706–711.

Federmeier, K., Kutas, M. & Schul, R. (2010). Age-related and individual differences in the use of prediction during language comprehension, *Brain & Language, 115*, 149–161.

Fitzgerald, P., & Leudar, I. (2010). On active listening in person-centred, solution-focused psychotherapy. *Journal of Pragmatics, 42*(12), 3188–3198.

Forbes-McKay, K. E., & Venneri, A. A. (2005). Detecting subtle spontaneous language decline in early Alzheimer's disease with a picture description task. *Neurological Sciences, 26*(4), 243–254.

Garrard, P., Maloney, L. M., Hodges, J. R., & Patterson, K. (2005). The effects of very early Alzheimer's disease on the characteristics of writing by a renowned author. *Brain, 128*(2), 250–260.

Gayraud, F., Lee, H., & Barkat-Defradas, M. (2011). Syntactic and lexical context of pauses and hesitations in the discourse of Alzheimer patients and healthy elderly subjects. *Clinical Linguistics & Phonetics, 25*(3), 198–209.

Goral, M., Clark-Cotton, M., Spiro, A, Obler, L. K, Verkuilen, J., & Albert, M. (2011). The contribution of set switching and working memory to sentence processing in older adults, *Experimental Aging Research, 37*, 516–538.

Goral, M., Spiro, A., Albert, M. L., Obler, L. K., & Connor, L. (2007). Changes in lexical retrieval ability during adulthood, *Mental Lexicon, 2*, 215–238.

Gordon-Salant, S. (2005). Hearing loss and aging: New research findings and clinical implications. *Journal of Rehabilitation Research and Development, 42*(4 Suppl 2), 9–24.

Gorno-Tempini, M., Hillis, A., Weintraub, S., Kertesz, A., Mendez, M. Cappa, S., Ogar, J., Rohrer, J., Black, S., Boeve, B., Manes, F., Dronkers, N, Vandenberghe, R., Rascovsky, K. Patterson, K. Miller, B., Knopman, D., Hodges, J., Mesulam, M., & Grossman, M. (2011). Classification of primary progressive aphasia and its variants, *Annals of Neurology, 76*, 1006–1004.

Goulet, P., Ska, B., & Kahn, H. (1994). Is there a decline in picture naming with advancing age? *Journal of Speech and Hearing Research, 37*, 629–644.

Hannah, A., & Murachver, T. (2007). Gender preferential responses to speech. *Journal of Language & Social Psychology, 26*(3), 274–290.

Harnish, S. M., & Neils-Strunjas, J. (2008). In search of meaning: Reading and writing in Alzheimer's disease. *Seminars in Speech & Language, 29*(1), 44–59.

Harris, J., Rogers, W., & Qualls, C. (1998). Written language comprehension in younger and older adults. *Journal of Speech, Language and Hearing Research, 41*, 603–617.

Harris, J. L., & Qualls, C. D. (2000). The association of elaborative or maintenance rehearsal with age, reading comprehension and verbal working memory performance. *Aphasiology, 14*(5–6), 515–526.

Hornstein, G. A. (1985). Intimacy in conversational style as a function of the degree of closeness between members of a dyad. *Journal of Personality and Social Psychology, 49*(3), 671–681.

Hough, M. (2004). Naming and category concept generation in older adults with and without dementia. *Aphasiology, 18*(5–7), 589–597.

Hubert, L., Scherr, P., Beckett, L., Albert, M. S., Pilgrim, D., Chown, M., Funkenstein, H., & Evans, D. (1995). Age-specific incidence of Alzheimer's disease in a community population. *Journal of the American Medical Association, 273*, 1354–1359.

Hyltenstam, K., & Abrahamsson, N. (2003). Maturational constraints in SLA. In C. J. Doughty & M. H. Long (Eds.), *The handbook of second language acquisition* (pp. 539–588). Oxford: Blackwell.

Hyltenstam, K., & Stroud, C. (1989). Bilingualism in Alzheimer's dementia: Two case studies. In K. Hyltenstam & L. K. Obler (Eds.), *Bilingualism across the lifespan: Aspects of acquisition, maturity, and loss*. Cambridge, UK: Cambridge University Press.

Jakobson, R. (1941/1968). *Child language, aphasia, and phonological universals.* The Hague: Mouton.

James, D., & Clark, S. (1993). Women, men, and interruptions: A critical review. In D. Tannen (Ed.), *Gender and conversational interaction* (pp. 231–280). New York: Oxford University Press.

James, D., & Drakich, J. (1993). Understanding gender differences in amount of talk: A critical review of research. In D. Tannen & D. Tannen (Eds.), *Gender and conversational interaction* (pp. 281–312). New York: Oxford University Press.

Janse, E. (2009). Processing of fast speech by elderly listeners. *The Journal of the Acoustical Society of America, 125*(4), 2361–2373.

Juncos-Rabadan, O., & Iglesias, F. (1994). Decline in the elderly's language: Evidence from cross-linguistic data. *Journal of Neurolinguistics, 8,* 183–190.

Juncos-Rabadan, O., Facal, D., Rodriguez, M., & Pereiro, A. (2010). Lexical knowledge and lexical retrieval in ageing: Insights from a tip-of-the-tongue (TOT) study. *Language & Cognitive Processes, 25*(10), 1301–1334.

Kahn, H., & Till, R. (1991). Pronoun reference and aging. *Developmental Neuropsychology, 7,* 459–475.

Kavé, G., Eyal, N., Shorek, A., Cohen-Mansfield, J. (2008). Multilingualism and cognitive state in the oldest old. *Psychology and Aging, 23,* 70–78.

Kelly, L., Keaten, J. A., & Finch, C. (2004). Reticent and non-reticent college students' preferred communication channels for interacting with faculty. *Communication Research Reports, 21*(2), 197–209.

Kemper, S. (1987). Syntactic complexity and the recall of prose by middle-aged and elderly adults. *Experimental Aging Research, 13,* 47–52.

Kemper, S., Rash, S., Kynette, D., & Norman, S. (1990). Telling stories: The structure of adults' narratives. *European Journal of Cognitive Psychology, 2,* 205–228.

Kemper, S., Thompson, M., & Marquis, J. (2001). Effects of aging and dementia on grammatical complexity and propositional content. *Psychology and Aging, 16,* 600–614.

Kempler, D., & Van Lancker, D. (1988). Proverb and idiom comprehension in Alzheimer's disease. *Alzheimer's Disease and Associated Disorders, 2,* 38–49.

Kemtes, K. A., & Kemper, S. (1997). Younger and older adults' on-line processing of syntactically ambiguous sentences. *Psychology and Aging, 12,* 362–371.

Kertesz, A., Jesso, S., Harciarek, M., Blair, M., & McMonagle, P. (2010). What is semantic dementia?: A cohort study of diagnostic features and clinical boundaries. *Archives of Neurology, 67*(4), 483–489.

Kiran, S., & Bassetto, G. (2008). Evaluating the effectiveness of semantic-based treatment for naming deficits in aphasia: What works? *Seminars in Speech and Language. 29,* 71–82.

Kynette, D., & Kemper, S. (1986). Aging and the loss of grammatical forms. *Language and Communication, 6,* 65–72.

Lambert, W. (1972). *Language, psychology, and culture.* Palo Alto, CA: Stanford University Press.

Lamm, O., & Epstein, R. (1999). Left-handedness and achievements in foreign language studies. *Brain and Language, 70,* 504–517.

Landro, L. (2010, July 6). Taking medical jargon out of doctors' visits. *Wall Street Journal, Eastern Edition,* pp. D1–D2.

Larsby, B., Hällgren, M., & Lyxell, B. (2008). The interference of different background noises on speech processing in elderly hearing impaired subjects. *International Journal of Audiology, 47,* Suppl 2S83–S90.

Lenneberg, E. (1967). *Biological foundations of language.* New York: Wiley.

Llewellyn, D. J., & Matthews, F. E. (2009). Increasing levels of semantic verbal fluency in elderly English adults. *Aging, Neuropsychology, and Cognition, 16*(4), 433–445.

Lorenzen, B., & Murray, L. L. (2008). Bilingual aphasia: A theoretical and clinical review. *American Journal of Speech-Language Pathology, 17*(3), 299–317.

Lyall, S. (2003, August 15). Britain: No love, dears. *New York Times.*

Mahoney, J. R., Verghese, J., Goldin, Y., Libton, R., & Holtzer, R. (2010). Alerting, orienting, and executive attention in older adults, *Journal of the International Neuropsychological Society, 16,* 877–899.

Martin, J. (2005). *Miss Manners' guide to excruciatingly correct behavior, freshly updated.* New York: Norton.

McFarland, K., Rhoades, D., Roberts, E., & Eleazer, P. (2006). Teaching communication and listening skills to medical students using life review with older adults. *Gerontology and Geriatrics Education, 27*(1), 81–94.

McNamara, P., Obler, L., Au, R., Durso, R. & Albert, M. (1992). Speech repair processes in Alzheimer's disease, Parkinson disease and normal aging. *Brain and Language, 42,* 35–51.

Meddeb, E. J., & Frenz-Belkin, P. (2010). What? I Didn't Say THAT!: Linguistic strategies when speaking to write. *Journal of Pragmatics, 42*(9), 2415–2429.

Menn, L., & Obler, L. K. (Eds.). (1990). Summary chapter. *Agrammatic aphasia: A cross-language narrative sourcebook.* Amsterdam: Benjamins.

Michel, J-B., Shen, Y. K., Aiden, A. P., Veres, A., Gray, M. K., Brockman, W., . . . & Aiden, E. L. (2011). Quantitative analysis of culture using millions of digitized books. *Science, 14,* 176–182

Miles, K. S., & Cottle, J. L. (2011). Beyond plain language: A learner-centered approach to pattern jury instructions. *Technical Communication Quarterly, 20*(1), 92–112.

Motschenbacher, H. (2007). Can the term "Genderlect" be saved? A postmodernist re-definition. *Gender and Language, 1*(2), 255–278.

Murray, L. L. (2008). Language and Parkinson's disease. *Annual Review of Applied Linguistics,* 28113–281127.

Murray, L. (2010). Distinguishing clinical depression from early Alzheimer's disease in elderly people: can narrative analysis help? *Aphasiology, 24*(6–8), 928–939.

Newman, R., & German, D. (2005). Life span effects of lexical factors on oral naming. *Language and Speech, 48,* 123–156.

Ngandu, T., von Strauss, F., Helkala, E., Winblad, B., Nissinen, A., Tuomilehto, J., & . . . Kivipelto, M. (2007). Education and dementia: What lies behind the association? *Neurology, 69*(14), 1442–1450.

Nicholas, M., Obler, L., Albert, M., & Goodglass, H. (1985). Lexical retrieval in healthy aging and in Alzheimer's dementia. *Cortex, 21,* 595–606.

Nicholas, M., Obler, L. K., Au, R., & Albert, M. L. (1996). On the nature of naming errors in aging and dementia: A study of semantic relatedness. *Brain and Language, 54,* 184–195.

Novoa, L., Fein, D., & Obler, L. (1988). A neuropsychological study of an exceptional second language learner. In L. Obler & D. Fein (Eds.), *The exceptional brain: The neuropsychology of talent and special abilities.* New York: Guilford Press.

Obler, L. (1980). Narrative discourse style in the elderly. In L. Obler & M. Albert (Eds.), *Language and communication in the elderly.* Lexington, MA: D.C. Heath.

Obler, L. K., & Albert, M. L. (1977). Influence of aging on recovery from aphasia in polyglots. *Brain and Language, 4,* 460–463.

Obler, L., Fein, D., Nicholas, M., & Albert, M. L. (1991). Auditory comprehension and aging: Decline in syntactic processing. *Journal of Applied Psycholinguistics, 12,* 433–452.

Obler, L., Nicholas, M., Albert, M. L., & Woodward, S. (1985). On comprehension across the adult life span. *Cortex, 21,* 273–280.

Papagno, C., Lucchelli, F., Muggia, S., & Rizzo, S. (2003). Idiom comprehension in Alzheimer's disease. The role of the central executive. *Brain, 126*(11), 2419–2430.

Patterson, K., Graham, N., & Hodges, J. R. (1994). Reading in dementia of the Alzheimer type: A preserved ability? *Neuropsychology, 8,* 395–407.

Rapp, A. M., & Wild, B. (2011). Nonliteral language in Alzheimer Dementia: A review. *Journal of the International Neuropsychological Society, 17*(2), 207–218.

Rebok, G. W., Carlson, M. C., & Langbaum, J. S. (2007). Training and maintaining memory abilities in healthy older adults: Traditional and novel approaches. *Journals of Gerontology Series B: Psychological Sciences & Social Sciences, 62B,* 53–61.

Reilly, J., Peelle, J. E., Antonucci, S. M., & Grossman, M. (2011). Anomia as a marker of distinct semantic memory impairments in Alzheimer's disease and semantic dementia. *Neuropsychology, 25,* 413–426.

Reilly, J., Rodriguez, A. D., Lamy, M., & Neils-Strunjas, J. (2010). Cognition, language, and clinical pathological features of non-Alzheimer's dementias: An overview. *Journal of Communication Disorders, 43*(5), 438–452.

Rochon, E., Waters, G., & Caplan, D. (2000). The relationship between measures of working memory and sentence comprehension in patients with Alzheimer's disease. *Journal of Speech, Language & Hearing Research, 43*(2), 395–413.

Romaine, S. (1984). *The language of children and adolescents: The acquisition of communicative competence.* Oxford, UK: Blackwell.

Ross, E. D., & Monnot, M. (2008). Neurology of affective prosody and its functional-anatomic organization in right hemisphere. *Brain and Language, 104*(1), 51–74.

Saddichha, S., & Pandey, V. (2008). Alzheimer's and non-Alzheimer's dementia: A critical review of pharmacological and nonpharmacological strategies. *American Journal of Alzheimer's Disease and Other Dementias, 23*(2), 150–161.

Shargorodsky, J., Curhan, S., Curhan, G., & Eavey, R. (2010). Change in prevalence of hearing loss in U.S. adolescents. *JAMA: The Journal of the American Medical Association, 304*(7), 772–778.

Shaw, S. (2000). Language, gender and floor apportionment in political debates. *Discourse & Society, 11,* 401–418.

Sherratt, S. (2007). Right brain damage and the verbal expression of emotion: A preliminary investigation. *Aphasiology, 21*(3–4), 320–339.

Skinner, B. F. (1983). Intellectual self-management in old age. *American Psychologist, 38,* 239–244.

Smith, B., Wasowicz, J., & Preston, J. (1987). Temporal characteristics of the speech of normal elderly adults. *Journal of Speech and Hearing Research, 30,* 522–529.

Smith, N., Tsimpli, I., Morgan, G., & Woll, B. (2011). *The signs of a savant: Language against the odds,* Cambridge, UK: Cambridge University Press.

Snow, C.E. (1998). Bilingualism and second language acquisition. In J. Berko Gleason & N Bernstein Ratner (Eds.), *Psycholinguistics* (2nd ed., pp. 391–416). New York: Harcourt Brace.

Sparks, R., Helm, N., & Albert, M. (1974). Aphasia rehabilitation resulting from melodic intonation therapy. *Cortex, 10*(4), 303–316.

Sparks, R. L., Patton, J., Ganschow, L., & Humbach, N. (2009). Long-term relationships among early first language skills, second language aptitude, second language affect, and later second language proficiency. *Applied Psycholinguistics, 30*(4), 725–755.

St-Pierre, M., Ska, B., & Beland, R. (2005). Lack of coherence in the narrative discourse of patients with dementia of the Alzheimer's type. *Journal of Multilingual Communication Disorders, 3*(3), 211–215.

Tannen, D. (1990). *You just don't understand: Women and men in conversation.* New York: Morrow.

Tomoeda, C., & Bayles, K. (1993). Longitudinal effects of Alzheimer's disease on discourse production. *Alzheimer Disease and Associated Disorders, 7,* 223–236.

Ulatowska, H., Cannito, M., Hayashi, M., & Fleming, S. (1985). Language abilities in the elderly. In H. Ulatowska (Ed.), *The aging brain: Communication in the elderly.* San Diego, CA: College-Hill Press.

U.S. Census Bureau (2009). *American FactFinder.* Retrieved February 2011 from www.census.gov/popest/national/asrh/NC-EST2009-sa.html

Vogel, I., Verschuure, H., & Van Der Ploeg, C. B. (2010). Estimating adolescent risk for hearing loss based on data from a large school-based survey. *American Journal of Public Health, 100*(6), 1095–1100.

Wagner, L., Greene-Havas, M., & Gillespie, R. (2010). Development in children's comprehension of linguistic register. *Child Development, 81,* 1678–1686.

Wharry, C. (2003). Amen and Hallelujah preaching: Discourse functions in African American sermons. *Language in Society, 32*(2), 203–225.

Wingfield, A., Prentice, K., Koh, C., & Little, D. (2000). Neural change, cognitive reserve and behavioral compensation in rapid encoding and memory for spoken language in adult aging. In L. Connor & L. K. Obler (Eds.), *Neurobehavior of language and cognition: Studies of normal aging and brain damage.* Boston: Kluwer Academic.

Glossary

This glossary defines key words as they are used in this book. When they first appear in the text, they are in **boldface,** and each chapter also contains a list of its key words. Many of the words (i.e., *competence, assimilation*) are technical terms in linguistics or psychology that have very different meanings in other contexts.

AAE (African American English), AAVE, BAE African American English, African American Vernacular English, Black American English. See *African American English.*

academic language Language, often required in school settings, that focuses on things that are not immediately present, for instance descriptions, definitions, and narratives.

actional verbs Verbs that describe a dynamic action and that have a volitionally acting agent (e.g., *take, hit, chase*). A more common term is *action verbs.*

activation nodes Processing units in parallel distributed processing (PDP) models that are meant to resemble or model individual neurons or assemblies of neurons in the brain.

additive bilingualism Acquisition of a second language while retaining one's original language.

affricates Sounds that are a combination of a stop and fricative, such as the voiced sound at the beginning of *judge* or the unvoiced sound at the beginning of *church*. The term "affricative" is sometimes used with the same meaning.

African American English (AAE) A variety of English spoken by many African Americans that is characterized by its phonological, syntactic, and pragmatic features.

agglutinative Characterizes languages like Turkish, which add separate inflectional suffixes for masculine, plural, and so on, in a predictable order. Contrasts with *synthetic.*

allomorph Any one of the possible phonetic forms of a morpheme; for example, the English possessive ending, spelled *s*, has three allomorphs: /s/, /z/, and /əz/. Which allomorph is used depends on the final sound of the word.

alphabetic principle The basic principle that underlies our orthographic system: Letters of the alphabet represent the sounds of our spoken language.

alveolar Refers to any consonant made with the tongue near or touching the alveolar ridge, behind the upper front teeth. English alveolar consonants include /t/, /d/, /n/, /s/, and /z/, as well as some varieties of /l/.

Alzheimer's disease (also DAT, Dementia of the Alzheimer's Type) A progressive dementia characterized by the presence of neuronal plaques and tangles in the cerebral cortex.

American Sign Language See *ASL.*

amplification The use of hearing aids to improve impaired hearing ability.

analytic style An early language acquisition strategy displayed by infants who have good comprehension and pay particular attention to individual words, rather than to phrases. Contrasts with *rote/ holistic style.*

anaphora Referring back to previous discourse through the use of pronouns, definite articles, and other linguistic devices. For example, "I saw a rainbow. *It* was beautiful."

anomia Aphasic difficulty in retrieving words.

anomic aphasia See *anomia*; the variety of aphasia whose most evident symptom is anomia.

aphasia Loss or impairment of language ability because of brain damage. Aphasic syndromes vary, depending on the site of the damage.

393

applied behavior analysis (ABA) A system based on the principles of learning theory that is designed to examine or change behavior in a measurable way; this typically includes interventions with clear objectives, based on an experimental design.

arcuate fasciculus A band of subcortical fibers connecting Broca's area and Wernicke's area in the left hemisphere of the human brain. See *conduction aphasia.*

articulatory phonetics The study of the types of sounds produced by different shapes of the vocal tract when people are speaking. This knowledge allows language teachers and speech-language pathologists to help students and clients pronounce words more accurately. (The study of the sound waves produced by speech sounds is called acoustic phonetics, and it allows scientists to synthesize speech by reproducing the acoustic patterns.)

ASD See *autism spectrum disorder*

ASL American Sign Language. A complete language, related historically to French, this is the manual language used by the Deaf community in the United States.

Asperger syndrome An autism spectrum disorder named for the Viennese physician who first described it. Affected individuals have normal IQs and may have exceptional talent in some domains, while at the same time lacking skills in pragmatics and social interaction.

assimilation Changing a sound in a word to make it more similar to an adjacent or nearby sound in that word or a neighboring word; for example, assimilation leads us to pronounce *greenbeans* as *greembeans* or a small child to produce *truck* as *guck.*

audiologist A professional who has the training and equipment to test the auditory acuity of a subject. If a child does not appear to be acquiring language in typical fashion, one of the first steps is to have her hearing tested by an *audiologist.*

auditory verbal therapy A therapy for children with hearing impairment that emphasizes the use of hearing (residual or that provided by hearing aids or cochlear implants) to listen to and use speech.

augmentative or alternative communication (AAC) Any of a number of ways, such as communication boards, designed to help individuals with disabilities to communicate.

aural rehabilitation The provision of therapy and training to individuals with hearing impairment.

autism A severe disorder, usually diagnosed in childhood and probably neurological in origin, characterized by stereotypic behavior and a broad range of social, communicative, and intellectual deficiencies.

autism spectrum disorder (ASD) A broad term that refers to autism as well as a number of other, related developmental disorders that share some of the characteristics of autism; these include conditions such as *Asperger syndrome* and *Rett syndrome.*

automaticity/automatized The potential of a process to be completed with great speed after long practice, without allocating conscious attention to it. When a cognitive process becomes automatic, it does not require extra time or processing capacity.

avoidance A strategy employed by some children as they acquire the phonology of their language: They may avoid some sounds or sound sequences, while exploiting others (see *exploitation*).

baby talk One of many names for the speech register used with young children (see *CDS*). The term is sometimes also used to refer to the speech of young children.

back-channel feedback Verbal and nonverbal behaviors that indicate to the speaker continuing attention and satisfactory comprehension or the lack thereof—for example, head nods, quizzical expressions, "uh-huh," "I see," "huh?"

basic-level category The level of abstraction that is most generally appropriate in a given situation or for the given speaker—for example, *dog* rather than *animal* or *collie.*

behavioral intervention Guiding one's own or another's overt behavior through the use of techniques based on the principles of learning (shaping, reinforcement, etc.).

bilabial A sound, such as /p/, /m/, or the /β/ of Cuba in Spanish, that is produced with the two lips touching or very close together.

bilingual Involving two languages; a person who speaks two languages.

bilingual/bicultural (bi-bi) approach to deaf education A philosophy of teaching that recognizes the authenticity and importance of both hearing and Deaf cultures, and that incorporates elements of both in the classroom. Programs are modeled on English as a Second Language (ESL) programs.

bimodal fitting of cochlear implants A method of improving deaf children's ability to hear prosody, intonation, or tone by providing a cochlear implant in one ear and a conventional hearing aid for the other ear.

binding principles According to government and binding theory, these are part of the rules of our grammar that dictate the relation between words such as pronouns and their referents.

biological capacity Innate factors, which are those present in the organism by virtue of its genetic makeup.

bottom-up models/processing A term taken from artificial intelligence research to depict the *direction* of processing. In bottom-up models of reading, the process of reading depends on accurate decoding of the letter strings that make up words.

bound morpheme A morpheme that must always be attached ("bound") to at least one other morpheme; it cannot stand alone (e.g., the *s* in *cats*).

Broca's aphasia See *Broca's area*.

Broca's area Area of the left hemisphere in the frontal region of the brain. Damage to this area usually results in aphasia characterized by difficulty in producing speech.

canonical form A sequence of phonological features (and perhaps one or two phonemes) expressing the properties that a group of highly similar words have in common, such as CVCV (consonant-vowel-consonant-vowel) or /CVs/ (consonant-vowel-/s/). Essentially the same concept as *template*.

categorical discrimination Two sounds with the same magnitude of acoustic difference are heard as different sounds (discriminated) if they fall into different phonemic categories, but they are heard as the same sound if they are from the same phonemic category.

CDS Child-directed speech. The special speech register used when talking to children, including short sentences, greater repetition and questioning, and higher and more variable intonation than that of speech addressed to adults. See *baby talk*.

center-embedded relative clause In English, a relative clause that modifies a main-clause subject and that therefore is positioned in the center of a main clause (i.e., between the head noun of the subject and the verb phrase, as in, for example, "The man *who lives next to my sister* is a doctor").

cerebral palsy A congenital motor disability that can affect an individual's ability to produce oral language. Various subgroups of individuals with cerebral palsy exist (e.g., ataxic, spastic), reflecting damage to distinct areas of the brain before or at birth.

CHAT Codes for the Human Analysis of Transcripts. CHAT is the part of *CHILDES* that contains rules for how to prepare transcripts of language that can be analyzed by computer programs.

child-directed speech See both *CDS* and *baby talk*.

CHILDES Child Language Data Exchange System. A major Web-based resource for language development researchers, containing rules for transcription (see *CHAT*), computer programs for analyzing language (see *CLAN*), and a database of language transcripts.

circumlocution A way of talking *about* something without naming it directly. For instance, saying "The thing you hit nails with" rather than *hammer*.

CLAN Acronym for the computerized Child Language Analysis programs that are part of the *CHILDES* system.

classical concept A concept that can be characterized by unchanging criteria; for instance, a *triangle* can be defined as a three-sided figure.

classical conditioning A form of associative learning in which previously neutral stimuli (e.g., words), through repeated pairing with other stimuli, come to elicit similar responses. First described by the Russian psychologist I. Pavlov, who used this method to condition dogs to salivate at the sound of a bell.

cleft palate A congenital disability (caused by defects in the bone or tissue separating the oral and nasal cavities) that impairs control of the oral air pressure necessary for the articulation of many speech sounds.

closed-class word In language, this is one of a small group of words with a role that is basically grammatical, such as articles and prepositions in English.

cluster reduction An early pronunciation strategy some children employ, in which they simplify consonant clusters in words by leaving some out, for instance saying "tore" or "sore" instead of "store."

cochlear implant Device that is surgically implanted in the inner ear to stimulate the acoustic/auditory nerve of a person who is deaf.

cohesive device A way to link the content of different parts of a conversation through the use of pronouns, ellipsis, connectives, anaphora, and other conversational strategies.

comment An early communicative function, also called a *declarative*, in which an infant calls a caregiver's attention to something in the surroundings, often by gesturing or pointing.

Communication and Symbolic Behavior Scales (CSBS) An assessment tool that appraises the communicative competence (use of eye gaze, gestures, sounds, words, understanding, and play) of children who are 6–24 months old, or who function at levels that are typically seen at ages between 6 and 24 months.

communicative competence Linguistic competence plus knowledge of the social rules for language use. The speaker has phonological, morphological, syntactic, and semantic knowledge and the additional pragmatic knowledge necessary to use language appropriately in social situations. See *pragmatics*.

communicative functions The purposes for which language, vocalizations, and gesture are used in conveying various kinds of information to other people.

For instance, even infants use pre-speech sounds and gestures to express rejection, requests, and comments.

communicative pointing   One of the roots of language in the gestural and usage-based theoretical approach to language development.

communicative temptation tasks   Tasks designed to elicit communication efforts from an infant.

comp   A functional syntactic category; the category of complementizers (e.g., *that, if, whether*)—words that are used to embed a clause inside of another clause (e.g., "I doubt *whether* my passport will arrive on time").

competence   Linguists' term for the inner knowledge one has of language and all of its linguistic rules and structures. Compare *communicative competence*.

competition model   A model of language development based on PDP networks that assumes that various cues in the language environment compete with one another. The most available and reliable cues will be learned first. Developed by Bates and MacWhinney.

compound word   A word composed of two or more free morphemes (e.g., *blackboard, merry-go-round*); it may contain bound morphemes in addition to the free morphemes (e.g., *blackboards*).

comprehension   The understanding of language. Comprehension typically precedes *production,* and is governed by a different set of constraints.

conduction aphasia   An aphasic syndrome characterized by inability to repeat; typically resulting from damage to the arcuate fasciculus.

confrontation naming   The ability to name items when provided with visual stimuli.

congenital   Present at birth, but not necessarily genetic in origin.

connectionist models   Models of language or other mental processes that are meant to represent the neural architecture and activity of the human brain.

consonant   Any speech sound made by constricting the vocal tract enough to impede or substantially reduce airflow through the mouth. Consonants include stops, affricates, fricatives, nasal stops, and liquids. Glides (semivowels) are sometimes grouped with consonants.

consonant clusters   Two or more consonants that occur together in a word, without intervening vowels. Permissible sequences and position within the word (initial, medial, or final) are dictated by the phonological constraints of the language.

constraints   Limits or biases that children bring to the task of acquiring language; also, limits in the sound patterns that a language uses. A constraint may dictate

a cognitive strategy in the interpretation of words. One early constraint leads children to assume that a new word refers to a whole object rather than to a part of the object.

constructivism   The view of cognitive psychologists who believe that children develop cognitively through their own active participation in the world around them.

content validity   A measure of the goodness of a test, based on the relation between the contents of the test and what it purports to be testing. A language test with high content validity will test many areas representing real language use.

contingent comments   Comments made by one conversational partner that follow the topic of the other speaker.

contrast   A principle employed by many children in word learning: They assume that words contrast in meaning; no two words have the same meaning. See also *phonological contrast*.

controlling interactional style   A way of talking to infants that is *intrusive,* constantly redirecting the child's attention, in contrast to a *responsive style*.

coordinations   Grammatical combinations that can involve two or more words, phrases, or sentences connected by conjunctions (e.g., "Sue and her mother ate and drank.").

cued speech   A manual system used by some deaf children and their teachers/parents, which uses hand shapes near the mouth to help make lipreading easier.

DAT   See *Alzheimer's disease*

decibel (dB)   A measure of the loudness of a sound.

declarative communicative function   See *comment*.

decontextualized language   Language that makes reference to people, events, and experiences that are not part of the immediate context. See *extended discourse*.

deep orthography   An orthography (spelling system) in which there is a relatively variable relation (e.g., more than one to one) between graphemes and phonemes (see *shallow orthography*).

Dementia of the Alzheimer's Type (DAT)   See *Alzheimer's disease*

dementia   Loss of mental ability, typically through neurological impairment, such as Alzheimer's disease.

dementing disease   Any disease that causes a loss of mental ability.

derivational morpheme   A morpheme that can be used to derive a new word. See *derived word*.

derived word   A complex word made from a base morpheme to which various affixes have been added; for example, *unhappiness* is derived from *happy* by the addition of the affixes *un-* and *-ness.*

descriptive adequacy   Characteristic of a model or theory that assures that it is capable of describing and cataloging all relevant behaviors and distinguishing them from those that are not relevant.

developmental disfluency   A stage of normal child language development during which many children demonstrate stuttering-like behaviors.

dialect   A systematic subvariety of a language spoken by a sizable group of speakers sharing characteristics such as geographic origin or social class.

disfluencies   Breaks in the ongoing rhythm of speech, such as those caused by hesitations, repetitions, or the use of fillers such as "um," "well," and so on.

Down syndrome   A congenital condition, usually caused by trisomy of the 21st chromosome, often characterized by short stature, typical epicanthic eyefolds, and intellectual disability of varying degrees.

d-structure   In linguistic theory, refers to the level of a grammar that captures the relationship between subject and object in a sentence.

dual-language learners   Children learning two languages, bilinguals

dyslexia (developmental dyslexia)   Any one of a number of conditions that lead to a specific impairment in learning to read; dyslexias are typically linguistic processing problems rather than difficulties with perception.

early language delay (ELD)   Difficulty with language production and failure to combine words by the age of 2 years, in the presence of good comprehension.

echolalia   Repetition of all or part of another's utterance as one's turn in a conversation; common in children with autism, but also seen in normally developing young children.

egocentrism/egocentric speech   Piaget's concept meaning the inability to take another person's perspective. Speech not adapted to listener needs; for example, using color terms to direct the action of a blindfolded listener.

electroencephalography (EEG)   The neurophysiological measurement of electrical activity generated by the brain, which is measured via electrodes on the scalp.

ellipsis   The omission of a word or words from an utterance that would be necessary for a complete syntactic construction, but that are not necessary for understanding. A *cohesive device* used when understanding rests on referring back to earlier parts of the conversation.

emergent literacy   Children's understanding about reading and writing before they actually acquire these skills; this understanding is enhanced in households that engage in many reading and writing activities.

environmental print   Writing found on traffic signs, food and household goods, packaging, and so on. Often the first written words a child recognizes.

epigenetic   A principle espoused by Piaget that complex cognitive processes arise from simpler functions and that at each stage the organism reorganizes. Development thus proceeds in stages that are qualitatively different from one another.

etiology   The cause of a particular problem, such as hearing loss, which may arise from a large number of genetic and environmental conditions.

event-related potentials (ERPs)   Changes in electrical voltage at the scalp that are time-locked to the presentation of a particular experimental event, such as the presentation of an unexpected word. They can be used to examine phonological, semantic, and syntactic processing, among other things.

evidence-based practice (EBP)   The use of systematic reviews of therapeutic outcomes to guide intervention in fields such as medicine, education, and speech language pathology, among others. Practitioners are expected to make use of current best evidence when making intervention decisions.

executive function   The cognitive abilities that control and regulate behavior; they include the ability to start and stop actions, to monitor and change one's behavior when required by circumstances, and to develop and adjust appropriate strategies when faced with new and unexpected tasks and situations.

expansion   A feature of child directed speech in which the adult repeats back a child's telegraphic utterance with the nearest likely grammatical version. For instance, "The doggie is eating" in response to the child's "Doggie eat."

expository writing   Writing that depends upon logic, rather than chronology, as its organizational principle. Hierarchically organized language that is associated with the paradigmatic mode of thinking.

expressive/expressive style   A style of language use observed in toddlers that is characterized by the use of many personal-social terms.

extended discourse   Multi-utterance discourse that makes reference to people, events, and experiences that are not part of the immediate context. Examples include narratives and explanations.

Extended Optional Infinitive account of SLI   The hypothesis that children with specific language impairment (SLI) have failed to progress beyond the early stage of typical development, during which children learning English appear to believe that marking of tense in main clauses is optional.

faithful, faithfulness One of the groups of constraints employed by children acquiring phonology: Be as faithful to each of the sounds of the adult model as possible. Other constraints might prevent the child from producing the exact adult form, but the pressure to be faithful will increase the similarity.

fast mapping Children's ability to form an initial hypothesis about a word's meaning very quickly, after hearing it only once or twice; in-depth learning requires multiple exposures to the word in many different contexts, however.

feature-blind aphasia A grammatical deficit characterized by difficulty in using grammatical morphemes, such as the forms of the past tense. Some researchers have claimed that this disability is genetically determined.

folk etymology An explanation of a word's origin that is not based on the historical record, but rather on common sense or custom, for instance, "It's called *Friday* because that's the day you eat fried fish."

format/scaffold In Vygotskyian theory, adults are thought to provide intellectual interaction that serves as a scaffold, or format, that makes it possible for children to develop at a much faster rate than they could without this helpful intervention.

fragile X (fra X) A genetic disorder, most often seen in males, in which the X chromosome is defective and the affected individual may have communication problems.

free morpheme A morpheme that can stand alone (e.g., *cat*), as opposed to a bound morpheme.

free variation Allophones that can appear in the same environment without changes in meaning are said to be in *free variation*. For instance, /t/ can be released, unreleased, aspirated, or unaspirated when one says *hat*.

free word association A word association in which the subject responds freely with the first word that comes to mind.

fricative A speech sound produced partly or wholly by airstream friction, such as /s/ or /v/.

functional analysis One of many methods used in the treatment of children with developmental disorders; children's inappropriate behaviors are examined for motivation or function and replaced with more appropriate responses.

functional category A grammatical category within the *d-structure* of a sentence, containing inflectional, complementizer, and other similar elements.

functional magnetic resonance imaging (fMRI) An imaging technique that reveals neural activity in the brain by measuring accompanying changes in blood oxygen levels.

GAE (General American English) A standardized dialect of American English that does not have easily detected regional pronunciations, such as those found in the South, the West, parts of the Northeast, etc. This is the dialect typically used by television newscasters.

generalization A learning principle whereby what is learned in specific context is extended to new instances.

generalized slowing hypothesis An explanation of specific language impairment (SLI) that is based on the observation that children with SLI need about one-third more time to execute a range of perceptual and motor functions than typically developing children. SLI is believed to be related to the children's limited processing capacity.

genre Discourse that is specific to particular contexts and functions. Genres are characterized by consistencies in form and content.

glide A speech sound made with slightly more vocal tract constriction than a vowel and having shorter duration than a vowel. The sounds /j/ and /w/ are glides. They are also referred to as semivowels.

global aphasia Aphasia resulting from extensive brain damage; the patient has poor comprehension and little voluntary language. See *aphasia*.

glottal Pertaining to the *glottis*.

glottis The opening at the upper part of the larynx, between the vocal folds.

government and binding theory (GB) A model of grammar descended from earlier transformational generative models. It proposes only one type of transformation (movement of elements), the specification of possible grammatical frames for lexical items and their mapping onto the syntax of sentences, and universal constraints on possible syntactic rules, among many other notions.

grapheme–phoneme correspondence rules Rules that define the relationship between a letter or group of letters and the sound they represent.

graphemes The actual graphic forms or elements of the writing system; the letters of the alphabet, for example.

head/head of a noun phrase A word (e.g., *dog, push, whether, will*) or abstract feature (e.g., *[past tense], [present tense]*) that is the central component of a phrase; the syntactic category of the head of a phrase determines the syntactic category of the phrase that contains it. For example, a noun must be the head of a noun phrase.

head-turn preference procedure (HPP) A method of testing very young infants' linguistic knowledge or preferences by measuring the amount of time they turn their heads in the direction of a sound file.

hearing impairment Loss or inability to hear sounds; children who cannot hear sounds below 60 decibels do not usually develop typical oral language.

high-amplitude sucking paradigm (HAS) A technique used to study infant perceptual abilities. Typically involves recording an infant's sucking rate as a measure of her attention to various stimuli.

hyperlexia Unusually advanced lexical ability. Often seen in children with Williams syndrome.

imitation The act of copying the behavior of another, either immediately or after a delay; no longer thought to be the mechanism whereby children acquire language. Imitation is one of the techniques used by therapists in helping children with language difficulties: The child is taught to imitate the productions of the therapist.

immersion Settings in which a group of learners are all taught a new language through the medium of the new language.

imperative communicative function An early communicative function, in which an infant indicates that she wants the caregiver to perform some action.

Index of Productive Syntax, IPsyn A method of evaluating children's spontaneous language that relies on scoring a sample for the presence of various grammatical forms.

indirect request A form of request whose surface structure does not indicate that the utterance is a request (e.g., a hint).

Individuals with Disabilities Education Act (IDEA) U.S. federal legislation that mandates that children with communicative disorders be treated in the least restrictive and most inclusive environments.

infant-directed speech Speech directed at infants that contains special modifications (e.g., high fundamental frequency, variable intonation). See *baby talk, CDS.*

Infl A functional syntactic category that is thought to be the head of a clause (an InflP) in some syntactic theories, and that contains information about the tense of the clause. The Infl position hosts tense-bearing auxiliary verbs like *could* and *will,* as well as abstract features such as *[past tense].*

inhibition In the sense used by cognitive psychologists, the ability to ignore irrelevant stimuli. This seems to become more difficult with advancing age.

innate Present at birth, part of an organism's essential nature.

intellectual disability A condition in which most cognitive abilities are depressed on standardized measures such as intelligence quotient (IQ) or other related measures, leading to functional limitations in both general learning and adaptive skills. The term replaces the former label *mental retardation.*

intentional communication Any communicative act that an individual engages in purposefully.

interdental Speech sound made by placing the tongue between the teeth; the initial sounds of *this* or *thing* in English.

internalized representation The mental, or inner cognitive image or map of external reality.

intonation contour The pattern of rhythmic stress and pitch across an utterance. In English, a falling pitch at the end of an utterance typically indicates a statement, whereas a final rising pitch usually marks an interrogative.

intrusive interactional style A way of interacting with an infant in which the caregiver is constantly controlling and redirecting the child's attention.

invented spelling Systematic, rule-governed spelling that is created (invented) by developing writers.

IPA International Phonetic Alphabet. A set of standardized symbols used to represent the speech sounds of the world's languages in an unambiguous way.

IPsyn See *Index of Productive Syntax.*

irony Using words to convey the opposite of their literal meaning, for example, "It's so clean in here," said of a messy dorm room.

jargon A term with several different meanings. In normal adults, *jargon* refers to a specialized vocabulary associated with the workplace or particular activities; in infants, *jargon* is a form of babbling with conversational intonation; in patients with aphasia, nonsense words are *jargon.*

joint attention Mutual attention between child and parent

joint focus Situation in which two individuals are paying attention to the same thing at the same time, as in reading a book together.

labial Any speech sound made by bringing the lips close together or making them touch one another. The English labials are /p/, /b/, and /m/.

labiodental Any speech sound made by bringing the lower lip close to or in contact with the upper teeth. The English labiodentals are the fricatives /f/ and /v/.

LAD Language acquisition device. The innate mental mechanism that, according to linguistic theorists, makes language acquisition possible.

language acquisition device See *LAD*.

language age (LA) A measure of a child's language development, based on her *mean length of utterance*.

language faculty A general term that refers to the innate ability to acquire language. Linguists believe that humans, and not other animals, possess a language faculty.

lateralization, lateralized The process whereby one side of the brain becomes specialized for particular functions; for instance, the left side becomes *lateralized* for language.

learnability The question as to whether something, like language, can be *learned*. See *learnability problem*.

learnability problem The fact that children master their native tongues across the world in spite of the supposed indecipherable nature of language has come to be called the *learnability problem* by nativists who believe that children cannot learn language from what they hear.

learnability theories Various models of language acquisition based on several assumptions concerning the nature of children, known learning mechanisms, and the structure of language and the logical inferences that may be drawn from these assumptions. Developed by Pinker, Wexler, and others.

letter recognition Detection of the features of a letter.

lexical category One of the categories of the *d-structure* that includes *content words* and their meanings, according to *government and binding theory*.

lexical selection A kind of preference that some young children have for particular sounds in their language. A child might, for instance, have many early words ending in /k/ because of a preference for this phoneme

limited-scope formulae Simple combinatorial rules followed by children at the two-word stage of language development.

linguistic competence See *competence*.

lipreading (speechreading) Decoding the language of a speaker by paying close attention to the face and mouth, without being able to hear the speaker's voice.

liquid A consonantal speech sound made with less oral constriction than a fricative but more constriction than a glide. The English liquids are /l/ and /r/.

logical form The component of the *s-structure* in *government and binding theory* that captures the meaning of the sentence and connects it to other parts of cognition.

long-distance question A question involving movement of the *wh*-word (e.g., *what, who*) across more than one clause, as in "What did Mary tell Jane that we should get?"

lower articulators In articulatory phonetics, the lower articulators are the lower parts of the mouth where sounds are made (articulated). This includes the lower teeth, lip, and tongue.

low-structured observation A method of studying young children that often relies upon free play with a standard set of toys.

MacArthur-Bates Communicative Development Inventories (CDI) Norms that are available for various aspects of language development, based on a large study that collected mothers' reports on their children's communicative behaviors. There are two scales, one for infants and one for toddlers.

magnetoencephalography (MEG) A brain imaging technique that measures the tiny magnetic changes that occur along with the electrical changes caused by cortical activation.

mainstreaming The practice of including children with disabilities into regular classrooms instead of keeping them apart in special classes.

manner of articulation In articulatory phonetics, the way in which a speech sound is produced. For instance, if the air stream is blocked completely (as in /p/ or /k/), the sounds are called *stops*.

Markov sentence models Processing models of sentence production that assume that the probability of the next word to appear in a sentence is determined by the words that have already occurred.

matched-guise model An experimental paradigm in which listeners make judgments about the characteristics of speakers of different languages or dialects, without knowing that the supposed speakers are actually just one person who is multilingual. This makes it possible to show attitudes toward the language, since the speaker is constant.

mean length of utterance See *MLU*.

mental age (MA) A measure of a child's intelligence, based on answers to age-graded questions (typical of standard IQ tests). For instance, a 6-year-old who can answer questions that are most typically answered only by 8-year-olds will be said to have a mental age of 8.

mental retardation See *intellectual disability*.

meta-analysis Analysis of the results a number of studies, for instance of the existing literature on gender differences in children's language.

metalinguistic knowledge (awareness) Knowledge about language, for example, an understanding of what a word is and a consciousness of the sounds of language. The ability to think about language.

metaphor Figure of speech in which one thing is called by the name of another to indicate the similarities between them, for example, "This room is a pigpen."

minimal pair A pair of words that differ in meaning and whose sounds are the same except for one phonetic segment. For example, *ram/ran* form a *minimal pair* that differ only in the final consonant; *ram/rim* form a minimal pair that differ only with respect to the vowel.

mirror neuron A neuron that fires both when performing an action and when observing the same action performed by another.

MLU Mean length of utterance. A measure applied to children's language to gauge syntactic development; the average length of the child's utterances is calculated in morphemes.

model adequacy Characteristic of a theory or model that includes principles that can account for the relevant behaviors.

modeling A therapeutic technique in which the therapist enacts the desired behavior as a model for the client.

monophthong Vowel sounds that do not change into glides as they are pronounced. In English, the vowel in *hot* is a monophthong, whereas the vowel in *hate* is *diphthongized*.

morpheme A minimal meaningful unit of language. A *free morpheme* (e.g., *cat*) can stand alone. A *bound morpheme* (e.g., the plural *s* in *cats*) must always be connected to another morpheme.

morphology The rules that govern the use of morphemes in a language; for instance, the *morphology* of English requires plural endings to be added after derivational endings like –ness or –ity, and their sound to vary according to the last sound of the word stem. The rules about the sounds of morphemes are also more specifically called *morphophonology*.

morphophonology The rules governing sound changes that accompany the combination of morphemes in a language.

motherese Speech addressed to language-learning infants and children, also called child-directed speech (CDS), characterized by distinctive prosodic, lexical, and syntactic differences from adult-directed speech (ADS). Most researchers in the field avoid this term.

mutual exclusivity A cognitive bias shown by young children, who typically avoid labeling anything at more than one level of generality; hence, they may refer to their pet as a "dog," but not also as an "animal."

narrative mode Thinking that reflects human intentions and is organized around chronology.

narrative writing Writing that uses the sequence of events in time as its organizational principle.

narratives Stories, usually about the past. A minimum narrative consists of two sequential clauses, temporally ordered, about a single past event.

nasal assimilation Changing a sound into a nasal sound that increases its similarity to other sounds in a word. A child might, for instance, say "mump" rather than "bump."

nasal/nasal stop A speech sound made with the velum lowered so that air can escape through the nose. A nasal stop lets air out only through the nose, not through the mouth. English nasal stops include /m/, /n/, and /ŋ/ (the sound at the end of *sing*).

nativism A theoretical approach emphasizing the innate, possibly genetic contributions to any behavior.

Near-Infrared Spectroscopy (NIRS) A brain imaging technique that measures cortical activity by detecting changes in hemoglobin levels.

negation The process of making a sentence negative, usually by adding *no* or *not* and auxiliary articles, when appropriate.

negative evidence Evidence concerning language errors or unacceptable combinations of sounds or words.

neglected children Children whose caregivers have not given them sufficient physical, emotional, or intellectual support to ensure healthy development.

neologism A new, made-up word, often not a word in the language, as when a Wernicke's aphasic patient refers to an ashtray as a "fremser."

nominal strategy Choice of words by young children who prefer to use nouns in their early two-word sentences, rather than pronouns.

nominalist fallacy The belief that simply naming a phenomenon also sufficiently explains that phenomenon.

nonreflexive vocalizations Describing a process that has some voluntary component. Reflexive crying in infants soon develops into nonreflexive crying.

nonword repetition (NWR) A task involving the ability to repeat nonsense words that differ in length. It is often impaired in specific language impairment and other communicative disorders.

null-subject parameter See *parameter*.

object-gap relative clause A relative clause in which there is a gap in the position of the object of the verb (e.g., the verb *ride* has no object in the phrase, "the horse *that the boy rode*"). In such structures, the understood object of the verb corresponds to the noun that the relative clause modifies (e.g., the horse).

obstruent Any speech sound that constricts the vocal tract enough to cause airstream friction or that closes it off entirely. The obstruents of a language consist of the stops, affricates, and fricatives.

onset and rime *Onset* refers to the initial consonant or group of consonants in a syllable, and *rime* refers to the remainder of the syllable.

ontological categories Concepts about how the world is organized that young children have before they begin to learn language.

open-class word A content word, such as a noun, verb, adjective, or adverb. Unlike closed-class words, new open-class words are often created.

optimality theory A phonological theory that outlines constraints on pronounceable sounds and sound sequences. It lists typical constraints that speakers prefer not to violate, such as "Every syllable should begin with one consonant followed by a vowel."

optional-infinitive stage A stage in early childhood (ages 2 to 3 years), during which children sometimes include tense inflections on their main clauses (unembedded clauses) and sometimes fail to include tense inflections in this context—producing infinitive verb forms instead.

oral/aural approach to deaf education An approach to deaf education that emphasizes auditory training, articulation ability, and *lipreading*.

ostension Pointing to referent; a technique used by mothers in teaching basic-level categories (e.g., "That's your *shoe*.").

otitis media Infections of the middle ear, which may, if chronic, affect a child's speech and language development.

overextension Used here to refer to a child's use of a word in a broader context than is permissible in the adult language; for instance, a young child may call all men "Daddy." Parents who call tigers "kitty" are also producing overextensions.

overregularization errors A common tendency among children and second language learners, overregularization involves applying regular and productive grammatical rules to words that are exceptions, for example, *hurted* and *mouses*.

overregularized An irregular form that has been (incorrectly) made regular (e.g., *foots, holded*).

palatal, pre-palatal A speech sound made with the blade or center of the tongue touching or very close to the hard palate. In English, the initial sound of *yes* (IPA /j/) is a palatal. The initial sound of *shirt* may also be called palatal, or, since it is made a little further front than y, it may be described more precisely as pre-palatal.

paradigmatic mode Thinking that is logical and scientific.

parallel distributed processing/parallel processing (PDP) An information theory term that refers to activity taking place at many levels at once, rather than sequentially, as in *serial processing*. PDP models explain grammatical development by analogy with the kinds of associative links that computers can forge.

parameter According to current theory, a parameter is a kind of linguistic switch that the young learner "sets" after exposure to the language—one of a finite number of values along which languages are free to vary. For example, the so-called pro-drop (null-subject) parameter distinguishes languages such as English and German, which do not permit omission of lexical subjects, from languages such as Spanish or Italian, which do.

Parkinson's disease A progressive disease, subcortical in nature, with primary effects on speech rather than language.

parsimony A principle in theory building that holds that theorists should use the simplest of the available alternative explanations if they all describe the data equally well.

passives Sentences in which the object of action is highlighted: "The *girl* was kissed by the chimpanzee."

Percent of Consonants Correct (PCC) A way of measuring the accuracy of a child's pronunciation, by computing the percent of correct consonants used, compared with standard adult pronunciation of the same words.

performance Linguist's term for the production of speech. Contrasts with *competence,* which is almost always greater than performance.

perseveration The tendency to respond with responses that were previously supplied but are no longer appropriate; also, a difficulty in shifting attention to a new focus.

pervasive developmental disorder (PDD) One of a number of generalized developmental syndromes related to autism but typically not as severe.

pervasive developmental disorder—not otherwise specified (PDD-NOS) Severe disorder, but children do not fulfill criteria for other subtypes.

phone An individual speech sound, the realization of a *phoneme* in a particular context.

phoneme A speech sound that can signal a difference of meaning. Two similar speech sounds, *p* and *b,* represent different phonemes in English because there are pairs of words with different meanings that have the same phonetic form except that one contains *b* where the other contains *p*, for example, *pet* and *bet*. See *minimal pair*.

phonetic form   A major component of the *s-structure*, according to *government and binding theory*. The phonetic form is the actual sound structure of the sentence.

phonetic inventory   In studying children's phonological development, a phonetic inventory is a list of the speech sounds used, without any reference to the adult system of the language.

phonological awareness   A form of metalinguistic knowledge that includes the ability to recognize the sounds of language and to talk about them; one of the basic skills that underlies literacy.

phonological contrast   A difference between two sounds that can signal a difference in meaning, such as the difference between the vowels of *lip* and *leap* in English. (In many other languages, including Spanish and French, the difference between these two sounds cannot signal a difference in meaning).

phonological idiom   See *progressive phonological idiom*.

phonological recoding   The process whereby a letter string (written word) is decoded into its phonological representation, which can then be recognized as a word.

phonology   Study of the sound system of language; the sounds the language uses, as well as the rules for their combination.

phonotactic constraints   The restrictions separating permissible sequences of sounds in a language from sequences that the language never uses; for example, Spanish has a phonotactic constraint against starting words with /s/ + consonant sequences, and English has a phonotactic constraint against starting words with /ŋ/ or ending them with /h/.

phrase structure rules   A major part of the *d-structure*, according to *government and binding theory*, that captures the relation between subjects and predicates.

physiological substrate for language   The anatomical structures involved in learning, understanding, and producing spoken or signed language: the brain and the relevant perceptual and motor systems.

pivotal response training (PRT)   An intervention technique for children with autism spectrum disorders that uses behavioral techniques in the context of ongoing interactions between the child and those around him to reinforce social interaction and imitation skills

that are considered important for the development of further skills.

place of articulation/position of articulation   The point or points in the vocal tract where the upper and lower articulators come closest together in the production of a particular phone.

polyglot   A person who speaks several, or many, languages.

poverty of imagination   In linguistic theory, the notion that just because one cannot imagine how language might be learned, this does not prove that it was not learned (is innate).

poverty of the stimulus   In linguistic theory, the claim that the language that children hear is too imperfect (impoverished) for them to be able to grammatical systems, which must, therefore, be innately specified.

pragmatics   The rules for the use of language in social context and in conversation or the study of these rules.

preferential-looking paradigm   An experimental design used with prelinguistic infants that tracks their eye movements when they are presented with verbal stimuli.

prelingually deaf   Hearing impairment that occurs before the infant has learned to speak. Such impairments are typically more devastating than a loss that occurs after language is established.

prelinguistic/preverbal   Occurring before the infant can speak.

pre-palatal   See *palatal*.

prime/priming   Presentation of a stimulus (verbal or pictorial) meant to facilitate the retrieval of a target response. A subject who has seen the words *hospital* and *doctor* will recognize the word *nurse* more quickly than a subject who has not been similarly primed.

principle of contrast   Children's assumption that no two words have the same meaning. Hence they assume that a new word will not refer to something for which they already have a name.

principle of mutual exclusivity   See *mutual exclusivity*.

principles   Rules or maxims. Basic tenets of a theory.

probabilistic concept   A concept that is characterized by a variable set of criteria, unlike a *classical concept*. For instance, *bird* is a probabilistic concept, because no criterion defines it exclusively: A creature need not fly or have a beak or feathers to qualify as a bird.

production   The process of speaking.

productive/productivity   Referring to the regular forms of a language that are used in the formation of new words—regular plural endings, for instance.

progressive phonological idiom A word in a child's vocabulary that is pronounced more accurately than most other words of the same general adult target form. Idioms are an exception to the child's current set of rules and are progressive in the sense that they anticipate the ability the child will soon have.

pronominal strategy A preference for pronouns, rather than nouns, exhibited by some young children in their early speech. See *nominal strategy*.

prosodic features Aspects of the speech stream, such as stress and intonation, that convey differences in the meaning of words or sentences.

prototype An instance of a category that best exemplifies it; for example, a robin is a prototypical member of the category *bird*, because it has all of the important defining features.

protoword A sequence of sounds (used by a child) that has a relatively consistent meaning but is not necessarily based on any adult word. The terms phonetically consistent form and vocable are also used for this general notion.

psychological verbs Verbs that describe a psychological or perceptual experience (e.g., *see, like, think*), rather than overt, observable actions.

reading as decoding (phonics) An approach to the teaching of reading that explicitly emphasizes mastery of the alphabetic principle and grapheme–phoneme correspondence rules.

reading for meaning An approach to reading instruction that emphasizes inferential skills and treating texts as sources of meaning.

recast, recasting A form of parental utterance that restates the child's immature utterance in acceptable adult form. See *expansion*.

reduplicated babble Babbling in which consonant–vowel combinations are repeated, such as "ba-baba." Also called repetitive babbling.

referent The actual thing to which a particular word alludes—an actual cat, for instance—as opposed to the meaning of the word, which is a mental construct.

referential communication The manner in which one talks about a particular referent among an array of possible referents.

referential style A speech style observed in toddlers that is characterized by the use of nouns, and few personal social terms. See *expressive style*.

referential Said of speech that makes reference to the outside world, for instance, speech that names objects, as contrasted with speech that is expressive, or more social in nature.

reflexive vocalization A sound made involuntarily, such as a vegetative sound, a burp, cough, newborn cry, and so on.

register A form of language that varies according to participants, settings, and topics, such as *CDS*.

regression hypothesis The theory (not currently upheld) that in aphasia, speech is lost in mirror-image fashion to the order of acquisition.

regression A change backward from behavior that is more adultlike to behavior that is a poorer approximation of the adult model and representative of earlier stages of development.

rejection One of the communicative functions seen in infants; the purposeful termination of an interaction, for example, pushing a toy away while vocalizing.

relative clause A dependent clause that begins with a relative pronoun (*that, where, who,* etc.).

request An early function of a child's prelinguistic gestures or sounds—infants want things or they want adults to do things (like pick them up).

response to intervention (RTI) An approach to helping children at risk for academic failure by adjusting the classroom curriculum. Children continue to have academic problems may subsequently be referred for special needs.

responsive interactional style Manner of interacting with an infant that allows the infant to set the pace and determine the topics engaged in.

Rett syndrome A severe developmental disorder with a neural basis, seen more frequently in girls, in which the infant appears to be developing normally but then regresses, often losing the ability to speak and engaging in stereotypic behaviors such as hand wringing.

riddles Word games, usually in the form of questions, that play on linguistic ambiguity.

right-branching relative clause A relative clause that modifies the noun phrase to the right of the verb, and that therefore expands the number of branches on the right side of a syntactic tree, for example, "The coach wonders *whether the team will win the game.*"

rote/holistic style A style of early language acquisition characterized by the child's learning a number of phrases or unanalyzed expressions. Contrasts with *analytic style*.

routine A speech form that occurs as part of a routinized event (e.g., a greeting of "Trick or treat" on Halloween).

rule In child phonology, a systematic relationship between adult target sounds and the child's pronunciation of them. Some children's phonology is very rule-governed; other children have more holistic and less systematic ways of rendering adult words that they cannot yet pronounce correctly.

sarcasm A use of language meant to wound others or convey contempt, often accomplished by the use of exaggerated intonation patterns and ironic devices (e.g., saying "Thank you SO MUCH!" to the person who sat on your hat and crushed it). See *irony*.

scaffold See *format*

SCERTS (Social Communication, Emotional Regulation, and Transactional Support) An intervention for children with autism spectrum disorder that emphasizes the development of spontaneous, functional social communication, emotional regulation to promote skill learning, and increasing the frequency of positive social experiences across a variety of settings (transactional support).

script Abstract knowledge about familiar, everyday events. For instance, a child may have a birthday party script.

segment One of the constituents of speech. See *segmentation*.

segmentation Separation of the stream of speech into its constituents, for instance, breaking words into syllables and phonemes.

selection See *lexical selection*.

semantic aggravator A word or phrase that intensifies a request (e.g., "or else," "right now").

semantic development The acquisition of words and their many meanings and the development of that knowledge into a complex hierarchical network of associated meanings.

semantic feature One of the criteria by which a concept is defined and distinguished from other concepts. For instance, + male and + relative are two features of the concept *brother*.

semantic knowledge See *semantic development*.

semantic mitigator Word or phrase that softens a request (e.g., "please," giving reasons).

semantic network A word and all of the words that are related to it through various hierarchies of meaning. See *semantic development*.

semantic relations Characterizing the limited set of meanings conveyed by children's early utterances.

semantic roles The way in which nouns or noun phrases are used in a sentence, for instance as agent, patient, object, or location. See *thematic role*.

semantic transparency Obvious meaning. One of the principles children use in making new words: "plant man" for *gardener,* for instance.

semantics The study of the meaning system of language.

semivowel See *glide*.

sensitive interactional style A way of interacting with a language-learning child that takes its lead from the child's interest. For instance, the parent labels what the child is pointing at.

sentence modalities The basic forms that sentences may take, including declaratives, questions, and imperatives.

serial processing An information-processing term that refers to linear cognitive activity (e.g., first seeing a letter, then the next one, then reading the word, then understanding it). Contrasts with *parallel processing*, in which cognitive activity takes place on many levels at once.

set task A verbal task in which the respondent is required to produce particular types of items; for instance, to name in a short period of time as many items of clothing as possible or words beginning with a particular letter.

shallow orthography An orthography in which there exists a close relationship (one to one) between graphemes and the phonemes they represent (see also *deep orthography*).

signifying A type of sarcastic or witty language play generally used by some African American youth to make indirect comments upon socially significant topics.

signs Manual representations of words, the individual units of sign systems. See *ASL*.

simplicity One of the principles children follow in creating new words. They extend forms they already know to cover new situations, creating words like *bicycler* for one who rides a bicycle.

SLI (specific language impairment) Delayed or deviant language development in a child who exhibits no obvious cognitive, neurological, or social impairment.

social cognition Knowledge about other people that makes interpersonal interaction possible.

social routine Routinized speech used in social settings, such as "bye-bye."

sociolinguistics An approach to the study of language variation and adaptation that considers the ways social constructs (class, gender role, status, etc.) affect language and that makes use of observation of natural conversations.

sound play See *reduplicated babble, variegated babble*.

species specific Refers to the fact that language as we know it is specific to our species and not to others.

species uniform   Refers to the observation that the major milestones of language occur in the same way and at the same general time in all members of the species.

specific language impairment   See *SLI*.

speech acts   Utterances used by speakers in order to accomplish things in the world (such as requesting or apologizing).

speech–language pathologist   A professional who had been trained to assess, diagnose, and treat speech and language problems.

speechreading   See *lipreading*.

speed of processing   The rate at which an individual manages information. One of the hallmarks of aging is a decrement in speed of processing.

s-structure   One of the major levels of a grammar, according to *government and binding theory*. The s-structure contains the linear arrangement of words in the sentence.

statistical learning   In language learning, the learner's ability to use general cognitive mechanisms to make use of distributional cues in the input to derive rules for correct ordering of linguistic elements and co-occurrence probabilities in the language without resort to innate linguistic knowledge.

stop   A speech sound characterized by the total interruption of air flow through the mouth, such as in the phonemes /t/ and /b/ in English. See also *nasal stop*.

stress   Greater prominence on one or more syllables in a word; this may be due either to greater actual loudness, a marked change (usually a rise) in pitch, or greater length of the syllable.

stress pattern   The arrangement of stressed and unstressed syllables in a word. English has many related noun-verb pairs, like *a reject/ to reject,* which differ primarily in their stress pattern: The noun is stressed on the first syllable and the verb on the second syllable.

structured observation   A research design that imposes some consistency on observation by keeping some things constant, for instance, by bringing children into a laboratory playroom and giving each of them the same toys.

stuttering   Lack of fluency in speech, characterized by prolonged or repeated segments, often produced with extreme tension.

subject-gap relative clause   A relative clause in which there is a gap in the position of the subject of the verb (e.g., the verb *tickle* has no subject in the phrase "the walrus *that is tickling the zebra*"). In such structures, the understood subject of the verb corresponds to the noun that the relative clause modifies (e.g., the walrus).

subtractive bilingualism   Bilingualism characterized by the loss of one's original language while learning a second language.

suprasegmental   Parts of the phonological system that extend beyond individual sounds; examples are stress and intonation patterns.

surface hypothesis model of SLI   The hypothesis that children with specific language impairment (SLI) have difficulty processing grammatical forms that are unstressed or have little salience.

syntagmatic–paradigmatic shift   The change in word association patterns seen when children reach the age of about 7; where previously they responded with a word that typically follows in conversation (*eat: dinner*), after the shift takes place they respond, like adults, with the same part of speech (*eat: drink*).

syntax   The rules by which sentences are made, such forms as passives, declaratives, interrogatives, imperatives.

synthetic   Characteristic of languages that combine several grammatical inflections (e.g., third person, plural, past) into one form. Contrasts with *agglutinative*.

tap   A sound made quickly with the tip of the tongue, such as the consonant in the middle of the Spanish word *pero,* which is a different phoneme from the trilled sound in *perro*. English has a similar tap or flap in the middle of the word *water*.

TEACCH   Treatment and Education of Autistic and related Communication-Handicapped Children. A therapy based on the model of normal parent–child interaction.

telegraphic speech   Speech that consists of content words without functors, much like a telegram.

template   A phonological output pattern that a given child apparently prefers to use, often regardless of whether it is a good match to the adult target word (if any). Templates are produced by vocal motor schemes, and often originate in preferred prelinguistic babbling patterns. *Canonical form* is another term for the same concept.

text presentation   According to *government and binding theory*, the type of language to which children learning language are exposed. It contains no *negative evidence*.

thematic roles (semantic roles)   The components of *government and binding theory* grammar that connect the lexicon to the logical form component of the *s-structure*, assigning noun phrases to roles such as agent or location.

theoretical adequacy   Characteristic of a theory or model that contains principles that not only account for observed behaviors, but are the actual principles individuals use to attain those behaviors.

theory of mind Assumptions individuals hold about the state of knowledge of others. Children must develop a theory of mind in order to speak to others at an appropriate level and to understand their intentions.

tongue root The part of the tongue that is at its far back. It continues down into the pharynx.

top-down (model) A term taken from artificial intelligence research to depict the direction of processing. *Top-down* (or concept-driven) indicates that processing moves from the level of concepts downward to basic-level data. Top-down reading models conceptualize reading as involving the generation and testing of hypotheses about which words are on the page.

topic-associating narrative Narrative that links several episodes thematically.

topic-focused narrative A narrative about a single person or event, which has a clear beginning, middle, and end. Contrasts with *topic-associating* style.

total communication A method of interacting with individuals with language impairments using a combination of spoken language and signs.

transformational rule In Chomsky's latest grammar, transformational rules, such as [move a]—meaning move any part of the sentence to a new position—applied to the *d-structure,* produce various syntactic surface forms while retaining the meaning or intent of the original.

transformational syntax A part of transformational generative grammar, developed by Noam Chomsky, in which surface structure is derived from deep structure by the application of transformational rules.

trill A speech sound produced by vibration or a series of rapid flaps of the articulator, such as the uvula or lips or tip of the tongue.

underextension Use or understanding of a word that does not include its full range—assuming, for instance, that *dog* refers only to collies.

universal grammar (UG) Hypothetical set of restrictions governing the possible forms all human languages may take.

universal newborn screening A program to test infants for a variety of problems and conditions early on; early identification of infants with hearing problems can greatly improve their prospects.

universality Property assumed to characterize all human languages.

unvoiced A sound produced without accompanying vibration of the vocal folds, for instance /p/ in English, as opposed to /b/, which is a similar but voiced sound.

upper articulators Upper parts of the mouth used in the production of speech, such as the upper lip, upper teeth, alveolar ridge, palate, etc.

variegated babble Babbling that includes a variety of sounds, such as "babideeboo." See *reduplicated babble.*

velar fricative A sound heard in words like the Scottish *loch* or German *Bach.* See *velar, fricative.*

velar Any speech sound produced by having the back of the tongue touch or come near the underside of the velum, or soft palate (see *velum*). The English velars are the consonants /k/, /g/, and /ŋ/.

velum Also called the soft palate; the soft rear extension of the hard palate. The velum plays two major roles as an articulator: First, it can be raised to close off the passage from the pharynx into the nasal cavity or lowered to open this passage; second, the back of the tongue rises to touch the velum in the production of the *velar stops* /k/, /g/,/ŋ/.

verbal humor Humor achieved through language.

vocabulary breadth The number of words a child knows.

vocabulary depth The richness of knowledge about words known, including pronunciation, spelling, multiple meanings, and connotations the word may have, and linguistic and pragmatic contexts in which it occurs.

vocabulary spurt A proposed stage in lexical development, usually at about 18 months of age, during which some young children's word learning expands rapidly.

vocal fold Often referred to as vocal cords, the portion of the larynx that vibrates and produces the sound that is the basis of the human voice.

vocal motor scheme A scheme or program of motor activity that underlies a canonical form. The scheme is a tightly linked sequence of articulatory gestures (including timing of jaw and tongue movements, velum position changes, and vocal cord vibration). The gestures of a vocal motor scheme are not completely specified; instead, certain details—for example, one position or manner of articulation—can be varied as the child tries to make the output resemble a particular adult target word. See *canonical form.*

vocal play babbling and other vocal behaviors seen in young infants to test their vocal capacity; it can include a variety of non-speech (e.g., growls, raspberries) as well as speech-like sounds.

voice onset time (VOT) A measure that describes the point during the production of a speech sound at which *vocal fold* vibration (voicing) begins.

voiced, voicing Said of a speech sound (stop, fricative, etc.) produced with *vocal fold* vibration: e.g., /a/,

/z/. In the case of English, this term is usually also extended to the stops /b/, /d/, /g/.

voiceless   See *unvoiced*.

vowel   A speech sound made with a relatively unobstructed flow of air. Semivowels have some restriction but the air is not stopped and there are no friction sounds—*w* or *y* (IPA /j/). See also *glide*.

weak central coherence   A term typically used in describing a profile in autism spectrum disorder that reflects the child's inability to bring together various details from perceived events or stimuli to make a meaningful whole.

Wernicke's aphasia   Aphasia characterized by fluent but relatively empty speech, poor comprehension, and neologisms in severe cases. See *aphasia*.

Wernicke's area   Speech area in the posterior region of the left hemisphere. Damage to *Wernicke's area* results in *Wernicke's aphasia*.

whole language (literature based)   A reading-for-meaning approach that stresses involvement with "whole," or meaningful, texts.

wh-question   A question preceded by a *wh-* word, such as *who, what, why, where, when* (or *how*), that requires specification of the missing element in the answer.

Williams syndrome (WS)   An inherited atypicality that includes elfin appearance, poor spatial ability, and hyperlexia.

word associations   Words that come to mind as a result of hearing other words. See *free word association*.

word family   A group of words sharing a common base, such as *drive, drives, driver, driving*, etc.

word recognition   The recognition that letter strings represent conventional words.

working memory   The part of memory that holds information in mind while it is being processed; working memory is limited in children with SLI and declines with age, and this has been linked to comprehension problems.

yes/no question   A question that may be responded to by saying "yes" or "no."

Name Index

Subject Index

Photo Credits

Page 8: Courtesy of Irene M. Pepperberg, the Alex Foundation. **Page 9:** Pam Gleason. **Page 20:** Dale G. Caldwell. **Pages 33, 36, 43:** Rochelle Newman. **Page 68:** Cindy Gongon. **Page 70:** Renata Osinska/Shutterstock. **Page 91:** Pam Gleason. **Page 98:** Paola Uccelli. **Page 103:** Monkey Business Images/Shutterstock. **Page 131:** yulya yurochka / Fotolia. **Page 133 both:** University of Maryland Infant Studies Laboratories. **Page 138:** Pam Gleason. **Pages 143, 151:** Photo by Andrea Zukowski. **Page 164:** Photography Through Your Eyes. **Page 170:** Ashley Armstrong/ Design Pics/Newscom. **Page 177:** bikeriderlondon/Shutterstock. **Page 216:** BlueOrange Studio/Shutterstock. **Page 226 from left to right:** Max S. Gerber; Brian MacWhinney; George Carnevale. **Page 242:** Aliaksei Lasevich/ Shutterstock. **Page 252:** auremar/Shutterstock. **Page 268:** Reprinted with the permission of the House Research Institute. **Page 278:** Edward Friedman. **Page 304:** UMD Speech and Hearing Clinic. **Page 333:** Tony Freeman/ PhotoEdit. **Page 335:** Deklofenak/Fotolia. **Page 339:** Jean Berko Gleason. **Page 343:** Suprijono Suharjoto/Fotolia. **Page 353:** iofoto/Shutterstock. **Page 372:** Adam Ratner. **Page 376:** The University of Maryland Speech and Hearing Clinic. Photo by Andrew Roberts.